Global Variation in Literacy Development

Bringing together an international team of scholars, this pioneering book presents the first truly systematic, cross-linguistic study of variation in literacy development. It draws on a wide range of cross-cultural research to shed light on the key factors that predict global variation in children's acquisition of reading and writing skills, covering regions as diverse as North and South America, Asia, Australia, Europe, and Africa. The first part of the volume deals with comprehensive reviews related to the variation of literacy in different world regions. The second part of the volume deals with comprehensive reviews related to the variation of literacy in different regions of the globe as a function of sociopolitical, sociocultural, and language and writing-system factors. Offering a pioneering new framework for global literacy development, this groundbreaking volume will remain a landmark in the fields of literacy development and literacy teaching and learning for years to come.

LUDO VERHOEVEN is Professor of Communication, Language, and Literacy in the Behaviour Science Institute at Radboud University Nijmegen and at the University of Curaçao.

SONALI NAG is Professor of Psychology and Education and Education Fellow of Brasenose College, University of Oxford.

CHARLES PERFETTI is Distinguished University Professor of Psychology and Director of the Learning Research and Development Center at the University of Pittsburgh.

KENNETH PUGH is Professor of Psychology at the University of Connecticut and Associate Professor of Linguistics and Medicine at Yale University, and is both President and Director of Research and Senior Scientist at Haskins Laboratories.

Global Variation in Literacy Development

Edited by

Ludo Verhoeven
Radboud University Nijmegen, and the University of Curaçao

Sonali Nag
University of Oxford

Charles Perfetti
University of Pittsburgh

Kenneth Pugh
Yale University

Shaftesbury Road, Cambridge CB2 8EA, United Kingdom

One Liberty Plaza, 20th Floor, New York, NY 10006, USA

477 Williamstown Road, Port Melbourne, VIC 3207, Australia

314–321, 3rd Floor, Plot 3, Splendor Forum, Jasola District Centre, New Delhi – 110025, India

103 Penang Road, #05–06/07, Visioncrest Commercial, Singapore 238467

Cambridge University Press is part of Cambridge University Press & Assessment, a department of the University of Cambridge.

We share the University's mission to contribute to society through the pursuit of education, learning and research at the highest international levels of excellence.

www.cambridge.org
Information on this title: www.cambridge.org/9781009242554

DOI: 10.1017/9781009242585

© Cambridge University Press & Assessment 2024

This publication is in copyright. Subject to statutory exception and to the provisions of relevant collective licensing agreements, no reproduction of any part may take place without the written permission of Cambridge University Press & Assessment.

First published 2024

A catalogue record for this publication is available from the British Library.

A Cataloging-in-Publication data record for this book is available from the Library of Congress.

ISBN 978-1-009-24255-4 Hardback

Cambridge University Press & Assessment has no responsibility for the persistence or accuracy of URLs for external or third-party internet websites referred to in this publication and does not guarantee that any content on such websites is, or will remain, accurate or appropriate.

Contents

List of Figures	*page*	vii
List of Tables		ix
List of Contributors		xi
List of Abbreviations		xiii

1 Introduction: Literacy Development – A Global Perspective   1
   LUDO VERHOEVEN, SONALI NAG, CHARLES PERFETTI, AND KENNETH PUGH

Part I   Regional Variations   31

2 Sociocultural Variation in Literacy Development in Canada and the United States   33
   MICHAEL J. KIEFFER AND ROSE VUKOVIĆ

3 Literacy Contexts and Literacy Development in South America   56
   ANA LUIZA NAVAS

4 Postcolonial Literacy Development in the Caribbean   70
   LUDO VERHOEVEN AND RONALD SEVERING

5 Literacy Development in Europe   90
   LUISA ARAÚJO AND PATRÍCIA COSTA

6 Literacy Education and Development in Russia   118
   OLGA VELICHENKOVA AND MARGARITA RUSETSKAYA

7 Literacy Development and Language of Instruction in Sub-Saharan Africa   133
   AMBER GOVE, KARON HARDEN, SIMON KING, JENNIFER PRESSLEY RYAN, SARRYNNA SOU, AND SUSAN EDWARDS

8 Literacy and Linguistic Diversity in Multilingual India   155
   POOJA R. NAKAMURA AND CHINMAYA U. HOLLA

9	Literacy Development in East Asia MICHELLE R. Y. HUO, XIN SUN, IOULIA KOVELMAN, AND XI CHEN	174
10	Literacy and Linguistic Diversity in Australia ANNE-MARIE MORGAN, NICHOLAS REID, AND PETER FREEBODY	203

Part II	**Neurobiological and Ecological Markers**	**239**
11	Writing Systems and Global Literacy Development CHARLES PERFETTI AND LUDO VERHOEVEN	241
12	Brain Foundations for Learning to Read PIETRA CASSOL RIGATTI, XIN CUI, KENNETH PUGH, MAILCE BORGES MOTA, AND AUGUSTO BUCHWEITZ	265
13	Genetics and Literacy Development ELENA L. GRIGORENKO	292
14	Role of Self-Regulation in the Transition to School FREDERICK J. MORRISON, JENNIE GRAMMER, WILLIAM J. GEHRING, LINDSAY BELL WEIXLER, AND MATTHEW H. KIM	316
15	Socioeconomic Status, Sociocultural Factors, and Literacy Development SONALI NAG	333
16	Sensitivity to Contextual Factors in Literacy Interventions in the Global South YONAS MESFUN ASFAHA AND SONALI NAG	353
17	How Teachers Contribute to Children's Literacy Success DAVID K. DICKINSON, CAROL MCDONALD CONNOR[†], AND ELIZABETH BURKE HADLEY	374
18	The Literacy Ecology of the Home: The Case of Rural Rwanda ELLIOTT FRIEDLANDER AND CLAUDE GOLDENBERG	402
19	Parental Literacy Support in Monolingual and Bilingual Contexts MILA SCHWARTZ	425
20	Global Literacy: Patterns and Variations CHARLES PERFETTI, SONALI NAG, KENNETH PUGH, AND LUDO VERHOEVEN	446

Index 469

Figures

1.1	Distribution of literacy throughout the world (see Roser & Ortiz-Ospina, 2016)	*page* 4
1.2	Model of how literacy development builds on the linguistic system and the writing system it represents	6
1.3	How writing systems map to languages	9
1.4	Interactive processes in reading (from written text to background knowledge) and writing (from background knowledge to written text)	11
1.5	General explanatory framework for the global variation of literacy	22
4.1	Means for the tests for receptive vocabulary, productive vocabulary, sentence reproduction, and narrative comprehension in Papiamentu and Dutch at the beginning (K1) and after one year (K2) and two years (K3) of kindergarten	79
4.2	Means for the tests for word decoding, reading vocabulary, sentence comprehension, and text comprehension in Papiamentu and Dutch at the beginning (B5) and the ends of Grades 5 (E5) and 6 (E6)	81
5.1	Average reading achievement by country and by SES in Grade 4 in twenty-two countries participating in the PIRLS 2016 EU-MS dataset	101
5.2	Average reading achievement according to alphabet knowledge and SES in Grade 4 in twenty-two countries participating in the PIRLS 2016 EU-MS dataset	102
5.3	Average reading achievement according to parental book reading and SES in Grade 4 in twenty-two countries participating in the PIRLS 2016 EU-MS dataset	103
5.4	Average reading achievement by country and by SES of fifteen-year-old students in twenty-five countries participating in the PISA 2018 EU-MS dataset	105

5.5	Average reading achievement by country, parental book reading, and SES of fifteen-year-old students in twenty-five countries participating in the PISA 2018 EU-MS dataset	106
7.1	Languages spoken matches language of instruction in Ghana and Zambia	
	a Ghana	
	b Zambia	143
7.2	Impact of L1 and LOI mismatch on students who could not read a word of connected text (estimates as odds ratios), Grade 2	145
7.3	Impact of L1 and LOI match on average reading fluency achievement (correct words per minute), Grade 2	146
7.4	Intervention impact of L1 and LOI match on average reading fluency gain (additional correct words per minute), Grade 2	146
10.1	Aboriginal languages map, Australian Institute of Aboriginal and Torres Strait Islander Studies, AIATSIS, Horton (1996)	206
11.1	The Cherokee syllabary invented by Sequoya. Each "letter" stands for a syllable in the spoken language	243
12.1	The brain subsystems for reading	269
14.1	Frequency distribution of teacher ratings of self-regulation for males and females at the beginning of the kindergarten year	319
14.2	In the top panel, there is a linear effect of age, but not schooling. This is typically seen for measures of vocabulary, which appear to be more sensitive to biological maturation compared to schooling	326
18.1	Flora's writing sample	410
18.2	Jolly writing in MT's notebook	410
18.3	Flora holding her exercise book	416
18.4	A stack of books in Jolly's house	417
20.1	The global literacy framework	457

Tables

2.1	Effect-size estimates of differences in vocabulary by SES at ages 4–5	*page* 40
2.2	Effect-size estimates of differences in reading achievement by SES in childhood	41
2.3	Effect-size estimates of differences in reading achievement by SES in adolescence	43
2.4	Effect-size estimates of vocabulary differences by home language at school entry (ages 4–5)	44
2.5	Effect-size estimates of reading achievement gaps by home language in childhood	45
2.6	Effect-size estimates of differences in reading comprehension by home language in adolescence	47
3.1	Total population, density, and Indigenous population estimates for countries in South America	57
3.2	Adjusted net enrollment rate (%), one year before the official primary entry age	60
3.3	Rate of enrollment (%) by age range (education level) in Brazil	60
3.4	Government expenditure on education as a percentage of GDP (%), South American countries	61
3.5	Percentages of students for PISA reading and science scores, by PISA proficiency levels and country, 2018	62
3.6	Distribution of Latin American countries compared to the average scores for the region for reading and mathematics for third- and sixth-grade students at the TERCE (2015)	63
7.1	Current language-of-instruction policies and degree of implementation for selected sub-Saharan Africa countries	136
7.2	Summary of country datasets consulted by research question	140
7.3	Descriptive variables included in the models for Ghana, Kenya, Liberia, Malawi, Tanzania, and Zambia	141

10.1	Some demographic features of selected countries (sources: International Monetary Fund, 2020; OECD, 2019a and b; United Nations Development Programme, 2019; World Bank, 2018)	204
10.2	Selected characteristics of ancestor groups in Australia, 2011 census (ABS, 2016b). Note that tallies may exceed 100 percent, as respondents can indicate more than one category	216
10.3	Mean (rounded) literacy-related scores for Years 3, 5, 7, and 9 on the National Assessment Program in Literacy and Numeracy (NAPLAN) 2019 results	218
10.4	OECD ranking of member nations scoring significantly above OECD mean for reading in PISA round 2018, and related national measures	219
11.1	The Cree Syllabary: Basic forms represent consonants. The orientation of the form represents a vowel	244
11.2	Five-way classification of writing systems	246
11.3	Example graphs from five writing systems with GraphCom complexity values	248
11.4	Five languages whose writing systems show some alignment with properties of the language	249
11.5	Comparisons of morphosyllabic and alphabetic literacy	252
11.6	Operating principles in literacy development	253
16.1	Included randomized controlled experiments by intervention focus, duration, student, and facilitator details	360
18.1	Variables loading onto each factor	406
18.2	Multivariate regressions using LE factors to predict reading achievement (N=466)	407
18.3	Evidence of the five LE factors in the qualitative data	411

Contributors

LUISA ARAÚJO, Institute of Education and Sciences (ISEC Lisboa and CETAPS)
LINDSAY BELL WEIXLER, University of Michigan
MAILCE BORGES MOTA, Universidade Federal de Santa Catarina
AUGUSTO BUCHWEITZ, University of Connecticut and Haskins Laboratories
ELIZABETH BURKE HADLEY, Vanderbilt University's Peabody College
PIETRA CASSOL RIGATTI, Universidade Federal de Santa Catarina
XI CHEN, University of Toronto
XIN CUI, Beijing Normal University
PATRÍCIA COSTA, Institute of Education and Sciences (ISEC Lisboa) and CEMAPRE
DAVID K. DICKINSON, Vanderbilt University's Peabody College
SUSAN EDWARDS, RTI International
PETER FREEBODY, The University of Sydney, Australia
ELLIOTT FRIEDLANDER, Stanford University
WILLIAM J. GEHRING, University of Michigan
CLAUDE GOLDENBERG, Stanford University
AMBER GOVE, RTI International
JENNIE GRAMMER, University of Michigan
ELENA L. GRIGORENKO, University of Houston
KARON HARDEN, RTI International Education Division, New York
CHINMAYA U. HOLLA, American Institutes for Research, Arlington
MICHELLE R. Y. HUO, University of Toronto
MICHAEL J. KIEFFER, New York University
MATTHEW H. KIM, University of Kentucky
SIMON KING, RTI International
IOULIA KOVELMAN, University of Michigan
CAROL MCDONALD CONNOR [†], University of California, Irvine
YONAS MESFUN ASFAHA, Asmara College of Education, Eritrea
ANNE-MARIE MORGAN, University of New England, Australia

FREDERICK J. MORRISON, University of Michigan
SONALI NAG, University of Oxford
POOJA R. NAKAMURA, American Institutes for Research, Arlington
ANA LUIZA NAVAS, School of Medical Sciences at Santa Casa de São Paulo
CHARLES PERFETTI, University of Pittsburgh
JENNIFER PRESSLEY RYANN, RTI International
KENNETH PUGH, University of Connecticut and Haskins Laboratories
NICHOLAS REID, University of New England, Australia
MARGARITA RUSETSKAYA, Pushkin State Russian Language Institute
MILA SCHWARTZ, Oranim Academic College of Education, Israel
RONALD SEVERING, University of Curaçao
SARRYNNA SOU, CEA Consulting, San Francisco
XIN SUN, University of Michigan
OLGA VELICHENKOVA, Pushkin State Russian Language Institute
LUDO VERHOEVEN, Radboud University Nijmegen and the University of Curaçao
ROSE VUKOVIĆ, University of Victoria

Abbreviations

ABS	Australian Bureau of Statistics
ACARA	Australian Curriculum, Assessment and Reporting Authority
ADHD	Attention Deficit Hyperactivity Disorder
AE	Aboriginal English
AFMLTA	Australian Federation of Modern Language Teachers Associations
ASER	Annual Status of Education Report
CDCV	Common Disorder–Common Variant hypothesis
CDRV	Common Disorder–Rare Variant hypothesis
CNV/SV	Copy Number Variation and Structural Variation
DLL	Dual-language learners
DNA	Deoxyribonucleic acid
EAL	English as an Additional Language
ECCE	Early Childhood Care and Education
ECLS-B	Early Childhood Longitudinal Study – Birth
ECLS-K	Early Childhood Longitudinal Study – Kindergarten
EEG	Electroencephalography
EF	Executive functioning
EGRA	Early Grade Reading Assessment
ELL	English-language learners
ELM	Emergent Literacy and Math program
ERN	Error-related negativity
ERP	Event-related potential
EU	European Union
FLLP	Family Language and Literacy Policy
FLP	Family Language Policy
GDP	Gross domestic product
GWA	Genome-wide association
HIA	Health Impact Assessment
HLE	Home literacy environment
HLLE	Home language and literacy environment
HTKS	Head-toes-knees-shoulders task

IFG	Inferior frontal gyrus
ILSA	International large-scale assessments
ILTS	International longitudinal twins study
ISI	Individualizing student instruction
L1	First language
L2	Second language
LBOTE	Language background other than English
LE	Literacy ecology framework
LH	Left hemisphere
LHA	Limited health abilities
LLECE	Latin American Laboratory for Assessment of the Quality of Education
LMTF	Learning Metrics Task Force
LOI	Language of instruction
MDAT	Malawi Emergent Literacy and Math test
MFG	Middle frontal gyrus
MGD	Millennium Development Goal
NAEP	National Assessment for Educational Progress
NAHR	Non-allelic homologous recombination
NAPLAN	National Program of Standardized Tests of Literacy and Numeracy
NCERT	National Council of Educational Research & Training
NCES	National Center for Education Statistics
NGO	Nongovernmental organization
NIRS	Near infrared spectroscopy
NLSCY	National Longitudinal Study of Children and Youth
NRP	National Reading Panel
NULP	Northern Uganda Literacy Project
OECD	Organisation for Economic Co-operation and Development
OP	Operating principle
OREALC	Oficina Regional de Educación para América Latina y el Caribe (Regional Office for Education in Latin America and the Caribbean)
PA	Phonological awareness
PCD	Ciliary dyskinesia
PIAAC	Programme for the International Assessment of Adult Competencies
PIRLS	Progress in International Reading Literacy Study
PISA	Programme for International Student Assessment
PLC	Professional Learning Community
PNAIC	Pacto Nacional pela Alfabetização na Idade Certa (National Pact for Literacy at the Right Age)

PNEP	Programa Nacional do Ensino do Português (National Program for Portuguese Teaching)
RCT	Randomized controlled trial
RDD	Regression discontinuity design
SAE	Standard Australian English
SES	Socioeconomic status
SICLE	Sydney Institute for Community Language Education
SIDS	Small Island Developing States
SISR	Sustained Independent Silent Reading program
SNP	Single nucleotide polymorphisms
SRD	Specific reading disability
STG	Superior temporal gyrus
SVR	Simple View of Reading
TERCE	Third Regional Comparative and Explanatory Study
TIMMS	Trends in International Mathematics and Science Study
UK	United Kingdom
UN	United Nations
UNDP	Human Development Index
UNESCO	United Nations Educational, Scientific and Cultural Organisation
UNICEF	United Nations International Children's Fund
VOT	Ventral occipitotemporal region
VWFA	Visual word form area
WLF	World Literacy Foundation
ZPD	Zone of proximal development

1 Introduction

Literacy Development – A Global Perspective

Ludo Verhoeven, Sonali Nag, Charles Perfetti, and Kenneth Pugh

Supporting children's literacy development is a major concern within the international community. Literacy is seen as conditional for school success and for participation in an increasingly print-heavy world. However, the acquisition of literacy is not a simple question of teaching a child to read. The acquisition of the written mode of language occurs within a complex of sociocultural processes affecting the transformation of societies as well as the development of individuals (see Olson, 2016). This basic idea has been elaborated by anthropological and sociological studies focusing on the effects of literacy on general modes of thinking, sociocultural transformations, and economic change (e.g., Smith & Kumi-Yeboah, 2015). Literacy thus contributes to individual empowerment and to social, economic, and political integration. Learning to read and write helps children to build knowledge and skills that are in turn refined throughout their schooling and career in preparation for full societal participation, including in the labor market and with sociopolitical institutions. Literacy provides the individual with opportunities for lifelong learning and tools to adapt to a constantly changing textual and digital world.

The importance of literacy draws attention to its distribution and prevalence around the world and to the consequences of being nonliterate. There is commonality across the globe. For one, children's schooling and adult literacy programs are implemented to support literacy worldwide. However, these programs not only vary internationally but also in ways that are embedded in cultural contexts that diverge historically and systemically. The cognitive task of literacy learning is also similar across the world: Individuals are confronted with the task of acquiring implicit knowledge of how a writing system works – how the written word reveals meaning through a layer of graphic forms – and to make this knowledge explicit. Here too, however, there are differences. The cognitive task is mediated by a layer of graphic forms whose properties vary worldwide in both their appearance and the typological levels of language the graphs represent: morphemes, syllables, and phonemes. Each writing system encodes language in one way or another, often mixing levels. Thus, literacy is both an achievement shared across the world and also varies substantially in sociocultural contexts, including languages and writing systems. In this volume, we address this global variability of literacy and the biological and ecological factors explaining this variation. In this introductory chapter, we examine the worldwide distribution of literacy, its development as it relates to that of schooling, and the sources of individual variation in literacy outcomes. In the final chapter, we will explain the patterns and variations in literacy development around the world as described in the present volume.

1.1 Global Variation in Literacy Attainments

1.1.1 Defining Literacy

Beyond its conventional conception as a set of reading and writing abilities, literacy must also be understood as a means of identification, understanding, interpretation, creation, and communication in an increasingly digital, text-mediated, fast-changing world (United Nations, 2014). According to the UN Strategic Development Goals, literacy can be considered a driver for sustainable development; enabling greater participation in the labor market; better opportunities to ensure child and family health, nutrition, and wellbeing; and the general expansion of life chances. As such, literacy may not only contribute to human capital but also to the flourishing of the child. Literacy can be defined as a lifelong, context-bound set of practices in which an individual's needs vary with time and place. Research has shown that the literacy practices through which individuals are socialized into various institutions can be extremely variable. Functionally, literacy not only involves the ability to read and write but also the ability to cope with literacy situations in everyday life. It comprises both literacy conventions and interrelated cultural and background knowledge. Literacy conventions are reflected in the types of documents that are used by social institutions such as letters, forms, legal briefs, political tracts, religious texts, expository texts, and narrative texts such as novels, comics, essays, and poems. Different types of documents may also call for different types of cultural background knowledge as well as different values and beliefs (e.g., Verhoeven, 1994; Wagner, 1993). Accordingly, one could also speak of multiple literacies (cf. Street, 2001), and therefore the importance of policies which enhance literacy education for all.

Literacy also reflects sociolinguistic positioning that specifically affects minority communities (cf. Fishman, 1999; Mohanty, 2000; Verhoeven, 2010. In a multiethnic society, for example, minority groups may use various written codes serving at least partially distinct sets of functions. Given the privileges of power, the written code with the highest status is primarily used by societal institutions such as the government and courts, whereas the written code of the minority language(s) is left to be used for intragroup communication and to express one's linguistic identity and ethnicity. Yet another written code may be used for religious practices. In light of such multilinguality, literacy competence must be understood in the context of language and cultural backgrounds as, for example, the multilingual and multicultural environments of children from ethnic minority communities. One must consider, therefore, whether an individual who is a member of an ethnic minority is literate in the ethnic group language, the language(s) of wider communication, or other language(s) (see Butvilovsky et al., 2021). An expansion of the conventional concept of literacy needs to include such multi-scriptal learning.

1.1.2 Demographics of Literacy

People are considered literate when they can both read and write, with understanding, a short simple statement about their everyday life. During the past two decades, literacy rates worldwide have increased by 12 percent. It is estimated that the literacy rate of people aged fifteen and older is 86 percent. In the population ranging from fifteen to twenty-four years of age, 90 percent of females and 93 percent of males now have basic literacy skills worldwide. Despite these gains, 750 million adults throughout the world are still unable to read and write, with almost two thirds of these being female (UNESCO, 2017).

Census data make it clear that literacy rates vary greatly around the globe (e.g., see Figure 1.1; Silberstein, 2021). The lowest literacy rates and greatest gender disparities are in low- and lower-middle income countries in sub-Saharan Africa and South Asia. Significant disparities in literacy attainments are also evident in countries with upper-middle-income economies like Brazil, India, and South Africa. It is estimated that, for example, more than a third of the population in India cannot read and write. Substantial variation in literacy levels is also reported within high-income countries. Data from periodic international surveys repeatedly demonstrate that substantial numbers of children in these countries leave school with significant literacy problems. As a case in point, the OECD "Programme for International Student Assessment" (PISA) evidenced in 2018 that 21.7 percent of fifteen-year-old pupils in Europe could be marked as underachievers in reading. This proportion of pupils failed to reach the minimum proficiency level necessary to participate successfully in society. What is more, the proportion of underachievers in reading has seen a steady increase in the past ten years (European Union, 2019).

Such demographics of literacy rates are important to track because low levels of literacy signal substantial costs. Reports from the World Bank, for example, clearly show that low literacy rates worldwide are associated with health problems and high crime rates (World Bank, 2019). Low rates are also associated with low incomes and low business profits, even more so in societies that are higher on the income scale (WLF, 2015). Increased awareness of the

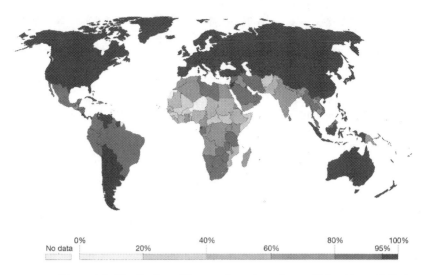

Figure 1.1 Distribution of literacy throughout the world (see Roser & Ortiz-Ospina, 2016)

personal, social, and economic value of literacy has fueled a broader recognition of the need for increased investment in literacy programs. Initiatives to develop and implement regional literacy have resulted in substantial gains in literacy levels for new generations (Wagner, 2017), but clearly more needs to be done.

1.1.3 Moderators of Literacy

To begin with, literacy achievement is moderated by economic status. There is a high association of lower levels of literacy attainment with poverty, showing that literacy is bound up with unequal structures and poor economies (Street, 2005). A substantial number of people with low literacy live in high-income countries (see UNESCO, 2017). In more than twenty low- and middle-income countries, the literacy rates are below 50 percent, with a large gender disparity. About two thirds of the low-literate population is female. In the lowest income communities, the proportion of literate women is estimated to be only about 20 percent. Schools can be seen as the main driver of literacy learning. Worldwide, 92 percent of children are enrolled in a primary school program and 84 percent are successful in completing it (UNESCO, 2019). Significant progress has been made toward achieving universal primary education. However, today's world statistics show that more than 260 million children up to age twelve have never had a chance to participate in elementary education and are at risk of stunted literacy development. In the most resource-poor societies, more than 50 percent of all school-aged children are not enrolled in a school program. As a case in point, 19 percent of children in sub-Saharan Africa are not enrolled in primary school and 37 percent do not complete it. Poverty (within the country, and for the individual family) is one important obstacle to school access, generally associated with a lack of trained teachers, impoverished classes with few learning materials, and child absences due to poor health and sanitation facilities. In some places, children that come to school are too hungry, sick, traumatized, or exhausted to benefit from instruction (Wagner, 2011).

In parallel, an increasing societal demand for text-mediated activities has steadily increased the standards of literacy needed on a daily basis – higher levels of literacy skills have become more urgent for the individual. Rapid social and technological changes in the past decades have contributed to these increased demands (Wickens & Sandlin, 2007). Also in parallel is the finding that even with the provision of compulsory primary education, many children do not reach a level of competence that is sufficient to cope with simplest everyday literacy demands. Literacy problems appear in various vulnerable groups, both Indigenous and non-Indigenous, urban and rural, mainstream and remote, newly arrived, native and settled (e.g., Nag, Chiat et al., 2014). A third parallel issue is with literacy problems among adults. In most high-income countries, the occurrence of such problems among adult citizens has historically been ignored. General educational policies have instead placed an emphasis on getting children into school and preventing school dropouts. Only in recent years has there been a realization that the establishment of a universal schooling system does not guarantee sufficient literacy attainments for all. Gradually, the need to support adult basic education with a literacy foundation is being recognized. One result of this recognition has been the publication of reports on parallel basic needs among adult populations in different countries (see Wagner, 2018).

1.2   Literacy Development across Languages and Writing Systems

Literacy is a broad concept. It includes the knowledge and skills for participation in cultural practices that use reading and writing. Because literacy builds on the foundation of learning to read, it is important to focus on what is involved in learning to read. The core achievement in all writing systems is learning how the written forms of a language map onto the forms and meanings of the spoken language. In terms of learning to write, the complementary core achievement is learning how the spoken forms of the language map onto the written forms of the language. However, much more effort is needed to develop reading and writing beyond these basic achievements. To focus on reading beyond functional literacy, we distinguish three main phases: (i) early literacy, which mainly involves the building of a mental lexicon along with an emergence of linguistic awareness; (ii) learning to read, which requires cracking the written code, and fluent reading with basic comprehension; and (iii) advanced literacy, with increased comprehension and interpretation skills. A similar range for writing should lead to the ability to write coherent and increasingly sophisticated texts.

The recognition of universals in the development of literacy gives rise to the proposal of a universal grammar of reading (see Perfetti, 2003) and writing (see Berman & Verhoeven, 2002; Nag, 2021). Writing systems can be typologically classified on the basis of the language constituents they represent: morphemes, syllables, and phonemes. Writing practice can intermix these types, as when Japanese is written in both syllable-based kana and morpheme-based kanji. Because of the linguistic constraints on writing – all writing systems encode language, not just concepts – the development of literacy is universally grounded in both the language and the writing system (cf. Nag, 2021; Perfetti, 2003; Verhoeven & Perfetti, 2017). Depending on the linguistic system and the system of orthography, the particulars of literacy development can be defined across languages and writing systems. Figure 1.2 shows how literacy development builds on the linguistic system and the writing system it represents. It should be acknowledged that from its early stages, reading fluency facilitates reading comprehension, and spelling facilitates writing.

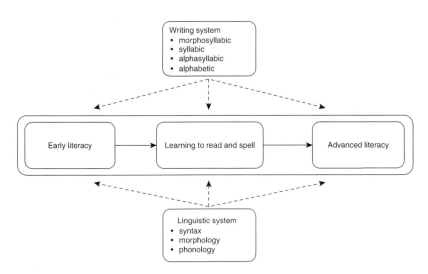

Figure 1.2 Model of how literacy development builds on the linguistic system and the writing system it represents

1.2.1 Early Literacy Development

Early literacy development is grounded in the development of early phonological abilities, such as speech decoding and speech production, and the emergence of a mental (orthographic) lexicon. Words are the carriers of meaning and therefore closely tied to word decoding, reading comprehension, and writing. Lexical development involves the correct linking of word meanings to word forms. Children start by overgeneralizing words as referring to a relatively large class of objects, acts, or events (cf. Clark, 2004). As their conceptual knowledge increases, they learn to refine the meanings of words. They use information from the context to make inferences about the semantic boundaries of the underlying concept of a word form. The richer the environment, the faster this lexical development will proceed. The quantity and quality of early social interactions with language and the richness of the language input shape language-learning trajectories. It is therefore generally assumed that vocabulary acquisition proves particularly successful when words are being offered in a context-rich environment (Rowe & Weisleder, 2020). Around one year of age, children develop a small number of lexical representations, which are holistic and undifferentiated (e.g., Jusczyk, 1997; Walley, 1993). As the number of words in the mental lexicon increases, the lexical restructuring hypothesis assumes there is pressure to make finer phonemic distinctions to accommodate this increase (Metsala & Walley, 1998). As a result, lexical representations become more specified through early childhood. Thanks to the increasing numbers of highly specified phonological representations, children may become phonologically aware (van Goch, McQueen, & Verhoeven, 2014). They gradually develop a metalinguistic awareness in which implicit knowledge of both the functions and structure of language are made explicit. By making language the object of their thinking, children learn to explicate their implicit knowledge of the functions and structure of language. In this type of knowledge, the emphasis shifts from the communicative content of their language to its morphophonological makeup.

Notwithstanding the complexity of written language, many children know a great deal about literacy before formal instruction starts. Conditions that strengthen the relevance and purpose of literacy turn out to be quite important for its early development. In becoming literate, the development of phonological awareness is particularly important. Phonological awareness, the ability to consciously attend to the components of spoken words (e.g., syllables, the onset-coda parts of syllables, and phonemes), gives the child a head start in learning to map written and spoken language. This ability is expressed when children can divide words up into syllables or phonemes, recognize rhyme (end rhyme and alliteration), use phonemes to form words, and omit, add, or replace phonemes in words. However, attention to meaningless functional units of spoken language, in particular the smallest unit, namely the phoneme, proves to be very difficult for children. In rich home-literacy environments with abundant meaningful interactions with adults, children discover the uses and functions of print, and learn how script is mapped onto language. From interactive storybook reading, more than from choral reading or silent listening, they learn new vocabulary and gain insight into the coherence and cohesion of narrative and expository texts (see Nag, Snowling, & Asfaha, 2016; Scarborough, 2005). The interactions between symbols in their environment and literate others help children to learn that print carries meaning, that written texts may have various forms and functions, and that ideas can be expressed with (non)conventional writing.

Although encouraging, the influential functions of literacy environments should not overshadow the crucial role of direct instruction in learning to read. It is obvious that there are dramatic disparities in home and neighborhood environments that affect the availability of literacy-supporting activities, and this opportunity gap is found even within high-income countries like Japan, Norway, the United States, and the United Kingdom. Schooling has the potential and responsibility to directly provide such opportunities in the form of systematic instruction. Accumulated research evidence indicates that to be able to grasp the written code, to acquire automaticity in word decoding, and to internalize appropriate strategies for word to text integration, children need formal reading instruction with sequentially structured activities managed by a skilled teacher (see Castles, Rastle, & Nation, 2018; McBride, 2016; Nag, 2017).

1.2.2   *Learning to Read and Spell*

In learning to read and spell, children are confronted with the task of acquiring implicit knowledge of how written language may reveal meaning through a layer of graphic forms. This involves learning how one's writing system encodes one's language. Writing systems involve minor but significant differences in the mapping of spoken units to written units (see Verhoeven & Perfetti, 2017). Figure 1.3 demonstrates how language units are related to graphic units across different writing systems and orthographies. Mapping occurs at the level of morpheme, syllable, or phoneme, either singularly (e.g., the syllabic and alphabetic systems) or in some combination (e.g., the alphasyllabic and morphosyllabic systems). In the Chinese writing system, for example, characters map to single syllables that are also morphemes, thus a morphosyllabic mapping. By comparison, there is mixed mapping in the Indic writing system, in which different *akshara* may map to one or more syllables and one or more phonemes.

Introduction

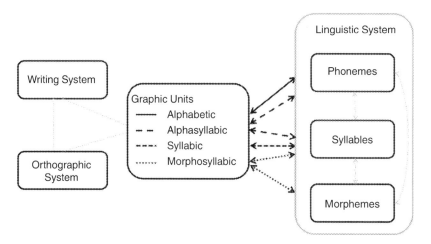

Figure 1.3 How writing systems map to languages

Cross-language research has shown that reading universally builds on language and that such universality accommodates properties of the writing system (Perfetti, 2003). This requires that children learn that words can be divided up in speech sounds that can be represented by written units (e.g., *akshara*: Nag & Narayanan, 2019; letters: Verhoeven et al., 2016). Moreover, children must learn the inventory of orthographic units for a language (Nag, 2017), and how these units map onto specific phonological and morphological units of the spoken language (Perfetti, 2003). As they acquire elementary decoding skills, children gradually learn to apply these skills with greater accuracy and speed in an increasingly automated process that recognizes multi-letter units (consonant clusters, and syllable- and morpheme-level strings) and whole words (Ehri, 2005). Automatic word recognition enables the devotion of mental resources to the meaning of a text and thus allows learners to use reading as a tool for the acquisition of new information and knowledge (Verhoeven & Perfetti, 2011). Spelling practice helps children to internalize relevant spelling rules in an efficient manner (Bhide et al., 2019; Graham et al., 2008) while text-reading practice produces gains in word-reading fluency, allowing cognitive resources to be redirected to reading comprehension (Verhoeven & van Leeuwe, 2008, 2012). It has been widely suggested that by the end of the third grade, children must be able to read basic texts fluently in order to make the step to reading to learn (e.g., NEP, 2020; NICHD, 2000).

Systematic explicit approaches are effective for all writing systems. In the case of alphabetic scripts, a variety of systematic phonics programs has been implemented to teach children word decoding and spelling (see Ehri et al., 2001). Such programs generally begin by teaching the alphabetic principle explicitly and follow a prespecified series of phonic elements sequentially. Synthetic phonics is the most common such program: It directly teaches the correspondence between specific letters to specific phonemes. In analytic phonics, children are taught sets of words with partly shared pronunciations to make them aware of individual sounds in words without sounding out phonemes in isolation. In embedded phonics, the emphasis is on orthographic patterns to be encountered in the context of predictable text. In a meta-analysis, Ehri et al. (2001) concluded that children who had been enrolled in systematic phonics instruction outperformed their peers in unsystematic phonics or nonphonics programs on both word reading and word spelling. Systematic approaches are also effective for nonalphabetic writing systems. To prepare for Chinese reading, children are taught character recognition by systematically showing the visual, semantic, and phonological features of a set of characters (McBride-Chang et al., 2008). For most Chinese children, formal reading instruction starts out with alphabetic reading; for example, on the Chinese mainland, Pinyin, a Roman alphabetic script representing the sounds of spoken Chinese, is used to lay the foundation for reading characters. In contrast, to prepare them to read Indic orthographies, children are taught to recite, write, and copy *akshara* families, which have been selected because they are phonologically related or are similarly high in frequency (Nag, 2017). Irrespective of the type of decoding instruction, however, a strong oral-language foundation is essential (e.g., alphabetic: Lervåg, Hulme, & Melby-Lervåg, 2018; *akshara*: Nag, Snowling et al., 2014).

1.2.3   Advanced Literacy Development

Literacy development is thus strongly dependent on the oral-language skills children have attained. Across different orthographies, research has shown that parallel gains in both word-reading accuracy and speed occur very rapidly after the outset of reading instruction, whereas a steady relationship between accuracy and speed of word decoding is maintained over the years (see Verhoeven & Perfetti, 2017). The growth in word decoding implies that children learn to make strong connections between graphs and sounds in a growing variety of words, and that frequent retrievals of word forms result in increases in fluency and automaticity of word representations. With this transition, children go from partially specified to fully specified representations of written words, with the strength of the association between print and sound (or sound and print, for that matter) also becoming increasingly automated. With sufficient reading practice, words are recognized by sight and the direct route to word decoding, without the need for letter–sound conversion to be activated, becomes more

Introduction 11

important (Coltheart et al., 2001). Successful reading practice and increased fluency of word identification facilitate the development of word-to-text integration, the continuously recurring basic comprehension process, generating a text model (verbal representation) and a situation model (conceptual representation) of the text which can be connected to the background knowledge of the reader. Figure 1.4 demonstrates how incremental word reading may facilitate word-to-text conversion, resulting into the construction of a text model and a situation model, both facilitating the elaboration of background knowledge.

According to the so-called "simple view of reading"(Hoover & Gough, 1990), reading comprehension can be seen as the product of word decoding and listening comprehension. More specifically, the simple view claims that listening comprehension or the linguistic processes involved in the comprehension of oral language strongly constrain reading comprehension. Importantly, the fundamental components of comprehension – parsing sentences into their constituent components, drawing inferences within and between sentences to support integration, and recognizing the underlying

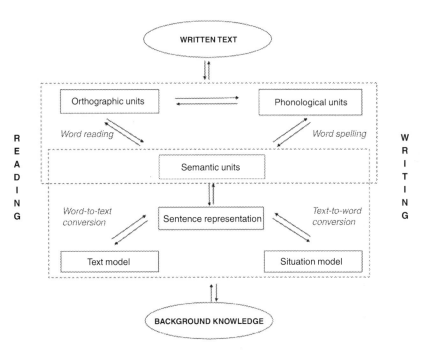

Figure 1.4 Interactive processes in reading (from written text to background knowledge) and writing (from background knowledge to written text)

meaning propositions within each section of text (microstructure), and the global gist (macrostructure) (see Perfetti & Stafura, 2014) – are all properties of language comprehension, not reading. Thus, written language will be understood as well as spoken language when written words can be identified and when language comprehension skills are well developed. Research has shown both younger and poorer readers have more problems with these language-comprehension processes than older and better readers (e.g., Cain & Barnes, 2017; Quinn & Wagner, 2018; Snowling et al., 2019; Verhoeven & van Leeuwe, 2008).

Once children have learned to use the basic written code, they increasingly experience the possibilities of written language use, and reading comprehension becomes more and more integrated with information processing related to distinct school subjects such as history, geography, and science. Major models of reading comprehension have evidenced that children learn to call on prior knowledge to construct new knowledge in these domains. Accordingly, literacy highly predicts the attainment of final school success in domains such as academic vocabulary and information-processing abilities. The use of incremental book series can lead to more proficient reading comprehension across languages and writing systems (McBride-Chang, 2004). In general, beyond reading practice, activities that drive deeper engagement with texts are to be recommended. Such engagement should lead the reader to use relevant knowledge and thus construct richer mental models of the text. Research has also shown that the advancement of literacy in the upper grades is highly dependent on literacy motivation (see Guthrie & Humenick, 2004). Consequently, high literacy levels are found to be associated with high levels of school motivation and school success (Verhoeven & Snow, 2001).

Learning to write is a complex process that evolves over an extended period during the primary and secondary grades (Berman & Verhoeven, 2002). Models of writing assume that the writing of texts involves multiple parallel processes focusing on transcription, planning of ideas generated from background knowledge, converting ideas into language, and writing and reviewing text (Chenoweth & Hayes, 2001; Hayes, 2012). Figure 1.4 shows that writing involves reverse processes to reading: Starting from background knowledge, ideas are converted into text and written down via coherence-building strategies and word spelling. Once word spelling becomes automatic, resources can be allocated to high-level writing processes. Research has shown that subprocesses of writing are supported by the learner's language skills, such as vocabulary and grammar; transcription skills, like handwriting, keyboarding, and spelling; and executive functions, such as inhibition control, cognitive flexibility, and working memory (e.g., see Berninger & Winn, 2006). The development of writing additionally involves a shift in writing strategies. Beginning writers tend to use an associative step-by-step writing strategy in which ideas are written down as they come to mind, without organizing the conceptual content or linguistic form. More advanced writers tend to use a more complex knowledge-transforming strategy, which involves the ability to adjust the text content according to rhetorical and pragmatic goals (see Berninger & Winn, 2006). In contemporary educational settings, Information Communications Technologies (ICT) offer additional ways of facilitating knowledge construction (cf. Verhoeven, Schnotz, & Paas, 2009). Although ICT is increasingly being integrated into the school curriculum through the convergence of instruction of school subjects and networked technologies, the evidence base on what works and for whom is still to be developed.

1.2.4 Problems in Attaining Literacy

The development of literacy is obviously at risk for children with developmental dyslexia. Research in the past decades has provided ample evidence that children with dyslexia have problems with decoding and spelling words and that a phonological-processing deficit underlies these problems (Seidenberg, 2017; Snowling, 2019). Brain-imaging studies have provided complementary evidence of early brain markers that predict reading outcomes and may yet help predict treatment outcomes (see Chapter 12). In alphabetic and alphasyllabic languages, poor readers tend to be less precise in phonemic discrimination, have problems in a variety of phoneme segmentation and awareness tasks (Nag & Snowling, 2011; Wagner, Torgeson, & Rashotte, 1994), and are slower in rapid naming of objects, digits, and letters (Wolf & O'Brien, 2001), as well as in producing rhyming words (Lundberg & Hoien, 2001). Failure to develop such aspects of language awareness can be considered early risk factors for developmental dyslexia, but the level of awareness that is critical for literacy development is dependent on the writing system. During the early stages of learning to read, a lack of phoneme awareness signals a risk for alphabetic reading, whereas for Chinese and alphasyllabic reading, reduced syllabic awareness is the more relevant signal. We thus observe a phonological component for developmental dyslexia across those languages with variation in the level of phonology that is encoded in the writing system (cf. Verhoeven, Perfetti, & Pugh, 2019). In addition, the research on dyslexia points to a biological source with genetic transmission, which at a very early age may result in a phonological deficit affecting learning to read (Grigorenko, 2022). In terms of the implications of this fact for global literacy, it is important to understand this: Despite a genetic component, the variability in reading achievement among poor readers and children with dyslexia is due to environmental factors that vary around the globe (Nag, 2022).

Obstacles to literacy vary with sociocultural and linguistic contexts. For example, it is important to take into account the sociolinguistic position of ethnic minorities when considering their literacy achievements (cf. Geva & Verhoeven, 2000). Lexical, grammatical, and discourse abilities are critical for people from ethnic minorities who must learn to read and write in an unfamiliar (second) language. In fact, individuals acquiring literacy in a second language are faced with a dual task. Besides the written code, they must learn the grammatical and discourse competencies specific to the second language. In many cases children learning to read in a second language are less efficient in the target language than are native-language-speaking peers. Thus, it can be hypothesized that L2 learners have difficulty in using (meta)linguistic cues while reading. Limited oral proficiency in a second language may also influence the various subprocesses of reading (cf. Droop & Verhoeven, 2003). With respect to word recognition and word spelling, there can be difficulties in the mediation of relevant phonological skills, resulting in a slow rate of acquisition of sound–symbol mapping rules. There can also be difficulties in the use of orthographic constraints due to a restricted awareness of phonotactic or phonological distribution rules in the second language. Furthermore, there may be differences between first- and second-language readers in the higher-order processes that follow the identification of words due to restricted lexical and syntactic knowledge, or limited background knowledge. These difficulties, as for first-language learners, impact reading and writing skills among L2 learners when parsing sentences into their constituents and finding the underlying propositions and vice versa.

1.3 Bio-ecological Markers of Literacy Development

On a global scale, the variation in literacy development can be explained by both innate child factors and environmental or ecological factors. A bio-ecological model highlighting the intermediate role of self-regulatory mechanisms in child development comes from Bronfenbrenner and Ceci (1994). This model recognizes direct learner and environmental measures and mechanisms of learner–environment interaction, called proximal processes (cf. Bronfenbrenner, 2005). These processes originate from the family or educational institutions, through which biological potentials are transformed into self-regulatory functions that determine children's social-communicative and cognitive growth. In this section, we first review the impact of learner characteristics, family support, educational support, and the role of sociopolitical context. We then describe an explanatory framework for the global variation in literacy.

1.3.1 Learner Characteristics

Genetics As we noted above, some of the variation in literacy development and, specifically, developmental dyslexia can be attributed to genetic predispositions. Literacy development and literacy problems are at least partly dependent on the transmission of the genomic information of DNA sequences from one generation to the other (Olson, 2016). The role of genetics in this intergenerational transmission has been evidenced in molecular genetic studies, behavioral genetic studies within twins and families, and more recently in imaging genetic studies. However, nongenetic factors play important roles in influencing gene functions and modifying heritability. In combination, the effects of these self-regulatory factors result in various phenotypes of literacy abilities (Hoeft & Wang, 2019).

Executive Functioning Neurobiological factors may not only affect literacy development directly, but also indirectly via learner executive functioning and language proficiency. Executive functions include sustained attention, working memory, inhibition, cognitive flexibility, and planning (Lehto et al., 2003; Miyake et al., 2000). There is research evidence that effortful control improves children's metalinguistic awareness and early literacy skills (cf. Goswami, 2000). Furthermore, Share (2004) showed that the emergence of early literacy skills can be seen as a self-teaching device that builds on children's self-regulated learning, which supports a growing phonological awareness and insight into the mapping principle of the writing system. Research highlights the importance of executive functions for reading comprehension after taking variance in decoding and language skills into account. It has also been found that working memory and planning uniquely contribute to reading comprehension whereas working memory and inhibition also support decoding (e.g., Cutting et al., 2009; Kieffer, Vukovic, & Berry, 2013).

Language Proficiency Learners' language proficiency can be seen as another prominent predictor of literacy development. Knowledge of word meanings, or in other words vocabulary skill, is particularly critical for advanced literacy skills, that is, reading comprehension and writing. Both the reading comprehension and writing of children and adults are supported by knowledge of words, which may include the precision of the reader's orthographic, phonological, and semantic representations. According to the lexical-quality hypothesis (Perfetti & Hart, 2001), both the quality of the reader's lexical representations and the quantity of words in the mental lexicon affect reading comprehension and writing. Several studies testing the "simple reading view" show a clear word decoding by listening comprehension interaction for beginning versus proficient readers. The role of word decoding in the explanation of reading comprehension is found to be large for beginning readers while the role of listening comprehension is found to be more prominent for proficient readers (cf. Carver, 1993; Tunmer & Hoover, 1993). In a similar vein, research testing the "simple view of writing" has evidenced that productive oral-language skills predict both the mechanics (handwriting and spelling) and higher-order-composition processes of writing (Berninger et al., 2002; Pressley et al., 2001).

Second-Language Proficiency Minority groups must often communicate in the dominant language of the majority environment to function in daily life. The dominant language is typically acquired as a second language. Importantly, minority children faced with the task of learning to read and write in a second language (L2) are confronted by a dual task: mastery of not only the basic written code for the second language but also the grammatical and discourse rules which characterize the second language. In many cases, minority children may have only a limited oral mastery of the second language – particularly when compared to their nonminority peers – which means that their use of oral cues from the second language to read and write may be limited as well. That is, limited oral proficiency in a second language may interfere with various literacy subprocesses. With respect to word decoding, for example, limited auditory discrimination of phonemes or tones may lead to slow acquisition of grapheme–phoneme correspondence rules or tone knowledge, and thus word decoding. Similarly, restricted lexical and syntactic knowledge may lead to problems with the parsing of sentences and the comprehension and production of written text (see Chen, Dronjic, & Helms-Park, 2016; Geva & Verhoeven, 2000).

1.3.2 Home Support

Socioeconomic Status Socioeconomic status (SES) has a great impact on children's school outcomes. A positive association between family wealth and background and children's achievement has been universally evidenced (e.g., Rolleston, James, & Aurino, 2013). However, the magnitude of the association is dependent on the social context and education system. In general, the achievement gap between students from different backgrounds appears more pronounced in education systems where overall inequality (e.g., income inequality) is strong (see Broer, Bai, & Fonseca, 2019). For example, Dolean et al. (2019) examined how SES is related to the development of reading skills in Roma children, who face severe poverty in comparison with mainstream children. They found that the Roma children had both poorer initial reading and a slower growth of their reading skills. They demonstrated that SES did explain growth in reading skills after controlling for other well-known cognitive and linguistic predictors of reading. However, the effects of SES on reading growth were partly mediated by school absence. This suggests that interventions directed to children facing severe poverty need to target both the quality of reading instruction and broader aspects of what prevents regular school attendance. In addition, a positive relationship between parents' education level and children's reading-comprehension achievement was found (Dearing et al., 2006; Hindman et al., 2010).

Language Exposure Another important indicator of family support is language exposure in the family. Language input in and outside the home environment affects children's L1 and L2 development (Lesaux & Geva, 2006). De Cat (2020) showed how various channels of language input in the home environment, such as communication between and with family members and communication with people outside the family, may influence children's second-language development. Socioeconomic status interacted in complex ways with language exposure: Only above a certain level of exposure to the school language did the benefits of a more privileged background have a tangible impact on school-language proficiency. In a survey of studies on children's literacy development in low- and middle-income countries, Nag et al. (2018) concluded that a match between linguistic experience in the child's home and the linguistic demands in the classroom is essential for academic progress. However, they found the home-language advantage to be context sensitive. Multiple risk factors, including feelings of unease and disempowerment, characterized a home- and school-language disconnection, and positive intervention effects following guided support were related to the amount of time spent on tutoring, and parents' increased confidence to home tutor.

Home Literacy Environment Research on the relationship between family characteristics and children's literacy development has focused on how and to what degree the family creates an effective home-learning environment (Dickinson & Neuman, 2006; Nag et al., 2018; Puglisi et al., 2017). Parental literacy expectations enhance children's reading-comprehension performance through literacy knowledge acquisition (cf. Englund et al., 2004). Furthermore, the supply of home literacy resources, such as the literacy environment and literacy materials available at home, contributes to children's literacy-knowledge development (Johnson et al., 2008; Strasser & Lissi, 2009). In a meta-analysis of fifty-nine studies Dong et al. (2020) examined the effects of home literacy environment (HLE) factors on children's reading comprehension. They found a moderate positive correlation between HLE and children's reading comprehension. Types of home literacy resources and parental involvement styles did not show a significant interaction effect between each HLE factor and children's reading outcomes. However, literacy expectations and parent involvement had a significantly higher association with children's reading comprehension than home literacy resources did.

The cross-national impact of home support on literacy development, including distributed home-tutoring roles in extended families, was evidenced by Borgonovi and Montt (2012) in the context of PISA data. They generally found that reading to young children and reading at home enhanced literacy at preschool and in the primary grades, and that engaging older children in discussions had a significant impact on their advanced literacy development. Involved parents were found to be more receptive to language and more adept at planning, monitoring, and evaluation of literacy activities, which helped children learn how to learn throughout the literacy curriculum. Interestingly, they found that levels of parental involvement varied across countries and economies, suggesting that high-quality parental involvement may help reduce performance differences across socioeconomic groups. Finally, it is important to note that parental interactive literacy involvement may particularly support children's literacy development in disadvantaged groups (Johnson et al., 2008; Manz et al., 2010; Mendive et al., 2020; Sénéchal, 2006) although not enough is known when parents cannot read or do not know the child's school language (Nag et al., 2018). From an intervention perspective, interventions that supplement school programmes with a home-based component targeting home tutoring, supply of materials, and/or parent–teacher meetings are becoming increasingly common. In studies that target the home environment through supply or skills training (e.g., library books, shared book-reading-skill training), results were promising. Most broad-based school/home/community interventions appear to have immediate effects on component skills of literacy and this effect is seen across preschool and the early grades (Nag et al., 2018).

1.3.3 School Support

Language of Instruction Due to continuous processes of migration, colonization, and decolonization, as well as of internationalization, the number of linguistic minorities continues to increase. For children of linguistic minorities, literacy can be taught in the home language and/or in the mainstream language spoken in the wider community. Answers to the questions of whether one or more languages are used for instruction, and which language and literacy abilities are educational objectives for minority children, depend on school policies. It can be argued that the acquisition of literacy will be facilitated when the instruction links up with the linguistic background of the child. Moreover, the child's motivation and self-concept may increase if the instruction is given in the native language. Importantly, there can be linguistic transfer in bilingual reading instruction. Children who have learned the mapping principle for one language and its writing system do not have to start from scratch in another language and writing system: What they do have to learn is a new mapping code. With respect to the acquisition of academic language skills, Cummins (1979: 233) has hypothesized the role of interdependence to be as follows:

To the extent that instruction in a certain language is effective in promoting proficiency in that language, transfer of this proficiency to another language will occur, provided there is adequate exposure to that other language (either in the school or environment) and adequate motivation to learn that language.

The interdependence hypothesis predicts that optimal input in one language leads not only to better skills in that language but also to a deeper conceptual and linguistic proficiency that can clearly facilitate the transfer of various cognitive and academic language skills across languages. A high level of linguistic competence in the first language may thus enhance the development of the second language. However, if skills in the first language are not well developed and education in the early years is in the second language, the further development of the second language may stagnate (see also Cummins, 1991). Importantly, most researchers currently accept the assumption of at least a partially overlapping organization of bilingual memory (Durgunoglu & Goldenberg, 2011; French & Jacquet, 2004) and the assumption of nonselective linguistic access, that is, the assumption that linguistic structures in both languages may be accessed simultaneously (Bialystok, 2001; Verhoeven, 2007).

Classroom Resources To improve the chances for universal literacy to be attained, providing basic education is a primary task. Classroom instruction presents children with a new set of interpersonal relationships and provide them with the opportunity to use language in a meaningful way and to receive feedback from professional teachers. It is essential to provide the child with continuous classroom resources while avoiding abrupt changes. To realize adequate education in functional literacy, appropriate curricula are needed. The pursuit of continuity in basic education requires that special attention is given to the transitional stages between preschool, junior or primary level, intermediate or middle-school level, and senior or secondary-school level. Close cooperation between preschool institutions in the area of home–school connections can help harmonize literary socialization (UNESCO, 2017). In the pursuit of continuity, the position of children from high-risk backgrounds requires more attention (Thompson et al., 2019). This includes children from socioeconomically weak communities, ethnic minority groups, and those with specific reading and writing problems. Korat (2005) examined the link between socioeconomic status and classroom instruction on emerging literacy skills in prekindergarten children. Compared with their higher-SES peers, low-SES children had poorer emergent literacy knowledge. However, later word recognition and emergent writing were predicted by phonemic awareness, knowledge of letter names, and concept of print knowledge, and not by SES group.

Teacher Responsivity Formal education is generally aimed at developing motivated, well-adjusted learners who are able to adapt to the changing demands and rules of the school system (see Verhoeven & Snow, 2001). The attainment of literacy can be stimulated and extended by offering children a school environment where children can enhance the positive literacy experiences they have had prior to school (Piasta & Wagner, 2010). School effectiveness can be considered an important outcome measure of teacher responsivity. Effective literacy teaching presupposes a balance between instructive learning situations in which direct instruction and exercises are required and constructive learning situations in which routines and anchors are used to deal with the learning questions of students (Kinzer & Verhoeven, 2007. Instructive learning situations ensure that knowledge and skills are learned and automatized. These more closed learning situations provide a program-oriented education in which the emphasis is on working with methodical materials in which the subject matter is offered in a more or less fixed order. For example, for the alphabetic languages, especially English, direct phonics instruction has been shown to be highly effective when students need to learn and automatize skills (Castles et al., 2018).

Constructive learning situations offer children the opportunity to use their knowledge and skills and apply strategies in a meaningful context; they also lay the foundation for a learning community and contribute to the advancement of functional literacy (Vágvölgyi et al., 2016). Seen in this light, responsiveness is the main quality of a competent teacher. By showing how to attack the coding or decoding of words, or by modeling problem-solving strategies, the teacher may enable children to master reading comprehension and writing. Through recurrent practice, teachers may learn to attune to the specific needs of children with literacy problems. Indeed, the teacher's educational level, teaching experience, language proficiency, and sociocultural orientation may have an impact on both their own responsiveness and the children's literacy learning (Lemberger & Reyes-Carrasquillo, 2011; Nag et al., 2016).

1.3.4 Sociopolitical Context

To advance literacy as an integral part of lifelong learning and the 2030 Agenda for Sustainable Development, UNESCO takes the following approaches to promoting literacy worldwide, with an emphasis on youth and adults: (1) providing quality basic education for all children; (2) building strong foundations through early childhood care and education; (3) scaling up functional

Introduction 21

literacy levels for youth and adults who lack basic literacy skills; and (4) developing literate environments. However, the worldwide support of literacy cannot be viewed without taking into account the sociopolitical context and the political will for system-wide change (e.g., Silberstein, 2021). National surveys in societies anywhere on the development scale show that literacy practices are embedded in unequal structures of power (e.g., Wickens & Sandlin, 2007). Even when literacy is viewed from an economic or technological point of view, its social context is important because it affects the engagement of cognitive processes, the outcome of economic measures, and individuals' quality of life. This importance lies in both sociopolitical aspects of development and the concerns of different communities and individuals (Street, 1994). Indeed, literacy practices occur within cultural and power structures in society and may function to serve those structures. Thus, literacy is a complex cultural and psychological process deeply affecting the transformation of societies and the development of individuals (e.g., Goody, 1968).

From a sociopolitical point of view, the debate on bilingual education must also be evaluated. Policymakers across the world have looked on home language instruction as a temporary support for low-SES minority children. Their focus has been on bridging the mismatch in language use in the home and at school while aiming at higher results in the majority language. However, home language instruction can also be conceived as a cultural policy in which minority languages are valued in their own right. From a cultural perspective, home language instruction can be defined as a structural support for children with a nonnative home language, independent of socioeconomic background. Contribution to first-language learning is then an autonomous goal, while first-language proficiency is seen as a school subject and accordingly evaluated (cf. Durgunoglu & Goldenberg, 2011).

1.3.5 Toward a General Explanatory Framework

To build a research agenda regarding the global variation in literacy we propose a general framework that organizes the systems that influence the development of literacy within larger sociocultural/economic/political contexts. In Figure 1.5, we show that literacy development involves gaining reading fluency and spelling to facilitate reading comprehension and writing, that it builds on language, and that child characteristics and home and school support factors combine to influence individual variation, within an indirectly influential sociopolitical context.

The framework assumes that multiple influences are operating across the stages of literacy development. Importantly, as we noted before, reading comprehension builds on reading fluency, and text writing on spelling, from the early stages on. The more proximal influences (e.g., child characteristics, teacher support) are embedded in a set of human ethology contexts ranging

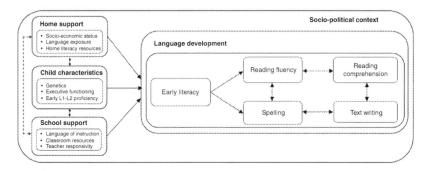

Figure 1.5 General explanatory framework for the global variation of literacy

across local communities to regional, national, and global economic and political structures. Because of this ethological embedding, these influences are not fully independent. As a case in point, there is continuous interaction between home-support and school-support factors in areas such as what is tutored and what is valued in each setting. It is thus necessary to examine not only the impact of isolated factors, but also the degree to which factors interact to affect literacy development.

1.4 The Present Volume

Cognitive and neurocognitive research has provided theoretical models for processes of literacy acquisition. In recent years, progress has come from a broadening of the research base to include literacy learning across languages and writing systems across country contexts. This progress has set the stage for the present goal of bringing together observations of the global variation in literacy development within cross-national, cross-linguistic and cross-writing systems perspectives. These perspectives allow considerations of literacy development in both its universal aspects and the variations that arise around the globe. The sources of variation – sociocultural, sociopolitical, socioeconomic, language background, educational opportunities – operate within regions and across regions.

In this volume, we bring together various perspectives on global variation while also aiming for a common framework to describe literacy development that recognizes demographic boundaries in the world, on the one hand, and its global variation as a function of bio-ecological markers on the other. In the first part of this volume (Part I), we draw attention to the wealth of recent research on variations in literacy development that arise across regions and that reflect multiple interrelated influences of individual, home, school, and societal factors. This regional focus includes literacy development in North America, Latin America and the Caribbean, Europe and Central Asia, sub-Saharan Africa, South Asia, East Asia, and the Pacific. The second part of the volume (Part II) brings together observations on the neurobiological and ecological markers related to global literacy as described in Part I. These include the role of writing systems, genetics, brain foundations, self-regulation, and sociocultural, contextual, teacher, and parental factors in global literacy development.

This volume closes with a final chapter highlighting the commonalities found in the research on the regional variations in global literacy development, and on the neurobiological and ecological factors explaining these variations.

References

Berman, R. A., & Verhoeven, L. (2002). Cross-linguistic perspectives on the development of text-production abilities. *Written Language and Literacy*, 5, 1–43.

Berninger, V. W., & Winn, W. D. (2006). Implications of advancements in brain research and technology for writing development, writing instruction, and educational evolution. In C. A. MacArthur, S. Graham, & J. Fitzgerald (eds.), *Handbook of writing research* (pp. 96–114). New York: The Guilford Press.

Berninger, V., Vaughan, K., Abbott, R. et al. (2002). Teaching spelling and composition alone and together: Implications for the simple view of writing. *Journal of Educational Psychology*, 94, 291–304.

Bhide, A., Luo, W., Vijay, N. et al. (2019). Improving Hindi decoding skills via a mobile game. *Reading and Writing: An Interdisciplinary Journal*, 32, 2149–2178. DOI: https://doi.org/10.1007/s11145-019-09934-x.

Bialystok, E. (2001). *Bilingualism in Development: Language, Literacy, and Cognition*. Cambridge: Cambridge University Press. DOI: https://doi.org/10.1017/CBO9780511605963.

Borgonovi, F., & Montt, G. (2012). Parental involvement in selected PISA countries and economies. OECD Education Working Papers 73. Paris: OECD Publishing. DOI: https://doi.org/10.1787/5k990rk0jsjj-en.

Broer, M., Bai, Y., & Fonseca, F. (2019) A review of the literature on socioeconomic status and educational achievement. In *Socioeconomic Inequality and Educational Outcomes*. IEA Research for Education. Series of In-depth Analyses Based on Data of the International Association for the Evaluation of Educational Achievement, vol 5. Cham: Springer. DOI: https://doi.org/10.1007/978-3-030-11991-1_2.

Bronfenbrenner, U. (2005). The developing ecology of human development: Paradigm lost or paradigm regained. In U. Bronfenbrenner (ed.), *Making Human Beings Human: Bioecological Perspectives on Human Development* (pp. 94–105). Thousand Oaks, CA: Sage.

Bronfenbrenner, U., & Ceci, S. J. (1994). Nature-nurture reconceptualized in developmental perspective: A bioecological model. *Psychological Review*, 101, 568–586.

Butvilovsky, S. A., Escamilla, K., Gumina,D., & Silva Diaz, E. (2021). Beyond monolingual reading assessments for emerging bilingual learners: Expanding the understanding of biliteracy assessment through writing. *Reading Research Quarterly*, 56, 53–70. DOI: https://doi.org/10.1002/rrq.292.

Cain, K., & Barnes, M. A. (2017). Reading comprehension: What develops and when? In K. Cain, D. Compton, & R. Parrila (eds.), *Theories of Reading Development* (pp. 257–282). Amsterdam: John Benjamins.

Carver, R. P. (1993). Merging the simple view of reading with rauding theory. *Journal of Reading Behavior*, 25(4), 439–455.

Castles, A., Rastle, K., & Nation, K. (2018). Ending the reading wars: Reading acquisition from novice to expert. *Psychological Science in the Public Interest*, *19*, 5–51. DOI: https://doi.org/10.1177/1529100618772271.

Chen, X., Dronjic, V., & Helms-Park, R. (2016). *Reading in a Second Language: Cognitive and Psycholinguistic Issues*. New York: Routledge.

Chenoweth, N. A., & Hayes, J. R. (2001). Fluency in writing generating text in L1 and L2. *Written Communication*, *18*, 80–98.

Clark, E. (2004). How language acquisition builds on cognitive development. *Trends in Cognitive Sciences*, *8*, 472–478.

Coltheart, M., Rastle, K., Perry, C., Langdon, R., & Ziegler, J. (2001). DRC: A dual route cascaded model of visual word recognition and reading aloud. *Psychological Review*, *108*, 204–256. DOI: https://doi.org/10.1037/0033-295X.108.1.204.

Cummins, J. (1979). Linguistic interdependence and the educational development of bilingual children. *Review of Educational Research*, *49*(2), 222–251. DOI: https://doi.org/10.2307/1169960.

Cummins, J. (1991). Interdependence of first- and second-language proficiency in bilingual children. In E. Bialystok (ed.), *Language Processing in Bilingual Children* (pp. 70–89). Cambridge: Cambridge University Press. DOI https://doi.org/10.1017/CBO9780511620652.006.

Cutting, L. E., Materek, A., Cole, C. A. S., Levine, T. M., & Mahone, E. M. (2009). Effects of fluency, oral language, and executive function on reading comprehension performance. *Annals of Dyslexia*, *59*, 34–54. DOI: http://dx.doi.org/10.1007/s11881-009-0022-0.

De Cat, C. (2020). Predicting language proficiency in bilingual children. *Studies in Second Language Acquisition*, *42*, 279–325. DOI: http://dx.doi.org/10.1017/S0272263119000597.

Dearing, E., Kreider, H., Simpkins, S., & Weiss, H. B. (2006). Family involvement in school and low-income children's literacy performance: Longitudinal associations between and within families. *Journal of Educational Psychology*, *98*, 653–664.

Dickinson, D. K., & Neuman, S. B. (2006). *Handbook of Early Literacy Research*. New York: Guilford Press.

Dolean, D., Melby-Lervag, M., Tincas, I., Damsa, C., & Lervag, A. (2019). Achievement gap: Socioeconomic status affects reading development beyond language and cognition in children facing poverty. *Learning and Instruction*, *63*, e0101218. DOI: https://doi.org/10.1016/j.learninstruc.2019.101218.

Dong, Y., Wu, S. X.-Y., Dong, W.-Y., & Tang, Y. (2020). The effects of home literacy environment on children's reading comprehension development: A meta-analysis. *Educational Sciences: Theory and Practice*, *20*, 63–82. DOI: http://dx.doi.org/10.12738/jestp.2020.2.005.

Droop, M., & Verhoeven, L. (2003). Language proficiency and reading comprehension in first and second language learners. *Reading Research Quarterly*, *38*, 78–103.

Durgunoglu, A., & Goldenberg, C. (2011). *Language and Literacy Development in Bilingual Settings*. New York: Guilford.

Ehri, L., Nunes, R. S., Willows, D. et al. (2001). Phonemic awareness instruction helps children learn to read: Evidence from the National Reading Panel's meta-analysis. *Reading Research Quarterly, 36*, 250–287.

Ehri, L. C. (2005). Learning to read words: Theory, findings and issues. *Scientific Studies of Reading, 9*, 167–189.

Englund, M. M., Luckner, A. E., Whaley, G. J. L., & Egeland, B. (2004). Children's achievement in early elementary school: Longitudinal effects of parental involvement, expectations, and quality of assistance. *Journal of Educational Psychology, 96* (4), 723–730. DOI: https://doi.org/10.1037/0022-0663.96.4.723.

European Union. (2019). *PISA 2018 and the EU*. Brussels: Directorate-General for Education, Youth, Sport and Culture.

Fishman, J. A. (1999). *Handbook of Language and Ethnic Identity*. New York: Oxford University Press.

French, R. M., & Jacquet, M. (2004). Understanding bilingual memory: Models and data. *Trends in Cognitive Sciences, 8*(2), 87–93. DOI: https://doi.org/10.1016/j.tics.2003.12.011.

Geva, E., & Verhoeven, L. (2000). Introduction: The development of second language reading in primary children. *Scientific Studies of Reading, 4*, 261–266.

Goody, J. (1968). *Literacy in Traditional Societies*. Cambridge: Cambridge University Press.

Goswami, U. (2000). Phonological and lexical processes. In M. L. Kamil, P. B. Rosenthal, P. D. Pearson, & R. Barr (eds.), *Handbook of Reading Research*, Vol. III, pp. 251–268). Mahwah, NJ: Lawrence Erlbaum Associates.

Graham, S., Morphy, P., Harris, K. R. et al. (2008). Teaching spelling in the primary grades: A national survey of instructional practices and adaptations. *American Educational Research Journal, 45*(3), 796–825. DOI: https://doi.org/10.3102/0002831208319722.

Grigorenko, E. L. (2022). The role of genetic factors in reading and its development across languages and writing systems. *Scientific Studies of Reading, 26*(2), 96–110. DOI:https://doi.org/10.1080/10888438.2022.2033244.

Guthrie, J. T., & Humenick, N. M. (2004). Motivating students to read: Evidence for classroom practices that increase reading motivation and achievement. In P. McCardle & V. Chhabra (eds.), *The Voice of Evidence in Reading Research* (pp. 329–354). Washington, DC: Paul H. Brookes Publishing Co.

Hayes, J. R. (2012). My past and present as writing researcher and thoughts about the future of writing research. In V. W. Berninger (ed.), *Past, Present, and Future Contributions of Cognitive Writing Research to Cognitive Psychology* (pp. 3-26). New York: Psychology Press.

Hindman, A. H., Skibbe, L. E., Miller, A., & Zimmerman, M. (2010). Ecological contexts and early learning: Contributions of child, family, and classroom factors during Head Start to literacy and mathematics growth through first grade. *Early Childhood Research Quarterly, 25*, 235–250.

Hoeft, F., & Wang, C. (2019). Intergenerational transmission in developmental dyslexia. In L. Verhoeven, C., Perfetti, & K. Pugh (eds.) *Developmental Dyslexia across*

Languages and Writing Systems (pp. 413–438). Cambridge: Cambridge University Press.

Hoover, W. A., & Gough, P. B. (1990). The simple view of reading. *Reading and Writing*, *2*, 127–160.

Johnson, A. D., Martin, A., Brooks-Gunn, J., & Petrill, S. A. (2008). Order in the house! Associations among household chaos, the home literacy environment, maternal reading ability, and children's early reading. *Merrill-Palmer Quarterly*, *54*, 445–472. DOI: https://doi.org/10.1353/mpq.0.0009.

Jusczyk, P. W. (1997). *The Discovery of Spoken Language*. Cambridge, MA: MIT Press.

Kieffer, M. J., Vukovic, R. K., & Berry, D. (2013). Roles of attention shifting and inhibitory control in fourth-grade reading comprehension. *Reading Research Quarterly*, *48*, 333–348.

Kinzer, C., & Verhoeven, L. (eds.) (2007). *Interactive Literacy Education: Facilitating Literacy Environments through Technology*. Mahwah, NJ: Lawrence Erlbaum Associates.

Korat, O. (2005). Contextual and non-contextual knowledge in emergent literacy development: A comparison between children from low SES and middle SES communities. *Early Childhood Research Quarterly*, *20*(2), 220–238. DOI: https://doi.org/10.1016/j.ecresq.2005.04.009.

Lehto, J. E., Juujärvi, P., Kooistra, L., & Pulkkinen, L. (2003). Dimensions of executive functioning: Evidence from children. *British Journal of Developmental Psychology*, *21*, 59–80. DOI: https://doi.org/10.1348/026151003321164627.

Lemberger, N., & Reyes-Carrasquillo, A. (2011). Perspectives on teacher quality: Bilingual education and ESL teacher certification, test-taking experiences, and instructional practices. *Journal of Multilingual Education Research*, *2*, Article 5. https://research.library.fordham.edu/jmer/vol2/iss1/5.

Lervåg, A., Hulme, C., & Melby-Lervåg, M. (2018). Unpicking the developmental relationship between oral language skills and reading comprehension: It's simple, but complex. *Child Development*, *8*, 1821–1838. DOI: https://doi.org/10.1111/cdev.12861.

Lesaux, N. K., & Geva, E. (2006). Synthesis: Development of literacy in language-minority students. In D. August & T. Shanahan (eds.), *Developing Literacy in Second-Language Learners: Report of the National Literacy Panel on Language-Minority Children and Youth* (pp. 53–74). Mahwah, NJ: Lawrence Erlbaum Associates.

Lundberg, I., & Hoien, T. (2001). Dyslexia and phonology. In A. Fawcett (ed.), *Dyslexia: Theory and Good Practice* (pp. 109–123). London: Whurr Publishers.

Manz, P. H., Hughes, C., Barnabas, E., Bracaliello, C., & Ginsburg-Block, M. (2010). A descriptive review and meta-analysis of family-based emergent literacy interventions: To what extent is the research applicable to low-income, ethnic-minority or linguistically- diverse young children? *Early Childhood Research Quarterly*, *25*, 409–431. DOI: http://dx.doi.org/10.1016/j.ecresq.2010.03.002.

McBride, C. A. (2016). Is Chinese special? Four aspects of Chinese literacy acquisition that might distinguish learning Chinese from learning alphabetic orthographies. *Educational Psychology Review*, *28*(3), 523–549. DOI: https://doi.org/10.1007/s10648-015-9318-2.

McBride-Chang, C., Tong, X., Shu, H., et al. (2008). Syllable, phoneme, and tone: Psycholinguistic units in early Chinese and English word recognition. *Scientific Studies of Reading*, 12, 171–194. DOI:https://doi.org/10.1080/10888430801917290.

Mendive, S., Lara, M. M., Aldoney, D., Perez, J. C. & Pezoa, J. P. (2020). Home language and literacy environments and early literacy trajectories of low-socioeconomic status Chilean children. *Child Development*, 91(6), 2042–2062.

Metsala, J. L., & Walley, A. C. (1998). Spoken vocabulary growth and the segmental restructuring of lexical representations: Precursors to phonemic awareness and early reading ability. In J. L. Metsala & L. C. Ehri (eds.), *Word Recognition in Beginning Literacy* (pp. 89–120). Mahwah, NJ: Lawrence Erlbaum Associates.

Miyake, A., Friedman, N. P., Emerson. M. J. et al. (2000). The unity and diversity of executive functions and their contributions to complex "Frontal Lobe" tasks: A latent variable analysis. *Cognitive Psychology*, 41, 49–100. DOI: http://dx.doi.org/10.1006/cogp.1999.0734. PMID: 10945922.

Mohanty, A. K. (2000). Perpetuating inequality: The disadvantage of language, minority mother tongues and related issues. In A. K. Mohanty & G. Misra (eds.), *Psychology of Poverty and Disadvantage* (pp. 104–117). New Delhi: Concept Publishing.

Nag, S. (2017). Learning to read alphasyllabaries. In K., Cain, D. Compton, & R. Parrila (eds.), *Theories of Reading Development* (pp. 75–98). Amsterdam: John Benjamins.

Nag, S. (2021). How children learn to use a writing system: Mapping evidence from an Indic orthography to written language in children's books. *Written Language and Literacy*, 24, 284–302.

Nag, S. (2022). Dyslexia and the dyslexia-like picture: Supporting all children in primary school. In M. A. Skeide (ed.), *The Cambridge Handbook of Dyslexia and Dyscalculia* (pp. 427–443). Cambridge: Cambridge University Press.

Nag, S., Chiat, S., Torgerson, C., & Snowling, M. (2014). *Literacy, Foundation Learning and Assessment in Developing Countries: Final Report*. London: EPPI-Centre, Social Science Research Unit, University of London. www.gov.uk/government/uploads/system/uploads/attachment_data/file/305150/Literacy-foundation-learning-assessment.pdf.

Nag, S., & Narayanan, B. (2019). Orthographic knowledge, spelling and reading development in Tamil: The first three years. In M. Joshi & C. McBride (eds). *Handbook of Literacy in Akshara Orthography* (pp. 55–83). Dordrecht: Springer.

Nag, S., & Snowling, M. (July 2011). Cognitive profiles of poor readers of Kannada. *Reading and Writing: an Interdisciplinary Journal*, 24(6), 657–676. DOI: http://dx.doi.org/10.1007/s11145-010-9258-7.

Nag, S., Snowling, M. J., & Asfaha, Y. (2016). Classroom literacy practices in low- and middle-income countries: An interpretative synthesis of ethnographic studies. *Oxford Education Review*, 42(1), 36–54. DOI: http://dx.doi.org/10.1080/03054985.2015.1135115.

Nag, S., Snowling, M., Quinlan, P., & Hulme, C. (2014). Child and symbol factors in learning to read a visually complex writing system. *Scientific Studies of Reading*, 18, 1–16. DOI: http://dx.doi.org/10.1080/10888438.2014.892489.

Nag, S., Vagh, S., Dulay, K., & Snowling, M. (2018). Home language, school language and children's literacy attainments: A systematic review of evidence from low- and middle-income countries. *Review of Education*, 1(1), 91–150. DOI:https://doi.org/10.1002/rev3.3130.

NEP (National Education Policy). (2020). Ministry of Human Resource Development, Government of India. www.education.gov.in/sites/upload_files/mhrd/files/NEP_Final_English_0.pdf.

NICHD (National Institute of Child Health and Human Development). (2000). *Teaching Children to Read: An Evidence-Based Assessment of the Scientific Research Literature on Reading and its Implications for Reading Instruction: Reports of the Subgroups*. (NIH Publication No. 00–4754). Washington, DC: US Government Printing Office.

Olson, D. R. (2016). *The Mind on Paper: Reading, Consciousness and Rationality*. Cambridge: Cambridge University Press. DOI: http://dx.doi.org/10.1017/CBO9781316678466.

Perfetti, C., & Stafura, J. (2014). Word knowledge in a theory of reading comprehension. *Scientific Studies of Reading*, *18*(1), 22–37. DOI: https://doi.org/10.1080/10888438.2013.827687.

Perfetti, C. A. (2003). The universal grammar of reading. *Scientific Studies of Reading*, *7*, 3–24.

Perfetti, C. A., & Hart, L. (2001). The lexical quality hypothesis. In L. Verhoeven, C. Elbro, & P. Reitsma (eds.), *Precursors of Functional Literacy* (pp. 189–214). Amsterdam: John Benjamins.

Piasta, S. B., & Wagner, R. K. (2010). Developing early literacy skills: A meta-analysis of alphabet learning and instruction. *Reading Research Quarterly*, *45*(1), 8–38. DOI: https://doi.org/10.1598/RRQ.45.1.2.

Pressley, M., Wharton-MacDonald, R., Allington, R., et al. (2001). A study of effective first grade literacy instruction. *Scientific Studies in Reading*, *5*, 35–58.

Puglisi, M. L., Hulme, C., Hamilton, L. G., & Snowling, M. J. (2017). The home literacy environment is a correlate, but perhaps not a cause, of variations in children's language and literacy development. *Scientific Studies of Reading*, *21*(6), 498–514. DOI: https://doi.org/10.1080/10888438.2017.1346660.

Quinn, J. M., & Wagner, R. K. (2018). Using meta-analytic structural equation modeling to study developmental change in relations between language and literacy. *Child Development*, *89*, 1956–1969. DOI: https://doi.org/10.1111/cdev.13049.

Rolleston, C., James, Z., & Aurino, E. (2013). *Exploring the Effect of Educational Opportunity and Inequality on learning Outcomes in Ethiopia, Peru, India and Vietnam*. Paris: United Nations Educational, Scientific and Cultural Organization (UNESCO). https://unesdoc.unesco.org/ark:/48223/pf0000225938.

Roser, M., & Ortiz-Ospina, E. (2016). Literacy. *OurWorldInData.org*. https://ourworldindata.org/literacy.

Rowe, M., & Weisleder, A. (2020). Language development in context. *Annual Review of Developmental Psychology 2*, 201–223.

Scarborough, H. S. (2005). Developmental relationships between language and reading: Reconciling a beautiful hypothesis with some ugly facts. In H. W. Catts & A. G. Kamhi (eds.), *The Connections between Language and Reading Disabilities* (pp. 3–24). Mahwah, NJ: Lawrence Erlbaum Associates.

Seidenberg, M. (2017). *Language at the Speed of Sight: How We Read, Why So Many Can't, and What Can Be Done About It*. New York: Basic Books.

Sénéchal, M. (2006). Testing the home literacy model: Parent involvement in kindergarten is differentially related to Grade 4 reading comprehension, fluency, spelling, and reading for pleasure. *Scientific Studies of Reading, 10*, 59–87. DOI: https://doi.org/10.1207/s1532799xssr1001_4.

Share, D. L. (2004). Orthographic learning at a glance: On the time course and developmental onset of reading. *Journal of Experimental Child Psychology, 87*, 267–298.

Silberstein, J. (2021). Measuring, visualising, and simulating solutions to the learning crisis: New evidence from learning profiles in 18 countries. *Research on Improving Systems of Education (RISE)*. 2021/029. DOI: https://doi.org/10.35489/BSG-RISE-RI_2021/029.

Smith, P., & Kumi-Yeboah, A. (2015). *Handbook of Research on Cross-Cultural Approaches to Language and Literacy Development*. Hershey, PA: IGI Global.

Snowling, M. J. (2019) *Dyslexia: A Very Short Introduction*. Oxford: Oxford University Press.

Snowling, M. J., Nash, H. M., Gooch, D. C., Hayiou-Thomas, M. E., & Hulme, C. (2019). Developmental outcomes for children at high risk of dyslexia and children with developmental language disorder. *Child Development, 90*: e548-e564. DOI: https://doi.org/10.1111/cdev.13216.

Strasser, K., & Lissi, M. R. (2009). Home and instruction effects on emergent literacy in a sample of Chilean kindergarten children. *Scientific Studies of Reading, 13*, 175–204. DOI: https://doi.org/10.1080/1088843090276952.

Street, B. (1994). The new literacy studies: Implications for education and pedagogy. *Changing English*, 1(1), 113–126. DOI: https://doi.org/10.1080/1358684940010109.

Street, B. V. (2001). *Literacy and Development: Ethnographic Perspectives*. London: Routledge.

Street, B. V. (2005). *Literacies across Educational Contexts: Mediating Learning and Teaching*. Philadelphia: Caslon Publishing.

Thompson, K., Richardson, L. P., Newman, H., & George, K. (2019). Interaction effects of socioeconomic status on emerging literacy and literacy skills among pre-kindergarten and kindergarten children: A comparison study. *Journal of Human Services: Training, Research, and Practice, 4*(1), Article 5. https://scholarworks.sfasu.edu/jhstrp/vol4/iss1/5.

Tunmer, W. E., & Hoover, W. A. (1993). Phonological recoding skill and beginning reading. *Reading and Writing: An Interdisciplinary Journal*, 5(2), 161–179. DOI: https://doi.org/10.1007/BF01027482.

UNESCO. (2019). *Global Literacy Figures*. Strasbourg: UNESCO Institute for Statistics.

United Nations. (2014). *Human Development Report*. Geneva: UN Office.

Vágvölgyi, R., Coldea, A., Dresler, T., Schrader, J., & Nuerk, H. C. (2016). A review about functional illiteracy: Definition, cognitive, linguistic, and numerical aspects. *Frontiers Psychology, 10*, 1617. DOI: http://dx.doi.org/10.3389/fpsyg.2016.01617. PMID: 27891100; PMCID: PMC5102880.

van Goch, M. M., McQueen, J. M., & Verhoeven, L. (2014). Learning phonologically specific new words fosters rhyme awareness in Dutch preliterate children. *Scientific Studies of Reading, 18*(3), 155–172. DOI: https://doi.org/10.1080/10888438.2013.827199.

Verhoeven, L. (1994). *Functional Literacy*. Amsterdam: John Benjamins.

Verhoeven, L. (2007). Early bilingualism, language transfer, and phonological awareness. *Applied Psycholinguistics*, *28*(3), 425–439.

Verhoeven, L. (2010). Second language reading acquisition. In M. L. Kamil, P. D. Pearson, E. B. Moje, & P. Afflerbach (eds.) *Handbook of Reading Research* (pp. 661–683). New York: Taylor & Francis.

Verhoeven, L., &van Leeuwe, J. (2008). Predictors of text comprehension development. *Applied Cognitive Psychology*, *22*, 407–423.

Verhoeven, L., & Perfetti, C. (2011). Vocabulary growth and reading skill. *Scientific Studies of Reading*, *15*, 1–7.

Verhoeven, L., & Perfetti, C. E. (2017). *Learning to Read across Languages and Writing Systems*. Cambridge: Cambridge University Press.

Verhoeven, L., Perfetti, C. & Pugh, K. (2019). *Developmental Dyslexia across Languages and Writing Systems*. Cambridge: Cambridge University Press.

Verhoeven, L., & Snow, C. (eds.) (2001). *Literacy and Motivation*. Mahwah, NJ: Lawrence Erlbaum Associates.

Verhoeven, L., Schnotz, W., & Paas, F. (2009). Cognitive load in interactive knowledge construction. *Learning and Instruction*, *19*(5), 369–375. DOI: https://doi.org/10.1016/j.learninstruc.2009.02.002.

Verhoeven, L. T. W., & van Leeuwe, J. (2012). The simple view of second language reading throughout the primary grades. *Reading and Writing*, *25*(8), 1805–1818.

Verhoeven, L. T. W., van Leeuwe, J., Irausquin, R. S., & Segers, P. C. J. (2016). The unique role of lexical accessibility in predicting kindergarten. *Reading and Writing*, *29*, 591–608.

Wagner, D. A. (1993). *Literacy, Culture and Development: Becoming Literate in Morocco*. Cambridge: Cambridge University Press.

Wagner, D. A. (2011). What happened to literacy? Historical and conceptual perspectives on literacy in UNESCO. *International Journal of Educational Development*, *31*, 319–323.

Wagner, D. A. (2017). Children's reading in low-income countries. *The Reading Teacher*, *71*(2), 127–133.

Wagner, D. A. (2018). *Learning as Development: Rethinking International Education in a Changing World*. New York: Routledge.

Wagner, R. K., Torgesen, J. K., & Rashotte, C. A. (1994). Development of reading-related phonological processing abilities: new evidence of bidirectional causality from a latent variable longitudinal study. *Developmental Psychology*, *30*, 73–87.

Walley, A. C. (1993). The role of vocabulary development in children's spoken word recognition and segmentation ability. *Developmental Review*, 13, 286–350.

Wickens, C., & Sandlin, J. (2007). Literacy for what? Literacy for whom? The politics of literacy education and neocolonialism in UNESCO and World Bank–Sponsored Literacy Programs. *Adult Education Quarterly*, *5*, 275–292. DOI: https://doi.org/10.1177/0741713607302364

WLF. (2015). *The Economic and Social Cost of Illiteracy: A Snapshot of Literacy in a Global Context*. Melbourne: World Literacy Foundation.

Wolf, M., & O'Brien, B. (2001). On issues of time, fluency, and intervention. In A. Fawcett (ed.), *Dyslexia: Theory and Good Practice* (pp. 124–140). London: Whurr.

World Bank. (2019). *Ending Learning Poverty: What Will it Take?* Washington, DC: World Bank. http://hdl.handle.net/10986/32553.

Part I

Regional Variations

2 Sociocultural Variation in Literacy Development in Canada and the United States

Michael J. Kieffer and Rose Vuković

2.1 Introduction

Large and growing economic inequalities have captured public attention in Canada and the United States. These economic inequalities do not exist in a vacuum, but track along the lines of structural inequalities resulting from historic and continuing racism, anti-immigrant sentiment and xenophobia, and oppression of Indigenous peoples (e.g., Fix, Papademetriou, & Sumption, 2013; Orfield & Lee, 2005; Truth and Reconciliation Commission of Canada, 2015). These broader structural inequalities lead to disparities in opportunities to develop the language and literacy skills privileged in schools, producing unequal outcomes in students' achievements in reading and writing (e.g., Duncan & Murnane, 2011; Shonkoff et al., 2012; Snow, Burns, & Griffin, 1998).

Although structural inequalities along socioeconomic, cultural, and linguistic lines have always been features of schooling in Canada and the United States, they have played out differently over time. Now that we are well into the twenty-first century, researchers from various disciplines have begun to reappraise the current magnitude and nature of achievement differences in terms of socioeconomic and sociodemographic factors (e.g., Duncan & Murnane, 2011; Gamoran, 2015; Shonkoff et al., 2012). In addition, researchers have begun to recently examine how these structural inequalities play out differently in the US and Canadian contexts, given their different histories, geographies, demographics, and social policies (e.g., Bradbury et al., 2015).

This chapter aims to synthesize evidence from large-scale studies on the magnitude of disparities between the literacy development of students from low socioeconomic and language-minority backgrounds and that of their more advantaged counterparts in the United States and Canada, particularly regarding reading skills. Among various structural inequalities that are relevant to reading, we focus on socioeconomic status (SES) differences and linguistic diversity (and their interrelationships). We explicitly acknowledge that extensive structural inequalities also exist for Indigenous peoples in both countries across a range of education, health, and social outcomes. We focus specifically on language-minority learners in this chapter primarily because the large-scale research that has examined disparities in reading development has provided valuable insight regarding students from immigrant backgrounds. By focusing on reading development in language-minority learners, we do not intend to minimize or obscure the very real barriers to equitable education in Indigenous communities, nor do we intend to convey that structural forces that affect immigrant students can be generalized to Indigenous communities. Instead, we echo previous calls to address the sociocultural context of reading development and education more broadly in Indigenous communities in both countries (Truth and Reconciliation Commission of Canada, 2015).

We primarily draw together evidence from nationally representative cross-sectional and longitudinal studies from early childhood through adolescence. When useful and appropriate, we provide comparisons between the two countries, but we also interpret findings for each country in the context of international benchmarks for high-income countries (e.g., countries in the Organisation for Economic Co-operation and Development; OECD). In measuring socioeconomic status, we focus primarily on two complementary indices – parental education and family income – while also using composites that incorporate parental occupation and home resources for learning when data are available.

In the sections that follow, we describe our theoretical framework that integrates ecological and developmental perspectives on reading. Next, we summarize key evidence describing differences by socioeconomic status and home-language background for each of the developmental periods. We end by commenting on some of the implications of this evidence and on what has not yet been possible to ascertain from large-scale studies of literacy development in Canada and the United States.

2.2 Ecological and Developmental Perspectives on Reading in Canada and the United States

2.2.1 Ecological and Developmental Framework

We take a perspective on reading that emphasizes ecological influences on child development, while integrating insights from neurocognitive, sociological, and economic perspectives. An ecological model of human development (e.g., Bronfenbrenner, 1994; Bronfenbrenner & Morris, 2006) helps us understand the development of individual children as influenced by the variety of social contexts in which they are growing, changing, and learning. Specifically, an ecological perspective on reading development acknowledges the central role of the "microsystem" – proximal processes (e.g., teacher's instructional practices, parent's interaction styles) in children's immediate contexts (e.g., classrooms, homes) – in their development of skilled reading.

At the same time, this perspective views these proximal processes and immediate context as shaped by multiple broader exosystems – family social networks, neighborhood contexts, school district practices – and macrosystems – overarching patterns characteristic of a given culture or, in the case of our analysis, a national context.

Applying an ecological perspective to reading, in particular, we focus on what Aaron et al. (2008) called the "ecological component" of reading in their Componential Model of Reading, which also includes a cognitive and a psychological component. Like these authors, we see this ecological component as influencing and interacting with the development of cognitive skills (i.e., word reading and linguistic comprehension) and psychological attributes (e.g., motivation, interest) required for successful reading (Kieffer & Vukovic, 2012). Neurocognitive research provides further insight into the nature of cognitive development required for reading. We share the perspective of many scholars that reading is a parasitic system on spoken language; that is, that reading written language is a culturally invented and "unnatural" activity, which draws on "natural" language systems that evolved to serve other purposes for *Homo sapiens*. Given that assumption, it is not surprising that acquiring language is a nearly universal human accomplishment, but that learning to read complex texts with comprehension is far from universal, even in countries like the United States and Canada with compulsory and free education through adolescence. Basic literacy rates are very high in both countries (e.g., 96 percent of fourth-grade students in each country reached the "low international benchmark" on the 2016 Progress in International Reading Literacy Study [PIRLS]; Mullis et al., 2017), but a large gap exists between these two countries in terms of the level of more advanced literary skills required in them for participation in the modern, global economy and democratic processes.

2.2.2 *Ecology of Education in the United States and Canada*

To apply these perspectives to a cross-national study of reading inequalities in the United States and Canada, we also start by acknowledging some key similarities and differences in the challenges associated with reading in these two countries. First, given the position of English as the common language in the United States and as one of two official languages in Canada, learning to read in these two contexts requires learning the same alphabetic writing system, with a deep orthography (i.e., a spelling system characterized by many inconsistencies and complexities in grapheme–phoneme correspondences; Seymour, Aro, & Erskine, 2003). Students learning to read in French in Canada are also learning an alphabetic writing system with a moderately deep orthography (e.g., Seymour et al., 2003). So, the cognitive challenges in learning to read are quite similar for

Anglophone students and roughly comparable for Francophone students in Canada as well. (That said, French readers may face particular challenges due to the language's higher frequency of historically preserved morphological patterns that produce speech-to-spelling inconsistencies; Deacon, Desrochers, & Levesque, 2017). Second, the United States and Canada, as OECD countries with long histories of stable government, have relatively similar levels of economic and institutional development. As a result, both countries offer free and compulsory education through secondary school, with relatively large levels of average investment in public education (e.g., NCES, 2016; UNESCO, 2016). Despite these similarities, the two countries differ in their ecologies of education in major ways. Importantly, these include major differences in the social services available, including the availability in Canada of universal, nationalized healthcare and more robust economic support in Canada than that found in the United States (e.g., Bradbury et al., 2015).

Third, as part of the legacy of settler colonization, the United States and Canada have both been defined by immigration since their founding. They have both varied over time in their treatment of new waves of immigrants – from encouragement through grudging acceptance to xenophobic rejection (Environics Institute for Survey Research, 2019; National Academies of Sciences, Engineering, and Medicine, 2015). As these broader forces inevitably affect schools, questions about the education of immigrants and the children of immigrants have been politically charged and answered differently over time. Foremost among these have been questions about schools' responsibilities as regards to meeting the language- and content-learning needs of language-minority learners, that is, students who speak a language other than the society's dominant language(s) at home. Of course, the other legacy of settler colonialism in both countries since their inception has been policies and practices that sought to eradicate Indigenous peoples and their ways of being. These have had the cumulative effect both of wiping out Indigenous languages and underfunding Indigenous education efforts, leading to significant education and opportunity gaps for Indigenous students in both countries (NCES, 2019; Truth and Reconciliation Commission of Canada, 2015).

In both countries, education for language-minority and immigrant learners has been defined by major tensions. In the United States, on one hand, these students benefit from civil rights protections, including the right to equal education opportunities guaranteed by the United States federal court decisions (*Lau* v. *Nichols*, 1974; *Castañeda* v. *Pickard*, 1981; *Plyler* v. *Doe*, 1982). On the other hand, US schooling has been characterized by persistent negative attitudes toward bilingual education and immigrant students that produce major inequalities in resources and opportunities to learn (e.g., Gandara et al., 2003). Canada has a more decentralized educational system, whereby each province has jurisdiction over education. Under this system, there has been relatively little federal attention to teaching language-minority learners in their native language, but the country also has official policies that embrace bilingualism (at least English/French bilingualism) and promote multiculturalism. There has also been a recent resurgence in Indigenous-language revitalization in Canada.

The immigration policies of the two countries have differed in major ways historically and continue to do so, with Canada accepting most immigrants using a points system that favors highly educated and skilled workers while the United States system prioritizes family reunification rather than education and skills (e.g., Bloemraad, 2006). It is worth noting that the geographic isolation of Canada from the rest of the world – surrounded by oceans to the east, west, and north, and sharing a border with only one other country – has also facilitated highly selective immigration criteria and policies. Given the two countries' demographic and political histories (and futures), describing the reading development of language-minority learners in the United States and Canada is central to understanding how diversity and structural inequalities in both countries play out in schools.

The two countries also have different histories and public rhetoric concerning multilingualism and multiculturalism. In Canada, French and English have had equal official status in government and all of the services it controls since the Official Languages Act of 1969; in the United States, there is no official language by law, but English remains the overwhelmingly predominant language in government and schooling, with only minor protections for other languages, most of which have been introduced as a result of civil rights actions rather than democratic processes (e.g., Crawford, 2004). Moreover, Canadian law (i.e., the 1982 Canadian Charter of Rights and Freedoms; the 1985 Canadian Multiculturalism Act) affirms an official policy of recognizing and promoting multiculturalism (Ambrose & Mudde, 2015). This proactive encouragement of multiculturalism goes beyond the prohibitions against discrimination that characterize the corresponding US laws (e.g., the 14th Amendment; the 1964 Civil Rights Act). (At the same time, Canada's Indian Act still engenders discriminatory practices and limits Indigenous sovereignty [Joseph, 2018], which contradicts the spirit of Canada's commitment to multiculturalism.) Finally, the two countries differ in the fundamental scale of their societies and educational systems. In the United States, roughly 50 million public K-12 students are taught by over 3 million teachers (NCES, 2015), whereas in Canada, roughly 5 million students are taught by approximately 700,000 teachers (Stats Canada, 2016). By point of comparison, New York City schools serve more students than those of every province and territory in Canada, except for the two largest, Quebec and Ontario.

2.2.3 Sociocultural Predictors of Reading Development

Understanding the ecological differences between the United States and Canada leads us to construct hypotheses about the two sociocultural predictors that are our focus: SES and linguistic diversity. Regarding SES, the stronger social safety net available to children living in poverty in Canada compared to that in the United States would suggest smaller effects of SES in the former country than in the latter, given the importance of health and well-being to reading development (e.g., Shonkoff et al., 2012; Snow et al., 1998). Regarding linguistic diversity, Canada's more selective immigration system is likely to result in language-minority learners with more resources and consequently better reading outcomes compared to their counterparts in the United States. That said, if these differences are associated primarily with differences in socioeconomic resources, we would expect smaller differences between language-minority learners in the two countries once we have taken SES into account.

Given our ecological perspective, we resist attributing differences by SES and home-language background to individual students' characteristics or to those of their families or teachers. Rather, we interpret these differences as the culmination of complex interactions among broad structural inequalities rooted in cultural and historical patterns of oppression and marginalization. These patterns play out in a variety of proximal processes in classrooms that constrain opportunities to learn and develop for some students, while maximizing these opportunities for others.

As we have seen, written text (from orthography through discourse patterns) is "unnatural" and culturally specific. Given this, it is not surprising that reading development will be linked to children's access to and opportunities to learn the oral language skills for the languages that are privileged in written school texts. For example, when language-minority learners enter kindergarten with limited oral proficiency in the language (or languages) of instruction, we can expect that their trajectories toward proficient reading will differ from those of their peers who enter with strong proficiency in the language of instruction. (That said, language-minority learners' trajectories often converge with those of language-majority students over time.) Moreover, language-minority students disproportionately come from low-income backgrounds, particularly in the United States (and to a much lesser extent in Canada), so disentangling the effects of poverty and home language on reading development is important to understanding these students' academic trajectories.

2.2.4 Evidence of Disparities in Reading Achievement

To synthesize evidence on the magnitudes of disparities in reading achievement by SES and home language, we leveraged existing published analyses and conducted new analyses of large-scale, nationally representative datasets.

Specifically, we leveraged analyses by an international team of scholars (Bradbury et al., 2011, 2015; Washbrook et al., 2012) of the US Early Childhood Longitudinal Study – Birth, 2001 cohort (ECLS-B) and Kindergarten, 1998 cohort (ECLS-K:98) as well as the Canadian National Longitudinal Study of Children and Youth (NLSCY) and analyses (Kieffer, 2008, 2011, 2012) of the ECLS-K:98 by one of this chapter's authors. We conducted new analyses using PIRLS 2006 and 2016 for fourth-grade reading in both countries. When possible, we report results from the most recent PIRLS administration, but rely on earlier datasets when they are the only administrations to include important variables of interest (e.g., parental education). We also conducted new analyses using the OECD Programme for International Student Assessment (PISA) data from 2018 as well as reports from PISA 2009 (which included useful analyses of home-language controlling for SES). Finally, we conducted new analyses with the US National Assessment for Educational Progress (NAEP) data from 2019 for SES and from 2015 for home language (the most recent year when the appropriate variable was available). All new analyses were conducted with online data explorers that appropriately account for weighting, matrix sampling, and other features of the datasets. All of the datasets are nationally representative, so include the full range of racial–ethnic and linguistic diversity in each country. In particular, the participating language-minority learners spoke a variety of languages, though the ability to conduct analyses separately by individual language group was limited.

In reporting and interpreting results, we present effect sizes, that is, standardized differences expressed in standard deviation units. In this way, we focus on the question of the size of the differences found, rather than simply whether differences exist. We interpret the effect sizes using Cohen's (1992) conventions, where 0.2 is small, 0.5 medium, and 0.8 large. This emphasis on magnitudes over statistical significance tests is appropriate because trivially small differences can be statistically significant in large datasets. In addition, effect sizes allow us to make rough comparisons across datasets for which statistical significance tests are not appropriate.

2.3   Differences by Socioeconomic Status

2.3.1   *Role of SES in Language Skills at School Entry*

Differences in students' language skills when they enter school provide key insights into the structural inequalities that will play out later, given the well-established role of early reading-related language skills in predicting later reading development (e.g., Snow et al., 1998). Fortunately, this is also a topic on which high-quality and highly comparable data has been collected in both the United States and Canada, particularly recent work by an international team of scholars (Bradbury et al., 2011, 2015; Washbrook et al., 2012). Specifically, they analyzed data from the Canadian NLSCY and from the US ECLS-K and ECLS-B. Here, we focus on their comparisons of the oral vocabulary skills of four- and five-year-olds in the two countries.

Their results indicated substantial differences in early vocabulary by SES in both countries, with much larger differences in the United States relative to Canada, as shown in Table 2.1. The difference in vocabulary scores between students with at least one college-educated parent and those with parents with high-school education or less was 1.22 standard deviations (SDs) in the United States and 0.66 SDs in Canada. Similarly, when estimated using family-income quintile, differences were large in both countries, but more so for the United States than Canada. Given the potential differences in structural inequalities caused by other demographic characteristics in the two countries, we also provide estimates from Bradbury et al., which have been adjusted for race/ethnicity and parental immigrant status in Table 2.1. These adjusted estimates remained large, but were more similar across the two countries. This suggests that these other structural inequalities, which are historically and fundamentally intertwined with economic inequality, explain some of the differences observed between the United States and Canada.

Table 2.1 *Effect-size estimates of differences in vocabulary by SES at ages 4–5*

Specific comparison	Data source	United States	Canada
By parental education (between at least one parent with a college degree and parents with a high-school degree or less)	Bradbury et al. (2011) using ECLS-B & NLSCY	1.21	0.66
	Bradbury et al. (2011) using ECLS-B & NLSCY; Adjusted for race/ethnicity and parent immigrant status	0.86	0.71
By income (between the highest and lowest quintile for income)	Bradbury et al. (2011) using ECLS-B & NLSCY	1.08	0.74
	Bradbury et al. (2011) using ECLS-B & NLSCY; Adjusted for race/ethnicity and immigration status	0.84	0.71

Note: Parental immigrant status was operationalized as dichotomous and referred to whether both the child's parents had been born in the country

2.3.2 Role of SES in Learning to Read

After four or five years of schooling, differences in reading achievement by SES continue to be moderate to large in both countries, as shown in Table 2.2. The available data did not allow direct comparisons between Canada and the United States, but nonetheless supported the general claim that differences in both countries are substantial. Consistent with results for early childhood, differences by parental education were moderate to large. For instance, for Canada, reading gaps by parental education in fourth grade on PIRLS 2006 were moderately sized (0.53 SDs), though smaller than the average for all countries participating in PIRLS 2006 (0.66 SDs) and slightly smaller than the corresponding gaps in early childhood vocabulary reported above. (We used PIRLS 2006 rather than PIRLS 2016 here because this was the last year in which parental education was measured.) Comparable PIRLS data were not

Table 2.2 *Effect-size estimates of differences in reading achievement by SES in childhood*

Comparison	Data source	United States	Canada	International average
By parental education (between at least one parent with a college degree and parents with a high-school degree or less)	PIRLS 2006 (Grade 4)	N/A	0.53	0.66[a]
	Bradbury et al. (2015) using ECLS-K (Grade 3)	0.99		
	Bradbury et al. (2015) using ECLS-K (Grade 5)	1.03		
By composite of home resources for learning (between students with different levels of home educational resources)	PIRLS 2016 (Grade 4)	N/A	0.48	0.66[b]
By income (between students receiving and not receiving free lunches)	NAEP 2019 (Grade 4)	0.71		
	NAEP 2019 (Grade 4); Adjusted for race/ethnicity	0.55		

a Average across all countries participating in PIRLS 2006.
b Average across OECD countries participating in PIRLS 2016.

available for the United States, which did not participate in all aspects of PIRLS data collection, but Bradbury et al. (2011) estimated these same gaps using ECLS-K data to be large in both third grade (0.99 SDs) and fifth grade (1.03 SDs).

Differences in reading by other SES indicators were also moderate to large. The PIRLS 2016 data for Canada include a home educational resource index, which included parental education and occupation, number of books in the home, and other study supports (i.e., having one's own room to study; having an internet connection). On this measure, achievement differences between Canadian children with different levels were moderate (0.48 SDs) and smaller than the average for thirty-one OECD countries which participated in PIRLS 2016 (0.66 SDs). Again, such analyses were not possible for the United States. Instead, if we look at differences by income on the Grade 4 NAEP 2019, reading differences by free- or reduced-price lunch status were large (Table 2.2). Similarly, on the Grade 3 and Grade 5 waves of ECLS-K, differences by an SES composite (i.e., a combination of parental education, income, and occupation and the school's percentage of students on free and reduced-price lunch) were also moderate to large in size for US children (Kieffer, 2012). Although these estimates are not strictly comparable across the two countries, they support the general conclusion that reading-achievement differences by SES in middle childhood are substantial in both countries.

Longitudinal studies corroborate these cross-sectional findings of substantial differences but also indicate some narrowing of SES gaps in each country between kindergarten and Grade 3. For the United States, Kieffer (2012) found that SES gaps in overall reading achievement narrowed by about 30 percent between kindergarten and Grade 3 (see also Bradbury et al., 2015). For Canada, a large epidemiological (but not nationally representative) study conducted in one city indicated a dramatic narrowing of gaps by neighborhood SES on a word-reading measure (D'Anguilli, Siegel, & Hertzman, 2004). The latter study was not comparable to Kieffer (2012) and Bradbury et al. (2015), due not only to differences in sampling and SES indicators but also to fundamental differences in the reading skills measured; the greater narrowing of gaps found by D'Anguilli et al. may be specific to word-reading skills, which would be consistent with constrained-skills theory (Paris, 2005). Nonetheless, these longitudinal findings suggest some degree of narrowing of SES gaps between early and middle childhood – though the cross-sectional results make it clear that large gaps remain.

2.3.3 Role of SES in Adolescent Reading Development

Similar to earlier developmental periods, evidence suggests moderate to large differences between levels of adolescent reading comprehension in both countries. On the most recent PISA in 2018, both countries demonstrated substantial

Literacy in Canada and the United States 43

Table 2.3 *Effect-size estimates of differences in reading achievement by SES in adolescence*

Comparison	Data source	United States	Canada	OECD average
By SES composite (between top and bottom national quarter)	PISA 2018 (age fifteen)	0.92	0.68	0.90
By parental education (between student-reported parent with college degree and parent without high-school diploma)	NAEP 2019 (Grade 8)	0.66		
	NAEP 2019 (Grade 8); Adjusted for race/ethnicity	0.53		
By income (between students receiving and not receiving free lunch)	NAEP 2019 (Grade 8)	0.67		
	NAEP 2019 (Grade 8); Adjusted for race/ethnicity	0.50		

differences between students in the top and bottom quartiles on an SES composite. As shown in Table 2.3, these large differences were somewhat greater in the United States (0.92 SDs) than in Canada (0.68 SDs), with the latter substantially smaller than the OECD average (0.90 SDs).

Other national datasets specific to the United States, including NAEP 2019, also suggest relatively large differences by SES indicators (Table 2.3). These gaps are reduced somewhat when adjusting for race/ethnicity, but remain substantial. Moreover, longitudinal studies using data from ECLS-K indicate that reading-achievement gaps widened between Grade 3 and Grade 8 (Kieffer, 2012; Bradbury et al., 2015), in contrast to these studies' findings that the same gaps narrowed between kindergarten and Grade 3.

2.3.4 *Summary of SES Differences*

Looking across early childhood, childhood, and adolescence, differences in reading by SES are moderate to large in magnitude, regardless of the SES indicator used. In early childhood, these differences are notably larger in the United States than in Canada. Childhood differences are also moderate to large in magnitude in both countries, but cannot be compared directly. Canada's differences are smaller than international averages in childhood. By adolescence, differences remain large in both countries, with larger differences again in the United States compared to Canada. In adolescence, Canada's SES differences are smaller than the international average, whereas the United States's differences are similar to this average.

2.4 Differences by Home Language Background

2.4.1 Linguistic Diversity at School Entry

Comparisons of national datasets indicate large differences in vocabulary (measured in the dominant language of English or French) between language-minority and language-majority students when they enter school in both the United States and Canada, as shown in Table 2.4. These results come from the same cross-national research team mentioned above (Washbrook et al., 2012). Here, language-minority students were defined as those who spoke a language other than the dominant language(s) at home and were either immigrants or native-born children of immigrants. Language-majority students were those who had native-born parents and spoke English (or French in the case of Francophone Canadians) primarily at home. As shown in Table 2.4, the differences in vocabulary scores were similar across the two countries. In addition, adjusting these estimates for income, parental education, and other SES indicators (see note, Table 2.4) did not lead to a substantial reduction in these differences, indicating that large gaps in early language are demonstrated between language-minority and language-majority students, even when comparing those from similar SES backgrounds. This is consistent with the findings of several US studies conducted with smaller samples of Spanish-speaking language-minority learners, which suggest that they enter school with underdeveloped English vocabularies, relative to national norms on standardized assessments (e.g., Mancilla-Martinez & Lesaux, 2011a, 2011b; Manis, Lindsey, & Bailey, 2004).

Table 2.4 *Effect-size estimates of vocabulary differences by home language at school entry (ages 4–5)*

Comparison	Data source	United States	Canada
By home language background (between children of immigrants who speak a nondominant language at home and children of native-born parents who speak the dominant language at home)	Washbrook et al. (2012) using ECLS-B and NLSCY	1.11 (0.04)	1.03 (0.09)
	Washbrook et al. (2012); adjusted for income, parental education, and other SES controls[1]	0.98 (0.04)	1.02 (0.05)

[1] Other SES controls included single parent household, number of children in the home, mother's age at birth, child gender, and low birth weight.

2.4.2 Linguistic Diversity and Learning to Read

In comparison to results for early childhood vocabulary, differences in reading achievement in Grade 4 between language-minority and language-majority learners appear to be much smaller, particularly in Canada, as shown in Table 2.5. On the 2016 PIRLS, differences in reading comprehension between language-majority and language-minority students were moderately sized in the United States (0.34 SDs) and small in Canada (0.04 SDs). Specific to this survey, the United States gap was similar to differences in other OECD countries (0.32), while the Canadian gap was notably smaller. It is worth noting that the definition of language minority was not identical to the one used so far. Here, language-minority students included those who reported "sometimes" speaking the dominant language(s) at home, while language-majority students include those who reported "always" speaking the dominant language(s) at home; only a trivial number of students (3 percent in Canada, 1 percent in the

Table 2.5 *Effect-size estimates of reading-achievement gaps by home language in childhood*

Comparison	Data source	United States	Canada	OECD average
By home language background (between children who sometimes vs. always speak the language of the test at home)	PIRLS 2016 (Grade 4)	0.34	0.04	0.32
	PIRLS 2016 (Grade 4); adjusted for home study supports	0.001	0.0001	
By home language background (between students with and without a primary language other than English at home at kindergarten entry)	Kieffer (2011) using ECLS-K (Grade 3)	0.48		
	Kieffer (2011) using ECLS-K (Grade 3); adjusted for family SES composite and school concentration of poverty	-0.005		
By home language background (between students reporting speaking a language other than English at home all or most of the time vs. never)	NAEP 2015 (Grade 4)	0.35		
	NAEP 2015 (Grade 4); Adjusted for free/reduced lunch status	0.15		

Note: Positive values indicate better performance for language-majority speakers, while negative values indicate better performance for language-minority learners. Home study supports include having one's own room to study in and having an internet connection.

United States) chose the other answer choice of "never" speaking the dominant language(s) at home, consistent with prior evidence that the vast majority of language-minority learners speak a combination of their home language and the dominant language, particularly after they enter school (e.g., Mancilla-Martinez & Kieffer, 2010; Mancilla-Martinez & Lesaux, 2011a). Although this definition is not strictly comparable to the one used by Washbrook et al. (2012), they likely capture roughly similar populations of students.

Given differences in immigration policies and patterns that in turn yield differences in the SES of immigrant families in the two countries, we also provide estimates adjusted for a comparable index of SES available from PIRLS 2016 (i.e., the presence of home study supports). The adjusted estimate was very close to 0 for both Canada and the United States, indicating that SES explained nearly all of the apparent differences between language-minority and language-majority students in both countries. This represented a much greater reduction for the United States, indicating greater confounding of SES and home-language backgrounds.

Similarly, United States-specific evidence from national datasets suggests moderately sized differences between language-minority and language-majority learners that decline to small or trivial magnitudes when adjusting for SES. Specifically, analyses of ECLS-K indicated a moderately sized reading achievement gap (0.48 SDs) in Grade 3 that became very close to 0 after adjusting for an SES composite and school concentration of poverty (see also Kieffer 2008, 2011). Results for the Grade 5 wave of ECLS-K were similar. NAEP 2015 results indicated a moderately sized gap (0.35 SDs) that became small when adjusting for students' eligibility for free or reduced-cost lunch (0.15 SDs). Across these datasets, US language-minority learners demonstrated reading levels that were substantially below national averages, but quite similar to those of their language-majority counterparts from similar SES backgrounds.

2.4.3 Linguistic Diversity and Adolescent Reading Development

In contrast to evidence for early childhood vocabulary and childhood reading, the PISA 2009 and 2018 data indicate relatively small US reading achievement differences by home language in adolescence (0.33 and 0.27 SDs, respectively); see Table 2.6. These differences were also somewhat smaller than OECD averages. Moreover, for the 2009 PISA, when adjusted for SES (using the PISA composite), this difference reversed in direction, such that language-minority learners outperformed language-majority learners to a small degree (-.10 SDs).[1] For Canada, PISA data indicated a small gap (0.13 in 2009, 0.24 in 2018) by home

---

[1] This analysis was not conducted for more recent PISA reports. It was also not possible to conduct this analysis with the PISA data explorer for the PISA 2018 data because the data explorer specifies the SES composite as an outcome, rather than a covariate to be used in multiple regression.

Table 2.6 *Effect-size estimates of differences in reading comprehension by home language in adolescence*

Comparison	Data source	United States	Canada	OECD average
By home language background (between students of immigrants who speak a nondominant language at home most of the time)	PISA 2009 (age fifteen)	0.33	0.13	0.57
	PISA 2009 (age fifteen) adjusted for SES composite	-0.10	0.08	0.35
By home language background (between students who speak a nondominant language at home most of the time and children who do not)	PISA 2018 (age fifteen)	0.27	0.24	0.57
By home language background (between students with and without a primary language other than English at home at kindergarten entry)	Kieffer (2011) using ECLS-K (Grade 8)	0.35		
	Kieffer (2011) using ECLS-K (Grade 8); adjusted for family SES composite and school concentration of poverty	-0.18		
By Home Language Background (between students reporting speaking a language other than English at home all or most of the time vs. never)	NAEP 2015 (Grade 8)	0.34		
	NAEP 2015 adjusted for free/reduced lunch status and parental education	0.02		

Note: Positive values indicate better performance for language-majority speakers, while negative values indicate better performance for language-minority learners.

language that was notably smaller than the OECD averages. Adjusting for SES, the 2009 gap was reduced somewhat (to 0.08 SDs). Here, language-minority children included those who spoke a language other than the dominant language(s) "most of the time" at home.

Similarly, United States-specific evidence from NAEP 2015 suggests a moderately sized reading-achievement gap in Grade 4 (0.34 SDs). As with PISA, the NAEP gap declined to a trivial size (0.02 SDs) when adjusting for SES (indexed by student eligibility for free or reduced-cost lunch and student-reported parental education). In additional converging evidence from ECLS-K, the United States reading-achievement gap by home language in Grade 8 was smaller than in earlier grades and reversed in direction to favor language-minority learners when adjusting for SES (Kieffer, 2011).

2.4.4 Summary of Home Language Differences

Looking across time, we see that large vocabulary differences between language-minority and language-majority students in both countries at kindergarten entry turn into moderate differences in reading in the United States and small differences in Canada by middle childhood. By adolescence, these differences become small-to-moderate in the United States and remain small in Canada. Moreover, while SES differences do not explain much of these initial vocabulary differences in kindergarten, they do explain a substantial proportion of later reading differences in middle childhood and adolescence. Comparing students from similar SES backgrounds in later grades, we find only small-to-trivial differences between language-majority and language-minority students, with some analyses indicating better performance for language-minority learners. Given the greater confounding of SES and language background in the United States, more of the observed differences are explained by the low SES, on average, for language-minority learners in the United States, compared to Canada.

2.5 Conclusions and Discussion

Despite some limitations in comparability across nationally representative datasets – both between countries and between developmental periods – some general conclusions emerge from this evidence. First, achievement differences by SES in both countries are large across early childhood, childhood, and adolescence, with larger differences in the United States than in Canada whenever comparisons are possible (i.e., early childhood and adolescence). Second, achievement differences by home language background in both countries are the largest for vocabulary in early childhood, moderate or small for reading in childhood, and relatively small for reading in adolescence. Third, for childhood and adolescent reading, differences by home language are much larger in the United States than in Canada, but this cross-country difference narrows or disappears when accounting for differences in students' SES. We discuss each of the general conclusions below.

2.5.1 Promoting Equity across SES Differences

Our conclusions regarding SES echo those of Bradbury et al. (2015) and provide further support for their suggestion that structural inequalities in both the United States and Canada prevent far too many students from low-SES backgrounds from reaching their potential to become skilled readers. As Reardon's (2011) analyses of national US datasets from the 1940s through the 2000s suggest, these inequalities are greater now than they have ever been since the government began collecting such data. Canada appears to have had some success relative to the United States, but does not escape notable SES differences. Indeed, achievement differences in both countries are large across early childhood, childhood, and adolescence. (For an international perspective, see Nag, Chapter 15 in this volume.)

From an ecological perspective, this relative success on the part of Canada in producing more equal outcomes might reflect influences at local levels (e.g., differences in childcare experiences) as well as influences at broader levels that prioritize social supports (e.g., maternity leave, universal healthcare). Bradbury et al. note these public investments in families as key levers that promote more equity in Canada and that should be considered in public policy discussion about education in the United States. Noting the larger differences by SES in the United States than in Canada at school entry, they argue for the particular importance of investment in early childhood development – including evidence-based preschool and parenting-support programs as well as income-support programs to reduce poverty and its associated stresses among families with young children. Historically, the United States has made large investments in K-12 education, while leaving working families on their own to pay for the education and development of children before age five – precisely the time at which children's brain development is most influenced by environmental affordances (e.g., Yoshikawa, Raver, & Morris, 2016).

At the same time, our results suggest that both countries could also do more to promote equity among elementary and secondary students. There is a strong and growing global research base on which to recommend specific instructional approaches for improving reading outcomes and how they can be tailored and implemented to meet the needs of students from low-SES backgrounds. From systematic phonics instruction to rich oral-language instruction, many curricula and instructional approaches have been found to be particularly beneficial to students from low-SES backgrounds (see Dickinson et al., Chapter 17, and Schwartz, Chapter 19, in this volume). Although instructional questions remain, we certainly know enough to improve classroom reading instruction in important ways.

2.5.2 *Understanding Linguistic Diversity in Relation to SES*

Our conclusions regarding language-minority learners underscore the long-term nature of the process of learning to become a proficient reader in a second language. The fact that language-minority students arrive at school with underdeveloped second-language vocabulary but many go on to catch up with their language-majority peers by adolescence aligns with a wide consensus that language learning is a long-term developmental process (National Research Council, 2017). Despite this widespread consensus, educational policies and practices continue to emphasize the short-term underperformance of language-minority learners in ways that may actually hurt their long-term success (e.g., Hopkins et al., 2013; Kieffer & Thompson, 2018). In particular, many US policies and practices focus attention on the subset of language-minority learners who are currently and temporarily classified as English learners. This group is defined by their current lack of proficiency in speaking, listening, reading, and writing English. Thus, differences between this selected subgroup and native English speakers is a "gap that can't go away" (Saunders & Marcelletti, 2013, p. 139). Recent analyses of NAEP data over time (Kieffer & Thompson, 2018) indicate that when one analyzes the entire population of language-minority or multilingual learners, one finds they have made substantial progress in reading and math that is not apparent when analyzing only current English learners.

At the same time, the data provide some support for the hypothesis that the process of learning the dominant language and catching up with language-majority peers is quicker in Canada than in the United States. Canadian gaps by home language are similar to US gaps in early childhood vocabulary, but much smaller by Grade 4. In addition to the social supports described in Section 2.5.1, these differences might reflect how Canadian provinces tend to have intentional educational policies in place to support immigrant students in learning the language of instruction (OECD, 2006). Such policies, in turn, might reflect macrosystem values as reflected in Canada's commitment to the protection and preservation of multiculturalism through federal law (i.e., Canadian Charter of Rights and Freedoms, 1982; Multiculturalism Act, 1985). That said, it is important to note that Canada is not immune to anti-immigrant and xenophobic sentiments; a recent report on Canadian public opinion revealed that 64 percent of respondents felt that Canada accepts too many immigrants from racial minority groups, and 50 percent felt too many immigrants coming into Canada were not adopting Canadian values (Environics Institute for Survey Research, 2019). Nonetheless, it does appear that Canada's commitment to multiculturalism creates a more conducive learning environment for immigrant students compared to countries without explicit educational integration policies (OECD, 2006); if so, this may be an example of policy making a difference in spite of countervailing popular sentiment. However, before one takes too rosy a view of Canada's relative success with language-minority learners, it is worth reiterating that its selective immigration policies favor highly educated and skilled parents.

In addition, our conclusions underscore how much the achievement of US language-minority learners may be constrained by structural inequalities associated with their disproportionately low SES. Although converging evidence suggests that US language-minority learners catch up with their peers from similarly low-SES backgrounds, this is a low bar, given the poor performance of those peers. One potential implication is that US educators may be overemphasizing the need for interventions specific to language-minority and English learners, rather than integrating such efforts into broader approaches to reduce inequalities by socioeconomic status.

This pattern of confounding SES and home language background does not appear to the same extent for Canada. This is likely due to the fact that very different immigration policies and practices are in place in Canada than those in the United States, but also perhaps to a variety of Canadian social policies that reduce the structural inequalities that would otherwise constrain the reading development of both language-minority learners and students from low-SES backgrounds.

2.5.3 What We Can't Learn from Current Large-Scale Datasets

Although the available data support some interesting conclusions, there remain many questions that cannot be easily answered from the existing large-scale datasets. First, although national and international assessments provide valuable insights into reading development, they pay little or no attention to writing development in either country. Given the importance of writing in college success and access to meaningful employment (e.g., Levy & Murnane, 2004), more attention to writing in large-scale research is warranted. Similarly, oral language is rarely assessed and when it is, it is assessed in superficial ways, despite its key role in literacy development (e.g., Snow et al., 1998). In addition, returning to the ecological approach we have described, there are many variables within the exosystems (e.g., neighborhood contexts, school practices) and microsystems (e.g., instructional practices) that cannot be captured effectively by national and international assessments.

Second, the differences between the United States and Canada in their systems and investment in collecting educational achievement data mean that we have more complete answers for many questions about achievement differences in the United States than we have for Canada. Unlike the United States, Canada maintains few national data-collection systems – in education or otherwise – leaving to individual provinces and territories the responsibility of identifying, collecting, and tracking relevant metrics, including demographic identifiers such as race/ethnicity or Indigenous status. In the context of education, individual provinces/territories implement regular testing programs that focus primarily on language arts and numeracy in both elementary and high school, with some provinces also assessing science and social studies in high school. However, there is little consistency across provinces/territories in what content is assessed or when, resulting in functional barriers to making comparisons across demographic groups even if such data were available. Canada also lacks longitudinal datasets, which limits the ability to monitor changes and trends over time.

Third and more problematic in terms of identifying and correcting for structural inequalities as a result of Canada's colonial history, provinces/territories have not devised a way to monitor achievement gaps between Indigenous and non-Indigenous Canadians, nor are provinces required to disaggregate data by demographic characteristics. Canada's legacy of the genocide of Indigenous peoples is well documented (Truth and Reconciliation Commission of Canada, 2015), but Canada also has a history of discrimination against immigrants of Asian and African descent (Ambrose & Mudde, 2015). The inability to comparably disaggregate data across provinces/territories obscures the successes of marginalized communities and failures of the education system for historically disenfranchised groups over time. This is especially concerning for Indigenous communities, who have experienced repeated neglect from the Canadian government. A recent call to action by Indigenous leaders explicitly summons the federal government to regularly publish educational attainments of Indigenous peoples compared with non-Indigenous peoples (Truth and Reconciliation Commission of Canada, 2015). There is also a need to move beyond standard testing programs that focus only on academic attainment to include outcomes that are important for Indigenous peoples, such as the social, physical, and spiritual wellbeing of individuals and communities (Friesen & Krauth, 2012). The most important message for Canadian policymakers is to work with Indigenous communities to ensure that the right data are collected, policies written, and programs implemented.

2.5.4 Structural Inequalities and Reading Development Revisited

Even now, decades into the twenty-first century, the promises of public education to be the great equalizer remain unfulfilled. In the United States and Canada, structural inequalities in opportunities to learn the complex reading skills required for the global economy persist. So, too, do the legacies – and continuing practices – of racism, classism, xenophobia, and oppression of Indigenous peoples, thereby perpetuating structural inequalities inside and outside of schools. To begin to address unequal outcomes in a real way, we must begin by considering how we make sense of the differences in achievement that we see (see also Navas, Chapter 3, Araújo and da Costa, Chapter 5, and Morgan et al., Chapter 10 in this volume). Too often, these are interpreted as evidence of how students from low-income or language-minority backgrounds are failing to reach the standards set by the educational system; too rarely are these differences interpreted as evidence of how the system is failing them.

References

Aaron, P. G., Joshi, R. M., Gooden, R., & Bentum, K. E. (2008). Diagnosis and treatment of reading disabilities based on the componential model of reading: An alternative to the discrepancy model of LD. *Journal of Learning Disabilities, 41*, 67–84.

Ambrose, E., & Mudde, C. (2015). Canadian multiculturalism and the absence of the far right. *Nationalism and Ethnic Politics, 21*, 213–236. DOI: http://dx.doi.org/10.1080/13537113.2015.1032033.

Bloemraad, I. (2006). *Becoming a Citizen: Incorporating Immigrants and Refugees in the United States and Canada*. Berkeley: University of California Press.

Bradbury, B., Corak, M., Waldfogel, J., & Washbrook, E. (2011). Inequality during the early years: Child outcomes and readiness to learn in Australia, Canada, United Kingdom, and United States. IZA Discussion Papers, No. 6120, Institute for the Study of Labor (IZA), Bonn. https://docs.iza.org/dp6120.pdf.

Bradbury, B., Corak, M., Waldfogel, J., & Washbrook, E. (2015). *Too Many Children Left Behind: The US Achievement Gap in Comparative Perspective*. New York: Russell Sage Foundation.

Bronfenbrenner, U. (1994). Ecological models of human development. In *International Encyclopedia of Education*, Vol. 3 pp. 37–43 (2nd edition). Oxford: Elsevier.

Bronfenbrenner, U., & Morris, P. A. (2006). The bioecological model of human development. In R. M. Lerner & W. Damon (eds.), *Theoretical Models of Human Development* (pp. 793–828). (Handbook of Child Psychology, Vol. 1). Hoboken, NJ: John Wiley & Sons.

Cohen, J. (1992). A power primer. *Psychological Bulletin, 112*(1), 155.

Crawford, J. (2004). *Educating English Learners: Language Diversity in the Classroom*. Portland, OR: Bilingual Education Services.

D'Angiulli, A., Siegel, L. S., & Hertzman, C. (2004). Schooling, socioeconomic context, and literacy development. *Educational Psychology, 24*, 867–883.

Deacon, S. H., Desrochers, A., & Levesque, K. (2017). Learning to read French. In L. Verhoeven & C. Perfetti (eds.)., *Learning to Read across Languages and Writing Systems* (pp. 243–269). Cambridge: Cambridge University Press.

Duncan, G. J., & Murnane, R. J. (eds.). (2011). *Whither Opportunity? Rising Inequality, Schools, and Children's Life Chances*. New York: Russell Sage Foundation.

Environics Institute for Survey Research. (2019). *Canadian Public Opinion about Immigration and Refugees*. Toronto, ON: Environics Institute for Survey Research.

Fix, M., Papademetriou, D. G., & Sumption, M. (eds.). (2013). *Immigrants in a Changing Labor Market: Responding to Economic Needs*. Washington, DC: Migration Policy Institute.

Friesen, J., & Krauth, B. (2012). *Key Policy Issues in Aboriginal Education: An Evidence-Based Approach*. Toronto: Council of Ministers of Education, Canada.

Gamoran, A. (2015). *The Future of Educational Inequality in the United States: What Went Wrong, and How Can We Fix It?* New York: WT Grant Foundation.

Gandara, P., Rumberger, R., Maxwell-Jolly, J., & Callahan, R. (2003). English learners in California schools: Unequal resources, unequal outcomes. *Education Policy Analysis Archives, 11*, 36.

Hopkins, M., Thompson, K. D., Linquanti, R., Hakuta, K., & August, D. (2013). Fully accounting for English learner performance: A key issue in ESEA reauthorization. *Educational Researcher, 42*(2), 101–108.

Joseph, B. (2018). *21 Things You May Not Know about the Indian Act: Helping Canadians Make Reconciliation with Indigenous Peoples a Reality.* Saanichton, BC: Indigenous Relations Press.

Kieffer, M. J. (2008). Catching up or falling behind? Initial English proficiency, concentrated poverty, and the reading growth of language minority learners in the United States. *Journal of Educational Psychology, 100*, 851–868.

Kieffer, M. J. (2011). Converging trajectories: Reading growth in language minority learners and their classmates, kindergarten to grade eight. *American Educational Research Journal, 48*, 1157–1186.

Kieffer, M. J. (2012). Before and after third grade: Longitudinal evidence for the shifting role of socioeconomic status in reading growth. *Reading and Writing: An Interdisciplinary Journal, 25*, 1725–1746.

Kieffer, M. J., & Thompson, K. D. (2018). Hidden progress of multilingual students on NAEP. *Educational Researcher, 47*(6), 391–398.

Kieffer, M. J., & Vukovic, R. K. (2012). Components and context: Exploring sources of reading difficulties for language minority learners and native English speakers in urban schools. *Journal of Learning Disabilities, 45*, 433–452.

Kymlicka, W. (2010). *The Current State of Multiculturalism in Canada and Research Themes on Canadian Multiculturalism 2008–2010* (Report No: Ci96-112/2010E-PDF). Department of Citizenship and Immigration.

Levy, F., & Murnane, R. J. (2004). *The New Division of Labor: How Computers Change the Way We Work.* New York: Princeton University Press.

Mancilla-Martinez, J., & Kieffer, M. J. (2010). Language minority learners' home language use is dynamic. *Educational Researcher, 39*(7), 545–546.

Mancilla-Martinez, J., & Lesaux, N. K. (2011a). Early home language use and later vocabulary development. *Journal of Educational Psychology, 103*(3), 535.

Mancilla-Martinez, J., & Lesaux, N. K. (2011b). The gap between Spanish speakers' word reading and word knowledge: A longitudinal study. *Child Development, 82*(5), 1544–1560.

Manis, F. R., Lindsey, K. A., & Bailey, C. E. (2004). Development of reading in grades K–2 in Spanish-speaking English-language learners. *Learning Disabilities Research & Practice, 19*(4), 214–224.

Mullis, I. V. S., Martin, M. O., Foy, P., & Hooper, M. (2017). *PIRLS 2016 International Results in Reading.* Chestnut Hill, MA: Boston College, TIMSS & PIRLS International Study Center. http://timssandpirls.bc.edu/pirls2016/international-results/.

National Academies of Sciences, Engineering, and Medicine. (2015). The integration of immigrants into American Society: Panel on the integration of immigrants into American society. In M. C. Waters and M. G. Pineau (eds.), *Committee on Population, Division of Behavioral and Social Sciences and Education.* Washington, DC: The National Academies Press. DOI: http://dx.doi.org/10.17226/21746.

NCES. (2015). Digest of educational statistics. https://nces.ed.gov/programs/digest/d15/tables/dt15_208.20.asp.

NCES. (2016). Education expenditures by country. https://nces.ed.gov/programs/coe/indicator_cmd.asp.

NCES. (2019). National Indian education study. https://nces.ed.gov/nationsreportcard/subject/publications/studies/pdf/2021018.pdf.

OECD. (2006). *Where Immigrant Students Succeed: A Comparative Review of Performance and Engagement in PISA 2003*. DOI: http://dx.doi.org/10.1787/9789264023611-en.

Orfield, G., & Lee, C. (2005). *Why Segregation Matters: Poverty and Educational Inequality*. Los Angeles: University of California Los Angeles, The Civil Rights Project/Proyecto Derechos Civiles. http://escholarship.org/uc/item/4xr8z4wb.

Paris, S. G. (2005). Reinterpreting the development of reading skills. *Reading Research Quarterly, 40*(2), 184–202.

Reardon, S. F. (2011). The widening academic achievement gap between the rich and the poor: New evidence and possible explanations. In G. J. Duncan & R. J. Murnane (eds.), *Whither Opportunity? Rising Inequality, Schools, and Children's Life Chances* (pp. 91–116). New York: Russell Sage Foundation.

Saunders, W. M., & Marcelletti, D. J. (2013). The gap that can't go away: The catch-22 of reclassification in monitoring the progress of English learners. *Educational Evaluation and Policy Analysis, 35*(2), 139–156.

Seymour, P. H., Aro, M., & Erskine, J. M. (2003). Foundation literacy acquisition in European orthographies. *British Journal of Psychology, 94*(2), 143–174.

Shonkoff, J. P., Garner, A. S., Siegel, B. S., et al. (2012). The lifelong effects of early childhood adversity and toxic stress. *Pediatrics, 129*(1), e232–e246.

Snow, C. E., Burns, M. S., & Griffin, P. (eds.) (1998). *Preventing Reading Difficulties in Young Children*. Washington, DC: National Academy Press.

Stats Canada. (2016). Back to school ... by the numbers. www.statcan.gc.ca/eng/dai/smr08/2016/smr08_210_2016#a8.

Truth and Reconciliation Commission of Canada. (2015). *Honouring the Truth, Reconciling for the Future: Final Report of the Truth and Reconciliation Commission of Canada*. https://publications.gc.ca/collections/collection_2015/trc/IR4-7-2015-eng.pdf.

UNESCO [United Nations Educational, Scientific, and Cultural Organization]. (2016). Country profiles for the United States and Canada. http://uis.unesco.org/country/us and http://uis.unesco.org/country/ca.

Washbrook, E., Waldfogel, J., Bradbury, B., Corak, M., & Ghanghro, A. A. (2012). The development of young children of immigrants in Australia, Canada, the United Kingdom, and the United States. *Child Development, 83*(5), 1591–1607.

Yoshikawa, H., Raver, C. C., & Morris, P. (2016). *Can Universal Pre-K Work? Education Solutions Initiative White Paper*. New York: New York University. http://steinhardt.nyu.edu/e/i2/edsolutions/201609/1PreK.pdf.

3 Literacy Contexts and Literacy Development in South America

Ana Luiza Navas

3.1 Introduction

According to UNESCO, some 250 million children worldwide are functionally illiterate, even if 50 percent of them have spent at least four years in school (UNESCO, 2014). Despite several efforts to achieve proper literacy development levels, challenges and obstacles remain for several developing countries, including most of South America. In this continent, underachievement encompasses sociocultural, economic, and political factors that affect education in general, and especially reading instruction policies, to different degrees. Substantial efforts have been made so far, and South America, with a diverse population of near 431 million (United Nations Department of Economic and Social Affairs, 2019), has achieved several educational goals in the past decade. Primary-school coverage has become almost universal, and average years of schooling approach those of the developed countries. Nevertheless, even if illiteracy has mainly decreased, the quality of literacy skills remains poor for both children and adults.

This chapter presents some detailed demographics on the status of literacy development in South America. It discusses public policies and the choice of reading instruction method, one aspect that likely has had a strong influence on the development of reading skills throughout several countries of this continent.

3.2 Demographics and Literacy Development in South America

South America is composed of thirteen countries (Argentina, Brazil, Bolivia, Chile, Colombia, Uruguay, Paraguay, Peru, Ecuador, Suriname, Guyana, French Guyana, and Venezuela). To set the stage for our discussion on literacy, it seems valuable to provide demographic data such as those on population estimates, density, socioeconomics, and, for our purposes, the sociolinguistic characteristics of the region.

The population density in South America, on average, is twenty-four per square kilometer, with considerable variation in this number according to locality. Brazil accounts for almost 50 percent of the population of the region; it is the sixth most populated country in the world, and the largest in size in South America (land area of 8,358,140 km^2). Table 3.1 presents population estimates and corresponding densities, as well as estimates of the Indigenous population of each country in South America (UNESCO Institute for Statistics, 2020).

Regarding the languages of the region, most countries have adopted Spanish as the official language except for Brazil, where Brazilian-Portuguese is the official language; Suriname, with Dutch; and Guyana, where English is the official language spoken. Portuguese and Spanish are represented by alphabetic orthographies, which are, for the most part, transparent; more so in Spanish than in Brazilian-Portuguese (Scliar-Cabral, 2012; Ijalba & Conner, 2006). Because of the large Indigenous population, especially in Bolivia, Ecuador, Peru, Chile, and Colombia, several native languages are spoken with no corresponding writing system. In Bolivia, for example, it is estimated by the National Institute of Statistics of Bolivia that 40.8 percent of children older than six years old are bilingual, 46.8 percent are monolingual in Spanish, and 11.1 percent are monolingual in an Indigenous language, with 27.6 percent speaking Quechua and 18.5 percent Aymara. Bolivia's constitution, in effect since February 2009 recognizes, thirty-six languages of the Indigenous people of Bolivia as official languages apart from Spanish (i.e., Aymara, Araona, Baure, Bésiro, Canichana, Cavineño, Cayubaba, Chácobo, Chimán, Ese Ejja,

Table 3.1 *Total population, density, and Indigenous population estimates for countries in South America*

Abbreviation	Country	Population 2020	Density (people per km^2)	Indigenous population
BR	Brazil	212,559,420	24.96	817,963
CO	Colombia	50,882,890	44.57	1,900,000
AR	Argentina	45,195,770	16.26	955,032
PE	Peru	32,971,850	25.65	5,900,000
VE	Venezuela	28,435,940	31.03	724,592
CL	Chile	19,116,200	25.28	2,100,000
EC	Ecuador	17,643,050	63.73	1,000,000
BO	Bolivia	11,673,020	10.63	4,100,000
PY	Paraguay	7,132,540	17.54	117,150
UY	Uruguay	3,473,730	19.19	76,452
GY	Guyana	786,550	3.66	78,492
SR	Suriname	586,630	3.58	20,344
GF	French Guiana	298,680	3.58	19,000

Source: United Nations, World Population Prospects 2020 (UNESCO Institute for Statistics, 2020)

Guaraní, Guarasu'we, Guarayu, Itonama, Leco, Machajuyai-Kallawaya, Machineri, Maropa, Mojeño-Trinitario, Mojeño-Ignaciano, Moré, Mosetén, Movima, Pacawara, Puquina, Quechua, Sirionó, Tacana, Tapiete, Toromona, Uru-Chipaya, Weenhayek, Yaminawa, Yuki, Yuracaré, and Zamuco). Therefore, Bolivian states must adopt Spanish officially, and at least one additional official language according to the preference of the region.

Across all countries in South America, laws and regulations aim to protect Indigenous languages and cultures and recognize the importance of intercultural bilingual education for Indigenous children. However, there is still a strong historical trend for Indigenous languages and cultures to vanish. Support for such education is a path to reversing this tendency, but it needs to be implemented carefully, which is often not the case. To worsen the scenario, of the Spanish-speaking countries 78 percent of the Indigenous child population live in poverty, as compared to 40 percent of those whose mother tongue is Spanish only (UNICEF, 2012). This inequality is more significant in the ethnic groups living in the Amazon basin, where almost half the children live in extreme poverty.

Throughout South America, educational reforms that promote intercultural bilingual education have been implemented in conjunction with national language policies that officially recognize Indigenous languages (King, 2008). There are some excellent examples of successful programs, even though the Indigenous population is still the least literate in the region. Education in Peru has historically ignored the first language of Indigenous children and has imposed Spanish as the primary language for reading instruction in schools. However, there have been some efforts to offer a Quechuan education for children of Quechua-speaking parents, and the comparison with Spanish-language education may play a role in ameliorating the Indigenous performance in national tests (Hynsjö & Damon, 2016).

Based on the data collected in the latest version of the Third Regional Comparative and Explanatory Study – TERCE, Delprato (2019) investigated whether Indigenous families have lower educational expectations than non-Indigenous families and whether lower Indigenous parental schooling expectations are linked to lower learning achievements by their children. The study included students attending sixth grade (UNESCO-OREALC, 2016) from the following countries: Argentina, Brazil, Chile, Colombia, Ecuador, Guatemala, Honduras, Mexico, Nicaragua, Panama, Paraguay, and Peru. Overall, the results showed that Indigenous parents educational expectations for their children are lower than those of non-Indigenous parents but, once external constraints are accounted for (at the family and school levels), the Indigenous parents' expectations gap tends to disappear.

The Indigenous population in South America still faces several obstacles to achieving adequate reading competence, whether related to the language of instruction, poverty, discrimination, or low educational expectations. Policymakers should focus on Indigenous students who speak native languages at home, since this group would benefit from intercultural and bilingual education. Such an approach to native language would lower the gaps in literacy achievement, particularly during the first grades, and would certainly help their transition to either the Spanish or Portuguese curriculum. In terms of the discussion of the Indigenous population's literacy levels in South American countries, it is crucial to consider the relevant points raised by Delprato (2019) on the concept of "indigenous literacy." The author illustrates the case of Quechuan literary practices, which were discontinued after colonization since they were contrary to European traditions (alphabetic writing). Furthermore, the pressure to impose a way to representing an Indigenous spoken language using a given writing system, such as the alphabet, may in itself exemplify the vulnerability of such minority groups. Any attempt to promote the literacy of Indigenous people should consider them essential to decision-making processes.

Another relevant aspect of the demographics of the region is the high variability of the socioeconomic status of South American countries, with substantial differences between private and public education systems, specially for the early years of schooling. This educational inequality is still a reality in South America, and it is evident that there are vast disparities across regions, and within each of the thirteen countries. In this scenario, the question of access to education has been a priority, and most countries have moved their figures to reasonable levels of enrollment in the past decade, as shown in Table 3.2. Uruguay has a total rate of 99.49 percent enrollment in all levels of education in the country with the highest enrollment rates. Guyana is the country with the lowest enrollment rate, with a value of 85.03 percent of the school-age population (UNESCO, 2014).

Some countries have adopted strong public policies to achieve these numbers, both for the general population and, more specifically, for the most vulnerable sectors. The Colombian school voucher program, PACES, aims to facilitate the enrollment and attendance of low-income students at better-quality schools (Angrist et al., 2002). In contrast, a comparable program in Chile (Anand et al., 2009) provides students with the financial resources to attend schools in more conducive environments. This program also aims to discuss the relevance of education to achieving proper professional training. In parallel, and as early as 1996, with the publication of the National Education Guidelines and Framework Law (the Lei de diretrizes e bases da educação, or LDB), Brazil implemented a basic curriculum in primary and secondary education, increased the number of teaching days, and created a system for the evaluation of educational institutions at all levels. These changes increased options for the integration of vocational education, with considerations for

Table 3.2 *Adjusted net enrollment rate (%), one year before the official primary entry age*

Country	2013	2014	2015	2016	2017	2018
Argentina	97.50	99.19	99.27	99.31	97.82	..
Bolivia	80.12	82.96	85.41	91.27	90.81	90.12
Brazil	89.55	92.25	90.87	97.45	98.05	..
Chile	93.13	95.65	95.10	95.52	93.60	..
Colombia	88.56	89.19	..	..	89.42	99.23
Ecuador	98.48	98.80	98.22	97.83	97.66	94.59
French Guiana						
Guyana						
Paraguay	..	..	..	69.49	..	..
Peru	92.40	96.54	99.47	99.59	99.38	99.23
Suriname	87.23	90.21	94.19	93.22	86.99	90.27
Uruguay	99.64	99.89	99.83	99.52	98.29	..
Venezuela (Bolivarian Republic of)	80.29	90.54	94.19	87.68	85.80	..

Note: There were no data available for Guyana and French Guiana
Source: World Bank 2015 (citing: UNESCO Institute for Statistics)

Table 3.3 *Rate of enrollment (%) by age range (education level) in Brazil*

Age/Year	2012	2013	2014	2015	2016	2017	2018	2019
6-14 y	98.4	98.5	98.6	98.7	99.2	99.2	99.3	99.7
15-17 y	61	62.3	64.2	65.4	67.3	67.5	68.7	71.1

Source: Ministério da Educação, BRASIL (2012).

special and Indigenous education. Since then, primary education has been mandatory, and states and municipalities have the legal obligation to provide openings in the public-school system for every child enrolled from first to ninth grade.

Table 3.3 takes a closer look at the advance of enrollment in the Brazilian education system. Even though the average enrollment rate is low for high-school level (71.1 percent), the figures are higher (up to 99.7 percent) for the age range corresponding to primary education (six to fourteen years old), which is mandatory in Brazil.

This picture reveals unambiguously that access to education has been dealt with seriously by South American governments. The next challenge is to increase the quality of education and to enhance investment into the different levels of education. Investments should range from infrastructure, better curricula for all levels of education, and better salaries to the promotion of evidence-based initial teacher training. What matters is not only the amount of public expenditure on education but also spending it better. Table 3.4 depicts the percentage of expenditure in relation to Gross Domestic Product (GDP) over the past few years for some countries. As a comparison, Finland saw an average of 7 percent of government expenditure on education in this period, whereas, for these countries in South America, the expenditure ranged from 3.30 to at most 6.32 percent of GDP.

Salazar-Cuéllar (2014) has provided a thorough analysis of investment in education digging deeper than the literal figures involved and describes the case of Colombia as an example of how and where money should be best invested to provide better educational outcomes. The main question is of how much better educational systems could perform, given the current public expenditure levels. Along these lines, some initiatives involve public policies aimed at improving reading-promotion activities across the country. One example comes, once again, from the Colombian government, which has increased the number of regular readers and access to books across the age range and promoted reading through the construction and organization of public libraries throughout the country. Between 2006 and 2014, 1,404 public libraries were built in Colombia (Ministerio de Cultura, COLOMBIA, 2006). Alvarez-Zapata et al. (2008) performed an analysis of the initial impact of public libraries in Colombia and showed positive effects on reading habits, recognizing the excellent quality of training programs for librarians and library personnel.

Table 3.4 *Government expenditure on education as a percentage of GDP (%), South American countries*

Country	2011	2012	2013	2014	2015	2016	2017	2018	2019
Argentina	5.29	5.35	5.44	5.36	5.78	5.55	5.46		
Brazil	5.74	5.86	5.84	5.95	6.24	6.31	6.32		
Chile	4.05		4.53	4.73	4.88	5.34	5.42		
Colombia	4.47	4.37	4.88	4.63	4.47	4.48	4.54	4.46	
Ecuador	4.73	4.64	5.00	5.26	5.00				
Guyana	3.59	3.18		5.85	5.21	6.06	6.23	5.49	
Peru	2.66	2.92	3.30	3.70	3.97	3.81	3.93	3.72	3.85
Paraguay	3.70	3.67				3.44			
Uruguay	4.36					4.76	4.84	5.05	

Note: There were no data available for Bolivia, French Guiana, Suriname, or Venezuela.
Source: UNESCO Institute for Statistics 2020 (www.uis.unesco.org). Data as of September 2020

To evaluate the impact of wealth inequalities on learning for six Latin American countries, Delprato, Köseleci, and Antequera (2015) used PISA data for 2000 and 2012. The authors used a multilevel analysis to assess the variability of achievement which accounted for student- and school-specific factors as well as heterogeneity of the types of inequalities across schools and time. The conclusion was that access alone did not guarantee an adequate level of academic achievement.

The data for PISA 2018 (OECD, 2019) also show better performance in reading and science for Chile. Overall, for reading and science scores, the six countries in South America that participate in PISA still show a higher number of students at the lowest levels (Levels 1 and 2). Colombia and Peru have improved their reading scores compared to their previous participation in PISA but are still far from the level of literacy expected (Table 3.5).

Another source of information on student achievement is the Third Regional Comparative and Explanatory Study (Latin American Laboratory for the Assessment of Quality in Education, 2015), an initiative of the Latin American Laboratory for Assessment of the Quality of Education (LLECE)

Table 3.5 *Percentages of students for PISA reading and science scores, by PISA proficiency levels and country, 2018*

Reading	Year	Country	Level 1	Level 2	Level 3	Level 4	Level 5	Level 6
	2018	Chile	28	33	24	12	2	#
		Colombia	48	30	16	6	1	#
		Argentina	51	27	16	5	1	#
		Brazil	50	25	16	7	2	#
		Peru	51	29	14	5	1	#
		Uruguay	39	31	20	8	1	#
Science	Year	Country	Level 1	Level 2	Level 3	Level 4	Level 5	Level 6
	2018	Chile	36	33	23	8	1	#
		Colombia	50	30	15	4	#	#
		Argentina	53	27	15	4	#	#
		Brazil	55	25	14	5	1	#
		Peru	55	29	13	3	#	#
		Uruguay	44	31	19	6	1	#

Rounds to zero. Level 1(1a, 1b, below1b)

Note: Percentages may not sum to 100 because of rounding. Some apparent differences between estimates may not be statistically significant.

Source: Organization for Economic Cooperation and Development (OECD), Program for International Student Assessment (PISA), 2018 Reading, and Science Assessment (OECD, 2019).

in conjunction with its member countries. This study seeks to evaluate the learning achievements of third- and sixth-grade students and identify the associated factors. The TERCE accessed skills in mathematics, reading, writing, and natural sciences, among third and sixth graders, across sixteen countries in Latin America. This institution also applies questionnaires to obtain information on students and their families, teachers, and schools, helping to identify the factors that have the most definite impact on pupils' learning. The results from the third-grade reading test show that 61 percent of students are within performance levels I and II, related to the comprehension of familiar texts and the use of explicit information from the text. The results of the sixth-grade reading test show that 70 percent of students are within performance levels I and II, related to the comprehension of text based on explicit and implicit elements that enable making inferences regarding the meaning of the text (Table 3.6).

An analysis of TERCE's main results corroborates that inequity in the distribution of learning across different social strata remains a continuing crucial issue, both between and within countries. A leading causal agent is the countries' economic status. Specifically, production and distribution of

Table 3.6 *Distribution of Latin American countries compared to the average scores for the region for reading and mathematics for third- and sixth-grade students at the TERCE (2015)*

Area	Grade	Below	At average	Above
Reading	3rd	Guatemala, Honduras, Nicaragua, Panama, Paraguay, Dominican Rep.	Argentina, Brazil, Colombia, Ecuador	Chile, Costa Rica, Mexico, Peru, Uruguay
Reading	6th	Ecuador, Guatemala, Honduras, Nicaragua, Panama, Paraguay, Dominican Rep.	Argentina, Peru	Brazil, Chile, Colombia, Costa Rica, Mexico, Uruguay
Mathematics	3rd	Guatemala, Honduras, Nicaragua, Panama, Paraguay, Dominican Rep.	Colombia, Ecuador	Argentina, Brazil, Chile, Costa Rica, Mexico, Peru, Uruguay
Mathematics	6th	Guatemala, Honduras, Nicaragua, Panama, Paraguay, Dominican Rep.	Brazil, Colombia, Ecuador	Argentina, Chile, Costa Rica, Mexico, Peru, Uruguay

Source: Student achievement in Latin America and the Caribbean – Results of the Third Regional Comparative and Explanatory Study (Latin American Laboratory for the Assessment of Quality in Education, 2015)

income might be a simple explanation of why higher-income countries such as Chile and Uruguay generally show better results, as seen in the performance of the Second Regional Comparative and Explanatory Study (2013). However, the relationship between socioeconomic status and reading outcomes is complex, and many other factors may play a role in this equation (Duncan & Magnuson, 2012).

3.3 Teacher Training and Reading Instruction in South America

One of the many aspects involved in the discussion of students' underachievement in international and local assessments in South American countries has been the deficient initial teacher training provided in those countries, especially for those in charge of the early stages of reading instruction. This discussion necessarily involves methods of instruction; a long-standing universal debate has concerned recommended approaches for reading instruction, for example, analytic versus synthetic methods.

The science of reading has produced a vast amount of evidence toward an understanding of the underlying mechanisms that support skilled reading, how reading should be taught, and the leading causes of reading difficulties in the contexts of many different languages and writing systems around the world (e.g., Seidenberg, 2013; Morais, 2014). Scientific evidence does suggest that a phonological approach is crucial in the early stages of visual word recognition in orthographies such as Spanish or Portuguese (Lieberman et al., 1974; Cardoso-Martins, 1991, 2013; Castro, Andrade, & Barrera, 2019; Manrique & Signorini, 1994). Duncan et al. (2013) investigated phonological development concerning native language and literacy in six alphabetic orthographies, including Portuguese and Spanish, at the beginning and end of the first year of reading instruction. Based on their results, they argue that phonics instruction promotes an early metaphonological capacity to manipulate phonemes. Additionally, based on another study comparing different orthographies, single-word reading level should be achieved among several languages after one year of formal instruction, especially in those with a transparent orthographic system (Seymour, Aro, & Erskine, 2003). However, for students in several countries in South America, performance in reading tasks was low, both at the decoding and comprehension levels. This is true even though the orthographies are transparent and straightforward, as in Portuguese or Spanish.

In the United States, the National Reading Panel (National Institute of Child Health and Human Development; NRP, 2000) performed a comprehensive evidenced-based review on how children learn to read. Over 100,000 studies published on reading since 1966–2000 were reviewed, and some areas were found to be crucial for reading instruction: for example, phonemic awareness, phonics, fluency, vocabulary, and comprehension. In the United States, where several public policies have emphasized the importance of language and phonological processing aspects in grasping the alphabetic principle, there is still a strong need for changes in the content of initial teacher-training programs. Information about the psychology of reading may be theoretical but also translate into practical situations in the classroom; in other words, there is still a need for teachers to acquire structured skills on the psychology of reading and apply this knowledge from research on reading instruction (Brady, 2018).

Godoy and Viana (2016) compared the linguistic content related to the teaching of reading in two training programs for literacy teachers in Brazil and Portugal. The researchers analyzed two official programs: (a) in Brazil, the National Pact for Literacy at the Right Age (Pacto Nacional pela Alfabetização na Idade Certa – PNAIC) and (b) in Portugal, the National Program for Portuguese Teaching (Programa Nacional do Ensino do Português – PNEP). Whereas the analysis showed similarities regarding duration, number of hours, and material provided, the theoretical approach differed. In Portugal, the program was rooted in theoretical cognitive psychology and linguistics, whereas the Brazilian equivalent lacked references to phoneme awareness or letter-sound correspondences, under a dominant constructivist approach. Hence, only in the former case was the importance of language and metalinguistic abilities for reading and writing development explicitly mentioned.

Other countries have also proposed revisions of initial teacher-training programs to guarantee that teachers implement oral language instruction and intervention based on precursors of reading development (Morales et al., 2015). In Chile, the program entitled "Aprendizaje Inicial de la Lectura Escritura y Matemáticas" still recommends explicitly integrating the contributions of the whole-language approach, which promotes immersion in a world of print, with contributions from the skills approach, including phonics.

Across South American countries, whole language is the dominant approach to teaching reading in the public educational system. Brazil, Argentina, and Colombia have favored top-down methods, such as whole language (Morais, 2014). In recent years, Chile and Uruguay have shifted to adopt a skill-based or a mixed approach in reading instruction, and even though the new policy is still recent, it may already have had some impact since both countries have since shown higher levels of achievement compared to their neighbors. In Brazil, the Ministry of Education released "The National Program for Reading at the Adequate Age" (Ministério da Educação, BRASIL, 2012), which proposes that third-grade students should have minimal reading skills. A couple of teacher-training programs have enhanced the initial reading instruction process, but according to Morais (2014), these programs misinterpreted phonics reading instruction and ignored the scientific evidence on learning to read. The main point of his criticism relates to the fact that teacher-training programs present wrong ideas on the concept of phonics instruction and promote the teaching of isolated sounds with no relation to letters.

Finally, Argentina's national public policies have moved from a whole-language to a synthetic approach, more specifically one with an emphasis on phonics instruction (Ministerio de Educación de la Nación, ARGENTINA, 2018). In 2019, the government changed the reading instruction policy in Brazil, strongly emphasizing the need to develop basic skills (Ministério da Educação, BRASIL, 2012), as proposed by the National Reading Panel (NRP, 2000), with adaptations for Brazilian-Portuguese language and orthography. It will be possible to estimate the effects of these changes in policies that are based on evidence-based teacher training in the years to come. The proposed program has received criticisms from teachers specially trained in whole language approach, reigniting the conflict between ideologies. Unfortunately, South American countries are far from ending the reading wars (Castles, Rastle, & Nation, 2018).

Although there are still some divergent discussions in terms of public policies, the research includes several studies that use evidence-based practices and consider the sociolinguistics characteristics of Portuguese and Spanish. However, there are a limited number of studies on reading for South American Indigenous languages, especially in the early stages (Latin-American and Caribbean Reads Capacity Program, 2016). In Chile, reading and language interventions show improvements after a twenty-seven-week program for low-income, vulnerable communities: The group that received the intervention showed better results than the control group on several skills, including reading comprehension (Mesa et al., 2020).

The most emblematic case of a stable public policy on successful reading instruction is found in Sobral, a city of around 207,000 inhabitants in the State of Ceara, Brazil. Since 2001 the students have undergone a process of systematic teaching of early reading and writing skills from kindergarten. The local teacher-training program emphasizes the cognitive sequence for precursors, such as oral language, acquisition of basic reading skills, and focus on reading fluency (Becskehazy, 2018). The fact that this has led to years of increasingly more effective evidence-based reading instruction are verified by the national basic-education ranking, on which Sobral has risen to number 1 out of the country's more than 5,000 municipalities. Furthermore, on the PISA, Sobral public schools showed higher scores than private schools in São Paulo.

3.4 Concluding Remarks

In the past decade, South America has faced advances and challenges in children's literacy development. Challenges range from problems related to demographic aspects of the countries (e.g., dense population, enrollment,

Indigenous languages) to political and socioeconomic factors (e.g., income-distribution inequality, extreme poverty, high vulnerability, low investment in education). However, there have been some promising advances in research on best practices in reading instruction, some successful experiences of Indigenous education, and the proposition of public policies that promote initial teacher training using evidence-based methods. Considering the complexity of reading instruction and the many challenges faced by the region, if we are to improve literacy development in South American countries, there is an urgent need to overcome socioeconomic barriers and increase the level of investment in primary education, including the establishment of public policies that protect the early development of the most vulnerable children (see also Nag, Chapter 15 in this volume). Moreover, it seems mandatory to improve initial teacher-training quality and continuous education programs focusing on scientifically based knowledge and warrant better opportunities to apply this theoretical knowledge in the form of efficient educational practices (see Dickinson et al., Chapter 17 in this volume).

References

Álvarez-Zapata, D., Nayrobis, G. Y., Santamaría, G. M. R., & Maricela, V. (2008). Acercamiento al estado actual de la promoción de la lectura en la Biblioteca Pública en Colombia. (Approach to the state of the art of reading promotion in Colombian public libraries).*Revista Interamericana de Bibliotecología, 31*(2), 13–43. SSRN: https://ssrn.com/abstract=2779607.

Anand, P., Mizala, A., & Repetto, A. (2009). Using school scholarships to estimate the effect of private education on the academic achievement of low-income students in Chile. *Economics of Education Review*, 28, 370–381. DOI: https://doi.org/10.1016/j.econedurev.2008.03.005.

Angrist, J., Bettinger, E., Bloom, E., & King, M. K. (2002). Vouchers for private schooling in Colombia: evidence from a randomized natural experiment. *American Economical Review*, 92(5), 1535–1558.

Becskehazy, I. (2018). *Institucionalização do direito à educação de qualidade: o caso de Sobral* (Institutionalization from rights to quality of education: The case of Sobral) (PhD. thesis, São Paulo: Universidade de São Paulo).

Brady, S. (2018). Efficacy of phonics teaching for reading outcomes: Indications from post-NRP research. In S. Brady, D. Braze, and C. Fowler (eds.), *Explaining Individual Differences in Reading: Theory and Evidence* (pp. 69–96). London: Psychology Press.

Cardoso-Martins, C. (1991). Awareness of phonemes and alphabetic literacy acquisition. *British Journal of Educational Psychology*, 61, 164–173.

Cardoso-Martins, C. (2013). Beginning reading acquisition in Brazilian Portuguese. In M. R. Joshi & P. G. Aaron (eds.), *Handbook of Orthography and Literacy* (pp. 171–188). London: Routledge.

Castles, A., Rastle, K., & Nation, K. (2018).Ending the reading wars: Reading acquisition from novice to expert. *Psychological Science in the Public Interest*, 19, 5–51.

Castro, D., Andrade S., & Barrera, S. D. (2019). The contribution of emergent literacy skills for early reading and writing achievement. *Trends in Psychology*, *27*(2), 509–522. DOI: https://doi.org/10.9788/tp2019.2-15.

Delprato, M. (2019). Parental education expectations and achievement for Indigenous students in Latin America: Evidence from TERCE learning survey. *International Journal of Educational Development*, *6*, 10–25.

Delprato, M., Köseleci, N., & Antequera, G. (2015). Education for all in Latin America: Evolution of the school inequality impact on education achievement. *Revista Latinoamericana de Educación Comparada*, *6*(8), 45–75.

Duncan, L. G., Castro, S. L., Defior, S., et al. (2013). Phonological development in relation to native language and literacy: Variations on a theme in six alphabetic orthographies. *Cognition*, *127*(3), 398–419.

Duncan G. J., & Magnuson, K. (2012). Socioeconomic status and cognitive functioning: moving from correlation to causation. *Wiley Interdisciplinary Reviews: Cognitive Science*, *3*, 377–386.

Godoy, D. M. A., & Viana, F. L. (2016). Conteúdos linguísticos como subsídio à formação de professores alfabetizadores – a experiência do Brasil e de Portugal. (Linguistic content as support to early teacher training – an experience from Brazil and Portugal). *Revista Brasileira de Estudos Pedagógicos*, *97*(245), 82–96.

Hynsjö, D., & Damon, A. (2016). Bilingual education in Peru: Evidence on how Quechua-medium education affects indigenous children's academic achievement. *Economics of Education Review*, *53*, 116–132.

Ijalba, E., & Conner, P. S. (2006). Multisensory identification-remediation of phonological- orthographic deficits in Spanish speakers learning English. (Paper presented at the annual convention of the American Speech-Language-Hearing Association, Miami.)

King, K. (2008). Language education policy in Latin America. In K. Brown (ed.) *Encyclopedia of Language & Linguistics* (pp. 453–457). Oxford:Elsevier, 2006.

Latin American and Caribbean Reads Capacity Program. (2016). *Early Grade Reading in Latin America and the Caribbean: A Systematic Review*. Washington, DC: United States Agency for International Development (USAID).

Latin American Laboratory for the Assessment of Quality in Education. (2015). *TERCE: Initial Background Information, Executive Summary*. Paris: UNESCO.

Liberman, I. Y., Shankweiler, D., Fischer, F.W., & Carter,B. (1974). Explicit syllable and phoneme segmentation in the young child. *Journal of Experimental Child Psychology*, *18*(2), 201–212.

Manrique, A. M. B., & Signorini, A. (1994).Phonological awareness, spelling and reading abilities in Spanish-speaking children. *British Journal of Educational Psychology*, *6*, 429–439.

Mesa, C., Newbury, D., Nash, M. et al. (2020). The effects of reading and language intervention on literacy skills in children in a remote community: An exploratory randomized controlled trial. *International Journal of Educational Research*. *100*. 101535. DOI: https://doi.org/10.1016/j.ijer.2020.101535.

Ministerio de Cultura, COLOMBIA. (2006). *Política pública de Fomento a la Lectura para el periodo 2006 – 2016*. (Public policy of reading promotion for 2006–2016). Decreto 133 del 21 de Abril de 2006.

Ministério da Educação, BRASIL. (2012). *Pacto Nacional pela Alfabetização na Idade Certa* (PNAIC). Brasília: Livreto de Apresentação.

Ministerio de Educación de la Nación, ARGENTINA. (2018). *Postítulo Alfabetización en la Unidad Pedagógica*. (Learning to read in pedagogical unit) Materiales. Coord. Gral: Dra. Mirta Castedo. Buenos Aires: Ministerio de Educación de la Nación.

Morais, J. (2014). *Alfabetizar para a democracia* (Learning to read for democracy). Porto Alegre: Penso Press.

Morales, L. M., Barrios, A. V., Moscoso, R. G., & Franco, V. G. (2015). Cómo enseñan a leer los profesores de 1° y 2° básico en un contexto de evaluación de desempeño docente en Chile? (How do teachers teach to read 1st and 2nd grades in a context of teachers performance evaluation in Chile?)*Estudios Pedagógicos 41*(1), 183–198.

NRP (National Reading Panel). (2000). *Teaching Children to Read: An Evidence-Based Assessment of the Scientific Research Literature on Reading and its Implications for Reading Instruction*. Washington, DC: NICHD.

OECD. (2019). *PISA 2018 Results (Volume I): What Students Know and Can Do*. Paris: PISA, OECD Publishing. DOI: https://doi.org/10.1787/5f07c754-en.

Salazar-Cuéllar, Andrés Felipe. (2014). The efficiency of education expenditure in Latin America and lessons for Colombia: La eficiencia del gasto público educativo en Latinoamérica y lecciones para Colombia. *Desarrollo y Sociedad*, (74), 19–67. DOI: https://dx.doi.org/10.13043/DYS.74.1.

Scliar-Cabral, L. (2012). Neuroscience applied to learning alphabetic principles: New proposals. *Ilha do Desterro: A Journal of English Language, Literatures in English and Cultural Studies* (63). DOI: http://doi.org/10.5007/21758026.2012n63p187.

Seidenberg, M. S. (2013). The science of reading and its educational implications. *Language Learning and Development: The Official Journal of the Society for Language Development*, 9(4), 331–360. http://doi.org/10.1080/15475441.2013.812017.

Seymour, P. H. K., Aro, M., & Erskine, J. M. (2003). Foundation literacy acquisition in European orthographies. *British Journal of Psychology*, 94, 143–174. DOI: http://doi.org/10.1348/000712603321661859.

World Bank. (2015). *Indigenous Latin America in the Twenty-First Century*. Washington, DC: World Bank.

UNESCO. (2014). *Teaching and Learning: Achieving Quality for All*. Education for All Global Monitoring Report. Paris: UNESCO,

UNESCO-OREALC. (2016). *Student Achievement in Latin America and the Caribbean: Results of the Third Regional Comparative and Explanatory Study*. Organization of the United Nations for Education, Science and Culture, Paris, France and the Regional Office of Education for Latin America and the Caribbean. Santiago: OREALC/UNESCO Santiago.

UNESCO Institute for Statistics (2020). Government expenditure on education as a percentage of GDP. Data extracted from UIS. www.uis.unesco.org

United Nations Department of Economic and Social Affairs. (2019). *World Population Prospects 2019: Highlights* (ST/ESA/SER.A/423). New York: United Nations.

4 Postcolonial Literacy Development in the Caribbean

Ludo Verhoeven and Ronald Severing

4.1 Introduction

During the past century, a far-reaching process of decolonization has taken place in the Caribbean, a region of insular territories with mostly native-Creole-speaking communities in between North and South America. However, the processes of the emancipation and liberalization of the colonies did not necessarily lead to self-government of these Caribbean communities. In many cases a political affiliation with the former colonizer remained, as characterized by the use of official languages linked to the colonial past. As a consequence, both indigenous Creoles and colonial languages, such as Spanish in Cuba, French in Haiti, English in Jamaica, and Dutch in Curaçao, are used in contemporary Caribbean societies. An important question is that of how literacy in the native language and second language(s) in Caribbean states develop in the context of the continued use of colonial languages. Literacy development in a postcolonial setting is not only obviously relevant in education; it can also be seen as a marker of identification and cultural distinctiveness as part of a growing autonomy (see also Navas, Chapter 3 and Morgan et al., Chapter 10 in this volume).

In the present chapter, we consider the postcolonial development of literacy in the Caribbean. First, we highlight the sociolinguistic background of language and literacy planning in native and (ex)colonial languages across Caribbean nations. Special attention is given to the use of these languages in education and the effects on the actual attainment of literacy levels in native and colonial languages across Caribbean states. In addition, the focus is on postcolonial literacy development in the Dutch Caribbean as an interesting case in which the Creole language Papiamentu has become highly valued in the media, education, and other social domains, replacing Dutch. We go into the gradual implementation of Papiamentu literacy in the curriculum, the literacy levels in native Papiamentu, and Dutch as a (foreign) colonial language throughout the primary grades and its relations with school success. Finally, we provide a future perspective on postcolonial literacy development in the Caribbean.

4.2 Literacy Development in the Caribbean

4.2.1 Sociolinguistic Background

Sociolinguistic studies provide evidence that the development of literacy has important consequences for individuals and societal communities. It guides personal and communal communication and serves social, economic, and political actions in society (cf. Stubbs, 2013). In the Caribbean context, as societies make the transition from colonization to autonomy, careful language planning is needed, as well as an appreciation of social and cultural resources which does not exclude the possibility of their utilization. The Caribbean islands are among the Small Island Developing States (SIDS), which were first recognized as a distinct group of developing countries at the United Nations Conference on Environment and Development in June 1992. They include countries that tend to share similar sustainable development challenges, including historical underachievement in terms of school success.

In many cases, a Creole variety is the native language of a location's inhabitants, or the predominant language heard at home. Creole languages derive from pidgins – language varieties that emerge when groups of people, mostly as a result of population movement, develop a new language by simplifying their own language(s) and adding words and phrases from other contact languages. In case a new generation of learners acquires the emerging variety as their home language, the pidgin is then redefined as a Creole (see Siegel, 2005). Creoles such as Papiamentu in the Dutch Caribbean and Kwéyòl in St. Lucia are autonomous in that the colonial language is not the lexifier language, whereas Creoles such as Jamaican and Trinidad Creoles can be considered more continuous. Creoles can be seen as contact languages in situations where groups of people have to communicate with each other without the availability of a common language (cf. Migge, Leglise, & Bartens, 2010a). The most widely spoken Creole is Haitian Creole with more than 10 million speakers. It is estimated that more than 75 million people speak a Creole as their native language, of which the majority develop literacy in a second language, often the colonial language (Siegel, 2005).

The focus of language planning in Caribbean societies during the past decades has been on the processes and individual variation of literacy and school success in L1 Creole and L2 colonial language(s). The low educational achievements of these societies can, to a large extent, be explained as resulting from a mismatch between the language of the population (mostly a Creole language) and the school language (mostly the ex-colonial language). Only gradually has investment been provided for the codification and further development of Creole languages. Reports of large numbers of class repeats and school dropouts have urged for a broad scientific evaluation of these countries' educational systems, with a special focus on the role of Creole language, not only as a school subject but also as a possible tool to enhance the development of literacy and school success in the second language (see Migge et al., 2010a). Programs of action have been proposed to assist the SIDS in their sustainable development efforts, with a strong focus on the development of human resources via education. Such programs vary widely and appear to be linked with the nature of the individual Caribbean country's remaining colonial ties, the nature of linguistic diversity, the developmental state of the indigenous language(s), and the language attitudes among the speakers. In most societies passing through a transitional period from colonial to postcolonial time, the tension between the position of indigenous languages and the colonial language brings about an upgrading of the mother tongues and even a takeover of the position of the colonial language (cf. Siegel, 2005). Decolonization involves not only the appreciation of the mother tongue over a colonial language, but also the strengthening of autonomy and political power. However, in many cases the drive to displace colonial languages tends to be softened because of economic or political forces, usually resulting in a slowing down of the pace of enactment of new laws. According to Churchill (1986), the strengthening of indigenous languages generally proceeds stagewise. It starts out with recognition of their existence as a vehicle for communication and education in the local community. Then it is followed by an extension, a consolidation, and an adaptation phase, leading to multilingual coexistence.

Depending on the situation in a society, language planning may take different forms (see Ager, 2001; Appel & Verhoeven, 1994). Usually, the first task in a postcolonial state is to determine which language(s) should fulfill the role of national language. In the vast majority of cases, the colonial language is abandoned in favor of one of the indigenous languages. In addition to processes of language selection, the position of minority languages must be dealt with. Accordingly, decisions need to be made about the developmental support of languages used in a society. A common procedure for language support is that of codification, which can be seen as a prerequisite for the standardization of a language. Codification includes at least an explicit statement of the model for standard language usage via dictionaries, grammars, spelling, punctuation, and pronunciation guides, and reference materials. It is important to note that any language variety is modifiable in such a way that orthographies can be developed and lexical elaboration provided. As Siegel (2010) has pointed out, the development of a standard form of a Creole differs from that of other language varieties in that the Creole needs to be made autonomous from its lexifier so that it is perceived as a separate language. Moreover, the standardized Creole needs to be accessible to the majority of its speakers.

4.2.2 Educational Background

Language policy primarily manifests itself in two domains: the mass media (including social media) and education. As to the mass media, it is a matter of policy to what extent the (post)colonial and indigenous language will perform public functions in the community. Measures in this domain concern the use of written language in institutions, periodicals, and libraries. As to education, different perspectives can be taken on the legal opportunities for both indigenous and (post)colonial literacy education (Siegel, 2005). There can be a monolingual approach focusing on the indigenous language, or the colonial language, only. There can also be a transitional model in which the indigenous language is used as a vehicle to better learn to become literate in the second language. Children who have learned the writing code in one language do not need to start from scratch in the other. Basic literacy skills can be easily transferred from one language to the other (Chen, Dronjic, & Helms-Park, 2015). Finally, there can be a model focusing on full biliteracy. In such a case, literacy instruction may start from the indigenous language, the colonial language, or simultaneously from both languages. For a review of the effects of alternative biliteracy instruction models, see Verhoeven (2010, 2017). Although evaluations of multilingual programs in the Caribbean are only beginning to emerge, it can be concluded that the implementation of Creole literacy in the school curriculum brings about an awareness that the native language can be seen as an educational resource for higher motivation and better learning outcomes among students (Pereira, 2018; Siegel, 2010).

With respect to literacy development in a Caribbean context, an important question is whether learning to read should be taught first in the child's indigenous language (L1) and then in the second language (L2); simultaneously; or the other way around. It can be argued that the acquisition of literacy will be facilitated when the instruction links up with the child's linguistic background (Cummins, 2001). Moreover, the child's motivation and self-concept may increase if the instruction is given in their native language (Spolsky, 2000). Importantly, there can be linguistic transfer in bilingual reading instruction in that children who have learned to read in one language do not have to start from scratch in another: What they do have to learn is a new written language code. With respect to the acquisition of academic language skills, Cummins (1991: 85) has hypothesized the role of interdependence as follows: "To the extent that instruction in a certain language is effective in promoting proficiency in that language, transfer of this proficiency to another language will occur, provided there is adequate exposure to that other language (either in the school or environment) and adequate motivation to learn that language." The interdependence hypothesis predicts that optimal input in one language leads not only to better skills in that language but also to a deeper conceptual and linguistic proficiency that can clearly facilitate the transfer of various cognitive and academic language skills across languages. A high level of proficiency in the first language may thus enhance the development of the second language. However, if skills in the first language are not well developed and education in the early years is in the second language, the further development of the second language may stagnate. Importantly, it is argued that certain aspects of bilingual development may also facilitate the more general cognitive and metalinguistic functioning of children (Bialystok, 2001; Verhoeven, 2007). However, the exact conditions under which language transfer typically occurs and just how particular patterns of bilingual development relate to children's levels of literacy in L1 and L2 are as yet unclear (Durgunoglu & Goldenberg, 2011; Verhoeven, 2010, 2017).

The sociocultural background of children in the Caribbean region may also have a large impact on their language and literacy learning. A first relevant aspect is language exposure. Language input in and outside the home environment may have an impact on children's L1 and L2 development (Lesaux & Geva, 2006; Nag et al., 2018). Likewise, the home literacy environment may have a differential effect on children's (bi)literacy development (Dickinson & Neuman, 2006; Dickinson et al., Chapter 17 in this volume,). Another relevant characteristic is the sociocultural orientation of the child and their parents (see Nag, Chapter 15 in this volume). Parental attitudes toward L1 maintenance and L2 learning may have an impact on the child's attitudes and motivation (Ager, 2001; Pereira, 2018). Apart from family-related characteristics, school-related sociolinguistic factors may also have an impact on children's language and literacy learning in L1 and L2, such as the teacher's educational level, teaching experience, language proficiency, and sociocultural orientation (Lemberger & Reyes-Carrasquillo, 2011; Nag et al., 2016; Dickinson et al., Chapter 17 in this volume).

Finally, initiatives must be taken to develop and implement (bi)literacy programs in schools. For such programs, two sets of curriculum materials should be made available, besides literary books and reference works in the two languages. For the Creole language, it is extremely important that the lexicon is continuously elaborated with new entries in order to enable the development of curricula for basic, secondary, and higher education. For the colonial language, it is critical that curriculum materials are an ethnically appropriate mirror of the local realities. Another important issue is the availability of qualified teachers. Teachers must be well trained in literacies in the language(s) of instruction in order to be able to offer the planned literacy programs. With reference to the teaching of Creole besides French in Guadeloupe, Bolus (2010) noted that there is a high load on teachers given the fact that the availability of curricular materials in the Creole languages is limited and they are in short supply, so that teachers have to develop their own curricular materials. Therefore, there is an urgent need for teacher training to ground teachers' knowledge on biliteracy development and apply this knowledge so as to make their literacy teaching more effective.

4.2.3 Literacy Levels in Caribbean Societies

UNESCO (2013) provided global literacy rates of the adult population (fifteen years and older) in Caribbean countries. Overall, the literacy rate in 2011 was estimated to be 92 percent as compared to 90 percent in 2000 and 86 percent in 1990. A breakdown by gender showed that 55 percent of illiterate people were women. Over the years, the literacy rate has grown faster among females, narrowing the gap with men. There is significant variation between the different territories. In Antigua and Barbuda, the Cayman Islands, Trinidad and Tobago, Aruba, and Costa Rica, the illiteracy rate is less than 5 percent; in Puerto Rico and the Dominican Republic, less than 10 percent; in Jamaica, Honduras, and Guyana less than 15 percent; and in Haiti about 50 percent. Trinidad and Tobago is one of the few countries in the region that has participated in the International Reading Literacy Study (PIRLS). Over the years 2006, 2011, and 2016, PIRLS results show a steady improvement in the global literacy benchmark, which may be due to the successful implementation of nationwide programs that were designed to increase literacy levels among students (Charles, 2013; George & Quamina-Aiyejina, 2003).

UNESCO data also show that throughout Caribbean territories there is large variation in school trajectories and in characteristics related to the child, the home environment, and schools in the region. With respect to school trajectories, literacy is often taught in the official (ex-colonial) language only. In some cases, literacy instruction in the Creole language is also being implemented (see Migge et al., 2010). In quite a few countries (e.g., Guadeloupe, Haiti, Jamaica), literacy is being taught in the Creole language from scratch. In a quasi-experimental study, Carpenter and Devonish (2010) showed that the implementation of a bilingual literacy program in the early primary grades with Jamaican Creole and English as languages of instruction yielded high literacy outcomes in Jamaican Creole with no cost for the development of English literacy (Phillipson, 1990). In another quasi-experimental study, Simmons-McDonald (2010) found that the introduction of French Creole as the language of instruction for literacy in primary schools in St. Lucia helped poor learners to develop literacy not only in French Creole but also in English as a second language. It is important to note that the pilot studies on bilingual literacy instruction that have been conducted so far have proved to be successful in developing literacy even in those children that show great variation in entrance levels of cognitive and linguistic abilities and cultural orientation, as well as in terms of the socioeconomic background of the family, the literacy practices in the home, and in the school support parents give to the child. Of course, it should be emphasized that experiments with bilingual literacy education can only be successful where there is full institutional support. Migge et al. (2010b) evaluated three projects on the implementation of local languages in primary schools in French Guiana. They concluded that only when long-term support from the authorities is provided, including the development and provision of curricula in the local languages and teacher training in bilingual literacy programs, can sustained levels of biliteracy be attained.

4.3 Creole Papiamentu Literacy Development in the Dutch Caribbean

4.3.1 Historical Context

The Dutch Caribbean comprises a group of islands, also named the Dutch Antilles, which were colonized by the Dutch in 1634. It is made up of the so-called Leeward Islands: Aruba, Bonaire, and Curaçao, with the Portuguese-based Creole Papiamentu as the generally used vernacular in a population of about 300,000; and the Windward Islands: Sint Maarten, Saba and St. Eustatius, with English as the common language of communication in a population of about 43,000. In this section, we focus on the development of literacy on the Leeward Islands, where Papiamentu is the language of children's primary socialization process (cf. Severing & Weijer, 2008). It is interesting to note that until the beginning of the twentieth century, education was offered by missionary posts, with Creole Papiamentu as the language of instruction. However, in 1936 Papiamentu was banned from schools after a renewed economic interest in the islands on the part of the Dutch authorities in the Netherlands, despite the fact that Papiamentu was spoken by the vast majority of the population. Since then, the use of Dutch in schools was prescribed, whereas Papiamentu was considered to be an obstacle to learning. Formal education could best be characterized as L2 submersion, with children who spoke Papiamentu as their main language being engaged in Dutch instruction. Not until 1986 was Papiamentu assigned a place in the primary school curriculum on Curaçao and Bonaire. Thanks to great efforts in language codification and curriculum development, the role of Papiamentu within schools greatly expanded, while the majority of the instruction nevertheless took place in Dutch. From 2008, Dutch, Papiamentu, and English were recognized as the three official languages on the islands.

According to estimates, Papiamentu is the mother tongue of almost 80 percent of the population on the Leeward Islands. Most children first come into contact with Dutch at school. As Dutch is not spoken or hardly spoken in the child's environment, it can be considered a foreign language. The language situation can best be characterized with the term "diglossia" (cf. Appel & Verhoeven, 1994; Managan, 2016). On the one hand, there is the Creole Papiamentu, which was traditionally held in relatively low esteem but functions as the general lingua franca. On the other hand, there is Dutch, which has a relatively high social status and is generally learned as a foreign language in school. However, as a result of increasing political independence, Papiamentu's status has increased dramatically in recent years, with the language being highly valued and increasingly used in formal situations. For example, most newspapers are published in Papiamentu and parliamentary debates also take place in that language (cf. Severing & Weijer, 2008). Moreover, serious attempts have been made to make Papiamentu suitable as a language for instruction by elaborating its lexicon with new entries, developing school curricula for language, literacy, and content matters, and by grounding teacher training in a multilingual perspective (Severing & Weijer, 2010). In a recent study, Pereira (2018) investigated how 108 teachers in Aruba valued the role of Papiamentu in education. The great majority of teachers promoted educational reform that gives an important place to Papiamentu in the curriculum. They also pointed to the necessity of specific in-service training of teachers to prepare them for multilingual education. Twelve teachers with experience in Scol Multilingual – an innovative bilingual-education experiment on the island – were also interviewed; they indicated improved learning attitudes and better academic outcomes on the part of their pupils. In another survey, Pereira interviewed 1,141 parents of children at primary education level. By far, most parents were extremely supportive of educational reform from monolingual Dutch toward bilingual Papiamentu–Dutch education.

4.3.2 Early Language and Literacy Development

In a recent survey, the exposure to Papiamentu and Dutch of 183 children aged nought to four years on the island of Bonaire was examined (Odenthal & Bouwman, 2016). The children's parents were interviewed as regarded their language of primary socialization, frequency of storybook reading, preferred television channels, and use of preschool facilities. It was found that the great majority of native parents from the Dutch Caribbean used Papiamentu as the primary home language, with only limited exposure to Dutch. Among a small minority of parents originating from other South American territories and from the Netherlands, the main languages in the home were reported to be Spanish and Dutch respectively, with limited contact with Papiamentu. With respect to storybook reading, parents reported reading to their child more often in Papiamentu than in Dutch. However, in one third of the cases, no storybook reading was reported by parents. Preschool facilities were reported to be widely used. In most cases the caretakers spoke Papiamentu or Papiamentu and Dutch, and the use of Dutch only was reported to be rare.

A quasi-experimental study examined the preliteracy development in Papiamentu and Dutch of eighty children aged four to six and living on the island of Curaçao (Narain, 1995; Narain & Verhoeven, 1994). Children's abilities in receptive and productive vocabulary, sentence reproduction, and narrative comprehension were assessed in Papiamentu and Dutch, and their phonological awareness in Dutch was also assessed. Children's performance on these tests were measured at three moments: at the beginning of kindergarten, and after one and two years of education in kindergarten. At the end of kindergarten, the children's phonological awareness was also measured. In order to explore the relationship between language proficiency and background features, sociocultural background characteristics (preschool duration, sociocultural orientation of the child and the parent, linguistic exposure, language used by the teacher) were also measured.

The results on the development of language abilities over time are presented in Figure 4.1. In all four linguistic skills examined in Papiamentu and Dutch, there was significant progress over time. Comparison of the two languages shows that participating children on Curaçao are significantly stronger in Papiamentu than in Dutch throughout the entire kindergarten school period and at all linguistic levels. Figure 4.1 also shows that the scores on productive vocabulary, sentence reproduction, and narrative comprehension were relatively low throughout the kindergarten period.

It is important to note that evidence of cross-language transfer was also found. Over the two years of kindergarten, the longitudinal relations between Papiamentu-language abilities on the one hand and Dutch-language abilities on the other turned out to be extremely strong. Interestingly, there was also evidence of significant relations from L1 Papiamentu to L2 Dutch over time, as assumed in the framework of linguistic transfer (e.g., Chen et al., 2015).

Two other important findings came out of the study. One is that sociocultural variables substantially predicted the children's first- and second-language proficiency. Duration of preschool and the child's cultural orientation combine to determine almost 40 percent of the variance in Papiamentu-language scores whereas the child's linguistic exposure and parents' cultural orientation explained 80 percent of the variance in Dutch-language scores. At the end of kindergarten, the language used by the teacher explained about 25 percent of the variance in Papiamentu-language scores. Simultaneously, language exposure at school and at home and the child's cultural orientation together determine 77 percent of the variance in Dutch-language scores.

The other finding was that the degree of bilingual competence in children predicted their phonological awareness, which can be seen as an important

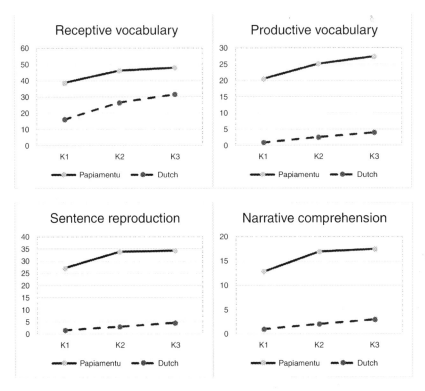

Figure 4.1 Means for the tests for receptive vocabulary, productive vocabulary, sentence reproduction, and narrative comprehension in Papiamentu and Dutch at the beginning (K1) and after one year (K2) and two years (K3) of kindergarten

precursor of their literacy development. The scores on phonological-awareness tasks were highest for children who scored above average in both languages, intermediate for children who scored above average in one language, and lowest for children who scored below average in the two languages. Apparently, a high level of bilingualism leads to good insight into the structure of language as such. This is in line with earlier research and theorizing (cf. Bialystok, 2001; Cummins, 1984).

4.3.3 Bilingualism and Learning to Read

With respect to the development of basic literacy skills, Prins-Winkel (1983) stated that Dutch-only language education on the island of Curaçao primarily leads to a high level of functional illiteracy. Children often prove to be able to perform reasonably well in the subject of Dutch as a foreign language, but have great difficulty using the language in everyday situations which require its written use. Recent evidence for this claim comes from a study by Odenthal and Bouwman (2016), who studied the language and literacy levels of 940 children in Bonaire in the age range of nine to eighteen. In a questionnaire, children reported that Papiamentu was spoken at home in almost 90 percent of families, in half of the cases in combination with Dutch. For half of the children, Papiamentu was the dominant language in school, while for 40 percent the dominant school language is Dutch. Outside school, children reported reading more books in Papiamentu than in Dutch. In Grades 2–5, children's word-decoding fluency (the number of isolated words read in one minute) and reading comprehension were assessed. It was found that children on Bonaire developed L2 word-decoding skills across the grades. However, they stayed behind their monolingual Dutch peers in the Netherlands. The children's reading-comprehension levels across the grades were extremely low compared to those of their Dutch peers. Finally, the literacy levels in Papiamentu and Dutch of 1,067 students at the end of secondary school were examined. The students from Bonaire remained behind in Dutch literacy compared with their peers in the Netherlands, whereas their level in Papiamentu literacy was higher than their Dutch. However, it should be noted that both in the Netherlands and in Bonaire there are three different educational tracks in the secondary school system (lower-vocational, higher-vocational, and pre-university level), with fewer students from Bonaire in the two higher tracks.

In several other studies attempts were made to examine the literacy development of children in both Papiamentu and Dutch. Severing (1997) and Severing and Verhoeven (1995) examined the development of word decoding, reading vocabulary, sentence comprehension, and text comprehension in written Papiamentu and Dutch from Grades 5 and 6 in primary school, with literacy being taught in Dutch and Papiamentu being taught as a subject for only half an hour a week. In Figure 4.2, the means of children's word decoding (number of words read aloud correctly in one minute), reading vocabulary, sentence comprehension, and text comprehension at the beginning and end of Grade 5 and at the end of Grade 6 are presented.

It was found that primary-school children on Curaçao learned to decode words significantly better in Dutch than in Papiamentu, but that their performance on reading vocabulary, sentence comprehension, and text comprehension was significantly better in Papiamentu than in Dutch. For word decoding, children were overall better in Dutch compared to Papiamentu, bearing in mind that reading instruction took place in Dutch. But the differences became smaller over time. For reading vocabulary, sentence comprehension, and reading comprehension, significant progress over the grades was also evidenced. The children scored higher overall in Papiamentu as compared to Dutch, and

Postcolonial Literacy Development in the Caribbean 81

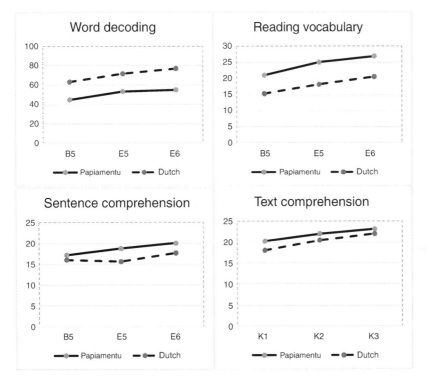

Figure 4.2 Means for the tests for word decoding, reading vocabulary, sentence comprehension, and text comprehension in Papiamentu and Dutch at the beginning (B5) and the ends of Grades 5 (E5) and 6 (E6)

even more so for reading vocabulary. Next, the researchers examined to what extent the children's reading abilities in Papiamentu and Dutch were related. In both Papiamentu and Dutch, word decoding, reading vocabulary, and reading comprehension abilities were not only longitudinally related but also cross-linguistically related to each other. Interestingly, the development of Papiamentu word-decoding ability could to a large extent be predicted from the level of Dutch word-decoding ability. This finding shows that the language of instruction has a high impact on the children's literacy development and that development of Papiamentu literacy skills takes place even without much formal instruction in school. However, it is interesting to note that for reading comprehension it was the other way around, with transfer going from Papiamentu (the strongest language) to Dutch (the weaker language) despite the lack of instruction in Papiamentu.

The study by Severing and Verhoeven also explored to what extent the variation in Papiamentu and Dutch reading abilities is associated with factors which can be related to the child or their family background. Papiamentu word decoding at the three testing times was negatively associated with grade repetition and positively with the child's reading behavior, whereas Papiamentu reading comprehension was negatively associated with grade repetition and positively with cognitive skills and socioeconomic status. For Dutch, word decoding and reading comprehension across the grades were negatively associated with class repeats and positively with cognitive skills, attitude toward Dutch, exposure to Dutch, and socioeconomic status. Dutch word decoding was also related to the child's reading behavior. These findings show that both child factors related to the child – such as cognitive skills, class repeating, and reading behavior – and background factors related to language exposure, language attitudes, and socioeconomic status contribute to the prediction of literacy in Papiamentu and Dutch.

In three recent studies, the variation of Papiamentu and Dutch reading in the Dutch Caribbean was further explored. Henderickx (2018) examined the effect of the order of literacy instruction on word-decoding and reading-comprehension abilities in Papiamentu and Dutch in 166 children from Grade 3 and 140 children from Grade 5. For half of the children in each cohort, the order of reading instruction was Papiamentu–Dutch (i.e., Papiamentu starting in Grade 1, Dutch starting by the end of Grade 2), and for the other half it was Dutch–Papiamentu. Overall, the word-decoding scores in the two grades were about the same in Papiamentu and Dutch. This may be because there is a great deal of overlap in the letters and literacy conventions used in the two languages. Importantly, the reading-comprehension scores in the two grades were found to be higher in Papiamentu. The instruction order Dutch–Papiamentu yielded higher scores on Dutch reading comprehension, with no impact on Papiamentu reading comprehension, in both grades. Apparently, a high reading proficiency in Dutch as a foreign language is largely dependent on the amount of reading instruction and reading exposure in that language.

Mercelina et al. (2023) examined the variation in early decoding development in Papiamentu (Creole L1) and Dutch (postcolonial L2) from kindergarten to second grade of 156 children while considering order of initial decoding instruction (L1 or L2), kindergarten precursors, and transfer effects. Results revealed that in the case of L1 decoding instruction, the development of letter knowledge and decoding was higher in Papiamentu and in the case of L2 decoding instruction it was higher in Dutch. When instruction started in L1, Papiamentu decoding development was statistically significantly predicted by phonological awareness and letter knowledge, and Dutch decoding development by letter knowledge only. When instruction started in L2, Dutch decoding development was statistically significantly predicted by phonological awareness, letter knowledge, short-term memory, and speech decoding, and Papiamentu decoding development by letter knowledge and vocabulary. Transfer effects were found from the language of decoding instruction to the other language with L1 precursors significantly predicting L2, but not the other way around. These results reveal the pivotal role and benefit of including the L1 in early bilingual decoding development in a postcolonial context.

Finally, Van der Elst-Koeiman et al. (2022) examined the Papiamentu (L1) and Dutch (L2) reading comprehension development of 293 fourth-grade students in postcolonial Dutch Caribbean schools. It was found that reading comprehension in Papiamentu and Dutch was predicted by initial language of alphabetization, on the one hand, and word decoding, receptive vocabulary, and grammatical ability on the other hand. There was also evidence of linguistic interdependencies for decoding and reading comprehension between languages. The results highlight the importance of language of instruction for Papiamentu and Dutch reading skills.

4.3.4 Literacy and School Success

A number of studies have examined the relationship between language skills and school success. A classic study is that of Prins-Winkel (1973). In the context of monolingual Dutch-language education, she related children's academic performance to their intelligence, their socioeconomic class, and their home language. General cognitive abilities and socioeconomic class proved to have a positive correlation with academic performance, a finding corroborated by other research in this field. Furthermore, the home language proved to be a predictor: The more Dutch was spoken at home, the better the academic performance at the Dutch-only school. On the other hand, Kook and Vedder (1989) found that Papiamentu-speaking children at middle-class schools scored as well in spelling and vocabulary tests as the Dutch-language children at those schools. They therefore concluded that the child's home language does not by itself have a decisive influence on academic performance. This is in line with findings in other parts of the world (cf. Nag et al., 2018). A few studies have revealed that the exclusive attention to Dutch in education did not lead to positive educational results. First, periodically gathered statistics proved how low the educational return was during the time of Dutch monolingual education. As a result of the high level of discontinuity between the language offered to children at home and at school, over 60 percent of the children were found to have repeated one or more years in primary education (Minister of Education and Culture, 1992). Oltheten (1980) examined the determinants of nonpromotion in primary education. Sociocultural characteristics and the family's socioeconomic position, regional differences, and the efficacy of the school proved to primarily predict children's nonpromotion. Finally, Severing (1997) examined the relation between word decoding and reading comprehension abilities in Papiamentu and Dutch in fifth and sixth grade on the one hand and educational success by the end of primary school on the other. Notwithstanding the fact that formal literacy instruction throughout the grades had been given to a large extent in Dutch and that educational success was measured in Dutch only, it was found that not only children's literacy attainment in Dutch but also their literacy development in Papiamentu significantly predicted their success in secondary education.

4.4 Future Perspectives on Literacy Development in the Caribbean

To conclude, research has evidenced an important impact of the role of Creole languages in enhancing literacy development and school success in Caribbean education. The studies carried out in the Dutch Caribbean and elsewhere show some important findings. To begin with, they show that at the onset of primary education, Papiamentu is by far the dominant language. This is educationally relevant since it has been well documented that, in a multilingual context, literacy is best taught in the strongest language children have at their disposal (Verhoeven, 2010). Research also showed that even in a Dutch school setting, reading comprehension scores in Papiamentu tended to be higher than in Dutch. Importantly, evidence of cross-language transfer was also evidenced in kindergarten and in the primary grades, showing that language and literacy skills learned in Papiamentu could be transferred to similar skills in Dutch. Moreover, a high level of bilingual proficiency was found to be associated with a high level of metalinguistic awareness, which is highly relevant for children's insight into the alphabetic principle. Another important research outcome was that the introduction of Papiamentu as a school language did result in substantial gains in that language without a cost of skills in L2 Dutch. Starting from a bilingual literacy curriculum it was found that the order of instruction did not affect word decoding outcomes. It did affect reading comprehension in that Dutch reading comprehension benefitted from an early start in the curriculum. Of course, research has only started to uncover the steps children in the Caribbean make in becoming literate in native Creole languages and second languages as it relates to their academic success. More research is needed to explain the large variation in linguistic skills and motivation that children bring to school in relation to the use of first and second language(s) in the school curriculum. Research should also focus on the language of higher education and how student success in academic languages there is affected by the patterns of language use in primary and secondary schools.

From the perspective of sustainability, the impact of Creole languages and of the teachers and parents in bilingual education can be regarded of utmost importance and should optimally be fostered in connection with cultural orientation and school success (Dijkhoff & Pereira, 2010). With a view to improving the success rate in education, it seems advisable to introduce Creoles or other indigenous languages as teaching languages in education on a large scale. The fact that census data report major numbers of class-repeat, students with low-level academic outcomes, and school dropouts suggests the need for investment related to the development of bilingualism, literacy, and school success (Delgado et al., 2016). At this point in time, Creole languages constitute the mother tongue of the vast majority of the population and are the languages of choice for all socioeconomic classes across a wide range of Caribbean territories. In many places, Creoles have already been accepted as teaching languages in infant school and special education and as the professional language in primary education. It seems plausible that with these educational reforms there will be fewer children repeating years and dropping out, and that the pupils' level of education will, on average, be higher at primary schools where the mother tongue is officially recognized as the language of instruction.

From a sociolinguistic point of view, it is clear that the development of the indigenous language(s) in a (post)colonial society can have a great impact on the individual child and its community. It provides a major socialization channel into the community and a means to get to know its historical roots. Accordingly, it can be seen as a cornerstone for the optimum attainment of both intragroup communication and ethnic continuity. Importantly, the mother tongue of children can be seen as the best vehicle to teach children academic subjects such as literacy and math (Verhoeven, 2017). Once children have learned these skills in their first language, they can be easily transferred to other languages, such as the colonial language. Of course, the colonial language can fulfill a role in intergroup communication and in schooling in higher-education settings. It can be argued that functional bilingualism in colonial settings can only be feasible if the language needs of speech communities are seriously taken into account by the authorities. With respect to language and educational planning, we recommend that policymakers analyze the language needs of communities by means of quantitative surveys and ethnographic interviews with teachers, parents, and students, as well as other community representatives. Such analyses of linguistic needs should yield guidelines for the determination of final objectives in education (see Pereira, 2018).

If there is a need to use the native language in education, adequate information and instructional materials in that language and qualified teachers must be made available in the native language. A distinction can be made between different kinds of educational arrangements. First of all, different roles can be acknowledged for the native language(s) and the (post)colonial language under consideration. These roles may vary from no encouragement to a short-term transitional medium, or a medium for language maintenance. When a bilingual program is foreseen, two sets of materials need to become available. For material in the indigenous language, the problems may be even greater. When the language is unstandardized, work on language standardization must be done beforehand. In addition, new instructional materials must be developed for all school subjects. Besides the development of curricula, literary books and reference works must be published and implemented (see Siegel, 2010). In case materials in the colonial language are still being used in schools, they should be carefully checked for cultural bias. Curricula in colonial languages often reflect the values of vernacular(s) country of origin, which makes it difficult for children to relate them to their local context. In order to arrive at a better connection between the child's background knowledge and the content of the foreign language curriculum, materials should be produced which reflect an ethnically and culturally appropriate picture of society.

The case of language planning in the Dutch Caribbean makes it clear that the standardization of a Creole and its implementation in education is feasible. However, a few words of caution are in order. First, the consequences of language planning usually bring about high costs. The poor socioeconomic background of (post)colonial states may hamper the execution of educational plans there. The provision of new instructional materials in the vernacular(s), as well as in the colonial language(s) – now being taught as a foreign language – will bring about high cost implications. Another important delimiting condition for bilingual literacy education is the availability of qualified teachers. Teachers must be well trained and competent enough to be able to offer literacy programs in primary and secondary education. An efficient administrative school board in charge of the implementation of innovative attempts in bilingual education should also be available. The success of innovations in bilingual education are not only dependent on the skills that teachers bring to the school; teacher attitudes are also extremely important in bringing about a fundamental renewal of education. Positive responses to educational renewal can be stimulated through intense school and community involvement during the process of curriculum development and implementation. All too often, implementation and evaluation have been neglected as necessary stages in language planning. In many cases intentions and orientations have been emphasized without attention being paid to the effects of proposed legislation. In this light, Pereira (2018) advocated an integrative approach to the use of Creole in the classroom with sustainable development as its major objectives, and affective rather than material and physical factors as the key to development.

References

Ager, D. (2001). *Motivation in Language Planning and Language Policy*. Bristol: Multilingual Matters.

Appel, R., & Verhoeven, L. (1994). Decolonization, language planning and education. In J. Arends, P. Muysken, & N. Smith (eds.), *Pidgins and Creoles: An Introduction* (pp. 65–74). Amsterdam: John Benjamins.

Bialystok, E. (2001). *Bilingualism in Development: Language, Literacy and Cognition.* Cambridge, MA: Cambridge University Press.

Bolus, M. (2010). The teaching of Creole in Guadeloupe. In B. Migge, I. Léglise, & A. Bartens (eds.), *Creoles in Education: An Appraisal of Current Programs and Projects* (pp. 81–106). Amsterdam: John Benjamins.

Carpenter, K., & Devonish, H. (2010). Swimming against the tide: Jamaican Creole in education. In B. Migge, I. Léglise & A. Bartens, (Eds.), *Creoles in Education: An Appraisal of Current Programs and Projects* (pp. 167–181). Amsterdam: John Benjamins.

Charles, J. (2013). An investigation into the experience of two reading specialists connected to the Caribbean Centre for Excellence in Teacher Training in enhancing student reading achievement in underperforming primary schools in Trinidad. (MA thesis, University of the West Indies.)

Chen, X., Dronjic, V., & Helms-Park, R. (2015). *Reading in a Second Language.* New York: Routledge.

Churchill, S. (1986). *The Education of Linguistic and Cultural Minorities in the OECD Countries.* Clevedon: Multilingual Matters.

Cummins, J. (1984). Wanted: A theoretical framework for relating language proficiency to academic achievement. In C. Rivera (ed.), *Language Proficiency and Academic Achievement.* Clevedon: Multilingual Matters.

Cummins, J. (1991). Conversational and academic language proficiency in bilingual contexts. *AILA Review, 8,* 75–89.

Cummins, J. (2001). *Language, Power and Pedagogy: Bilingual Children in the Crossfire.* Clevedon: Multilingual Matters.

Delgado, S., Lecompte, P., Lao, H., Mopsus, D., Echteld, L., Severing, R., & Faraclas, N. (2016). Education, languages in contact, and popular culture in the Hispanophone, Francophone and Dutch Caribbean. In N. Faraclas, R. Severing, C. Weijer, L. Echteld, W. Rutgers, & R. Dupey, (eds.) *Embracing Multiple Identities: Opting Out of Neocolonial Monolingualism, Monoculturalism and Mono-identification in the Dutch Caribbean* (pp. 85–94). Curaçao: University of Curaçao.

Dickinson, D. K., & Neuman, S. B. (2006). *Handbook of Early Literacy Research.* New York: Guilford Publications.

Dijkhoff, M., & Pereira, J. (2010). Language and education in Aruba, Bonaire and Curaçao. In: B. Migge, I. Leglise, & A. Bartens (2010). *Creoles in Education: An Appraisal of Current Programs and Projects* (pp. 211–226). Amsterdam: John Benjamins.

Durgunoglu, A., & Goldenberg, C. (eds.) (2011). *Language and Literacy Development in Bilingual Settings.* New York: Guilford.

George, J., & Quamina-Aiyejina, L. (2003). *An Analysis of Primary Teacher Education in Trinidad and Tobago.* DFID Educational Paper 49E. London: Department for International Development.

Henderickx, I. (2018). *Effecten van instructievolgorde bij tweetalig leesonderwijs op Curaçao.* (MA thesis, Radboud University Nijmegen.)

Kook, H., & Vedder, P. H. (1989). *Antiano I Arubano den skol; de onderwijssituatie van Antilliaanse en Arubaanse kinderen en van hun klasgenoten.* Utrecht: P. O. A.

Lemberger, N., & Reyes-Carrasquillo, A. (2011). Perspectives on teacher quality: Bilingual education and ESL teacher certification, test-taking experiences, and instructional practices. *Journal of Multilingual Education Research, 2,* 57–79.

Lesaux, N.K., & Geva, E. (2006). Synthesis: Development of literacy in language minority learners. In D. L. August & T. Shanahan (eds.) *Developing Literacy in a Second Language: Report of the National Literacy Panel* (pp. 53–74). Mahwah, NJ: Lawrence Erlbaum Associates.

Managan, K. (2016). The sociolinguistic situation in Guadeloupe: Diglossia reconsidered. *Journal of Pidgin and Creole Languages,* 31, 253–287. DOI: https://doi.org/10.1075/jpcl.31.2.02man.

Mercelina, G., Segers, E., Severing, R., & Verhoeven, L. (2023). Variation in early decoding development in a post-colonial Caribbean context. *Learning and Individual Differences,* 102. DOI: https://doi.org/10.1016/j.lindif.2023.102257

Migge, B., Léglise, I., & Bartens, A. (2010a). Creoles in education: A discussion of pertinent issues. In B. Migge, I. Léglise & A. Bartens (eds.), *Creoles in Education: An Appraisal of Current Programs and Projects* (pp. 1–30). Amsterdam: John Benjamins.

Migge, B., Leglise, I., & Bartens, A. (2010b). *Creoles in Education: An Appraisal of Current Programs and Projects.* Amsterdam: John Benjamins.

Minister of Education and Culture. (1992). *Het basisonderwijs op de Nederlandse Antillen.* Willemstad: Ministry of Education and Culture.

Narain, G. (1995). *Een studie naar het Papiamentu en het Nederlands van kleuters op Curaçao en Nederland.* (Doctoral dissertation, Tilburg University.)

Narain, G., & Verhoeven, L. (1994). *Ontwikkeling van tweetaligheid bij allochtone kleuters.* Tilburg: Tilburg University Press.

Odenthal, L., & Bouwman, A. (2016). *Geletterdheid op Bonaire.* Bonaire: Stichting Lezen en Schrijven.

Oltheten, T. (1980). *Overgaan of zittenblijven: Een sociologische verkenningsstudie van factoren die invloed hebben op de leerprestaties van het Curaçaose volkskind in het basisonderwijs.* The Hague: UNA.

Pereira, J. (2018). *Valorization of Papiamentu in Aruban Society and Education.* (Doctoral dissertation, University of Curaçao.)

Prins-Winkel, A. C. (1973). *Kabes duru? Verslag van een onderzoek naar de onderwijssituatie op de Benedenwindse Eilanden van de Nederlandse Antillen in verband met het probleem van de vreemde voertaal bij het onderwijs.* Zeist: Dijkstra.

Prins-Winkel, A. C. (1983). Educational myths, ideals and realities on the A-B-C-islands of the Netherlands Antilles: A century of educational efforts and failures in Dutch-colonial schools. In E. Muller (ed.), *Papiamentu: Problems and Possibilities* (pp. 9–22). Zutphen: De Walburg Pers.

Severing, R. (1997). *Geletterdheid en onderwijssucces op Curaçao.* (Doctoral dissertation, Nijmegen.)

Severing, R., & Verhoeven, L. (1995). Tweetaligheid en schoolsucces van kinderen op Curaçao. *Pedagogische Studiën, 72,* 357–373.

Severing, R. & Weijer, C. (2008). The fundashon pa planifikashon di idioma: Language planning and language policy in Curaçao (p. 247–260). In N., Faraclas, R. Severing, & C. Weijer (eds.), *Linguistic Studies on Papiamentu*. Curaçao: Fundashon pa Planifikashon di Idioma.

Severing, R., & Weijer, C. (2010). Gaining perspective on Papiamentu: Milestones and achievements. In N. Faraclas, R. Severing, C. Weijer & L. Echteld (eds.), *Crossing Shifting Boundaries* (pp. 13–28). Willemstad: Fundashon pa Planifikashon di Idioma, Universiteit van de Nederlandse Antillen.

Siegel, J. (2005). Literacy in pidgin and creole languages. *Current Issues in Language Planning, 6*(3), 143–163.

Siegel, J. (2010). Bilingual literacy in creole contexts. *Journal of Multilingual and Multicultural Development, 31*(4), 383–402.

Simmons-McDonald, H. (2010). Introducing French Creole as a language of instruction in education in St. Lucia. In B. Migge, I. Léglise & A. Bartens (eds.), *Creoles in Education: An Appraisal of Current Programs and Projects* (pp. 183–210). Amsterdam: John Benjamins.

Spolsky, B. (2000). Anniversary article: Language motivation revisited. *Applied Linguistics, 21*, 157–169. DOI: https://doi.org/10.1093/applin/21.2.157.

Stubbs, M. (2013). *Language and Literacy: The Sociolinguistics of Reading and Writing*. London: Routledge.

UNESCO. (2013). *Never Too Late to Complete School*. UIS Information Paper, 15. Paris: UNESCO.

Van der Elst-Koeiman, M., Segers, E., Severing, R., & Verhoeven, L. (2022). Learning to read in mother tongue or foreign language: Comparing Papiamento-Dutch reading skills in the post-colonial Dutch Caribbean. *Learning and Individual Differences, 95*, 102–138. DOI: https://doi.org/10.1016/j.lindif.2022.102138.

Verhoeven, L. (2007). Early bilingualism, language transfer, and phonological awareness. *Applied Psycholinguistics, 28*, 425–439.

Verhoeven, L. (2010). Second language reading acquisition. In M. L. Kamil, P. D. Pearson, E. B. Moje & P. Afflerbach (eds.) *Handbook of Reading Research* (pp. 661–683). New York: Taylor & Francis.

Verhoeven, L. (2017). Learning to read in a second language. In K. Cain, D. L. Compton, & R. K. Parilla (eds.) *Theories of reading development* (pp. 215–235). Amsterdam: John Benjamins.

5 Literacy Development in Europe

Luisa Araújo and Patrícia Costa

5.1 Introduction

The European Union (EU) is a political and economic union of twenty-seven Member States (MS).[1] Its members are industrialized nations that value inclusion and allow free movement of its citizens within the union (Charter of Fundamental Rights of the European Union, European Union, 2016). In most countries in the EU, primary education starts at age six and compulsory education lasts between nine and ten years, but in many countries, students are required to attend vocational programs until they reach eighteen (European Commission/EACEA/Eurydice, 2016). The EU has common educational benchmarks, such as the reduction of the number of low achievers in reading, mathematics, and science in secondary school, and a minimum tertiary education completion rate. The latter stood at 41,2% in 2021, and the 2030 target is 45% (European Commission, 2022). These targets reflect common agreement on what is deemed important to achieve in education and schooling, namely the appropriate qualifications for jobs that should be acquired in professional training and/or via a university degree. Good skills in reading, mathematics, and science are viewed as a prerequisite for integration in the knowledge society (European Commission, 2020), but challenges remain. In the EU, socioeconomic status is still a determinant of education achievement (see also Kieffer & Vuković, Chapter 2, and Nag, Chapter 15 in this volume). Immigrant students have lower achievement levels in reading, mathematics, and science in secondary school (OECD, 2017), and the foreign-born have lower tertiary attainments than native students (European Commission, 2020).

This chapter offers an overview of literacy development in Europe. The focus is on indicators of reading-literacy achievement in countries that are members of the EU and participate in International Large-Scale Assessments (ILSAs).

---

[1] The European Union (EU) is an economic and political union of twenty-seven countries also called Member States: Austria, Belgium, Bulgaria, Croatia, Republic of Cyprus, Czech Republic, Denmark, Estonia, Finland, France, Germany, Greece, Hungary, Ireland, Italy, Latvia, Lithuania, Luxembourg, Malta, Netherlands, Poland, Portugal, Romania, Slovakia, Slovenia, Spain, Sweden.

Literacy Development in Europe

First, we present evidence related to the spread of literacy in Europe and discuss current notions about the relationship between schooling and literacy abilities and about the role of skills for full integration in society. Second, we summarize the evidence on the variation of reading acquisition and development in different linguistic systems. Third, we give an overview of variations in literacy achievement and their relationship with home and school factors. Next, we present current literacy achievement levels in primary and secondary school and discuss their association with home background factors captured in ILSAs. Finally, we summarize the role of ecological factors and conclude by discussing how ILSAs can contribute to our understanding of reading development in Europe and inform policy decisions.

5.2 Literacy and Schooling in Europe

5.2.1 Historical Perspective

Educational attainment grew enormously from 1960 to 1995 in most of the Western world, with the average number of years of schooling nearly doubling (Heckman & Jacobs, 2009). In 2015, in the European Union,[2] 80 percent of youngsters under twenty-five completed upper-secondary education or the equivalent of twelve years of schooling (OECD, 2017). This average is for twenty-two EU countries; the available data still includes the United Kingdom but excludes Bulgaria, Croatia, Cyprus, Lithuania, Malta, and Romania. It is possible that if data were available for the current twenty-seven EU Member States this average would be slightly different. For the EU22, it reflects wide variation among countries in terms of progress over time and differences in recent education attainment rates. For example, while in Portugal the secondary-school completion rate grew from 51 percent in 2005 to 83 percent in 2012, in Hungary it increased only two percentage points, from 80 to 82 percent, during the same time interval. In 2015, in Spain 68 percent of young adults completed secondary school compared to 87 percent in Finland.

The expansion of schooling is a major factor influencing the spread of literacy worldwide and three major periods have been identified in the diffusion of literacy (UNESCO, 2005). Before 1800, reading was already widespread in northern Europe in countries like Denmark, Finland, England, and France, but was confined to the upper classes. In Germanic-language countries and German-speaking regions, more than 50 percent of males were already literate

---

[2] The European Union average – EU22 – for upper-secondary completion rate includes the following countries: Austria, Belgium, the Czech Republic, Denmark, Estonia, Finland, France, Germany, Greece, Hungary, Ireland, Italy, Latvia, Luxembourg, the Netherlands, Poland, Portugal, the Slovak Republic, Slovenia, Spain, Sweden, and the United Kingdom (OECD, 2017, p. 63).

before 1790 (Diebolt & Hippe, 2017). In contrast, in southern European countries like Spain, Portugal, and Italy, illiteracy was the norm. Between 1800 and 1860, little progress in literacy rates was registered in these countries, while in northern Europe modest progress was achieved. Several European countries introduced compulsory education in the first half of the nineteenth century, but actual enrollment in primary schools was very low (Hippe & Fouquet, 2015). After 1860, literacy levels improved in much of Europe because of the introduction of legislation regulating compulsory education, although literacy levels in Hungary, Italy, Spain, and the Balkan countries remained low even around 1900. Following low literacy levels in most of nineteenth-century Europe, schooling became more available to all but social elites after the mid-nineteenth century. This change was rooted in the need for record keeping and for skillful labor linked to the use of new technologies, such as the steam engine, that required workers who could maintain and fix machinery. However, the spread of literacy remained a challenge (Hippe & Fouquet, 2015) and the situation in the following century was as follows:

During the early twentieth century, literacy levels increased throughout Europe, with few changes in the ranking of countries. By mid-century, central, and northern Europe were reported to have achieved over 95% literacy; Western Europe, over 80%; Austria and Hungary, over 70%; and Italy, Poland, and Spain, over 50% literacy. In Portugal and the Eastern Orthodox countries, adult literacy rates were not above 25%; only after 1945 did the ability to use written languages extend to the masses. (UNESCO, 2005, p. 191)

Different factors may account for the cross-country and within-country regional differences in adult literacy rates from the 1800s to the twenty-first century. These include literacy traditions (Elley, 2001), geographical location, and linguistic background. For example, during the 1800s, geographical proximity appears to have played a role in the spread of literacy from Germany, Switzerland, and the Netherlands to neighboring regions in Belgium, France, and northern Italy (Diebolt & Hippe, 2017). Furthermore, regional discrepancies in literacy rates within a country were often associated with linguistic variations. This may have been the case in Brittany, where French was not widely spoken before the nineteenth century, and which registered much lower literacy rates than other French regions in the 1800s (Diebolt & Hippe, 2017).

The beginning of the twentieth century clearly marked the widespread attendance of all children at least at primary school in most of the industrialized world (Weber, 2001), although in some countries the literacy rate of all citizens did not significantly increase until the second half of the century (UNESCO, 2005). During this latter period, the spread of schooling in most of Europe was clearly linked to the attainment of more sophisticated levels of literate ability and to greater economic returns. Put differently, while in earlier periods an individual could be considered literate if he or she could only sign his or her name (Venezky, 1991) schooling in the second half of the twentieth century made it possible for individuals to further develop reading and writing abilities, and this rise in education levels translated into better jobs and higher salaries (Heckman & Jacobs, 2009). The accumulation of knowledge through schooling, often referred to as human capital, paid off in economic terms. However, at the turn of the century and into the twenty-first century the picture is more complex, because studies show that more school attainment does not translate directly and unequivocally into higher literate abilities.

Research conducted in the last decades has shown that quality of education is a better indicator of life outcomes than quantity of education, as measured in years of schooling (Heckman & Jacobs, 2009). This suggests that "School attainment is not a very good proxy for knowledge" (p. 27) and that, as Hanushek and Woessmann (2015) contend, "direct measures of cognitive skills offer a superior approach to understanding how human capital affects the economic fortunes of nations" (p. 28). In relation to literacy attainment, children who fail to develop the basic reading skills needed to comprehend what they read by the fourth grade are likely to face reduced educational opportunities (Adams, 2009; Chall & Jacobs, 2003). This, in turn, will affect their chances of acquiring the skills that are essential for full participation in society and in the labor force (Hanushek & Woessmann, 2015).

As we have discussed, schooling and associated literacy rates in Europe vary from country to country and this variation has been present since the 1800s. While the relation between years of schooling and literacy abilities is not well documented prior to the twentieth century, in the 1800s someone with the ability to sign his or her name would have been considered a literate individual (UNESCO, 2005). If the ability to sign one's name was already considered a literate behavior in the 1800s, and a useful one in terms of signing a work commitment or property possession (Venezky, 1991), what reading-literacy skills characterize the European student population of the twenty-first century, and how do children develop them?

5.2.2 *Reading Development in Different Orthographies*

Several cross-linguistic and/or cross-national studies have looked at how children develop reading skills in different orthographies (Seymour, Aro, & Erskine, 2003; Vaessen et al., 2010; Ziegler et al., 2010). In the case of alphabetic writing systems, orthographic depth explains different rates of reading development and children seem to acquire reading faster in transparent orthographies (Pollatsek & Treiman, 2015). The facilitating effect transparent orthographies have in reading development has mostly been established in the first stages of learning to read, first and second grades, and confirmed by studies that ask children to read words and nonwords (Seidenberg, 2013). In a comparative study of reading acquisition in twelve different languages, Seymour et al. (2003) found that English and Danish first-graders take longer than Finish, Spanish, or Italian ones to master word-decoding skills.

In a transparent or shallow orthography, such as Finnish, there is a one-to-one phoneme-to-grapheme mapping whereby one letter represents one sound and vice versa. Research indicates that there is a continuum, with English being one of the most opaque alphabetic languages – different pronunciations for the same spelling patterns – while French and Danish are positioned somewhere in the middle of the orthographic-depth continuum (Schmalz et al., 2015). For example, in French, spelling-to-sound relations are reasonably predictable, but sound-to-spelling relations are more ambiguous (Schmalz et al., 2015). Among Western European languages, English has the most inconsistent orthography, and this impacts the rate at which English-speaking children develop literacy (Sproat, 2016). A child learning to read in English is confronted with the task of learning inconsistent print-to-speech correspondences, such as "ea" having one sound in "bread" and another in "leak" (Schmalz et al., 2015). To a lesser extent, a Portuguese first-grader is also confronted with a phonological inconsistent orthography; for example, "ca" can correspond to /ka/ or /kɐ/ (Ventura et al., 2019). In contrast, a child learning to read in Spanish does not encounter many words that have graphemes that share the same spelling but can be pronounced differently in different words. This facilitates learning to an extent that a child's ability to name letters and segment speech sounds in kindergarten are not such strong determiners of that child's reading ability in second grade and beyond (Caravolas et al., 2012).

Other studies specifically addressing the impact of predictors of reading ability, for example the ability to segment speech sounds or phonological awareness (PA), indicate that reading development is modulated by orthography transparency. PA is a stronger predictor in less transparent orthographies, such as French and Portuguese, than in more transparent ones like Dutch, Hungarian, and Finish (Ziegler et al., 2010). Although researchers have questioned the relevance of PA as a reading predictor in different languages because most studies have been conducted in English (Share, 2008), current evidence suggests that PA is a predictor of reading ability across European alphabetic languages (Vaessen et al., 2010). Perfetti and Verhoeven (2017) concluded that this association of PA and reading development holds for fourteen European languages. Some studies indicate that accuracy in word recognition is a better predictor of reading ability in less consistent orthographies, whereas variations in speed in more consistent orthographies explain reading performance (Landerl et al., 2013; Pollatsek & Treiman, 2015; Vaessen et al., 2010). However, the cognitive processes involved in word decoding – accuracy and speed – are identical in orthographies that vary along the transparency continuum (Hulme & Snowling, 2013; Vaessen et al., 2010), and this has been observed also in Grades 3 to 6 of primary school (Moll et al., 2014).

As children move beyond the initial stages of learning to read, knowledge of other aspects of language beyond accurate and fluent word reading, namely grammar and vocabulary knowledge, are associated with reading comprehension (Hulme & Snowling, 2013; Seidenberg, 2013; Sénéchal, 2012). During the learning-to-read phase (Chall, 1996) fast word-identification skills serve as the foundation for text comprehension (Perfetti, 1992), but as the ability to decode words develops, other factors, such as vocabulary knowledge, support reading to learn (Chall & Jacobs, 2003). In fact, "research indicates that reading with comprehension depends on understanding at least 95% of the words of the text" (Adams, 2009, p. 172). This understanding of the meaning of words develops, for example, when preschool-age children are exposed to book reading and parents explore the meaning of print with them. Later, the oral comprehension they developed early in life will assist them in comprehending what they will read by themselves (Sénéchal et al., 2012). For example, Sénéchal, Ouellette, and Rodney (2006) found that preschool Canadian children's vocabulary knowledge, acquired from parental book reading, predicts reading comprehension in Grade 3. The influence of this home-literacy practice of shared reading on future reading achievement has been found in studies with English- and French-speaking children (Sénéchal, 2006), as well as in studies in other more transparent languages. For instance, in Greek (Manolitsis, Georgiou, & Parrila, 2011; Lithuanian (Silinskas et al., 2021); German (Lehrl, Ebert, & Roßbach, 2013; Niklas & Schneider, 2017; Rose et al., 2018), and Finnish (Silinskas et al., 2012; Silinskas et al., 2020). As Kalb and Van Ours (2014) put it, reading to young children gives them a head start in life. In their study of the impact of book reading by Australian parents they found that children who are read to in the home frequently, three-to-five days a week and six-to-seven days a week, obtain the equivalent of between six-to-twelve months' higher scores in literacy at eight/nine years of age. Smaller effects of reading to children were found for numeracy skills.

Sénéchal's home-literacy model (2012) postulates that during the preschool years both meaning-based interactions during shared reading and code-based teaching by parents, like naming alphabet letters, contribute to later reading achievement, and this view is consistent with theories of reading development (Mol & Bus, 2011; Perfetti, Landi, & Oakhill, 2005). More specifically, shared reading supports vocabulary knowledge (Sénéchal, 2012) and code-based teaching by parents during shared reading can also assist children in learning to read. Nonetheless, "achievement-based skills such as early reading, early math, and letter recognition skills appear to be more sensitive to Head Start intervention attendance than cognitive skills such as IQ, vocabulary, and attention which are less sensitive to classroom instruction" (Shager et al., 2013, p. 90).

In summary, country variations in reading development are associated with linguistic differences related to orthographic depth in the early years of reading instruction and individual variations in reading achievement are linked to different levels of language knowledge and to the specific contexts, at home and/or at school, where this knowledge is acquired.

5.2.3 Variation in Reading Achievement

Home and school socioeconomic and linguistic contexts are relevant in explaining differences in reading achievement that are already present during the primary-school years. In the United States, for example, the reading gap between students from high- and low-income families and between students of different ethnic and linguistic backgrounds has been well documented (Seidenberg, 2013; Kieffer & Vuković, Chapter 2 in this volume). Similarly, in Europe data from comparative education surveys show that there is a relationship between socioeconomic and linguistic backgrounds and achievement.

Large-scale studies, such as the Progress in International Reading Literacy Study (PIRLS), offer unique information about fourth-graders' comprehension of authentic texts – the goal of learning to read – and related predictors of reading ability. The contextual information collected in different participant countries via student, home, school, and teacher questionnaires in PIRLS makes it possible to look at reading achievement from an international comparative perspective. This information can be used to study both student-background factors and environmental ones and to explore variations across countries in terms of reading-related literacy universals and particulars (Lenkeit, et al., 2015). In this sense, PIRLS allows us to characterize the reading-literacy skills of fourth-grade students in European countries and to understand their relationship with different sociolinguistic contexts.

Measures of socioeconomic status (SES) can include income, number of books and children's books at home, parental education level or occupation level, or a combination of these and other variables indicative of available home resources such as possession of an internet connection and one's own room (Araújo & Costa, 2015; Caro, Sandoval-Hernández & Lüdtke, 2014). Features of supportive literacy environments, such as having books at home, have been conceptualized as a measure of cultural capital and have been found to explain reading-score differences among students (e.g., Park, 2008). Moreover, both a school's intake of children from a certain range of socioeconomic status levels and the school's average of students' cultural capital account for part of the reading-score differences between schools (Caro et al., 2014; Myrberg & Rosén, 2006). This indicates that there is a school compositional effect whereby students in schools with a higher SES composition have higher reading achievement and this trend has been found in Germany, France, and Denmark (Stancel-Piatak, Mirazchiyski, & Desa, 2013). Similarly, Myrberg and Rosén (2006) found that in PIRLS 2001, students' cultural capital accounted for a great part of the reading-score differences between Swedish independent and public schools. In Sweden the share of students with a migrant background is higher in public schools, and this explains their lower reading achievement scores when compared to private schools. This has been corroborated in Dutch studies that also use PIRLS data and show that students who speak Dutch as a second language have lower achievement levels (Netten et al., 2014; Netten et al., 2016).

Literacy achievement in PIRLS in European countries reveals that common underlying factors such as socioeconomic and linguistic backgrounds are associated with student achievement. Nonetheless, the strength of the association between reading achievement and SES and between achievement and family/student characteristics varies across countries. For instance, a positive correlation of parents' socioeconomic status and children's fourth-grade reading achievement level is present in all European countries participating in PIRLS 2006 and 2011 (Araújo & Costa, 2015; Park, 2008). However, score-point differences between students from high and from low SES backgrounds are wider in some countries than in others and both home-literacy activities and students' early literacy skills also seem to mediate results (Costa & Araújo, 2017). In a PIRLS study that considered aspects of the home-literacy model proposed by Sénéchal (2012), Myrberg and Rosén (2009) found that parental book reading and storytelling during preschool made a positive contribution to reading achievement, and that book reading was mediated by cultural capital, as measured by the number of books at home. Additionally, this study showed that Swedish students' early literacy skills had a positive impact on their subsequent reading attainment, without any mediating effect of cultural capital or number of books at home. Other studies with PIRLS data that include several European countries (e.g., Martin et al., 2013; Stancel-Piatak et al., 2013) also support the notion that early literacy skills, such as recognizing letters of the alphabet and being able to write some words, exert a positive influence on achievement. However, Netten et al. (2014) examined PIRLS data for the Netherlands and found a positive influence of early literacy activities, but not of early literacy skills, on achievement.

In short, students who enter elementary school knowing how to name letters of the alphabet and how to write some words score higher in PIRLS. This has been observed in most European countries, after controlling for SES, except in the Netherlands (Netten et al., 2014). Nevertheless, the studies reviewed suggest that variations in reading achievement in PIRLS may be related to sociocultural and linguistic factors, as well as to individual literacy abilities and skills.

Furthermore, PIRLS studies suggest that individual reading habits and reading for pleasure are related to achievement in Denmark, Sweden, and France (Costa & Araújo, 2017), after accounting for SES. Similar findings are reported in a Dutch study that assessed reading ability using the PIRLS variable that measures reading motivation (Netten, Droop, & Verhoeven, 2011).

With respect to school factors, analyses of PIRLS data have shown that adequate resources for teaching reading are related with increased reading achievement (Mullis et al., 2017), as is a school's emphasis on academic success (Costa & Araújo, 2017; Martin et al., 2013). Considering instructional factors, PIRLS studies do not show a strong relation with reading scores. For instance, an emphasis on reading skills in first grade is only positively related to achievement in Grade 4 in one European country – Germany (Martin et al., 2013). However, this may be due to a restriction of range in reading curricula (see Perfetti & Verhoeven, Chapter 11 in this volume). Similarly, no relationships have been reported between reading achievement and types of reading instruction – whole group vs. small group or individualized instruction and time spent on reading (Shiel & Eivers, 2009). Reading literacy achievement in PIRLS 2011 compared with PIRLS 2006 has been associated with a decline in students' ability to answer questions that require higher-order comprehension processes, such as understanding text structure and main idea (Netten et al., 2014). However, this finding has not been linked to teachers' instructional strategies or, more specifically, to a different emphasis in reading processes. It remains difficult to ascertain cause-and-effect relations between the way teachers teach comprehension and reading achievement in PIRLS, but studies suggest that reading instruction influences reading ability (Hulme & Snowling, 2013). For example, comprehension instruction that focuses on practicing making inferences from text enhances reading attainment (Elbro & Buch-Iverson, 2013).

Turning next to secondary-school attainments, observed variations in reading achievement level reveal that similar student-background factors are associated with achievement and that schools can also make a difference. All rounds of the Program for International Student Assessment (PISA) show, for example, that the higher the SES the higher students score in reading, and that migrant students' scores are lower than those of native students. In PISA, the reading achievement gap between immigrant and native students is observed even after controlling for SES (Lenkeit, Caro, & Strand, 2015). Nonetheless, students' achievement levels reveal that European immigrant students perform better in reading-test items that mirror educational situations or contexts where reading serves the purpose of learning or acquiring information (Costa & Araújo, 2012). Moreover, they perform better than native students in test items linked to occupational reading or reading that involves accomplishing a task, such as looking for a job in a newspaper or following directions in the workplace. Conversely, native students perform better in personal and public situations that imply reading for recreational purposes as well as attending public events (e.g., a concert). Last, at the European level immigrant students perform better in exposition and instruction types of text, which again are text types likely found in textbooks used in school (Costa & Araújo, 2012).

Additional student-background factors related to students' reading achievement in PISA include parental book reading and students' reading for enjoyment. Results show that the parent effect in reading is present because students whose parents report reading to them frequently during first grade score higher (OECD, 2012). Furthermore, they show that resilient students, as defined by those who score above what would be expected given their SES background, read frequently outside of school.

The school factors associated with reading achievement in PISA are like those found in PIRLS studies. Besides emphasis on academic success, PISA results highlight that school climate – discipline – and student–teacher relations are associated with higher achievement. Students in schools where there is a good disciplinary climate, where teachers support students and emphasize academic achievement, score higher (OECD, 2012, 2013a, 2016). School compositional effects are also present in PISA. For example, students attending schools with a socioeconomically advantaged intake tend to perform better than those attending schools with more disadvantaged peers (OECD, 2010b).

It is with the PISA surveys that the European Commission monitors progress in the EU goal of reducing the share of low achievers in reading, mathematics, and science. However, PISA 2015 results indicate that, on average, the percentage of low achievers in reading has increased slightly from 17.8 percent in 2012 to 22.5 percent in 2018 in the EU (European Commission, 2020). This indicates that almost one fifth of fifteen-year-olds in the EU do not attain a satisfactory level of reading ability that would enable them to interpret texts effectively, although there are wide variations among countries (e.g., the share of low achievers is 26 percent in Hungary, but only 8 percent in Estonia).

In the following section, we present research evidence on literacy levels in the EU based on PIRLS primary-school data and PISA secondary-school data. The analyses illustrate the association of SES and home-literacy practices with reading scores in both surveys and the relation between early literacy skills and reading achievement in PIRLS.

5.3 Literacy Levels across European Societies

5.3.1 *Literacy Levels in Children*

The International Association for the Evaluation of Educational Achievement (IEA) runs PIRLS every five years to measure trends in the reading achievement of fourth-grade students. At this point in their schooling, students have moved from learning to read to reading to learn (Chall, 1996), and PIRLS tests students' ability to comprehend both literary and informational texts. Its assessment framework defines reading literacy as "the ability to understand and use those written language forms required by society and/or valued by the individual. Young readers can construct meaning from a variety of texts. They read to learn, to participate in communities of readers in school and everyday life, and for enjoyment" (Mullis et al., 2006, p. 103). Reading comprehension is tested in questions that ask students to do the following: (1) focus on and retrieve explicitly stated information; (2) make straightforward inferences; (3) interpret and integrate ideas and information; and (4) evaluate and critique content and textual elements (Mullis et al., 2017).

The first cycle of PIRLS was carried out in 2001 and in 2016 recorded the participation of fifty countries and eleven regional entities. Twenty-four EU Member States (EU-MS)[3] collected representative data on the reading literacy skills of their fourth-grade students in 2001. The PIRLS achievement scale is based on item response theory (IRT) and scores are scaled to have an international average of 500 and a standard deviation of 100 points.

Figure 5.1 presents the average reading achievement by country and SES of fourth-graders in the twenty-two EU-MS that participated in PIRLS 2016. The graph shows that in 2016, Ireland, Finland, and Poland were the top-performing countries in Europe. Conversely, Malta, French Belgium, and France were the countries with the lowest reading scores in Europe.

When we look at the reading scores of low SES students, using low parental educational level as a proxy, we see that those students whose parents have up to a high-school education have lower achievement than students whose parents have gone on to complete higher education. Differences in students' reading achievement vary from about sixteen to seventy-three points, favoring students with a high parental education level, although the associations differ by country. Larger differences in reading achievement are found in Bulgaria and Hungary, and the smallest in Malta, Spain, and Denmark (Figure 5.1).

Turning next to variables prior to school entry, we use items from the PIRLS home questionnaire which asks parents to indicate how well their children were able to name letters of the alphabet before starting school and how often they or someone in the household read to their children. Evidence from studies with PIRLS data indicate that both greater alphabet knowledge and more frequent book reading at home before the start of compulsory education are associated with students' achievement in Grade 4 (Alivernini, 2013; Araújo & Costa, 2012, 2015; Myrberg & Rosén, 2009). Furthermore, good knowledge of the alphabet and high book-reading frequency benefit children from both high- and

---

[3] Educational systems referring to regions (i.e., Belgium-French and Belgium-Flemish areas) are considered.

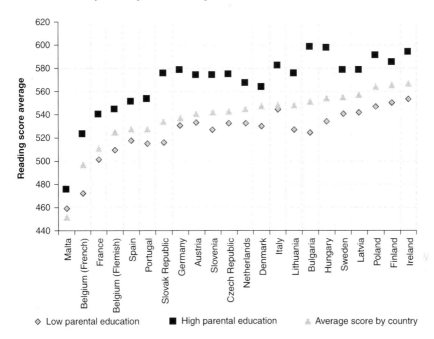

Figure 5.1 Average reading achievement by country and by SES in Grade 4 in twenty-two countries participating in the PIRLS 2016 EU-MS dataset
Source: PIRLS, 2016, authors' calculations
Notes: Countries are ranked in ascending order of the reading-score average. High parental education denotes completion of tertiary education or higher education, and low parental education denotes completion of up to upper-secondary education.

low-SES backgrounds across countries. These data are consistent with trends reported in several small-scale studies: Children's ability to name letters of the alphabet before formal reading instruction begins is one of the strongest predictors of children's reading ability (Bond & Dykstra, 1967; Riley, 1996, Piasta & Wagner, 2010), because naming letters shares a reciprocal relation with phonological awareness (Adams, 1990; Verhoeven et al., 2016). Similarly, parental book reading promotes reading development because when preschool-age children are exposed to book reading, they develop an understanding of vocabulary that is not commonly used in daily oral interactions (Kalb & Van Ours, 2014; Sénéchal, 2012).

Figure 5.2 presents the reading-score average according to alphabet knowledge and students' SES. High alphabet knowledge is positively associated with student scores. For students from low SES, Austria shows the smallest

102   *Luisa Araújo & Patricia Costa*

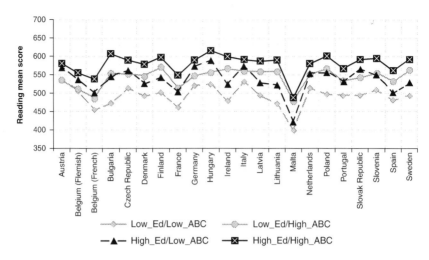

Figure 5.2 Average reading achievement according to alphabet knowledge and SES in Grade 4 in twenty-two countries participating in the PIRLS 2016 EU-MS dataset
Source: PIRLS, 2016, authors' calculations
Notes: Grey lines and symbols correspond to low parental education. Black corresponds to high parental education. Dotted lines correspond to low alphabet knowledge and solid to high alphabet knowledge.

difference (one point) and Lithuania shows the largest, difference between high alphabet knowledge and low alphabet knowledge (eighty-seven points). For students whose parents have tertiary education, Austria is again the country with the lowest difference in student scores (thirteen points) and Ireland is the country with highest difference (seventy-five points).

Overall, except for Austria, Spain, and Belgium (Flemish speaking), and France, the differences in reading scores related to alphabet knowledge are larger for the low-parental-education group. That is, children whose parents have a low educational level seem to reap more benefits from knowing the letters of the alphabet very well than children whose parents have higher levels of education. However, as Figure 5.2 shows, within the same SES background knowing the letters of the alphabet very well is consistently related to higher student achievement.

Figure 5.3 shows the association between frequency of book reading before the start of compulsory education and the reading achievement of fourth-grade students whose parents have high and low education levels (SES). It clearly shows that within an SES band, high frequency of home book reading is always

Literacy Development in Europe 103

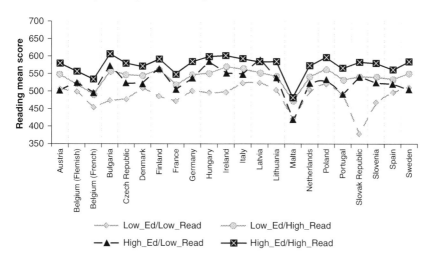

Figure 5.3 Average reading achievement according to parental book reading and SES in Grade 4 in twenty-two countries participating in the PIRLS 2016 EU-MS dataset
Source: PIRLS 2016, authors' calculations
Notes: Grey lines and symbols correspond to low parental education. Dark Black corresponds to high parental education. Dotted lines correspond to low book-reading frequency and solid to high book-reading frequency.

related to higher student achievement, although there are country-wise variations in the range within each band. For students whose parents have low educational levels, the Slovak Republic shows the largest effect of preschool book reading (160 points); for students whose parents have high educational levels, Sweden has the largest effect (79 points). The graph also reveals that the contribution of home reading to the achievement of students from distinct SES backgrounds is different in different countries. In particular, in a group of ten countries – Bulgaria, the Czech Republic, Finland, France, Hungary, Ireland, Latvia, the Slovak Republic, Slovenia, and Belgium Flemish – the magnitude of the reading score difference between high and low home-reading exposure is larger for students with low SES. In contrast, in Austria, Denmark, Germany, Italy, Lithuania, Malta, the Netherlands, Poland, Portugal, Spain, Sweden, and Belgium Flemish, the magnitude of the reading-score difference between high parental book reading and low parental book reading is larger for students with high SES.

5.3.2 Literacy Levels in Adolescents

PISA is a cross-sectional survey launched in 2000 by the Organisation for Economic Co-operation and Development (OECD). Its purpose is to assess how ready youngsters are to either enter the workforce or continue further studies, enabling countries to monitor their progress in meeting key learning objectives (OECD, 2013a). The OECD has been running this international large-scale assessment of fifteen-year-old students' skills in reading, mathematics, and science every three years. Each assessment cycle focuses on a main domain or knowledge area and reading was the main domain in 2000, 2009, and 2018, whereas science was the focus in 2006 and in 2015 and mathematics the focus in 2003 and 2012. In PISA, students' scores are computed according to IRT and standardized with an OECD mean of 500 and a standard deviation set at 100 in 2000.

In PISA 2018, "reading literacy is understanding, using, evaluating, reflecting on and engaging with texts in order to achieve one's goals, to develop one's knowledge and potential and to participate in society" (OECD, 2019, p. 28). In much the same way as PIRLS does, PISA examines the extent to which students are able to understand and integrate the information in informational and literary texts by including the following dimensions in its assessment framework: (1) Retrieve texts and access them; (2) interpret and integrate texts; and (3) reflect and evaluate texts. In addition to the achievement score, PISA also collects information on students' sociodemographic and dispositional characteristics, students' home environments, and teaching and learning contexts in schools (Lenkeit, et al., 2015) through the application of student and school questionnaires.

In order to examine the reading achievement of fifteen-year-old European students we focus on the most recent PISA 2018 data, which had reading as a main domain. Figure 5.4 shows the average reading score by country and SES across the PISA 2018 participating EU-MS, for which data are publicly available. The graph shows that there is great variation in students' reading scores, with the difference in scores among EU-MS reaching about 100 points (Estonia vs Bulgaria). Estonia, Finland, and Ireland are the top performers, while the EU-MS with the lowest performance in reading are Bulgaria, Romania, and Malta.

When comparing the reading scores for high- and low-SES students, using parental educational level as a proxy, we see that students whose parents have tertiary education perform better in reading than the ones whose parents have not completed higher education. Differences in students' reading achievement vary from about one, in Croatia, to fifty-three points in Poland, favoring the students with a higher parental education level. These findings are in line with those from the previous section showing that differences in reading achievement according

Literacy Development in Europe 105

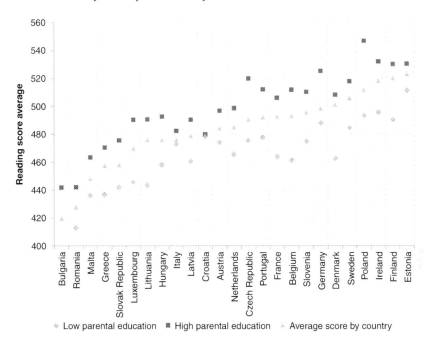

Figure 5.4 Average reading achievement by country and by SES of fifteen-year-old students in twenty-five countries participating in the PISA 2018 EU-MS dataset
Source: PISA 2018, authors' calculations
Notes: Countries are ranked in ascending order of the reading score average. High parental education denotes completion of tertiary education or higher education and low parental education denotes completion of up to upper-secondary education.

to students' SES are already present in primary education. Additionally, this is in line with evidence from OECD that uses PISA 2009 data. In particular, across OECD countries students with a higher socioeconomic status outperform disadvantaged students in reading on average by thirty-eight score points, or about one year's worth of education (OECD, 2010b). This corroborates evidence that there is an association between parents' educational attainment, used as a proxy of students' SES (Jerrim & Micklewright, 2014), and students' achievement (Pokropek, Borgonovi, & Jakubowski, 2015).

With respect to the home environment, and in accord with Sénéchal's home literacy model, the PISA home questionnaire implemented in some countries in 2009 and 2018 asked parents how often they read to their children during their first year in primary education (OECD, 2012). Figure 5.5 presents the

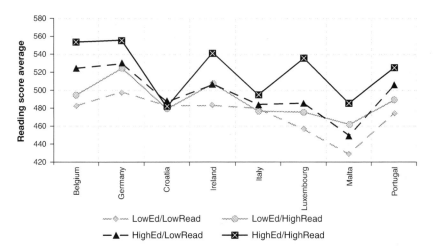

Figure 5.5 Average reading achievement by country, parental book reading, and SES of fifteen-year-old students in twenty-five countries participating in the PISA 2018 EU-MS dataset
Source: PISA 2018, authors' calculations
Notes: Grey lines and symbols correspond to low parental education. Black corresponds to high parental education. Dotted lines correspond to low book-reading frequency and solid to high-Book-reading frequency. The graph includes EU-MS for which PISA 2018 data is available for the variable "home book reading."

association between frequency of book reading and the reading achievement of fifteen-year-old students by parental educational level in EU-MS. It is evident that, in general and irrespective of parental educational level, high frequency of home book reading is associated with higher student achievement. The highest contribution of home reading for the achievement of students is found in Luxembourg and Belgium and the lowest difference is found in Croatia. These results are in line with those found using PIRLS data (Araújo & Costa, 2015), showing that a higher frequency of home book reading is related to higher student achievement in the same MS, although these results do not pertain to the same cohort of students.

A comparison of home literacy in PIRLS and PISA shows that reading to young children gives them a head start in reading achievement, as retrospectively reported by parents in PIRLS (e.g., how often children were read to before the start of compulsory education) and during the first year of primary education in PISA (e.g., how often children were read to at the start of compulsory education).

Overall, the analyses presented in this chapter show that in PIRLS students are better readers in fourth grade when they were read to during the preschool years (Araújo & Costa, 2015). Similarly, PISA 2018 students who were read to when in first grade are better readers at age fifteen, and this is in line also with findings using the PISA 2009 dataset (OECD, 2011). This highlights the positive reading outcomes accrued from home reading at a young age, a significant finding also with Australian children (Kalb & van Ours, 2014) and with Canadian children (Sénéchal, 2012). Clearly, ILSAs such as PIRLS and PISA provide rich data for cross-country comparative analyses and the contextual information they collect allows us to understand what factors are associated with variations in the reading literacy performance of students. Although they are not longitudinal studies, the findings related with book reading in European countries converge with evidence from longitudinal research in Australia and Canada (Kalb & van Ours, 2014, Sénéchal, 2012). The PISA results, however, also suggest that different European countries present particular relations between reading achievement and home book reading. In Croatia, for example, student scores change very little according to frequency of parental book reading with SES level. In contrast, in Poland, Belgium, and Bulgaria, score differences are much wider according to SES level. It is possible that children's exposure to shared book reading in preschool kindergarten classrooms also varies among countries and that frequent exposure reduces the effects of home variables, but PIRLS and PISA do not collect such data. Research supports this conjecture and there is evidence that this effective early instruction practice promotes fourth-grade language and reading abilities (Dickinson & Porche, 2011).

5.4 Role of Ecological Factors

5.4.1 *Role of Socioeconomic Status*

The analyses we present show that there are variations in achievement across countries and that socioeconomic variations within and across countries are associated with differences in reading achievement. High-SES students surveyed in PIRLS and PISA show higher achievement than low-SES students in all EU Member States. In addition, our analyses show that home book reading and early literacy skills can contribute to increased reading achievement in PIRLS for both groups of students. In this sense, early literacy skills and home practices before the start of primary school can help improve the reading abilities of students with different SES.

PIRLS research also shows that a school's SES composition explains variation in students' reading achievement in EU-MS (Martin et al., 2013). The study by Stancel-Piatak et al. (2013) found that in three PIRLS-2011-participating

European countries – Denmark, Germany, and France – a school's average of students' cultural capital, measured by the number of books at home, was one of the most relevant variables in explaining variation in reading scores. Myrberg and Rosén's study (2006) found that in PIRLS 2001, students' cultural capital accounted for a large part of reading score differences between independent and public schools. These findings suggest that it is not only individual/home SES that matters, but that to a lesser extent a school's SES compositional effect also shapes reading achievement in PIRLS (Araújo & Costa, 2012; Costa & Araújo, 2017). PISA findings corroborate this with adolescents (OECD, 2013b).

5.4.2 Role of Home Literacy Experiences

Different analyses of PIRLS confirm that both early literacy skills and practices, such as home book reading, in conjunction with other characteristics of effective schools, have a positive influence on achievement (Araújo & Costa, 2012, Costa & Araújo, 2017). Moreover, PIRLS studies suggest that motivational factors, like students' enjoyment of reading, are positively related to achievement (Costa & Araújo, 2017; Stancel-Piatak et al., 2013).

The home literacy environment, namely home book reading during the preschool years and the first year of primary school, contributes to higher reading achievement in PIRLS and PISA. This is in accord with Sénéchal's (2012) home literacy model. In addition, and in accord with Sénéchal (2012) and with findings from research that looks at predictors of reading ability, the ability of young children to recognize the letters of the alphabet contributes to reading achievement in PIRLS. In this survey, parents are asked how well their children recognized the letters of the alphabet before the start of compulsory education. Children could have learned them at school or at home or in both settings. In this sense, this predictor of reading attainment in fourth grade is not restricted to the home literacy environment and research indicates that alphabet knowledge can be successfully acquired in school (Shager et al., 2013).

Findings from other studies that use PIRLS and PISA data and the information collected in student and parental questionnaires reveal interesting links between achievement and students' sociodemographic and dispositional characteristics (Lenkeit, Caro, & Strand, 2015). For example, in PIRLS reading for enjoyment outside of school contributes to higher achievement in Denmark, Sweden, and France, after controlling for SES (Costa & Araújo, 2017). Similarly, in all EU countries, secondary students who enjoy reading perform significantly better than students who have not developed an interest in reading (OECD, 2010a). This suggests that literacy practices can partially compensate for students' socioeconomically disadvantaged backgrounds.

5.4.3 Role of Educational Factors

While the relationship of SES and home literacy practices with achievement is similar in all EU-MS, the relation of school-related literacy practices with achievement is more particular in terms of variation across countries. Similarly, for other school-level characteristics, such as emphasis on academic success, there is more variation across countries.

For example, research with PIRLS data shows that a school's emphasis on academic success is related to higher achievement in France, but not in Denmark or Germany, which suggests that school effects are country specific (Stancel-Piatak et al., 2013). Martin et al. (2013) used PIRLS 2011 data to study the characteristics of effective schools and their findings corroborate the positive influence of good discipline and of emphasizing academic success. However, a school's early emphasis on reading skills is only positively related to achievement in one European country – Germany. Conversely, the index of early literacy skills, which includes the ability to name alphabet letters before the start of compulsory education, is positively associated with higher achievement in all European countries (Martin et al., 2013).

Other factors related to schools and teachers have been found to also influence the achievement levels of fifteen-year-old students in PISA. For instance, students attending schools with a better disciplinary climate and better teacher–student relations perform better in reading (OECD, 2010c). This is supported by school effectiveness research, which suggests that school climate is a factor that explains variance in students' achievement in reading (OECD, 2013b).

Clearly, PIRLS and PISA-related research has called attention to the school factors that seem to make a difference or that have "an effect on student achievement over and above" student/home predictors (Martin et al., 2013, p. 111). Nonetheless, evidence of a school's added value linked to student–teacher relations and instructional practices is limited, especially in PIRLS studies. Moreover, existing PIRLS studies suggest that factors like a school's academic climate and literacy practices and their relationship with students' achievement are more country specific than those factors associated with student-background variables (Stancel-Piatak et al., 2013).

5.5 Conclusions and Discussion

This chapter began by offering a historical overview of the spread of literacy in Europe and by discussing current notions about schooling and literacy abilities. Good literacy and numeracy skills equate with good life outcomes (Heckman & Jacobs, 2009) and current ILSAs at the primary- and secondary-school levels offers indicators of these cognitive skills. PIRLS has received considerably less attention as a survey that can tell us how well the world's fourth-graders read, yet the information it provides can be useful in that it shows the value of early intervention to promote reading achievement (Choi & Jerrim, 2016). Given the interdependence between reading and learning, it is important to monitor whether young readers develop good comprehension skills during primary education. Those who do not are at risk of school failure (Adams, 2009).

The analyses presented for EU-MS show that Finland is a top performer in both PIRLS and PISA. This only partially supports the notion that results vary according to historical patterns of the spread of literacy in Europe. Literacy was already widespread in Finland in the 1900s, but this was also the case in France, which displays a much lower reading achievement in PIRLS and PISA. In PIRLS, Italy ranks higher than France, but in France literacy was more widespread in the 1900s. Regarding orthographic depth, Irish and English fourth-graders score higher than Spanish and Italian students, but the latter learn to read in quite transparent writing systems. Thus, no facilitating effect of language transparency is observable.

The cross-linguistic studies reviewed indicate that linguistic variations associated with orthographic depth can facilitate or make more difficult the acquisition and development of reading abilities. However, in PIRLS we do not observe a pattern of achievement in different countries indicating that children learning more opaque orthographies have lower reading achievement than those that learn more transparent languages. Different reasons may account for this. Perhaps the effects associated with orthographic depth are only observable at the beginning stages of learning to read. It could also be that because PIRLS uses authentic texts, this produces reading-comprehension results that differ from those observed when word and pseudoword fluency and cloze comprehension tests are used (Cutting & Scarborough, 2006). As Catts (2009) argues, we should not underestimate the complexity of reading comprehension, which is "not a skill like word recognition that can be mastered in a relative short time, but rather a collection of knowledge and processes that takes many years to acquire" (Catts, 2009, p. 178). In this chapter we highlighted how early literacy skills and practices can affect reading achievement, but other variables related to reading instruction, namely reading comprehension, in different countries may also modulate student performance.

The results also highlight that some countries, such as Latvia, are better positioned in PISA than in PIRLS. Nevertheless, different countries participate in the two surveys, and reading-score averages are calculated for the specific participating countries. In addition, we must keep in mind that the reading assessment frameworks of PIRLS and PISA are similar, but not identical. PIRLS, in particular, seems to assess very basic reading-comprehension processes. When compared to the National Assessment of Educational Progress (NAEP), for example, PIRLS asks for the retrieval of text information that matches verbatim the questions asked while NAEP includes more questions that require higher levels of interpretation (U.S. Department of Education, 2003). Moreover, NAEP passages are written at a seventh-grade level, whereas PIRLS passages are written at a fifth-to-sixth-grade level (U.S. Department of Education, 2003).

Importantly, the research evidence presented based on PIRLS suggests that although SES is a determinant of reading achievement, home book reading and alphabet knowledge can contribute to increased reading scores. PISA data based on parental questionnaires in some participating countries also corroborate the positive influence of book reading to young children. This suggests that what parents do is important. Additional research suggests that both in PIRLS and PISA autonomous, recreational reading outside of school is a factor that relates to higher reading achievement. School factors, such as a positive disciplinary climate and good teacher–student relations, also contribute to increased student scores. Thus, teachers and what teachers do are also important in boosting reading achievement. However, PIRLS and PISA variables present limitations in terms of unraveling possible links between reading instruction and achievement. For example, the role of preschool teachers in exposing children to the same types of home shared-reading experiences is not captured in these surveys.

Still, International Large-Scale Assessments provide a rich basis for designing evidence-based policies and for monitoring achievement trends over time in a comparative perspective. The comprehensive information provided in these surveys and the high number of participating countries make it possible to investigate commonalities and differences in reading achievement and their relationship with student background and ecological factors. In the case of the EU, this is even more relevant because of common educational goals. The results we present suggest, for instance, that to reduce the influence of SES background, countries should encourage interactions around books. Curricula that contemplate teaching the alphabet before the start of compulsory education may also give children a head start in reading. Building a supporting school environment that encourages academic success should also be a priority.

Future research using ILSA should build on the existing evidence about the factors that are related to reading-achievement levels and try to confirm or disconfirm universals and particulars – what is country specific and what is more universal across countries. Most studies conducted thus far are correlational in nature and more research is needed to disentangle cause-and-effect relationships. Additionally, our knowledge of the development of reading skills and their relationship with reading achievement would gain much from observational studies that document how reading curricula are implemented and how reading comprehension strategies are taught in different educational systems.

References

Adams, M. J. (1990). *Beginning to Read: Thinking and Learning about Print*. Cambridge, MA: MIT Press.

Adams, M. J. (2009). The challenge of advanced texts: The interdependence of reading and learning. In E. Hiebert (ed.), *Reading More, Reading Better* (pp. 163–189). New York: Guilford Press.

Alivernini, F. (2013). An exploration of the gap between highest and lowest ability readers across 20 countries. *Educational Studies*, *39*(4), 399–417.

Araújo, L., & Costa, P. (2012). Reading literacy in PIRLS 2006: What explains achievement in 20 EU countries? EUR 66894 EN.

Araújo, L., & Costa, P. (2015). Home book reading and reading achievement in EU countries: the Progress in International Reading Literacy Study 2011 (PIRLS). *Educational Research and Evaluation*, *21*, 422–438. DOI: http://dx.doi.org/10.1080/13803611.2015.1111803.

Bond, G. L., & Dykstra, R. (1967). The cooperative research program in first-grade reading instruction. *Reading Research Quarterly*, *2*, 10–141. DOI: http://dx.doi.org/10.2307/746948.

Caravolas, M., Lervåg, A., Mousikou, P. et al. (2012). Common patterns of prediction of literacy development in different alphabetic orthographies. *Psychological Science*, *23*, 678e686. DOI: http://dx.doi.org/10.1177/0956797611434536.

Caro, D. H., Sandoval-Hernández, A., & Lüdtke, O. (2014). Cultural, social, and economic capital constructs in international assessments: An evaluation using exploratory structural equation modelling. *School Effectiveness and School Improvement*, *25*, 433–450. DOI: https://doi.org/10.1080/09243453.2013.812568.

Catts, H. W. (2009). The narrow view of reading promotes a broad view of comprehension. *Language, Speech, and Hearing Services in the Schools*, *40*, 178–183.

Chall, J. (1996). *Learning to Read: The Great Debate* (revised ed.). New York: McGraw-Hill.

Chall, J., & Jacobs, V. A. (2003). Poor children's fourth-grade slump. *American Educator*, *27*, 14–17.

Choi, A., & Jerrim, J. (2016). The use (and misuse) of PISA in guiding policy reform: The case of Spain. *Comparative Education*, *52*, 230–245.

Costa, P., & Araújo, L. (2012). Differential Item Functioning (DIF): What functions differently (EUR 25565 – 2012). Luxembourg: Publications Office of the European Union. DOI: http://dx.doi.org/10.2788/60811.

Costa, P., & Araújo, L. (2017). Skilled students and effective schools: Reading achievement in Denmark, Sweden and France. *Scandinavian Journal of Educational Research*, *50*(2), 185–205. DOI: http://dx.doi.org/10.1080/00313831.2017.1307274.

Cutting, L., & Scarborough, H. S. (2006). Prediction of reading comprehension: Relative contributions of word recognition, language proficiency, and other cognitive skills can depend on how comprehension is measured. *Scientific Studies of Reading*, *10*(3), 277–299.

Dickinson, D. K., & Porche, M. V. (2011). Relation between language experiences in preschool classrooms and children's kindergarten and fourth-grade language and reading abilities. *Child Development*, *82*, 870–886. DOI: https://doi.org/10.1111/j.1467-8624.2011.01576.x.

Diebolt, C., & Hippe, R. (2017). Regional human capital inequality in Europe in the long run, 1850–2010. *Région et Développement, 45*, 5–30.

Elbro, C., & Buch-Iverson, I. (2013). Activation of prior knowledge for inferences making: Effects on reading comprehension. *Scientific Studies of Reading, 17*, 435–452.

Elley, W. (2001). Literacy in the present world: Realities and possibilities. In L. Verhoeven & C. Snow (eds,). *Literacy and Motivation: Literacy Engagement in Individuals and Groups* (pp. 225–242). Mahwah, NJ: Lawrence Erlbaum Associates.

European Commission. (2022). Education and Training Monitor. https://education.ec.europa.eu/about-eea/education-and-training-monitor

European Commission. (2020). Education and Training Monitor. www.bit.ly/3MHFMcT.

European Commission/EACEA/ Eurydice. (2016). *Compulsory Education in Europe – 2016/17. Eurydice Facts and Figures.* Luxembourg: Publications Office of the European Union.

Hanushek, E., & Woessmann, L. (2015). *The Knowledge Capital of Nations: Education and the Economics of Growth.* Cambridge, MA: MIT Press.

Heckman, J. J., & Jacobs, B. (2009). Policies to create and destroy human capital in Europe. IZA Discussion Papers, No. 4680. Bonn: Institute for the Study of Labor (IZA). http://hdl.handle.net/10419/36102.

Hippe, R., & Fouquet, R. (2015). The human capital transition and the role of policy. The Centre for Climate Change Economics and Policy (CCCEP). Working Paper No. 185.

Hulme, C., & Snowling, M. J. (2013). Learning to read: What we know and what we need to understand better. *Child Development Perspectives, 7*(1), 1–5.

Jerrim, J., & Micklewright, J. (2014). Socio-economic gradients in children's cognitive skills: Are cross-country comparisons robust to who reports family background? *European Sociological Review, 30*(6), 766–781. DOI:https://doi.org/10.1093/esr/jcu072

Kalb, G., & van Ours, J. C. (2014). Reading to young children: A head-start in life? *Economics of Education Review, 40*, 1–24.

Landerl, K., Ramus, F., Moll, K., et al. (2013). Predictors of developmental dyslexia in European orthographies with varying complexity. *Journal of Child Psychology and Psychiatry, 54*(6), 686–694.

Lehrl, S., Ebert, S., & Roßbach, H.-G. (2013). Facets of preschoolers' home literacy environments: What contributes to reading literacy in primary school? In M. Pfost, C. Artelt, & S. Weinert (eds.), *The Development of Reading Literacy from Early Childhood to Adolescence* (pp. 35–62). Bamberg: University of Bamberg Press.

Lenkeit, J., Caro, D. H., & Strand, S. (2015). Tackling the remaining attainment gap between students with and without immigrant background: An investigation into the equivalence of SES constructs. *Educational Research and Evaluation, 21*(1), 60–83.

Lenkeit, J., Chan, J., Hopfenbeck, T. N., & Baird, J. (2015). A review of the representation of PIRLS related research in scientific journals. *Educational Research Review, 16*, 102–115.

Manolitsis, G., Georgiou, G., & Parrila, R. (2011). Revisiting the home literacy model of reading development in an orthographically consistent language. *Learning and Instruction, 21*, 496–505. DOI: https://doi.org/10.1016/j.learninstruc.2010.06.005.

Martin, M. O., Foy, P., Mullis, I. V. S., & O'Dwyer, L. M. (2013). Effective schools in reading, mathematics, and science at the fourth grade. In M. O. Martin & I. V. S. Mullis (eds.), *TIMSS and PIRLS 2011: Relationships among Reading, Mathematics, and Science Achievement at the Fourth Grade – Implications for Early Learning*. Chestnut Hill, MA: TIMSS & PIRLS International Study Center, Boston College.

Mol, S. E., & Bus, A. G. (2011). To read or not to read: A meta-analysis of print exposure from infancy to early adulthood. *Psychological Bulletin, 137*, 267–296. DOI: https://doi.org/10.1037/a0021890.

Moll, K., Ramus, F., Bartling, J. et al. (2014). Cognitive mechanisms underlying reading and spelling development in five European orthographies: Is English an outlier orthography? *Learning and Instruction, 29*, 65–77.

Mullis, I. V. S., Kennedy, A. M., Martin, M. O., & Sainsbury, M. (2006). *PIRLS 2006 Assessment Framework and Specification* (2nd ed.). TIMSS & PIRLS International Study Center Lynch School of Education. Chestnut Hill, MA: Boston College.

Mullis, I. V. S., Martin, M. O., Foy, P., & Hooper, M. (2017). PIRLS 2016 International Results in Reading. *Boston College, TIMSS & PIRLS International Study Center* (website). http://timssandpirls.bc.edu/pirls2016/international-results/

Myrberg, E., & Rosén, M. (2006). Reading achievement and social selection into independent schools in Sweden – Results from IEA PIRLS 2001. *Scandinavian Journal of Educational Research, 50*(2), 185–205. DOI: https://doi.org/10.1080/00313830600576005.

Myrberg, E., & Rosén, M. (2009). Direct and indirect effects of parents' education on reading achievement among third graders in Sweden. *British Journal of Education Psychology, 79*, 695–711. DOI: https://doi.org/10.1348/000709909X453031.

Netten, A., Droop, M., & Verhoeven, L. (2011). Predictors of reading literacy for first and second language learners. *Reading & Writing, 23*, 413–425.

Netten, A. R., Luyten, J. W., Droop, M., & Verhoeven, L. T. W. (2016). Role of linguistic and sociocultural diversity in reading literacy achievement: A multilevel approach. *Journal of Research in Reading, 39*(2), 189–208. DOI: https://doi.org/10.1111/1467-9817.12032.

Netten, A. R., Voeten, M. J. M., Droop, M., & Verhoeven, L. T. W. (2014). Sociocultural and educational factors for reading literacy decline in the Netherlands in the past decade. *Learning and Individual Differences, 32*, 9–18.

Niklas, F., & Schneider, W. (2017). Home learning environment and development of child competencies from kindergarten until the end of elementary school. *Contemporary Education Psychology, 49*, 263–274. DOI: https://doi.org/10.1016/j.cedpsych.2017.03.006.

OECD. (2010a). *PISA 2009 Results: Executive Summary*. www.oecd.org/pisa/pisaproducts/46619703.pdf.

OECD. (2010b). *PISA 2009 Results: Overcoming Social Background – Equity in Learning Opportunities and Outcomes* (Volume II). http://dx.doi.org/10.1787/9789264091504-en.

OECD. (2010c). *PISA 2009 Results: What Makes a School Successful? – Resources, Policies and Practices* (Volume IV). DOI: http://dx.doi.org/10.1787/9789264091559-en.

OECD. (2011). *What Can Parents Do to Help Their Children Succeed in School?* Pisa in Focus No. 10. www.oecd.org/pisa/49012097.pdf.
OECD. (2012). *Let's Read Them a Story: The Parent Factor in Education.* Paris: OECD Publishing. DOI: http://dx.doi.org/10.1787/9789264176232-e.
OECD. (2013a). *PISA 2012 Assessment and Analytical Framework: Mathematics, Reading, Science, Problem Solving and Financial Literacy.* Paris: OECD Publishing.
OECD. (2013b). *PISA 2012 Results: Ready to Learn: Students' Engagement, Drive and Self-Beliefs* (Volume III). Paris: OECD Publishing. DOI: http://dx.doi.org/10.1787/9789264201170-en.
OECD. (2017). *Education at a Glance 2017: OECD Indicators.* Paris: OECD Publishing. DOI: http://dx.doi.org/10.1787/eag-2017-en.
OECD. (2019). *PISA 2018 Assessment and Analytical Framework, PISA.* Paris: OECD Publishing. DOI: https://doi.org/10.1787/b25efab8-en.
Park, H. (2008). Home literacy environments and children's reading performance: A comparative study of 25 countries. *Educational Research and Evaluation, 14,* 489–505. DOI: http://dx.doi.org/10.1080/13803610802576734.
Perfetti, C. A. (1992). The representation problem in reading acquisition. In P. B. Gough, L. C. Ehri, & R. Trieman (eds.), *Reading Acquisition* (pp. 145–174). Hillsdale, NJ: Erlbaum.
Perfetti, C. A., Landi, N., & Oakhill, J. (2005). The acquisition of reading comprehension skills. In M. J. Snowling & C. Hulme (eds.), *The Science of Reading: A Handbook* (pp. 227–274). Oxford: Blackwell.
Perfetti, C., & Verhoeven, L. (2017). Epilogue: Universals and particulars in learning to read across seventeen orthographies. In L. Verhoeven & C. Perfetti (eds.), *Learning to Read across Languages and Writing Systems* (pp. 455–466). Cambridge: Cambridge University Press.
Piasta, S. B., & Wagner, K. (2010). Developing early literacy skills: A meta-analysis of alphabet learning and instruction. *Reading Research Quarterly, 45*(1), 8–38. DOI: https://doi.org/10.1598/RRQ.45.1.2.
Pollatsek, A., & Treiman, R. (2015). *The Oxford Handbook of Reading.* New York: Oxford University Press.
Pokropek, A., Borgonovi, F., & Jakubowski, M. (2015). Socio-economic disparities in academic achievement: A comparative analysis of mechanisms and pathways, *Learning and Individual Differences, 42,* 10–18. DOI: https://doi.org/10.1016/j.lindif.2015.07.011.
Riley, J. (1996). *The Teaching of Reading: The Development of Literacy in the Early Years of School.* London: Sage Publications.
Rose, E., Lehrl, S., Ebert, S., & Weinert, S. (2018). Long-term relations between children's language, the home literacy environment, and socioemotional development from ages 3 to 8. *Early Education and Development, 29,* 342–356. DOI: https://doi.org/10.1080/10409289.2017.1409096.
Schmalz, X., Marinus, E., Coltheart, M. & Castles, A. (2015). Getting to the bottom of orthographic depth. *Psychonomic Bulletin & Review, 22,* 1614–1629. DOI: https://doi.org/10.3758/s13423-015-0835-2.
Seidenberg, M. S. (2013). The science of reading and its educational implications. *Language Learning and Development, 9*(4), 331–360. http://dx.doi.org/10.1080/15475441.2013.812017.

Sénéchal, M. (2012). Child language and literacy development at home. In B. Wasik (ed.), *Handbook of Family Literacy* (pp. 38–50). London: Taylor and Francis.

Sénéchal, M., Ouellette, G., & Rodney, D. (2006). The misunderstood giant: On the predictive role of early vocabulary to future reading. In S. B. Neuman & D. K. Dickinson (eds.), *Handbook of Early Literacy Research*, Vol. 2 (pp. 173-184). New York: Guilford Press.

Seymour, P., Aro, M., & Erskine, J. M. (2003). Foundation literacy acquisition in European orthographies. *British Journal of Psychology*, *94*, 143–174.

Shager, H. M., Schindler, H. S., Magnuson, K. A. et al. (2013). Can research design explain variation in head start research results? A meta-analysis of cognitive and achievement outcomes. *Educational Evaluation and Policy Analysis*, *35*, 76–95. DOI: https://doi.org/10.3102/0162373712462453.

Share, D. L. (2008). On the Anglocentricities of current reading research and practice: The perils of overreliance of on an "outlier" orthography. *Psychological Bulletin*, *134*, 584–615.

Shiel, G. & Eivers, E. (2009). International comparisons of reading literacy: What can they tell us? *Cambridge Journal of Education*, *39*(3), 345–360.

Silinskas, G., Aunola, K., Lerkkanen, M.-K., & Raiziene, S. (2021). Parental teaching of reading and spelling across the transition from kindergarten to Grade 1. *Frontiers in Psychology*, 11, Article 610870. DOI: https://doi.org/10.3389/fpsyg.2020.610870.

Silinskas, G., Lerkkanen, M. K., Tolvanen, A. et al. (2012). The frequency of parents' reading-related activities at home and children's reading skills during kindergarten and Grade 1. *Journal of Applied Developmental Psychology*, *33*, 302–310. DOI: https://doi.org/10.1016/j.appdev.2012.07.004.

Silinskas, G., Torppa, M., Lerkkanen, M. K., and Nurmi, J. E. (2020). The home literacy model in a highly transparent orthography. *School Effectiveness and School Improvement*, *31*, 80–101. DOI: https://doi.org/10.1080/09243453.2019.1642213.

Sproat, R. (2016). English among the writing systems of the world. In V. Cook & D. Ryan (ed.), *The Routledge Handbook of the English Writing System* (pp. 3–40). New York: Routledge.

Stancel-Piatak, A., Mirazchiyski, P., & Desa, D. (2013). Promotion of reading and early literacy skills in schools: A comparison of three European Countries. *European Journal of Education*, *48*, 449–510. DOI: https://doi.org/10.1111/ejed.12050.

UNESCO. (2005). *Education for All Global Monitoring Report 2006 – Literacy for Life*. Paris: UNESCO.

U.S. Department of Education, National Center for Education Statistics. A Content Comparison of the NAEP and PIRLS Fourth-Grade Reading Assessments, NCES 200310, by Marilyn Binkley and Dana Kelly. Project Officer: Marilyn Binkley. Washington, DC: 2003

Vaessen, A., Bertrand, D., Toth, D. et al. (2010). Cognitive development of fluent word reading does not qualitatively differ between transparent and opaque orthographies. *Journal of Educational Psychology*, *102*(4), 827–842. DOI: https://doi.org/10.1037/a0019465.

Venezky, R. L. (1991). The development of literacy in the industrialized nations of the West. In R. Barr, M. L., Kamil, P. Mosenthal, & D. Pearson (eds.), *Handbook of Reading Research*, Vol. 2, (pp. 46–67). Mahwah, NJ: Lawrence Erlbaum Associates.

Ventura, P., Fernandes, T., Leite, I., Pereira, A., & Wong, A. (2019). Is holistic processing of written words modulated by phonology? *Acta Psychologica, 201*. www.researchgate.net/publication/337050574_Is_holistic_processing_of_written_words_modulated_by_phonology.

Verhoeven, L., van Leeuwe, J., Irausquin, R., & Segers, E. (2016). The unique role of lexical accessibility in predicting kindergarten emergent literacy. *Reading and Writing*, 29(4), 591–608. DOI: https://doi.org/10.1007/s11145-015-9614-8.

Weber, R. M. (2001). Historical perspectives on promoting reading: The early Soviet effort. In L. Verhoeven & C. Snow (eds.), *Reading Engagement in Individuals and Groups* (pp. 275–290).Mahwah, NJ: Lawrence Erlbaum Associates.

Ziegler, J. C., Bertrand, D., Tóth, D. et al.(2010).Orthographic depth and its impact on universal predictors of reading: A cross-language investigation. *Psychological Science, 21*(4), 551–559.

6 Literacy Education and Development in Russia

Olga Velichenkova and Margarita Rusetskaya

6.1 Introduction

The understanding of literacy in Russia requires the analysis of several issues. To begin with, historical changes in the provision of education in the region, and the introduction of a modern educational system in preschool (kindergarten age four–six years) and primary school (Grades 1–4) need to be considered. This is because, in recent years, a transformation has been recorded in both the number of educational institutions and the nature of the educational process. Furthermore, the Russian scholarship on writing and reading disorders requires examination in view of several internal contradictions and inconsistencies in the approaches to psychological and pedagogical support available for children with these disorders. The situation may be described as a disconnection between the diagnostic processes and remedial methods used in Russia and the international experience. This chapter will start out with a description of the Russian writing system. This will be followed by an overview of teaching and assessment methods over the past decades. Finally, a reflection will be provided on the identification of children with reading problems and strategies for remediation.

6.2 Features of the Russian Orthography

The Russian orthography is alphabetical, with thirty-three letters representing forty-two phonemes. The relationship between sound and letter is not unambiguous. One letter can correspond to several sounds and vice versa, with one sound indicated by a letter or letters in different ways. In literacy instruction, the main and secondary letter sounds are distinguished and highlighted. In addition, there are elements of syllable writing involved. In the initial stages, children become acquainted with *graphics* as possible options for designating sounds with letters. In the process of decoding and coding words, problems of different complexity need to be solved. First, as with any alphabetic system, a novice reader is forced to update letter–sound correspondences as they encounter various aspects of the orthography. However, with certain cognitive deficits it may become difficult to identify a letter, since there are several visually similar letters in Russian and acoustically similar sounds as well (e.g., within phonological oppositions). In addition, the syllabic principle of reading requires a consonant postposition analysis. The phonological opposition of the softness–hardness of consonants can be conveyed by letter soft signs or by follow-up vowels. This "economizes" the size of the letter system but creates difficulties for the child, since it is a departure from the principle of *one sound–one letter* correspondences.

By reading aloud syllable by syllable, novice readers may put a word together, but they may get a phonological variant that does not correspond to a valid pronunciation of the word. This may be due to confusion in letter–sound correspondence, with the main rather than the secondary sound value available for the target letter. For example, the Russian pronunciation is characterized by devocalization of voiced consonants at the end of words, but in writing these sounds are determined by their strong (intervocal) phonetic position: *дуб* (oak) is vocalized as [dup] in its singular form, but due to its strong, intervocal position in the plural it is written as *дубы* (oaks) where it sounds voiced [duby]. Thus, even though a uniform spelling for a family of morphemes that are carriers of shared meaning may create decoding challenges, it may optimize reading by providing quick lexical access in an experienced reader's case. Children need training and the opportunity to build up a sight vocabulary to be able to take advantage of it. At the initial stages, when reading aloud they tend to repeatedly try to choose the closest phonetic word from memory or rely on the available context (Egorov, 2006).

The process of learning to spell in Russian is somewhat different from learning to read. Russian spelling is not only based on orthographic but also on morphological and grammatical principles (Shcherba, 1983; Zinder, 1987). The morphological principle dominates Russian spelling, involving prefixes, roots, suffixes, which are written consistently. For the child it is important to learn, for example, how to find a word with an explicit, unambiguous spelling among words with the same root. In such case, the learner will have to check the spelling of the last letter in the word *сад* ('garden'), comparing it with the word *сады* (gardens), and will need to proceed vice versa to check the spelling of the unstressed root vowel in the word *сады* ('gardens'), comparing it to the word *сад* ('garden'), in which this vowel is stressed. There are several morphological principles that underpin Russian spelling, and it may be expected that children will require a high level of morphological awareness to learn to spell in Russian. The grammatical principle governs spellings that convey a particular grammatical meaning. For example, *строится* and *строиться* ('is being built' and 'be built') are the indicative and infinitive grammatical forms of the same verb; they have a different spelling but are pronounced the same way. And finally, unlike the morphological and grammatical principles, some words have deep historical roots such that their contemporary spelling is based only on tradition. In such instances, the child must simply remember the spelling of words or morphemes.

6.3   Teaching Russian Literacy

6.3.1   Analytic and Global Methods

Russian literacy instruction is dominated by the analytical-synthetic method, which is focused on sound units in a word (Lvov, Goretsky, & Sosnovskaya, 2000). Methods that are based on global reading do not have wide popularity nor official recognition. They were relatively popular in the early 2000s, mainly in the parental environment: such methods include those outlined by Doman (1998), Reznichenko (2012), and Zaitsev (2000), as well as Chaplygin's cubes (2019).[1] The first two approaches are global in the full sense, with children being introduced to a word as a whole. Doman's method is more often used in kindergarten or even preschool. By contrast, Reznichenko's method is designed for six–eight-year-old learners, gradually guiding them from a global to an analytical approach to decoding and coding the Russian orthography. The contemporary use of such strongly global methods was "tested" in Russia in the 1920s (Lvov et al., 2000). The syllabic teaching method (Zaitsev, 2000; Chaplygin's cubes) can be classified as "semi-global"; its historical roots go back to the late nineteenth and early twentieth centuries. In this method, letter–sound correspondences are not explicitly taught; children practice syllable lists instead. This makes it easier to switch to analytical reading.

There are also many variations of the analytical-synthetic method. Russian creators of ABC books have gone from invariant models of teaching to the practical implementation of different technologies. In the Soviet period, from the end of the 1930s to the beginning of the 1980s, the literacy-teaching methodology was quite invariant. Children began school at the age of seven, with primary education for three years. The teacher had one common primer, and the only significant change that occurred during this period was the introduction of separate reading and writing lessons, that is, the transition from co-teaching reading and writing to parallel learning (Lvov et al., 2000). The teaching of the Russian language at school was characterized by a transition from practical language experiences to language generalizations, with literacy teaching based on moving from letter to sound. The sound values of a letter were simply communicated, and after a few exercises in which children were asked to find the target sound in a word, they were introduced to reading syllables and then words. These practice exercises began

---

[1] Chaplygin's cubes, https://umnitsa.ru/cat/chitaju-legko/ (2019).

immediately after the introduction of letters, which made it possible for young learners to form implicit conclusions based on experience. The use of a special order in which to introduce the letters helped preserve the rule of simplicity in the lesson and not overload the child. The longest period in Soviet literacy studies is associated with the idea of the gradual introduction of those letters that are difficult in terms of their lack of transparency in letter–sound correspondences. For example, the letter M has only two sound values in any position in the word: [m] and [m ']. Paired consonants, based on voiceless and voiced features, have four sound values, and the sound values of some vowels depend on their position. Therefore, in the Soviet school primers, the sonorants (*m, n, r, l*) were introduced first, then the paired unvoiced consonants, followed by voiced ones, with the complex vowels studied last.

From the early 1980s onward, reforms in the primary education system popularized the idea of the need for earlier literacy instruction (Silchenkova, 2006). This acceleration was perceived as a challenge to teaching practitioners. A gradual transition to four-year schooling began for six-year-old children. During this time, the literacy curriculum also changed by accounting for letter frequency in the Russian language. According to the curriculum developers (Lvov et al., 2000), this created the opportunity to offer full, lexically rich texts for reading earlier in the learning program, in order to contribute to a more comprehensive development of children's literacy skills. However, this frequency-based approach led to the early introduction of complex letters. This problem of complexity was solved by increasing the proportion of exercises for phonological analysis, and by using detailed sound schemes that highlighted sound properties as follows: vowels, consonants, hard sounds, soft sounds, stressed sounds, and unstressed sounds. In our opinion, Goretsky's curriculum of 1982 strengthened the phonics component in the Russian literacy education by instructing first-graders to master sound–letter connections and to make abstract generalization from these connections in words. Another systemic change in the 2000s was a transition from a unified to a more variable education program, with Russian schools receiving new primers and alphabet books. The elementary school began to be seen as a "school of cultural-activity pedagogy of variative education," "the basic stage of designing universal educational activities," the main task of which was to learn how to learn (Asmolov, 2013, p. 9).

Proponents of developmental education's polemic against proponents of the traditional pedagogy had already been going on for a long time. Almost in parallel with the appearance of Goretsky's alphabet book was the appearance of the school primer by Elkonin and collaborators based on the idea of development-centered child education (Elkonin, 1992, 1997). Its structure and content are founded on the principle of a functional meaning of letters and their role in Russian writing, and on the position-oriented principle. The position-oriented principle, on which Russian orthography is based, is actively deduced by students together with the teacher before reading. The path used is from sound to letter. First, sounds from a word are distinguished, then consonant characteristics (hard or soft) are clarified, after which a decision is made as to a letter that should represent the softness of the consonant and the actual vowel. This phonemic analysis precedes word decoding, and children only begin reading the first syllables several months later. This way of teaching literacy is based on the principle of ascent from the abstract to the concrete (Zuckerman, 2011). Even the introduction of the child to the rules of Russian morphology remains a subject of pedagogical discussion. And literacy is one of the most controversial issues here. It has been assumed that a preschooler with their syncretic perception of speech is faced with the need to be aware of complex linguistic phenomena and should therefore be exposed to a rich range of complex phonology in a structured way (Velichenkova, 2018b). However, it has also been argued that a "language model developed for scientific purposes and a didactic model that is a way of presenting a language in the educational process are not required to coincide" (Leontiev, 2016, p. 140).

Currently, Elkonin's system is implemented in two school primers: Zhurova and Evdokimova's (2014) and Repkin, Vostorgova, and Levin's (2019), with the former the most widely used (Glagoleva, Arkhipova, & Boykina, 2019).[2] A recent federal list of textbooks that schools may use includes six school primers (Order of the Ministry of Education; 2019). The most popular is Goretsky's textbook, which is used by about 40–60 percent of teachers (Glagoleva et al., 2019). Although Goretsky's book is perceived by the pedagogical community as a traditional textbook, all the features of the new school methodology are inherent in it, including an increased role for analytical sound exercises and for the teaching of relevant knowledge in the field of phonetics.

6.3.2 Role of the Home Environment

In the contemporary Russian education system, we have started to observe phenomena very similar to the trends in Russia at the turn of the nineteenth and twentieth centuries: individual home-schooling flourishes in the context of state-education differentiation (Shtets, 2009). These phenomena are especially characteristic in the initial stage of the child's education. At the same time, one gets the feeling that the vectors of official and family approaches to teaching reading are regarded as opposites (Velichenkova, 2018a; Velichenkova & Gorilko, 2019). In the case of home literacy support, there is usually a parent acting as a teacher, and the book that is used by this "naive methodologist" is of particular importance. An approach often adopted by families who are trying to

---

[2] Data on the frequency of educational and methodological kits; https://schoolguide.ru/index.php/polls.html (2019).

get away from the school primer is to look for a preschool one. Preschool textbooks do not require examination and testing; the choice to purchase them is the parents' private matter. While only six school primers are on sale, there are about sixty preschool ones available. Despite such a huge selection and the significance of preschool family education, a comparative analysis of the manuals and methods in Russia has not been carried out.

Even more surprisingly, almost half of preschool primers are logopedic, with roots in speech therapy. It seems likely that there are objective factors that make logopedic textbooks attractive for parents. We attempted a comparative analysis of seven modern logopedic ABC books (Batyaeva, 2017; Ilyina, 2015; Kosinova, 2006; Krylova, Pisareva, & Ipatova, 1989; Nischeva, 2004; Zhukova, 2016; Zhukova, 2017). These primers usually emphasize that they have been compiled based on the authors' extensive experience, but there is no scientific justification of this experience in peer-reviewed publications. Most authors highlight the traditional nature of the literacy-teaching methodology used in the textbook, and that it is supplemented by speech-therapy technologies. Parents wanting to find an alternative to the modern school primer and relying on their own experience of school accept this message and buy a traditional primer. For example, in the most popular "logopedic ABC book" by Zhukova (2017), the order in which letters are introduced keeps to the traditions of the Soviet period: The letters that come first are those that are unequivocal in terms of sound meaning. Other logopedic primers use a different order. Back in the 1960s, the idea emerged of postponing the study of late-mastered sounds (e.g., *r, l, sh, s*) to assist the literacy of children with a speech pathology. Since, in the case of speech disorders, these sounds are not being pronounced correctly by the time the child enters school, the corresponding letters are postponed to a later part of the curriculum.

Logopedic ABC-book preschool primers do not usually include many exercises for sound analysis and linguistic schematization. After all, they are focused on family education, and subtleties of phonology are inaccessible to the parent. If we compare the volume of speech material of three types (syllables, words, sentences), then it turns out that the logopedic ABC books on average are more extensive than, for example, the school primer by Goretsky et al. (2012) in terms of the numbers of syllables and words for reading. However, in terms of text volume, they are still behind due to the greater level of attention paid by their authors to reading a syllable and a word, and to their use of adapted texts that are shorter and simpler. Thus, in contradiction to the approach of strengthening the role of analytical strategy in schools, training in logopedic ABC books is being built rather more synthetically and at the same time more intuitively.

6.4 Monitoring of Preschool and Primary-Education Outcomes

6.4.1 Monitoring Literacy Education

Preschool literacy teaching is a common phenomenon that is not regulated by the state. Let us try to briefly describe the state system of preschool and school education organization and education quality data. Preschool education is not obligatory; parents can use the services of the state kindergarten when their child reaches three years of age. There are state standards for preschool and school education that describe the requirements for the structure of educational programs, their implementation conditions, and how results should be assessed. The preschool standard (Federal State Educational Standards, 2019) emphasizes preschool education optionality in the Russian Federation. The educational program formulates its targets, but not children's specific educational achievements. The program is compiled by the educational institution itself based on a sample program which the Ministry of Education has approved and posted on its website (Inventory of Sample Main Basic Education Programs, 2019). In addition to the development of all components of speech, it must only include the formation of sound analytical-synthetic activity as a precondition for literacy teaching. This means that in Russian kindergartens, literacy is not taught in an explicit way. A kindergarten teacher is not confronted with such a task. However, the teacher can conduct classes with children according to the chosen standard textbook, which to some degree develops sound-analytic and synthetic activity, whereas in some cases letters, syllables, and words are presented for literacy development.

Primary education starts at around seven years of age and lasts for four years. There are two state standards for elementary schools: general (valid since 2010) and those for children with special health needs (Health Impact Assessment HIA) (valid since 2016). The programs' content formulates concrete targets for children to master in which reading literacy occupies a significant place. The disciplines in the philological block include the Russian language, literary reading, and a foreign language. At the time of writing, there are seven textbook series for teaching the Russian language and five for literary reading. The school carries out the assessments to establish whether students have mastered the program. This is done by means of marks attained at an intermediate stage in combination with the results of the final test. There is a state system for the monitoring of education quality. The marks received by schoolchildren through any such monitoring do not affect their final marks; they only serve as a tool for identifying problem areas and the education level in schools as well as in regions.

6.4.2 Literacy Outcomes

Russia has been participating in the PIRLS (Progress in International Reading Literacy Study) since 2001. From sixteenth place in its ranking, Russia has since climbed close to the top, where it has remained since 2006, which may be due to greater parental involvement. Research has consistently shown that Russian parents are the most active participants in the formation of children's reading literacy among all the participating countries (Mullis et al., 2007 [PIRLS-2006]).

In PISA, reading literacy results have been extremely low. Starting in 2000 at twenty-seventh place, Russia kept worsening its position until 2012 (forty-second place), and then in 2015 returned to twenty-seventh place. The discussion about the poor results of Russian children in this study is ongoing (Zuckerman, Kovaleva, & Kuznetsova, 2011). Obviously, students' initial reading competency is well formed, but the complex of competencies that are usually described as making up functional literacy are not sufficiently developed.

The All-Russian Test Work initiative is compulsory in elementary schools; its tests are held once a year on the main subjects (the Russian language in all classes). As to outcomes on the All-Russian Test Work over the past five years, 4.6 percent of the population showed literacy problems.[3] For writing, 7.8 percent of primary-school graduates could not cope with the test, as shown from their performances on the ability to copy a text, use of spelling and punctuation norms, and independent writing.

6.5 Children with Learning Disabilities

6.5.1 Assistance for Children with Disabilities

Recently, progress has been made in the assistance system for children with learning disabilities. The system has undergone significant changes since 2013, especially in schools. The Law on Education was adopted in 2013 and introduced the concepts of "children with limited health abilities" and "adapted educational programs" (Federal Law of December 29, 2012). A child with limited health abilities (LHA) is defined as "an individual with physical and/or psychological developmental deficiencies confirmed by a psychological, medical and pedagogical commission as hindering education if special arrangements are not in place" (Federal Law of December 29, 2012). Adapted educational programs were created to teach children with disabilities, taking into account the peculiarities of their psychophysical development, individual

---

[3] All-Russian Test Work: https://rcoko.khb.ru/oko/monitoring/verification-work.

capabilities, and social adaptation. These programs were focused on children with vision, speech, hearing, and motor impairments, as well as delayed mental development. It is important to note that reading and writing impairments are not specifically distinguished from each other (Volkova & Shakhovskoy, 1998). Reading and writing disorders are considered only because of either a phonological processes deficiency or general underdevelopment of speech. The terms dyslexia and dysgraphia are simply absent from the school standard, although, as we will see later, they are widely used in professional support systems.

Children who have difficulty in mastering reading and writing are often diagnosed as having a speech disorder or a delay in mental development. Their parents are advised to apply for an adapted program for the child based on a more intensive standard program or an approximate adapted program, (partly) outside the classroom. This new assistance system differs from the one that existed before primarily by virtue of its strengthening of the mediating role of medical-psychological-pedagogical commissions. Unfortunately, there are many unsolved problems with this system. The most important one is personnel. There are no mechanisms to encourage schools to employ a speech therapist. Furthermore, parents tend to mistrust the input of this new institute of medical-psychological-pedagogical commissions.

6.5.2 Public Perception of Children with Reading Disabilities

In 2019, on the initiative of the Association of Parents and Children with Dyslexia and with the financial support of the Our Future Foundation and the Ministry of Education of the Russian Federation, an independent research agency (MAGRAM MR) carried out an unprecedented survey to determine the level of awareness and attitudes toward problems with writing and reading in society and among professionals. Our role was to expertly evaluate the results. The all-Russian population survey included 2,516 telephone interviews (the sample represented the population of the Russian Federation by socio-demographic characteristics). The survey of professionals was carried out using an online questionnaire. The support of the Ministry of Education of the Russian Federation made it possible to collect data on 32,406 school specialists.

The survey found that only 17 percent of the Russian population understands what dyslexia or dysgraphia are. Eighty-three percent do not know these terms: 61 percent of these respondents do not know anything about the problem; 22 percent have heard of the terms but cannot explain their meaning. Young participants (from eighteen to thirty-four years old) demonstrate a higher level of knowledge of the terms in question than representatives of the older age groups. According to almost half of participants (49 percent), one of the main causes of dyslexia/dysgraphia is parents' neglect their children and failing to provide the necessary participation in their upbringing and education. Thus, the child's health problem is "shifted" onto the parents. Only a quarter to a third of respondents said that the cause of the problem relates to the child's neurobiological characteristics. A fourth of respondents indicated that the causes of the problem under consideration lie in the irregularly organized school educational process, including a high level of high teacher workload (28 percent), high-school requirements (25 percent), and insufficient attention from support specialists (24 percent). More than a third of respondents (38 percent) believed that dyslexia in children is quite widespread. However, only 2 percent noted that their family had a child with dyslexia, and less than half of these children received specialized assistance.

To explore professional support for children with dyslexia, school staff were interviewed: primary-school teachers (23,849) school-department managers (3,497), psychologists (2,851), speech therapists (1,549) and speech pathologists (660). Ninety-eight percent of the speech therapists, 87 percent of the speech pathologists, 80 percent of the psychologists, 73 percent of the head-teachers, and 66 percent of the teachers were familiar with the problem. Among causes for children's writing and reading disabilities, teachers mentioned the child's individual characteristics (63 percent). Half of the survey participants noted parents' insufficient attention to the problem – rejection of the problem (54 percent) and lack of proper participation in education and training (49 percent). Fifty-three percent also mentioned lack of timely access to specialists. Among the professionals surveyed, the prevalence of the problem was rated as high by most specialists. Content-wise, 67 percent of pedagogical community representatives indicated that remedial classes with underachieving children were held. But many of them (38 percent) stated that classes were held much less frequently than required. Seventy-three percent of the professional representatives interviewed pointed out the insufficient number of psychological and pedagogical support specialists working with children with dyslexia, and 38 percent of them indicated that a substantial replenishment of specialized professionals is necessary. It can thus be concluded that the gap in awareness between the general population and professionals concerning learning disabilities in children and assessing their prevalence is significant.

6.5.3 Research on Developmental Dyslexia

The terms dyslexia and dysgraphia are widely used in the clinical and pedagogical classification of speech disorders. In Russia it is customary to consider reading and writing disorders as separate from each other (Akhutina, 2018; Grigorenko & Elliott, 2012; Sadovnikova, 2011; Tokareva, 1971; Volkova & Shakhovskoy, 1998). And this relates to the greater difficulty of mastering the

Russian coding than decoding. Dyslexia is generally defined as persistent difficulties in reading. The diagnostic inclusion criterion for dyslexia is the same as for dysgraphia. However, most authors simply indicate the absence of intellectual disability as an important symptom for diagnosis (Sadovnikova, 2011; Velichenkova & Rusetskaya, 2015; Volkova & Shakhovskoy, 1998). Kornev (1995, 2004, 2010) insisted on the need to apply the criterion of reading level and level of mental development discrepancy. Defining dysgraphia, specialists normally name diagnostic criteria for inclusion (Kornev, 1995; Sadovnikova, 2011; Velichenkova & Rusetskaya, 2015). The main criterion for inclusion is the presence of errors associated with nonmastery of the graphics and a high frequency of such errors. The term *dysorthography* has been actively used in scientific and pedagogical practice (Kornev, 1995; Prishchepova, 2006; Velichenkova & Rusetskaya, 2015), alongside the term dysgraphia, referring to the lack of spelling understanding. The diagnostic criteria remain the same for these conditions except for the higher frequency and different type of spelling errors associated with dysgraphia; these indicate a failure to master the morphological, grammatical, and traditional principles of writing.

Standardized reading assessment methods are based on the accuracy and speed of single-word reading (Korneev, Akhutina, & Matveeva, 2019; Rybchinskaya, Korneev & Akhutina, 2018) and text reading as well as reading comprehension (Akhutina & Inshakova, 2008; Rybchinskaya et al., 2018). In a study by Rusetskaya (2018), students in Grades 1–4 were given the same texts to read. It was shown that on average, correct scores increased from 91 percent in the first grade to 97 percent in the fourth grade. Reading efficiency as measured by the words read correctly in one minute increased from 45 words in the first grade to 67 words in the second grade, 84 words in the third grade, and 101 words in the fourth grade. These data show that reading problems in Russian are mainly a matter of reading speed. A psychometric procedure for assessing reading comprehension was proposed by Akhutina and Inshakova (2008). They assessed the integrity and coherence of retelling and comprehension in 197 third-graders by addressing accuracy, semantic adequacy of retelling, its deployment, and lexical-grammatical design. It was found that 11 percent of the children showed reading-comprehension problems.

With respect to dysgraphia, we obtained data on the average number of dysgraphic errors in the dictations of sixty-six third-graders in two Moscow schools in 2018. In total, about 600 control dictations of 45–70 words written by the children over one year were analyzed. Dysgraphic errors (2.01 on average) included omissions of letters, mixing graphically similar letters (*m-n, б-д, u-y*), mixing by acoustic-articulation similarity, rearrangement, perseveration, anticipation of letters, and violation of soft-consonants designation in writing. Furthermore, the development of writing in dictation, copying from printed material, and handwritten text was examined in 216 children from Grades 1 to 4 (Inshakova, 2013). It was found that children made the most errors in dictation and that the numbers of errors remained constant throughout the grades.

6.6 Conclusions and Discussion

Consideration of literacy achievement in Russia is impossible without considering the changes in the country that have affected the whole education system. The diversification and humanization of contemporary Russian education have led to the search for new teaching methods and changes in the way the system is organized, as well as changes in content at the preschool and school levels. Schools expect new levels of achievement from children that would have seemed inaccessible to previous generations. School teams seek to teach literacy using sophisticated learning tools, and parents and children expect to meet modern educational trends. The way that society has changed in response to these changes in the Russian education system is obvious. It seeks to meet the system's expectations by strengthening parental support for the educational process, even encouraging parents to get involved in the more accessible aspects of children's education (see also Schwartz, Chapter 19 in this volume). For example, home preschool literacy support is universally perceived as the norm, and the number of textbooks addressed to parents is growing exponentially. In these conditions, pedagogy should analyze the main vectors of the development of the home methodology in order to understand what the official methodology lacks, given parent expectations. There is an urgent need to assess the social and economic value of such a significant contribution on the part of adults to children's education.

It can be concluded that in the past decades the system of psychological and pedagogical support for children with writing and reading disabilities in Russia has also undergone changes. However, further reorganization of education for children with special literacy needs is warranted. There is still a lack of personnel and textbooks, while there are also inconsistencies in the legislation, as has been indicated by both school staff and parents. Monitoring of literacy outcomes in Russia is also seen as important. It is now carried out constantly and in all regions. Its results can be compared with those of international projects such as PIRLS and PISA. This trend makes it possible to evaluate the national monitoring, and to control and influence the results in the context of interregional differences, to monitor positive and negative trends. Nowadays, children in Russia demonstrate an adequate reading level by the end of their primary-school education. However, more research is needed to assess the variation in reading literacy of students in secondary education and beyond.

References

Akhutina, T. V. (2018). Neuropsychological analysis of errors in writing. In O. A. Velichenkova (ed.), *Writing and Reading Disorders in Children: Study and Correction* (pp. 76–95). Moscow: Logomag.

Akhutina, T. V., & Inshakova, O. B. (eds.). (2008). *Neuropsychological Diagnostics: Examination of Writing and Reading of Primary School Students*. Moscow: SFERA: V. Sekachev.

Asmolov, A. G. (2013). Variational education in a changing world: Sociocultural perspective. *Education and Science*, *8*, 3–13.

Batyaeva, S. V. (2017). *Logopedic Primer: Comprehensive Author's Methodology for Teaching Reading: For Preschool Age*. Moscow: AST [in Russian].

Doman, G. (1998). *How to Teach a Child to Read*. Moscow: AST.

Egorov, T. G. (2006). *Psychology of Reading Skill*. Saint Petersburg: KARO.

Elkonin, D. B. (1992). *School Primer* [test textbook for four-year-old school beginners]. Moscow: Education.

Elkonin, D. B. (1997). How to teach children to read. In D. I. Feldstein (ed.), *Mental Development in Childhood*. Moscow: Institute of Practical Psychology.

Federal Law of December 29, 2012, N 273-FZ. "On Education in the Russian Federation." (2012). *Garant.ru*. https://base.garant.ru/70291362/.

Federal State Educational Standards. (2019). https://fgos.ru/.

Glagoleva, Y. I., Arkhipova, Y. I., & Boykina, M. V. (2019). The choice of textbooks and teaching materials for primary school students in state educational institutions of St. Petersburg: Analytical note. https://grot-school.ru/images/doc/fgos-noo/documenty/metodicheskie-rekomendacii.pdf.

Goretsky, V. G., Kiryushkin, V. A., Vinogradskaya, L. A. et al. (2012). *ABCs. Textbook for General Education in 2 parts*. Moscow: Education.

Grigorenko, E. L., & Elliott, J. J. (2012). *Reading about Reading*. Voronezh: Aist.

Ilyina, T. G. (2015). *Game Primer: For Children of 5–7 Years Old Having Speech Impairments: Reading Instruction According to the Method of G. A. Kashe*. Moscow: GNOM.

Inshakova, O. B. (2013). *Multidisciplinary Analysis of Phonemic Writing Skill Formation in Younger Students*. Moscow: V. Sekachev.

Inventory of Sample Main Basic Education Programs. (2019). http://fgosreestr.ru/.

Korneev, A. A., Akhutina, T. V., & Matveeva E. Y. (2019). Peculiarities of third graders reading with different levels of skill development: Analysis of eye movements. *Moscow University Physics Bulletin. Series 14: Psychology*, *2*, 64–87.

Kornev, A. N. (1995). *Dyslexia and Dysgraphia in Children*. St. Petersburg: Hippocrates.

Kornev A. N. (2004). Dyslexia and Its Twins: Criteria for Differentiation. In *Materials of the Conference Studies on Reading and Writing Disorders:Results and Prospects*. (pp. 117–125). Moscow: Publishing House of Moscow Social and Humanitarian Institute.

Kornev, A. N., & Ishimova, O. A. (2010). *A Technique for Diagnosing Dyslexia in Children: A Methodological Guide*. St. Petersburg: Publishing House of the Polytechnic University.

Kosinova, E. M. (2006). *Logopedic School Primer*. Moscow: Machaon.

Krylova, N. L., Pisareva, I. B., & Ipatova, N. L. (1989). *Primer: For Training. First School Graders: For Children with Severe Speech Disorders (1st Department)*. Moscow: Education.

Leontiev, A. A. (ed.) (2016). *Pedagogy of Common Sense: Selected Works on the Philosophy of Education and Pedagogical Psychology*. Moscow: Smiysl.

Lvov, M. R., Goretsky, V. G., & Sosnovskaya, O. V. (2000). *Methods of Teaching Russian Language in Primary School: Textbook for Students of Pedagogical Institutions Studying the Specialty "Pedagogy and Methods of Elementary Education"* (2nd, advanced ed.). Moscow: Akademia.

Mullis, I. V. S., Martin, M. O., Kennedy, A. M., & Foy, P. (2007). *PIRLS 2006: INTERNATIONAL REPORT, IEA's Progress in International Reading Literacy Study in Primary Schools in 40 Countries*. Chestnut Hill, MA: Boston College. http://author-club.org/media/files/Report_PIRLS2006_ENG.pdf.

Nischeva, N. V. (2004). *My School Primer: Textbook for Teaching Preschoolers to Read*. St. Petersburg: CHILDHOOD-PRESS.

Prishchepova, I. V. (2006). *Dysorthography of Elementary School Students: Textbook. Study Guide*. St. Petersburg: KARO.

Repkin, V. V., Vostorgova, E. V., & Levin, V. A. (2019). *Primer: Textbook for Grade 1: In Two Parts*. [system of D. B. Elkonin – V. V. Davydov]. Moscow: Binom. Knowledge Laboratory.

Reznichenko, T. S. (2012). *Entertaining Primer*. Moscow: GNOM.

Rusetskaya, M. N. (2018). Diagnosis and correction of dyslexia on the basis of competent approach to teaching reading. In O. A. Velichenkova (ed.), *Writing and Reading Disorders in Children: Study and Correction* (pp. 151–65) [in Russian]. Moscow: Logomag.

Rybchinskaya, E. V., Korneev, A. A., & Akhutina, T. V. (2018). Reading regular and irregular words by younger students. In A. K. Krylov, V. D. Soloviev, & A. A. Kibrik (eds.), *Eighth International Conference on Cognitive Science: Abstracts of reports. Svetlogorsk. October 18–21. 2018* (pp. 1246–1248). Moscow: Institute of Psychology, Russian Academy of Sciences.

Sadovnikova, I. N. (2011). *Dysgraphia. Dyslexia: Technology of Overcoming*. Moscow: Paradigm.

Shcherba, L. V. (1983). *Theory of Russian Writing: Executive Editor and Foreword Author*, edited by L. R. Zinder. Leningrad: Science: Leningrad Department.

Shtets, A. A. (2009). Literature as self-developing methodological system. (Doctoral thesis [pedagogical sciences], Chelyabinsk State University.)

Silchenkova, L. S. (2006). *Teaching Russian Literacy Traditions and Innovations*. Moscow: APKiPRO.

Tokareva, O. A. (1971). Disorders of writing in different groups of abnormal children and the principles of work to eliminate them. *Speech Pathology: Scientific Notes MGPI Named after Lenin, 406,* 63–98.

Velichenkova O. A. (2018a). Logopedic support of first graders with special educational needs in literacy teaching. In O. A. Velichenkova (ed.), *Writing and Reading Disorders in Children: Study and Correction* (pp. 237–260). Moscow: Logomag.

Velichenkova, O. A. (2018b). Phonemic perception: Linguistic, psychological and pedagogical aspects. In O. A. Velichenkova (ed.), *Writing and Reading Disorders in Children: Study and Correction* (pp. 40–66). Moscow: Logomag.

Velichenkova, O. A., & Gorilko, M. O. (2019). Logopedic primer as child's first textbook. In N. A. Borisenko (ed.), *All-Russian Scientific Conference Psychodidactics of Modern Textbook: Continuity of Traditions and Development Vectors* (pp. 93–100). Moscow: Institute of Psychology of the Russian Academy of Education.

Velichenkova, O. A., & Rusetskaya, M. N. (2015). *Speech Therapy Work to Overcome Reading and Writing Disorders in Primary School Students*. Moscow: National Book Center.

Volkova, L. S., & Shakhovskoy, S. N. (eds.) (1998). *Logopedia: A Textbook for Students of Defectology Faculties in Pedagogical Universities*. Moscow: VLADOS.

Zaitsev, N. A. (2000). *Writing. Reading. Counting: Textbook of a New Type for Teachers. Educators. Parents*. Saint Petersburg: Lan.

Zhukova, N. S. (2017). *Primer: Textbook for Teaching Preschoolers to Read Correctly*. Moscow: Exmodetstvo.

Zhukova, O. S. (2016). *Logopedic School Primer*. Moscow: AST.

Zhurova, L. E., & Evdokimova, A. O. (2014). *School Primer: Textbook for Students of General Educational Institutions: In 2 Parts*. Moscow: Ventana-Graf.

Zinder, L. R. (1987). *Essay on General Theory of Writing*. Leningrad [Saint Petersburg]: Nauka.

Zuckerman, G. A. (2011). Developmental education: A genetic modelling experiment. *Journal of Russian and European Psychology, 49*, 45–63. DOI: https://doi.org/10.2753/RPO1061-0405490603.

Zuckerman, G. A., Kovaleva, G. S., & Kuznetsova, M. I. (2011). Victory in PIRLS and defeat in PISA: Fate of readers' literacy of 10–15-year-old students. *Voprosy Obrazovaniya* [Education Issues], *2*, 123–150.

7 Literacy Development and Language of Instruction in Sub-Saharan Africa

Amber Gove, Karon Harden, Simon King, Jennifer Pressley Ryan, Sarrynna Sou, and Susan Edwards

7.1 Introduction

The Sustainable Development Goals (SDGs) adopted in 2015 represent an important opportunity to improve learning globally. For the first time in the history of the successive promises made under global goals, countries have pledged not only to improve learning outcomes but also to measure and report on the percentage of children reaching proficiency in reading and math (UNESCO, 2015). Although learning was mentioned under the prior goal frameworks – Education for All (World Conference on Education for All, 1990) and the Millennium Development Goals (UNESCO, 2000) – much of the two decades of subsequent efforts centered on ensuring access to school, with the assumption that learning would naturally follow (Gove et al., 2015). Since those first promises were made, low- and middle-income countries, particularly those in sub-Saharan Africa, have nearly caught up with their wealthier peers in enrolling children in primary school (UNESCO Institute for Statistics [UIS], 2017). But commensurate gains in learning have proved elusive. UNESCO estimates that more than 250 million children around the world are not learning basic reading and math skills, with African children accounting for roughly 40 percent of this total (UNESCO, 2012). Why has closing the learning gap proved so difficult in so many African countries?

Researchers and practitioners point to a variety of factors to explain the persistent lag in learning outcomes, including lack of teacher preparation (Akyeampong et al., 2011), a dearth of teaching and learning materials (RTI International, 2016a–d), and persistent poverty and its associated ills, such as malnutrition and stunting (Black et al., 2017; Engle et al., 2007). Often lacking in these explanations is the role of language (Williams, 2014, and see Verhoeven & Severing, Chapter 4 and Nag, Chapter 15 in this volume). Many children who go to school in Africa receive classroom instruction in a language that is not their own. Estimates vary, but every day, millions of schoolchildren are instructed in a language other than their primary home language. While many children can and do learn to read in a language that is not a home language, this does not happen automatically and the mismatch between home language and language of instruction (LOI) can be a source of significant barriers.

This chapter draws on a unique set of early literacy assessment results and demographic information from six African countries (Ghana, Kenya, Liberia, Malawi, Tanzania, and Zambia) to better understand the role that language plays in influencing early reading outcomes. While these data have been published in individual country reports, the information has not been analyzed and released prominently in the narrative surrounding learning outcomes in the region, although data like those presented in this chapter have begun to reverse this tendency. Following this introduction, we provide a brief history of postcolonial trends in literacy acquisition and language policy in sub-Saharan Africa from about 1960 to the present day, and document current language-of-instruction policies for twenty countries. We outline key questions driving our interest in better understanding the variation in literacy acquisition in a selection of the target countries for which we have data, then document the data and methods used and results. Finally, we discuss the implications of this work for future policy and planning in order to achieve the promises made under the SDGs.

7.2 Language, Literacy, and Schooling in Sub-Saharan Africa

Language and literacy are intricately interconnected. Learners' familiarity with the language in which they learn to read has important implications for the literacy acquisition process and overall learning outcomes. Narrowing this point geographically, sub-Saharan Africa is densely multilingual, and historical, political, and sociolinguistic factors have heavily influenced each country's selection of LOI(s). All regional governments face the challenge of balancing the benefits of home-language instruction with the logistical constraints of offering instruction in multiple (often underresourced) languages, the desire for national unity through a common language, and the advantages of access to the global community through international languages. However, governments also differ in how they ultimately resolve these tensions. Frequently in sub-Saharan Africa, the language of the former European colonial power serves as the sole LOI at the secondary and tertiary levels of education, but there is greater variety in LOI(s) at the primary level as well as in the timing of any transitions between LOIs.

As described in Albaugh (2014), LOI policies in sub-Saharan Africa have fluctuated over the years. For example, precolonial and colonial missionary work included the transcription of many previously unwritten African languages; many Protestant missions used local languages as a pragmatic means of promulgating their message to the largest audience possible, resulting in mother-tongue-based education. In the colonial era, the British favored the use of local languages in early primary with transition to English in late primary, while the French valorized assimilation and instruction exclusively in French from the beginning. At independence, most countries continued with the inherited colonial model; thus, whereas the former British colonies experimented widely with African LOIs, most former French colonies held fast to a French-only model through the 1990s. Since then, many francophone countries have become increasingly open to African LOIs (at least in principle), while anglophone countries have vacillated ambivalently. LOI policy remains controversial and continues to shift; many countries are currently in policy transitions, often with a disconnection between the official written policy and actual implementation; reasons range from language attitudes to training and resource shortfalls (Trudell, 2007). The evolution of literacy acquisition and language policy for an entire continent is beyond the scope of this chapter; however, we refer the reader to the works of Albaugh, 2014; Ouane and Glanz, 2011; and Trudell 2016a and 2016b. To describe the current state of the art, Table 7.1 illustrates the variety of current LOI policies and their implementation in twenty of the forty-six countries in sub-Saharan Africa for which we were able to find information; policies prescribing use of an African language are shaded in vertical stripes, a bilingual model (African and European language together) in diagonal stripes, and a European language in gray.

The LOI policies described above can be categorized into five different types: (1) *exclusive home language (L1) immersion* – students learn in their home language throughout all cycles of education. This is the norm in many high-income countries, but in sub-Saharan Africa it is applicable only to the minority of students who are native speakers of one of the LOIs offered throughout all cycles (e.g., Kiswahili in Tanzania, English in Liberia or South Africa, French in Cameroon); (2) *second- or additional language (L2/LX) immersion* – students learn in an unfamiliar language (i.e., not the home or community language) for the whole education cycle, e.g., for most students in Angola, Liberia, and Cameroon; (3) *early-exit transitional bilingual* – students learn in a familiar language for a relatively short time (e.g., one to four years) before transitioning to an additional language as the sole LOI – for example, in Ghana, Kenya, Nigeria, Uganda, and Zambia; (4) *late-exit transitional bilingual* – students learn in a familiar language (L1) for a longer period of time (e.g., five to eight years) before transitioning to L2/LX as the sole LOI, for example Democratic Republic of Congo (DRC), Ethiopia, Mali, and Mozambique; (5) *additive bilingual* – students begin in and maintain learning in L1 while eventually adding a simultaneous L2.

Although recent trends have favored increased use of African languages as LOIs, particularly in early-exit transitional bilingual models, most communities – and therefore schools – are linguistically heterogeneous, especially in urban areas; as a result, even systems implementing an African language LOI

Table 7.1 Current language-of-instruction policies and degree of implementation for selected sub-Saharan Africa countries

Country	N languages[a]	1	2	3	4	5	6	7	8	9–12	Degree of implementation
Angola	40	Portuguese (but Angolan languages are permitted as LOI)[b]									wide with Portuguese[c]
Burundi	3	Kirundi and French[d]				French					wide
Cameroon	279	French (in 8 provinces) or English (in 2 provinces)[e]									wide with rare exceptions using Cameroonian languages as LOI at primary level
DRC	210	Kikongo, Lingala, Swahili, Tshiluba, or a "language of the locality"[f]				French					data not readily available
Eritrea	15	One of nine Eritrean languages[g]				English					wide[h]
Ethiopia	88	The "nationality" (Ethiopian) language chosen by each regional state[i]							English		wide though timing of transition to English varies[j]
Ghana	81	One of 11 Ghanaian languages and English[k]				English					partial[l]
Kenya	67	The "language of the catchment area" or Kiswahili (urban areas)[m]				English					generally low in lower primary where English is widely used as LOI[n]
Liberia	31	English[o]									wide
Malawi	16	English[p]									generally low in lower primary where Chichewa is widely used as LOI[q]
Mali	68	One of 13 national languages and French[r]							French		partial[s]
Mozambique	43	One of 16 Mozambican languages and Portuguese[t]							Portuguese		partial implementation (policy in transition)[u]
Namibia	27	The predominant local language (or English, with permission)[v]						English			wide with some exceptions[w]

Nigeria	520	"... Initially the mother tongue or language of the immediate community"[x]	"... at a later stage, English" (the timing of the transition is not specified)	English	partial, but English widely used as LOI in lower primary, especially in urban and private schools[y]
Rwanda	3	Kinyarwanda[z]		English	wide
South Africa	30	Student's choice of Zulu, Xhosa, Sepedi, Setswana, Sesotho, Xitsonga, Swati, Tshivenda, Ndebele, English, Afrikaans, or Sign Language[aa]			wide but LOIs vary in availability; majority of schools offer English as LOI starting in grade 4[ab]
Tanzania	125		Kiswahili[ac]		wide at primary level; partial at secondary level (policy in transition)[ad]
Uganda	43	"Local language"[ae]	idem + English	English	wide [af]
Zambia	46	A "familiar" language (the local language of the community)[ag]		English	partial[ah]
Zimbabwe	21	Shona, Ndebele, or a minority indigenous language[ai]		English	generally low in lower primary, where English is widely used as LOI[aj]

Note: Adapted from RTI International, 2016d.

a All living language statistics are taken from Simons and Fennig, 2017.
b Lei de Bases do Sistema de Educação [Basic Education System Law], No. 13/01 (Angola).
c Trudell, 2016b.
d Mazunya and Habonimana, 2010.
e Rosendal, 2008.
f Democratic Republic of Congo, 2014, 2005.
g Provisional Government of Eritrea, 1991; Woldemikael, 2003.
h Asfaha et al., 2009.
i Federal Democratic Government of Ethiopia, 1994; Ethiopia Ministry of Education, 2002.
j Heugh, 2010; Piper, 2010; Vujich, 2013.
k Ansah, 2014; Ansah and Agyeman, 2015; Erling et al., 2016.
l Addy et al., 2012; Arkorful, 2013; RTI International, 2016c; Diesob, 2017.
m Republic of Kenya, 2012.
n Begi, 2014; Piper and Miksic, 2011; Spernes, 2012; Wangia, Furaha, and Kikech, 2014.
o The 2010–2020 Liberian Education Sector Plan has a medium-to-long-term goal to "[e]stablish mother tongue to English bilingual education programs in indigenous language communities" and to "[w]ork towards the use of the local community language as the language of instruction in Kindergarten, Grades 1 and 2 of primary schooling" (Republic of Liberia, 2010), but this has not yet been enacted.

[p] Malawi's official LOI policy contains some ambiguity. From 1996 to 2014, the policy prescribed the "mother tongue" as LOI for Grades 1–4, with a full transition to English in Grade 5 (Secretary for Education's letter Ref. No. IN/2/14, March 28, 1996, as shown in Issa & Yamada, 2013). In 2014, the Minister of Education announced that English was to become the LOI beginning in Grade 1, in accordance with the new Education Act passed in 2013 (Masina, 2014). However, the new policy is subject to different interpretations and has not yet been widely implemented; also the National Reading Strategy (2014–2019) of the Ministry of Education, Science, and Technology prescribes language and literacy instruction in both English and Chichewa in early primary (Malawi MoEST, 2014).

[q] Issa and Yamada, 2013.

[r] Canvin, 2007.

[s] Agence Française de Développement (AFD) and Ministère de l'Éducation, de l'Alphabétisation et des Langues Nationales (MEALN), Mali, 2010; Varly, 2010; Rhodes, 2012.

[t] A new policy scheduled to take effect in 2017 prescribes that one of sixteen Mozambican languages be used as LOI alongside Portuguese at the primary level (Ensino primário moçambicano, 2015).

[u] Portuguese is currently used as the sole LOI throughout all cycles in urban schools and in many rural schools (Henriksen, 2010). Pilot projects in rural areas using a Mozambican language and Portuguese bilingually at the primary level began in the 1990s and are ongoing. As of 2015, an estimated 80,000 children in nearly 500 primary schools were learning in 2 languages (ASSECOM, 2015).

[v] Namibia Ministry of Basic Education, Sport and Culture, 2003.

[w] Batibo, 2014; Tötemeyer, 2010.

[x] National Policy on Education as cited in Adegbija, 2004, p. 211.

[y] Okebukola, Owolabi, and Okebukola, 2012; Duze, 2011.

[z] Rwanda Ministry of Education, 2008.

[aa] Students choose their preferred LOI from among the twelve approved languages (where available); school governing bodies determine the LOI(s) offered at each school based primarily on local demand (South Africa Department of Basic Education, 2010; Hazeltine, 2013).

[ab] South Africa Department of Basic Education, 2010.

[ac] Tanzania Ministry of Education and Vocational Training, 2014; Trudell, 2016a; Lugongo, 2015.

[ad] A new policy in 2015 replaced English with Kiswahili as the LOI at the secondary level. It is expected that this policy will take years to fully implement (Lugongo, 2015); however, Kiswahili has long been used informally as the de facto LOI alongside or instead of English (Kinyaduka & Kiwara, 2013).

[ae] Uganda Ministry of Education, Science, Technology, and Sports, 2010; Altinyelken, Moorcroft, and van der Draai, 2014.

[af] Piper and Miksic, 2011.

[ag] Zambia Ministry of Education, Science, Vocational Training and Early Education, 2013.

[ah] Trudell, 2016b.

[ai] Education Act 25 04 (Zimb.).

[aj] Gotosa, Rwodzi, and Mhlanga, 2013; Chivhanga and Chimhenga, 2013.

policy are not able to offer every child instruction in his or her home language. This becomes evident when we compare the number of living languages in each country in Table 7.1 with the far fewer languages that the country offers as LOI. For example, although Kiswahili is now the official LOI throughout all cycles in Tanzania, during the 2016 nationally representative Early Grade Reading Assessment (EGRA), 44.5 percent of students reported speaking one of the other 124 Tanzanian languages at home (see Table 7.2).

Research suggests that learners need at least six–eight years of instruction in L1, as in late-exit transitional or additive bilingual models, and at least five–seven years of instruction in L2 *as a subject* before they are adequately prepared to transition to L2 as the LOI (Ball, 2011; Cummins, 1979; Dutcher & Tucker, 1995; Ouane & Glanz, 2011). Given that many countries still offer four years or fewer of instruction in the home language, either in official policy or in practice, and given the underlying linguistic heterogeneity in even the best-case scenarios, it is reasonable to conclude that most children in sub-Saharan Africa spend inadequate time learning in L1.

7.3 Learning to Read in Sub-Saharan Countries

Given this complex, continually evolving language context, we used data from several previously collected national and large-scale regional assessments of early literacy outcomes to explore how language influences early literacy acquisition in the region, with Ghana, Kenya, Liberia, Malawi, Tanzania, and Zambia as target countries. Although the data were originally collected for other purposes, most notably to inform and improve early reading instruction and policy within each context, the review of results and language differences for multiple countries is a novel and (we hope) useful application of the data. The research questions driving our analyses for the six target countries for which we had appropriate data were: (1) What are the key characteristics of children learning to read in the early grades of primary school? (2) Do children who learn to read in L1 perform differently than children learning to read in an L2/LX? and (3) Do children who learn to read in L1 have greater *learning gains* than children who learn to read in L2/LX?

The data utilized draw from six studies conducted between 2010 and 2016. Student reading results were collected through EGRAs developed for each language and country. The EGRA is an open-source test of early reading skills, with adaptations developed for each country and language following published guidelines and specifications (Dubeck & Gove, 2015; RTI International, 2016b). Trained enumerators conduct fifteen-minute individual oral interviews during which students read from paper stimulus sheets or respond to questions read aloud by the administrator. Tasks include letter-name and letter-sound identification, word reading, and passage reading, as well as comprehension questions.

Table 7.2 *Summary of country datasets consulted by research question*

Research questions	Country	Level of representation	Year	Grades	Students	Report reference
1 and 2	Ghana	National	2015	2	7,311	Ghana Education Service and RTI International, 2014
3	Kenya	Project	2013	1 and 2	4,222	Piper and Mugenda, 2014
3	Liberia	Project	2011 and 2013	1, 2, and 3	6,680	King et al., 2015
1 and 2	Malawi	National	2012	2 and 4	5,240	Pouezevara, Costello, and Banda, 2012a
3	Malawi	Project	2010 and 2012	2 and 4	3,290	Pouezevara, Costello, and Banda, 2012b
1 and 2	Tanzania	National	2014	2	2,266	RTI International, 2016a
1 and 2	Zambia	National	2014	2	4,850	Brombacher et al., 2015

Enumerators record student responses on a tablet using an open-source software package designed to capture both student responses and time elapsed (for more information see Tangerine specifications at www.tangerinecentral.org). The assessment is typically accompanied by a demographic questionnaire of student characteristics, including student age, grade, home language, home literacy practices, socioeconomic status, and other key variables. Detailed information for each country-specific dataset, including sampling frame, instruments, and questionnaires, are provided in each of the country reports. Data on Ghana originate from Ghana Education Service and RTI International (2014); on Kenya from Piper and Mugenda (2014); on Liberia from King et al. (2015); on Malawi from both Pouezevara, Costello, and Banda (2012a) and Pouezevara, Costello and Banda (2012b); on Tanzania from RTI International (2016a–d); and on Zambia from Brombacher et al. (2015).

To address pupil characteristics in the six countries, we relied on self-reported data from demographic surveys conducted in conjunction with the EGRA. As noted, each EGRA survey incorporated questionnaires administered to the student participants, teachers, and school directors (the number of individuals interviewed varied according to the research objectives of the study). Students were asked to indicate the languages they spoke in the home. Table 7.3 provides summary demographic results for key variables for each of the six countries included in subsequent models.

Table 7.3 Descriptive variables included in the models for Ghana, Kenya, Liberia, Malawi, Tanzania, and Zambia

Demographic	Ghana (2015)	Kenya (2013) *	Liberia (2013) *	Malawi (2012)	Tanzania (2016)	Zambia (2014)
Sample size %	**7,311**	**1,592**	**457**	**3,388**	**7,743**	**4,855**
Percentage of students receiving instruction in their home language (self-reporting)	51.0	73.7	25.7	83.5	55.5	73.0
"Does someone help you with your homework?": Yes (self-reporting)	76.2				60.4	69.5
"Do you read to someone at home?": Yes (self-reporting)	62.6			57.3	75.6%	53.4
"Do you have the school reading textbook?": Yes (self-reporting)	53.1			10.4		14.7
"Does someone read to you at home?": Yes (self-reporting)	71.1			57.4		58.3
Urban	27.9					25.7

Note: Gray cells indicate question was not asked.

Other than the urban classification, all the demographic estimates are created from student responses. The most concerning estimates presented are the percent of students reporting that they have a school reading textbook; students reported having a reading textbook only 10.4 and 14.7 percent of the time in Malawi and Zambia, respectively. On further investigation, it was discovered that in Zambia a new curriculum had been implemented and that at the time of the survey (November 2014) very few students had indeed received a reading textbook. Malawi has the highest percentage of students receiving instruction in their home language (83.5 percent), and from Table 7.1 we can see that the country only has one official language of instruction in the early grades, namely Chichewa.

As a further illustration of the complex role language plays in shaping literacy outcomes, we prepared a detailed mapping of the match between L1 and LOI in two of our target countries: Ghana and Zambia. Each country uses several languages for classroom instruction in the early grades, but their language of instruction policies differ substantially. Zambia – a country with seven officially recognized languages, but an official count of forty-six different languages spoken by the population (Simons & Fennig, 2017) – declares a school's LOI based on province. In contrast, Ghana boasts eighty-one different living languages (Simons & Fennig, 2017), but only eleven are recognized as national languages. However, Ghana's policy allows LOI to be chosen by the head teacher on a school-by-school basis. This policy, in theory, allows head teachers to better serve their specific population. So, it is surprising that only 51 percent of students in Ghana report receiving instruction in their home language (see Table 7.3). These different language of instruction policies provide a rich setting in which to understand policy impact and how it relates to reading-skills acquisition.

The maps shown in Figure 7.1 below, originally prepared by Pressley, Sou, and Edwards (2016), illustrate country regions where L1 matched the LOI. Figure 7.1a shows the country regions and the geographic location of the eleven official LOIs for Ghana; Figure 7.1b does so for the 7 official LOIs in Zambia. Maps were generated by superimposing documentation regarding the official LOI for each region on Ethnologue maps of regional majority L1s (Lewis, Simons, & Fennig, 2016). In both cases, areas in white indicate language mismatch, while shaded areas indicate a match between the L1 of the majority of inhabitants and LOI. Students in Zambia reported receiving instruction in their home language 73 percent of the time (from Table 7.3) and it is important to note that Figures 1a and 1b do not include population density; while many students in rural areas do not receive instruction in their home language, urban migration has created a situation where many students have moved into a region that uses an unfamiliar language of instruction. Despite the use of African languages in the classroom in the early grades in both Ghana and Zambia, these maps illustrate

Literacy Acquisition in Sub-Saharan Africa

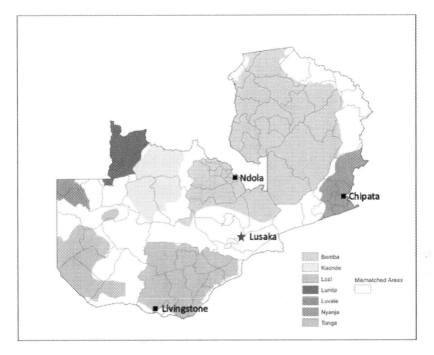

Figure 7.1a: Languages spoken matches language of instruction in Ghana

that this approach can only be classified as a partial implementation, given the wide swaths of the mismatch between L1 and LOI.

7.4 Learning to Read in L1 vs L2

The follow-up question we sought to answer is whether a mismatch on L1 and LOI results in performance differences, that is, whether or not language mismatch correlates with the child being unable to read a single word of text. Figure 7.2 shows an analysis using odds ratios for predicting oral reading fluency (ORF) results from Tanzania, Zambia, Ghana, and Malawi. Odds ratios predict the likelihood that an outcome will occur (in this case that students would score zero on the ORF portion of the EGRA) given a particular condition of interest, in this case L1–LO1 mismatch. On the oral reading fluency section of EGRA, students are asked to read aloud a grade-level passage; results are scored in correct number of words read per minute.

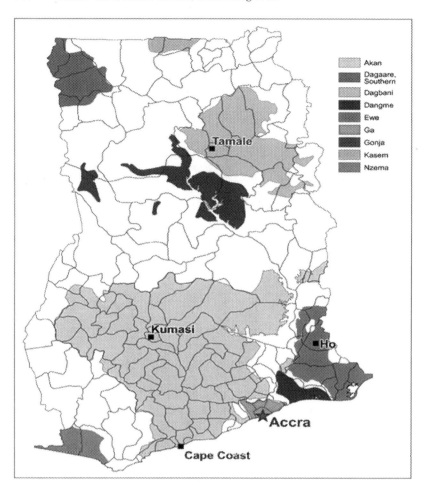

Figure 7.1b: Languages spoken matches language of instruction in Zambia

The results indicate that Grade 2 students in Tanzania were 1.56 times (95 percent confidence interval [1.25, 1.95]) more likely to be unable to read a single word if their LOI was not their mother tongue. Similarly, Grade 2 children in Ghana were 1.23 times (95 percent confidence interval [1.02, 1.48]) more likely not to be able to read a word of connected text. The same analysis in Malawi and Zambia, on the other hand, did not find similar associations that were significant. One explanation for this difference is that average results in Tanzania and Ghana appear to be higher than those of Malawi and Zambia;

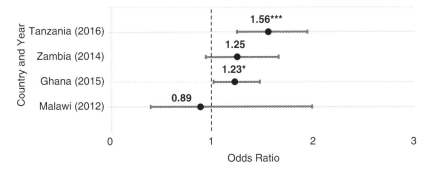

Figure 7.2 Impact of L1 and LOI mismatch on students who could not read a word of connected text (estimates as odds ratios), Grade 2
Note: * p < 0.05, ** p < 0.01, *** p < 0.001

more students reading at a higher skill level means that more variability existed in the data used to detect differences. In other words, if all students are performing poorly, language match or mismatch does not make much of a difference.

This analysis has some limitations, however. For example, the indicator of mother tongue (L1) was self-reported by Grade 2 students (typically seven or eight years of age); thus, response bias is possible. In addition, the students were assessed at school, which means that the research population did not include children not attending school. It is not unreasonable to hypothesize that many children who face an L1–LOI mismatch do not attend school precisely because of those language difficulties. Finally, the indicator is binary – that is, either the child's L1 is the same as the LOI, or not, although we know that language acquisition for children in African multilingual societies is far more complex than this model can support. That is, the indicator effectively places a child who cannot speak the LOI at all in the same category as a child who speaks it well albeit as an L2/LX, which we acknowledge is a limitation owing to the proficiency measures this dataset relies on. These conclusions are reinforced by assessing an L1–LOI match on average oral reading fluency for Grade 2 students. Figure 7.3 shows the association between better reading fluency and L1–LOI match in Tanzania (p<0.001), Zambia (p<0.05), and Ghana (p<0.05), but not Malawi. Average reading fluency in Malawi is poor for Grade 2 students; thus, while the control model shown attempts to account for socioeconomic status, it is difficult to fully disentangle its impact from mother tongue because students from all socioeconomic backgrounds are demonstrating low reading fluency.

146 *Amber Gove, Karon Harden, Simon King et al.*

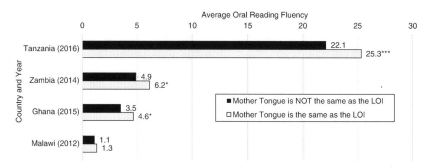

Figure 7.3 Impact of L1 and LOI match on average reading fluency achievement (correct words per minute), Grade 2
Note: * p < 0.05, ** p < 0.01, *** p < 0.001

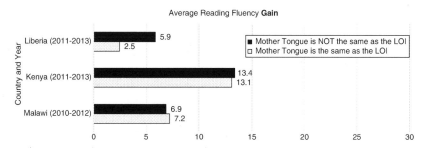

Figure 7.4 Intervention impact of L1 and LOI match on average reading fluency gain (additional correct words per minute), Grade 2
Note: * p < 0.05, ** p < 0.01, *** p < 0.001

Even accounting for the limitations of the school-based data, it is not surprising that one sees an association between student reading achievement and students who report speaking the LOI as their L1. What now becomes of interest is the impact of L1–LOI mismatch on learning (in this case, gain scores in oral reading fluency). An analysis of three intervention programs in Liberia, Kenya, and Malawi (shown in Figure 7.4) through the interaction of L1–LOI match and treatment year indicates a lack of association between average oral reading fluency gain and L1–LOI match in Liberia ($p = 0.321$), Kenya ($p = 0.861$), and Malawi ($p = 0.674$). That is, the effect of language match is not found to be as important in determining the average learning gains as other key variables such as quality teaching and learning. This is unsurprising considering the challenges of learning in these countries and the influence of the quality of teaching above all other factors (see country-level reports as specified in Table 7.2). Clearly, individual students will have challenges with learning to read in a language in which they are not orally fluent, but on average it is less of an issue in these countries than barriers such as poverty and receiving poor-quality instruction in the classroom.

7.5 Conclusions and Discussion

The present chapter explores the important question of the relation of language match to learning outcomes in sub-Saharan Africa. Language match is defined as the condition in which a student's primary language of instruction is the same as the student's self-reported mother tongue or L1. Analysis of the characteristics of children learning to read in six target countries of study revealed substantial variation. This, coupled with the myriad policies and educational models, highlights the need for country-specific solutions to the challenge of improving literacy outcomes. It can be concluded that there is no one-size-fits-all policy response to the complex language environment that characterizes many countries in the region. What is clear from the learning-outcomes data is that the current policy response across sub-Saharan countries is not producing acceptable learning outcomes. This is only partly due to a mismatch between the language of the child and the language of the curriculum, with many other factors contributing to low learning results (see Nag, , Chapter 15; Asfaha & Nag, Chapter 16; and Friedlander & Goldenberg, Chapter 18 in this volume. While these other factors affect the low overall outcomes in the region, language should not be an additional barrier to children learning to read. Even when the language of the child matches the language of instruction, the gain in oral reading fluency can be considered small.

While acknowledging the limitations of the data, including reliance on child self-report for identification of home language and other key variables, the results provide new insight into the complex challenge of language and learning. We evidenced a large variation in both policy and educational practice across the six target countries. As just one example, the share of students receiving instruction in their L1 ranged from 26 percent in Liberia to 83 percent in Malawi. Language mismatch was shown to have a substantive and significant effect on the probability that a student would perform poorly on the assessment: Students in Ghana and Tanzania whose L1 did not match the LOI scored substantially lower on text-reading abilities. Furthermore, the absence of the effect of language match on intervention impact on learning gains is an indication that the language effect is outweighed by other key issues, such as poverty, instructional quality, and the availability of teaching and learning materials.

As governments map a pathway to 2030 and plot their approach to meeting their obligations under the Sustainable Development Goals, we expect that language-of-instruction policies will increasingly be examined as a possible avenue for learning improvement. These results show that in many cases policy and practice do not match, meaning whatever parameters policymakers think they have put in place are getting subverted by practitioners in schools. In some contexts, when examining which policy levers are the easiest to move, language policy will need to be compared to other options over which governments can exert influence and change. This can be considered a complex process, as getting language policy right requires careful examination of context, resources, beliefs, and practice. As we endeavor to collect additional information about the impact of language policy on learning, the issue will continue to challenge practitioners and policymakers throughout the region for generations to come.

References

Addy, N., Kraft, R., Carlson, S., & Fletcher, B. (2012). *Synthesis Report: Transforming Learning Outcomes through a Learner Centred Pedagogy: Moving Toward a Ghanaian Activity Based Learning Concept and Framework*. https://assets.publishing.service.gov.uk/media/57a08a78ed915d3cfd0007a2/61003-IDEVREAN11016G H_ABL_Report_Final_with_appendices_300413.pdf.

Adegbija, E. (2004). Language policy and planning in Nigeria. *Current Issues in Language Planning*, 5(3), 181–246. DOI: http://dx.doi.org/10.1080/14664200408668258.

Agence Française de Développement (AFD) & Ministère de l'Éducation, de l'Alphabétisation et des Langues Nationales (MEALN), Mali. (2010). *Étude sur le curriculum de l'enseignement fondamental: Rapport 3 développement du scénario privilégié*. www.education.gov.ml/IMG/pdf/Etude_sur_le_Curriculum_de_l_enseignement_fondamental.pdf.

Akyeampong, K., Pryor, J., Westbrook, J., & Lussier, K. (2011). *Teacher Preparation and Continuing Professional Development in Africa: Learning to Teach Early Reading and Mathematics*. Brighton: Centre for International Education, University of Sussex. www.sussex.ac.uk/webteam/gateway/file.php?name-tpa-synthesis-report-july2011.pdf&site=320.

Albaugh, E. A. (2014). *State-Building and Multilingual Rducation in Africa*. New York: Cambridge University Press. DOI: http://dx.doi.org/10.1017/CBO9781107323735.

Altinyelken, H. K., Moorcroft, S., & van der Draai, H. (2014). The dilemmas and complexities of implementing language in education policies: Perspectives from urban and rural contexts in Uganda. *International Journal of Educational Development*, 36, 90–99. DOI: http://dx.doi.org/10.1016/j.ijedudev.2013.11.001.

Ansah, G. N. (2014). Re-examining the fluctuations in language in-education policies in post-independence Ghana. *Multilingual Education*, 4(1), 12. DOI: http://dx.doi.org/10.1186/s13616-014-0012-3.

Ansah, M. A., & Agyeman, N. A. (2015). Ghana language-in-education policy: The survival of two South Guan minority dialects. *Per Linguam*, 31(1), 89–104. DOI: http://dx.doi.org/10.5785/31-1-592.

Arkorful, K. (2013). Complementary Education Programme and the opportunity to learn in the northern region of Ghana. (Unpublished doctoral dissertation,

University of Sussex). http://sro.sussex.ac.uk/45242/1/Arkorful%2C_Kingsley_K_D.pdf.
Asfaha, Y. M., Beckman, D., Kurvers, J., & Kroon, S. (2009). L2 reading in multilingual Eritrea: The influences of L1 reading and English proficiency. *Journal of Research in Reading*, *32*(4), 351–365. DOI: http://dx.doi.org/10.1111/j.1467-9817.2009.01399.x.
ASSECOM. (2015, July 23). Aprovado uso de línguas moçambicanas nas assembleias provinciais. Universidade da Integração Internacional da Lusofonia Afro-Brasileira. www.unilab.edu.br/noticias/2015/07/23/mocambique-aprovado-uso-de-linguas-mocambicanas-nas-assembleias-provinciais/.
Ball, J. (2011). *Enhancing Learning of Children from Diverse Language Backgrounds: Mother Tongue-Based Bilingual or Multilingual Education in the Early Years*. Paris: UNESCO. http://unesdoc.unesco.org/images/0021/002122/212270e.pdf.
Batibo, H. M. (2014). Searching for an optimal national language policy for sustainable development. In H. McIlwraith (ed.), *The Cape Town Language and Development Conference: Looking Beyond 2015* (pp. 16–20). London: British Council.
Begi, N. (2014). Use of mother tongue as a language of instruction in early years of school to preserve the Kenyan culture. *Journal of Education and Practice*, *5*(3), 37–49.
Black, M. M., Walker, S. P., Fernald, L. C. H. et al. (2017). Early childhood development coming of age: Science through the life course. *Lancet*, *389*(10064), 77–90. DOI: http://dx.doi.org/10.1016/S0140-6736(16)31389-7. PubMed.
Brombacher, A., Bulat, J., King, S., Kochetkova, E., & Nordstrum, L. (2015). *National Assessment Survey of Learning Achievement at Grade 2: Results for Early Grade Reading and Mathematics in Zambia*. Washington, DC: USAID. https://shared.rti.org/content/national-assessment-survey-learning-achievement-grade-2-results-early-grade-reading-zambia#.
Canvin, M. (2007). Language and education issues in policy and practice in Mali, West Africa. In N. Rassol (ed.), *Global Issues in Language, Education and Development: Perspectives from Postcolonial Countries* (pp. 157–186). Clevedon: Multilingual Matters Ltd.
Chivhanga, E., & Chimhenga, S. (2013). Language planning in Zimbabwe: The use of indigenous languages (Shona) as a medium of instruction in primary schools. *Journal of Humanities and Social Science*, *12*(5), 58–65.
Cummins, J. (1979). Linguistic interdependence and the educational development of bilingual children. *Review of Educational Research*, *49*(2), 222–251. DOI: http://dx.doi.org/10.3102/00346543049002222.
Democratic Republic of the Congo. (2005). Constitution, Article 1, §1. www.constitutionnet.org/sites/default/files/DRC%20-%20Congo%20Constitution.pdf.
Democratic Republic of the Congo. (2014). Loi-cadre nombre 14/004 du 11 Février 2014 de l'enseignement national. www.leganet.cd/Legislation/Droit%20Public/enseignement/Loi14.004.11.02.2004.htm.
Diesob, C. (2017, March 1). Mother tongue language policy in education needs supervision. *Ghana News Agency*. www.ghananewsagency.org/social/mother-tongue-language-policy-in-education-needs-supervision-113787.
Dubeck, M. M., & Gove, A. (2015). The early grade reading assessment (EGRA): Its theoretical foundation, purpose, and limitations. *International Journal of Educational Development*, *40*, 315–322. DOI: https://doi.org/10.1016/j.ijedudev.2014.11.004.

Dutcher, N., & Tucker, R. (1995). *The use of First and Second Languages in Education: A Review of International Experience*. Pacific Islands Discussion Paper Series Number 1. http://documents.worldbank.org/curated/en/131161468770987263/pdf/multi-page.pdf.

Duze, C. O. (2011). Implementation of the mother-tongue/language component in the National Policy in Education in Nigeria. *Lwati: A Journal of Contemporary Research*, 8(1). www.ajol.info/index.php/lwati/article/view/79716.

Education Act 25 04 (Zimb.). www.parlzim.gov.zw/acts-list/education-act-25-04.

Engle, P. L., Black, M. M., Behrman, J. R. et al. (2007). Strategies to avoid the loss of developmental potential in more than 200 million children in the developing world. *Lancet*, *369*(9557), 229–242. DOI: http://dx.doi.org/10.1016/S0140-6736(07)60112-3.

Ensino primário moçambicano será ministrado nas 16 línguas nativas a partir de 2017. (2015, March 19). *Voz de América*. www.voaportugues.com/a/ensino-primario-mocambique-linguas-nativas/2686803.html.

Erling, E. J., Adinolfi, L., Hultgren, A. K., Buckler, A., & Mukorera, M. (2016). Medium of instruction policies in Ghanaian and Indian primary schools: An overview of key issues and recommendations. *Comparative Education*, *52*(3), 294–310. DOI: http://dx.doi.org/10.1080/03050068.2016.1185254.

Ethiopia Ministry of Education. (2002). *The Education and Training Policy and Its Implementation*. Addis Ababa. www.moe.gov.et/documents/20182/23015/The+Education+and+Training+Policy+and+its+Implementation/770c9d55-eace-42f4-8fa5-f2878cf8f4b1.

Federal Democratic Government of Ethiopia. (1994). *Education and Training Policy*. Addis Ababa. www.unesco.org/education/edurights/media/docs/8bee116313a86cc53420f01a7fa052bd5e40bf3d.pdf.

Ghana Education Service & RTI International. (2014). Ghana 2013 – Early Grade Reading Assessment and Early Grade Mathematics Assessment: Report of findings. Unpublished draft prepared under the USAID Education Data for Decision Making (EdData II) project, Task Order No. AID-641-BC-13-00001 (RTI Task 21). Porto-Novo.

Ghana Education Service & RTI International. (2016). *Early Grade Reading Assessment and Early Grade Mathematics Assessment: Report of Findings*. Porto-Novo. : USAID. http://pdf.usaid.gov/pdf_docs/pa00mhmt.pdf.

Gotosa, K., Rwodzi, M., & Mhlanga, G. (2013). Language in education: A critical review of current proposals for official mother tongue use in Zimbabwean classrooms. *International Journal of Humanities and Social Science*, *3*(14), 88–94. www.ijhssnet.com/journals/Vol_3_No_14_Special_Issue_July_2013/11.pdf

Gove, A., Chabbott, C., Dick, A. P. et al. (2015). *Early Learning Assessments: A Retrospective. Paper Commissioned for the EFA Global Monitoring Report 2015*. Education for All. New York: United Nations. http://unesdoc.unesco.org/images/0023/002324/232419e.pdf.

Hazeltine, R. (2013). Language policy and education in multilingual South Africa. *Hohonu*, *11*, 26–29. https://hilo.hawaii.edu/academics/hohonu/documents/LanguagePolicyandEducationinMultilingualSouthAfricaRachelHazeltine.pdf.

Henriksen, S. M. (2010). Language attitudes in a primary school: A bottom-up approach to language education policy in Mozambique (Unpublished doctoral dissertation, Roskilde University)

Heugh, K. (2010). Productive engagement with linguistic diversity in tension with globalized discourses in Ethiopia. *Current Issues in Language Planning, 11*(4), 378–396. DOI: http://dx.doi.org/10.1080/14664208.2011.541867.

Issa, M. D., & Yamada, S. (2013). *Stakeholders' Perceptions of the Language of Instruction Policy in Malawian Primary Schools and Its Implications for the Quality of Education*. Hiroshima: Center for the Study of International Cooperation in Education at Hiroshima University.

King, S., Korda, M., Nordstrum, L., & Edwards, S. (2015). *Liberia Teacher Training Program: Endline assessment of the impact of early grade reading and mathematics interventions*. Prepared for USAID and FHI 360 under Contract No. 669-A-00-10-00116.00. Research Triangle Park, NC: RTI International. https://globalreadingnetwork.net/eddata/endline-assessment-impact-early-grade-reading-and-mathematics-interventions-liberia

Kinyaduka, B. D., & Kiwara, J. F. (2013). Language of instruction and its impact on quality of education in secondary schools: Experiences from Morogoro Region, Tanzania. *Journal of Education and Practice, 4*(9), 90–95.

Lei de Bases do Sistema de Educação [Basic Education System Law]. (2001). No. 13/01 (Angola).

Lewis, M. P., Simons, G. F., & Fennig, C. D. (eds.). (2016). *Ethnologue: Languages of the world* (19th ed.). Dallas, TX: SIL. www.ethnologue.com.

Lugongo, B. (2015, February 14). Bye Std VII exams, English; Karibu Kiswahili in studies. *The Citizen*. www.thecitizen.co.tz/News/national/Bye-Std-VII-exams–English-Karibu-Kiswahili-in-studies/-/1840392/2623428/-/2krj4x/-/index.

Malawi MoEST (Ministry of Education, Science, and Technology). (2014). *National Reading Strategy (2014–2019)*. Lilongwe: MoEST.

Masina, L. (2014, August 21). Malawi schools to teach in English. *Aljazeera*. www.aljazeera.com/news/africa/2014/08/malawi-schools-teach-english-local-debate-colonial-201482184041156272.html.

Mazunya, M., & Habonimana, A. (2010). *Les Langues de scolarisation dans l'enseignement fondamental en Afrique subsaharienne francophone: Le cas du Burundi*. http://docplayer.fr/12812507-Les-langues-de-scolarisation-dans-l-enseignement-fondamental-en-afrique-subsahariennefrancophone-cas-du-burundi.html.

Namibia Ministry of Basic Education, Sport and Culture (MBESC). (2003). *The Language policy for schools in Namibia: Discussion document*. Windhoek: MBESC.

Okebukola, P. A., Owolabi, O., & Okebukola, F. O. (2012). Mother tongue as default language of instruction in lower primary science classes: Tension between policy prescription and practice in Nigeria. *Journal of Research in Science Teaching, 50*(1), 62–81. DOI: https://doi.org/10.1002/tea.21070.

Ouane, A., & Glanz, C. (eds.). (2011). *Optimising Learning, Education and Publishing in Africa: The Language Factor: A Review and Analysis of Theory and Practice in Mother-Tongue and Bilingual Education in Sub-Saharan Africa*. Hamburg: UNESCO.

Piper, B. (2010). *Ethiopia Early Grade Reading Assessment. Data Analytic Report: Language and Early Learning*. Prepared for USAID under the EdData II project Task

Number 7 and Task Number 9. Washington, DC: USAID. http://pdf.usaid.gov/pdf_docs/pnady834.pdf.

Piper, B., & Miksic, E. (2011). Mother tongue and reading: Using early grade reading assessments to investigate language-of-instruction policy in East Africa. In A. Gove & A. Wetterberg (eds.), *The Early Grade Reading Assessment: Application and Intervention to Improve Basic Literacy* (pp. 139–182). Research Triangle Park, NC: RTI Press. www.rti.org/sites/default/files/resources/bk-0007-1109-wetterberg.pdf.

Piper, B., & Mugenda, A. (2014). *Primary Math and Reading (PRIMR) Initiative: Endline Impact Evaluation*. Washington, DC: USAID. http://pdf.usaid.gov/pdf_docs/pa00k27s.pdf.

Pressley, J., Sou, S., & Edwards, S. (2016). Assessing the impact of language on pupil learning utilizing GIS data to map ethnologue with school language of instruction to further investigate the impact of language on reading skills acquisition. Poster presented at the 2016 Comparative and International Education Society Conference, April 2016, Vancouver, Canada.

Provisional Government of Eritrea. (1991). Declaration of policies on education in Eritrea. Legal Notice, Number 2–1991 (Oct. 2). Asmara: Department of Education. www.academia.edu/9508712/Language_Education_and_Public_Policy_in_Eritrea.

Republic of Kenya. (2012). Policy framework for education and training. www.kemi.ac.ke/index.php/downloads/category/2-kemi-library?download=4:policy-framework-for-education-2012.

Republic of Liberia. (2010). Education Sector Plan 2010–2020. www.globalpartnership.org/content/liberia-education-sector-plan.

Rhodes, R. (2012). Moving towards bilingual education in Mali: Bridging policy and practice for improved reading instruction [PowerPoint presentation]. *MTB-MLE Network* (website). http://mlenetwork.org/sites/default/files/Moving%20towards%20bilingual%20education%20in%20Mali.o_0.pdf.

Rosendal, T. (2008). *Multilingual Cameroon: Policy, Practice, Problems and Solutions*. Gothenburg: University of Gothenburg. www.pol.gu.se/digitalAssets/1328/1328399_no-7_final-multilingual-cameroon-081101.pdf.

RTI International. (2016a). *Assistance to Basic Education: All Children Reading (ABE-ACR), Findings Report, Tanzania National Early Grade Reading Assessment (EGRA)*. Washington, DC: USAID. https://www.edu-links.org/sites/default/files/media/file/2016%20TZ%20EGRA%20Findings%20Report.pdf

RTI International. (2016b). *Early Grade Reading Assessment (EGRA) Toolkit*, 2nd ed. Washington, DC: USAID. https://shared.rti.org/content/early-grade-reading-assessment-egra-toolkit-second-edition#modal-29-560.

RTI International. (2016c). *Ghana 2015 Early Grade Reading Assessment and Early Grade Mathematics Assessment: Report of Findings*. Prepared for USAID under the EdData II project, Task Order No. AID-641-BC-13-00001 (RTI Task 21). Washington, DC: USAID. http://pdf.usaid.gov/pdf_docs/pa00mhmt.pdf.

RTI International. (2016d). *Survey of Children's Reading Materials in African Languages in Eleven Countries: Final Report*. Prepared for USAID under the EdData II project, Task Order No. AID-OAA-12-BC-00004 (RTI Task 19). Washington, DC: USAID. http://pdf.usaid.gov/pdf_docs/pbaaf466.pdf.

Rwanda Ministry of Education. (2008). *Nine Years Basic Education Implementation: Fast Track Strategies*. Kigali. ww.academia.edu/7708703/REPUBLIC_OF_RWAN

DA_MINISTRY_OF_EDUCATION_NINE_YEARS_BASIC_EDUCATION_IMP LEMENTATION_FAST_TRACK_STRATEGIES_NOVEMBER_2008.

Simons, G. F., & Fennig, C. D. (eds.). (2017). *Ethnologue: Languages of the World* (20th ed.). Dallas, TX: SIL International. www.ethnologue.com.

South Africa Department of Basic Education. (2010). *The Status of the Language of Learning and Teaching (LOLT) in South African Public Schools: A Quantitative Overview.* Pretoria: Department of Basic Education. www.education.gov.za/Portals/0/Documents/Reports/Status%20of%20LOLT.pdf?ver=2011-03-30-231358-000.

Spernes, K. (2012). "I use my mother tongue at home and with friends – not in school!" Multilingualism and identity in rural Kenya. *Language, Culture and Curriculum, 25* (2), 189–203. DOI: http://dx.doi.org/10.1080/07908318.2012.683531.

Tanzania Ministry of Education and Vocational Training. (2014). Education and training policy. www.pmoralg.go.tz/noticeboard/tangazo-1027-21050223-Sera-ya-Elimu-na-Mafunzo-2014/Sera-ya-Elimu-na-Mafunzo-2014.pdf.

Tötemeyer, A. (2010). Multilingualism and the language policy for Namibian schools. PRAESA Occasional Papers No. 37. Cape Town: PRAESA.

Trudell, B. (2007). Local community perspectives and language of education in sub-Saharan African communities. *International Journal of Educational Development, 27*(5), 552–563. DOI: http://dx.doi.org/10.1016/j.ijedudev.2007.02.002.

Trudell, B. (2016a). Language choice and education quality in Eastern and Southern Africa: a review. *Comparative Education, 52*(3), 281–293. DOI: http://dx.doi.org/10.1080/03050068.2016.1185252.

Trudell, B. (2016b). *The Impact of Language Policy and Practice on Children's Learning: Evidence from Eastern and Southern Africa.* New York: United Nations Children's Fund (UNICEF). www.unicef.org/esaro/UNICEF(2016)LanguageandLearning-FullReport(SingleView).pdf.

Uganda Ministry of Education, Science, Technology, and Sports. (2010). *Uganda Updated Education Sector Strategic Plan 2010–2015.* Kampala: Uganda Ministry of Education, Science, Technology, and Sports.

UNESCO. (2000). *Education for All: Meeting Our Collective Commitments.* (Text adopted by the World Education Forum, April 26–28, 2000, Dakar, Senegal). Paris: UNESCO. http://unesdoc.unesco.org/images/0012/001211/121147e.pdf.

UNESCO. (2012). At least 250 million children of primary school-age are failing to learn the basics. Technical note prepared for the *Education for All Global Monitoring Report 2012: Youth and Skills: Putting Education to Work.* Paris: UNESCO. http://unesdoc.unesco.org/images/0021/002193/219349E.pdf.

UNESCO. (2015). Sustainable Development Goals (webpage). http://en.unesco.org/sdgs.

UNESCO Institute for Statistics (UIS). (2017). *Net Enrolment Rate by Level of Education* [Interactive data set]. Montreal: UIS. http://uis.unesco.org/indicator/edu-part-er-ner.

Varly, P. (2010). *The Monitoring of Learning Outcomes in Mali: Language of Instruction and Teachers' Methods in Mali Grade 2 Curriculum Classrooms.* The William and Flora Hewlett Foundation Grant #2008-3367. RTI International Project No. 0212014. Research Triangle Park, NC: RTI International. www.researchgate.net/publication/278390729_The_Monitoring_of_Learning_Outcomes_in_Mali_Language_of_Instruction_and_Teachers%27_Methods_in_Mali_Grade_2_Curriculum_Classrooms

Vujich, D. (2013). Policy and practice on language of instruction in Ethiopian schools: Findings from the young lives school survey. https://assets.publishing.service.gov.uk/media/57a08a21ed915d3cfd0005de/wp108_vujich_language-of-instruction.pdf.

Wangia, J., Furaha, M., & Kikech, B. (2014). The language of instruction versus learning in lower primary schools in Kenya. In D. O. Orwenjo, M. C. Njoroge, R. W. Nudng'u, & P. W. Mwangi (eds.), *Multilingualism and Education in Africa: The State of the State of the Art* (pp. 8–23). Newcastle upon-Tyne: Cambridge Scholars Publishing.

Williams, E. (2014). *Bridges and Barriers: Language in African Education and Development* (Vol. 8). London: Routledge.

Woldemikael, T. M. (2003). Language, education, and public policy in Eritrea. *African Studies Review*, 46(1), 117–136. DOI: http://dx.doi.org/10.2307/1514983.

World Conference on Education for All. (1990). *World Conference on Education for All: Meeting Basic Learning Needs, Final Report*. Inter-Agency Commission, WCEFA. http://unesdoc.unesco.org/images/0009/000975/097551e.pdf.

Zambia Ministry of Education, Science, Vocational Training and Early Education. (2013). *Medium of Instruction in the Early Education and Lower Primary: National Guide*. Lusaka: Zambia Ministry of Education, Science, Vocational Training and Early Education.

8 Literacy and Linguistic Diversity in Multilingual India

Pooja R. Nakamura and Chinmaya U. Holla

8.1 Introduction

In India, only 44 percent of students in government schools can read Grade 2 texts in Grade 5 fluently, as measured by the ASER test, which focuses on decoding skills (Annual Status of Education Report [ASER Centre, 2018]). According to India's national census conducted in 2011, 74 percent of the total population of India were considered literate, defined as having the ability to "both read and write with understanding in any language" (Education for All in India, 2011). Within India, there is, however, wide variation, with literacy rates being significantly higher in private schools (Pal & Kingdon, 2010) and in urban areas (Agrawal, 2014).

India – and the entire South and Southeast Asian region – is home to different types of writing systems and linguistic situations; however, literacy acquisition in the region is often defined by the use of alphasyllabic akshara orthographies and multilingualism. Both these characteristics have significant implications for the theory, practice, and policy of literacy acquisition in India. Although the scientific foundations and corresponding practical applications of reading development in monolingual contexts of alphabetic languages have been relatively conclusively established (Castles, Rastle, & Nation, 2018; Rayner et al., 2001; Seymour, Aro, & Erskine, 2003; Tunmer & Hoover, 2019), there is less research examining the psycholinguistic underpinnings of literacy acquisition in alphasyllabic akshara writing systems. The recent literature in akshara reading acquisition lends credibility to the universal mapping principle that learning to read depends on learning how a writing system encodes a spoken language (Perfetti, 2003; Verhoeven & Perfetti, 2017), by highlighting the very specific reading processes necessary to decode the particularities of the akshara scripts (Joshi & McBride, 2019; Nag & Perfetti, 2014). The research on biliteracy acquisition has also grown over the past several years, especially in cases of literacy acquisition in two alphabetic language (August & Shanahan, 2006), but also in cases of morphosyllabic–alphabetic biliteracy acquisition (Wang, Perfetti, & Liu, 2005; Zhang & Koda, 2014). However, the research on akshara-alphabetic biliteracy acquisition in functionally multilingual contexts – especially wherein educational resources are very limited – remains relatively uncharted territory (see also Nag, Chapter 15 in this volume).

Our chapter focuses on literacy and linguistic diversity in the most populous nation in the world. We begin with a brief description of the historical and contemporary state of multilingual education policy and practice in India. In addition, the psycholinguistic underpinnings of learning to read in akshara orthographies and of biliteracy acquisition with at least one akshara orthography will be uncovered. Finally, future directions related to literacy development research and practice among diverse populations in India will be discussed.

8.2 Multilingual Education Policy and Practice in India

Functional multilingualism – as Bhatia and Ritchie (2004) call it – is widespread in India. Functional multilingualism refers to the ability for people to "function" in different domains of society using different languages. This has complex and multifaceted implications for improving reading outcomes due to large variances and mismatches between students' oral-language abilities and the media of instruction in schools, as well as a lack of access to education in a child's home language (Ball, 2011; Pinnock, 2009).

At a national level, multilingualism forces India's education decision makers to craft policies that appropriately sequence the introduction of languages used as media of instruction. According to the 2011 census, there are 1,369 languages from at least 5 different language families spoken in India, and 121 of them have more than 10,000 speakers; however, more than 95 percent of the population speak one of 22 regional languages (Census; Government of India, 2011). In 1946, when India was drafting its Constitution, debate raged over whether to include languages other than Hindi as a national language (Jayasundara, 2014). While the Hindi-only camp declared that "people who do not know Hindustani have no right to stay in India" (Dhulekar, 1946, as cited by Jayasundara, 2014), several South Indian scholars and activists from non-Hindi-speaking regions of India pushed to maintain English as a national language as well, which resulted in both English and Hindi becoming official languages of the nation. In 1968, the National Policy in Education instated an education policy called the Three-Language Formula, which mandated that by the end of secondary school, all students should be learning three languages (Vaish, 2008). In Hindi-speaking states, the three languages are Hindi, English, and another modern Indian language, preferably a South Indian one; and in non-Hindi-speaking states, the three languages are that state's regional language, English, and Hindi.

In 2019, the central government of India released a draft New Education Policy, which makes amendments to the 1968 policy in that it refers to the "mandatory" teaching of Hindi in states where Hindi is not spoken, as well as inclusion of Hindi from the primary levels. These new directions have led to a backlash and widespread protests in non-Hindi-speaking regions (Dasgupta, 2019; Shankaran, 2019; Venkataramanan, 2019), reflecting past protests against Hindi dominance in India. At the pre-primary level, the Draft National Early Childhood Care and Education (ECCE) Policy (Government of India, 2012) argues that the "mother tongue or home language of the child will be the primary language of interaction in the ECCE programs. However, given the young child's ability at this age to learn many languages, exposure to the national language English in oral form, as required, will also be explored." These policies reflect the decades-long tensions around this issue of the need to promote multilingual education policies in India, as well as highlighting the necessity for more research to be undertaken to inform the construction of effective multilingual education policies in the country.

At a regional level, there is a need to reconcile the increasingly strong parental and community preference for schools that emphasize English learning earlier in the elementary grades (Nag, 2014) with the multifaceted positive benefits of learning in the local language for a longer period of time. The preference for English stems mainly from the perception that English is crucial to enhancing a child's life outcomes (National Council of Educational Research & Training [India], 2005), and from the growing evidence that English is indeed linked with socioeconomic mobility in India (Azam, Chin, & Prakash, 2013; Chakraborty & Bakshi, 2016; Shastry, 2012). In response to these parental preferences, some government schools, NGO-run schools, and private affordable schools in India have changed their policies and started using English as the medium of instruction from Grade 1 (Indo-Asian News Service, 2019; Kurrien, 2004; Press Trust of India, 2020). Yet research conducted on biliteracy acquisition in India indicates that students must attain a threshold level of reading skills in the local or regional language for a more effective transfer of skills from the local language to English and thus better biliteracy acquisition; it further indicates that this threshold level was not reached until Grade 4 or 5 by most students in a sample of thirteen urban and rural low-income schools in South India (Nakamura, de Hoop, & Holla, 2019). Research also shows that about 80 percent of children from nursery to Grade 7 in one sample of low-income schools in urban South India had very small English vocabularies (Nag, Rankumar, et al., 2014). International studies highlight a significant link between learning in the mother tongue and a positive sense of identity and self-worth (Tollefson & Tsui, 2003; Trudell, 2005). There is also a rising call from regional activists in India (Gejji, 2019), and the international education community (Ball, 2011; Bender et al., 2005; Benson, 2005) to maintain regional languages as the media of instruction for longer periods of time in early education. Clearly, more research is needed to inform an effective multilingual education practice that allows for a reconciliation between these complex, competing forces of increasing demand for earlier English learning vis-à-vis an increasing evidence base supporting the later teaching of English.

Also, regionally, policymakers and frontline workers in India face different sets of challenges in urban settings as compared to rural areas while implementing multilingual education policies. A typical child in Bangalore, an urban area in the south of India, may be exposed to – and use – up to four or five languages on a daily basis: a home language which may not be used in the school system at all (in some cases two home languages); a regional language different from the home language, which may or may not be used in schools; one school language as the language of instruction; a second regional school language; and a third language in school, such as Hindi (Reddy, 2011). Indeed, it is common for students in low-income community schools in Bangalore to come from several different L1 backgrounds, including commonly Telugu, Tamil, Hindi, Urdu, Tulu, and Malayalam, with only 15–20 percent speaking the regional language of Kannada (Nag, Snowling, et al., 2014; Reddy, 2011), making mixed mother-tongue-language classrooms relatively common. Mohanty, Panda, and Pal (2010) note that language heterogeneity within classrooms leads to teachers and field-level educational administrators having difficulties navigating prescribed curricular and pedagogic practices alongside the realities of the children's language capabilities.

In contrast, in rural areas, most children are likely to speak the same language, but they may come from homes that speak marginalized languages and dialect varieties, especially in states with significant tribal populations such as Jharkhand and Chhattisgarh. In these cases, the mismatch between the state language and the children's mother tongue results in well-documented negative consequences, such as a lack of opportunity to learn in a language the child understands that leads to stunted learning outcomes as well as high rates of dropouts (Jhingran, 2005) (see also Asfaha & Nag, Chapter 16 and Friedlander & Goldenberg, Chapter 18 in this volume).

At the household level, parents and the home literacy environment play a crucial role in children's language acquisition (Sénéchal & LeFevre, 2002), mainly through students' exposure to a language outside of school (Nag-Arulmani, 2000). There is significant variation in degrees of adult literacy and proficiency in different languages (including the languages of school instruction), and thus there are gaps in the language abilities of parents as well as children, especially in reading, which also hinders the ability of parents to support their children's literacy acquisition. Likewise, there is also evidence from a sample of about 500 students from 6 low-income communities in South India that there is a dire lack of print materials in *any* language in many homes (Reddy, 2011). When print was found in homes, the most common print-related items were religious books or decorative or functional items, such as calendars or newspapers used for wrapping goods.

Another key factor determining the success of multilingual education policy in India is the capabilities of the teachers. Nag-Arulmani (2000) found that one of the most important factors in English learning in India is the teacher's English-language proficiency. Kurrien (2005) identified four types of schools: (a) English-medium middle-high-cost private schools, where teachers are proficient in English, but students have differing levels of knowledge of English; (b) English-medium low-cost private schools, where teachers and students have limited proficiency in and exposure to English, but parents view English as an instrument for upward mobility; (c) government-aided regional schools, where teachers have varying levels of English proficiency, with students from a variety of backgrounds; and (d) government regional schools run by district and municipal education authorities, where both teachers' and students' English proficiency and exposure are limited. The National Council of Educational Research & Training (2005) argues that the language proficiency of teachers varies remarkably across schools, with a strong difference observable between government and private schools. Thus, depending on the type of school, the English proficiency levels of teachers differ and, arguably, the teachers' proficiency, in turn, differentially affects the language proficiency of the child (Shenoy & Wagner, 2019).

Curricular pace and pedagogical practices are another manifestation of how language choices play out in the classrooms of low-income communities in India. Despite some evidence from private unaided English-medium schools in urban low-income communities that phonics is a more effective teaching method for early decoding and encoding outcomes (Dixon, Schagen, & Seedhouse, 2011), these methods are rarely used in low-income urban communities in Bangalore (Shenoy, Wagner, & Rao, 2020). In an in-depth qualitative observation of four students in an English-medium school in India, Gupta (2013) reveals that pedagogical practice proceeds through the following stages: teaching isolated letters; then spelling individual words, without any explicit connections to meaning or context; learning grammar by copying sentences and recitation; and finally learning grammatical explanations and terms such as "proposition" and "conjunction" at age five. The study also showed that there was no focus on storytelling, storybooks, or any print support in the classroom other than the textbook. Nag, Ramkumar et al. (2014) find similar trends at the preschool level, with disproportionate time spent on copying texts by hand and no activities including storytelling or dialogue or interactive sessions, and short bursts of teaching in both the regional language (Kannada) and English. These findings also highlighted that Kannada was used mainly for punitive commands and teachers were not confident in teaching even in Kannada – which was the teachers' native language, but a later-acquired language for the students – because of their perception that the students did not have enough linguistic knowledge in that language to learn concepts.

Finally, a paucity in schools of appropriate learning materials that support and augment learning also adversely affects the practice of multilingual education. There are two ways in which this scenario of resource deprivation operates: (1) schools are under-resourced and are not able to provide adequate learning materials such as books and other print materials to their students in *any* language, and (2) learning materials in a particular language – most likely the regional languages or dialectical varieties – are not available in the learning ecosystem due to the lack of demand from parents and communities for teaching in these languages to take place, and thus the limited supply of such materials. Nag-Arulmani (2003) notes that there could be wide variations between different types of schools (government vs. private) in terms of learning opportunities, class libraries, culture, and management, which eventually lead to a similar divide in students' levels of oral-language and reading proficiency. Additionally, a lack of learning materials in vernacular languages, especially in science, can hinder learning among children (Mohanty, 2006).

In sum, there are immense challenges to the successful implementation of the Three-Language Formula in India's complex multilingual environment; however, there are also significant opportunities for success with multilingual education in a country that is dedicated to the teaching of more than one language in its policy.

8.3 Psycholinguistic Processes Underpinning Akshara Literacy Acquisition

While many early classification frameworks put forth the notion that there are three main categories of writing systems logographic (now more commonly called morphosyllabic), syllabic, and alphabetic (Gelb, 1952)– more recent frameworks also include the West Semitic abjad as well as the alphasyllabary (Nag & Perfetti, 2014; Perfetti, 2003). The akshara writing system, along with Korean Hangul and the Ethiopian Ge'ez scripts, commonly fall into the latter category.

Share and colleagues (Share, 2014; Share & Daniels, 2016) go a step further in unpacking the alphasyllabary category to highlight some of the key features that distinguish the ancient Brahmi-derived orthographies of the Dravidian and Sanskrit languages, akshara,[1] from alphabetic and syllabic scripts. Examples of such distinction from *both* alphabetic and syllabic writing systems include the

---

[1] Akshara is a Sanskrit word that means "syllable" (Ramanujan & Weekes, 2019). It is the term used in the most recent literature on the Brahmi-derived Indic orthographies (Joshi & McBride, 2019; Nag & Perfetti, 2014); however, the precise term varies by language (*akshara* in Kannada, *akshar* in Hindi, and *aksharamu* in Telugu)

visual prominence of the consonant in the syllabic clusters; the lack of visual resemblance between primary word-initial vowel forms, or their nondiacritic forms, and their secondary diacritic forms (for example, the difference between ಅ, the primary vowel form of /a/ versus ಾ, the secondary diacritic form of /a/); the lack of any graphical representation of the common schwa following consonants (which is hence called the inherent vowel); and the lack of case (majuscule and minuscule letters).

The basic orthographic representations of akshara are vowels and consonants, with the mid central vowel (schwa) inherent to each consonant. Consonants and vowels can be added to the base akshara consonant while keeping the syllabic form intact and prominent. Thus, each syllabic orthographic representation can be a vowel (V) ಅ /a/, a consonant with schwa (Cə) ಸ /sə/, a consonant plus a vowel diacritic marker (CV) ಸಾ /s/+/a/, a consonant with a consonant diacritic marker and vowel diacritic marker (CCV) ಶ್ರಿ /sh/+/r/+/i/, or even a consonant with a consonant diacritic marker, a second consonant diacritic marker, a vowel diacritic marker, and a long vowel diacritic marker (CCCVV) ಸ್ತ್ರೀ /s+th+r+i+long vowel marker/. Each of these configurations are represented as single symbol blocks that are visually approximately the same size, retaining syllabic prominence in the orthography (Nag, 2017).

Reflecting these orthographic features of the akshara, studies are beginning to unpack the psycholinguistic mechanisms that underlie early akshara reading acquisition. One of the central themes in most recent studies is that there is a need for dual syllabic and phonemic sensitivity in order to successfully acquire akshara-decoding ability (Nag, 2007; Nakamura, Joshi, & Ji, 2018; Reddy & Koda, 2013; Sircar & Nag, 2013; Vaid & Gupta, 2002; Vasanta, 2004; Winskel & Iemwanthong, 2010), as there is for decoding skills in other alphasyllabaries such as Korean Hangul and the *fidäl* symbols used in the Ge'ez scripts of Ethiopia (Asfaha, Kurvers, & Kroon, 2009; Cho & McBride-Chang, 2005; Kim & Davis, 2004; Kim & Petscher, 2011). Interestingly, however, the precise nature of the sublexical phonological sensitivity required at different stages of early akshara acquisition is still emerging and the evidence is inconclusive. For instance, due to the salience of the syllabic structure in the orthography, studies demonstrate that syllabic sensitivity remains a stronger predictor through the akshara-decoding acquisition process (Nakamura et al., 2018), and phonemic awareness is slower to emerge (Nag, 2007). However, studies are also highlighting that phonemic-level sensitivity is significant for the mastery of the entire repertoire of symbols (Nesan, Sadeghi, & Everatt, 2019; Wijayathilake et al., 2019). Accordingly, there is a wide consensus that akshara-decoding skills require dual syllable–phoneme phonological sensitivity, but the degree to which both are needed in different stages of the acquisition of decoding skills in akshara is a question that remains ripe for further investigation.

A second key feature of akshara is the size of the orthographic registry that needs to be learned. The "extensive" symbol set size (Nag, 2014), the large set of complex diacritic ligaturing rules, and the need for dual syllable and phoneme awareness lead to a longer acquisition trajectory of approximately four–five years to master decoding skills in the Indic akshara compared to approximately one–two years in most alphabetic languages (Nag, 2007, 2014; Reddy & Koda, 2013). Scholars have recently begun referring to this as the "orthographic breadth" (Inoue et al., 2017; Nag, 2014), adding a critical dimension of breadth to the much-researched implications of the depth spectrum (Katz & Frost, 1992; Seymour, Aro, & Erskine, 2003) on early decoding-acquisition ability.

Another key feature of akshara orthographies that makes them distinct from alphabetic orthographies, as well as leading to some challenges for young readers, is the nonlinear arrangement of the symbols. While alphabetic languages spatially arrange their letters in the same sequence as their corresponding sounds, noninitial vowel or consonant phonemic components of akshara are ligatured to the primary consonant in positions above, below, to the right of, and even to the left of the consonant (Share & Daniels, 2016). For instance, in the word हिन्दी /hindi/ the िo diacritic /i/ appears before the ह /h/ consonant, leading to nonlinear spatial configurations of the phonological sequence. This mismatch between spatial and temporal sequencing of sounds and symbols leads to challenges in decoding acquisition and adds to word-reading acquisition time (Kandhadhai & Sproat, 2010; Vaid & Gupta, 2002; Winskel, Padakannaya, & Pandey, 2013).

Akshara are also visually complex in unique ways. While most cross-orthography comparative research has focused on sound–symbol mapping correspondence differences (Katz & Frost, 1992; Perfetti, 2003; Ziegler & Goswami, 2005), visual-form differences also have consequences for recognition and learning (Chang, Chen, & Perfetti, 2018; Nag, Snowling et al., 2014). Visual-form differences are most often manifested in terms of the degree of discriminability of graphic symbols (Pelli et al., 2006). Chang et al. (2018) propose a measure of visual complexity, which takes into account perimetric complexity (the ratio of the space taken up by the graph to the background unused space of the graph) and other features that amount to the inventory size that needs to be acquired. In this categorization of the complexity of the world's writing systems, the akshara writing system tends to rank as more complex than alphabetic writing systems but as less complex than morphosyllabic writing systems. Similarly, Nag, Snowling, et al. (2014) demonstrated that the pixel density of Kannada led to significant differences in early reading acquisition. Share and Daniels (2016) also point out the differences between the initial and noninitial forms of vowels and consonantal diacritics in the Indic scripts as a potential source of confusion for beginning readers. Together, the visual complexity of the akshara writing system uniquely constrains early reading acquisition.

Taken collectively, there are key differences between akshara literacy acquisition and literacy acquisition in alphabetic, syllabic, morphosyllabic, and even other alphasyllabic orthographies. Each of these differences have critical implications for the precise cognitive and linguistic subskills that are required for acquisition of word-reading skills, and the timing of the acquisition of each of these skills.

8.4 Biliteracy Acquisition in Akshara and Other Languages

Biliteracy acquisition is a qualitatively different process from monolingual literacy acquisition primarily because there is dual language involvement in biliteracy acquisition (Koda, 2013). Early theoretical formulations of this dual language involvement centered on the notion of a "common underlying proficiency" that accounted for the significant correlations between reading ability in one's first language (L1) and one's second language (L2) (Cummins, 1979, 1991). More recent models have disentangled various reading subcomponent skills as being more or less susceptible to transfer – depending on their language-neutrality or language-specificity. Critically, metalinguistic skills are generally pinned down as those being shared across language, and decoding skills are those most likely to transfer, while certain orthographic constraints and oral-language skills are the least likely to be related across languages (Geva & Siegel, 2000; Koda, 2013). One conceptualization of transfer is synthesized in the compelling Transfer Facilitation Model (Koda, 2005; 2008; 2013) as follows: previously acquired literacy subskills, primarily decoding skills, transfer and affect the development of L2 reading through shared metalinguistic awareness, primarily metalinguistic skills; however, this transfer facilitation is dependent upon the linguistic and orthographic distance between the two languages, as well as L2 print and oral-language input and experience.

Chung, Chen, and Geva (2019) provide an interactive framework for cross-linguistic transfer in L2 reading, in which they reiterate that the relationship between L1 and L2 reading skills is influenced by cognitive, linguistic, and metalinguistic factors such as language-specific constructs (orthographic mapping, vocabulary knowledge, and oral-language skills) versus language-neutral constructs (e.g., phonological awareness, morphological awareness, conceptual knowledge, background knowledge), L1–L2 distance, and L1–L2 proficiency and complexity. However, they extend the model to argue that transfer itself is also impacted by sociocultural factors such as age of beginning acquisition of the L2, immigration experience, educational settings, and extent of exposure to the L1 and L2.

Several studies provide empirical support for the tenets of these theoretical frameworks of transfer. Studies across an array of typologically diverse language pairs have shown significant correlations between phonological awareness skills in both languages (Abu-Rabia & Siegel, 2002 in Arabic–English; Bialystok, McBride-Chang, & Luk, 2005; Gottardo et al., 2001; Wang, Perfetti, & Liu, 2005, in Chinese–English; Schaefer & Kotzé, 2019 in isiZulu and Siswati and English; Nakamura, Koda, & Joshi, 2014; Reddy & Koda, 2013 in Kannada–English; Wawire & Kim, 2018 in Kiswahili–English; da Fontoura & Siegel, 1995 in Portuguese–English; Kim, 2009 in Korean–English; Durgunoğlu, Nagy, & Hancin-Bhatt, 1993; Goodrich, Lonigan, & Farver, 2017 in Spanish–English). Some of these studies and others have also demonstrated that through the cross-linguistic sharing of phonological skills, there is not only an association with improved L2 reading (Kuo et al., 2016; Melby-Lervåg & Lervåg, 2011; Reddy & Koda, 2013; Schaefer & Kotzé, 2019); but also a causal impact on L2 early reading subskills (Goodrich et al., 2017; Wawire & Kim, 2018). Morphological awareness has also been identified as a prime candidate for cross-linguistic resource sharing in both morphosyllabic–alphabetic biliteracy pairs such as Mandarin/Cantonese and English (Lam et al., 2012; Wang, Cheng, & Chen, 2006; Zhang, 2013) and in alphabetic–alphabetic biliteracy acquisition, such as Spanish and English (Ramírez, Chen, & Pasquarella, 2013).

While metalinguistic awareness and decoding skills are often correlated between L1 and L2, the relationship between orthographic skills tend to be less significantly related in languages that are typologically more distant (Abu-Rabia, 1997; Geva & Siegel, 2000; Geva, Wade-Woolley, & Shany, 1997; Wade-Woolley & Geva, 2000 for Hebrew–English bilinguals; and Wang, Park, & Lee, 2006 for Korean–English bilinguals). In addition, L2 linguistic and orthographic input is also critical for L2 word reading (Wang & Koda, 2007).

In multilingual contexts wherein more than two languages are being acquired, it has also been demonstrated that biliteracy skills themselves significantly predict L3 reading ability (Schwartz et al., 2007). The directionality of transfer is also questioned in contexts where children have limited input to print in their L1, and studies show that in these cases L2 print input not only supports L2 reading but also reverse transfers to support L1 reading (Asfaha et al., 2009; Pretorius & Mampuru, 2007). Finally, cross-linguistic transfer effects reduce, and within-language effects increase, across grades (Nakamoto, Lindsey, & Manis, 2008; Nakamura et al., 2014). Taken together, as evidenced by the meta-analysis by Melby-Lervåg and Lervåg (2011), there are stronger cross-linguistic relations between L1 and L2 phonological awareness and decoding skills than between L1 and L2 oral-language skills. Crucially, both medium of instruction and writing-system distance also moderate the cross-linguistic effects. Both these moderators play an important role in teaching and learning reading on the Indian subcontinent.

There are few studies that focus specifically on biliteracy acquisition in an Indic akshara language and English. In one example, Reddy and Koda (2013) examined whether and how the dual syllable and phoneme encoding of phonology in the Kannada orthography might transfer and facilitate reading acquisition in L2 (or more precisely, later-acquired Lx) English. Their results, reflective of other biliteracy studies with typologically differing languages, showed that only the phonemic aspect of phonological awareness from Kannada supported cross-linguistic facilitative effects, suggesting significant orthographic constraints to the biliteracy acquisition process in this case. Also consistent with previous studies, Nakamura, Koda, and Joshi (2014) revealed that in the case of Kannada–English biliteracy acquisition in Grade 3–8 students, the cross-linguistic relationships that were evident in decoding scores in the earlier grades faded as literacy development progressed, highlighting the increasing role of L2 oral-language skills in the later grades.

In an attempt to apply this cross-linguistic transfer research to the practice and policy question in India of when to introduce a child to literacy instruction in English, Nakamura, de Hoop, and Holla (2019) tested whether there was a structural break in the relationship – or a point of "sufficient" mastery – between L1 akshara (Kannada or Telugu) decoding scores and L2 English decoding scores in students in Grades 1–5. Building on the akshara–English biliteracy studies that showed that the independent, significant predictors of reading development in L2 English in India were L1 decoding skills and L2 oral-language skills (Nakamura et al., 2013; Reddy & Koda, 2013) and that phonemic awareness in Kannada specifically accounted for variance in English decoding, it was hypothesized that after the mastery of the phonemic components within the akshara (a constrained skill, as opposed to oral vocabulary language, which can be considered an unconstrained skill; Snow & Matthews, 2016), L1 decoding ability is at a threshold level of mastery and transfer occurs. This transfer, in turn, leads to exponential improvements in English after the threshold has been achieved. In other words, it was predicted that there would be an L1 decoding transfer "tipping" point after which English decoding acquisition was significantly easier for the child. The results clearly demonstrated that in fact there was such a structural break in the correlation between Kannada or Telugu (depending on the region of study), and English decoding skills, suggesting that an empirical basis for transfer "readiness" can be identified. Furthermore, this study also theoretically contributed to our understanding of biliteracy transfer as a likely nonlinear process.

In sum, it is evident that there are cross-linguistic relations between L1 and L2 reading subskills, primarily through the sharing of metalinguistic skills and transfer of early word-reading skills. This is apparent in akshara–English biliteracy acquisition as well. Furthermore, there is emerging evidence for the possible nonlinearity of the transfer relationship in akshara and English biliteracy, wherein, based on the orthographic properties of the L1, there is a point at which a child has sufficient decoding ability to be considerably better prepared for literacy acquisition in English.

8.5 Conclusions and Discussion

With hundreds of languages, dozens of scripts, multiple writing systems, literacy acquisition in three languages formally required in all schools, and wide variances in socioeconomic groups and access to quality educational programs, India has one of the most diverse, complex, multilingual educational contexts in the world. Although private schools and certain sectors of society excel globally in terms of educational quality and outcomes, those less privileged in urban and rural poor communities continue to struggle to reach even minimal levels of literacy achievement (ASER Centre, 2018).

Multilingualism and multiscriptal learning in India are fraught with challenges as well as issues that make that country's education system unamenable to the straightforward application of monolingual or even bilingual education research from Western nations and contexts of only alphabetic language learning. Literacy and biliteracy acquisition research from India and South and Southeast Asia, though nascent, are revealing that there are identifiable and teachable cognitive resources and opportunities in multilingual learning that need to be taken into consideration for more effective literacy education. One of the strongest candidates for this is the cross-linguistic transfer of resources from a known or familiar language. For the most part, there are normal distributions in oral-language skills and metalinguistic skills in a native or familiar language – and in contexts of not much else, these resources form a foundation for L1 or mother-tongue literacy acquisition, which in turn can transfer and act as one of the strongest predictors of success of literacy acquisition in a new or later-acquired language. Thus, if drawn upon efficiently, cross-linguistic resource sharing may provide an important opportunity for overcoming some of the challenges and limited resources of multilingual education in low-income communities in India.

In order to begin addressing the Indian literacy crisis and making a dent in global "learning poverty" (World Bank, 2019), it is critical to not only look at macro and systemic education issues but also recognize the importance of the cognitive foundations of learning in diverse multilingual and multiscriptal societies. Programmatic and policy theories of change that are founded in these realities (multiple and varying scripts, bi- and multilingualism, and multiple language involvement in learning to read) are critical to efforts to move the needle on the learning crisis (see also Nag, Chapter 15 and Asfaha &

Nag, Chapter 16 in this volume). The research insights from the literacy diversity and multilingualism in India could potentially support this endeavor.

References

Abu-Rabia, S. (1997). Reading in Arabic orthography: The effect of vowels and context on reading accuracy of poor and skilled native Arabic readers. *Reading and Writing, 9*, 65–78.

Abu-Rabia, S., & Siegel, L. S. (2002). Reading, syntactic, orthographic, and working memory skills of bilingual Arabic-English speaking Canadian children. *Journal of Psycholinguistic Research, 31*, 661–678.

Agrawal, T. (2014). Educational inequality in rural and urban India. *International Journal of Educational Development, 34*, 11–19.

ASER Centre. (2018). *Annual Status of Education Report (Rural) 2018*. New Delhi: ASER. http://img.asercentre.org/docs/ASER%202018/Release%20Material/aserreport2018.pdf.

Asfaha, Y. M., Beckman, D., Kurvers, J., & Kroon, S. (2009). L2 reading in multilingual Eritrea: The influences of L1 reading and English proficiency. *Journal of Research in Reading, 32*, 351–365.

Asfaha, Y. M., Kurvers, J., & Kroon, S. (2009). Grain size in script and teaching: Literacy acquisition in Ge'ez and Latin. *Applied Psycholinguistics, 30*, 709–724.

August, D., & Shanahan, T. (eds.). (2006). *Developing Literacy in Second-Language Learners: Report of the National Literacy Panel on Language-Minority Children and Youth*. Washington, DC: Center for Applied Linguistics.

Azam, M., Chin, A., & Prakash, N. (2013). The returns to English-language skills in India. *Economic Development and Cultural Change, 61*, 335–367.

Ball, J. (2011). *Enhancing Learning of Children from Diverse Language Backgrounds: Mother Tongue-Based Bilingual or Multilingual Education in the Early Years*. Paris: UNESCO.

Bender, P., Dutcher, N., Klaus, D., Shore, J., & Tesar, C. (2005). *In Their Own Language: Education for All*. Education Notes 38906. Washington, DC: World Bank Group. http://documents.worldbank.org/curated/en/374241468763515925/In-their-own-language-education-for-all.

Benson, C. (2005). The importance of mother tongue-based schooling for educational quality. Paper commissioned for the EFA Global Monitoring Report 2005, The Quality Imperative. www.unesco.org/en/efareport/reports/2005-quality/.

Bhatia, T., & Ritchie, W. C. (2004). Bilingualism in South Asia. In T. K. Bhatia & W. Ritchie (eds.), *The Handbook of Bilingualism* (pp. 780–807). Oxford: Blackwell.

Bialystok, E., McBride-Chang, C., & Luk, G. (2005). Bilingualism, language proficiency, and learning to read in two writing systems. *Journal of Educational Psychology, 97*, 580.

Castles, A., Rastle, K., & Nation, K. (2018). Ending the reading wars: Reading acquisition from novice to expert. *Psychological Science in the Public Interest, 19*, 5–51.

Chakraborty, T., & Bakshi, S. K. (2016). English language premium: Evidence from a policy experiment in India. *Economics of Education Review, 50*, 1–16.

Chang, L. Y., Chen, Y. C., & Perfetti, C. A. (2018). GraphCom: A multidimensional measure of graphic complexity applied to 131 written languages. *Behavior Research Methods, 50,* 427–449.

Cho, J. R., & McBride-Chang, C. (2005). Levels of phonological awareness in Korean and English: A 1-year longitudinal study. *Journal of Educational Psychology, 97,* 580–590.

Chung, S. C., Chen, X., & Geva, E. (2019). Deconstructing and reconstructing cross-language transfer in bilingual reading development: An interactive framework. *Journal of Neurolinguistics, 50,* 149–161.

Cummins, J. (1979). Linguistic interdependence and the educational development of bilingual children. *Review of Educational Research, 49,* 222–251.

Cummins, J. (1991). Interdependence of first-and second-language proficiency in bilingual children. In E. Bialystok (ed.), *Language Processing in Bilingual Children* (pp. 70–89). Cambridge: Cambridge University Press.

Da Fontoura, H. A., & Siegel, L. S. (1995). Reading, syntactic, and working memory skills of bilingual Portuguese-English Canadian children. *Reading and Writing, 7,* 139–153.

Dasgupta, K. (2019, June 3). The three-language formula is a bad idea. *Hindustan Times.* www.hindustantimes.com/analysis/why-the-three-language-formula-is-a-bad-idea/story-xkmnLInWyJGq6Pale1RdhJ.html.

Dixon, P., Schagen, I., & Seedhouse, P. (2011). The impact of an intervention on children's reading and spelling ability in low-income schools in India. *School Effectiveness and School Improvement, 22,* 461–482.

Durgunoğlu, A. Y., Nagy, W. E., & Hancin-Bhatt, B. J. (1993). Cross-language transfer of phonological awareness. *Journal of Educational Psychology, 85,* 453.

Education for All in India. (2011). State of literacy. (Online chapter.) www.education forallinindia.com/chapter6-state-of-literacy-2011-census.pdf.

Gejji, A. (2019, September 7). Karnataka: Scrap English medium in govt schools, writers urge govt. *The Times of India.* https://timesofindia.indiatimes.com/city/bengaluru/karnataka-scrap-english-medium-in-govt-schools-writers-urge-govt/articleshow/71028126.cms.

Gelb, I. J. (1952). *A Study of Writing: The Foundations of Grammatology.* Chicago: University of Chicago Press.

Geva, E., & Siegel, L. S. (2000). Orthographic and cognitive factors in the concurrent development of basic reading skills in two languages. *Reading and Writing, 12,* 1–30.

Geva, E., Wade-Woolley, L., & Shany, M. (1997). Development of reading efficiency in first and second language. *Scientific Studies of Reading, 1,* 119–144.

Goodrich, J. M., Lonigan, C. J., & Farver, J. M. (2017). Do early literacy skills in children's first language promote development of skills in their second language? An experimental evaluation of transfer. *Journal of Educational Psychology, 105,* 414–426.

Gottardo, A., Yan, B., Siegel, L. S., & Wade-Woolley, L. (2001). Factors related to English reading performance in children with Chinese as a first language: More evidence of cross-language transfer of phonological processing. *Journal of Educational Psychology, 93,* 530.

Government of India. (2011). Census of India. New Delhi: Ministry of Home Affairs.

Government of India. (2012). *Draft National Early Childhood Care and Education (ECCE) Policy*. https://shodhganga.inflibnet.ac.in/bitstream/10603/234067/4/13%20appendix.pdf.

Gupta, R. (2013). More than ABC: Instructional practices and children's understanding of literacy through English. *Contemporary Education Dialogue, 10*, 37–65.

Indo-Asian News Service. (2019, September 11). English to be medium of instruction in Andhra government schools. *India TV*. www.indiatvnews.com/news/india/english-medium-of-instruction-andhra-government-schools-548970.

Inoue, T., Georgiou, G. K., Muroya, N., Maekawa, H., & Parrila, R. (2017). Cognitive predictors of literacy acquisition in syllabic Hiragana and morphographic Kanji. *Reading and Writing, 30*, 1335–1360.

Jayasundara, N. S. (2014). The development of language education policy: An Indian perspective; a view from Tamil Nadu. *International Journal of Scientific and Research Publications, 4*, 1–4.

Jhingran, D. (2005). *Language Disadvantage: The Learning Challenge in Primary Education*. New Delhi: APH Publishing.

Joshi, R. M., & McBride, C. (2019). Introduction: Handbook of literacy in akshara orthography. In R. M. Joshi & C. McBride (eds.), *Handbook of Literacy in Akshara Orthography* (pp. 3–9). Cham: Springer.

Kandhadai, P., & Sproat, R. (2010). Impact of spatial ordering of graphemes in alpha-syllabic scripts on phonemic awareness in Indic languages. *Writing Systems Research, 2*, 105–116.

Katz, L., & Frost, R. (1992). The reading process is different for different orthographies: The orthographic depth hypothesis. In R. Frost & L. Katz (eds.), *Orthography, phonology, morphology, and meaning* (pp. 45–66). Amsterdam: Elsevier.

Kim, J., & Davis, C. (2004). Characteristics of poor readers of Korean Hangul: Auditory, visual and phonological processing. *Reading and Writing, 17*, 153–185.

Kim, Y. S. (2009). Crosslinguistic influence on phonological awareness for Korean–English bilingual children. *Reading and Writing, 22*, 843.

Kim, Y. S., & Petscher, Y. (2011). Relations of emergent literacy skill development with conventional literacy skill development in Korean. *Reading and Writing, 24*, 635–656.

Koda, K. (2005). *Insights into Second Language Reading*. Cambridge: Cambridge University Press.

Koda, K. (2008). Impacts of prior literacy experience on second language learning to read. In K. Koda & A. M. Zehler (eds.), *Learning to Read across Languages: Cross-Linguistic Relationships in First- and Second Language Literacy Development* (pp. 68–96). New York: Routledge.

Koda, K. (2013). Development of second language reading skills: Cross-linguistic perspectives. In S. M., Gass, & A. Mackey (eds.), *The Routledge Handbook of Second Language Acquisition* (pp. 303–318). New York: Routledge.

Kuo, L. J., Uchikoshi, Y., Kim, T. J., & Yang, X. (2016). Bilingualism and phonological awareness: Re-examining theories of cross-language transfer and structural sensitivity. *Contemporary Educational Psychology, 46*, 1–9.

Kurrien, J. (2004, April 30). The English juggernaut: Regional medium schools in crisis. *The Times of India*, pp. 1–12.

Kurrien, J. (2005). Notes for the meeting of the National Focus Group on Teaching of English, and note on introduction of English at the primary stage. Unpublished manuscript. (New Delhi: National Council of Educational Research and Training.)

Lam, K., Chen, X., Geva, E., Luo, Y. C., & Li, H. (2012). The role of morphological awareness in reading achievement among young Chinese-speaking English language learners: A longitudinal study. *Reading and Writing, 25*, 1847–1872.

Melby-Lervåg, M., & Lervåg, A. (2011). Cross-linguistic transfer of oral language, decoding, phonological awareness and reading comprehension: A meta-analysis of the correlational evidence. *Journal of Research in Reading, 34*, 114–135.

Mohanty, A. (2006). Multilingualism of the unequals and predicaments of education in India: Mother tongue or other tongue? In O. Garcia, T. Skutnabb-Kangas, & M. Torres-Guzman (eds.), *Imagining Multilingual Schools: Languages in Education and Glocalization* (pp. 262–283). Clevedon: Multilingual Matters.

Mohanty, A. K., Panda, M., & Pal, R. (2010). Language policy in education and classroom practices in India: Is the teacher a cog in the policy wheel? In K. Menken & O. Garcia (eds.), *Negotiating Language Policies in Schools: Educators as Policymakers*, (pp. 211–231). London: Routledge.

Nag, S. (2007). Early reading in Kannada: The pace of acquisition of orthographic knowledge and phonemic awareness. *Journal of Research in Reading, 30*, 7–22.

Nag, S. (2014). Alphabetism and the science of reading: From the perspective of the akshara languages. *Frontiers in Psychology, 5*, 1–3.

Nag, S. (2017). Learning to read alphasyllabaries. In K. Cain, D. L. Compton, & R. K. Parrila (eds.), *Theories of Reading Development* (pp. 75–98). Amsterdam: John Benjamins.

Nag, S., & Perfetti, C. A. (2014). Reading and writing: Insights from the alphasyllabaries of South and Southeast Asia. *Writing Systems Research, 6*, 1–9.

Nag, S., Ramkumar, S., Miranda, R. et al. (2014). Home and school learning environment: Field notes from eight urban, public-funded nursery and primary schools. Working paper. Bangalore: The Promise Foundation.

Nag, S., Snowling, M., Quinlan, P., & Hulme, C. (2014). Child and symbol factors in learning to read a visually complex writing system. *Scientific Studies of Reading, 18*, 309–324.

Nag-Arulmani, S. (2000). Types and manifestations of learning difficulties in Indian classrooms. In paper presented at the First Orientation Programme for Schoolteachers, National Institute for Public Co-operation and Child Development (NIPCCD), Bangalore, India.

Nag-Arulmani, S. (2003). Reading difficulties in Indian languages. In N. Ghoulandris (ed.), *Dyslexia in Different Languages: Cross Linguistic Comparisons*. (pp. 235–254). London: Whurr.

Nakamoto, J., Lindsey, K. A., & Manis, F. R. (2008). A cross-linguistic investigation of English language learners' reading comprehension in English and Spanish. *Scientific Studies of Reading, 12*, 351–371.

Nakamura, P. R., de Hoop, T., & Holla, C. U. (2019). Language and the learning crisis: evidence of transfer threshold mechanisms in multilingual reading in South India. *The Journal of Development Studies, 55*, 2287–2305.

Nakamura, P. R., Joshi, R. M., & Ji, X. R. (2018). Investigating the asymmetrical roles of syllabic and phonemic awareness in akshara processing. *Journal of Learning Disabilities, 51*, 499–506.

Nakamura, P. R., Koda, K., & Joshi, R. M. (2014). Biliteracy acquisition in Kannada and English: A developmental study. *Writing Systems Research*, *6*, 132–147.

National Council of Educational Research & Training. (2005). *National Curriculum Framework 2005*. National Council of Educational Research and Training (India).

Nesan, M., Sadeghi, A., & Everatt, J. (2019). Literacy acquisition in the Malayalam orthography: Cognitive/linguistic influences within a multilingual context. In R. M. Joshi & C. McBride (eds.), *Handbook of Literacy in Akshara Orthography* (pp. 85–101). Cham: Springer.

Pal, S., & Kingdon, G. G. (2010). Can private school growth foster universal literacy? Panel evidence from Indian districts. IZA Discussion Paper 5274.

Pelli, D. G., Burns, C. W., Farell, B., & Moore-Page, D. C. (2006). Feature detection and letter identification. *Vision Research*, *46*, 4646–4674.

Perfetti, C. A. (2003). The universal grammar of reading. *Scientific Studies of Reading*, *7*, 3–24.

Pinnock, H. (2009). *Language and Education: The Missing Link, How the Language Used in Schools Threatens the Achievement of Education For All*. London: Save the Children.

Press Trust of India. (2020, May 28). AP CM says firm in resolve to introduce English medium in primary schools. *The Times of India*. https://timesofindia.indiatimes.com/home/education/news/ap-cm-says-firm-in-resolve-to-introduce-english-medium-in-primary-schools/articleshow/76061600.cms.

Pretorius, E. J., & Mampuru, D. M. (2007). Playing football without a ball: language, reading and academic performance in a high-poverty school. *Journal of Research in Reading*, *30*, 38–58.

Ramanujan, K., & Weekes, B. S. (2019). What is an Akshara? In R. M. Joshi, & C. McBride (eds.), *Handbook of Literacy in Akshara Orthography*. Cham: Springer.

Ramírez, G., Chen, X., & Pasquarella, A. (2013). Cross-linguistic transfer of morphological awareness in Spanish-speaking English language learners: The facilitating effect of cognate knowledge. *Topics in Language Disorders*, *33*, 73–92.

Rayner, K., Foorman, B. R., Perfetti, C. A., Pesetsky, D., & Seidenberg, M. S. (2001). How psychological science informs the teaching of reading. *Psychological Science in the Public Interest*, *2*, 31–74.

Reddy, P. R. (2011). Biliteracy development in middle-school students from the slums of India (Unpublished doctoral dissertation, Carnegie Mellon University, Pittsburgh, PA.)

Reddy, P. R., & Koda, K. (2013). Orthographic constraints on phonological awareness in biliteracy development. *Writing Systems Research*, *5*, 110–130.

Schaefer, M., & Kotzé, J. (2019). Early reading skills related to Grade 1 English second language literacy in rural South African schools. *South African Journal of Childhood Education*, *9*, 1–13.

Schwartz, M., Geva, E., Share, D. L., & Leikin, M. (2007). Learning to read in English as third language: The cross-linguistic transfer of phonological processing skills. *Written Language & Literacy*, *10*, 25–52.

Sénéchal, M., & LeFevre, J. A. (2002). Parental involvement in the development of children's reading skill: A five-year longitudinal study. *Child Development*, *73*, 445–460.

Seymour, P. H., Aro, M., Erskine, J. M. (2003). Foundation literacy acquisition in European orthographies. *British Journal of Psychology*, *94*, 143–174.

Shankaran, S. (2019, June 3). Is the three-language formula really implementable now? *The Times of India*. https://timesofindia.indiatimes.com/blogs/cash-flow/is-the-three-language-formula-really-implementable-now/.

Share, D. L. (2014). Alphabetism in reading science. *Frontiers in Psychology*, *5*, 752. DOI: https://doi.org/10.3389/fpsyg.2014.00752.

Share, D. L., & Daniels, P. T. (2016). Aksharas, alphasyllabaries, abugidas, alphabets and orthographic depth: Reflections on Rimzhim, Katz and Fowler (2014). *Writing Systems Research*, *8*, 17–31.

Shastry, G. K. (2012). Human capital response to globalization education and information technology in India. *Journal of Human Resources*, *47*, 287–330.

Shenoy, S., & Wagner, R. K. (2019). Language and literacy practices that influence bilingual and bi-Literate acquisition in L1 Kannada and L2 English in Bangalore, India. In R. M. Joshi & C. McBride (eds.), *Handbook of Literacy in Akshara Orthography* (pp. 373–388). Cham: Springer.

Shenoy, S., Wagner, R. K., & Rao, N. M. (2020). Factors that influence reading acquisition in L2 English for students in Bangalore, India. *Reading & Writing*, *33*, 1809–1838.

Sircar, S., & Nag, S. (2013). Akshara–syllable mappings in Bengali: A language-specific skill for reading. In S. Winskel & P. Padakannaya (eds.), *South and Southeast Asian Psycholinguistics* (pp. 202–211). Cambridge: Cambridge University Press.

Snow, C. E., & Matthews, T. J. (2016). Reading and language in the early grades. *The Future of Children*, *26*, 57–74.

Tollefson, J. W., & Tsui, A. B. (2003). The centrality of medium-of-instruction policy in sociopolitical processes. In J. W. Tollefson & A. B. M. Tsui (eds.), *Medium of Instruction Policies: Which Agenda? Whose Agenda?* (pp. 1–18). London: Lawrence Erlbaum Associates.

Trudell, B. (2005). Language choice, education and community identity. *International Journal of Educational Development*, *25*, 237–251.

Tunmer, W. E., & Hoover, W. A. (2019). The cognitive foundations of learning to read: A framework for preventing and remediating reading difficulties. *Australian Journal of Learning Difficulties*, *24*, 75–93.

Vaid, J., & Gupta, A. (2002). Exploring word recognition in a semi-alphabetic script: The case of Devanagari. *Brain and Language*, *81*, 679–690.

Vaish, V. (2008). *Biliteracy and Globalization: English Language Education in India*. Clevedon: Multilingual Matters.

Vasanta, D. (2004). Processing phonological information in a semi-syllabic script: Developmental data from Telugu. *Reading and Writing*, *17*, 59–78.

Venkataramanan, K. (2019, June 8). What is the three-language formula? *The Times of India*. https://timesofindia.indiatimes.com/blogs/cash-flow/is-the-three-language-formula-really-implementable-now/.

Verhoeven, L., & Perfetti, C. (eds.). (2017). *Learning to Read across Languages and Writing Systems*. Cambridge: Cambridge University Press.

Wade-Woolley, L., & Geva, E. (2000). Processing novel phonemic contrasts in the acquisition of L2 word reading. *Scientific Studies of Reading*, *4*, 295–311.

Wang, M., Cheng, C., & Chen, S. W. (2006). Contribution of morphological awareness to Chinese-English biliteracy acquisition. *Journal of Educational Psychology, 98*, 542.

Wang, M., & Koda, K. (2007). Commonalities and differences in word identification skills among learners of English as a second language. *Language Learning, 57*, 201–222.

Wang, M., Park, Y., & Lee, K. R. (2006). Korean-English biliteracy acquisition: Cross-language phonological and orthographic transfer. *Journal of Educational Psychology, 98*, 148–158.

Wang, M., Perfetti, C. A., & Liu, Y. (2005). Chinese–English biliteracy acquisition: Cross-language and writing system transfer. *Cognition, 97*, 67–88.

Wawire, B. A., & Kim, Y. S. G. (2018). Cross-language transfer of phonological awareness and letter knowledge: Causal evidence and nature of transfer. *Scientific Studies of Reading, 22*, 443–461.

Wijayathilake, M. A. D. K., Parrila, R., Inoue, T., & Nag, S. (2019). Cognitive predictors of word reading in Sinhala. *Reading and Writing, 32*, 1881–1907.

Winskel, H., & Iemwanthong, K. (2010). Reading and spelling acquisition in Thai children. *Reading and Writing, 23*, 1021–1053.

Winskel, H., Padakannaya, P., & Pandey, A. (2013). Eye movements and reading in the alphasyllabic scripts of South and Southeast Asia. In H. Winskel & P. Padakannaya (eds.), *South and South-East Asian Psycholinguistics* (pp. 315–328). Cambridge: Cambridge University Press.

World Bank. (2019). *Ending Learning Poverty: What Will It Take?* Washington, DC. World Bank. https://openknowledge.worldbank.org/handle/10986/32553.

Zhang, D. (2013). Linguistic distance effect on cross-linguistic transfer of morphological awareness. *Applied Psycholinguistics, 34*, 917–942.

Zhang, D., & Koda, K. (2014). Awareness of derivation and compounding in Chinese–English biliteracy acquisition. *International Journal of Bilingual Education and Bilingualism, 17*, 55–73.

Ziegler, J. C., & Goswami, U. (2005). Reading acquisition, developmental dyslexia, and skilled reading across languages: A psycholinguistic grain size theory. *Psychological Bulletin, 131*, 3–29.

9 Literacy Development in East Asia

Michelle R. Y. Huo, Xin Sun, Ioulia Kovelman, and Xi Chen

9.1 Introduction

East Asia, the eastern region of the Asian continent, includes China, Japan, South Korea, North Korea, Mongolia, and Taiwan. East Asia is densely populated; its 1.7 billion people make up approximately 22 percent of the world's population (United Nations World Population Prospects; United Nations, 2019). China has the largest population in the world, with 1.398 billion people (World Bank, 2019). The populations are 126.26 million in Japan, 51.70 million in South Korea, 25.55 million in North Korea, and 3.23 million in Mongolia (World Bank, 2019). Taiwan is estimated to have 23.78 million people (Worldometer, 2020). Several East Asian countries, such as South Korea and China, have experienced rapid economic growth in the past few decades, whereas Japan's economy consistently ranks among the top three in the world (Sarel, 1997). The 2018 Human Development Index (UNDP, 2018) classified Japan and South Korea as developed countries, and China and Mongolia as developing countries.[1]

Students in most East Asian countries/regions perform well on literacy. The reading scores of Chinese,[2] Japanese, South Korean, and Taiwanese students were higher than average according to the 2018 Programme for International Student Assessment (PISA), administered to fifteen-year-old students across sixty-five countries (OECD, 2018).[3] Notably, migrant communities still face many struggles in East Asia. For example, ethnic minorities, such as Filipinos, Indonesians, and South Asians, make up about 8 percent of the population in Hong Kong (Population By-Census, 2016). These minority groups experience both poverty and low education attainment (Chu, 2019; Population By-Census, 2016). Similarly, in China, migrant children and children who reside in the

---

[1] Hong Kong ranks as a developed country, but it is a region of China. North Korea is not on the list.
[2] The PISA was only administered in four cities/regions: Beijing, Shanghai, Zhejiang, and Jiangsu in China.
[3] Mongolia had not participated in PISA previously but was expected to participate from 2021. North Korea does not participate in PISA.

countryside consistently perform less well than those who reside in the city (Ren & Zhou, 2019).

East Asia has a very long history of literary practice. With China being the largest and oldest country in East Asia, its writing system has a profound impact in the region. Written language first appeared in China on oracle bones in around 1400 BC. Since then, the Chinese writing system has undergone a long period of evolution to transform into the characters used today. The modern Chinese writing system is used not only by the 1.4 billion people in Mainland China but also in Chinese-speaking regions such as Hong Kong, Macau, and Taiwan. It is further used by Chinese-heritage speakers in Singapore, Malaysia, and countries around the world. Historically, Chinese characters were the standard written symbols used in Japan and Korea (Feather & Sturges, 2003). However, most East Asian countries are biscriptal. Both Japan and Korea eventually developed their own scripts due to the mismatch between their spoken languages and Chinese characters. Today, the Japanese writing system consists of both kanji (Chinese characters) and kana; in Korea, Hanja (based on Chinese characters) has largely been replaced by Hangul. Mongolia also has a captivating history of coexisting scripts. It adopted the Cyrillic script under the influence of the Soviet Union in the 1940s. While the Cyrillic script is now the only official script in the country, the older Mongolian script has been kept, representing the traditional culture.

In what follows, we first present an overview of the writing systems used in China, Japan, Korea, and Mongolia, followed by a description of the educational system in relation to literacy in each country. We dedicate the rest of the chapter to individual variation, neurological foundations, and environmental factors related to literacy development in Chinese, because of the language's long-standing history, diverse populations of speakers, and major impacts on other East Asian languages and writing systems.[4] We conclude the chapter by presenting a brief comparison of the factors related to literacy development in Chinese, Japanese, and Korean.

9.2 Writing Systems in East Asia

Modern Chinese characters originated from pictograms that resembled the shape of the object described. In this sense, they share some resemblance to other ancient writing systems in the world such as Egyptian hieroglyphs. The Chinese script now relies on morphosyllabic coding to map print onto speech and meaning (Leong & Tamaoka, 1995). Each character typically represents a syllable and a morpheme. While there are approximately 90,000 characters in

---

[4] For a review of literacy development in Japanese see Koda (2017), in Korean see Wang et al. (2017).

modern Chinese (Xu & Wang, 2004), a college-educated person typically recognizes 5,000 characters (Hue, 2003). About 80 to 90 percent of commonly used characters are semantic-phonetic compound characters formed by combining a phonetic radical and a semantic radical (Shu et al., 2003). For example, the character 粒 /li 4/ (a grain of rice) consists of the phonetic radical 立 /li4/, which provides information about the pronunciation, and the semantic radical 米 /mi 3/ (rice), which provides clues for the meaning. The other three common types of characters are pictographs, ideographs, and semantic-semantic compounds. Pictographs are simple characters originated from drawings of objects, for example, 山 /shan 1/ (mountain). Ideographs are modified pictographs used to express abstract ideas in iconic forms, for example, 上 /shang 4/ (up). Semantic-semantic compound characters are formed by combining two semantic radicals. For example, the character 明 (brightness) is formed by combining 日 (sun) and 月 (moon), both of which contribute to the meaning.

The Chinese writing system was brought to Japan in the fourth and fifth centuries. It was introduced to the elites to familiarize them with Chinese culture. Since then, the development of Japanese has been heavily influenced by Chinese in both script and vocabulary (Loveday, 1996). The Modern Japanese writing system consists of two scripts, syllable-based kana (hiragana and katakana) and morpheme-based Chinese characters, Kanji (Taylor & Taylor, 1995). The Japanese hiragana and katakana orthographies consist of five vowels, and each vowel has a short and long version. Hiragana is mostly used for words that are not represented in kanji and for verbs and adjective conjugations with kanji. Most loan words from English and other European languages are written in katakana. For example, the word *restaurant* has been adapted into Japanese as Resutoranto/ (ラストランと). On the other hand, kanji characters are used extensively to represent words borrowed from Chinese. While a kanji character keeps the original monosyllabic Chinese pronunciation, the spoken sound of the Japanese word is also added to represent its lexical identity. As such, most kanji characters consist of two or more readings. For example, the character 森 uses its Japanese pronunciation /mori/ when it appears alone, but it adopts the Chinese pronunciation /sin/ in the word forest (森林 /sinrin/).

For a long time, Korean was a spoken language without any written scripts. Chinese characters were brought to Korea around the third century. Upper-class Koreans have since used Chinese characters in royal and historical documents (Holcombe, 2017). However, many poorly educated Koreans were nonliterate due to the fundamental differences between the Korean and Chinese languages. To solve this problem, King SeJong invented the Korean script so that people with little education could have access to literacy (Feather & Sturges, 2003). The Korean script was officially published in 1446, and was named Hangul (or "Hunminjeongeum"), meaning "the correct sounds to instruct the people."

Hangul was initially opposed by the literary elite, and Hanja remained the prestige script for the next few hundred years. Hangul became the official writing system in the 1880s due to the efforts of the nationalist movement. The use of Hanja has been in decline since the 1970s and it was banned in North Korea completely (Kim-Renaud, 1997; Lee, 1990).

Hangul is a syllabic alphabet consisting of seventeen vowels and eleven consonants. The letters were carefully designed to indicate the shape of the mouth and placement of the tongue when articulating the respective sound. For example, the letter /n/ represents the tongue touching the upper larynx (ㄴ) inside the mouth when articulating the /n/ sound, and the letter /m/ (ㅁ) shows the closed mouth shape when pronouncing the /m/ sound. Hangul is arranged in a nonlinear fashion orthographically. Its letters are shaped into square-like blocks, and the alphabet letters are arranged from left to right, then top to bottom (example: /감/, pronounced as /kam/) (Taylor & Taylor, 1995). Modern Korean includes native Korean words and loan words. More than 70 percent of the loan words come from Chinese and can be written in Hangul or Chinese characters (Hanja). Native Korean words and loan words with European roots are only written using Hangul. Although it remains debatable when and how Chinese scripts were first introduced to Korea, Chinese culture and scripts gained their popularity in Korea during the Han and Tang dynasties (approximately 108 BC to AD 677). Western loan words, on the other hand, were introduced to Korea through Japanese mostly from 1890 to 1945 (Sohn, 2006).

Modern-day Mongolia uses two scripts. The Cyrillic script was introduced in the 1940s, when Mongolia was a satellite state of the Soviet Union. It is a phonemic writing system that includes all the letters from the Russian alphabet with an additional two letters representing vowels unique to the Mongolian language (Grivelet, 2001; Sanders, 2013). The Mongolian script boasts a much longer history – it was created at the end of the twelfth century, shortly before the start of the Yuan dynasty. The Mongolian script is considered as an abugida script, with its writing arranged in vertical columns and from left to right on a page. While the adoption of the Cyrillic script dramatically improved the literacy rate in Mongolia, the Mongolian script was nearly extinct around the same time. This script was only used in Inner Mongolia in Northern China and continues to be used there today. Despite several attempts to revitalize the Mongolian script in the 1980s and 1990s, the Cyrillic script remains the only official script in Mongolia. The Mongolian script is taught as a school subject but rarely used in daily life (Grivelet, 2001). The two writing systems represent different attributes. The Mongolian script is associated with Mongolia's traditional culture and history. The Cyrillic script, on the other hand, is appreciated for its ease of learning and regarded as an instrument for communication (Grivelet, 1999).

9.3 Literacy Education in China, Japan, and Korea

Literacy education is highly valued in East Asian societies due to the Confucian tradition of student enlightenment (Cheng, 2014; Sheng, 2014).[5] Literacy also served practical functions in feudal times – when the general public was mostly illiterate, it was important to have a literate member to handle a family's business affairs in the written form (Lee, 2000; Seeberg, 1990). Furthermore, achieving a high level of literacy was nearly the only way for students to excel in the imperial examination (科举) and become "scholar bureaucrats" (士大夫) (Zuo, 2003). In today's China, education continues to be perceived as an effective way to move up the social ladder. For children of farmers, for example, a university degree enables them to escape from the harsh living conditions of the countryside to resettle in cities; for city residents, good education helps them find high-paying jobs (Seeberg, 1990; Seeberg, 1993). The history of the imperial examination shows a widespread and enduring impact on education across East Asia. Japan was the first country to follow China in adopting the imperial examination system, whereas Korea had the longest-standing and most complete system outside of China (Liu, 2006). Even today, education is regarded as a high priority in Japanese and Korean families. Students put extensive amounts of effort into studying to prepare themselves for university entry exams, as attending university improves one's socioeconomic level (Kell & Kell, 2013; Mani & Trines, 2018).

Modern-day China has a nine-year compulsory education system from Grades 1 to 9 (Li & Rao, 2005). Children officially learn to read when they enter Grade 1. Beginning readers learn to read Chinese using Pinyin, a transliteration system that denotes character pronunciation. Pinyin contains mostly the same letters as the Roman alphabet, and it is completely regular in letter–sound correspondences. A similar phonetic system called Zhuyin Fuhao is used in Taiwan, except that the symbols in this system come from radicals and subcomponents of ancient characters (Huang, 2019). In Mainland China, initially, Pinyin syllables are printed above all characters. As children's literacy improves, use of Pinyin in children's text becomes limited to unfamiliar characters and then entirely disappears (Leong & Tamaoka, 1995). By the end of Grade 6, a child is expected to recognize 3,000 characters and to spell 2,500 of them (Li & Rao, 2000). Due to the high memory load of learning to read a morphosyllabic script, dictation and repeated copying of characters are commonly used in literacy instruction. In Hong Kong, children start to learn to read Chinese characters as early as in the first year of kindergarten, at the age of three (McBride-Chang et al., 2008). The "look and say" method is commonly used to teach Chinese characters without the help of any phonemic coding

---

[5] Mongolia is not included in this section due to a lack of relevant information in the literature.

system (Yeung et al., 2016a). Education in Hong Kong highlights the importance of "bi-literacy and tri-lingualism," meaning children are required to become trilingual in Cantonese, Mandarin, and English, and biliterate in Chinese and English (Lee & Leung, 2012).

The compulsory education system is also nine years in Japan (Foreign Press Center, Japan, 2010). Japanese students learn 105 kana in the forms of hiragana and katakana as well as 1,006 kanji in elementary school. It is common for Japanese children to start formal schooling with basic mastery of hiragana. Students begin to learn katakana and kanji from first grade. Students are expected to master katakana symbols by Grade 3 and to acquire 1,006 kanji characters by Grade 6, and an additional 1,130 kanji characters by the end of junior high school, in Grade 9.

The South Korean Ministry of Education is currently expanding its nine-year compulsory education to twelve years and is expected to achieve this goal for the entire country in the near future. Similar to Japan, Korean children often begin formal schooling with a basic understanding of Hangul. By elementary school, children are expected to master basic grapheme-to-phoneme correspondences for Hangul letters and learn more complex concepts that alter the phonology of some words such as resyllabification, consonantal assimilation, and the simplification of multiple coda. Currently, 1,800 "common Chinese characters" designated by the ministry of education in Korea are included in the school curriculum. Students are required to master 1,300 Chinese characters by Grade 9. North Korea, on the other hand, implements an eleven-year compulsory education system. Starting from the ages of four to five, students attend one year of kindergarten, four years of elementary school, and six years of middle school (Reed, 1997). However, Chinese is excluded from the education curriculum in primary and secondary schools in North Korea (Reed, 1997; Song, 2002).

9.4 Literacy Development: Focus on China

The Chinese writing system is among the oldest in the world. Unlike many other ancient scripts that were buried in the long course of history, Chinese characters are still in use today, and are used by the largest population in the world (Shu, 2003). Logographic symbols were encrypted on pottery about 4,800 years ago (Boltz, 1994). Around the fourteenth century BC, writing symbols were inscribed in oracle bones. These oracle-bone inscriptions contain more than 3,000 words, including nouns, verbs, adjectives, and pronouns. In the late Shang dynasty (approximately 1,000 BC), writing started to appear on bronze. The script form on the bronzes is very similar to the oracle-bone inscription sand that gained its popularity in the times of the West Zhou, the dynasty that followed Shang (Li, 2002).

From 259 to 210 BCE, the Qin Empire, the first united dynasty in China, standardized writing, currency, and metric systems across the country. The emperor modified Chinese characters and their writing structure so they could be used consistently. This unified writing system is named Xiao Zhuan (小篆). Xiao Zhuan then evolved into a more simplified script called Li Shu[6] (隶书) in the Han dynasty (approximately 200 BC). Li Shu was originally used by slaves and peasants due to its simplified form. As its popularity increased among the general public, this form of writing was adopted by the elite class and became the official system across the country. The number of characters significantly increased in the Han Dynasty, with more than 9,000 characters identified in the earliest Chinese dictionary, "Shuo Wen Jie Zi" (说文解字) (Lan & Matsuoka, 2018). Later in the East Han dynasty (approximately AD 25–200), Li Shu gradually evolved into Cao Shu (草书), Kai Shu (楷书), and Xing Shu (行书), all of which are still practiced by calligraphers today.

In 1964, the government in Mainland China simplified 2,238 commonly used characters. These simplified characters have also been adopted in Singapore, whereas traditional characters continue to be used in Hong Kong, Macau, and Taiwan (Bökset, 2006). Because Chinese characters were simplified based on a set of principles, and many simplified characters bear a resemblance to corresponding traditional characters, a fluent reader educated in one script is typically able to read the other (Liu & Hsiao, 2012; Bökset, 2006). However, the simplification of the Chinese script remains highly controversial. Some scholars argue that simplified characters are less aesthetically pleasing and are disconnected from Chinese history and culture (Goodman et al., 2012). Supporters contend that simplification promoted literacy among Chinese people, as more than half of the Chinese population were illiterate or semiliterate at the time.

9.5 Individual Variation in Chinese Reading Development

9.5.1 Role of Phonological Awareness

China is a country where many different dialects are spoken.[7] These varieties are generally classified into seven major groups: Mandarin, Wu, Xiang, Gan, Hakka, Min, and Yue (Li & Thompson, 1981). Among these, Mandarin is the standard language of China and used by the largest percentage of the population. Unlike English, which contains more than 6,000 syllables, Mandarin has only about 400 basic syllables and a total of 1,300 syllables when different

---

[6] Shu (书) refers to the form of writing in Chinese calligraphy.
[7] While the different varieties in Chinese are typically referred to as dialects, they may be different to the point of being mutually unintelligible, though all of them are represented by the same Chinese writing system.

tones are considered (Duanmu, 2007). Mandarin consists of twenty-one initial consonants, two final consonants, three glides, and six vowels (Duanmu, 2007). Possible syllable combinations in Mandarin include V (爱, /ai4/), CV (大, /da4/), VC (安, /an1/), and CVC (晚, /wan3/) (Yang, 1988). Mandarin is a tonal language; when the tone of a syllable changes, it turns into a different morpheme. For example, 妈 /ma1/ means *mother*, whereas 马 /ma3/ means *horse*. Mandarin has four different tones – high level, rising, fall-rise and high falling. Tones are usually indicated by either tone marks or the numbers 1, 2, 3, and 4 for ease of writing. A small number of syllables (e.g., 了 /le/) can be marked with a neutral tone, also called a zeroth tone. These syllables are shorter and less meaningful than other syllables. Chinese has a large number of homophones. On average, each tone syllable corresponds to five morphemes. These morphemes share the same pronunciation but are represented by idiosyncratic characters in print (e.g., 言, 岩, 盐, 颜, 严, 研, 阎, /yan2/) (Duanmu, 2007).

Cantonese is a dialect mainly spoken in Southeast China, including the provinces of Guangdong and Guangxi, and Hong Kong and Macao. Cantonese has a more complex phonological structure than Mandarin (Chen et al., 2004). It consists of nineteen initial consonants, eight final consonants, and eight vowels (So & Dodd, 1995, Zeng, 1994). There are six tones in Cantonese: high level, high rising, mid-level, low falling, low rising, and low level. There are also three "entering tones," the high-, mid- and low-stopped tones, which appear with syllables ending with /p/, /t/, and /k/. These tones are much shorter in duration and are considered allotones of the three level tones (Bauer & Benedict, 1997; So & Dodd, 1995). Despite the considerable differences between Cantonese and Mandarin, the two dialects, as well as all other dialects in China, are represented by the same written text, based on Mandarin. In other words, all Chinese children learn to read in Mandarin, though for many it is not their native dialect. This situation creates unique challenges that are currently understudied and need to be addressed by future research.

Phonological awareness refers to the ability to reflect on and manipulate smaller units of sounds in spoken words (Goswami, 2000). Phonological awareness consists of three different levels – syllable, onset-rime, and phoneme in most languages (Lin, Cheng, & Wang, 2018; Yoon et al., 2002). Tone awareness is a unique aspect of phonological awareness in Chinese (Chen & Pasquarella, 2017; Treiman & Zukowski, 1991). There is a one-to-one association between syllables and morphemes in Chinese, and both correspond to characters. For this reason, syllable awareness is salient for children at an early age (Pan et al., 2016; Zhang et al., 2014). In Mainland China, when beginning readers learn to read characters using Pinyin, a syllable is usually split into two basic components: an onset (声母 /sheng1mu3/), which is the initial consonant of the syllable, and a rime (韵母 /yu4mu3/), which includes the rest of the syllable (Třísková, 2011). As a result, onset-rime awareness is also important for reading characters. Finally, because Chinese is a tonal language, Chinese speakers must possess tone awareness to distinguish morphemes with the same syllable but different tones (少 /shao3/ -less, and 勺/shao2/-spoon).

An extensive body of research has found phonological awareness to be critical for success in word reading in alphabetic languages (Lesaux & Siegel, 2003; Linan-Thompson et al., 2006). Chinese, as a morphosyllabic script, differs substantially on orthography–phonology correspondences from alphabetic languages (i.e., Korean, English) or languages based on alphasyllabaries (i.e., Japanese). The link between phonological awareness, particularly phonemic awareness, and reading is less straightforward due to the lack of grapheme–phoneme correspondences in Chinese. However, given the use of Pinyin and phonetic radicals to denote character pronunciations, some aspects of phonological awareness, such syllable and tone awareness, may still play an important role in Chinese reading (e.g., Ruan et al., 2018). It has been found that learning a phonetic alphabet such as Pinyin enhances phonological awareness among Chinese children. Children from Mainland China and Taiwan perform better on phonological-awareness measures compared to their peers from Hong Kong, who read without the assistance of a transliteration system (Huang & Hanley, 1995; McBride-Chang et al., 2004). Furthermore, research has shown that syllable and tone awareness are both significant predictors of word reading in Chinese (McBride-Chang et al., 2008; Tong et al., 2015). For example, syllable awareness was found to act as a stronger predictor of Chinese word reading than onset-rime awareness in the early grades (Pan et al., 2016; Shu, Peng, & McBride-Chang, 2008). By contrast, research examining onset-rime awareness has generated mixed findings. While some studies found onset-rime awareness to predict Chinese word reading (e.g., Ho & Bryant, 1997; Wang et al., 2014), others did not (e.g., McBride-Chang et al., 2008).

9.5.2 Role of Morphological Awareness

Morphemes are the smallest units of meaning. They are combined to build complex words in a language. A root carries the meaning of a word, whereas affixes are auxiliary components that attach to a base.[8] Affixes can be further divided into inflectional and derivational affixes. Inflectional affixes denote grammatical functions (e.g., *book-books*). Derivational affixes form a new word from the base unit, and this new word often belongs to a different word class (e.g., *book-bookish*). The morphological system in Chinese has many distinct features. Chinese does not have grammatical agreement, morphological paradigms, and morphophonemic alternation (Packard, 2000). About 70 percent of Chinese words are lexical compounds formed by combining two

---

[8] A base may be a root word or a complex word that already contains an affix.

roots (e.g., *cow: beef meat*) (Packard, 2000). In Chinese, one morpheme is typically represented by one syllable in its spoken form and one character in print, for example 天/tian1/ "sky" (DeFrancis, 1984). Occasionally, loan words consist of more than one syllable, for example, 咖啡/ka1fei1/ "coffee," because characters are used to indicate sounds. In addition to homophonic morphemes, Chinese contains homographic morphemes, which have the same pronunciation and orthographic form. In other words, the same character can correspond to different morphemes. For example, 面 /mian4/ means *flour* in 面粉/mian4-fen3/ (flour powder) but *surface* in 桌面/zhuo1mian4/ (desk top).

Morphological awareness can be defined as the awareness of the morphological makeup of words and the ability to reflect on and manipulate their constituent morphemic parts. Due to the prominence of lexical compounding and a high density of homophony in Chinese, researchers have examined the role of compound awareness and homophone/homograph awareness in children's reading development. A morphological construction task is often used to measure compound awareness (Chen et al., 2009; McBride-Chang et al., 2003). Children are first presented with the definition of a familiar word and are then asked to create a novel word that has the same morphological structure. For example, "Striped horse (zebra) is a horse with stripes on its body. What should we call a cow with stripes on its body?" (斑马是身上有斑纹的一种马，那么身上有斑纹的牛我们叫什么?). The correct answer is "striped cow" (斑牛). Homophone/homograph awareness is often assessed with a morpheme-judgment task. For example, in a homophone-awareness task, children are aurally presented with a word containing the target morpheme (e.g., /hua4/ in 画家 /hua4jia1/ – "paint artist: painter") and then are asked to choose the word that contains the same morpheme from several options (e.g., 话剧/hua4ju4/– "speech opera: drama"; and 画布 /hua4bu4/ – "paint fabric: canvas") (McBride-Chang et al., 2003; McBride-Chang et al., 2005; Shu et al., 2006). In a homograph-awareness task, children are aurally presented with a compound word containing a target morpheme (e.g., /hua1/ in 花园 /hua1yuan2/ – "flower yard: garden"), then asked to produce two words with the target morpheme having different meanings in the words (e.g., /hua1/ in 花朵 /hua1-duo3/ – "flower blossom" and /hua1/ in 花钱 /hua1qian2/ – "spend money") (Xie et al., 2019).

Both lexical compounding awareness and homophone/homograph sensitivity have been found to predict reading outcomes among Chinese children (Chen et al., 2009; Tong, Tong, & McBride, 2017). As the majority of Chinese words are compound words, it is crucial to understand how morphemes can be legally combined to form morphologically complex words (Chan, 2013). Studies have found that after controlling for other relevant variables, compound awareness has significant effects on Chinese character reading (e.g., Liu & McBride-Chang, 2010), vocabulary (e.g., Liu & McBride-Chang,

2010; Liu, McBride-Chang et al., 2013), and reading comprehension (e.g., Li et al., 2017; Xie et al., 2019). In addition, the high density of homophones and homographs requires children to distinguish among characters that have the same pronunciation (and sometimes also the same orthographic form) but represent different morphemes. Research shows that children who are more sensitive to homophones (Chung & Hu, 2007) and homographs (Li et al., 2009) perform better on Chinese character reading and vocabulary tasks (Cheng et al., 2017; ; Ku & Anderson, 2003; Liu, McBride-Chang et al., 2013; Shu et al., 2006; Wu et al., 2009). Due to the one-to-one mapping between syllables and morphemes in Chinese, studies comparing morphological and phonological awareness simultaneously often report that the former plays a larger role in reading (e.g., Li et al., 2002; McBride-Chang et al., 2005; Pan et al., 2015). This pattern is confirmed by a meta-analysis by Ruan et al. (2018), who reported that morphological awareness was more strongly associated with word reading and reading comprehension than with phonological awareness in Chinese. Interestingly, the same study found phonological awareness to play a stronger role than morphological awareness in reading English.

9.5.3 Role of Orthographic Knowledge

Characters are composed of strokes, which are the smallest units of written form in Chinese. A stroke is usually a line (一) or a dot (、). A stroke can be straight or curved (丿), vertical (丨), horizontal, or diagonal (\), and it can contain a "hook" (亅) (Taylor & Taylor, 1995). The visual complexity of a character is usually identified by the number of individual strokes within the character. Characters of higher frequency usually contain fewer strokes, whereas those of lower frequency have more strokes (Li et al., 2016; Shu et al., 2003). On average, the total number of strokes in characters written in the simplified script is approximately 22.5 percent fewer than those written in the traditional script (Gao & Kao, 2002). Interestingly, readers who have been exposed to traditional Chinese characters showed higher visual-perception skills than those who have been exposed to simplified characters (Chang, Chen, & Perfetti, 2018). Radicals, formed by stroke combinations, are functional units of Chinese characters. There are approximately 800 phonetic and 200 semantic radicals in Chinese (Hoosain, 1992). Most radicals are independent characters with their own meanings and pronunciations; a small number of them are in bound forms that can only appear as a part of a character (Shu et al., 2003). Among the four common types of characters, pictographs and ideographs are simple characters without an internal structure. Semantic-phonetic and semantic-semantic compound characters are complex characters made up of radicals. The majority of compound characters consist of a left–right structure (e.g, 彩 /cai3/); others have a top–

bottom structure (e.g, 菜 /cai4/) or an inside–outside (surrounding) structure (困 /kun4/) (Zhang et al., 2016).

Orthographic knowledge in Chinese refers to knowledge of the internal structure of Chinese characters (Ho, Ng, & Ng, 2003). This knowledge includes the position, function, and legal combination of phonetic and semantic radicals that form compound characters. With respect to position, semantic radicals usually appear on the left (75 percent) or top (15 percent) of a character (Feldman & Siok, 1999), whereas the common positions for phonetic radicals are right or bottom. Most radicals always appear in the same position, but a small number of them appear in different positions across different characters. Functionally, semantic and phonetic radicals provide cues to meaning and pronunciation respectively. The Chinese writing system is more accurate in representing meaning than phonology. Semantic radicals are generally informative of character meaning. In contrast, a phonetic radical has the same syllable as the character in only about 40 percent of the characters (Shu, 2003). The percentage is even lower when tone is considered. Finally, not all semantic and phonetic radicals can combine to form characters. Simply combining a semantic radical and a phonetic radical in their legal positions may or may not form a real character together.

Due to the unique characteristics of the Chinese writing system, a variety of measures have been designed to assess orthographic knowledge. For example, in an orthographic judgment task, children are presented with different types of "novel" characters and asked to judge whether each one could be a real character (Li et al., 2012). These items may include line drawings with no conventional stroke patterns (▦), noncharacters with real radicals in illegal positions (悸), pseudo-characters with real radicals that appear in legal positions but do not combine together (栱), pseudo-characters with subcomponents that do not exist in Chinese (江). Furthermore, specific tasks have been designed to assess children's awareness of the position and function of phonetic (Ho, Yau, & Au, 2003; Yeung et al., 2016a) and semantic radicals (Yeung et al., 2011; Zhang et al., 2016). For example, in a phonetic radical knowledge task, a pseudo-compound character (砵) is paired with three real characters, one with the same semantic radical (破), one with the same phonetic radical (味), and one that does not share any radicals in common (埋). Children are asked to choose the character (味) that has the same pronunciation as the target character. In a semantic radical knowledge task, each item is paired with four pictures, and children are asked to choose the picture that best represents the meaning of the semantic radical (Ho, Ng, & Ng, 2003).

Research has shown that children start to form mental representations of radical forms and positions in Grade 1, and these representations are well established by Grade 3 (Chan & Nunes, 1998; Ho, Yau, & Au, 2003; Li et al., 2012). Children are faster at rejecting noncharacters that violate legal radical positions than pseudo-characters that follow the legality of radical positions in lexical-decision tasks (Qian et al., 2015; Wang, Perfetti, & Liu, 2005). Children are able to derive meanings of unfamiliar compound characters using familiar semantic radicals (Anderson et al., 2003; Ho, Ng, & Ng, 2003; Shu & Anderson, 1997) and pronunciations using phonetic radicals (Anderson et al., 2003; Ho & Bryant, 1997). The pronunciation of an unfamiliar character (e.g, 蜻 /qing1/) can also be predicted by making an analogy to a character (e.g., 清 /qing1/) with the same phonetic radical (e.g., 青 /qing1/) (Ho, Ng, & Ng, 2003). Importantly, research shows that orthographic knowledge of both semantic and phonetic radicals is related to word reading (Leong et al., 2011; Peng, Li, & Yang, 1997; Yeung et al., 2016b) and spelling (Yeung et al., 2016b). For example, two studies (Ho, Ng, & Ng, 2003; Yeung et al., 2011) observed that semantic radical knowledge predicted word reading in Grades 1 and 3, and phonetic radical knowledge predicted word reading in Grades 1, 3, and 5. Yeung et al. (2016a) found that both types of radical knowledge predicted word spelling in Grades 2 and 4. Finally, knowledge of semantic radicals has been found to contribute to reading comprehension (Ho, Ng, et al., 2003). Because the majority of the compound characters introduced in the elementary school curriculum are semantically transparent, semantic radicals provide reliable information about character meaning (Shu et al., 2003). For example, Yeung et al. (2016a) reported that semantic radical knowledge uniquely contributed to reading comprehension among Chinese children in Grade 4.

9.5.4 Word Reading and Spelling

According to the lexical-quality hypothesis (Perfetti, 2007), word identity consists of orthography, phonology, grammar, and meaning, and these features are bound together to secure coherence (binding). Studies have provided evidence in support of the lexical-quality hypothesis in Chinese (Guan & Wang, 2017). Accordingly, phonological awareness, morphological awareness, and orthographic knowledge have all been found to contribute to word reading in Chinese children. With respect to phonological awareness, research has shown that both syllable and tone awareness play an important role in Chinese word reading due to the salience of these linguistic units (McBride-Chang et al., 2008; Tong et al., 2015). In terms of morphological awareness, both lexical compounding awareness (Liu & McBride-Chang, 2010) and homophone/homograph sensitivity (Chung & Hu, 2007) predict word reading because Chinese consists of a large number of compound words and homophones/homographs. In addition, the knowledge of the position, function, and legal combination of phonetic and semantic radicals of compound characters is a reliable contributor to Chinese word reading (Ho, Yau, & Au, 2003; Leong et al., 2011;

Peng et al., 1997; Yeung et al., 2016a). Metalinguistic skills have also been found to contribute to spelling. Previous studies have shown that phonological awareness (Tong et al., 2009; Yeung et al., 2011), orthographic processing (Ho et al., 2003; Yeung et al., 2015), and morphological awareness (Tong et al., 2009; Yeung et al., 2016a) are all related to spelling acquisition in Chinese.

Because Chinese characters are visually complex, repetition of character writing, following the correct stroke order, is a popular approach to fostering children's literacy development (Lam & McBride, 2018; Pine, Ping'an, & Ren Song, 2003). Several recent studies have examined the role of visual-motor integration in reading and spelling Chinese characters. Visual-motor integration refers to the ability to coordinate visual information and hand movement (Longcamp et al., 2005) and is measured by character-copying tasks in Chinese children. This small body of research has provided evidence that visual-motor integration is related to both reading (McBride-Chang et al., 2011; Meng, Wydell, & Bi, 2019) and spelling (Lam & McBride, 2018) in Chinese. For example, Wang, McBride-Chang, and Chan (2014) observed that after controlling for age and nonverbal intelligence, the ability to copy unfamiliar scripts (Korean, Vietnamese, and Hebrew) uniquely contributed to spelling in kindergarteners (Wang et al., 2014). McBride-Chang et al. (2011) reported that this ability differentiated Chinese children in Grades 3 and 4 with and without dyslexia and uniquely contributed to reading in the combined sample. In addition, orthographic working memory, measured using a delayed copying task (where children were briefly presented with unfamiliar characters and then asked to write them down from memory), was found to predict both word reading (Chung et al., 2011) and spelling (Mo, McBride, & Yip, 2018; Wang et al., 2014) among kindergartners in Hong Kong.

9.5.5 Reading Comprehension

The simple view of reading model (SVR) proposes that reading comprehension is the cross product of two main components, decoding and listening comprehension (Gough & Tunmer, 1986; Hoover & Gough, 1990). Skilled decoding is defined by Hoover and Gough (1990) as the ability to "rapidly derive a representation from printed input that allows access to the appropriate entry in the mental lexicon" (p. 130), whereas listening comprehension refers to the ability to use phonological, semantic, syntactic, and discourse information to understand language (Hogan et al., 2014). Although Chinese is represented by a logographic writing system, there is evidence supporting the SVR model in Chinese (Ho et al., 2017; Joshi et al., 2012; Yeung et al., 2016b). Since characters cannot be read through grapheme–phoneme correspondences, the decoding component in the SVR model is measured by character- and word-reading accuracy and fluency. As for listening comprehension, studies have measured children's vocabulary knowledge, morphological awareness, morphosyntactic skills, and discourse skills (Chik et al., 2012; Yeung et al., 2013). Generally speaking, studies examining the SVR model in Chinese have found that decoding and listening comprehension explain a significant amount of variance in reading comprehension, confirming the applicability of the SVR model (Ho et al., 2017;Yeung et al., 2016b; Zhang et al., 2012). For example, in Yeung et al. (2016b), the best-fitting model with decoding and listening comprehension explained 83 percent of the variance in reading comprehension among Grade 1 children in Hong Kong, with decoding and listening comprehension accounting for 37 and 46 percent of the variance respectively.

As mentioned in the previous sections, research has examined the contribution of metalinguistic skills (morphological awareness, phonological awareness, and orthographic knowledge) to reading comprehension in Chinese. Studies have demonstrated that morphological awareness, including compound awareness and homophone awareness, contribute to both concurrent and longitudinal reading comprehension, even after controlling for phonological awareness and speed naming (Tong et al., 2009; Xie et al., 2019; Zhang et al., 2012; Zhang et al., 2014). Phonological awareness is also shown to play an significant role in reading comprehension among Chinese children (Lau & Chan, 2007; Ruan et al., 2018; Zhang et al., 2012; Zhang et al., 2014). Orthographic knowledge, especially knowledge of the semantic radical, is related to reading comprehension in Chinese due to its contribution to character meaning (Ho, Ng, & Ng, 2003; Yeung et al., 2011). In addition to metalinguistic skills, cognitive skills such as working memory have been found to predict reading comprehension among Chinese children (Jing & Lu, 2009; Lu & Zhang, 2007). Jing and Lu (2009), for example, observed that higher working-memory capacity was associated with better Chinese reading comprehension.

9.6 Neurocognitive Foundations

The unique features of Chinese orthography have intrigued neuroscientists for many decades. Researchers often use the comparisons between Chinese and English, or between character- and sound-based orthographic systems within Japanese and Korean, to understand the universality and cross-linguistic diversity made possible by the human mind (see also Rigatti et al., Chapter 12 in this volume).

There has been some disagreement in the field as to the extent to which Chinese speakers engage and develop the phonological network in the process of learning to read. An example of a phonological-awareness task is a rhyme-judgment task, such as the question "Do *cat* and *hat* rhyme?" In a milestone study of phonological awareness and dyslexia in Chinese, Siok et al. (2008) used a rhyme-judgment task and found that Chinese-speaking children recruited left inferior and middle frontal gyrus (IFG/MFG) regions but did not significantly activate the left superior temporal gyrus (STG) regions, classically associated with phonological processing. Similarly, Brennan et al. (2013) showed that only English speakers (and no Chinese speakers) showed a developmental increase in activation in the left temporal and parietal regions associated with phonological processes. Thus, literacy development and dyslexia in Chinese are indeed associated with the development of neural pathways for phonological processing.

Phonological development has also been found to be closely associated with morphological development. The neuroimaging task commonly used to study morphological awareness in Chinese and other languages is a semantic-relatedness task. For example, the words *class<u>room</u>–bed<u>room</u>* are morphologically related whereas *class<u>room</u>–mush<u>room</u>* are morphologically unrelated. Using this paradigm, Liu, Tao et al. (2013) observed that only typically developing readers (and no children with dyslexia) showed stronger activation for related versus unrelated pairs in left inferior frontal regions. Interestingly, the magnitude of this activation was stronger in typical readers with better reading proficiency, but weaker in children with dyslexia with better reading proficiency. The authors interpreted the finding as suggesting that reading success in Chinese dyslexics is associated with whole-word rather than morphological deconstruction strategies. In other words, neuroimaging evidence suggests that Chinese speakers develop distinct neural mechanisms for whole-word recognition versus phonological as well as morphological word processing and that the latter two might be especially affected by dyslexia in Chinese (Zou et al., 2019).

Importantly, Chinese characters are more visually complex than English words and their complexity may influence children's neural organization for orthographic processing. Indeed, research evidenced that English-speaking children show stronger activation for line drawings than printed words in brain regions associated with orthographic processing, including occipitotemporal regions and Visual Word Form Area (VWFA). In contrast, Chinese learners show similar patterns of brain activity for both (Krafnick et al., 2016). Furthermore, as Chinese children become better readers, they develop a stronger neural association between VWFA and brain regions supporting language (left Inferior Fusiform Gyrus, Supra-Marginal Gyrus) and handwriting (Exner's area; Li et al., 2017). The findings are taken to support the idea that universally, learning to read is associated with the emergence of a tightly interconnected neural network that supports language in speech and in print (Marks et al., 2019). In other words, universally, learning to read is associated with the development of visual word processing regions as well as a tight interconnection between those regions and regions for spoken language processing. Specific to Chinese, there might be a tighter interconnection between neural processes for phonology and morphology as well as more extensive engagement of occipitotemporal regions and motor systems that support recognition and writing of characters (Cao & Perfetti, 2016).

9.7 Environmental Factors Related to Chinese Literacy Development

Literacy environment in early childhood education differs across different regions in China. Following the "readiness" approach, educators in Mainland China believe that children need to be physically and neurologically ready for formal literacy education (Liang et al., 1997). As a result, formal literacy education only starts when children enter Grade 1 at age six (Li & Rao, 2000). Nevertheless, young children are often exposed to informal literacy activities at home or other early-childhood-education settings. Chinese parents are usually heavily involved in creating home literacy environments (Li & Rao, 2005). A survey showed that about 50 percent of Chinese households possessed 20 to 100 books for children, and most parents from urban households carried out shared book-reading activities with their children (Zhu & Yang, 2003). Studies have found that informal literacy experiences at home, including shared book reading and storytelling, contribute to children's vocabulary development (Chen et al., 2010; Zhao, Zhou, & Chen, 2008). Educators in Hong Kong, on the other hand, believe that formal literacy education should start as early as possible. This formal approach focuses on character learning. Hong Kong children are introduced to formal literacy education upon entering kindergarten at age three (Li & Rao, 2005).

Although the Chinese government has made continuous efforts to guarantee fundamental education among school-aged children, including implementing the nine-year compulsory educational system from 1986 onward, and investing 4 percent of its GDP in education (Zhu, 2018), the rural–urban literacy gap remains large in China (Wang, Li, & Wang, 2018). For example, in Gansu province, 56.7 percent of students from rural regions did not pass the minimum literacy curriculum requirements, whereas only 4.7 percent of students from urban regions failed the requirements. Wang et al. (2018) observed significant rural–urban gaps in literacy attainment in Grades 1, 3, and 5 among students from Shandong and Guizhou provinces. This literacy gap was mediated by parental education level and family literacy. A national survey conducted in 2010 showed that parents who resided in rural areas completed 6.3 years of education, compared to 9.5 years of education by those who resided in urban areas (Zhang, Li, & Xue, 2015). Moreover, parents from rural areas are less able to provide books and extracurricular activities for their children, and are thus unable to create an optimal home environment for literacy development (Hu et al., 2018; Wang et al., 2018; Zhao & Shen, 2010). In addition to home literacy environments, schools in rural areas are confronted with problems that hinder quality education. Schools are located in old or unsafe buildings, with outdated or no technology, and have limited curricular resources. Teachers in rural areas receive lower salaries than their colleagues in the city. As a result, teachers who work in rural schools tend to be less qualified and enthusiastic (Yang et al., 2011).

Migrant children represent another vulnerable group in China. With a large number of people migrating from rural areas to large cities to seek employment opportunities, their children face significant challenges in receiving proper education. Public schools in the city are typically only open to local residents. As a result, children of migrant workers either have to pay expensive fees to enroll in public schools, or attend private schools designated for nonresidents. The quality of education is poor in these private schools, and children are required to pay for their tuition, which brings a financial burden to their families (Ren & Zhou, 2019; Shen, 2008; Yang et al., 2011). Studies have found the quality and continuity of education among migrant children are adversely affected by the instability caused by frequent moving, limited educational resources both at home and school, poor qualifications of teachers, and low expectations (Yang et al., 2011). Yet another group that faces challenges in receiving quality education is that of the "left-behind" children. As parents migrate from rural areas to seek work in cities, their children are often left behind to live with grandparents or other relatives (Hu et al., 2018). Compared to migrant children in urban centers, left-behind children in rural areas have even fewer educational resources at home and, because of the rural setting, in school. They are also more likely to experience anxiety and depression due to the absence of their parents (Fan et al., 2018; Hu et al., 2018; Zhao & Shen, 2010).

9.8 Conclusions and Discussion

To summarize, this chapter describes the writing systems, literacy education, and literacy development in East Asian countries. We focus on Chinese when we discuss literacy development because much less is known about this process in Japanese or Korean. Generally speaking, literacy development in Japanese and Korean shares many similarities with that of Chinese in that phonological awareness, morphological awareness, and orthographic knowledge have been shown to predict literacy skills in these two languages (see Koda, 2017; Wang, Cho, & Li, 2017 for reviews). However, because each language has unique features, the ways in which these aspects of metalinguistic awareness operationalize in Japanese and Korean are not identical to the ways they do so in Chinese. For example, with respect to morphology, both Japanese and Korean have well-developed inflectional and derivational systems (Koda, 2017; Wang et al., 2017), and as such, inflectional and derivational awareness have been shown to contribute to reading in Japanese (Inoue et al., 2017; Muroya et al., 2017) and Korean (Wang, Ko, & Choi, 2009). In contrast, neither inflectional nor derivational awareness plays a major role in reading Chinese. On the other hand, compound awareness may be a significant predictor of literacy skills across the three languages, as all of them are rich in compounds. Although this relationship has been reported by a considerable number of studies in Chinese (e.g., Chen et al., 2009) and Korean (e.g., McBride-Chang et al., 2005), empirical studies still need to be carried out in Japanese.

Indeed, each of the East Asian languages faces unique challenges in literacy acquisition. A major challenge for Chinese is the lack of grapheme–phoneme correspondences. Chinese children must memorize thousands of complex characters to become fluent readers. In addition, the large number of homophones in Chinese adds complexity. Beginning readers struggle with distinguishing homophonic morphemes both in oral language and reading. The Japanese language consists of two scripts, kana and kanji. The combined use of the two scripts makes learning to read a complicated task, as beginning learners must memorize three types of symbols (hiragana, katakana, and kanji) (Koda, 2017). Learning to read Korean also possesses its own challenges. Although Korean is a highly transparent orthography, its orthography is non-linear. Korean characters are arranged in syllable blocks in six different ways. The complex variation in its syllable-block patterns requires greater visual-spatial skills for reading and spelling than those required in Japanese (McBride-Chang et al., 2011; Wang et al., 2017).

Regarding the neural bases of literacy in Japanese and Korean, research suggests that learners develop semi-independent neural pathways for the languages' phonological and character-based writing systems. The neural development and processing of phonological systems closely mirrors those developed for English and other alphabetic languages. For instance, Kita et al. (2013) found greater recruitment of left superior temporal gyrus regions in adults than children while performing on phonological tasks in kana. Furthermore, children with developmental dyslexia showed less left activation in these regions than typically developing children. In contrast, kanji incurs greater engagement of inferior-temporal and VWFA regions associated with complex sound-to-print mappings and orthographic processes (Coderre et al., 2008; Nakamura et al., 2005; Sakurai et al., 2000; Thuy et al., 2004). As in Japanese, comparisons between Hanja and Hangul in Korean also yield evidence of greater engagement of the visual neural systems (bilateral occipital and VWFA) during Hanja reading and greater engagement of the phonological neural systems (frontal and temporoparietal) during Hangul reading (Cho et al., 2014; Lee, 2004; Yoon et al., 2005; Yoon, Cho & Park, 2005). Thus, within-language comparisons between alphabetic and character-based reading systems in Japanese and Korean resemble findings obtained for cross-linguistic comparisons between English and Chinese, suggesting that the developing brain makes special adaptations for learning to read characters that are visually complex and more consistent in their meaning-to-print than sound-to-print mappings (see also Perfetti & Verhoeven, Chapter 11 in this volume).

The literacy rate in East Asia has improved significantly since the beginning of the last century. From 1910 to 2016, the adult literacy rate rose from less than 50 to 96 percent, whereas the youth literacy rate rose from 80 to close to 100 percent (UNESCO, 2016). A report from UNESCO in 2016 showed that the overall literacy rate in China was 96.4 percent, with 98.2 percent among males and 94.5 percent among females. Both South Korea and North Korea are reported to have a 100 percent literacy rate among both genders, and Mongolia also has a high literacy rate of 98 percent, with females having a higher literacy rate than males. The literacy rates of Japan and Taiwan were not included in the report, but Japan is generally believed to have a near-100-percent literacy rate, and the Ministry of Education of Taiwan reported a 98.87 percent literacy rate (Ministry of Education Taiwan, 2017). Research on literacy development in East Asian languages has turned into a rapidly growing field. Clearly, extensive research has been conducted on Chinese, but more research on other East Asian languages is urgently needed to inform theory and practice.

References

Anderson, R. C., Li, W., Ku, Y. M., Shu, H., & Wu, N. (2003). Use of partial information in learning to read Chinese characters. *Journal of Educational Psychology*, *95*(1), 52–57.

Bauer, R. S., & Benedict, P. K. (1997). *Modern Cantonese Phonology* (pp. 109–276). Berlin: Mouton de Gruyter.

Bökset, R. (2006). Long story of short forms: The evolution of simplified Chinese characters. (Doctoral dissertation, Institutionen för orientaliska spark, Stockholm.)

Boltz, W. G. (1994). *The Origin and Early Development of the Chinese Writing System*, Vol. 78. New Haven, CT: American Oriental Society.

Brennan, C., Cao, F., Pedroarena-Leal, N., McNorgan, C., & Booth, J. R. (2013). Reading acquisition reorganizes the phonological awareness network only in alphabetic writing systems. *Human Brain Mapping*, *34*(12), 3354–3368.

Cao, F., & Perfetti, C. A. (2016). Neural signatures of the reading-writing connection: greater involvement of writing in Chinese reading than English reading. *PloS One*, *11*(12), e0168414.

Chan, L., & Nunes, T. (1998). Children's understanding of the formal and functional characteristics of written Chinese. *Applied Psycholinguistics*, *19*(1), 115–131.

Chan, Y. C. (2013). Learning to read Chinese: The relative roles of phonological awareness and morphological awareness. (Doctoral dissertation, University of Kansas.)

Chang, L. Y., Chen, Y. C., & Perfetti, C. A. (2018). GraphCom: A multidimensional measure of graphic complexity applied to 131 written languages. *Behavioral Research*, *50*, 427–449.

Chen, X., Anderson, R. C., Li, W. et al. (2004). Phonological awareness of bilingual and monolingual Chinese children. *Journal of Educational Psychology*, *96*(1), 142–151.

Chen, X., Hao, M., Geva, E., Zhu, J., & Shu, H. (2009). The role of compound awareness in Chinese children's vocabulary acquisition and character reading. *Reading and Writing*, *22*(5), 615–631.

Chen, X., & Pasquarella, A. (2017). Learning to read Chinese. In L. Verhoeven & C. Perfetti (eds.), *Learning to Read across Languages and Writing Systems* (pp. 31–56). Cambridge: Cambridge University Press.

Chen, X., Zhou, H., Zhao, J., & Davey, G. (2010). Home literacy experiences and literacy acquisition among children in Guangzhou, South China. *Psychological Reports*, *107*(2), 354–366.

Cheng, K. M. (2014). Does culture matter? Education reforms in East Asia. *Revue internationale d'éducation de Sèvres*. (online). DOI: https://doi.org/10.4000/ries.3804.

Cheng, Y., Wu, X., Liu, H., & Li, H. (2017). The developmental trajectories of oral vocabulary knowledge and its influential factors in Chinese primary school students. *Acta Psychologica Sinica*, *50*(2), 206–215.

Chik, P. P. M., Ho, C. S. H., Yeung, P. S. et al. (2012). Contribution of discourse and morphosyntax skills to reading comprehension in Chinese dyslexic and typically developing children. *Annals of Dyslexia*, *62*(1), 1–18.

Cho, Z. H., Kim, N., Bae, S. et al. (2014). Neural substrates of Hanja (Logogram) and Hangul (Phonogram) character readings by functional magnetic resonance imaging. *Journal of Korean Medical Science*, *29*(10), 1416–1424.

Chu, R. (2019, October 8). Hong Kong's education gap hurts ethnic minorities as much as society at large. *Hong Kong Free Press*. https://hongkongfp.com/2019/10/08/hong-kongs-education-gap-hurts-ethnic-minorities-much-society-large/.

Chung, K. K., Ho, C. S. H., Chan, D. W., Tsang, S. M., & Lee, S. H. (2011). Cognitive skills and literacy performance of Chinese adolescents with and without dyslexia. *Reading and Writing*, *24*(7), 835–859.

Chung, W. L., & Hu, C. F. (2007). Morphological awareness and learning to read Chinese. *Reading and Writing*, *20*(5), 441–461.

Coderre, E. L., Filippi, C. G., Newhouse, P. A., & Dumas, J. A. (2008). The Stroop effect in kana and kanji scripts in native Japanese speakers: An fMRI study. *Brain and Language*, *107*(2), 124–132.

DeFrancis, J. (1984). *The Chinese Language: Fact and Fantasy*. Honolulu: University of Hawaii Press.

Duanmu, S. (2007). *The Phonology of Standard Chinese*. Oxford: Oxford University Press.

Fan, X., Fang, X., Huang, Y., Chen, F., & Yu, S. (2018). The influence mechanism of parental care on depression among left behind rural children in China: A longitudinal Study. *Acta Psychologica Sinica [in Chinese]*, *50*(9), 1029–1040.

Feather, J., & Sturges, P. (2003). *International Encyclopedia of Information and Library Science*. London: Routledge.

Feldman, L. B., & Siok, W. W. (1999). Semantic radicals contribute to the visual identification of Chinese characters. *Journal of Memory and Language*, *40*(4), 559–576.

Foreign Press Center, Japan. (2010). *Facts and Figures about Japan*. https://web.archive.org/web/20130616132127/http://fpcj.jp/modules/news22/index.php?page=article&storyid=18&topicid=1.

Gao, D. G., & Kao, H. S. R. (2002). Psycho-geometric analysis of commonly used Chinese characters. In H. S. R. Kao (ed.), *Cognitive Neuroscience Studies of the Chinese Language* (pp. 195–206). Hong Kong: Hong Kong University Press.

Goodman, K. S., Wang, S., Iventosch, M., & Goodman, Y. M. (eds.). (2012). *Reading in Asian Languages: Making Sense of Written Texts in Chinese, Japanese, and Korean*. New York: Routledge.

Goswami, U. (2000). Phonological representations, reading development and dyslexia: Towards a cross-linguistic theoretical framework. *Dyslexia*, *6*(2), 133–151.

Gough, P. B., & Tunmer, W. E. (1986). Decoding, reading, and reading disability. *Remedial and Special Education*, *7*, 6–10.

Grivelet, S. (1999). Scriptal environment in Mongolia. *Studia Orientalia Electronica*, *87*, 101–108.

Grivelet, S. (2001). Digraphia in Mongolia. *International Journal of the Sociology of Language*, *2001*(150), 75–93.

Guan, C. Q., & Wang, Y. (2017). The effect of handwriting training on language learning among deaf children and their matched hearing peers in China. *American Annals of the Deaf*, *162*(3), 265–276.

Ho, C. S. H., & Bryant, P. (1997). Phonological skills are important in learning to read Chinese. *Developmental psychology*, *33*(6), 946–951.

Ho, C. S. H., Ng, T. T., & Ng, W. K. (2003). A "radical" approach to reading development in Chinese: The role of semantic radicals and phonetic radicals. *Journal of Literacy Research*, *35*(3), 849–878.

Ho, C. S. H., Yau, P. W. Y., & Au, A. (2003). Development of orthographic knowledge and its relationship with reading and spelling among Chinese kindergarten and primary school children. In C. McBride-Chang & H. C. Chen (eds.), *Reading Development in Chinese Children* (pp. 51–71). Westport, CT: Praeger.

Ho, C. S. H., Zheng, M., McBride, C. et al. (2017). Examining an extended simple view of reading in Chinese: The role of naming efficiency for reading comprehension. *Contemporary Educational Psychology*, *51*, 293–302.

Hogan, T. P., Adlof, S. M., & Alonzo, C. N. (2014). On the importance of listening comprehension. *International Journal of Speech-Language Pathology*, *16*(3) (June): 199–207. DOI: https://doi.org/10.3109/17549507.2014.904441. PMID: 24833426; PMCID: PMC4681499.

Holcombe, C. (2017). *A History of East Asia*. Cambridge: Cambridge University Press.

Hoosain, R. (1992). Psychological reality of the word in Chinese. In H. C. Chen & O. J. L. Tzeng (eds.), *Language Processing in Chinese* (Vol. 90, pp. 111–130). Amsterdam, NY: North-Holland.

Hoover, W. A., & Gough, P. B. (1990). The simple view of reading. *Reading and Writing*, *2*(2), 127–160.

Hu, Y., Fang, X., Liu, S. et al. (2018). Heterogeneity in anxiety felt by left-behind children in rural areas: Based on latent profile analysis. *Psychological Development and Education* 34(3), 346–352 [in Chinese].

Huang, H. S., & Hanley, J. R. (1995). Phonological awareness and visual skills in learning to read Chinese and English. *Cognition*, *54*(1), 73–98.

Huang, K. (2019). Language ideologies of the transcription system Zhuyin fuhao: a symbol of Taiwanese identity. *Writing Systems Research*, *11*(2), 159–175.

Hue, C. W. (2003). Number of characters a college student knows. *Journal of Chinese Linguistics*, 31(2), 300–339.

Inoue, T., Georgiou, G. K., Muroya, N., Maekawa, H., & Parrila, R. (2017). Cognitive predictors of literacy acquisition in syllabic Hiragana and morphographic Kanji. *Reading and Writing*, *30*(6), 1335–1360.

Jing, L., & Lu, H. (2009). The effects of self-explaining and working memory on Chinese reading comprehension. *Psychological Science*, *32*(4), 1009–1011.

Joshi, R. M., Tao, S., Aaron, P. G., & Quiroz, B. (2012). Cognitive component of componential model of reading applied to different orthographies. *Journal of Learning Disabilities*, *45*(5), 480–486.

Kell, M., & Kell, P. (2013). *Literacy and Language in East Asia: Shifting Meanings, Values and Approaches*, Vol. 24. Berlin: Springer Science & Business Media.

Kim-Renaud, Y. K. (ed.). (1997). *The Korean Alphabet: Its History and Structure*. Honolulu: University of Hawaii Press.

Kita, Y., Yamamoto, H., Oba, K. et al. (2013). Altered brain activity for phonological manipulation in dyslexic Japanese children. *Brain*, *136*(12), 3696–3708.

Koda, K. (2017). Learning to read Japanese. In L. Verhoeven & C. Perfetti (eds.), *Learning to Read Across Languages and Writing Systems*. Cambridge: Cambridge University Press.

Krafnick, A. J., Tan, L. H., Flowers, D. L. et al. (2016). Chinese character and English word processing in children's ventral occipitotemporal cortex: fMRI evidence for script invariance. *Neuroimage*, *133*, 302–312.

Ku, Y. M., & Anderson, R. C. (2003). Development of morphological awareness in Chinese and English. *Reading and Writing*, *16*(5), 399–422.

Lam, S. S. Y., & McBride, C. (2018). Learning to write: The role of handwriting for Chinese spelling in kindergarten children. *Journal of Educational Psychology*, *110*(7), 917–930.

Lau, K. L., & Chan, D. W. (2007). The effects of cognitive strategy instruction on Chinese reading comprehension among Hong Kong low achieving students. *Reading and Writing*, *20*(8), 833–857.

Lee, H. B. (1990). Differences in language use between North and South Korea. *International Journal of the Sociology of Language*, *1990*(82), 71–86.

Lee, K. M. (2004). Functional MRI comparison between reading ideographic and phonographic scripts of one language. *Brain and Language*, *91*(2), 245–251.

Lee, K. S., & Leung, W. M. (2012). The status of Cantonese in the education policy of Hong Kong. *Multilingual Education*, *2*, 1–22.

Lee, T. H. (2000). *Education in Traditional China: A History*, Vol. 13. Leiden: Brill.

Leong, C. K., & Tamaoka, K. (1995). Use of phonological information in processing kanji and katakana by skilled and less-skilled Japanese readers. *Reading and Writing: An Interdisciplinary Journal*, *7*, 377–393.

Leong, C. K., Tse, S. K., Loh, K. Y., & Ki, W. W. (2011). Orthographic knowledge important in comprehending elementary Chinese text by users of alphasyllabaries. *Reading Psychology, 32*(3), 237–271.

Lesaux, N. K., & Siegel, L. S. (2003). The development of reading in children who speak English as a second language. *Developmental Psychology, 39*(6), 1005–1019.

Li, C., & Thompson, S. (1981). *A Functional Reference Grammar of Mandarin Chinese*. Berkeley, CA: University of California Press.

Li, H., Dong, Q., Zhu, J., Liu, J., & Wu, X. (2009). The role of morphological awareness in language skills development of kindergartens. *Psychological Science* 32(6), 1291–1294 [in Chinese].

Li, H., Dronjic, V., Chen, X. I. et al. (2017). Morphological awareness as a function of semantics, phonology, and orthography and as a predictor of reading comprehension in Chinese. *Journal of Child Language, 44*(5), 1218–1247.

Li, H., & Rao, N. (2000). Parental influences on Chinese literacy development: A comparison of preschoolers in Beijing, Hong Kong and Singapore. *International Journal of Behavioral Development, 24*(1), 82–90.

Li, H., & Rao, N. (2005). Curricular and instructional influences on early literacy attainment: Evidence from Beijing, Hong Kong and Singapore. *International Journal of Early Years Education, 13*(3), 235–253.

Li, H., Shu, H., McBride-Chang, C., Liu, H., & Peng, H. (2012). Chinese children's character recognition: Visuo-orthographic, phonological processing and morphological skills. *Journal of Research in Reading, 35*(3), 287–307.

Li, H., Zhang, J., Ehri, L. et al. (2016). The role of orthography in oral vocabulary learning in Chinese children. *Reading and Writing, 29*(7), 1363–1381.

Li, W., Anderson, R. C., Nagy, W., & Zhang, H. (2002). Facets of metalinguistic awareness that contribute to Chinese literacy. In W. Li, J. Gaffney, & J. Packard (eds.), *Chinese Children's Reading Acquisition: Theoretical and Pedagogical Issues* (pp. 87–106). Boston, MA: Springer. DOI: https://doi.org/10.1007/978-1-4615-0859-5.

Li, X. (2002). The Xia-Shang-Zhou chronology project: methodology and results. *Journal of East Asian Archaeology, 4*(1), 321–333.

Li, Y., Zhang, L., Xia, Z. et al. (2017). The relationship between intrinsic couplings of the visual word form area with spoken language network and reading ability in children and adults. *Frontiers in Human Neuroscience, 11*, 327–338.

Lin, C. Y., Cheng, C., & Wang, M. (2018). The contribution of phonological and morphological awareness in Chinese–English bilingual reading acquisition. *Reading and Writing, 31*(1), 99–132.

Linan-Thompson, S., Vaughn, S., Prater, K., & Cirino, P. T. (2006). The response to intervention of English language learners at risk for reading problems. *Journal of Learning Disabilities, 39*(5), 390–398.

Liu, H. F. (2006). Chinese influence on the imperial exam in Japan, Korea, and Vietnam. *Academic Monthly* 38(12), 136–142 [in Chinese].

Liu, H. Q., Lu, C., An, C. et al. (2013). *The Present Situation and Future Development Trend of Rural Education in China*. Beijing: 21st Century Educational Research Institute [in Chinese].

Liu, L., Tao, R., Wang, W. et al. (2013). Chinese dyslexics show neural differences in morphological processing. *Developmental Cognitive Neuroscience, 6*, 40–50.

Liu, P. D., & McBride-Chang, C. (2010). What is morphological awareness? Tapping lexical compounding awareness in Chinese third graders. *Journal of Educational Psychology, 102*(1), 62–73.

Liu, P. D., McBride-Chang, C., Wong, T. T. Y., Shu, H., & Wong, A. M. Y. (2013). Morphological awareness in Chinese: Unique associations of homophone awareness and lexical compounding to word reading and vocabulary knowledge in Chinese children. *Applied Psycholinguistics, 34*(4), 755–775.

Liu, T., & Hsiao, J. (2012). The perception of simplified and traditional Chinese characters in the eye of simplified and traditional Chinese readers. The 34th Annual Conference of the Cognitive Science Society (CogSci 2012), Sapporo, Japan, August, 1–4, 2012. *Proceedings of the Annual Meeting of the Cognitive Science Society* 34, 689–694.

Longcamp, M., Anton, J. L., Roth, M., & Velay, J. L. (2005). Premotor activations in response to visually presented single letters depend on the hand used to write: A study on left-handers. *Neuropsychologia, 43*(12), 1801–1809.

Loveday, L. J. (1996). *Language Contact in Japan: A Sociolinguistic History.* Oxford: Clarendon Press.

Lu, Z., & Zhang, Y. (2007). The effects of phonological loop of the working memory in Chinese reading comprehension. *Acta Psychologica Sinica, 39*(05), 768–776.

Mani, D., & Trines, S. (2018, October 16). Education in South Korea. *World Education News Reviews.* https://wenr.wes.org/2018/10/education-in-south-korea.

Marks, R. A., Kovelman, I., Kepinska, O. et al. (2019). Spoken language proficiency predicts print-speech convergence in beginning readers. *NeuroImage, 201,* 116021.

McBride-Chang, C., Bialystok, E., Chong, K. K., & Li, Y. (2004). Levels of phonological awareness in three cultures. *Journal of Experimental Child Psychology, 89*(2), 93–111.

McBride-Chang, C., Cho, J. R., Liu, H. et al. (2005). Changing models across cultures: Associations of phonological awareness and morphological structure awareness with vocabulary and word recognition in second graders from Beijing, Hong Kong, Korea, and the United States. *Journal of Experimental Child Psychology, 92*(2), 140–160.

McBride-Chang, C., Shu, H., Zhou, A., Wat, C. P., & Wagner, R. K. (2003). Morphological awareness uniquely predicts young children's Chinese character recognition. *Journal of Educational Psychology, 95*(4), 743–751.

McBride-Chang, C., Tong, X., Shu, H. et al. (2008). Syllable, phoneme, and tone: Psycholinguistic units in early Chinese and English word recognition. *Scientific Studies of Reading, 12*(2), 171–194.

McBride-Chang, C., Zhou, Y., Cho, J. R. et al. (2011). Visual spatial skill: A consequence of learning to read? *Journal of Experimental Child Psychology, 109*(2), 256–262.

Meng, Z. L., Wydell, T. N., & Bi, H. Y. (2019). Visual-motor integration and reading Chinese in children with/without dyslexia. *Reading and Writing,* 32(2), 493–510.

Ministry of Education Taiwan. (2017). *Literacy Rate Report Y02-02.* https://english.moe.gov.tw/mp-1.html.

Mo, J., McBride, C., Yip, L. (2018). Identifying the unique role of orthographic working memory in a componential model of Hong Kong kindergarteners' Chinese written spelling. *Reading and Writing,* 31(5), 1083–1108. DOI: https://doi.org/10.1007/s11145-018-9829-6.

Muroya, N., Inoue, T., Hosokawa, M. et al. (2017). The role of morphological awareness in word reading skills in Japanese: A within-language cross-orthographic perspective. *Scientific Studies of Reading*, *21*(6), 449–462.

Nakamura, K., Dehaene, S., Jobert, A., Bihan, D. L., & Kouider, S. (2005). Subliminal convergence of Kanji and Kana words: Further evidence for functional parcellation of the posterior temporal cortex in visual word perception. *Journal of Cognitive Neuroscience*, *17*(6), 954–968.

OECD (Organization for Economic Co-operation and Development). (2018). *PISA 2018 Results*. Paris: OECD.

OECD (Organization for Economic Co-operation and Development). (2020). *Economic Outlook for Southeast Asia, China and India 2020*. Paris: OECD.

Packard, J. L. (2000). *The Morphology of Chinese: A Linguistic and Cognitive Approach*. Cambridge: Cambridge University Press.

Pan, J., Shu, H., Wang, Y., & Yan, M. (2015). Parafoveal activation of sign translation previews among deaf readers during the reading of Chinese sentences. *Memory & Cognition*, *43*(6), 964–972.

Pan, J., Song, S., Su, M. et al. (2016). On the relationship between phonological awareness, morphological awareness and Chinese literacy skills: Evidence from an 8-year longitudinal study. *Developmental Science*, *19*(6), 982–991.

Peng, D. L., Li, Y. P., & Yang, H. (1997). Identification of Chinese characters. In H.-C. Chen (ed.), *Cognitive Processing of Chinese and Related Asian Languages*, 85–108. Hong Kong: The Chinese University of Hong Kong.

Perfetti, C. (2007). Reading ability: Lexical quality to comprehension. *Scientific Studies of Reading*, *11*(4), 357–383.

Pine, N., Ping'an, H., & Ren Song, H. (2003). Decoding strategies used by Chinese primary school children. *Journal of Literacy Research*, *35*(2), 777–812.

Population By-Census. (2016). *Thematic Report: Ethnic Minorities*. www.bycensus2016.gov.hk/data/16bc-ethnic-minorities.pdf.

Qian, Y., Song, Y. W., Zhao, J., & Bi, H. Y. (2015). The developmental trend of orthographic awareness in Chinese preschoolers. *Reading and Writing*, *28*(4), 571–586.

Reed, G. G. (1997). Globalisation and education: The case of North Korea. *Compare*, *27*(2), 167–178.

Ren, Y., & Zhou, X. (2019). The "not learning" subculture: Educational isolation and reproduction of migrant children. *Research on Youth Phenomena and Problems*, *2*(220), 87–99 [in Chinese].

Ruan, Y., Georgiou, G. K., Song, S., Li, Y., & Shu, H. (2018). Does writing system influence the associations between phonological awareness, morphological awareness, and reading? A meta-analysis. *Journal of Educational Psychology*, *110*(2), 180–202.

Sakurai, Y., Momose, T., Iwata, M. et al. (2000). Different cortical activity in reading of Kanji words, Kana words and Kana nonwords. *Cognitive Brain Research*, *9*(1), 111–115.

Sanders, A. (2013). Mongolian transliteration: From a Latin alphabet to romanisation of Cyrillic. *Inner Asia*, *15*(1), 165–175.

Sarel, M. (1997). Growth and productivity in ÚSEAN countries. IMF Working Paper 97/97. Washington, DC: IMF.

Seeberg, V. (1990). *Literacy in China: The Effect of the National Development Context and Policy on Literacy Levels, 1949–79*. Bochum: Brockmeyer.

Seeberg, V. (1993). Access to higher education: Targeted recruitment reform under economic development plans in the People's Republic of China. *Higher Education*, 25(2), 169–188.

Shen, J. (2008). Development and environmental role of mobile and left-behind children. *Contemporary Youth Research*, 10, 9–16 [in Chinese].

Sheng, X. (2014). *Higher Education Choice in China: Social Stratification, Gender and Educational Inequality*. New York: Routledge.

Shu, H. (2003). Chinese writing system and learning to read. *International Journal of Psychology*, 38(5), 274–285.

Shu, H., & Anderson, R. C. (1997). Role of radical awareness in the character and word acquisition of Chinese children. *Reading Research Quarterly*, 32(1), 78–89.

Shu, H., Chen, X., Anderson, R. C., Wu, N., & Xuan, Y. (2003). Properties of school Chinese: Implications for learning to read. *Child Development*, 74(1), 27–47.

Shu, H., McBride-Chang, C., Wu, S., & Liu, H. (2006). Understanding Chinese developmental dyslexia: Morphological awareness as a core cognitive construct. *Journal of Educational Psychology*, 98(1), 122–133.

Shu, H., Peng, H., & McBride-Chang, C. (2008). Phonological awareness in young Chinese children. *Developmental Science*, 11(1), 171–181.

Siok, W. T., Niu, Z., Jin, Z., Perfetti, C. A., & Tan, L. H. (2008). A structural–functional basis for dyslexia in the cortex of Chinese readers. *Proceedings of the National Academy of Sciences*, 105(14), 5561–5566.

So, L. K., & Dodd, B. J. (1995). The acquisition of phonology by Cantonese-speaking children. *Journal of Child Language*, 22(3), 473–495.

Sohn, H. M. (ed.). (2006). *Korean Language in Culture and Society*. Honolulu: University of Hawaii Press.

Song, J. J. (2002). The Juche ideology: English in North Korea. *English Today*, 18(1), 47–52.

Taylor, I., & Taylor, M. M. (1995). *Writing and Literacy in Chinese, Korean and Japanese*, Vol. III. John Benjamins.

Thuy, D. H. D., Matsuo, K., Nakamura, K. et al. (2004). Implicit and explicit processing of kanji and kana words and non-words studied with fMRI. *Neuroimage*, 23(3), 878–889.

Tong, X., Lee, S. M. K., Lee, M. M. L., & Burnham, D. (2015). A tale of two features: Perception of Cantonese lexical tone and English lexical stress in Cantonese-English bilinguals. *PloS One*, 10(11), e0142896.

Tong, X., McBride-Chang, C., Shu, H., & Wong, A. M. (2009). Morphological awareness, orthographic knowledge, and spelling errors: Keys to understanding early Chinese literacy acquisition. *Scientific Studies of Reading*, 13(5), 426–452.

Tong, X., Tong, X., & McBride, C. (2017). Unpacking the relation between morphological awareness and Chinese word reading: Levels of morphological awareness and vocabulary. *Contemporary Educational Psychology*, 48, 167–178.

Treiman, R., & Zukowski, A. (1991). Levels of phonological awareness. In S. A. Brady & D. P. Shankweiler (eds.), *Phonological Processes in Literacy: A Tribute to Isabelle Y. Liberman* (pp. 67–83). Mahwah, NJ: Lawrence Erlbaum Associates, Inc.

Třísková, H. (2011). The structure of the Mandarin syllable: Why, when and how to teach it. *Archiv orientální, 79*(1), 99–134.

UNDP. (2018). *Human Development Reports: Statistical Update 2018.* http://hdr.undp.org/en/content/human-development-indices-indicators-2018-statistical-update.

UNESCO. (2016). *EFA Global Monitoring Report 2016: Education for People and Planet: Creating Sustainable Futures for All.* http://unesdoc.unesco.org/images/0024/002457/245752e.pdf.

United Nations. (2019). *2019 Revision of World Population Prospects.* https://population.un.org/wpp/.

Wang, J., Li, H., & Wang, D. (2018). Bridging the rural-urban literacy gap in China: A mediation analysis of family effects. *Journal of Research in Childhood Education, 32* (1), 119–134.

Wang, M., Cho, J., & Li. C. (2017). Learning to read Korean. In L. Verhoeven & C. Perfetti (eds.), *Learning to Read Across Languages and Writing Systems.* Cambridge: Cambridge University Press.

Wang, M., Ko, I. Y., & Choi, J. (2009). The importance of morphological awareness in Korean–English biliteracy acquisition. *Contemporary Educational Psychology, 34* (2), 132–142.

Wang, M., Perfetti, C. A., & Liu, Y. (2005). Chinese–English biliteracy acquisition: Cross-language and writing system transfer. *Cognition, 97*(1), 67–88.

Wang, Y., McBride-Chang, C., & Chan, S. F. (2014). Correlates of Chinese kindergarteners' word reading and writing: The unique role of copying skills? *Reading and Writing, 27*(7), 1281–1302.

World Bank. (2019). *World Development Annual Report 2019.* Washington, DC: World Bank.

Worldometer. (2020). Real Time World Statistics (website). www.worldometers.info.

Wu, X., Anderson, R. C., Li, W. et al. (2009). Morphological awareness and Chinese children's literacy development: An intervention study. *Scientific Studies of Reading, 13*(1), 26–52.

Xie, R., Zhang, J., Wu, X., & Nguyen, T. P. (2019). The relationship between morphological awareness and reading comprehension among Chinese children. *Frontiers in Psychology, 10,* 54–67.

Xu, J., & Wang, H. (2004). *An Introduction to Modern Chinese.* Beijing: Global Publishing [in Chinese.]

Yang, C., Yu, B., Zhao, F., & Lei, Z. (2011). The logistic model analysis of influencing factors for education continuity of migrant children. *Journal of Hebei University of Economics and Business,* 11(2), 106–109 [in Chinese].

Yeung, P. S., Ho, C. S. H., Chan, D. W. O., & Chung, K. K. H. (2016a). Orthographic skills important to Chinese literacy development: The role of radical representation and orthographic memory of radicals. *Reading and Writing, 29*(9), 1935–1958.

Yeung, P. S., Ho, C. S. H., Chan, D. W. O., & Chung, K. K. H. (2016b). A componential model of reading in Chinese. *Learning and Individual Differences, 45,* 11–24.

Yeung, P. S., Ho, C. S. H., Chan, D. W. O., Chung, K. K. H., & Wong, Y. K. (2013). A model of reading comprehension in Chinese elementary school children. *Learning and Individual Differences, 25,* 55–66.

Yeung, P. S., Ho, C. S. H., Chik, P. P. M. et al. (2011). Reading and spelling Chinese among beginning readers: What skills make a difference? *Scientific Studies of Reading*, *15*(4), 285–313.

Yoon, H. K., Bolger, D. J., Kwon, O. S., & Perfetti, C. A. (2002). Subsyllabic units in reading. *Precursors of Functional Literacy*, *11*, 139–163.

Yoon, H. W., Cho, K. D., Chung, J. Y., & Park, H. (2005). Neural mechanisms of Korean word reading: A functional magnetic resonance imaging study. *Neuroscience Letters*, *373*(3), 206–211.

Yoon, H. W., Cho, K. D., & Park, H. W. (2005). Brain activation of reading Korean words and recognizing pictures by Korean native speakers: A functional magnetic resonance imaging study. *International Journal of Neuroscience*, *115*(6), 757–768.

Zeng, Z. (1994). 广东话普通话的对比与教学 (Comparison between and instruction of Cantonese and Mandarin). Hong Kong: Joint Publishing.

Zhang, J., Li, H., Dong, Q., Xu, J., & Sholar, E. (2016). Implicit use of radicals in learning characters for nonnative learners of Chinese. *Applied Psycholinguistics*, *37*(3), 507–527.

Zhang, D., Li, X., & Xue, J. (2015). Education inequality between rural and urban areas of the People's Republic of China, migrants' children education, and some implications. *Asian Development Review*, *32*(1), 196–224.

Zhang, J., Lin, T. J., Wei, J., & Anderson, R. C. (2014). Morphological awareness and learning to read Chinese and English. In X. Chen, Q. Wang, C. L. Yang (eds.), *Reading Development and Difficulties in Monolingual and Bilingual Chinese Children* (pp. 3–22). Dordrecht: Springer.

Zhang, J., McBride-Chang, C., Tong, X. et al. (2012). Reading with meaning: The contributions of meaning-related variables at the word and subword levels to early Chinese reading comprehension. *Reading and Writing*, *25*(9), 2183–2203.

Zhao, J., & Shen, J. (2010). An ecological model for left-at-home rural children's development and its implications for their education. *Chinese Journal of Special Education*, *7*(121), 65–76 [in Chinese].

Zhao, J., Zhou, H., & Chen, X. (2008). Quantity of family shared reading as a predictor of young children's oral vocabulary. *Psychological Development and Education*, *1*, 14–18 [in Chinese].

Zhu, C., & Yang, L. H. (2003). Investigation about the early home reading education. *Early Education*, *7*, 2–3.

Zhu, Y. (2018, October 15). China's government spending on education has exceeded 4 percent of GDP for six consecutive years. *Xinhua News Agency*. www.gov.cn/xinwen/2018-10/15/content_5330998.htm.

Zou, L., Packard, J., Xia, Z., Liu, Y., & Shu, H. (2019). Morphological and whole-word semantic processing are distinct: ERP evidence from spoken word recognition in Chinese. *Frontiers in Human Neuroscience*, *13*, 133.

Zuo, J. (2003). From revolutionary comrades to gendered partners: Marital construction of breadwinning in post-Mao urban China. *Journal of Family Issues*, *24*(3), 314–337.

10 Literacy and Linguistic Diversity in Australia

Anne-Marie Morgan, Nicholas Reid, and Peter Freebody

10.1   Introduction

Literacy educators in Australian schools work in the midst of conditions, opportunities, and challenges comparable to those facing their colleagues in many other settings. These include increasing cultural and linguistic diversity among students, communities, and workplaces, variable support from governments in fiscally unstable times, and continual professional and public debates over curriculum, pedagogy, and assessment, and over the role of research and policy. But Australian educators also encounter distinctive, and some at least distinctively inflected historical, cultural, and economic features that bear on their literacy efforts.

To background our discussion of those efforts, we open with a selection of Australia's demographic and administrative characteristics. We then describe the less-frequently discussed challenges and opportunities presented to research, practice, and policy by educational engagements with Aboriginal and migrant communities, and the often noteworthy, but generally patchy track record of achievements in literacy and language education arising from those engagements. We advance some lessons that this track record offers on literacy's relationship to community languages, to pedagogy, to policy formation and maintenance, and to research. We summarize international perspectives on Australian literacy education, including those based on national and international assessment programs, discuss the varied history of research traditions that have both informed and divided the field of literacy education in Australia, and conclude with some observations about the research, policy, and media environments in which literacy is an object of policy, inquiry, and public anxiety.

A selection of features of Australia that provide some background to the following discussion is shown in Table 10.1. We can draw some general inferences: Australia is a large and sparsely populated country, so many Australian schools operate in remote areas or in regions that are far away from the centers of educational policy direction and institutes of teacher education; in general, Australian society is comparatively affluent and moderately equitable; and

Table 10.1 *Some demographic features of selected countries (sources: International Monetary Fund, 2020; OECD, 2019a and b; United Nations Development Programme, 2019; World Bank, 2018)*

	Australia	Brazil	Canada	Germany	Japan	OECD mean
Area (m km^2)	7.7	8.5	10	.4	.4	1
Population (m)	25	209	38	83	127	35
Per-capita productivity (Adj. US $k)	55	17	52	50	47	43
Equity (GINI)	.33	.54	.31	.29	.34	.33
Urbanization (%)	86	87	81	77	92	68
Population density / sq km	3	25	4	208	317	35
Mean years schooling	12.7	7.8	13.3	14.1	12.8	12.4
~% with tertiary qualifications	44	17	55	30	52	36

Australians generally attend senior high school, and many have tertiary qualifications, suggesting a general belief in institutionalized education.

There are three types of schools in Australia. In 2019, 67 percent of Australian school students attended government-run schools, 19 percent attended Catholic schools, and 14 percent attended independent schools, many affiliated with religious organizations. Catholic and independent schools are accountable to government-mandated curriculum policies, and are funded, to varying degrees, by contributions from government and parents. The implications of these funding arrangements for equity and quality have long been matters of debate among economists and educationists (see, e.g., Bonnor & Connors, 2018; Connors & McMorrow, 2015; Gonski, 2011). Assessments of the literacy capabilities of students have figured prominently in these debates.

The functions of government in Australia are divided between federal, state, and local bodies. Traditionally, it is states that take responsibility for school policies and curriculums. Beginning in 2008, however, the Australian government created the Australian Curriculum, Assessment and Reporting Authority (ACARA) to develop and implement a national curriculum. Literacy appears in three places in ACARA's curriculum: as a strand in the Foundation year (prior to Year 1 of formal schooling) to Year 10 English curriculum (the other two strands are "language" and "literature"); in a national program of standardized tests of literacy and numeracy (NAPLAN); and as one of the seven "General Capabilities" to be applied across all curriculum areas (e.g., numeracy and information and communication technology capability). In addition, ACARA further stipulates three 'Cross-Curriculum Priorities': sustainability, Asia and

Australia's engagement with Asia, and Aboriginal and Torres Strait Islander histories and cultures. We turn to two of these "cross-curriculum" accountabilities and to their implications for the teaching and learning of literacy.

10.2 Australian Aboriginal Languages and Literacy

10.2.1 History of Aboriginal Culture and Languages

The first European visitors to the Australian continent were Dutch, and the European name for the continent from about 1620 until well into the 1800s was New Holland. One of the earliest British maps of New Holland was made in 1790, two years after the British settlement at Port Jackson. The map shows details of the geographical features and European settlements of the coastal and an empty interior. The British administration was aware of the significant Aboriginal presence on the continent, but nonetheless deemed it to be "terra nullius" – "nobody's land" – a legal mechanism that afforded lawful annexation and settlement, and that declared, effectively, that whatever it was that the new settlers were doing, they were *not* invading (Goot & Rowse, 2007).[1]

Evidence from archaeology and genetics (e.g., Clarkson, Smith Marwick et al., 2015; Malaspinas, Westaway, Muller et al., 2016) indicates that, beginning about 60,000 years before the visitors arrived from Europe, the first Australians crossed from the Sunda Peninsula, later to become the Indonesian archipelago, into Sahul, a single continent subsuming what are now mainland Australia, Tasmania, and Papua New Guinea. Genetic research suggests that these first Australians traveled around the coast in both directions with surprising rapidity, filled the interior, and then largely remained *in situ*; the gene-flow picture of Aboriginal Australia is one of remarkable stability (Malaspinas, Westaway, Muller et al., 2016).

The tentative coastal outlines of the earliest maps made by Europeans provide the initial impressions of outsiders peering into a continent from the edge. For the most part the travelers and settlers who followed them over the next century inherited the restricted gaze of the newcomer, literally unable to see beyond their coastal settlements, and metaphorically unable to see the locals' unfamiliar social organizations, or their sophisticated systems of land tenure, religious belief, and cultural practice. As for talk and inscription, effectively, what was heard across the land in 1788, and for a long time afterwards, was *lingua nullius*, nobody's voice. Two centuries after settlement we now understand that, throughout Australia, Aboriginal people had developed thriving cultures, and filled the continent with at least 250 different

---

[1] We refer here to these groups collectively as Aboriginal Australians, while we acknowledge the ongoing debate surrounding the appropriate nomenclature.

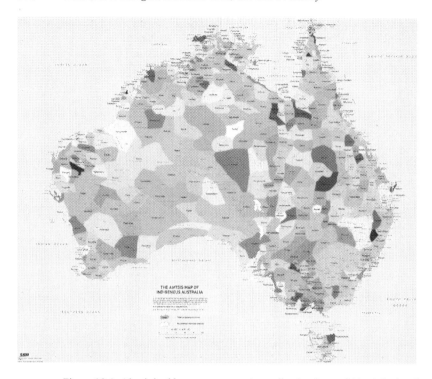

Figure 10.1 Aboriginal languages map, Australian Institute of Aboriginal and Torres Strait Islander Studies, AIATSIS, Horton (1996)
This map attempts to represent the language, social or nation groups of Aboriginal Australia. It shows only the general locations of larger groupings of people, which may include clans, dialects, or individual languages in a group. It used published resources from 1988 to 1994 and is not intended to be exact, nor the boundaries fixed. It is not suitable for native title or other land claims. David R. Horton (creator), © Aboriginal Studies Press, AIATSIS, 1996. No reproduction without permission. To purchase a print version visit: www.aiatsis.ashop.com.au/.

languages, each as sophisticated as all other human languages. Figure 10.1 shows linguists' and historians' best current mapping of the regions and languages of Australia in 1788.

This map shows the extraordinary linguistic diversity and complexity evident on the continent before the European arrival. For tens of thousands of years, the first Australians needed to be competent in several languages in order to communicate and intermarry with neighboring communities, and to accommodate additional language expectations among their children (Clyne, 2005,

2011; Jupp & Clyne, 2011). Recent research suggests that the stability of populations, the development of rich narrative cultures, and culture-specific mechanisms of intergenerational transmission, have combined to make Australian Aboriginal people the custodians of the world's oldest orally transmitted memories, recording, for instance, late-Holocene inundations of the continental shelf that occurred about 10,000 years ago (Nunn & Reid, 2016), a narrative feat of human memory probably unparalleled on other continents.

In his encyclopedic history of writing, Fischer defined it as "the sequencing of standardized symbols (characters, signs or sign components) in order to graphically reproduce human speech, thought and other things in part or whole" (Fischer, 2001, p. 12). For over 50,000 years Aboriginal Australians have produced inscriptions that depicted land features, origin myths, and ideas about land, ancestors, social organization, customs, and moral responsibilities. While not representing speech phonemically, they used painting and sculpture on rocks, wood, and leaves, employing symbols that retained similar meanings over long periods of time within and across regions (e.g., Taylor, 1996). Depictions of animals that were extinct almost 40,000 years ago have been discovered, as have paintings of the arrival of ships, presumably from Europe less than a few hundred years ago (Kleinert & Neale, 2000).

These rich precolonial linguistic assets of Australia, however, were quickly lost. Estimates vary, but the Australian Aboriginal population prior to the arrival of the British settlers seems to have been between 500,000 and 750,000. Since then, as Burnley (1988) pointed out,

whatever the actual population level before 1788, the Aboriginal population was decimated with European contact through mortality from diseases which Europeans brought with them, from starvation resulting from dislocation of traditional man-habitat relations, with malnutrition rendering Aborigines more susceptible to contagious diseases, and deaths from conflict with colonial police and settlers. It is estimated that, by 1891, the Aboriginal population had fallen to 40,000 persons, and even by 1981 there had been a recovery to only some 170,000 persons. (Burnley, 1988, p. 263)

Most estimates are that the Aboriginal population on the continent returned to precolonial levels only after about 220 years. But by 2018, of the 250 languages of 1788, more than 100 had become extinct, about 130 were critically endangered (spoken only by the oldest generations and no longer learned by children), and only 13 were currently being learned as first languages by children (AIATSIS, 2019). Those thirteen languages are often classed, in Australia, as "healthy," using "intergenerational language transmission" as a diagnostic of "health"; but crucially, all thirteen, at the time of writing, fail to meet most of the other key diagnostic factors employed in UNESCO's *Language Vitality and Endangerment* report (UNESCO, 2003) for determining language vitality – in particular, "absolute number of speakers" and "proportion of speakers existing within the total (global) population." They can, therefore, be accurately classified as "critically endangered."

Researchers have documented grammars, dictionaries, and collections of texts in most of the languages still spoken (Australian Research Council Centre of Excellence on the Dynamics of Languages, e.g., Simpson, McConvell, & Thieberger, 2019; Simpson, 2019; Eades, 2014). A rich understanding has emerged of historical relationships within the "Australian language family" (Bowern & Koch, 2004; Simpson, 2019). Theoretical linguists around the world have long mined the richness and complexity of Aboriginal languages in pursuing answers to theory-driven questions about the nature and limits of human language in general (e.g., Evans & Sasse, 2002; Koch & Nordlinger, 2014).

For much of the last two centuries Aboriginal people and their languages were largely ignored. White Australian nation building advanced on the assumption that Aboriginality would be absorbed and assimilated into the new Anglo-Australia. Instead, we now find a vibrant and growing Aboriginal population across Australia, ranging from metropolitan, urban living people to those living in rural and remote locations, speaking one or more of the following languages and/or language varieties:

- Traditional Aboriginal languages, of which about 130 are still spoken (Purdie et al., 2008; Simpson, 2019);
- Standard Australian English, a descriptor used for a variety of English spoken by most Australians (Collins & Peters, 2004);
- Aboriginal English, a nonstandard variety of English, usefully conceived of as a continuum ranging from light acrolectal varieties (closer to standard), with only subtle differences from Standard Australian English, to heavy basilectal varieties that are closer to creoles (Kaldor & Malcolm, 1991; Eades, 1991);
- One of two creole languages, Kriol and Broken, largely English-lexified, but with substrate influence from Aboriginal languages (Harris & Sandefur, 1984).

10.2.2 Aboriginal Literacy and Schooling

Despite the obvious cultural importance of Aboriginal languages to the identity of modern Australia, there has generally been little provision or sustained political support for the learning of Aboriginal languages by non-Aboriginal Australians (Oldfield & Lo Bianco, 2019; Simpson, 2019). As we outline below, additional language learning in Australian schools, for most of the last century, has remained mostly focused on French, German, Italian, Japanese, Indonesian, and Chinese. Only since 2006 has there been an effort to teach Aboriginal languages in public schools. As a result, in 60 target schools in New

South Wales, for instance, about 5,000 primary and secondary students, of whom two thirds are non-Aboriginal, were learning an Aboriginal language in 2008 (Purdie et al., 2008), with recent increases to around 7,000 in 2018.

In 2019, of the top fifteen non-English languages learned in New South Wales schools, three were Aboriginal languages (NSW Department of Education, 2019). At the national level, the Australian curriculum includes language-specific curricula for so-called "world" languages, and a *Framework for Aboriginal Languages and Torres Strait Islander Languages* (ACARA, 2016a, b; Disbray, 2019; Simpson, Disbray, and O'Shannessy, 2019; and see First Languages Australia, 2020), which aimed to increase students' learning of Aboriginal and Torres Strait Islander languages. By 2008 there were 16,000 Aboriginal students and 13,000 non-Aboriginal students in 260 Australian schools participating in Aboriginal language and literacy programs (Purdie et al., 2008). These programs ranged from bilingual programs to second-language-learning programs to revival and language-awareness programs. Here we focus on the history of bilingual education and the use of creoles and Aboriginal English in schools, before turning to literacy outcomes.

There were sporadic attempts through the 1800s, often by missionaries, to teach Aboriginal children through the use of their own languages, notably Kaurna, Diyeri, and Arrernte (Gale, 1994). Up until the 1970s, however, most Aboriginal children were educated in English-only schools, and faced the task of acquiring literacy skills in a language other than their mother tongue. The 1970s saw the introduction of bilingual education in about twenty communities, mostly in the Northern Territory, and typically in public schools (Devlin, 2009; Gale, 1994). These were transitional programs, intended to introduce literacy and numeracy using the child's first language and then to transfer those skills to English, via graduated increases, across each school year. All of these programs explicitly nominated English literacy, rather than traditional language maintenance, as their immediate goal (Gale, 1994). They exemplify what Baker and Wright (2017, Reid, 2010) described as the "subtractive" model of bilingualism, in which the first language gradually disappears.

Bilingual schooling of Aboriginal children in Australia has a troubled history. Funded by the Australian government but administered by the Northern Territory's Education Department, the scheme's support from governments has vacillated. As a scheme affecting only a relatively small number of students, its rationale and details have often been poorly articulated and understood, including by many of those who have made decisions about its direction and funding. Administrators of bilingual education have often failed to understand that learning an Aboriginal language, like learning any additional language, complements rather than hinders developing proficiency in English (Simpson, Caffery, & McConvell, 2009). Critically, support for bilingual education never fully embraced the principle that children learning English as an additional language (EAL) need to be taught by EAL-trained teachers (Nicholls, 2005), preferably bilingual teachers who understand the processes entailed in additional language learning (Ellis, 2016). Nationally standardized English literacy assessments for children in bilingual schools have failed to assess students' first-language literacy. Further, evidence that these students were performing at levels lower than nonbilingual schoolchildren in Standard Australian English literacy testing has regularly been used to discredit the scheme by those seeking to reduce its funding (Simpson et al., 2009).

Bilingual schools, mostly in remote locations, have struggled to find enough appropriately trained first-language-speaking teachers, have been frequently staffed by non-Aboriginal teachers whose professional training did not prepare them specifically for bilingual classroom practices, and have experienced levels of teacher turnover far higher than mainstream schools (Simpson et al., 2009). Despite high levels of multilingualism and oral literacy, the parents of most children in bilingual schools have low levels of written literacy themselves, and, for many children in these remote communities, books and writing play no role in their lives outside of school. Since 2008 the Northern Territory Education Department has mitigated its involvement in a bilingual approach by reintroducing a "Talk English" focus and calling on bilingual schools to focus on English literacy for the first four hours of each school day. Some bilingual programs have complied while others have ignored the department's directive and insisted on maintaining a "two-way education" balance. In these latter cases, the general aim has been to value both languages equally (Devlin, 2009; Sellwood & Angelo, 2013). There are promising aspects of this story, with some individual bilingual schools achieving excellent results in the national English literacy tests, the only measure for literacy outcomes available. But bilingual and biliterate education for Aboriginal Australia has a history of policy somersaults and fluctuating levels of funding, support, and commitment.

Most Aboriginal children speak Standard Australian English, Aboriginal English, or a creole variety, whereas the bilingual programs described above cater to only the minority of Aboriginal children who speak an Aboriginal language as their first language. There is clear evidence that Aboriginal English and the two creole varieties, Kriol and Broken, while predominantly English-lexified, are distinct from Standard Australian English. The degree of distinctiveness is greater in the case of the creoles, which in their "heavier" forms are not mutually intelligible. At the acrolectal end of the Aboriginal English spectrum, the lexical, grammatical, and phonological differences from Standard Australian English are comparatively minor (Kaldor & Malcolm, 1991). But a range of more subtle pragmatic differences, ranging from forms of knowledge organization (Sharifian, 2005) to culturally significant ways of using silence and eye contact and to methods of eliciting information through

Literacy and Linguistic Diversity in Australia   211

questioning techniques (Eades, 1991) still create difficulties in communication between Standard Australian English and Aboriginal English speakers.

Apart from a single Standard Australian English–Kriol bilingual program that ran at one school in the 1980s, there has been little use of either creoles or Aboriginal English as mediums of education in Australia. Due to the apparent similarities of these languages with Standard Australian English, speakers of the creoles and Aboriginal English are typically not identified as learning Standard Australian English as an additional language (Wigglesworth, Billington, & Loakes, 2013). A history of attitudes that characterize Aboriginal English as "bad English," held by both teachers and speakers of Aboriginal English, has further functioned to make Aboriginal English unacceptable as a language of instruction in many community schools. Because Standard Australian English is widely associated with vocational advantage (Disbray & Loakes, 2013), and because there is a continuum of creole-to-Aboriginal English varieties that makes it difficult to choose one language variety over another for schooling purposes (Siegel, 1999), Standard Australian English has remained unchallenged as the language of both instruction and assessment in Australian schools.

10.2.3 *Aboriginal Literacy Outcomes*

Aboriginal children in remote communities are outperformed on standardized literacy tests across all English literacy skills by non-Aboriginal children in metropolitan centers (ACARA, 2017). According to the *Closing the Gap* report (Australian Department of Prime Minister and Cabinet, 2015), school attendance rates have been as low as 14 percent in some remote schools, and in 2014 only 34 percent of Aboriginal students in remote communities met the national minimum standard for Year 7 reading. Similar findings come from the 2017 NAPLAN results: 25 percent of students in remote parts of Australia are achieving at or above minimum standards for reading in Year 3, increasing only to 27 percent in Year 9 (ACARA, 2017). In the "very remote" geographical location category, only 15 percent are at minimum standard by Year 9; and over 80 percent of Aboriginal students across the Northern Territory achieved below the minimum standard for Year 3 reading, spelling, grammar and punctuation, results that are lower than preceding years (ACARA, 2017).

The Programme for International Student Assessment (PISA 2012) report showed a 2.5–3-year gap between non-Aboriginal and Aboriginal literacy rates in Australia (Thomson, De Bortoli, & Buckley, 2012). Similarly, the *Progress in International Reading Literacy Study* (PIRLS 2016), drawing on data from fifty countries, points to significant literacy gaps between Indigenous and non-Indigenous Australians: "Australia's Aboriginal and Torres Strait Islander students attained an average score of 483 points, which was 67 points lower than the average score for non-Indigenous students ... In 2016 ... students with an Aboriginal or Torres Strait Islander background had almost four times the odds of being a poor reader compared to non-Indigenous students" (Thomson et al., 2017). Findings such as these have been used by successive governments to criticize bilingual education, and to justify the shift of resources to developing English-only literacy skills. Australian linguists and literacy specialists have noted that the real issue is "the cost and complexity of lifting both performance standards and attendance rates across remote schools. Bilingual education is a decoy" (Devlin, 2010, p. 3). The recent removal of bilingual programs in many areas has not yielded any increase in English literacy levels.

Those schoolchildren speaking Indigenous forms of English and creoles have also long been recognized to be disadvantaged (Hudson & Taylor-Henley, 1995), and their failure to achieve expected outcomes, especially in literacy, is well documented (OECD, 2011; Sharifian, 2001; Wigglesworth et al., 2013). Prominent among the drivers of disadvantage are structural differences between Aboriginal English and Standard Australian English, such as:

- gender undifferentiated third singular pronoun "ee";
- hypercorrective initial "h" as in "huncle Henry"; and
- zero copula usages like "ee gone."

Such grammatical differences are routinely interpreted by speakers of Standard Australian English as "errors," and can result in teachers overlooking demonstrated content knowledge (Dixon, 2013; Wigglesworth, Simpson, & Loakes, 2011).

A meaningful response to the challenges and opportunities involved in engaging Aboriginal Australian school students will emerge when the current invisibility of Aboriginal English and creoles in Australian education systems is recognized. Murtagh (1982) assessed the single Kriol bilingual program and found that explicit teaching of, and in, both languages resulted in increased oral proficiency in both English and Kriol (Murtagh, 1982, cited in Siegel, 1999, and see the collection of studies in Rennie & Harper, 2019). Similarly, various researchers have pointed out that the directions that will help the Australian schooling system address the disadvantage that Aboriginal students currently experience include: teaching that explicitly addresses the differences between Standard Australian English and the students' own variety, be it a creole, Aboriginal English, or a traditional Aboriginal language; teaching that understands and reinforces the contextual appropriateness of each (e.g., Shinkfield & Jennings, 2019); and teaching that supports students in learning Standard Australian English as an additional variety (e.g., Sellwood & Angelo, 2013; Siegel, 1999; Wigglesworth et al., 2013).

To summarize, the subtractive focus of bilingual education, the overlooking of creoles and Aboriginal English as varieties to be used in school, and the unfounded suspicion that the teaching of traditional languages, creoles, and Aboriginal English is incompatible with English literacy acquisition, have together contributed to a large gap between the literacy outcomes of Aboriginal and non-Aboriginal Australians. An acknowledgment of the language and literacy resources and needs of Australia as a *country* calls for a much more nuanced reaction to the realities of European–Aboriginal history, rather than the apathy, tokenism, and capricious educational and social policies that have characterized much of Anglo-Australia's reaction for generations.

10.3 Community Languages and Literacy

10.3.1 Historical Perspectives

Analogous patterns in practice and policy arise in any consideration of community and migrant education in literacy. British colonials arriving in Australia promoted the norm of English monolingualism and monoliteracy as both a gift and an instrument of empire (Clyne, 2011; Ellis, 2008). The expectation that English would be the national language was such that the need has never been felt to declare an official language for Australia: English is the language of politics, law, education, and of everyday social life more broadly, and so the de facto national language.

The history of Australian migrant settlement, however, tells a different story. Apart from the original hundreds of Australian Aboriginal languages described above, significant numbers of the earliest migrant settlers spoke Irish, Gaelic, and Welsh as first languages, and during the nineteenth century settlers came from across Europe and Asia, attracted by discoveries of gold and readily available land. There were many urban and rural communities that used spoken and written languages other than English (Clyne, 2011). Multilingual and bilingual educational activities were more prevalent in the nineteenth century than at any other time in Australia's history. Many migrant communities used their languages for everyday and business purposes, and to teach their children in schools (Lo Bianco & Slaughter, 2009).

During the seven decades following the First World War, a period in which the population of Australia grew from about 5 to 14 million, the use of languages other than English was considered undesirable, and their active usage decreased. The dominant political and social paradigm was "integration," a project to which the learning of English was seen as central. Over this period waves of large-scale immigration to Australia from nations across Europe, the Middle East, and Asia brought a wide range of languages and cultures, but these migrants were actively encouraged to learn English, and discouraged from using their own languages, even in their homes (Clyne, 2011; Lo Bianco & Slaughter, 2009).

The large influx of migrants to Australia that followed the Second World War led to efforts to link migration with English literacy capability, and thereby to Australia's most consequential language policy instruments, the Adult Migration Education Program and the subsequent 1969 Child Migrant Education Act. Via these, a national policy of teaching English to all children was systematically enacted (Hajek & Slaughter, 2014). Additional language education practices "favoured choices and methods of instruction dictated by attachment to the western canon of literary prestige, principally for reading and cultivation rather than active use" (Lo Bianco & Slaughter, 2009, p. 15). So French and German, as well as Latin and Classical Greek, as languages of literature and academic prestige, were popular in elite schools and universities. There was little effort to promote or retain the use of active community languages (e.g., Modern Greek, Italian, German, Chinese, Polish, Turkish, Lithuanian), despite the substantial communities of migrants for whom these were first languages.

Since the late 1970s overseas military and political conflicts have led to a surge in immigration from southern Asian nations (e.g., Vietnam, Cambodia, East Timor, and China), and stimulated the emergence of a more pluralistic cultural policy. Australians developed an image of their nation as a "multicultural" nation, but nonetheless monolingual (Clyne, 2011), celebrating this image in the popular media and in policy (Hajek & Slaughter, 2014). It is a self-representation that has persisted to the present and is frequently announced to the global community as an example of the peaceful nature of such multicultural identity building. It ignores, however, the multilingual or plurilingual possibilities that arise from such diversity.

By the late 1980s increasing support for learning the languages of neighbors and new trade partners, the balance of which had shifted to Asia from Britain following Britain's accession to the Common European Market, was beginning to take hold in schools and universities (Hajek & Slaughter, 2014; Lo Bianco & Slaughter, 2009; Morgan, Kohler, & Harbon, 2011). The Federal Government began to implement policies promoting and supporting Asian language studies. Japanese surpassed French as the most studied additional language, and Chinese, Indonesian, Japanese, and Korean were promoted as priority languages (Harrington, 2012).

The study of "community" languages (Clyne, 2005) was pushed out of mainstream schools into "community" or "ethnic" schools operating outside of school hours. Community groups tried to maintain heritage languages and cultures by running these schools. Despite pressures to reduce the use of heritage languages, by 2018 there were about eighty languages offered by the Ethnic Schools Association for students from Foundation to Year 10 and over forty languages at Years 11 and 12. These were offered across all states and territories, with almost 120,000 students participating in over 1,400 venues (Australian Federation of Ethnic Schools, 2016; Community Languages Australia, 2019; Migration Heritage Centre, NSW, Powerhouse Museum, n.d.; Scrimgeour et al., 2019). Such practices remained politically and professionally marginalized, operating principally through "Saturday schools," and attracting little political or media recognition. In 2019 an effort was made to formalize these community provisions and to begin a process of educationally credentialing the community members doing the teaching work, via the creation of the Sydney Institute for Community Language Education (SICLE, n. d.). The Institute's initiatives include introducing community languages into mainstream primary schools, with programs in nine community languages – Arabic, Assyrian, Chinese, Greek, Hindi, Korean, Macedonian, Tamil, and Turkish – and the development of full syllabuses for New South Wales schools in Hindi, Macedonian, Persian/Dari, Punjabi, and Tamil. Over 400 languages are spoken in homes and communities across Australia (Australian Bureau of Statistics (ABS), 2016a; Scrimgeour et al., 2019; Slaughter & Hajek, 2014). No current data exist on levels of written literacy for these languages, however, and children commencing school who are fluent in spoken community languages vary substantially in how well they read and write in those languages.

There has been a gradual acknowledgment of multilingualism and its value for literacy generally (see Wilks-Smith, 2017), and multicultural policies to promote cultural diversity exist at all levels of government. The prevalent message of the media, and of populist political comment in relation to literacy capability, however, remains firmly focused on English. The view is that English literacy, assessed through standardized testing programs, remains key to Australia's economic success, and should therefore be the educational imperative. In some jurisdictions it occupies, by policy mandate, the prime teaching time in elementary schools, in so-called "literacy blocks" each morning. This is at the expense of learning areas such as additional languages, or other subjects taught through additional languages.

Australia's history indicates that it is one of the world's major immigrant nations, with over 7.5million settlers since 1945 in a national population of about 26 million (Phillips & Simon-Davies, 2016). The estimated overseas-born population in 2016 was 28.6 percent, with a further 21 percent having at least one overseas-born parent (in total, half the population), a rate considered high compared to those of other OECD nations (ABS, 2016a; Phillips & Simon-Davies, 2016). It is therefore a prime site for historical analyses of immigrant processes, and for educational research and development relating to the teaching and learning of language and literacy.

Historically, most migrants have come to Australia from Europe, but there are increasing numbers from Asia. Of the 189,700 migrants arriving in 2016–2017, around 21 percent were from India, 15 percent from China, 6.3 percent from the Philippines, 3.5 percent from Pakistan, and 3 percent each from Vietnam and Nepal. China and India, both at about 8 percent, now rank highest as Australians' countries of birth after the UK and New Zealand (ABS, 2016b). Many of these immigrants are first-generation Chinese and Indians. Table 10.2 summarizes Australian ancestry data, showing high rates of first-generation Chinese (74.3 percent) and Indian (79.8 percent) citizens, who bring their first languages with them and who also have large existing communities of speakers.

Humanitarian migration for refugees and others who cannot return to their country of origin currently accounts for an average of around 14,000 people a year (out of 60,000–70,000 annual applications). These come from a range of countries, with an additional 12,000 from the ISIS conflict for the year 2015–2016 (Australian Government, Department of Immigration and Border Protection, 2016a, 2016b). While some of the 14,000 or so in the standard program were currently, controversially, housed offshore, their needs remained the responsibility of the Australian government. These needs entail the maintenance of education and health, and communication in their own languages. While these refugee numbers are low in terms of the overall Australian population, their linguistic and cultural diversity contributes significantly to the complexity of the educational challenges facing Australian language and literacy educators.

Table 10.2 *Selected characteristics of ancestor groups in Australia, 2011 census (ABS, 2016b). Note that tallies may exceed 100 percent, as respondents can indicate more than one category*

Ancestry			Generations in Australia		
	Persons '000	Of total population %	First generation %	Second generation %	Third-plus generation %
English	7,236	36	19	20	61
Australian	7,099	35	2	18	80
Irish	2,088	10	13	14	73
Scottish	1,793	9	17	19	64
Italian	916	5	24	41	35
German	899	5	17	20	63
Chinese	866	4	74	21	4
Indian	391	2	80	18	2
Greek	378	2	31	45	24
Dutch	336	2	36	43	24

10.3.2 Mainstream Literacy, Multilingualism, and Schooling

Recent research from a variety of sources – magnetic resonance imaging, psychological and cognitive testing, literacy testing at national and international levels, and across a range of curriculum areas – together indicates that bilingual or multilingual capacity is a significant aid to improved literacy outcomes (see also Nakamura & Holla, Chapter 8 and Schwartz, Chapter 19 in this volume). As well as establishing the benefits in personal, cognitive, academic, and social domains, many studies have identified language use and general literacy benefits from bilingual education (e.g., ACARA, 2014; Alban, 2016; Bak et al., 2014; Baker & Wright, 2017; Bialystok, 2014; Bialystok, 2016; Bialystok et al., 2014; Clyne, Hunt, & Isaakidis, 2004; Delistrati, 2014; Pinter, 2015; Rubio-Fernández & Glucksberg, 2012). These benefits include increased communicative capacity, including alternate expression in both (or all) languages; increased engagement in moving across languages, and agility in lexical choice; increased literacy skills in first and additional languages; equivalent or better performance in standardized literacy and numeracy tests; enhanced understanding of symbolic representation of print; and enhanced sense of identity and self-esteem (Morgan et al., 2016).

Despite these identified benefits, policymakers' remedy of choice for any apparent shortcomings in literacy standards has generally been to increase time allocations to English literacy instruction. This view compounds the challenges presented by such a linguistically and culturally diverse nation, where learners need to engage with a globalized, multilingual and "super diverse" world (Vertovec, 2010).

The challenges for educators, including literacy researchers, are to increase awareness of the benefits of a bilingual or multilingual approach to literacy in mainstream schooling, to address the needs of an increasingly diverse population, and to give recognition to Aboriginal and migrant populations and their language and literacy needs that go beyond English. As we have seen, assessment results for Aboriginal students in English literacy testing remain low and are compounded by social history and lack of access to learning in their first languages in the critical first few years of schooling. This situation, however, is not reflected in migrant communities: Results from the national assessment program, NAPLAN, regularly show a consistent advantage for students from non-English-speaking backgrounds (termed 'Language background other than English' [LBOTE] in these tests). These students or their parents are born overseas. Table 10.3 summarizes the 2019 results.

The findings from the standardized national assessment are consistent and unequivocal: Students with an additional language, who are likely to speak that language at home, rather than "underperforming" in fact surpass (or, in one

Table 10.3 *Mean (rounded) literacy-related scores for Years 3, 5, 7, and 9 on the National Assessment Program in Literacy and Numeracy (NAPLAN) 2019 results*

Student group	Year 3 LBOTE*	Year 3 AUST**	Year 5 LBOTE	Year 5 AUST	Year 7 LBOTE	Year 7 AUST	Year 9 LBOTE	Year 9 AUST
Reading	436	432	506	506	548	546	582	581
Writing	431	420	483	471	521	511	554	547
Grammar	447	439	507	497	548	540	580	572

Source: https://nap.edu.ay/docs/default3source/resources/naplan320193national3report.pdf?sfvsn=2

* LBOTE= results for students with language backgrounds other than English
** AUST= results for all Australian students

case match) non-LBOTE on all of these literacy measures. Left out of this program are assessments of the substantial cognitive, social, and cultural advantages, as we have seen, that LBOTE students enjoy.

10.4 A National Literacy Profile

10.4.1 International Test Results

Along with national processes for assessing literacy among school students, Australia has taken part in OECD's international literacy assessments programs for both high-school students (PISA) and adults (PIAAC, the Programme for the International Assessment of Adult Competencies). The results of these are widely reported in the media and are often brought to bear in debates about teaching, policy, and research. The rankings of the OECD nations scoring significantly above the OECD mean for reading in PISA, round 2018, and for PIAAC, round 2012, along with some related national characteristics, are summarized in Table 10.4.

Comparing the Australian profile, we see Australia rating at about the midpoints on some measures (relationship between literacy score and socioeconomic status, and expenditure per student as percent of GDP spent on schooling), and above average on other measures (overall literacy, percentage of adults with tertiary education, and inequality-adjusted education index). In its PISA 2018 "Country Note: Australia," the OECD highlighted these issues:

While Australia's reading performance in PISA 2018 was similar to that observed in 2015, when considering a longer period, mean performance in reading has been steadily declining, from initially high levels, since the country first participated in PISA in 2000 ... students' performance in reading ... was less strongly associated with

Table 10.4 OECD ranking of member nations scoring significantly above OECD mean for reading in PISA round 2018, and related national measures

Country	Mean reading score	% variance reading associated with SES	Per student expenditure '000 ** Age 6L15	InequalityL Adjusted Education index (HDR, 2019)	% GDP per cap on schools	Rank in OECD PIAAC literacy	PIAAC*** literacy ranking for category "school teachers"
Estonia	523	6	8	.87	5	8	20
Canada	520	7	11	.87	5	12	10
Finland	520	9	11	.92	7	2	3
Ireland	518	11	6	.92	4	21	11
S Korea	514	8	11	.94	5	15	14
Poland	512	12	8	.86	5	20	13
Sweden*	506	11	15	.94	8	4	9
New Zealand*	506	13	9	.86	6	5	NA
USA*	505	12	15	.85	5	18	16
UK*	504	9	11	.90	6	16	18
Japan*	504	8	10	.96	3	1	1
Australia	503	10	11	.89	5	5	2
Denmark*	501	10	7	.89	8	14	17
Norway*	499	7	15	.93	8	6	7

Table 10.4 (cont.)

Country	Mean reading score	% variance reading associated with SES	Per student expenditure '000 Age 6L15	InequalityL Adjusted Education index (HDR, 2019)	% GDP per cap on schools	Rank in OECD PIAAC literacy	PIAAC literacy ranking for category "school teachers"
Germany*	498	17	10	.91	5	17	6
Slovenia	495	12	9	.91	5	27	15
Belgium	493	17	12	.82	7	11	8
France	493	17	10	.93	5	24	19
Mean, OECD	487	12	9	.78	3.4		

* Mean reading score not significantly different from Australia's.

** In $US adjusted for purchasing power parity.

*** As reported in Freebody and Freebody (2017); the category covers early years, primary, and secondary schooling.

Sources: HDR and United Nations Development Programme. World Bank. October http://hdr.undp.org/en/content/expenditure3education3public3gdp;OECD Education Report https://data.oecd.org/eduresource/education3spending.htm; OECD 2019a PISA report: 2016, PIAAC, OECD, 2019c, www.oecd.org/skills/piaac/Skills_Matter_Further_Results_from_the_Survey_of_Adult_Skills.pdf, p. 45

socioeconomic status in Australia than on average across OECD countries. (OECD, 2019a–b, p. 1)

The rightmost columns of Table 10.4 refer to the literacy rankings of Australian adults on the tests administered as part of OECD's PIAAC program. Clearly, Australian adults rank highly on the PIAAC literacy test. In 2015 Australia's national government announced the implementation of a program of literacy testing for initial teacher-education students, as a reaction to the declining performance of Australian school students in the immediately preceding PISA tests. The government claimed that students' unsatisfactory performance was partly explained by inadequate literacy levels among Australian schoolteachers. Freebody and Freebody (2017) examined this claim using OECD's PIAAC literacy test, selecting the literacy scores of participants, from Australia and the twenty-three other participating OECD countries, who nominated "teaching" as their profession, or "teacher education" as their highest qualification. They also compared Australian teachers' scores with the scores of those of Australian participants from five comparable professional groups. They drew two main conclusions: "first, that Australian teachers, as determined by their highest qualification or their current professional status, are in the highest performing group of countries on OECD's literacy tests, and second, that Australian teachers have literacy test scores statistically comparable to other professional practitioners in Australia" (2017, p. 5). It is informative to examine OECD's own interpretation of Australian students' performance on PISA and on the national assessment program, NAPLAN. The OECD made these six recommendations concerning the teaching and assessment of literacy in Australia (*OECD Country Report Australia*, OECD 2011, pp. 152ff):

- establish national strategies for strengthening the linkages to classroom practice within the overall evaluation and assessment framework;
- promote greater national consistency while giving room for local diversity;
- reinforce the assessment validity of the national testing program and establish safeguards against an overemphasis on it;
- strengthen teachers' capacity to assess student performance against the Australian curriculum and use student assessment data;
- maintain the centrality of teacher-based assessment while ensuring the diversity of assessment formats;
- clearly establish what the country takes to be the fundamental purpose of external school evaluation – either it can "bring about general improvement across all schools or, more narrowly, it can focus on 'failing schools'" (p. 156).

Remarkable here is the notice taken of this set of recommendations by Australian governments responsible for literacy education over the intervening years: These authorities have, by acts of both omission and commission, continued to move in precisely the opposite direction on all six counts.

Perhaps the most striking aspect of the findings from PISA and PIAAC is how deeply Australian literacy educators – classroom practitioners, school leaders, teacher educators, researchers, and policymakers – are divided on the validity of these metrics and comparisons, and on their usefulness in improving the quality of literacy efforts (e.g., Freebody, 2017, 2019; Lingard, Thompson, & Sellars, 2016). The degree of attention paid by policymakers, politicians, and the media to literacy has resulted in the spectacle of recurring crises and "literacy wars" in Australia (Castles, Rastle, & Nation, 2018; Lo Bianco & Freebody, 2001; Snyder, 2008). But there have also been collaborations, summarized in Subsection 10.4.2, that have resulted in attempts to "balance" various approaches in light of the varying needs of Australian students (e.g., Cox, Feez, & Beveridge, 2019; Wyatt-Smith & Gunn, 2007).

10.4.2   A History of Opportunities, Challenges, and Dynamism

The history of Australia's institutional efforts in education has presented distinctive challenges and opportunities to literacy educators. The inconsistent management of Aboriginal and migrant education figures prominently. More recent, abrupt institutional changes in education over the period of the late 1980s and early 1990s were also influential: The institutes responsible for teacher education in Australia were amalgamated into universities, or, in some cases, combined to form aggregations that were renamed as universities. These amalgamations meant that academics in faculties or schools of educational studies in most existing universities were joined by significant numbers of colleagues from teacher-education institutions. In this relatively sudden way, different kinds of professional expertise were conjoined under the one set of institutional expectations and incentives. While teacher education and research had gone on in both university schools and colleges, the institutional emphases had been generally different; so the amalgamations called for new kinds of - and new priorities for – undergraduate teaching for some staff, and research activity and supervision for others.

These new configurations, mixing school-based "guild" experience and disciplinary-based approaches to teaching and research, brought to the surface differences around basic questions such as the nature of good teaching, how best to prepare teachers for the practical work of schools (Connell, 2009), and the research–practice relationship. New forms of debate and new opportunities for collaboration arose. Literacy education was center stage in many of these debates partly because long-standing research programs in reading and writing had developed in some university schools of psychology, linguistics, and English, as well as in some schools of education.

These amalgamations also led to ownership skirmishes across disciplinary boundaries. At worst, discipline- or site-based groups have tended to become aware of conceptual, practical, or policy developments in their professional neighborhoods. At best, more productive cross-discipline and cross-method approaches to literacy education have occurred than in some other comparably sized research settings (e.g., in the psychology of reading, Byrne, Freebody, & Gates, 1992; in reviews of literacy education, e.g., Australian Department of Employment, Education and Training, 1991, and in extended research collaborations such as Morgan et al., 2014).

The competitive dynamism that has developed within and across the various scholarly disciplines that address literacy education is evident in the volume and range of published Australian empirical and theoretical work. A well-developed line focuses on the cracking of graphic codes as they map onto speech and the educational implications of those processes (e.g., phonics teaching, alphabetic knowledge, phonemic awareness). This area has been developed largely by educational psychologists (e.g., Buckingham, Beaman, & Wheldall, 2014; Byrne, 1998, 2010; Castles et al., 2018; Coltheart, 2005; Commonwealth of Australia, 2005; Cox et al., 2019; Fielding-Barnsley & Hay, 2012). There has also been a body of research in theory within the Australian setting based on constructivist or so-called whole language approaches to the teaching of reading and writing, emphasizing Piagetian and other growth and development approaches and arguing against the pervasive use of explicit teaching and segmented, atomized skills development (e.g., Cambourne, 1988; and see the summary in Wyatt-Smith & Gunn, 2007).

A distinctive contribution to literacy education has arisen from the application of systemic functional linguistics (SFL), developed by Halliday (1985) and his students and colleagues. This contribution includes documentations and analyses of the formal curriculum-based reading and writing demands on students across the school years (most prominently Christie & Derewianka, 2008), and applications of approaches based on SFL to classroom work (Gibbons, 2014; Gray, 2007; Hammond, 2016; Martin, 1985). One application of SFL to classroom teaching and teacher professional development, called *Reading to Learn*, is summarized in Rose (2017). He outlined these key elements of the program: (i) engagement of students in curriculum texts that may be beyond their independent reading levels, (ii) interrogation of passages from texts that models comprehension processes, (iii) recognition of language usages and their related purposes, (iv) recruiting these language resources into students' writing, and (v) constructing effective, purposeful, and appropriately organized texts.

Rose (2017) summarized several research application phases demonstrating the efficacy of this program over five grade-level bands from kindergarten to Grade 8. Accuracy levels on five features of students' writing were assessed:

overall generic structure, appropriate use of register, discourse, grammar, and graphic features. Composite assessment over these phases showed not only major gains at all grade levels after six months of the program's use, but also a reduction of the gaps between previously designated literacy achievement bands within each grade level (see MacRae et al., 2000; Rose & Martin, 2013). Systemic functional linguistics has also been applied to questions about how multiple modalities and media can be put to work in literacy learning settings (e.g., Macken-Horarik et al., 2017; Painter, Martin, & Unsworth, 2013). Unsworth and Macken-Horarik (2015), for example, documented three progression points among school students' understandings of picture–language relations in multimodal texts across the elementary and secondary years:

- a "tactical orientation": early-years students describe in a variety of nonrational ways how illustrators choose to represent the language (the tactic is simply finding something apparently relevant to say);
- "diegetic orientation": images are interpreted in terms of the apparent reality of the story's world, where illustrators' choices are tied to the thoughts or feelings of the characters; and
- a "semiotic orientation": students orient to the explicit crafting of the text, the deliberate construction of the multimodal to shape the responses of readers, and an awareness of the kinds of options the illustrator exercised to represent emotion and power relations.

These researchers concluded that teachers need to work with the learners' "shifts from more idiosyncratic responses to images, on from those that attend primarily to the experiential world 'inside' the text, and toward those that respond to the shaping power of the text itself" (p. 75). Sociological approaches have also been evident in the Australian tradition of literacy research. These have included critical approaches to literacy materials used in schools (Baker & Luke, 1991; Gilbert, 1989; Green & Beavis, 2012; Luke, 1988, 2018) as well as approaches based on the rapidly changing social, technological, and vocational conditions in which schools operate, and in which increasingly diverse groups of students need to participate (Cope & Kalantzis, 2013; Farrell, 2009; Kalantzis et al., 2016; Lankshear & Knobel, 2014; Luke, Dooley, & Woods, 2011).

As a large-scale example, a series of studies in this tradition was conducted by Hill et al. (2002, and see Hill, 2002). Through a compilation of detailed case studies, they documented the literacy learning experiences of 100 children from a range of cultural and socioeconomic backgrounds, including a remote Aboriginal community. They first followed the children from preschool into school, and followed up on the same children five years later. Among many other findings, some key conclusions were that:

- most children increased their literacy capabilities substantially;

- nonetheless the range of reading and writing achievement within age groups was extensive;
- significantly lower levels of literacy were found overwhelmingly in schools serving poor communities;
- findings overall indicated that, within those patterns, the teaching that has a substantial positive effect on children's literacy learning, first, does not rely on a narrow set of teaching strategies or prepackaged curriculum content, and second, is dynamic and based on a detailed, "data-driven responsive" focus on individual students' needs. (Hill, 2002, p. 1)

In her 2002 summary, Hill concluded:

there is a need for a second safety net at 8–9 years of age for children who do not have automatic and independent literacy strategies and repertoires needed to reach their learning potential in primary school. Good first teaching, effective early intervention and a second safety net require teachers who are knowledgeable and energetic, and practise culturally responsive literacy teaching. (Hill, 2002, p. 3)

Collaborations across these fields have also included multidisciplinary focuses on the interactional details of classroom activity and learning (e.g., Edwards-Groves & Grootenboer, 2015; Martin & Maton, 2013), on new technologies, critical online analysis, and multimodal literacy activities in the middle years of schooling (e.g., Morgan et al., 2014), and on technology and diversity-oriented pedagogies (e.g., Mills et al., 2018; New London Group, 1996; SICLE, n. d.). Rapidly growing is a research base aimed at capitalizing on students' out-of-school activities in digital, online, and mobile contexts. This includes work on how classrooms can be constructed that capitalize on the new literacy affordances of these technologies (e.g., Reimann et al., & Wasson, 2016; Wells & Auld, 2014); how new media can reshape literate communications (e.g., Green & Beavis, 2013); and how literacy learning can be reliably evaluated in online, "big data" settings (e.g., Mills, 2019).

So-called C21 lines of work continue to develop along with "literacy education," conventionally construed. The real conceptual, methodological, and professional advances on offer from an integration of print and digital literacy efforts, especially in Aboriginal, community, remote, and equity settings, are yet to fully emerge in Australian education. These topics present educators and researchers with challenges in learning from literacy education's past and applying that knowledge to its future, in a unique combination of community, state, and national settings. Finally, how the various curriculum areas put literacy to work in gradually more specialized and divergent ways has assumed increasing prominence in Australian work (e.g., Christie & Maton, 2011; Martin, Maton, & Doran, 2019; Muspratt & Freebody, 2013). This may be one outcome of increased collaboration among the various groups of scholars, policymakers, and classroom practitioners, in periods of national and state curricular reform.

The influential *Alice Springs (Mparntwe) Declaration* (Education Council, 2019), for instance, identifies languages, especially Asian and Aboriginal languages, as key learning, along with English. In the national languages curriculum, a strong case is made for the benefits of students' literacy improvement in all languages through engagement in learning and using additional languages, as well as for the rights of Australian children to bilingual capabilities (ACARA, 2011, 2020). While programs managed at state and territory levels vary widely, there are positive signs: The increase of bilingual school programs is the biggest growth area in languages programs. This growth is most evident in programs that use a Content and Language Integrated Learning approach, in which specific, high-status curricular areas are taught in a second or additional language (Cross, 2015; Morgan et al., 2016). In a recent initiative, the Australian government contracted the Australian Federation of Modern Language Teachers Associations (AFMLTA, lead investigators Morgan & Scrimgeour) to develop a national plan and strategy for languages education. These initiatives indicate emerging levels of understanding of the need for bilingual and multilingual programs to support literacy learning.

10.5 Conclusions and Discussion

Australian school students and adults have performed at moderate-to-strong levels in international assessments of literacy. Australian literacy researchers have contributed significantly over several decades to debates about the nature of literacy learning and the ways in which it can be enhanced both in and out of school settings. But, as our discussion shows, there remain enduring shortcomings in the capacity and willingness of Australian education systems to address some of the dramatic variations in the quality and efficacy of current literacy education efforts.

At the time of writing, the Australian population includes about 97 percent settler and migrant groups, and there is increasing immigration from geographically neighboring countries whose cultures are far removed from those of the linguistic and social settings of the still-dominant Anglo ethnos. So one possible explanation for the continued shortcomings in effective, wholehearted multilingual or bilingual literacy education efforts on the part of a succession of Australian administrations is that, by enveloping English-only literacy within the self-evidently innocent goal of national economic productivity, the generally muffled background of xenophobia that a small, but electorally consequential minority exhibits toward Aboriginal and non-European migrant communities is channeled. A visible and relatively sudden disjunction has appeared, however, between the long-standing Anglo-centric cultural identity of Australia and the new economic and cultural dealings of Australians with their thriving local, Asian neighbors. Combined with the growing body of research on the individual and community benefits beyond monolingualism, this reorientation, based partly as it is on pragmatism, may usher in a generational change in approaches to language and literacy education.

The Australian literacy education community also encompasses several drivers of caution and conservatism when it comes to innovating practices and assessments. One is the relatively recent commercialization of programs for use in schools and homes on phonics, phonemic awareness, and alphabetic knowledge. These programs have attained the status of commodities and compete in a growing marketplace, such that the research accompanying them runs the risk of becoming, or coming to be seen as, more resistant to independent critical scrutiny and adaptation than might otherwise be the case.

This commodification of literacy learning in turn interacts with a second feature of the current literacy research field in Australia – a gradual retreat from the pressure to collaborate across disciplines and toward an intensification of methodological and citation cadres, initially stimulated by the amalgamation of the colleges and universities, and a return to a more independent, foundational disciplinary control of the research topic. For example, research on the teaching and learning of reading was traditionally a prerogative of university departments of psychology or educators working with psychological concepts and methods in the domain of "special needs" (e.g., see the extensive review in Castles et al., 2018). Similar "repossessions" may apply to departments of English and linguistics and the teaching and learning of writing (such as, e.g., creativity, composition, text construction, and so on).

A final driver of caution and conservatism is the suspicion among some groups that Anglo-Australian values and cultural mores are weakening, and the ready allocation of blame to education, specifically to education in English literacy, as the cause of this vague sense of cultural deterioration. These essentially nostalgic motivations are often exploited by conservative sections of the media, and connected simplistically to a hankering for a lost, mythical era of internal social stability and external economic competitiveness. The attribution to literacy of an almost magical relation to the economic and cultural wellbeing of the country continues to result in a growing investment in literacy as an apparently effective short-term solution, at the expense of other more patient, more carefully and consensually developed, and potentially more relevant policy options. These material and psychological investments in literacy can present a challenge to communities' and funding bodies' support for the development of useful traditions of research in literacy education. If the signifier "literacy" continues to trigger, among researchers and policymakers alike, an apparently irresistible temptation to overpromise – in terms of quality, speed, durability, and scale – then that temptation can itself become an ongoing educational liability.

But against these cautionary urges, the field of Australian literacy education – its teachers, school leaders, policymakers, teacher educators, and researchers – displays at least three sources of dynamism and optimism, and it is these that have organized our discussion in this chapter. The first is the current urge to rewrite and reread the Australian "origin narrative" – and thereby to encourage broader rights of access to those retellings. Despite the retreats and partly filled aspirations that we have related here, there are more literate Aboriginal children in schools, and more Aboriginal parents involved in school and community educational activities than ever before. These gains have been hard earned by Aboriginal activists and educators, and, as happened to Aboriginal native land title aspirations through the 1998 "amendment act," they can be eroded; but a third gain – more non-Aboriginal youngsters learning Aboriginal languages and culture than before – may make community interest in a more inclusive origin narrative harder to deflect.

A second source of dynamism and optimism in Australian literacy education arises from the reconstitution of settler culture via changing patterns of migration. The diversity and multiplicity of Australian society is continuously being renewed, and the cultural significance of migration is being made increasingly visible and, through language, audible. It offers literacy educators and researchers challenges and opportunities that potentially involve changing technologies for literate communication, increasingly complex patterns of mono-, bi-, and multilingualism, an ethic of productive inclusiveness, and a direct connection to cultural fluency and thereby to relations with geographic and trading neighbors.

These two sources of dynamism and optimism call into play a third: the need for more intensive within-and-across-discipline collaborations among researchers, using methodologies that build in deeper engagement with the teaching and educational policy professions, and with the diverse communities they serve. As with Australian culture at large, so in Australian research on language and literacy education: Fractiousness can sustain dynamism. In a weaponized commercial and sociopolitical environment, however, fractiousness can present the end users of research – educators and policymakers – with a troubling array of options. What remains abidingly clear is the need for researchers, educators, and policymakers to commit to incorporating the diversity of the users, uses, and purposes of literacy, acknowledging the complex language and culture communities that are Australia's durable endowment, rather than its burden.

References

Alban, D. (2016). The brain benefits of learning a second language. Be Brain Fit (web page). https://bebrainfit.com/benefits-learning-second-language/.

ABS (Australian Bureau of Statistics). (2016a). *Census of Population and Housing*. www.abs.gov.au/census.

ABS (Australian Bureau of Statistics). (2016b). Ancestry. www.abs.gov.au/websitedbs/censushome.nsf/home/factsheetsa?opendocument&navpos=450.

ACARA (Australian Curriculum, Assessment and Reporting Authority). (2011). *Shape of the Australian Curriculum: English*. www.acara.edu.au/_resources/Australian_Curriculum_-_English.pdf.

ACARA (Australian Curriculum, Assessment and Reporting Authority). (2014). *The Shape of the Australian Curriculum: Languages*. www.acara.edu.au/_resources/Languages_-_Shape_of_the_Australian_Curriculum_new.pdf.

ACARA (Australian Curriculum, Assessment and Reporting Authority). (2016a). *Framework for Aboriginal Languages and Torres Strait Islander Languages*. www.australiancurriculum.edu.au/languages/framework-for-aboriginal-languages-and-torres-strait-islander-languages/rationale.

ACARA (Australian Curriculum, Assessment and Reporting Authority). (2016b). *Australian Curriculum*. www.australiancurriculum.edu.au/.

ACARA (Australian Curriculum, Assessment and Reporting Authority). (2017). *2017 National Assessment Program: Literacy and Numeracy (NAPLAN), National Report 2017*. www.nap.edu.au/docs/default-source/default-document-library/naplan-national-report-2017_final_04dec2017.pdf?sfvrsn=0.

ACARA (Australian Curriculum, Assessment and Reporting Authority). (2020). *Australian Curriculum: Languages*. www.australiancurriculum.edu.au/f-10-curriculum/languages/.

Australian Department of Employment, Education and Training. (1991). *Teaching English literacy: A Project of National Significance on the preservice preparation of teachers for teaching English literacy*. 3 vols. (F. Christie, Chair). Canberra: Department of Employment, Education and Training.

Australian Department of Prime Minister and Cabinet. (2015). *Closing the Gap: Prime Minister's Report*. www.dpmc.gov.au/sites/default/files/publications/Closing_the_Gap_2015_Report.pdf.

Australian Federation of Ethnic Schools. (2016). Community Languages Australia. Website. www.communitylanguagesaustralia.org.au/.

Australian Government Department of Immigration and Border Protection. (2016a). *Fact sheet- Australia's refugee and humanitarian programme*. www.border.gov.au/about/corporate/information/fact-sheets/60refugee.

Australian Government Department of Immigration and Border Protection. (2016b). *Australia's Response to the Syrian and Iraqi Humanitarian Crisis*. www.border.gov.au/Trav/Refu/response-syrian-humanitarian-crisis.

AIATSIS (Australian Institute of Aboriginal and Torres Strait Islander Studies). (2019). Indigenous Australian languages. Web page. https://aiatsis.gov.au/explore/articles/indigenous-australian-languages.

Bak, T. H., Nissan J. J., Allerhand M. M., & Deary, I. J. (2014). Does bilingualism influence cognitive aging? *Annals of Neurology*, 75, 959–963.

Baker, C. D., & Luke, A. (eds.). (1991). *Toward a Critical Sociology of Reading Pedagogy*. Amsterdam: John Benjamins Publishing.

Baker, C. & Wright, W. E. (2017). *Foundations of Bilingual Education and Bilingualism*, 6th ed. Bristol: Multilingual Matters.

Bialystok, E. (2014). Neuroplasticity as a model for bilingualism: Commentary on Baum and Titone. *Applied Psycholinguistics, 35*, 899–902.

Bialystok, E. (2016). Aging and bilingualism: Why does it matter? *Linguistic Approaches to Bilingualism, 6*, 1–8.

Bialystok, E., Poarch, G., Luo, L, & Craik, F. I. M. (2014). Effects of bilingualism and aging on executive function and working memory. *Psychology and Aging, 29*, 696–705.

Bonnor, C., & Connors, L. (2018). Labor's $250 m promise to Catholic schools reveals a funding horror story. *Australian Education Section, Guardian*, March. www.theguardian.com/commentisfree/2018/mar/11/labors-250m-promise-to-catholic-schools-reveals-a-funding-horror-story.

Bowern, C., & Koch, H. (2004). *Australian Languages: Classification and the Comparative Method*. Current Issues in Linguistic Theory Series. Amsterdam: John Benjamins Publishing.

Buckingham, J., Beaman, R., & Wheldall, K. (2014). Why poor children are more likely to become poor readers: The early years. *Educational Review, 66*, 428–446.

Burnley, I. (1988). The population geography of Australia: Trends and prospects. *Geoforum, 19*, 263–276.

Byrne, B. (1998). *The Foundations of Literacy: The Child's Acquisition of the Alphabetic Principle*. New York: Psychology Press.

Byrne, B. (2010). Reading and reading acquisition. In M. J. Bates & M. N. Maack (eds.), *Encyclopedia of Library and Information Sciences*, 3rd edition (pp. 4404–4413). London: Taylor & Francis.

Byrne, B. B., Freebody, P., & Gates, E. A. (1992). Longitudinal data on the relations of word-reading strategies to comprehension, reading time, and phonemic awareness. *Reading Research Quarterly, 27*, 140–151.

Cambourne, B. (1988). *The Whole Story: Natural Learning and the Acquisition of Literacy in the Cassroom*. Sydney, NSW: Ashton Scholastic.

Castles, A., Rastle, K., & Nation, K. (2018). Ending the reading wars: Reading acquisition from novice to expert. *Psychological Science in the Public Interest, 19*, 5–51.

Christie, F., & Derewianka, B. (2008). *School Discourse*. London: Continuum.

Christie, F., & Maton, K. (eds). (2011). *Disciplinarity: Functional Linguistic and Sociological Perspectives*. London: Continuum.

Clarkson, C., Smith, M., Marwick, B. et al. (2015). The archaeology, chronology and stratigraphy of Madjedbebe (Malakunanja II): A site in northern Australia with early occupation. *Journal of Human Evolution, 83*, 46–64.

Clyne, M. (2005). *Australia's Language Potential*. Sydney, NSW: University of New South Wales Press.

Clyne, M. (2011). Multilingualism, multiculturalism and integration. In J. Jupp & M. Clyne (eds.), *Multiculturalism and Integration: A Harmonious Relationship*, pp. 53–71. Canberra: Australian National University Press.

Clyne, M., Hunt, C. & Isaakidis, T. (2004). Learning a community language as a third language. *International Journal of Multilingualism, 1*, 33–52.

Collins, P. C., & Peters, P. (2004). Australian English: morphology and syntax. In B. Kortmann & E. W. Schneider (eds.) *A Handbook of Varieties of English*, pp. 593–610. Berlin: Mouton de Gruyter.

Coltheart, M. (2005). Modeling reading: The Dual-Route approach. In M. J. Snowling & C. Hulme (eds.), *The Science of Reading: A Handbook*, pp. 6–23. Malden, MA: Blackwell Publishing.

Commonwealth of Australia. (2005). *Teaching Reading: National Inquiry into the Teaching of Literacy.* (K. Rowe, Chair). Australian Council for Educational Research. http://research.acer.edu.au/tll_misc/5/.

Community Languages Australia. (2019). *Project Report 2017–2018.* www.communitylanguagesaustralia.org.au/aboutus.

Connell, R. (2009). Good teachers on dangerous ground: Towards a new view of teacher quality and professionalism. *Critical Studies in Education, 50*, 213–229.

Connors, L., & McMorrow, J. (2015). *Imperatives in School Funding: Equity, Sustainability and Achievement.* Australian Education Review, Number 60, Camberwell, VIC: Australian Council for Educational Research. http://research.acer.edu.au/aer/14/.

Cope, B., & Kalantzis, M. (2013). "Multiliteracies": New literacies, new learning. In M. R. Hawkins (ed.), *Framing Languages and Literacies: Socially Situated Views and Perspectives*, pp. 105–135. New York: Routledge.

Cox, R., Feez, S., & Beveridge, L. (eds.) (2019). *The Alphabetic Principle and Beyond: Surveying the Landscape.* Newtown, NSW: Primary English Teaching Association of Australia.

Cross, R. (2015). Defining content and language integrated learning for languages education in Australia. *Babel, 49*, 4–12.

Delistrati, J. (2014). The cognitive benefits of multilingualism. *The Atlantic.* www.theatlantic.com/health/archive/2014/10/more-languages-better-brain/381193/.

Devlin, B. (2009). Bilingual education in the Northern Territory and the continuing debate over its effectiveness and value. Paper presented to AIATSIS Research Symposium, Canberra. www.abc.net.au/4corners/special_eds/20090914/language/docs/Devlin_paper.pdf.

Devlin, B. (2010). Evidence, policy, and the step model of bilingual education in the Northern Territory: A brief outline. Paper presented to public forum "Bilingual Education in the Northern Territory," Charles Darwin University. www.ns.uca.org.au/wp-content/uploads/2010/09/Evidence-in-Bilingual-Education.pdf.

Disbray, S. (2019). Realising the Australian curriculum framework for Aboriginal languages and Torres Strait Islander languages. *Babel, 54*(1/2), 21–25.

Disbray, S., and Loakes, D. (2013). Writing Aboriginal English and creoles: Five case studies in Australian educational contexts. *Australian Review of Applied Linguistics, 36*, 285–301.

Dixon, S. (2013). Educational failure or success: Aboriginal children's non-standard English utterances. *Australian Review of Applied Linguistics, 36*, 302–315.

Eades, D. (1991). Communicative strategies in Aboriginal English. In S. Romaine (ed.) *Language in Australia* (pp 84–93). Sydney: Cambridge University Press, pp. 84–93.

Eades, D. (2014). Aboriginal English. In H. Koch and R. Nordlinger (eds.), *The Languages and Linguistics of Australia: A Comprehensive Guide* (pp. 417–447). Berlin: Walter de Gruyter.

Education Council. (2019). Alice Springs (Mparntwe) Education. https://docs.education.gov.au/documents/alice-springs-mparntwe-education-declaration.

Edwards-Groves, C., & Grootenboer, P. (2015). Practice and praxis in literacy education. *Australian Journal of Language and Literacy, 38*, 150–161.

Ellis, E. (2008). Defining and investigating mono-lingualism. *International Journal Sociolinguistic Studies*, *2*, 173–196.

Ellis, E. (2016). The pluri-lingual TESOL teacher. *Trends in Applied Linguistics*, Vol. 25. Berlin: de Gruyter Mouton.

Evans, N., & Sasse, H-P. (eds.) (2002). *Problems of Polysynthesis*. Studia Typologica, Neue Reihe. Berlin: Akademie Verlag.

Farrell, L. (2009). Testing the future: Work, literacies, and economies. In M. Baynham & M. Prinsloo (eds.), *The Future of Literacy Studies* (pp. 181–198). London: Palgrave Macmillan.

Fielding-Barnsley, R., & Hay, I. (2012). Comparative effectiveness of phonological awareness and oral language intervention for children with low emergent literacy skills. *Australian Journal of Language and Literacy, 35*, 271–286.

First Languages Australia. (2020). www.firstlanguages.org.au/projects/schools.

Fischer, S. R. (2001). *A History of Writing*. London: Reaktion.

Freebody, P. (2017). Evidence and culture in the global literacy education competition – and other possibilities. In A. Lian, P. Kell, P. Black, & Lie, K-Y. (eds.), *Challenges in Global Learning: Dealing with Education Issues from an International Perspective* (pp. 70–94). Cambridge: Cambridge Scholars Publishing.

Freebody, P. (2019). What kind of knowledge can we use? Scoping an adequate program for literacy education. In R. Cox, S. Feez, & L. Beveridge (eds.), *The Alphabetic Principle and Beyond: Surveying the Landscape* (pp. 32–47). Newtown, NSW,: Primary English Teaching Association of Australia.

Freebody, S., & Freebody, P. (2017). Australian teachers' literacy levels: Comparisons from the OECD international Survey of Adult Skills. *Hot topics in literacy education*, (pp. 1–9). Australian Literacy Educators Association, www.alea.edu.au/publicresources/alea-hot-topics.

Gale, M. (1994). Bi-lingual education programs in Aboriginal schools. In D. Hartman and J. Henderson (eds.), *Aboriginal Languages in Education* (pp. 192–203). Alice Springs: Institute for Aboriginal Development.

Gibbons, P. (2014). *Scaffolding Language, Scaffolding Learning*. London: Heinemann.

Gilbert, P. (1989). *Writing, Schooling and Deconstruction: From Voice to Text in the Classroom*. London: Routledge.

Gonski, D. (Chair). (2011). *Review of Funding for Schooling – Final Report*. Canberra: Department of Education, Employment and Workplace Relations. https://docs.education.gov.au/system/files/doc/other/review-of-funding-for-schooling-final-report-dec-2011.pdf.

Goot, M., & Rowse, T. (2007). *Divided Nation: Indigenous Affairs and the Imagined Public*. Melbourne: Melbourne University Publishing.

Gray, B. (2007). *Accelerating the Literacy Development of Indigenous Students*. Darwin: Charles Darwin University Press.

Green, B., & Beavis, C. (2012). *Literacy in 3D: An Integrated Perspective in Theory and Practice*. Camberwell, Vic.: Australian Council for Educational Research.

Green, B., & Beavis, C. (2013). Literacy education in the age of new media. In K. Hall, T. Cremin, B. Comber, & L. Moll (eds.), *International Handbook of Research on Children's Literacy, Learning, and Culture* (pp. 42–53). Oxford: Wiley-Blackwell.

Hajek, J., & Slaughter, Y. (eds.) (2014). *Challenging the Monolingual Mindset*. London: Multilingual Matters.

Halliday, M. A. K. (1985). *An Introduction to Functional Grammar*. London: Edward Arnold.

Hammond, J. (2016). Dialogic space: intersections between dialogic teaching and systemic functional linguistics. *Research Papers in Education*, *31*, 5–22.

Harrington, M. (2012). Australia in the Asian Century: Asian Studies in Schools. Parliament of Australia. www.aph.gov.au/About_Parliament/Parliamentary_Departments/Parliamentary_Library/FlagPost/2012/November/Australia_in_the_Asian_Century_Asian_studies_in_schools.

Harris, J., & Sandefur, J. (1984). The creole language debate and the use of creoles in Australian schools. *Aboriginal Child at School*, *12*, 8–29.

Hill, S., Comber, B., Louden, B., Rivalland, J., & Reid, J. (2002). *100 Children Turn 10: A Longitudinal Study of Literacy Development from the Year Prior to School to the First Four Years of School*. Canberra: Department of Education, Science and Training.

Horton, D. R. (1996). *Map of Aboriginal Australia, Circa 1788*. Australian Institute of Aboriginal and Torres Strait Islander Studies (AIATSIS). Canberra: Aboriginal Studies Press.

Hudson, P., & Taylor-Henley, S. (1995). First Nations child and family services: Facing the realities. *Canadian Social Work Review*, *12*, 72–84.

International Monetary Fund. (2020). *World Economic Outlook, 2019*. Washington, DC: International Monetary Fund. www.imf.org/en/Publications/WEO/Issues/2019/10/01/world-economic-outlook-october-2019.

Jupp, J., & Clyne, M. (eds.). (2011). *Multiculturalism and Integration: A Harmonious Relationship*. Canberra: Australian National University Press.

Kalantzis, M., Cope, B., Chan, E., & Dalley-Trim, L. (2016). *Literacies*, 2nd ed. Melbourne: Cambridge University Press.

Kaldor, S., and Malcolm, I. (1991). Aboriginal English: An overview. In S. Romaine (ed.), *Language in Australia*, pp. 67–83. Sydney: Cambridge University Press.

Kleinert, S., & Neale, M. (eds.) (2000). *The Oxford Companion to Aboriginal Art and Culture*. Melbourne: Oxford University Press.

Koch, H., and Nordlinger, R. (2014). *The Languages and Linguistics of Australia*. Amsterdam: Mouton de Gruyter.

Lankshear, C., & Knobel, M. (2014). Englishes and digital literacy practices. In C. Leung & V. Street (eds.), *The Routledge Companion to English Studies*, pp. 451–463. London: Routledge.

Lingard, B., Thompson, G., & Sellar, S. (2016). *National Testing in Schools: An Australian Assessment*. Abingdon: Routledge.

Lo Bianco, J., & Freebody, P. (2001). *Australian Literacies: Informing National Policy on Literacy Education*, revised 2nd ed. Canberra: Language Australia.

Lo Bianco, J., & Slaughter, Y. (2009). *Second Languages and Australian Schooling*. Melbourne: Australian Council for Educational Research.

Luke, A. (1988). *Literacy, Textbooks, and Ideology: Postwar Literacy and the Mythology of Dick and Jane*. London: Falmer Press.

Luke, A. (2018). *Critical Literacy, Schooling, and Social Justice: The Selected Works of Allan Luke*. London: Routledge.

Luke, A., Dooley, K., & Woods, A. (2011). Comprehension and content: Planning literacy in low socioeconomic and culturally diverse schools. *Australian Educational Researcher, 38*, 149–166.

Macken-Horarik, M., Love, K., Sandiford, C., & Unsworth, L. (2017). *Functional Grammatics: Re-conceptualizing Knowledge about Language and Image for School English*. London: Routledge.

Malaspinas, A., Westaway, M. C., Muller, C. et al. (2016). A genomic history of Aboriginal Australia. *Nature, 538*, 207–214.

Martin, J. R. (1985). *Factual Writing: Exploring and Challenging Social Reality*. Geelong: Deakin University Press.

Martin, J. R., & Maton, K. (eds.). 2013. Special Issue on Cumulative Knowledge-Building in Secondary Schooling. *Linguistics and Education*, 24.

Martin, J. R., Maton, K., & Doran, Y. J. (2019). *Accessing Academic Discourse: Systemic Functional Linguistics and Legitimation Code Theory*. London: Routledge.

Migration Heritage Centre, NSW, Powerhouse Museum. (n. d.). Objects through Time: 1616 Dirk Hartog Plate. www.migrationheritage.nsw.gov.au/exhibition/objects throughtime/hartog/.

Mills, K. A. (2019). *Big Data for Qualitative Research*. London: Routledge.

Mills, K. A., Stornaiuolo, A., Smith, A., & Pandya, J. (2018). Handbook of Writing, *Literacies, and Education in Digital Cultures*. London: Routledge.

Morgan, A-M., Comber, B., Freebody, P., & Nixon, H. (2014). *Literacy in the Middle Years: Learning from Collaborative Classroom Research*. Sydney: Primary English Teachers' Association of Australia.

Morgan, A-M, Kohler, M., & Harbon, L. (2011). Developing intercultural language learning textbooks: Methodological trends, engaging with the intercultural construct, and personal reflections on the process. *International Association for Research on Textbooks and Educational Media, 4*, 20–51.

Morgan, A-M., Scrimgeour, A., Farmer, K., Dodd, C., & Saunders, S. (2016). *Effective Practice in Early Years (Prep-Year 2) Languages Programmes*. Commissioned report for the Queensland Department of Education and Training. www.afmlta.asn.au/documents/item/192.

Murtagh, E. J. (1982). Creole and English as languages of instruction in bilingual education with Aboriginal Australians: Some research findings. *International Journal of the Sociology of Language, 36*, 15–33.

Muspratt, S., & Freebody, P. (2013). Understanding the disciplines of science: Analysing the language of science textbooks. In M. S. Khine (ed.), *Critical Analysis of Science Textbooks: Evaluating Instructional Effectiveness* (pp. 33–60). Dordrecht: Springer Science.

New London Group. (1996). A pedagogy of multiliteracies: Designing social futures. *Harvard Educational Review, 66*, 60–92.

New South Wales Education Department. (2019). *Annual Report 2018*. Sydney: NSW Department of Education. https://education.nsw.gov.au/content/dam/main-education/about-us/strategies-and-reports/media/documents/2018-annual-report.pdf.

Nicholls, C. (2005). Death by a thousand cuts: Indigenous language bilingual education programs in the Northern Territory of Australia, 1972–1998. *International Journal of Bilingual Education and Bilingualism*, 8, 160–177.

Nunn, P., & Reid, N. (2016). Aboriginal memories of inundation of the Australian coast dating from more than 7000 years ago: Analysis of the complete dataset and its implications. *Australian Geographer*, 47, 11–47.

OECD. (2011). Policy outlook. *OECD Country Report on Australia*. Paris: OECD Publishing. www.oecd.org/edu/EDUCATION_POLICY_OUTLOOK_AUSTRALIA_EN.pdf.

OECD. (2019a). *PISA 2018 Results (Volume I): What Students Know and Can Do*. Paris: OECD Publishing. DOI: https://doi.org/10.1787/5f07c754-en.

OECD. (2019b). *Country Note, PISA 2018: Australia*. OECD. Website. https://apo.org.au/node/270241?utm_source=APOfeed&utm_medium=RSS&utm_campaign=rss-all.

OECD. (2019c). Programme for the International Assessment of Adult Competencies (PIAAC). OECD. Website. www.oecd.org/skills/piaac/about/piaac.

Oldfield, J., & Lo Bianco, J. (2019). A long unfinished struggle: Literacy and Indigenous cultural and language rights. In J. Rennie & H. Harper (eds.), *Literacy and Indigenous Australians: Theory, Research, and Practice*, pp. 165–184. Dordrecht: Springer Nature.

Painter, C., Martin, J. R., & Unsworth, L. (2013). *Reading Visual Narratives: Image Analysis of Children's Picture Books*. London: Equinox Publishing.

Phillips, J., & Simon-Davies, J. (2016). *Migration to Australia: A quick guide to the statistics*. Parliament of Australia. Web page. www.aph.gov.au/About_Parliament/Parliamentary_Departments/Parliamentary_Library/pubs/rp/rp1516/Quick_Guides/MigrationStatistics.

Pinter, A. (2015). *Teaching Young Language Learners*. Oxford: Oxford University Press.

Purdie, N., Frigo, T., Ozolins, C. et al. (2008). *Indigenous Language Programs in Australian Schools: A Way Forward*. Australian Council for Educational Research Report. ACEResearch. Website. http://research.acer.edu.au/indigenous_education/18/.

Reid, N. (2010). Maintenance and revival strategies for Indigenous languages: Lessons from Australia. In K. Sengupta (ed.), *Proceedings of the 2009 Symposium on Intangible Cultural Heritage*. New Delhi: Indian National Trust for Art and Cultural Heritage.

Reimann, P., Bull, B., Kickmeier-Rust, M., Vatrapu, R., & Wasson, B. (eds.), (2016). *Measuring and Visualizing Learning in the Information-Rich Classroom*, (pp. 137–153). New York: Routledge.

Rennie, J., & Harper, H. (eds.). (2019). *Literacy Education and Indigenous Australians: Theory, Research, and Practice*. Dordrecht: Springer Nature.

Rose, D. (2017). *Evaluating the Task of Language Learning*. In B. Miller, P. McCardle, & V. Connelly (eds.), *Writing Development in Struggling Learners: Understanding the Needs of Writers Across the Lifecourse* (pp. 161–181). Leiden: Brill Academic Publishers.

Rose, D., & Martin, J. R. (2012). *Learning to Write, Reading to Learn: Genre, Knowledge and Pedagogy in the Sydney School*. Sheffield: Equinox.

Rubio-Fernández, P., & Glucksberg, S. (2012). Reasoning about other people's beliefs: Bilinguals have an advantage. *Journal of Experimental Psychology: Learning, Memory, and Cognition*, *38*, 211–217.

Scrimgeour, A., Morgan, A., Cruikshank, K., & Hajek, J. (2019). Refocusing on community languages. *Babel*, *53*, 5–16.

Sellwood, J., & Angelo, D. (2013). Everywhere and nowhere: The invisibility of Aboriginal and Torres Strait Island contact languages in education and indigenous language contexts. *Australian Review of Applied Linguistics*, *36*, 250–266.

Sharifian, F. (2001). Aboriginal English in the classroom: An asset or a liability? *Language Awareness*, *17*, 131–138.

Sharifian, F. (2005). Cultural conceptualizations in English words: as study of Aboriginal children in Perth. *Language and Education*, *19*, 74–88.

Shinkfield, A., & Jennings, B. (2019). Family story time in the Ngaanyatjarra Early Years program. In J. Rennie & H. Harper (eds.), *Literacy Education and Indigenous Australians* (pp. 71–86). Language Policy Series, vol. 19, series eds. J. Lo Bianco & T.G. Wiley. Dordrecht: Springer Nature.

Siegel, J. (1999). Creoles and minority dialects in education: An overview. *Journal of Multilingual and Multicultural Development*, *20*, 508–531.

Simpson, J. (2019). The Horwood Memorial Lecture: Learning and speaking first Nations Languages in Australia. *Babel*, *54*, 7–11.

Simpson, J., Caffery, J., & McConvell, P. (2009). Gaps in Australia's Indigenous language policy: Dismantling bilingual education in the Northern Territory. AIATSIS. www.aiatsis.gov.au/research/publications/discussion_papers.

Simpson, J., Disbray, S., & O'Shannessy, C. (2019). Setting the scene: Aboriginal and Torres Strait Islander languages learning and teaching. *Babel*, *54*, 7–10.

Simpson, J., McConvell, P., & Thieberger, N. (2019). Languages past and present. In W. Arthur & F. Morphy (eds.), *Macquarie Atlas of Indigenous Australia*, 2nd ed. (pp. 76–85). Sydney: Pan Macmillan.

Slaughter, Y., & Hajek, J. (2014). Mainstreaming of Italian in Australian schools: The paradox of success? In J. Hajek & Y. Slaughter (eds.), *Challenging the Monolingual Mindset* (pp. 182–198). Bristol: Multilingual Matters.

Snyder, I. (2008). *The Literacy Wars: Why Teaching Children to Read and Write Is a Battleground in Australia*. Sydney: Allen & Unwin.

Sydney Institute for Community Language Education (SICLE). (n. d.). The Sydney Institute for Community Language Education. Website. www.sydney.edu.au/arts/our-research/centres-institutes-and-groups/sydney-institute-community-languages-education.html.

Taylor, L. (1996). *Seeing the Inside: Bark Painting in Western Arnhem Land*. Oxford: Oxford University Press.

Thomson, S., De Bortoli, L., & Buckley, S. (2012). *PISA 2012: How Australia Measures Up: The PISA 2012 Assessment of Students' Mathematical, Scientific and Reading Literacy*. Melbourne: Australian Council for Educational Research (ACER). http://research.acer.edu.au/cgi/viewcontent.cgi?article=1015&context=ozpisa.

Thomson, S., Hillman, K., Schmid, M., Rodrigues, S., & Fullarton, J. (2017). *Highlights from PIRLS 2016: Australia's Perspective*. Melbourne: Australian Council for Educational Research (ACER).

UNDP (United Nations Development Program). (2019). *Human Development Report*. New York: UNDP. http://hdr.undp.org/en/2019-report.

UNESCO (2003). *Language Vitality and Endangerment*. www.unesco.org/culture/ich/doc/src/00120-EN.pdf.

Unsworth, L., & Macken-Horarik, M. (2015). Interpretive responses to images in picture books by primary and secondary school students: Exploring curriculum expectations of a "visual grammatics." *English in Education*, *49*(1), 56–79.

Vertovec, S. (2010). Towards post-multiculturalism? Changing communities, conditions and contexts of diversity. *International Social Science Journal*, *61*, 83–95.

Wells, M., & Auld, G. (2014). Literacy teaching and learning in digital times: Tales of classroom interactions. In B. Doecke, G. Auld, & M. Wells (eds.), *Becoming a Teacher of Language and Literacy* (pp. 63–82). Melbourne: Cambridge University Press.

Wigglesworth, G., Billington, R., & Loakes, D. (2013). Teaching creole-speaking children: Issues, concerns and resolutions for the classroom. *Australian Review of Applied Linguistics*, *36*, 234–249.

Wigglesworth, G., Simpson, J., & Loakes, D. (2011). NAPLAN language assessments for Indigenous children in remote communities: Issues and problems. *Australian Review of Applied Linguistics*, *34*, 320–343.

Wilks-Smith, N. (2017). The place of learners' languages in literacy programs: Bringing learners' home languages in through the school gate. *Babel*, *52*, 27–35.

World Bank. (2018). GDP per person employed (constant 2017 PPP $). Online data. https://data.worldbank.org/indicator/SL.GDP.PCAP.EM.KD?view=chart.

Wyatt-Smith, C., & Gunn, S. (2007). Evidence-based research for expert literacy teaching. Paper Number 12. Melbourne: Victorian Department of Education and Early Childhood Development. www.education.vic.gov.au/Documents/school/teachers/teachingresources/discipline/english/proflearn/litsumm.pdf.

Part II

Neurobiological and Ecological Markers

11 Writing Systems and Global Literacy Development

Charles Perfetti and Ludo Verhoeven

11.1 Introduction

A global perspective on literacy compels our attention to global variation in languages and writing systems. The history of writing involves processes of discovery, borrowing, and modification, which language communities go through when they move toward a literate society. These processes require choices regarding the graphic forms of that writing system and how they connect to the spoken language, as well as choices regarding broader cultural and educational considerations, including how new generations can learn this writing to understand their language. Across the globe, writing systems have developed varying solutions to how to represent their spoken language, that is, its phonological, morphological, and semantic properties. In what follows, we examine some of the solutions to this mapping problem using invention and variation and suggest how general principles aid the process of learning to read across languages and writing systems.

11.2 Inventing a Writing System

A single hypothetical situation can set the stage for the invention of a writing system: Suppose a preliterate people want to bring literacy to their language and come to an expert – a reading scientist, a linguist, or a writing scholar – for advice on how to design the writing system. What should the advice be – about the graphic forms? About how these forms relate the spoken language? About how people will learn to use this writing to understand their language? Before we turn to these questions, we consider the plausibility of this hypothetical situation.

Of course, written language did not usually come into existence through the advice of expert counsel, but through cultural and technological developments mediated by social transactions within and between language communities. In other words, written language evolved. Nevertheless, there have been many inventions of writing systems, or, more carefully, rediscoveries involving language-specific and culturally specific adaptations of the basic systems described by writing scholars (e.g., Daniels, 1990; 1996; Gelb, 1952). One of the most widely noted of these inventions is the creation of the alphabetic Hangul for the Korean language by King Sejong in the fifteenth century (De Francis, 1989; Kim-Renaud, 2000), which has now served the Korean language for about 470 years. However, the survival of an invented writing system to multigenerational use is relatively rare. The overwhelming majority of invented systems were limited in use and survive mainly as curiosities. For example, Benjamin Franklin, a prolific inventor, tried his hand at improving the English alphabet by getting rid of the consonants c, j, q, w, x, and y, and, adding some vowel letters, keeping the number of letters at twenty-six. Dozens of similar examples exist.

More relevant for a global perspective on universal literacy are cases of invention in nonliterate societies. For example, in regions of West Africa, some twenty scripts have been developed since 1830, including one in 2002 (Kelly, 2019). Among cases in which the development was led by nonliterate speakers, some systems survived – for example, the Vai language (Mande family) spoken in present-day Sierra Leone and Liberia, for which a syllabary was invented. Other inventions by nonliterates did not survive. For example, the Kpelle syllabary was developed in 1935 to write another West African language, Kpelle (also Mande family), and was used in Liberia and Guinea for a time before succumbing to the fate of a "failed script" (Unseth, 2011).

Especially interesting is the suggestion by Daniels (1992) that the kind of writing developed was different when it was invented by illiterates, as syllabaries were chosen more often than when the system was created by a person who was literate. As noted by Kelly (2019), this suggestion resonates with the conclusion that syllables are perceptually salient and are more manageable speech units for mapping to writing than those used in other systems (e.g., Liberman, 1973). A literate mind is aware of other possibilities for mapping, including the less perceptually accessible phoneme. Indeed, the application of alphabetic systems on nonliterate languages seems to arise only when those who develop the system are not only literate, but alphabetically literate. Additionally, the replacement of existing systems also occurs, and when this happens it is usually replacement by alphabet. This occurred, for example, when Portuguese missionaries introduced alphabetic writing for the Vietnamese language, which had been written in the Chinese system. This led eventually to the replacement of the Chinese system by the Portuguese version of the Latin alphabet, leading to its modern form of Chữ Quốc Ngữ, which requires diacritics to represent additional phonemes and the five tones of Vietnamese.

Consistent with the idea of the basic discoverability of syllabaries are the inventions of syllabaries for indigenous peoples of North America. An especially informative case is the invention of a syllabary for Cherokee, provided by Sequoyah, a member of the Cherokee nation. Sequoyah began by developing a pictorial or meaning symbol for each word in Cherokee. However, he

Writing Systems and Global Literacy Development 243

eventually abandoned this solution because of the excessive demand of creating pictures and more abstract symbols. According to an entry in the Chronicles of Oklahoma (Davis, 1930, p. 160):

Sequoyah at last discovered that the language was made up of a number of recurring sounds, that there were certain voiced sounds with which the words ended and other less pronounced sounds to go with these to make up the word. He set to work to analyze the language, to go to all public gatherings and to listen attentively to all speeches and conversations in order to be sure that no sound was overlooked.

To map this inventory of sounds to writing, Sequoyah developed a graph for each syllable, arriving at a system of eighty-six characters. To quote again from Davis's entry in the *Chronicles of Oklahoma* (p. 160):

He obtained an old English book, and, although he had no idea of the sounds represented by the English characters, he decided to adapt these characters to his use. The forms were simpler and more distinct than the ones he had been making, they were more easily read and remembered and were easier to make. After taking some of the letters, modifying others, and inventing some forms of his own, Sequoyah had ... a syllabary, with which he could write any word in his native language.

The resulting Cherokee syllabary is illustrated in Figure 11.1, where one can see a combination of familiar Latin letters and some less familiar invented forms. Thus, we see here the recapitulation of the ordering of writing system mapping levels (syllables before phonemes) that developed over a period of time between 5,000 and 3,000 years ago.

A realization that written graphs can represent ideas comes relatively easily, beginning with the idea of using pictures (pictographs). When followed later by

Figure 11.1 The Cherokee syllabary invented by Sequoya. Each "letter" stands for a syllable in the spoken language. Courtesy of Rob Ferguson, Jr – Public Domain, https://commons.wikimedia.org/w/index.php?curid=6771856

the insight that abstract symbols can also refer to ideas, this allows even more ideas to be expressed. But the challenge of the large inventory of symbols required for this solution is daunting enough to eventually prompt the idea of having the graphs represent sounds instead of meanings. The speech sounds that are the most accessible are syllables. Hence, the syllabary is likely to be the form invented by the nonliterate mind, although there are some examples of alphasyllabaries being invented (Kelly, 2019).

Other indigenous languages in North America also created syllabaries. The Cree syllabary is used by about 70,000 Algonquian-speaking people in Canada. Its form as an invented script was influenced by the Cherokee example. Unlike the case of Cherokee, the inventor of Cree, James Evans, a missionary and amateur linguist, was far from illiterate. He was familiar with the alphasyllabic (abugida) Devanagari as well as shorthand. The Cree forms, shown in Table 11.1, suggest an adaptation of an alphasyllabary form, using the orientation of a consonant graph (rather than a diacritic) to represent the vowel.

We have highlighted some examples of invented systems with an emphasis on the tendency for invented writing systems to be syllabaries when the inventor is nonliterate. In contrast, there is a tendency for alphabets to be adapted to the language when the inventors are literate. The history of writing is dominantly one of discovery, borrowing, and modification over long periods of time. However, the processes of invention and adaptation of existing systems have been rather common, for both a language that is not yet written and also a language that already has a writing system. Invention and adaptation, in addition to simple adoption, are the two avenues open to language communities seeking to move from nonliterate to literate.

Table 11.1 *The Cree Syllabary: Basic forms represent consonants. The orientation of the form represents a vowel*

	a	E	I	o
-	◁	▽	△	▷
p	⋖	∨	∧	⋗
t	⊂	∪	∩	⊃
k	┕	┑	┍	┙
ch	∪	∩	∩	∪
m	∟	┐	┌	┘
n	◖	┬	σ	◗
s	↘	↙	↗	↖
y	↳	↲	↱	↰

11.3 Variations in How Language Is Written

The preceding section highlighted just a few of the variations in writing that have come through invention and adaptation. In this section, we provide a general account of the relevant features of writing that might matter for literacy.

11.3.1 Graphic Forms and Mapping Solutions in Writing Systems

When one examines the writing of a specific language or reviews the large inventory of invented writing, one is struck by the variety of visual forms. On further examination, one is impressed by the relative complexity of possible mapping solutions. The job of classification of writing, as with any taxonomy, is a balancing act. The need to provide principled structure to the variety of what is found must be balanced against the obligation to respect significant differences. The balance point differs in alternative classification schemes. The three-way classification scheme (Gelb, 1952) struck the balance on the side of the broadest principles that could characterize solutions to the mapping problem. The five-way classification of Daniels (1996) struck a balance that added differentiation, partly reflective of analyses of the historical development of writing and arguably more accurately reflecting the differences among syllabaries, alphabets, and systems that represent consonant phonemes only and that represent some syllabic information blended into phoneme representation.

The mapping problem to solve is how the written graphs will be related to units in the spoken language. The mapping solutions have been to map graphs onto (1) morphemes (meaning forms), (2) syllables or (3) phonemes, often mixing at least two of these three solutions, with more weight on one or the other. The solution to the mapping problem faces multiple constraints. Meaning mapping presents a simple solution that gets from a graphic form to a meaning, but leads to an enormous number of graphs, even when the graphs for meanings can be combined for new meanings, as they can be in Chinese meaning compounds. Mapping to speech units is much more productive: Relatively few graphs allow the expression in writing of any idea that can be expressed in the language. Thus, speech-level mapping allows the written language to attain the full productivity of the spoken language.

A system of five mapping solutions (Daniels, 1990; Daniels and Bright, 1996) provides a useful balance between simplicity and differentiation. This system, using terms introduced by Daniels (1990), refines the broader category of alphabetic writing used by Gelb (1952), adding consonant-based systems: abjads, the consonant systems that originated in the Middle East (and were the forbearers of

Table 11.2 *Five-way classification of writing systems*

Mapping type	Written language examples
Morphosyllabary	Chinese, Japanese Kanji
Syllabary	Cree, Japanese Kana
Abjad	Arabic, Amharic, Hebrew,
Alphasyllabary (abugida)	Hindi, Telugu
Alphabet	Spanish, Korean, English

alphabets) and serve West Semitic languages, and the abugida or alphasyllabaries[1] that serve many languages of South Asia. Table 11.2 shows these five types.

All systems represent speech to some extent. Syllable-based mapping is seen in the syllabary system, in which graph-to-syllable mapping is direct and exclusive; that is, the graphs do not generally map onto morphemes. In contrast, the morphosyllabary system that evolved in China, spreading also to other areas in East and Southeast Asia, maps the graphs to syllables that are also morphemes, with the syllable pronunciation of complex graphs (characters) inconsistently signaled by components within the character. The abjad system is consonant-based, with root consonants that represent morphemes and that are spatially distributed rather than necessarily contiguous. The abugida orthographies combine syllabic and alphabetic features with graphs that represent consonant–vowel sequences; as in the abjads, the consonant is the obligatory element.

These five types appear to sample the full range of implemented solutions to the mapping problem. They all meet the fundamental constraint on writing systems, that they connect graphs with units of language. Pictographs and ideographs are possible, but because they are not practical, they have not survived the pressure for efficiency that is provided by language mapping. Pure logography, mapping graphs to words, is an inefficient option that does not survive among modern writing systems; despite the recurring use of this term to refer to Chinese, it is only roughly approximated by the Chinese morphosyllabary. Thus, writing maps to language, to its phonology (always), and to its morphology (often, and in variable ways).

---

[1] Abugida and alphasyllabaries refer to functionally identical but technically different categories (Bright, 2000). Daniels's (1990) term "abugida" reflects the Ethiopian names for key consonant letters.

11.3.2 Scripts and Layouts of Writing

It is important not to be misled by the simplicity of these solutions to the mapping problem. If we shift attention from what matters for classification to what matters for reading, we find there are more things to consider than whether a graph maps to a morpheme, a syllable, or a phoneme. Daniels and Share (2018; also Share & Daniels, 2015) describe ten dimensions of writing variation that may be important in characterizing the complexity of a writing system and its impact on reading. Most of these dimensions concern the details of the orthography, or the specific way in which a written language implements its writing systems. The orthographic features center on phonographic challenges that have been a focus of much discussion, for example, the failure of spellings to change when pronunciations do. Others are about visual-spatial factors that arise from the choice of graphs and their arrangement for the reader, for example, the distorting of standalone graph shapes when they are joined together though ligature.

The visual forms of the graphs, along with conventions for displaying the graphs, constitute the script of a writing system. Compared with issues of mapping, i.e., the differences between alphabetic and nonalphabetic systems, differences between scripts have received less attention, even though the visual appearance of the script is initially the most salient feature confronting the learner. The forms of the graphs, which reflect their intrinsic visual complexity and their discriminability from other graphs, could potentially affect the identification of written units – single letters and letter combinations in alphabets and abjads, akshara (consonant–vowel combinations) in alphasyllabaries, syllables in syllabaries, and characters in morphosyllabaries (Pelli et al., 2006). Thus, the visual complexity of graphs is a prime candidate for a nonmapping factor that could make a difference in reading.

One proven measure of a graph's visual demands is perimetric complexity, which captures the overall configurational complexity of a graph (Pelli et al., 2006)[2]. Another is a multidimensional approach, which uses perimetric complexity and additional graph-design measures (Chang, Chen, & Perfetti, 2017). GraphCom, the measure described by Chang et al. (2017), consists of four dimensions applied to a graph: perimetric complexity, number of disconnected components, number of connected points, and number of simple features (strokes). Chang et al. applied GraphCom to 131 written languages representing the 5 major writing systems of Table 11.2.

Table 11.3 shows an example of GraphCom's complexity dimensions applied to a representative orthography from each of the five systems. One can see relatively simple graphs, from abjads and alphabets, compared with

---

[2] Perimetric complexity is the ratio of the square of the sum of inside and outside perimeters to 4π x the area of the foreground, the space occupied by the graph.

Table 11.3 *Example graphs from five writing systems with GraphCom complexity values**

Writing system	Abjad	Alphabet	Syllabary	Alphasyllabary	Morphosyllabary
Written language	Hebrew	Russian	Cree	Telugu	Chinese
Example grapheme	ב	3	△·	ఌః	面
PC	6.02	7.83	12.04	18.06	20.85
DC	2	1	3	3	1
CP	1	1	3	2	14
SF	3	3	6	5	9

* PC = Perimetric complexity, DC = number of disconnected components, CP = number of connected points, SF = number of simple features. Based on Chang et al. (2017).

much more complex graphs from alphasyllabaries and the Chinese morphosyllabary. Further, one can see that while Telugu and Chinese are fairly close in perimetric complexity, Chinese is more complex in its use of connected points and the total number of simple features.

GraphCom has been validated through correlations with performance on perceptual tasks, and provides an ordering of graphic complexity across 131 languages that aligns with intuitive judgments and demonstrates differences among writing systems. Chinese has by far the highest average complexity in its graphs; abjads and alphabets have the least complexity. The number of disconnected components is generally the most important distinguisher among writing systems.

Although visual complexity might be considered a factor independent of the writing system, in fact it is not. What drives graphic complexity is the number of graphs in the writing system. The more graphs are required, the more complex graphs must become to distinguish them from other graphs. And writing systems differ substantially in the number of graphs required. A writing system based on meaning units requires more than a system based on syllables, which in turn requires more than a system based on phonemes. The correlation between the number of graphs and the average complexity in each of the 131 languages in Chang et al. is r=.78. Thus, written Chinese stands alone in its average complexity, as well as in the size of its graphic inventory. Both factors can affect the time and effort required for learning to read.

11.4 How Language Matters in Considering a Writing System

We next ask whether the choice of a writing system reflects the properties of the language. The wide variety of languages and the relatively limited options for writing systems suggest that any adaptation will be at the broad systems level.

The adaptation must also reflect understanding writing as encoded language, not just encoded speech (Perfetti & Harris, 2013). If a writing system tends to be somehow adaptive for its spoken language, the adaptations are based on the linguistic system, not just its phoneme inventory.

The idea that "languages get the writing systems they deserve" has a history dating back at least to Halliday (1977) with more recent claims by Frost (2012) and by Seidenberg (2011). This idea, when applied to mapping solutions, is that writing systems make the trade-off between morphology and phonology in response to relevant properties of the language (Seidenberg, 2011). Perfetti and Harris (2013) argued that specific language factors (phoneme inventory, syllable inventory, morphological complexity) were consistent with the choice of writing systems across a sample of languages. In Table 11.4, we show five languages to illustrate how writing systems may be well suited for the languages they serve. (See also a summary table of seventeen languages whose linguistic and writing systems features were reviewed in Perfetti & Verhoeven in *Learning to Read across Languages and Writing Systems*, Verhoeven & Perfetti, 2017.)

The languages shown in Table 11.4 appear to be reasonably well aligned with properties of their writing systems. Within the three alphabetic languages, there are significant differences in the trade-off between phonology and morphology. If such cases of apparent accommodation proved to be widespread across the world's thousands of languages, this would be impressive, indeed. We might, as Frost (2012) suggested, refer to optimization; that is, each language gets the writing system that is optimal for its linguistic features. This degree of

Table 11.4 *Five languages whose writing systems show some alignment with properties of the language*

Chinese	Syllable/morpheme units. Extensive homophony. Alphabets and syllabaries not adaptive to the language. Characters can distinguish between homophones.
Japanese	Simple syllable types (V and CV) and small number of syllables. Prevalence of multisyllabic words. These factors favor a syllabary.
Finnish	Extensive homophony avoided, despite a small number of phonemes, through long words of several syllables. Transparent alphabet adapts to complex inflectional morphology.
English	Phonological complexity and a large number of syllables make an alphabet efficient. Simple inflectional morphology and morphophonemes favor morpheme spellings. A mismatched letter-to-phoneme ratio keeps phonological transparency low.
Spanish	Phonologically simple; open syllables; Inflectional morphology (typical of Romance languages); transparent orthography with one-to-one mapping (except for three graphemes and multiple use of consonant letters).

optimization seems unlikely given counter-pressures for the adoption of specific writing systems, especially alphabetic systems. Instead, it seems more plausible that languages tend to get a good-enough writing system. As Japanese shows, a writing system that seems very well suited (kana) can be replaced by one that, at least in its implementation, may seem less well suited (kanji).

Moreover, cases in which writing systems are imposed on nonliterate languages do not reflect an adaptive strategy, except by chance. The two large indigenous languages of South America that have gained official recognition, Queschua and Guarni, are written only in the Latin alphabet, as imposed by European missionaries. Cases in which one writing system is replaced by another also provide a different perspective: Turkish, following the end of the Ottoman Empire, moved from the Arabic abjad to the Latin alphabet. Korean and Vietnamese moved from morphosyllabic Chinese to nonlinear alphabetic and linear alphabetic, respectively. Such changes occur in cultural-political contexts that may (Korean) or may not be more adaptive to the language. Phonemically rich languages with tones or large numbers of vowels, if they move to Latin-based linear alphabets, may gain simplicity in some ways while taking on complexity in additional graphs or diacritics. Although it is an interesting exercise to imagine a different writing system for a given language, it seems more useful to explore how a different system would affect literacy.

11.5   Impact of Written Language on Literacy Development

Although many cross-language comparisons are important for considering the impact of writing systems on literacy development, a case of high contrast is especially useful.

11.5.1   A High-Contrast Case: Comparing Morphosyllabic and Alphabetic Literacy

The question of whether the form of the writing system influences the way we read and write is a long-standing one. In contrasting morphosyllabic literacy (e.g., Chinese) with alphabetic literacy, a popular view, based on the differences in the mapping principles and the script was that Chinese is read directly, from graphs to meaning; in contrast, on this view, alphabetic writing is read indirectly, from graphs to speech to meaning. An example from an online discussion board illustrates this view:

I feel English is a reading language, if you are reading an English book, you watch the word and make sound in your brain. *But Chinese can be a watching language, take a Chinese book, I can watch over a paragraph and get the meaning of most part.* (https://chinese.stackexchange.com/questions/2003/can-chinese-readers-scan-large-amounts-of-text-faster-more-accurately-than-their, March 31, 2020)

It is usually wise to consider that an opinion held by so many might contain an element of correctness. The broad endorsement – in reading research (e.g., Smith, 1979) as well as popular opinion – of Chinese as a system that allows a very direct meaning-based reading suggests this opinion deserves serious attention. However, the results of research on morphosyllabic-alphabetic literacy comparisons present a different picture, with more complexity. One of the chapter's authors (CP) carried out a research program that targeted the specific question of whether reading Chinese for meaning evaded phonology. The answer was "no" according to studies of character-meaning decisions and Stroop-based color naming. These studies led us to propose the Universal Phonological Principle (Perfetti, 2003; Perfetti, Zhang, & Berent, 1992), that reading activates phonology in all writing systems. The conclusion concerning phonology in Chinese reading specifically has continued to be upheld in more recent research (e.g. Ma, Wang, & Li, 2016).

The picture gets more complex when we consider a different component of reading, familiarity-based word identification. Reading experience promotes the establishment of word-specific representations, based on increasingly familiar orthographic objects. This applies to all written languages and does not depend on a reduced role for phonology, because both orthographic identification and phonological activation become automatic. With the experience that brings familiarity-based identification comes increasing use of the lexical-level phonology that is partly redundant (and thus helpful) with sublexical phonology in retrieving word pronunciations. This growth of familiarity-based reading with reading experience comes through context-sensitive orthographic-phonological mappings (Perfetti, 1992) than can be acquired through self-teaching (Share, 1995).

Thus, there are two issues involving the large contrast between morphosyllabic and alphabetic literacy, both of which work against the idea of profound differences. In both systems, phonology is part of reading. In both systems, reading increasingly becomes familiarity-based with skilled experience. However, that is not the end of the story.

Differences between morphosyllabic and alphabetic literacy lead to differences in the procedures that produce orthographic identification and phonology. These differences have been discussed in a number of papers and in some detail by Perfetti, Cao, and Booth (2013). Alphabetic reading allows cascade-style identification, as alphabetic constituents activate corresponding phonemes during the process of identification. Morphosyllabic reading, which allows character embedding and thus lexical-level facilitation or competition, is better understood as a threshold system in which orthographic identification of the character precedes a resolved phonological identity. Table 11.5 summarizes some of these differences.

Table 11.5 *Comparisons of morphosyllabic and alphabetic literacy*

	Alphabetic	Morphosyllabic	
Sublexical graphic units	Hierarchically compositional	Embedded lexical units	Both systems reflect statistical regularities in the relation of subunits to lexical units.
Basic phonological unit	Phoneme	Syllable	
Phonological activation	Cascade style	Threshold style diffuse because of homophones	For both systems, activation of phonology is rapid and supports identification
Meaning activation	May be "mediated" by phonology	Less mediation by phonology	

We highlight morphosyllabic-alphabetic comparisons because the two systems maximally contrast in their mapping systems. If there are similarities between these two systems in literacy (and there are), then we conclude that more similar writing systems must also produce similarities in literacy processes. However, there are some differences, as we noted. Those in Table 11.5 arise from orthographic mapping. Others arise from the perceptual and memory processes that stem from the differences in script. The large number of characters required for morphosyllabic literacy challenges perceptual discrimination and memory inventories. Familiarity-based identification is continuously required in morphosyllabic literacy.

11.5.2 Operating Principles in Literacy Development across Languages and Writing Systems

If literacy development implies learning how a writing system encodes language, we can ask whether there are general, universal procedures to support this learning. We have proposed a set of operating principles that do this, enabling children to perceive, analyze, and use written language in ways that support the mastery of a particular orthography. Two recent volumes on learning to read (Verhoeven & Perfetti, 2017a) and dyslexia (Verhoeven, Perfetti, & Pugh, 2019) across languages and writing systems examined reading across seventeen different languages and five writing systems. The authors of specific language chapters reviewed research and provided insights that could be used to probe for evidence for universal aspects of reading and differences associated with specific languages and writing systems. Here we draw on some of the generalizations that were supported by the evidence gathered from a close study of these languages, which represent all of the

Writing Systems and Global Literacy Development 253

five major writing systems. (The languages are Arabic, Hebrew, Chinese [Mandarin], Japanese, Korean, Kannada, Greek, Italian, French, Spanish, Czech-Slovak, Russian, Finnish, Turkish, German, Dutch, English.) Verhoeven and Perfetti (2017b) proposed a universal set of operating principles that support the acquisition of implicit knowledge of how a given writing system relates to a learner's spoken language. These are shown in Table 11.6.

The first three operating principles concern the development of awareness of linguistic elements conveyed through speech, which are the foundation of written forms onto which reading is built.

OP1 holds that children must attend to salient stretches of speech indicated by stress, intonation, rhythm. The acquisition of literacy is supported by a learned sensitivity to the units of spoken language. To the extent that visual word identification in a language requires the connection of a familiar phonological form to a familiar or to-be-learned orthographic form, the quality of the child's phonological knowledge and processing is essential. This is most clearly the case when the phonological grain size is at the level of the phoneme, as for alphabetic reading. Acquiring the alphabetic principle requires representations of phonemes. But the speech signal is continuous and rapid, with sharp modulations in both frequency and amplitude. Moreover, the same phoneme can manifest itself differently in the speech stream, depending on the phonetic environment, speaker, and rate of speech. With exposure to speech, infants begin to parse the incoming acoustic signal into consistent, replicable chunks that come to represent phonemes (cf. Kuhl et al., 1997). By continuing to attend to salient stretches of speech, which are typically indicated by stress,

Table 11.6 *Operating principles in literacy development*

Becoming linguistically aware
OP1: Attend to salient stretches of speech as indicated by stress, intonation, rhythm
OP2: Attend to any salient syllabic, onset-rime, or phoneme boundaries in words
OP3: Attend to written language signals for their connection to language

Developing word identification and spelling
OP4: Increase the orthographic inventory
OP5: Increase the inventory of familiar words through reading and spelling
OP6: Read to gain word-identification fluency

Developing reading comprehension and writing
OP7: Attend to morphological affixes
OP8: Use knowledge of language as you read and write
OP9: Mobilize executive skills to supplement text with relevant background knowledge and inferences

intonation, and rhythm, children can build high-quality speech-based lexical representations. And stable and precise representations at the level of the phoneme are what are needed for the retrieval and discrimination of word identities.

OP2 asserts the importance of attending to salient syllabic, onset-rime, or phoneme boundaries in words. Becoming literate builds upon a child's vocabulary and phonological awareness. Children need to increase their knowledge of word forms and their associated meanings, increasing both the size of their vocabularies and their quality of knowledge of the meaning of individual words. As the number of words in the spoken lexicon increases, so does pressure to make finer phonological representations to accommodate this increase, according to the phonological restructuring hypothesis (Metsala & Walley, 1998). In this account, words are initially underspecified phonemically, until a growing lexicon that applies pressure for increased discriminability among words forces greater phonological specification. The growth of the spoken lexicon is important for later literacy development and also supports the preliterate linguistic awareness that aids the early stages of learning to read. Syllable awareness universally emerges earlier than phonemic awareness, and a failure to acquire it predicts difficulty in learning to read. Phonemic awareness prior to literacy enables easy learning of the alphabetic principle. However, phoneme awareness typically develops reciprocally with the beginning of instruction in alphabetic reading. Not showing phoneme awareness prior to literacy instruction does not predict difficulties in learning to read; but a lack of phonemic awareness after literacy instruction has begun does. The role of phonemic awareness in alphabetic reading does not significantly depend on the transparency of the orthography; its role in more transparent Dutch and Czech is comparable to its role in English. There is a writing system factor, however: Phoneme-level awareness is not uniformly important for learning to read syllabaries and morphosyllabaries, where other factors may matter more, for example syllable awareness and tone awareness in Chinese (Shu, Peng, & McBride-Chang, 2008).

OP3 stresses the importance of children's attention to written language signals that connect to their spoken language. Interactions with symbols in the environment and with literate others help children learn that print carries meaning, that written texts may have various forms and functions, and that ideas can be expressed with spontaneous (non)conventional writing (Yaden, Rowe, & MacGillivray, 2000). Such attention can set the stage for learning that printed words consist of graphs that not only link to spoken language but also allow the discovery of phonological recoding (Ehri, 2014). During a period of early emerging literacy, children may acquire only a limited collection of written words that have personal meaning. However, attending to the sounds and letters of these words supports the child's insight that written language codes spoken language, and can lead to self-teaching of orthography, as the child associates graphs with sounds as they attempt to read a word (see Share, 2004). The research suggests that more is needed for most children: a systematic approach that directly instructs children on the mapping principle and on specific correspondences between graphic units and sound units.

To summarize, emerging literacy growth is supported by the first three operating principles, which focus on attention to first spoken and then written language in ways that build a foundation for reading. This foundation provides the basic linkage between spoken and written language and may bring a small inventory of familiar written words. Additional operating principles are critical for the continued development of word identification and spelling.

OP4 supports the development of word identification as a generalized skill built on what is required by the writing system. In productive systems with small graphic inventories, such as alphabets, abjads, and syllabaries, there is some learning of additional graphic forms along with the primary learning of mappings between specific graphic forms and their language units (syllables, phonemes) and the ability to use these mappings to read words. However, in alphasyllabaries there is prolonged multiyear learning of graphic forms and their associations with spoken language (Nag, 2007). Chinese requires six years to teach a curriculum of 2,570 characters, a standard of basic reading (Shu et al., 2003). An important practice that supports the beginning of this character learning is the use of an alphabet (e.g., Pinyin) prior to the introduction of learning, although learning also occurs without this first step in some Chinese-speaking areas (e.g., Hong Kong). For alphabets, learning grapheme-to-phoneme mappings and their variations across words comprises the primary learning. This learning is affected by the consistencies of the grapheme-phoneme mappings, which varies across alphabetic languages and is lower in English than other alphabetic languages. Spelling in alphabetic languages tends to lag behind reading, even for consistent orthographies, and benefits from specific instruction beyond reading practice.

OP5. The ability to access language through orthography, the systematic structuring of basic graphic units, is the heart of skilled reading. It enables the language system to use information from the visual system with astonishing speed. It is accompanied, subjectively, by a sense that one can see the language through the print. This ability does not come automatically with the learning required by OP4. Instead, it requires an increase of the inventory of highly familiar words that is acquired through reading and spelling experience. This development marks a shift of reading from computation to memory-based retrieval for words that have become familiar. In all languages, written words can become familiar perceptual objects that are recognized quickly. Learning to read fluently builds on this increasing familiarity. Turning the unfamiliar into the familiar is relatively simple in a consistent orthography. The first encounter with a new written word leads to decoding of the written form into its phonological form and establishes initial familiarity with the word's orthography (Share, 1995). Relatively few additional exposures may be needed to establish an orthographic memory for the word; for inconsistent orthographies, more exposures are needed. The resulting high-quality orthographic representation supports familiarity-based memory retrieval. Gaining familiarity is especially important in systems that lack explicit phonological composition, as in Chinese and in Japanese kanji. Abugidas (alphasyllabaries) are phonologically compositional, but fluent recognition of consonant–vowel combinations requires considerable practice that also brings about familiarity-based reading.

OP6 also targets the effects of reading experience and provides a link to reading comprehension. It emphasizes that beyond establishing words as familiar, reading experience produces gains in reading fluency that arise from the automatization of word decoding, familiarity-based memory retrieval, and experience in connected text reading. These developments allow cognitive resources to be directed to comprehension (Perfetti, 1992; Stanovich, 2000; Verhoeven & van Leeuwe, 2008). Across different orthographies, parallel developmental gains in word decoding occur very rapidly after the start of explicit reading instruction, while steady improvements in the speed and accuracy of word decoding continue in the years thereafter. With effective reading practice, children advance from having partially specified to more fully specified representations of written words, as the strength of the association between print and sound becomes increasingly automated and words come to be retrieved as familiar orthographic objects (Coltheart et al., 2001). This provides mental resources for text meaning and makes reading a tool for the acquisition of knowledge.

The final two operating principles apply to the development of reading comprehension and writing.

OP7 captures the importance of attending to morphological affixes. Current models of reading and writing have focused on how letter strings are mapped onto phonological strings (pronunciations), essentially ignoring any internal structure that words have as morpheme units. Morphological processes, including some decomposition of written forms into their constituent morphemes, may be a part of word identification and they are essential in cueing meaning information (case, tense, number, aspect). Morphological knowledge is variably associated with reading success across languages and writing systems. We expect the relevant morphological knowledge to depend on the writing system. Chinese word formation demands knowledge of compounding morphology; Finnish word formation demands knowledge of inflectional morphology. The explicit teaching of morphology is increasingly part of instruction in some languages.

OP8 reflects the importance of the learner's mobilizing knowledge of language (oral language skill) to build meaning structures from words in text and vice versa. This involves sentence processes and processes across sentences. Within a sentence, meaning-related constituent structures are built from words, immediately attaching each word to a meaningful syntactic phrase. In reading and writing, word meanings, meaningful phrases, and sentence meanings are connected to a continuously updated representation of the text. These integrative processes take place throughout the reading and writing of a text, both within a sentence and across sentences. This integration is necessary to maintain a coherent understanding and production. Models of text comprehension (Kintsch, 1988) and text production (Berman & Verhoeven, 2002) incorporate the conclusion that comprehension and production of text cannot be accomplished on the basis of text information alone, but require the use of prior knowledge.

Finally, *OP9* highlights the importance of mobilizing executive functions (attention, inhibition, working memory, cognitive flexibility) to supplement the literal meaning of the text with relevant background knowledge. Because texts are never fully explicit, inferences are needed both to maintain the coherence of the text and to establish more referentially rich situational meanings, thus supplementing the basic propositional meanings expressed in the text. Activation of knowledge from the reader's memory occurs rapidly and automatically, but not all activated knowledge is relevant for a veridical understanding or production of the text. The selection of text-relevant knowledge builds a veridical situation model, one that is consistent with the meaning of the text. A situation model can help readers and writers identify and define problems, specify options for solving identified problems, generate problem-solving strategies, and observe the results of attempted solutions (cf. Zwaan et al., 2001).

11.6 The Universal Brain Network for Literacy

Although the most important information on becoming literate comes from behavioral research, there is by now substantial research on the neural correlates of reading and writing. This research has led to the identification of functional brain networks that link functionally defined areas of specialization. The research suggests that neural networks for reading are largely shared across languages and writing systems; to that extent, one can speak of a universal network. However, the writing system appears to influence the detailed functionality of the reading network through the demands it places on reading procedures.

In reading, the brain connects visual input to the posterior regions with language areas in the frontal regions. For alphabetic reading, three nodes in the left hemisphere are prominent. The visual recognition of graphic strings is supported by neural structures in the posterior temporal lobe, adjacent to visual cortex, the posterior fusiform gyrus. This occipital-temporal "visual word form" area connects to frontal areas through both a ventral and a dorsal pathway. The ventral pathway connects to anterior brain areas, the middle/inferior temporal gyrus, while the dorsal pathway connects upward to temporal-parietal cortex, the posterior superior temporal gyrus, and the inferior parietal lobule and its angular and supramarginal gyri. The anterior component of the reading network is the left inferior frontal gyrus (IFG), Broca's region, which, in its different parts, is involved in multiple language functions, including phonological processes during reading. The dorsal pathway is engaged by more complex phonological analysis, whereas the ventral pathway is engaged when reading is simpler or more automatized. This relatively simple network has been observed across many studies (Shuai et al., 2017), achieving the status of a "standard view," although refinements of the network have highlighted additional components (Richlan, Kronbichler, & Wimmer, 2009).

Research on reading East Asian writing systems has produced results for Chinese, both Japanese kanji and kana, and the alphabetic but nonlinear Korean. Imaging studies of Chinese readers find areas of brain activation that overlap with alphabetic reading, as well some differences, as shown in early metanalyses (Bolger, Perfetti, & Schneider, 2005 and Tan et al., 2005). The left fusiform gyrus (posterior temporal lobe) is universally observed in reading, because it functions in coding graphic input to connect with left hemisphere language areas. This is a consequence of the fact that true writing encodes language, whatever the written forms or their mapping levels. Frontal, temporal, and parietal areas also function in all languages, although not always within precisely the same anatomical subregions. A recent candidate for a universal function is the left inferior parietal lobule (IPL), observed in alphabetic reading (Richlan et al., 2009) and in Chinese (Cao et al., 2006). The development of reading skill in both Chinese and English seems to lead to the increased functionality of the left IPL, which may function as part of an integrating network for orthography, phonology, and meaning (Perfetti, Cao, & Booth, 2013)

The most noted difference between Chinese and alphabetic reading is the greater role of the left middle frontal gyrus (LMFG) in Chinese, although its activation during reading is observed across languages. One idea about its greater role in Chinese is that it reflects the more intimate connection between reading and writing as a result of Chinese literacy education, which traditionally emphasizes character writing. On this hypothesis, reading Chinese characters may evoke a premotor memory trace of its writing sequence. Cao & Perfetti (2017) found not only that the LFMG was more active in Chinese than English, but also that its activation showed more overlap between writing and reading in

Chinese than it did in English. Nakamura et al. (2012) also investigated handwriting across alphabetic (French) and Chinese writing. Their experiments led them to conclude that there are two intimately connected subsystems in reading, one for word shape and one for handwriting gestures, and these two subsystems are universal.

There is much more to consider if we are to form a fuller picture of the brain networks for reading across languages and writing systems (see recent reviews by Shuai et al., 2017; Rigatti et al., Chapter 12 in this volume). Also of interest for reading across writing systems are the neural bases of learning to read a second language and its possible assimilation into the L1 network (Perfetti et al., 2007). A study of L1 Korean trilinguals who were equally proficient in L2 English and L2 Chinese by Kim et al. (2016) found that brain areas overlap more for Korean–English, both of which are alphabetic but different in spatial layout, than for Korean–Chinese. This adds to the picture that reading is affected by writing-system differences, even when the high-level view is one of universality.

11.7 Educational Relevance

Writing systems and the orthographies and scripts that implement them matter for reading and learning to read. Meaning-weighted systems like Chinese require a larger inventory of graphs than do writing systems that are phonology weighted. Alphasyllabaries, which are phonology weighted, also require longer periods for the acquisition of basic reading levels. Behavioral and brain data suggest the reading processes show differences due both to the mapping levels of writing and to script factors (visual complexity and layout).

Within the family of alphabetic writing, cross-language comparisons show that English-speaking children lag behind children who speak German (Wimmer & Goswami, 1994), Spanish and French (Goswami, Gombert, & de Barrera, 1998), Greek (Goswami, Porpodas, & Wheelwright, 1997), and Dutch (Patel, Snowling, & de Jong, 2004). Seymour, Aro, and Erskine's (2003) comparison of children after one year of instruction found that English children showed only a 40 percent accuracy rate in reading words and nonwords. Most other European samples were above 90 percent, and the worst among the remainder, France and Denmark, were much higher on word reading.

The invited inference is that the disadvantages of English are due to English orthography; and they may be. However, it is useful to keep in mind the many factors that vary across national and regional settings – the language, the culture and its emphasis on literacy, variations among children and families, instructional method, and the familiarity of specific words used to test reading. In studies that are able to control for these factors by research on a single bilingual population reading two different orthographies, the evidence does suggest that learning English produces a reading strategy that is less phonetic than learning Welsh, a transparent orthography (Ellis & Hooper, 2001).

We can conclude that the writing system and orthographies matter for reading. However, to place this difference in the context of other considerations for emerging literacy, the question is how much this matters compared with other factors. Perhaps not so much. Learning to read is, in part, learning how one's writing system works. Thus, we can suggest that sound instruction – instruction that is designed to teach (directly or indirectly) the mapping properties of the writing system – can succeed. To suggest the obvious, teaching a syllabary requires focus on the syllabic principle, teaching an alphabet requires focus on the alphabetic principle, teaching an abjad requires focus on both the alphabetic principle and the consonantal root principle; teaching an abugida requires focus on the alphabetic principle and the akshara principle. Across all systems, effective practice in real reading is needed to shift reading procedures to become familiarity based.

11.8 Conclusion and Discussion

We began by pointing out that a global perspective on literacy compels attention to the possible variations in how language is written, whether the language matters in considering a writing system, and whether variation in written language leads to important differences in learning and teaching to read. Our conclusion is that writing systems follow the same set of operating principles in learning to read but that the differences between them do matter for understanding the weighting of reading procedures and different educational challenges. We also emphasize that the existence of a variety of flourishing systems means that all writing systems are learnable, and instruction effectively geared toward their specific properties will be successful for most children.

We also posed a hypothetical, in which a preliterate people come to an expert for help in designing a writing system to bring literacy to their language. Nearly all experts read an alphabetic system in either a second or first language. Accordingly, the advice from most of these experts may be "use an alphabet"; not any old alphabet, but a perfect one with one-to-one mappings between graphs and phonemes. If the phoneme inventory is not too large, this will work very well and would be highly productive. Others, drawn to the primacy of the syllable, might suggest a syllabary. If the language has a simple syllable structure and not too many syllables, this would work very well. Importantly, it would be the easiest to learn, at least at the beginning. The fact that syllabaries are what tend to be invented by nonexperts who are also nonliterate stands in support of this approach. The most accessible unit of speech becomes the basis for an easy-to-learn writing system.

Finally, the hypothetical gives way to the reality that the abundance of orthographies within both alphabetic and syllabic systems, as well as the enormous variety in alphasyllabaries, gives us many choices for models. The creation of a new system is less likely than the adaptation of an existing system. One guiding principle for invention or adaptation is to consider the fundamental phonological and morphological structures of the language. These really do matter.

References

Berman, R. A., & Verhoeven, L. (2002). Cross-linguistic perspectives on the development of text-production abilities: Speech and writing. *Written Language and Literacy*, 5(1), 1–43. DOI: https://doi.org/10.1075/wll.5.1.02ber.

Bolger, D. J., Perfetti, C. A., & Schneider, W. (2005). A cross-cultural effect on the brain revisited: Universal structures plus writing system variation. *Journal of Human Brain Mapping*, 25(1), 92–104.

Bright, B. (2000). A matter of typology: Alphasyllabaries and abugidas. *Studies in the Linguistics Sciences*, 30(1), 63–71.

Cao, F., Bitan, T., Chou, T. L., Burman, D. D., & Booth, J. R. (2006). Deficient orthographic and phonological representations in children with dyslexia revealed by brain activation patterns. *Journal of Child Psychology and Psychiatry*, 47, 1041–1050.

Cao, F., & Perfetti, C. A. (2017). Neural signatures of the reading-writing connection: Greater involvement of writing in Chinese reading. *PlosOne* 11(12), e0168414. DOI: https://doi.org/10.1371/journal.pone.0168414.

Chang, L.-Y., Chen, Y.-C., & Perfetti, C. A. (2017). GraphCom: A multidimensional measure of graphic complexity applied to 131 written languages. *Behavior Research Methods*, 50, 427–449.

Coltheart, M., Rastle, K., Perry, C., Langdon, R., & Ziegler, J. (2001). DRC: A dual route cascaded model of visual word recognition and reading aloud. *Psychological Review*, 108, 204–256.

Daniels, P. T. (1990). Fundamentals of grammatology. *Journal of the American Oriental Society*, 119(4), 727–731. DOI: https://doi.org/10.2307/602899, JSTOR 602899.

Daniels, P. T. (1992). The syllabic origin of writing and the segmental origin of the alphabet. In P. Downing, S. D. Lima, & M. Noonan (eds.), *The Linguistics of Literacy* (pp. 83–110). Amsterdam: John Benjamins.

Daniels, P. T. (1996). The invention of writing. In P. T. Daniels & W. Bright (eds.), *The World's Writing Systems*. New York: Oxford.

Daniels, P. T., & Bright, W. (1996). *The World's Writing System*. New York: Oxford.

Daniels, P. T., & Share, D. L. (2018). Writing system variation and its consequences for reading and dyslexia. *Scientific Studies of Reading*, 22(1), 101–116. DOI:https://doi.org/10.1080/10888438.2017.1379082.

Davis, J. B. (1930). *The Life and Work of Sequoyah: Chronicles of Oklahoma*, vol. 8, no. 2. https://web.archive.org/web/20171028175529/http://digital.library.okstate.edu/chronicles/v008/v008p149.html.

DeFrancis, J. (1989). *Visible Speech: The Diverse Oneness of Writing Systems.* Honolulu: University of Hawaii Press.

Ehri, L. C. (2014). Orthographic mapping in the acquisition of sight word reading, spelling memory and vocabulary learning. *Scientific Studies of Reading, 18,* 5–21.

Ellis, N. C., & Hooper, A. M. (2001). Why learning to read is easier in Welsh than in English: Orthographic transparency effects evinced with frequency-matched tests. *Applied Linguistics, 22*(4), 571–599.

Frost, R. (2012). Towards a universal model of reading. *Behavioral and Brain Sciences, 35*(5), 263–79. DOI: https://doi.org/10.1017/S0140525X11001841.

Gelb, I. J. (1952). *A Study of Writing.* Chicago: University of Chicago Press. (Rev. ed., 1963.)

Goswami, U., Gombert, J. E., & de Barrera, L. F. (1998). Children's orthographic representations and linguistic transparency: Nonsense word reading in English, French, and Spanish. *Applied Psycholinguistics, 19*(10), 19–52.

Goswami, U., Porpodas, C., & Wheelwright. S. (1997). Children's orthographic representations in English and Greek. *European Journal of Psychology of Education, 12,* 273.

Halliday, M. A. K. (1977). Ideas about language. In *Aims and Perspectives in Linguistics. Occasional Papers, No. 1* (pp. 32–55). Applied Linguistics Association of Australia. (Reprinted in *On Language and Linguistics: Collected Works of M. A. K. Halliday, vol. 3,* ed. Jonathan Webster, pp. 92–115. London: Bloomsbury Publishing.)

Kelly, P. (2019). The invention, transmission and evolution of writing: Insights from the new scripts of West Africa. In S. Ferrara & M. Valerio (eds.), *Paths Into Script Formation in the Ancient Mediterranean* (pp. 189–209). New England: Studi Micenei ed Egeo-Anatolici.

Kim, S. Y., Qi, T., Feng, X., Ding, G., Liu, L., & Cao, F. (2016). How does language distance between L1 and L2 brain network? An fMRI study of Korean-Chinese-English trilinguals. *Neuroimage, 129*(1), 25–39.

Kim-Renaud, Y.-K. (2000). Sejong's theory of literacy and writing. *Studies in the Linguistic Sciences, 30*(1), 13–45.

Kintsch, W. (1988). The use of knowledge in discourse processing: A construction-integration model. *Psychological Review, 95,* 163–182.

Kuhl, P. K., Andruski, J. E., Chistovich, I. A. et al. (1997). Cross-language analysis of phonetic units in language addressed to infants. *Science, 277,* 684–686.

Liberman I. Y. (1973). Segmentation of the spoken word and reading acquisition. *Bulletin of the Orton Society* 23, 65–77.

Ma, B., Wang, X., & Li, D. (2016). The processing of visual and phonological configurations of Chinese one- and two-character words in a priming task of semantic categorization. *Frontiers in Psychology, 6,* 1918. DOI: https://doi.org/10.3389/fpsyg.2015.01918.

Metsala, J. L., & Walley, A. C. (1998). Spoken vocabulary growth and the segmental restructuring of lexical representations: Precursors to phonemic awareness and early reading ability. In J. L. Metsala & L. C. Ehri (eds.), *Word Recognition in Beginning Literacy* (pp. 89–120). Mahwah, NJ: Lawrence Erlbaum Associates.

Nag, S. (2007). Early reading in Kannada: The pace of acquisition of orthographic knowledge and phonemic awareness. *Journal of Reading in Research, 30,* 7–22.

Nakamura, K., Kuo, W.-J., Pegado, F. et al. (2012). Universal brain systems for recognizing word shapes and handwriting gestures during reading. *Proceedings of the National Academy of Sciences (PNAS)*, *109*(50), 20762–20767.

Patel, T. K., Snowling, M. J., & de Jong, P. F. (2004). A cross-linguistic comparison of children learning to read in English and Dutch. *Journal of Educational Psychology*, *96*(4), 785–797.

Pelli, D. G., Burns, C. W., Farell, B., & Moore-Page, D. C. (2006). Feature detection and letter identification. *Vision Research*, *46*(28), 4646–4674.

Perfetti, C. A. (1992). The representation problem in reading acquisition. In P. B. Gough, L. C. Ehri, & R. Treiman (eds.), *Reading Acquisition* (pp. 145–174). Hillsdale, NJ: Lawrence Erlbaum Associates.

Perfetti, C. A. (2003). The universal grammar of reading. *Scientific Studies of Reading*, *7*(1), 3–24.

Perfetti, C. A., Cao, F., & Booth, J. (2013). Specialization and universals in the development of reading skill: How Chinese research informs a universal science of reading. *Scientific Studies of Reading*, *17*(1), 5–21.

Perfetti, C. A., & Harris, L. N. (2013). Universal reading processes are modulated by language and writing system. *Language Learning and Development*, *9*(4), 296–316.

Perfetti, C. A., Liu, Y., Fiez, J. et al. (2007). Reading in two writing systems: Accommodation and assimilation in the brain's reading network. *Bilingualism: Language and Cognition*, *10*(2), 131–146. Special issue on "Neurocognitive approaches to bilingualism: Asian languages," P. Li (Ed.).

Perfetti, C. A., & Verhoeven, L. (2017). Epilogue: Universals and particulars in learning to read across seventeen orthographies. In L. Verhoeven & C. A. Perfetti (eds.), *Learning to Read across Languages and Writing Systems* (pp. 455–480). Cambridge: Cambridge University Press.

Perfetti, C. A., Zhang, S., & Berent, I. (1992). Reading in English and Chinese: Evidence for a "universal" phonological principle. In R. Frost & L. Katz (eds.), *Orthography, Phonology, Morphology, and Meaning* (pp. 227–248). Amsterdam: North-Holland.

Richlan, F., Kronbichler, M., & Wimmer, H. (2009). Functional abnormalities in the dyslexic brain: A quantitative meta-analysis of neuroimaging studies. *Human Brain Mapping*, *30*(10), 3299–3308.

Seidenberg, M. S. (2011). Reading in different writing systems: One architecture, multiple solutions. In P. McCardle, J. Ren, O. Tzeng, & B. Miller (eds.), *Dyslexia across Languages: Orthography and the Brain-Gene-Behavior Link* (pp. 146–168). Baltimore, MD: Brookes.

Seymour, P. H. K., Aro, M., & Erskine, J. M. in collaboration with COST Action A8 network (2003). Foundation literacy acquisition in European orthographies. *British Journal of Psychology*, *94*, 143–174.

Share, D. L. (1995). Phonological recoding and self-teaching: Sine qua non of reading acquisition. *Cognition*, *55*, 151–218.

Share, D. L. (2004). Orthographic learning at a glance: On the time course and developmental onset of reading. *Journal of Experimental Child Psychology*, *87*, 267–298.

Share, D. L., & Daniels, P. T. (2015). Aksharas, alphasyllabaries, abugidas, alphabets, and orthographic depth: Reflections on Rimzhim, Katz, and Fowler (2014). *Writing Systems Research*, *8*(1), 17–31. DOI: https://doi.org/10.1080/17586801.2015.1016395.

Shu, H., Chen, X., Anderson, R. C., Wu, N., & Xuan, Y. (2003). Properties of school Chinese: Implications for learning to read. *Child Development*, *74*(1), 27–47.

Shu, H., Peng, H., & McBride-Chang, C. (2008).Phonological awareness in young Chinese children. *Developmental Science*, *11*, 171–181.

Shuai, L., Frost, S. J., Landi, M., Mencl, W. E., & Pugh, K. R. (2019). Neurocognitive models of skilled and impaired reading from a cross-language perspective. In L. Verhoeven, C. A. Perfetti, & K. Pugh (eds.), *Developmental Dyslexia across Languages and Writing Systems*. Cambridge: Cambridge University Press.

Smith, F. (1979). *Reading without Nonsense*. New York: Teachers College Press.

Stanovich, K. E. (2000). *Progress in Understanding Reading: Scientific Foundations and New Frontiers*. New York: Guilford Press.

Tan, L. H., Spinks, J. A., Eden, G., Perfetti, C. A., & Siok, W. T. (2005). Reading depends on writing, in Chinese. *Proceedings of the National Academy of Sciences (PNAS)*, *102*, 8781–8785.

Unseth, P. (2011). Invention of scripts in West Africa for ethnic revitalization. In J. A. Fishman & O. Garcia (eds.), *Handbook of Language and Ethnic Identity: The Success-Failure Continuum in Language and Ethnic Identity Efforts, Volume 2* (pp. 23–32). New York: Oxford University Press.

Verhoeven, L., & Perfetti, C. A. (2017b). Operating principles in learning to read. In L. Verhoeven & C. A. Perfetti (eds.), *Learning to Read across Languages and Writing Systems* (pp. 1–30). Cambridge: Cambridge University Press.

Verhoeven, L., & Perfetti, C. A. (eds.). (2017a). *Learning to Read across Languages and Writing Systems*. Cambridge: Cambridge University Press.

Verhoeven, L., Perfetti, C. A., & Pugh, K. (eds.) (2019). *Developmental Dyslexia across Languages and Writing Systems*. Cambridge: Cambridge University Press.

Verhoeven, L., & van Leeuwe, J. (2008). Prediction of the development of reading comprehension: A longitudinal study. *Applied Cognitive Psychology*, *22*, 407–423.

Wiley, J., & Rayner, K. (2000). Effects of titles on the processing of text and lexically ambiguous words: Evidence from eye movements. *Memory and Cognition*, 28(6), 1011–1021.

Wimmer, H., & Goswami, U. (1994). The influence of orthographic consistency on reading development: Word recognition in English and German children. *Cognition*, *51*(1), 91–103.

Yaden, D., Rowe, D., & MacGillivray, L. (2000). Emergent literacy: A matter (polyphony) of perspectives. In M. L. Kamil, P. B. Mosenthal, P. D. Pearson, & R.. Barr (eds.), *Handbook of Reading Research*, vol. 3 (pp. 425–454). Mahwah, NJ: Erlbaum.

Zwaan, R. A., Kaup, B., Stanfield, R. A., & Madden C. J. (2001). Language comprehension as guided experience. http://cogprints.soton.ac.uk/documents/.

12 Brain Foundations for Learning to Read

Pietra Cassol Rigatti, Xin Cui, Kenneth Pugh, Mailce Borges Mota, and Augusto Buchweitz[*]

12.1 Introduction

The development of early literacy can be adversely impacted by neurodevelopmental disorders and socioeconomic disparities that have lasting effects on child and adolescent cognition (Merz et al., 2020; Noble et al., 2015). The goal of this chapter is to address the continuum of literacy development in two critical stages – birth to six years old and six to ten years old – and their respective language and brain milestones: the development of the hardwired brain networks for speech, and the adaptation of brain regions for reading. The discussion attempts to disentangle neurodevelopmental disorders and socioeconomic factors that influence early literacy, and the associated effects on brain function and structure (Duryea, 2019; Gracco, Tremblay, & Pike, 2005; Merz, Wiltshire, & Noble, 2019; Preston et al., 2015). We underscore emerging evidence for a near-universal brain system that develops with learning to read across writing systems, and address the dynamic relations among brain networks for reading, speech, and writing across the two age spans.

Early-literacy-skills awareness of letter–sound relationships and concepts about print make up the building blocks of learning to read (Castles, Rastle, & Nation, 2018; Ehri, 2005; National Reading Panel, 2000). These skills support the child in learning to break the code of writing systems, which does not come naturally to children, as a result of their first acquiring oral language (see also Perfetti & Verhoeven, Chapter 11 in this volume) The development of early literacy skills depends on instruction and is influenced both by neurodevelopmental factors and socioeconomic status (SES). Low SES is associated with poor early literacy skills, which follow from disadvantages at home – that is, high-SES homes have language advantages – and at school – that is, low-SES children receive nonsystematic classroom practices more frequently, and are thus more dependent on incidental learning (Hoff, 2003; Hoff & Tian, 2005; Nag et al., 2016, 2019). As a case in point, Brazil is among the countries that are

---

[*] This study was financed in part by the Coordenação de Aperfeiçoamento de Pessoal de Nível Superior – Brasil (CAPES) – Finance Code 001 and the Conselho Nacional de Desenvolvimento Científico e Tecnológico (CNPq), Brasil, process number 311632/2019-0.

most unequal in distribution of income (Cruz & Loureiro, 2020) and the country's third-grade-level national reading assessment shows 50 percent of students reading in its Tier 2, inadequate for grade and age; moreover, in the poorer regions of the country, the assessment shows 40–60 percent of third graders reading in Tier 1, the lowest level of basic decoding skills (INEP, 2017).

Of course, low SES directly influences other constructs, such as school-readiness and associated cognitive, motor, and socioeconomic skills (Wolf & McCoy, 2019). Recent studies also show the effects of poverty on brain development (Dufford et al., 2020; Merz, Maskus, et al., 2019; Noble et al., 2015). In this sense, SES disadvantages not only result in developmental outcome disparities but are also associated with unequal opportunity for effective early instruction practices.

Early literacy skills, including alphabet knowledge, phonological awareness, and rapid naming, are among the most predictive precursors of reading outcomes. They are the "what" of early literacy. Code-focused instruction strategies, in turn, have the largest effect size on literacy outcomes (Shanahan & Lonigan, 2010). They are the most effective "how-to" in literacy instruction (Ehri et al., 2001; Shanahan & Lonigan, 2010). But the literacy "what" and "how-to" still stand to benefit from a better understanding of the brain dynamics associated with development and instruction. The neuroscience of reading has the potential to inform prediction of reading achievement, identification of risk for reading difficulties, and possibly, choice of intervention and identification of the age ranges that are more amenable to treatment. Understanding why some children respond to treatment better than others from the point of view of the brain mechanisms of success and struggle may inform policy decisions and teaching practices, especially when it comes to interventions for underachieving children. It may be possible to replace teaching to the test with teaching to the brain. In sum, the contribution of the neuroscience of reading may be to understand how neurodevelopmental and environmental factors combine to hold children back, and thus to better inform the first steps toward overcoming these factors; we consider all this in this chapter.

12.2 Frontotemporal Network for Speech and Posterior System Adapted for Reading

Spoken language is a uniquely human capacity and the human brain is hardwired for the development of perception and production skills (Gracco et al., 2005). The brain areas hardwired for oral language include the well-known frontal and temporal regions. By contrast, written language is a unique cultural invention. Since Huey's (1908) studies were published, it has been known that the human brain is not hardwired for the ability to decode and understand print (Dehaene, 2009; Seidenberg, 2017). Noninvasive brain-imaging methods have allowed for an emerging consensus: the "reading brain" develops as posterior regions of the brain take on new roles to adapt to the new medium, and as the frontotemporal speech areas that underpin superior cognitive processes of language, in their turn, also do so for reading (Ferstl et al., 2008; Friederici, 2012; Rueckl et al., 2015).

From the identification of brain indices that suggest risk of learning disorders to identification of those brain indices associated with fluent reading, modern structural and functional brain-imaging methods have afforded *in vivo* studies of reading where only postmortem evaluations were once possible (Altarelli et al., 2014; Galaburda et al., 1985). As a result, the posterior systems and the temporal and frontal regions that make up the subsystems of the reading brain have been identified across diverse writing systems, including Portuguese, Polish, German, English, Chinese, Japanese, Hebrew, Spanish, French, and Italian (Bolger, Perfetti, & Schneider, 2005; Buchweitz et al., 2009, 2019; Kamykowska et al., 2013; Kronbichler et al., 2006; Paulesu et al., 2000; Paulesu, Démonet, & Fazio, 2001; Rueckl et al., 2015; Szwed et al., 2014; Twomey et al., 2013). These studies establish a cross-cultural understanding of the neurobiological nature of learning to read. To note, there are extended networks of brain areas associated with the specific properties that are characteristic of writing systems around the world (Bolger et al., 2005; Buchweitz et al., 2009; Paulesu et al., 2000; Tan et al., 2001; see also Huo et al., Chapter 9 in this volume).

The development of language is intertwined with that of literacy skills. Although being different in nature, the speech and reading networks merge as reading experience increases. The dynamic hierarchy of the natural process of language development shares features with the instruction-dependent process of developing literacy skills (Whitehurst & Lonigan, 1998). Early literacy skills include awareness of language sounds and of their relationship with print, which are among the building blocks for learning to read. The higher-level skills, in turn, include reading as well as drawing meaning from words, sentences, and connected text (Frith, 1985; Whitehurst & Lonigan, 1998). In general, this set of skills is largely universal, despite the specific differences across writing systems. For example, early morphological awareness skills in spoken Arabic are related to later reading fluency in standard Arabic (Schiff & Saiegh-Haddad, 2018). Moreover, the contribution of phonological awareness is modulated by phonological distance of this diglossic language pair (Saiegh-Haddad, Shahbari-kassem, & Schiff, 2020). It is also worthy of note that the Chinese logographic writing system is quite unique relative to alphabetic systems (McBride, 2016). Nonetheless, the time course of word-semantic processing by Chinese children is similar to the time course of visual word processing in alphabetic languages (Lo et al., 2019).

For decades now, studies have shown causal relations among early literacy-related skill phonological development and later reading outcomes. The link between early literacy skills such as phonological awareness and lexical access (e.g., rapid naming) and successful reading outcomes has been clearly established (Cardoso-Martins & Pennington, 2004; Ehri, 2005; House of Commons, 2009; National Reading Panel, 2000; Rose, 2006; Scarborough, Dobrich, & Hager, 1991). Phonological awareness is predictive of reading outcomes across writing systems with varying letter–sound mappings, to the extent that a universal phonological principle of reading has been postulated (Perfetti, 1992; Perfetti & Tan, 1998; Ziegler et al., 2010). The precursors of reading show remarkable predictive power for reading achievement. Early literacy skills measured at age four years (preschool) have been shown to explain a great deal of the variance in later reading attainment at age seven years (Hjetland et al., 2019). Brain-imaging studies, as we will show in the following sections, have also provided complementary evidence of early brain markers that predict reading outcomes and may yet help predict treatment outcomes. In sum, successfully teaching children to read is strongly associated with teaching the right precursors early on and continuously stimulating the next stage (see, e.g., countries that successfully teach children to read and their varying ages at first grade; OECD, 2019). In the interest of parsimony and by drawing on the most common age milestone for formal schooling (i.e., six years; The World Bank Group, 2020), we divided the discussion of brain, language, and literacy development into two age groups: birth to six years old and six to ten years old.

12.3 Universal Network for Reading in the Brain

A general neurobiological model of reading (see Figure 12.1), first proposed by Pugh et al. (2001) and Sandak et al. (2004) and refined by others (Richlan, 2012, 2014), postulates the involvement of three general left-hemisphere subsystems that develop with reading instruction: a ventral occipitotemporal region that makes up the ventral circuit of reading in the brain (lexical route), a temporo-parietal region that makes up the dorsal circuit of reading in the brain (phonological route), and a frontal network of regions that makes up the anterior circuit. Meta-analyses of brain-imaging studies of children and adults (Houdé et al., 2010; Martin et al., 2015) show early speech-print convergence on the left superior temporal and left ventral occipitotemporal subsystems; the presence of these two subsystems has been identified across writing systems as a hallmark of early and proficient reading (Centanni et al., 2019; Cohen et al., 2002; Gabrieli, 2009; McCandliss, Cohen, & Dehaene, 2003; Pleisch et al., 2019; Wang, Joanisse, & Booth, 2018; Yamada et al., 2011; Yu et al., 2018), with minor variations explained by differences in, for example, letter–sound correspondence (Chyl et al., 2018).

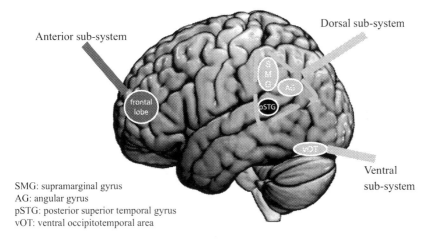

SMG: supramarginal gyrus
AG: angular gyrus
pSTG: posterior superior temporal gyrus
vOT: ventral occipitotemporal area

Figure 12.1 The brain subsystems for reading

The dorsal subsystem region includes the angular, supramarginal, and posterior superior temporal gyri. More activation of this subsystem is associated with better word-level reading and mapping print to sound in good readers relative to poor readers (Hoeft et al., 2011; Meyler et al., 2007; Rueckl et al., 2015; Sandak et al., 2004; Shaywitz et al., 2002). Activation, and increasingly focal activation, of the ventral occipitotemporal region (vOT), in turn, signals the brain is tuning to print (Brem et al., 2010; Dehaene-Lambertz, Monzalvo, & Dehaene, 2018; Kubota et al., 2019; Saygin et al., 2016). Not unlike the universal phonological principle of reading, the specialized activation of the vOT cortex for print is found across alphabetic and logographic writing systems (i.e., it is script invariant); and, as we will see in the section dedicated to developmental dyslexia (Section 12.4), abnormal activation of the vOT is associated with dyslexia and poor reading achievement across writing systems (Bach et al., 2013; Bolger et al., 2005; Buchweitz et al., 2019; Krafnick et al., 2016; Kronbichler et al., 2006; Rueckl et al., 2015; Szwed et al., 2014). In sum, the universality of brain networks of language in its oral and print forms may stem from a similar hardwiring of the brain for speech and a relatively similar process of adaptation of posterior brain systems to reading.

12.3.1 Birth to Six: Brain Adapts to the Relations between Print and Sound

One of the most influential models of reading development in alphabetic systems proposes three stages for reading development: from children's early identification of symbols and visual objects (the logographic stage), to decoding print–sound relationships (the alphabetic stage), and reading at a morphological level (the orthographic stage; Frith, 1985). Children's understanding that print encodes meaning and their ability to decode print to sound and access that meaning, in the alphabetic stage, is tuned to activation of the dorsal subsystem, as seen in the introduction of Section 12.3. As speech and print merge, so do the brain networks for speech and print (Rueckl et al., 2015; Seidenberg, 2017; Seidenberg, Borkenhagen, & Kearns, 2020). A question emerges as to how these systems continue to develop and predict later reading comprehension attainment, the ultimate goal of teaching children to read; this is discussed in a subsection 12.3.2.

The development of reading is influenced by brain response to spoken language processing early on. Delays in language milestones are associated with less activation in basal ganglia, insular cortex, and auditory cortex (left superior temporal gyrus) in late talkers relative to early talkers (Preston et al., 2010). Readers, relative to prereaders, were better able to recognize words and showed more activation of the vOT and frontal and temporal areas of the brain (Chyl et al., 2018). Activation of the dorsal subsystem is also predictive of reading achievement. A study of rhyme and phonemic awareness showed brain activation in the superior posterior temporal region predicted reading skill 1.5 years later (Wang, Joanisse, & Booth, 2020). The birth-to-six stage is underscored by neural adaptability and plasticity for language. It is also a stage in which the brain development tells a story: in children born preterm, relative to those born full-term, there were differences in white-matter tracts associated with language-skill attainment (Bruckert et al., 2019); in preschool children, in turn, early word learning, another important skill, was predicted by the quality of language-related white-matter tracts (Ekerdt et al., 2020). The brain activation and tuning to print–sound relationships in the years from birth to six is predictive of later achievement. The early specialization of the vOT and other subsystems to reading and language sounds holds promise for the prediction of typical or atypical reading acquisition and/or treatment response for struggling learners.

12.3.2 Six to Ten: Posterior Brain Networks Specialize for Reading

The following statement can always be repeated: Learning to read does not emerge from simple exposure to print and oral language (Marks et al., 2019; Moulton et al., 2019; Verhoeven & van Leeuwe, 2012). Instead, learning to read involves developing fundamental skills from birth to age six, as discussed in the previous section and requires systematically continuing to learn sound and print associations in order to climb the ladder of complexity (Torgesen, 2000, 2002). The dynamic relation between ventral and dorsal subsystem activations and reading achievement, as we have seen, is also reflected in later periods. A gradient of activation has been found for the occipitotemporal cortex: adults activate more anterior and lateral areas, while ten-year old children show more posterior and mesial activation portion (Olulade et al., 2013). An influential theory of reading in the brain proposes that the vOT, also called the visual word form area (VWFA), undergoes a process of neuronal recycling and stores abstract representations of words (Cohen et al., 2002; Dehaene, 2009; Dehaene-Lambertz et al., 2018). With instruction, the VWFA tunes to the prelexical function of identification of abstract letter strings (Cohen et al., 2002). Around the ages of six to seven, children stop mirroring letters when they write, an achievement associated with the specialization of the occipitotemporal cortex to print (Dehaene, 2009; Dehaene et al., 2010; Pegado et al., 2014).

Studies with children in the early elementary school years show that the consolidation of early literacy skills paves the way to the development of higher-level reading skills, and these processes are reflected in the brain. Poor readers show less activation of the dorsal and ventral subsystems in word- and sentence-level reading tasks (Hoeft, Meyler et al., 2007; Meyler et al., 2007, 2009). Improvement in reading skill following remediation, in turn, shows an increase in activation of these systems (Meyler et al., 2009; Temple et al., 2003). Children who are successfully learning to read show a strong specialization of the vOT for words, for example, relative to faces, whereas children who are struggling to learn to read show that words and faces compete for vOT brain activation (Kubota et al., 2019). A longitudinal study of brain activation for words and symbols at age six showed that left occipitotemporal sensitivity, or tuning, to print and behavioral data predicts 88 percent of the variance in reading achievement two years later (Bach et al., 2013). Reflecting the importance of the integration of oral and written language domains early on, longitudinal findings (Frost et al., 2009; Preston et al., 2015) found that brain convergence of neural networks for print and speech processing in left-hemisphere (LH) fronto-temporal networks in emergent readers (at age seven) predicts reading outcomes two years later.

Reading instruction for ages six to ten is aimed at consolidating early literacy skills and laying the foundation for developing much-desired higher-level skills. To become fluent readers, children need to automatize early literacy skills. It is only by overcoming the challenge of learning to read that the ultimate goal of reading to learn, to comprehend, and to become avid readers is fulfilled. High-level processes of discourse (i.e. connected text) comprehension, such as inference making and ambiguity resolution, among others, tax brain resources (Buchweitz et al., 2014; Ferstl et al., 2008; Keller, Carpenter, & Just, 2001; Lillywhite et al., 2010; Mason & Just, 2006). Arguably, low-level processes must be automated to free up resources for their higher-up counterparts. Studies of struggling readers in early elementary school show the atypical brain function associated with persistent difficulties in learning to read (e.g., developmental dyslexia), which corroborates the nonspecialization of the subsystems found in struggling readers.

12.4 Brain Function and Morphology in Developmental Dyslexia

Developmental dyslexia is a neurodevelopmental disorder that presents with a persistent and unexpected difficulty in learning to read that cannot be accounted for by, for example, intelligence or inadequate schooling (APA, 2014; Asbury & Plomin, 2013; Mitchell, 2014, 2018). Dyslexia is diagnosed only after formal schooling starts, usually at the age of eight. Thus, the dyslexia paradox, which refers to waiting for children to reach at least eight years of age, causes us to miss a window of brain plasticity and opportunity for remediation (Ozernov-Palchik & Gaab, 2016). In low-income countries, studies suggest an older average age at diagnosis, especially among low-SES children: for example, age ten to eleven in Brazil (Buchweitz et al., 2019; Costa et al., 2016).

There is consistent evidence of alterations in brain morphology associated with developmental dyslexia. From early postmortem studies (Galaburda et al., 1985; Galaburda & Kemper, 1979; Hier et al., 1978) to studies in the 1980s and 1990s (Galaburda & Eidelberg, 1982; Humphreys, Kaufmann, & Galaburda, 1990; Rumsey et al., 1986), and finally to more recent studies of gray- and white-matter morphology *in vivo* (Altarelli et al., 2014; Eckert, 2004; Eckert et al., 2005; Franco et al., 2013; Frye et al., 2010; Langer et al., 2017; Raschle, Chang, & Gaab, 2011; Yeatman et al., 2012), the evidence accumulates in favor of the neurodevelopmental nature of dyslexia. Although structural imaging studies have identified localized, posterior brain differences associated with developmental dyslexia, a recent metanalysis of neuroanatomical differences found that smaller overall brain volume is the only difference that replicates consistently across studies (Ramus et al., 2018). It remains to be seen whether more fine-grained anatomical differences are generalizable across developmental dyslexia studies.

Neurofunctional alterations, in turn, have been replicated across different languages (Buchweitz et al., 2019; Cao et al., 2017; Cattinelli et al., 2013; Kronbichler et al., 2006; Paulesu et al., 2001; Paulesu, Danelli, & Berlingeri, 2014; Seki et al., 2001). The most common alterations include hypoactivation of left-hemisphere occipitotemporal and temporoparietal regions associated with dyslexia and poor reading (Centanni et al., 2019; Hoeft et al., 2011; Hoeft, Ueno et al., 2007; McCandliss et al., 2003; Meyler et al., 2007, 2009; Raschle, Zuk, & Gaab, 2012; Richlan et al., 2009; Richlan, Kronbichler, & Wimmer, 2011; Shaywitz et al., 2002). Functional and connectivity alterations of the posterior ventral and dorsal brain subsystems are potential neural markers of developmental dyslexia and language-related deficits (Cao et al.,

2017; Gabrieli, 2009; van den Bunt et al., 2018) and hold promise for informing treatment response.

The alterations associated with developmental dyslexia extend to the white-matter tracts of the brain. These tracts make up the "cables" that connect the brain's information superhighway. The quality of these neural connections can be evaluated by fractional anisotropy, an index of orientation of water molecules obtained with diffusion-weighted imaging and associated with quality of myelination. Studies show consistent lower fractional anisotropy, construed as poorer connections, in the arcuate and superior longitudinal fasciculi, which connect temporal and frontal language areas, and in the inferior longitudinal fasciculus, which connects occipital and temporal areas (Langer et al., 2017; Ramus et al., 2018; Wandell & Yeatman, 2013; Yeatman et al., 2012). There is emerging evidence of white-matter changes associated with improved reading skills following reading treatment (Huber et al., 2018).

Dyslexia falls in the same category of clinical neurodevelopmental disorders as autism spectrum and attention deficit disorders. These disorders present as highly heritable, but complex, heterogeneous genetics (i.e., different from single-mutation disorders) (Mitchell, 2014; Grigorenko, Chapter 13 in this volume). Thus, alterations in the neural architecture of dyslexia likely result from a combination of heritability and the subsequent execution of the information in the genes, that is, the neurodevelopmental processes. But dyslexia is diagnosed at age eight, or older, and thus there may be brain function and structure differences that result from contextual factors such as having read fewer books, or none at all, as a result of struggling with reading since early preschool and elementary years. A two-year longitudinal study of a cohort of children identified aberrant activation to print in left inferior gyrus and left fusiform gyrus prior to reading instruction and also found prereading morphological and connectivity differences in the auditory and occipitotemporal cortices (Berninger & Richards, 2002; Berninger & Winn, 2006; Pugh et al., 2006). These findings help disambiguate the underlying cause of brain alterations of reading subsystems, which were reliably predicted before school (Kuhl et al., 2020).

12.5 Impact of a Poor Literacy Environment

Language and reading development are also influenced by a myriad of factors other than those discussed up to this point, including socioeconomic factors and language exposure (see also Nag, Chapter 15 and Schwartz, Chapter 19 in this volume). For example, the quality of nutrition and food security can influence risk for infant delays in language development (Nieto-Ruiz et al., 2020). Children who live in food-insecure households also show low levels of literacy and numeracy attainment, and lower short-term memory capacity (Aurino, Wolf, & Tsinigo, 2020). Poor language development at twenty-four months is also linked to low SES (Spann et al., 2020). A series of recent studies have also shown the effects of poverty on brain and language development (Merz et al., 2020; Noble et al., 2015; Pavlakis et al., 2015; Piccolo et al., 2016).

The educational level of mothers and literacy practices shared with children and guardians at home can positively influence emergent literacy (Morais, 2013; Snow & Ninio, 1986; Whitehurst & Lonigan, 1998) and brain development (Shonkoff, 2000). Home literacy environment and child health predict school-readiness for children with family risk of dyslexia (Dilnot et al., 2016). The better the reading ability of mothers, the better the brain connections in children: Maternal reading ability positively correlates with better maturation, construed as higher fractional anisotropy, of language-related tracts in preschool children (Farah et al., 2020). Also, functional connectivity among reading-related areas of the brain in four-year-old children correlates with the reading ability of their mothers (Greenwood et al., 2019).

The positive effects of stimulating language and reading can extend beyond literacy. Reading aloud and storytelling are well known for their positive effects on socioemotional development and early literacy (Irwin & Moore, 2015; Morais, 2013). The amount of reading aloud to children aged 1–2.5 is linked to language and literacy outcomes (Duursma, Augustyn, & Zuckerman, 2008). Reading to children enables enriched use of vocabulary, language sounds, and syntax (Ece Demir-Lira et al., 2019). A recent study also showed the positive effects of sleep and sensory stimulation for overcoming mirror confusion in writing (Torres et al., 2020). Reading to children boosts emergent literacy, but it alone does not pave the road to literacy (Seidenberg, 2017).

Possible effects of low maternal reading ability, thus, *are not* to be misconstrued as mothers' fault, as was the discredited "refrigerator mother" theory of the 1940s, which attributed autism to the emotional distance of mothers. One of the goals of the science of reading is to understand how to strengthen literacy by studying various potential factors. Teachers reading books aloud helps improve the receptive vocabulary of preschool children from low-income families (Dickinson et al., 2019). Moreover, the educational policymaking decisions need to be taken into account as partly responsible for low achievement among low-SES children. If low-SES classrooms are using few evidence-based practices (Nag et al., 2016), the educational system is helping to perpetuate inequality in reading achievement. In sum, the findings briefly discussed in this section corroborate those of the social science concerning the returns on investments in early childhood (Beddington et al., 2008; Heckman, 2006; Heckman & Mosso, 2014; Kautz et al., 2014). We underscore that it is up to public policy and education systems to mitigate language-development gaps brought on by economic and educational disparities. Examples from Brazil, so far, have shown the negative results of a lack of responsibility by the authorities. But a well-known municipality in the poorer northeastern region of the country has shown how evidence-based literacy can help low-SES children learn to read, and read better than their high-SES peers in other regions of the country (Cruz & Loureiro, 2020).

12.6 Brain Systems for Reading, Spelling, and Writing

There is some degree of overlap of brain areas involved in typical and atypical development of reading, spelling, and writing (Berninger & Richards, 2002; Berninger & Winn, 2006; Pugh et al., 2006). Since this overlap is not absolute, component processes of reading (e.g., orthographic, phonologic, or semantic coding) are partially associated with distinct subsystems. These specific features are also true for handwriting (James & Gauthier, 2006; Katanoda, Yoshikawa, & Sugishita, 2001; Menon & Desmond, 2001) and spelling (Booth et al., 2001; Richards, Berninger, & Fayol, 2009; Tokunaga et al., 1999). For instance, Menon & Desmond (2001) examined writing-to-dictation tasks with functional magnetic resonance imaging (fMRI) and implicated left-hemisphere inferior and superior parietal lobes and the supplementary motor area in this task; the parietal regions are similar to those implicated in reading disorders. James and Gauthier (2006) investigated reading and writing in the brain and found a distributed network of posterior (perception) and motor-control regions (production) simultaneously involved in perception and action.

Print is mapped to units of spoken language such as phonemes (e.g., alphabetic systems) and syllables, including syllables that are morphemes (e.g., logographic systems). Alphabetic systems also vary in the regularity of the relations among print and sounds (Katz & Frost, 1992; Seymour et al., 2003; Tan et al., 2001; Yap & Balota, 2015). The properties of writing systems influence computational processes of reading and modulate brain function. For example, English readers, relative to Italian readers, show more activation of the ventral system of the brain; Italian monolinguals, relative to English monolinguals, on the other hand, show more activation in the dorsal system (Paulesu et al., 2000). Moreover, logographic systems relative to alphabetic systems have been associated with more activation of right-hemisphere visual-processing areas (Buchweitz et al., 2019; Higuchi et al., 2015; Perfetti et al., 2007). But just as differences emerge across different writing systems, similarities in dorsal and ventral networks' activation for core processing of print/speech integration are seen, strongly suggesting universality in these core processes (Rueckl et al., 2015). Spelling has been associated with left inferior frontal gyrus (pars opercularis) and bilateral temporal and inferior premotor areas when words are spelled orally (Planton et al., 2017). Moreover, Booth and colleagues (2001) presented auditory word pairs in a spelling overlap judgment task. They showed that left-hemisphere language regions were largely involved in this task.

There are few studies about the brain networks for (hand) writing. In a nutshell, learning to write requires development of automatic fine motor skills. It begins with greater involvement of somatosensory and visual systems in children, which reflect more programmed, stroke-by-stroke movements (Palmis et al., 2017), and it develops to more automated processes, in adults, which involve the superior parietal cortex and right cerebellum, associated with control and retention of fine motor skills in writing (Kadmon Harpaz, Flash, & Dinstein, 2014). The adult network for writing – which is composed of the left dorsal premotor cortex and superior parietal cortex and of the right cerebellum – encodes abstract information about motor planning for writing: Activation is not modulated by switching hands, by writing with one's foot, by writing faster, nor by larger or smaller fonts (Palmis et al., 2017). In other words, the evidence suggests the brain encodes abstract information about letter (letter shapes), which is independent of the variation of, for example, visual and spatial traits of the actual writing out of letters and words.

The development of writing putatively involves four stages. It begins with lower-level motor processes and ends with higher-level orthographic processes. The low-level motor processes evolve from (1) large movements with little skill to adjust the ongoing trace, usually at age six to seven, to (2) a second stage of controlled movements that rely on visual feedback to adjust the ongoing trace but still draw heavily on attentional processes, around age seven to eight, to (3) a memorization of spatial and kinematic information, from age 9 and older, and finally to (4) automated, fast, accurate movements that no longer tax attention (Palmis et al., 2017).

It is worthy of note that the occipitotemporal cortex, ubiquitous in the reading brain, is also involved in writing. Lesions in the occipitotemporal cortex have been shown to affect writing and spelling ability (Palmis et al., 2017; Purcell, Jiang, & Eden, 2017). Also, more activation of the occipitotemporal cortex is associated with fluent writing (Richards et al., 2011), much like fluent reading. The take-home message of this brief discussion of reading and writing in the brain is that overlapping left-hemisphere networks support both aspects. Thus, it is unsurprising that difficulties on one are usually mirrored on the other and that reading interventions which support writing may facilitate general gains in reading, and vice versa (Berninger & Winn, 2006).

12.7 Promises of Neuroscience for Reading Instruction

It is reasonable to ask at this point: What have we learned to date from cognitive science and neuroscience research? It has been argued (Bowers, 2016) that at present the state of evidence linking reading to the brain is correlational. The field has generated a fair amount of evidence about which brain networks are associated with typical or atypical development. Yet the discipline is only beginning to unveil how the brain changes with treatment, as briefly introduced, and whether learning about these changes can be brought to bear on informing treatment. There is a still a lack of developed causal mechanistic models that directly inform novel approaches to educational practices. Indeed, as noted by Bowers, it is difficult to point to any direct contributions from neuroscience findings to teaching, the "how-tos," although the findings do corroborate how critical it is to teach the "what," that is, the precursors of literacy.

The present chapter has addressed the evidence that has been amassed over the past years. We suggest that continued investment in the neuroscience of reading, while critical for advancing basic science, should also aim to fulfill the promise of educational neuroscience: to inform educational practices and policymaking. How and if brain-based approaches to instruction and remediation might impact the classroom or clinic are not conceived of at present, but the sensitivity to individual differences that gene-brain-cognitive measurement affords promises better understanding of what works for whom and why. A particularly exciting new focus is on brain-guided learning and treatment, or teaching to the brain, which has been implemented in autism treatment studies (LaMarca et al., 2018). This is a hot topic for neuroimaging technical development at present (Watanabe et al., 2018). In these approaches, the child is given varied experiences and learning/treatment contexts with concurrent brain-imaging measures. Unveiling how the brain adapts to learning may inform the likelihood of treatment success before learning translates into tangible behavioral improvements.

Another way neuroimaging shows promise for education and clinical practice is the growing focus on measuring the brain in its social context. New research focuses on how the individual brain adapts and synchronizes with other brains in the act of communication and learning. To illustrate this, Hirsch and colleagues (2018) have used Near Infrared Spectroscopy (NIRS) imaging to examine joint brain activity between two individuals as they interact in conversation. They show that efficient communication involves a kind of synchrony between the two brains, with correlated activation patterns in the language areas of the speaker and listener. Other research with larger groups of individuals interacting in a classroom setting, all while wearing electroencephalogram (EEG) caps, has shown preliminary evidence of how an individual entrains to the environment or to other individuals, and how this entrainment to the outside world impacts learning and approaches to learning (Dikker et al., 2017). This focus on entrainment between the learner and teacher in different social contexts will continue to be a hot topic in educational neuroscience going forward. This approach may lead to novel learning paradigms steeped in individuated and brain-guided learning, approaches that match the learning protocols to the learner's relative strengths/weaknesses.

The neuroscience of reading needs to move beyond the largely descriptive neuroimaging results that have been produced to date toward more comprehensive neuromechanistic models (Hancock, Pugh, & Hoeft, 2017). In this sense, emerging evidence from neurochemical studies begins to associate metabolic differences in posterior brain systems with dyslexia, in adults and children (del Tufo et al., 2018; Pugh et al., 2014). There is also a call for research on early or late treatments and interventions for language impairments (see e.g. the paradox of dyslexia, mentioned above). Children with dyslexia outperformed controls in spelling and decoding accuracy and speed after twelve weeks of grapheme–phoneme conversion instruction (Tilanus, Segers, & Verhoeven, 2016). The interaction between type of intervention, duration of intervention, and effectiveness is still not fully understood (Soodla, Tammik, & Kikas, 2019). The variables addressed in this chapter indicate that learning to read is a dynamic and multidimensional process underpinned by similarly dynamic brain function. In addition, learning to read was shown to feed back upon the brain's speech and reading dynamics themselves (van den Bunt et al., 2016, 2018). In the long term, the way forward will involve facing these challenges of translating research findings to the classroom and treatment practices.

References

Altarelli, I., Leroy, F., Monzalvo, K. et al. (2014). Planum temporale asymmetry in developmental dyslexia: Revisiting an old question. *Human Brain Mapping*, *35*(12), 5717–5735. DOI: https://doi.org/10.1002/hbm.22579.

APA. (2014). *Diagnostic and Statistical Manual of Mental Disorders, 5th Edition: DSM-5*. Washington, DC: American Psychological Association.

Asbury, K., & Plomin, R. (2013). *G Is for Genes: The Impact of Genetics on Education and Achievement*. Wiley-Blackwell. DOI: https://doi.org/10.1002/9781118482766.

Aurino, E., Wolf, S., & Tsinigo, E. (2020). Household food insecurity and early childhood development: Longitudinal evidence from Ghana. *PLoS ONE*, *15*(4), 1–20. DOI: https://doi.org/10.1371/journal.pone.0230965.

Bach, S., Richardson, U., Brandeis, D., Martin, E., & Brem, S. (2013). Print-specific multimodal brain activation in kindergarten improves prediction of reading skills in second grade. *NeuroImage*, *82*, 605–615. https://doi.org/10.1016/j.neuroimage.2013.05.062.

Beddington, J., Cooper, C. L., Field, J. et al. (2008). The mental wealth of nations. *Nature*, *455*(7216), 1057–1060. DOI: https://doi.org/10.1038/4551057a.

Berninger, V. W., & Richards, T. L. (2002). *Brain Literacy for Educators and Psychologists*. Washington, DC: Academic Press.

Berninger, V. W., & Winn, W. D. (2006). Implications of advancements in brain research and technology for writing development, writing instruction, and educational evolution. In C. MacArthur, S. Graham, & J. Fitzgerald (eds.), *The Writing Handbook* (pp. 96–114). New York: The Guildford Press.

Bolger, D. J., Perfetti, C., & Schneider, W. (2005). Cross-cultural effect on the brain revisited: universal structures plus writing system variation. *Human Brain Mapping*, *25*(1), 92–104. DOI: https://doi.org/10.1002/hbm.20124

Booth, J. R., Burman, D. D., van Santen, F. W. et al. (2001). The development of specialized brain systems in reading and oral language. *Child Neuropsychology: A Journal on Normal and Abnormal Development in Childhood and Adolescence*, *7*(3), 119–141. DOI: https://doi.org/10.1080/09297049508400221.

Bowers, J. S. (2016). The practical and principled problems with educational neuroscience. *Psychological Review*, *123*(5), 600–612. DOI: https://doi.org/https://doi.org/10.1037/rev0000025.

Brem, S., Bach, S., Kucian, K. et al. (2010). Brain sensitivity to print emerges when children learn letter-speech sound correspondences. *Proceedings of the National Academy of Sciences of the United States of America*, *107*(17), 7939–7944. DOI: https://doi.org/10.1073/pnas.0904402107.

Bruckert, L., Borchers, L. R., Dodson, C. K. et al. (2019). White matter plasticity in reading-related pathways differs in children born preterm and at term: A longitudinal analysis. *Frontiers in Human Neuroscience*, *13*. DOI: https://doi.org/10.3389/fnhum.2019.00139.

Buchweitz, A., Costa, A. C., Toazza, R. et al. (2019). Decoupling of the occipitotemporal cortex and the brain's default-mode network in dyslexia and a role for the cingulate cortex in good readers: A brain imaging study of Brazilian children. *Developmental Neuropsychology*, *44*(1), 146–157. DOI: https://doi.org/10.1080/87565641.2017.1292516.

Buchweitz, A., Mason, R. A., Hasegawa, M., & Just, M. A. (2009). Japanese and English sentence reading comprehension and writing systems: An fMRI study of first and second language effects on brain activation. *Bilingualism*, *12*(2), 141–151. DOI: https://doi.org/10.1017/S1366728908003970.

Buchweitz, A., Mason, R. A., Meschyan, G., Keller, T. A., & Just, M. A. (2014). Modulation of cortical activity during comprehension of familiar and unfamiliar text topics in speed reading and speed listening. *Brain and Language*, *139*, 49–57. DOI: https://doi.org/10.1016/j.bandl.2014.09.010.

Cao, F., Yan, X., Wang, Z. et al. (2017). Neural signatures of phonological deficits in Chinese developmental dyslexia. *NeuroImage*, *146*(March 2016), 301–311. DOI: https://doi.org/10.1016/j.neuroimage.2016.11.051.

Cardoso-Martins, C., & Pennington, B. F. (2004). The relationship between phoneme awareness and rapid serial naming skills and literacy acquisition: the role of developmental period and reading ability. *Scientific Studies of Reading*, *8*(1), 27–52. DOI: https://doi.org/10.1207/s1532799xssr0801_3.

Castles, A., Rastle, K., & Nation, K. (2018). Ending the reading wars: Reading acquisition from novice to expert. *Psychological Science in the Public Interest*, *19* (1), 5–51. DOI: https://doi.org/10.1177/1529100618772271.

Cattinelli, I., Borghese, N. A., Gallucci, M., & Paulesu, E. (2013). Reading the reading brain: A new meta-analysis of functional imaging data on reading. *Journal of Neurolinguistics*, *26*(1), 214–238. DOI: https://doi.org/10.1016/j.jneuroling.2012.08.001.

Centanni, T. M., Norton, E. S., Ozernov-Palchik, O. et al. (2019). Disrupted left fusiform response to print in beginning kindergartners is associated with subsequent reading. *NeuroImage: Clinical*, *22*, 101715. DOI: https://doi.org/10.1016/j.nicl.2019.101715.

Chyl, K., Kossowski, B., Dębska, A. et al. (2018). Prereader to beginning reader: Changes induced by reading acquisition in print and speech brain networks. *Journal of Child Psychology and Psychiatry and Allied Disciplines*, *59*(1), 76–87. DOI: https://doi.org/10.1111/jcpp.12774.

Cohen, L., Lehéricy, S., Chochon, F. et al. (2002). Language-specific tuning of visual cortex? Functional properties of the Visual Word Form Area. *Brain*, *125*(Pt 5), 1054–1069. www.ncbi.nlm.nih.gov/pubmed/11960895.

Costa, A. C., Toazza, R., Bassôa, A., Portuguez, M. W., & Buchweitz, A. (2016). Ambulatório de aprendizagem do projeto ACERTA (Avaliação de Crianças em Risco de Transtorno da Aprendizagem): métodos e resultados em dois anos. *Neuropsicologia Do Desenvolvimento*, *33*, 151–157.

Cruz, L., & Loureiro, A. (2020). Achieving world-class education in adverse socioeconomic conditions: The case of Sobral in Brazil. *World Bank Group Education*, June, pp. 1–37.

Dehaene, S. (2009). *Reading in the Brain: The New Science of How We Read*. New York: Penguin Books.

Dehaene, S., Pegado, F., Braga, L. W. et al. (2010). How learning to read changes the cortical networks for vision and language. *Science*, *330*(6009), 1359–1364. DOI: https://doi.org/10.1126/science.1194140.

Dehaene-Lambertz, G., Monzalvo, K., & Dehaene, S. (2018). The emergence of the visual word form: Longitudinal evolution of category-specific ventral visual areas during reading acquisition. *PLoS Biology*, *16*(3), 1–34. DOI: https://doi.org/10.1371/journal.pbio.2004103/.

del Tufo, S. N., Frost, S. J., Hoeft, F. et al. (2018). Neurochemistry predicts convergence of written and spoken language: A proton magnetic resonance spectroscopy study of cross-modal language integration. *Frontiers in Psychology*, *9*(SEP), 1–17. DOI: https://doi.org/10.3389/fpsyg.2018.01507.

Dickinson, D. K., Collins, M. F., Nesbitt K. et al. (2019). Effects of teacher-delivered book reading and play on vocabulary learning and self-regulation among low-income preschool children. *Journal of Cognition and Development*, *20*(2), 136–164. DOI: https://doi.org/10.1080/15248372.2018.1483373.

Dikker, S., Wan, L., Davidesco, I. et al. (2017). Brain-to-brain synchrony tracks real-world dynamic group interactions in the classroom. *Current Biology*, *27*(9), 1375–1380. DOI: https://doi.org/10.1016/j.cub.2017.04.002.

Dilnot, J., Hamilton, L., Maughan, B., & Snowling, M. J. (2016). Child and environmental risk factors predicting readiness for learning in children at high risk of dyslexia. *Development and Psychopathology*, 1–10. DOI: https://doi.org/10.1017/S0954579416000134.

Dufford, A. J., Kim, P., & Evans, G. W. (2020). The impact of childhood poverty on brain health: Emerging evidence from neuroimaging across the lifespan. *International Review of Neurobiology*, *150*, 77–105. DOI: https://doi.org/10.1016/bs.irn.2019.12.001.

Duryea, T. K. (2019). Emergent literacy including language development. In J. E. Drutz & M. Augustyn (eds.), *UpToDate*. Website. www.uptodate.com/contents/emergent-literacy-including-language-development?search=emergent

Duursma, E., Augustyn, M., & Zuckerman, B. (2008). Reading aloud to children: the evidence. *Archives of Disease in Childhood*, *93*(7), 554–557. DOI: https://doi.org/10.1136/adc.2006.106336.

Ece Demir-Lira, Ö., Applebaum, L. R., Goldin-Meadow, S., & Levine, S. C. (2019). Parents' early book reading to children: Relation to children's later language and literacy outcomes controlling for other parent language input. *Developmental Science*, *22*(3). DOI: https://doi.org/10.1111/desc.12764.

Eckert, M. (2004). Neuroanatomical markers for dyslexia: A review of dyslexia structural imaging studies. *Neuroscientist*, *10*(4), 362–371. DOI: https://doi.org/10.1177/1073858404263596.

Eckert, M. A., Leonard, C. M., Wilke, M. et al. (2005). Anatomical signatures of dyslexia in children: Unique information from manual and voxel based morphometry brain measures. *Cortex*, *41*(3), 304–315. DOI: https://doi.org/10.1016/S0010-9452(08)70268-5.

Ehri, L. C. (2005). Learning to read words: Theory, findings, and issues. *Scientific Studies of Reading*, *9*(2), 167–188. DOI: https://doi.org/10.1207/s1532799xssr0902.

Ehri, L. C., Nunes, S. R., Willows, D. M. et al. (2001). Phonemic awareness instruction helps children learn to read: evidence from the national reading panel's meta-analysis. *Reading Research Quarterly*, *36*(3), 250–287. DOI: https://doi.org/10.1598/RRQ.36.3.2.

Ekerdt, C. E. M., Kühn, C., Anwander, A., Brauer, J., & Friederici, A. D. (2020). Word learning reveals white matter plasticity in preschool children. *Brain Structure and Function*, *225*(2), 607–619. DOI: https://doi.org/10.1007/s00429-020-02024-7.

Farah, R., Dudley, J., Hutton, J., & Horowitz-Kraus, T. (2020). Maternal reading and fluency abilities are associated with diffusion properties of ventral and dorsal white matter tracts in their preschool-age children. *Brain and Cognition*, *140*(January), 105532. DOI: https://doi.org/10.1016/j.bandc.2020.105532.

Ferstl, E. C., Neumann, J., Bogler, C., von Cramon, D. Y., & Cramon, D. Y. von. (2008). The extended language network: a meta-analysis of neuroimaging studies on text comprehension. *Human Brain Mapping*, *29*(5), 581–593. DOI: https://doi.org/10.1002/hbm.20422.

Franco, A. R., Mannell, M. V., Calhoun, V. D., & Mayer, A. R. (2013). Impact of analysis methods on the reproducibility and reliability of resting-state networks. *Brain Connectivity*, *3*(4), 363–374. DOI: https://doi.org/10.1089/brain.2012.0134.

Friederici, A. D. (2012). The cortical language circuit: From auditory perception to sentence comprehension. *Trends in Cognitive Sciences*, *16*(5), 262–268. DOI: https://doi.org/10.1016/j.tics.2012.04.001.

Frith, U. (1985). Surface dyslexia: Neurological and cognitive studies of phonological reading. In K. Patterson, J. Marshall, & M. Coltheart (eds.), *Surface Dyslexia* (pp. 301–330). Erlbaum.

Frost, S. J., Landi, N., Mencl, W. E. et al. (2009). Phonological awareness predicts activation patterns for print and speech. *Annals of Dyslexia*, *59*(1), 78–97. DOI: https://doi.org/10.1007/s11881-009-0024-y.

Frye, R. E., Liederman, J., Malmberg, B. et al. (2010). surface area accounts for the relation of gray matter volume to reading-related skills and history of dyslexia. *Cerebral Cortex, 20*(11), 2625–2635. DOI: https://doi.org/10.1093/cercor/bhq010.

Gabrieli, J. D. E. (2009). Dyslexia: A new synergy between education and cognitive neuroscience. *Science, 325*(5938), 280–283. DOI: https://doi.org/10.1126/science.1171999.

Galaburda, A., & Eidelberg, D. (1982). Symmetry and asymmetry in the human posterior thalamus: II. Thalamic lesions in a case of developmental dyslexia. *Archives of Neurology, 39*(6), 333–336. DOI: https://doi.org/10.1001/archneur.1982.00510180011002.

Galaburda, A., & Kemper, T. L. (1979). Cytoarchitectonic abnormalities in developmental dyslexia: a case study. *Annals of Neurology, 6*(2), 94–100. DOI: https://doi.org/10.1002/ana.410060203.

Galaburda, A., Sherman, G. F., Rosen, G. D., Aboitiz, F., & Geschwind, N. (1985). Developmental dyslexia: Four consecutive patients with cortical anomalies. *Annals of Neurology, 18*(2), 222–233. DOI: https://doi.org/10.1002/ana.410180210.

Gracco, V. L., Tremblay, P., & Pike, B. (2005). Imaging speech production using fMRI. *NeuroImage, 26*(1), 294–301. DOI: https://doi.org/10.1016/j.neuroimage.2005.01.033.

Greenwood, P., Hutton, J., Dudley, J., & Horowitz-Kraus, T. (2019). Maternal reading fluency is associated with functional connectivity between the child's future reading network and regions related to executive functions and language processing in preschool-age children. *Brain and Cognition, 131*(November 2018), 87–93. https://doi.org/10.1016/j.bandc.2018.11.010.

Hancock, R., Pugh, K. R., & Hoeft, F. (2017). Neural noise hypothesis of developmental dyslexia. *Trends in Cognitive Sciences*, 21(6), 434–448. DOI: https://doi.org/10.1016/j.tics.2017.03.008.

Heckman, J. J. (2006). Skill formation and the economics of investing in disadvantaged children. *Science, 312*(5782), 1900–1902. DOI; https://doi.org/10.1126/science.1128898.

Heckman, J. J., & Mosso, S. (2014). The economics of human development and social mobility. *Annual Review of Economics, 6*(1), 689–733. DOI: https://doi.org/10.1146/annurev-cconomics-080213-040753.

Hier, D. B., LeMay, M., Rosenberger, P. B., & Perlo, V. P. (1978). Developmental dyslexia: Evidence for a subgroup with a reversal of cerebral asymmetry. *Archives of Neurology, 35* (2), 90–92. DOI: https://doi.org/10.1001/archneur.1978.00500260028005.

Higuchi, H., Moriguchi, Y., Murakami, H. et al. (2015). Neural basis of hierarchical visual form processing of Japanese Kanji characters. *Brain and Behavior, 5*(12), e00413. DOI: https://doi.org/10.1002/brb3.413.

Hirsch, J., Noah, J. A., Zhang, X., Dravida, S., & Ono, Y. (2018). A cross-brain neural mechanism for human-to-human verbal communication. *Social Cognitive and Affective Neuroscience, 13*(9), 907–920. DOI: https://doi.org/10.1093/scan/nsy070.

Hjetland, H. N., Lervåg, A., Lyster, S. A. H. et al. (2019). Pathways to reading comprehension: A longitudinal study from 4 to 9 years of age. *Journal of Educational Psychology, 111*(5), 751–763. DOI: https://doi.org/10.1037/edu0000321.

Hoeft, F., McCandliss, B. D., Black, J. M. et al. (2011). Neural systems predicting long-term outcome in dyslexia. *Proceedings of the National Academy of Sciences of the United States of America, 108*(1), 361–366. DOI: https://doi.org/10.1073/pnas.1008950108.

Hoeft, F., Meyler, A., Hernandez, A. et al. (2007). Functional and morphometric brain dissociation between dyslexia and reading ability. *Proceedings of the National Academy of Sciences of the United States of America*, *104*(10), 4234–4239. DOI: https://doi.org/10.1073/pnas.0609399104.

Hoeft, F., Ueno, T., Reiss, A. L. et al. (2007). Prediction of children's reading skills using behavioral, functional, and structural neuroimaging measures. *Behavioral Neuroscience*, *121*(3), 602–613. DOI: https://doi.org/10.1037/0735-7044.121.3.602.

Hoff, E. (2003). The specificity of environmental influence: Socioeconomic status affects early vocabulary development via maternal speech. *Child Development*, *74* (5), 1368–1378. DOI: https://doi.org/10.1111/1467-8624.00612.

Hoff, E., & Tian, C. (2005). Socioeconomic status and cultural influences on language. *Journal of Communication Disorders*, *38*(4), 271–278. DOI: https://doi.org/10.1016/j.jcomdis.2005.02.003.

Houdé, O., Rossi, S., Lubin, A., & Joliot, M. (2010). Mapping numerical processing, reading, and executive functions in the developing brain: an fMRI meta-analysis of 52 studies including 842 children. *Developmental Science*, *13*(6), 876–885. DOI: https://doi.org/10.1111/j.1467-7687.2009.00938.x.

House of Commons. (2009). "House of Commons – Evidence Check 1: Early Literacy Interventions – Science and Technology Committee" (2009 HC). https://publications.parliament.uk/pa/cm200910/cmselect/cmsctech/44/4402.htm.

Huber, E., Donnelly, P. M., Rokem, A., & Yeatman, J. D. (2018). Rapid and widespread white matter plasticity during an intensive reading intervention. *Nature Communications*, *9*(1), 1–13. https://doi.org/10.1038/s41467-018-04627-5.

Huey, E. B. (1908). *The Psychology and Pedagogy of Reading*. New York: Macmillan.

Humphreys, P., Kaufmann, W. E., & Galaburda, A. M. (1990). Developmental dyslexia in women: Neuropathological findings in three patients. *Annals of Neurology*, *28*(6), 727–738. DOI: https://doi.org/10.1002/ana.410280602.

INEP. (2017). *Avaliação Nacional da Alfabetização*. Ministério da Educacao. http://portal.mec.gov.br/docman/outubro-2017-pdf/75181-resultados-ana-2016-pdf/file.

Irwin, J., & Moore, D. (2015). *Preparing Children for Reading Success* (1st edition). New York: Rowman & Littlefield.

James, K. H., & Gauthier, I. (2006). Letter processing automatically recruits a sensory-motor brain network. *Neuropsychologia*, *44*(14), 2937–2949. DOI: https://doi.org/10.1016/j.neuropsychologia.2006.06.026.

Kadmon Harpaz, N., Flash, T., & Dinstein, I. (2014). Scale-invariant movement encoding in the human motor system. *Neuron*, *81*(2), 452–462. DOI: https://doi.org/10.1016/j.neuron.2013.10.058.

Kamykowska, J., Haman, E. W. A., Latvala, J.-M., Richardson, U., & Lyytinen, H. (2013). Developmental changes of early reading skills in six-year-old Polish children and GraphoGame as a computer-based intervention to support them. *L1 Educational Studies in Language and Literature*, *13*, 1–17. DOI: https://doi.org/10.17239/L1ESLL-2013.01.05.

Katanoda, K., Yoshikawa, K., & Sugishita, M. (2001). A functional MRI study on the neural substrates for writing. *Human Brain Mapping*, *13*(1), 34–42. DOI: https://doi.org/10.1002/hbm.1023.

Katz, L., & Frost, R. (1992). The reading process is different for different orthographies: The orthographic depth hypothesis. *Advances in Psychology*, *64*, 67–84.

Kautz, T., Heckman, J. J., Diris, R., Weel, B. ter, & Borghans, L. (2014). *Fostering and Measuring Skills: Improving Cognitive and Non-cognitive Skills to Promote Lifetime Success*. Paris: OECD. DOI: https://doi.org/10.1787/5jxsr7vr78f7-en.

Keller, T. A., Carpenter, P. A., & Just, M. A. (2001). The neural bases of sentence comprehension: A fMRI examination of syntactic and lexical processing. *Cerebral Cortex*, *11*(3), 223–237. www.ncbi.nlm.nih.gov/pubmed/11230094.

Krafnick, A. J., Tan, L. H., Flowers, D. L. et al. (2016). Chinese character and English word processing in children's ventral occipitotemporal cortex: FMRI evidence for script invariance. *NeuroImage*, *133*, 302–312. DOI: https://doi.org/10.1016/j.neuroimage.2016.03.021.

Kronbichler, M., Hutzler, F., Staffen, W. et al. (2006). Evidence for a dysfunction of left posterior reading areas in German dyslexic readers. *Neuropsychologia*, *44*(10), 1822–1832. DOI: https://doi.org/10.1016/j.neuropsychologia.2006.03.010.

Kubota, E. C., Joo, S. J., Huber, E., & Yeatman, J. D. (2019). Word selectivity in high-level visual cortex and reading skill. *Developmental Cognitive Neuroscience*, *36* (April 2018), 100593. DOI: https://doi.org/10.1016/j.dcn.2018.09.003.

Kuhl, U., Neef, N. E., Kraft, I. et al. (2020). The emergence of dyslexia in the developing brain. *NeuroImage*, *211*(January). https://doi.org/10.1016/j.neuroimage.2020.116633.

LaMarca, K., Gevirtz, R., Lincoln, A. J., & Pineda, J. A. (2018). Facilitating neurofeedback in children with autism and intellectual impairments using TAGteach. *Journal of Autism and Developmental Disorders*, *48*(6), 2090–2100. DOI: https://doi.org/10.1007/s10803-018-3466-4.

Langer, N., Peysakhovich, B., Zuk, J. et al. (2017). White matter alterations in infants at risk for developmental dyslexia. *Cerebral Cortex*, *27*(2), 1027–36. DOI: https://doi.org/10.1093/cercor/bhv281.

Lillywhite, L. M., Saling, M. M., Demutska, A. et al. (2010). The neural architecture of discourse compression. *Neuropsychologia*, *48*(4), 873–879. https://doi.org/10.1016/j.neuropsychologia.2009.11.004.

Lo, J. C. M., McBride, C., Ho, C. S., & Maurer, U. (2019). Event-related potentials during Chinese single-character and two-character word reading in children. *Brain and Cognition*, *136*, 103589. DOI: https://doi.org/10.1016/j.bandc.2019.103589.

Marks, R. A., Kovelman, I., Kepinska, O. et al. (2019). Spoken language proficiency predicts print-speech convergence in beginning readers. *NeuroImage*, *201*(February), 116021. DOI: https://doi.org/10.1016/j.neuroimage.2019.116021.

Martin, A., Schurz, M., Kronbichler, M., & Richlan, F. (2015). Reading in the brain of children and adults: A meta-analysis of 40 functional magnetic resonance imaging studies. *Human Brain Mapping*, *36*(5), 1963–1981. https://doi.org/10.1002/hbm.22749.

Mason, R. A., & Just, M. A. (2006). Neuroimaging contributions to the understanding of discourse processes. In M. Traxler & M. A. Gernsbacher (eds.), *Handbook of {Psycholinguistics}* (pp. 765–799). New York: Elsevier.

McBride, C. A. (2016). Is Chinese special? Four aspects of Chinese literacy acquisition that might distinguish learning Chinese from learning alphabetic orthographies. *Educational Psychology Review*, *28*, 523–549. DOI: https://doi.org/10.1007/s10648-015-9318-2.

McCandliss, B. D., Cohen, L., & Dehaene, S. (2003). The visual word form area: Expertise for reading in the fusiform gyrus. *Trends in Cognitive Sciences*, *7*(7), 293–299. DOI: https://doi.org/10.1016/S1364-6613(03)00134-7.

Menon, V., & Desmond, J. E. (2001). Left superior parietal cortex involvement in writing: Integrating fMRI with lesion evidence. *Cognitive Brain Research*, *12*(2), 337–340. DOI: https://doi.org/10.1016/S0926-6410(01)00063-5.

Merz, E. C., Maskus, E. A., Melvin, S. A., He, X., & Noble, K. G. (2020). Socioeconomic disparities in language input are associated with children's language-related brain structure and reading skills. *Child Development*, *91*(3), 846–860. DOI: https://doi.org/10.1111/cdev.13239.

Merz, E. C., Wiltshire, C. A., & Noble, K. G. (2019). Socioeconomic inequality and the developing brain: Spotlight on language and executive function. *Child Development Perspectives*, *13*(1), 15–20. DOI: https://doi.org/10.1111/cdep.12305.

Meyler, A., Keller, T. A., Cherkassky, V. L., Gabrieli, J. D. E. E., & Just, M. A. (2009). Modifying the brain activation of poor readers during sentence comprehension with extended remedial instruction: A longitudinal study of neuroplasticity. *Neuropsychologia*, *46*(10), 2580–2592. DOI: https://doi.org/10.1016/j.neuropsychologia.2008.03.012.

Meyler, A., Keller, T. A., Cherkassky, V. L. et al. (2007). Brain activation during sentence comprehension among good and poor readers. *Cerebral Cortex*, *17*(12), 2780–2787. DOI: https://doi.org/10.1093/cercor/bhm006.

Mitchell, K. J. (2014). The genetic architecture of neurodevelopmental disorders. Preprint. bioRxiv DOI: https://doi.org/10.1101/009449.

Mitchell, K. J. (2018). *Innate: How the Wiring of Our Brains Shapes Who We Are*. Princeton, NJ: Princeton University Press. https://press.princeton.edu/titles/13255.html.

Morais, J. (2013). *Criar leitores – para professores e educadores*. Barueri, SP: Minha editora.

Moulton, E., Bouhali, F., Monzalvo, K. et al. (2019). Connectivity between the visual word form area and the parietal lobe improves after the first year of reading instruction: A longitudinal MRI study in children. *Brain Structure and Function*, *224*(4), 1519–1536. DOI: https://doi.org/10.1007/s00429-019-01855-3.

Nag, S., Vagh, S. B. Dulay, K. M & Snowling M. J. (2019). Context and Implications: Home language, school language and children's literacy attainments: A systematic review of evidence from low- and middle-income countries. *Review of Education*, *7* (1), 151–155. DOI: https://doi.org/10.1002/rev3.3132.

Nag, S., Snowling, M. J., & Asfaha, Y. M. (2016). Classroom literacy practices in low- and middle-income countries: An interpretative synthesis of ethnographic studies. *Oxford Review of Education*, *42*(1), 1–15. DOI: https://doi.org/10.1080/03054985.2015.1135115.

National Reading Panel. (2000). Teaching children to read: An evidence-based assessment of the scientific research literature on reading and its implications for reading instruction. *NIH Publication No. 00–4769*, *7*, 35. DOI: https://doi.org/10.1002/ppul.1950070418.

Nieto-Ruiz, A., Diéguez, E., Sepúlveda-Valbuena, N. et al. (2020). Influence of a functional nutrients-enriched infant formula on language development in healthy children at four years old. *Nutrients*, *12*(2). DOI: https://doi.org/10.3390/nu12020535.

Noble, K. G., Houston, S. M., Brito, N. H. et al. (2015). Family income, parental education and brain structure in children and adolescents. *Nature Neuroscience, 18* (5), 773–778. DOI: https://doi.org/10.1038/nn.3983.

OECD. (2019). *PISA 2018 Assessment and Analytical Framework: Vol. I*. Paris: OECD. DOI: https://doi.org/10.1787/b25efab8-en.

Olulade, O. A., Flowers, D. L., Napoliello, E. M., & Eden, G. F. (2013). Developmental differences for word processing in the ventral stream. *Brain and Language, 125*(2), 134–145. DOI: https://doi.org/10.1016/j.bandl.2012.04.003.

Ozernov-Palchik, O., & Gaab, N. (2016). Tackling the "dyslexia paradox": Reading brain and behavior for early markers of developmental dyslexia. *Wiley Interdisciplinary Reviews Cognitive Science, 7*(2), 156–176. DOI: https://doi.org/10.1002/wcs.1383.

Palmis, S., Danna, J., Velay, J.-L., & Longcamp, M. (2017). Motor control of handwriting in the developing brain: A review. *Cognitive Neuropsychology, 34*(3–4), 187–204. DOI: https://doi.org/10.1080/02643294.2017.1367654.

Paulesu, E., Danelli, L., & Berlingeri, M. (2014). Reading the dyslexic brain: Multiple dysfunctional routes revealed by a new meta-analysis of PET and fMRI activation studies. *Frontiers in Human Neuroscience, 8*. DOI: https://doi.org/10.3389/fnhum.2014.00830.

Paulesu, E., Démonet, J. F., & Fazio, F. (2001). Dyslexia: Cultural diversity and biological unity. *Science, 291*(5511), 2165–2167. DOI: https://doi.org/10.1126/science.1057179.

Paulesu, E., McCrory, E., Fazio, F. et al. (2000). A cultural effect on brain function. *Nature Neuroscience, 3*(1), 91–96. DOI: https://doi.org/10.1038/71163.

Pavlakis, A. E., Noble, K., Pavlakis, S. G., Ali, N., & Frank, Y. (2015). Brain imaging and electrophysiology biomarkers: Is there a role in poverty and education outcome research? *Pediatric Neurology, 52*(4), 383–388. DOI: https://doi.org/10.1016/j.pediatrneurol.2014.11.005.

Pegado, F., Nakamura, K., Braga, L. W. et al. (2014). Literacy breaks mirror invariance for visual stimuli: A behavioral study with adult illiterates. *Journal of Experimental Psychology General, 143*(2), 887–894. DOI: https://doi.org/10.1037/a0033198.

Perfetti, C. A. (1992). The representation problem in reading acquisition. In P. B. Gough, L. C. Ehri, & R. Treiman (eds.), *Reading Acquisition* (pp. 145–174). Mahwah, NJ: Lawrence Erlbaum Associates.

Perfetti, C. A., Liu, Y., Fiez, J. et al. (2007). Reading in two writing systems: Accommodation and assimilation of the brain's reading network. *Bilingualism, 10* (2), 131–146. DOI: https://doi.org/10.1017/S1366728907002891

Perfetti, C. A., & Tan, L. H. (1998). The time course of graphic, phonological, and semantic activation in Chinese character identification. *Journal of Experimental Psychology: Learning, Memory, and Cognition, 24*(1), 101–118. DOI: https://doi.org/10.1037/0278-7393.24.1.101.

Piccolo, L. R., Merz, E. C., He, X., Sowell, E. R., & Noble, K. G. (2016). Age-related differences in cortical thickness vary by socioeconomic status. *PLoS One, 11*(9), e0162511. DOI: https://doi.org/10.1371/journal.pone.0162511.

Planton, S., Longcamp, M., Péran, P., Démonet, J. F., & Jucla, M. (2017). How specialized are writing-specific brain regions? An fMRI study of writing, drawing and oral spelling. *Cortex, 88*, 66–80. DOI: https://doi.org/10.1016/j.cortex.2016.11.018.

Pleisch, G., Karipidis, I. I., Brauchli, C. et al. (2019). Emerging neural specialization of the ventral occipitotemporal cortex to characters through phonological association learning in preschool children. *Neuroimage*, *189*, 813–831. DOI: https://doi.org/10.1016/j.neuroimage.2019.01.046.

Preston, J. L., Frost, S. J., Mencl, W. E. et al. (2010). Early and late talkers: School-age language, literacy and neurolinguistic differences. *Brain*, *133*(8), 2185–2195. DOI: https://doi.org/10.1093/brain/awq163.

Preston, J. L., Molfese, P. J., Frost, S. J. et al. (2015). Print-speech convergence predicts future reading outcomes in early readers. *Psychological Science*, *27*(1), 75–84. https://doi.org/10.1177/0956797615611921.

Pugh, K. R., Frost, S. J., Rothman, D. L. et al. (2014). Glutamate and choline levels predict individual differences in reading ability in emergent readers. *The Journal of Neuroscience: The Official Journal of the Society for Neuroscience*, *34*(11), 4082–4089. DOI: https://doi.org/10.1523/JNEUROSCI.3907-13.2014.

Pugh, K. R., Mencl, W. E., Jenner, A. R. et al. (2001). Neurobiological studies of reading and reading disability. *Journal of Communication Disorders*, *34*(6), 479–492. DOI: https://doi.org/10.1016/S0021-9924(01)00060-0.

Pugh, K. R., Sandak, R., Frost, S. J., Moore, D., & Mencl, W. E. (2006). Examining reading development and reading disability in diverse languages and cultures: Potential contributions from functional neuroimaging *Journal of American Indian Education*, *45*(3), 60–76.

Purcell, J. J., Jiang, X., & Eden, G. F. (2017). Shared orthographic neuronal representations for spelling and reading. *Neuroimage*, *147*, 554–567. DOI: https://doi.org/10.1016/j.neuroimage.2016.12.054.

Ramus, F., Altarelli, I., Jednoróg, K., Zhao, J., & Scotto di Covella, L. (2018). Neuroanatomy of developmental dyslexia: Pitfalls and promise. *Neuroscience and Biobehavioral Reviews*, *84*(August 2017), 434–452. DOI: https://doi.org/10.1016/j.neubiorev.2017.08.001.

Raschle, N. M., Chang, M., & Gaab, N. (2011). Structural brain alterations associated with dyslexia predate reading onset. *Neuroimage*, *57*(3), 742–749. DOI: https://doi.org/10.1016/j.neuroimage.2010.09.055.

Raschle, N. M., Zuk, J., & Gaab, N. (2012). Functional characteristics of developmental dyslexia in left-hemispheric posterior brain regions predate reading onset. *Proceedings of the National Academy of Sciences of the United States of America*, *109*(6), 2156–2161. DOI: https://doi.org/10.1073/pnas.1107721109.

Richards, T. L., Berninger, V. W., & Fayol, M. (2009). fMRI activation differences between 11-year-old good and poor spellers' access in working memory to temporary and long-term orthographic representations. *Journal of Neurolinguistics*, *22*(4), 327–353. DOI: https://doi.org/10.1016/j.jneuroling.2008.11.002.

Richards, T. L., Berninger, V. W., Stock, P. et al. (2011). Differences between good and poor child writers on fMRI contrasts for writing newly taught and highly practiced letter forms. *Reading and Writing*, *24*(5), 493–516. DOI: https://doi.org/10.1007/s11145-009-9217-3.

Richlan, F. (2012). Developmental dyslexia: Dysfunction of a left hemisphere reading network. *Frontiers in Human Neuroscience*, *6* (May 2012), 1–5. DOI: https://doi.org/10.3389/fnhum.2012.00120.

Richlan, F. (2014). Functional neuroanatomy of developmental dyslexia: The role of orthographic depth. *Frontiers in Human Neuroscience*, *8*(MAY), 1–13. DOI: https://doi.org/10.3389/fnhum.2014.00347.

Richlan, F., Kronbichler, M., & Wimmer, H. (2009). Functional abnormalities in the dyslexic brain: A quantitative meta-analysis of neuroimaging studies. *Human Brain Mapping*, *30*(10), 3299–3308. DOI: https://doi.org/10.1002/hbm.20752.

Richlan, F., Kronbichler, M., & Wimmer, H. (2011). Meta-analyzing brain dysfunctions in dyslexic children and adults. *NeuroImage*, *56*(3), 1735–1742. DOI: https://doi.org/10.1016/j.neuroimage.2011.02.040.

Rose, J. (2006). *Independent Review of the Teaching of Early Reading: Final Report*. London: Department for Education and Skills.

Rueckl, J. G., Paz-Alonso, P. M., Molfese, P. J. et al. (2015). Universal brain signature of proficient reading: Evidence from four contrasting languages. *Proceedings of the National Academy of Sciences of the United States of America*, *112*(50), 15510–15515. DOI: https://doi.org/10.1073/pnas.1509321112.

Rumsey, J. M., Dorwart, R., Vermess, M. et al. (1986). Magnetic resonance imaging of brain anatomy in severe developmental dyslexia. *Archives of Neurology*, *43*(10), 1045–1046. DOI: https://doi.org/10.1001/archneur.1986.00520100053014.

Saiegh-Haddad, E., Shahbari-kassem, A., & Schiff, R. (2020). Phonological awareness in Arabic: The role of phonological distance, phonological-unit size, and SES. *Reading and Writing*, *33*(6), 1649–1674. DOI: https://doi.org/10.1007/s11145-020-10019-3.

Sandak, R., Mencl, W. E., Frost, S. J., & Pugh, K. R. (2004). The neurobiological basis of skilled and impaired reading: Recent findings and new directions. *Scientific Studies of Reading*, *8*(3), 273–292. DOI: https://doi.org/10.1207/s1532799xssr0803.

Saygin, Z. M., Osher, D. E., Norton, E. S. et al. (2016). Connectivity precedes function in the development of the visual word form area. *Nature Neuroscience*, *19*(9), 1250–1255. DOI: https://doi.org/10.1038/nn.4354.

Scarborough, H. S., Dobrich, W., & Hager, M. (1991). Preschool literacy experience and later reading achievement. *Journal of Learning Disabilities*, *24*(8), 508–511. DOI: https://doi.org/10.1177/002221949102400811.

Schiff, R., & Saiegh-Haddad, E. (2018). Development and relationships between phonological awareness, morphological awareness and word reading in spoken and standard Arabic. *Frontiers in Psychology*, *9*, 1–13. DOI: https://doi.org/10.3389/fpsyg.2018.00356.

Seidenberg, M. (2017). *Language at the Speed of Sight: How We Read, Why So Many Can't, and What Can Be Done About It*. New York: Basic Books.

Seidenberg, M., Borkenhagen, M. C., & Kearns, D. M. (2020). Lost in translation? Challenges in connecting reading science and educational practice. Preprint. PsyArxiv DOI: https://doi.org/10.31234/osf.io/sq4fr.

Seki, A., Koeda, T., Sugihara, S. et al. (2001). A functional magnetic resonance imaging study during sentence reading in Japanese dyslexic children. *Brain and Development*, *23*(5), 312–316. DOI: https://doi.org/10.1016/S0387-7604(01)00228-5.

Seymour, P. H. K. K., Aro, M., Erskine, J. M. et al. (2003). Foundation literacy acquisition in European orthographies. *British Journal of Psychology*, *94*(Pt 2), 143–174. DOI: https://doi.org/10.1348/000712603321661859.

Shanahan, T., & Lonigan, C. J. (2010). The National Early Literacy Panel: A summary of the process and the report. *Educational Researcher, 39*(4), 279–285. DOI: https://doi.org/10.3102/0013189X10369172.

Shaywitz, B. A., Shaywitz, S. E., Pugh, K. R. et al. (2002). Disruption of posterior brain systems for reading in children with developmental dyslexia. *Society of Biological Psychiatry, 3223*(02), 101–110. DOI: https://doi.org/10.1016/S0006-3223(02)01365-3.

Shonkoff, J. P. (2000). Science, policy, and practice: Three cultures in search of a shared mission. *Child Development, 71*(1), 181–187. DOI: https://doi.org/10.1111/1467-8624.00132.

Snow, C. E., & Ninio, A. (1986). The contracts of literacy: What children learn from learning to read books. In W. H. Teale & E. Sulzby (eds.), *Emergent literacy: Writing and reading* (pp. 116–138). Norwood, NJ: Ablex.

Soodla, P., Tammik, V., & Kikas, E. (2019). Is part-time special education beneficial for children at risk for reading difficulties? An example from Estonia. *Dyslexia*. DOI: https://doi.org/10.1002/dys.1643.

Spann, M. N., Bansal, R., Hao, X., Rosen, T. S., & Peterson, B. S. (2020). Prenatal socioeconomic status and social support are associated with neonatal brain morphology, toddler language and psychiatric symptoms. *Child Neuropsychology, 26*(2), 170–188. DOI: https://doi.org/10.1080/09297049.2019.1648641.

Szwed, M., Qiao, E., Jobert, A., Dehaene, S., & Cohen, L. (2014). Effects of literacy in early visual and occipitotemporal areas of Chinese and French readers. *Journal of Cognitive Neuroscience, 26*(3), 459–475. DOI: https://doi.org/10.1162/jocn_a_00499.

Tan, L. H., Liu, H.-L., Perfetti, C. A. et al. (2001). The neural system underlying Chinese logograph reading. *NeuroImage, 13*(5), 836–846. DOI: https://doi.org/10.1006/nimg.2001.0749.

Temple, E., Deutsch, G. K., Poldrack, R. A. et al. (2003). Neural deficits in children with dyslexia ameliorated by behavioral remediation: Evidence from functional MRI. *Proceedings of the National Academy of Sciences of the United States of America, 100*(5), 2860–2865. DOI: https://doi.org/10.1073/pnas.0030098100.

The World Bank Group. (2020). DataBank. The World Bank Group (web page). https://databank.worldbank.org/reports.aspx?source=2&series=SE.PRM.AGES&country=.

Tilanus, E. A. T., Segers, E., & Verhoeven, L. (2016). Responsiveness to intervention in children with dyslexia. *Dyslexia, 22*(3), 214–232. DOI: https://doi.org/10.1002/dys.1533.

Tokunaga, H., Nishikawa, T., Ikejiri, Y. et al. (1999). Different neural substrates for Kanji and Kana writing: A PET study. *NeuroReport: An International Journal for the Rapid Communication of Research in Neuroscience, 10*(16), 3315–3319. DOI: https://doi.org/10.1097/00001756-199911080-00012.

Torgesen, J. K. (2000). Individual differences in response to early interventions in reading: The lingering problem of treatment resisters. *Learning Disabilities Research & Practice, 15*(1), 55–64. www.tandfonline.com/doi/abs/10.1207/SLDRP1501_6#.VXH15s-jNcY.

Torgesen, J. K. (2002). The prevention of reading difficulties. *Journal of School Psychology, 40*(1), 7–26. DOI: https://doi.org/10.1016/S0022-4405(01)00092-9.

Torres, A. R., Mota, N. B., Adamy, N. et al. (2020). Selective inhibition of mirror invariance for letters consolidated by sleep doubles reading fluency. *Current Biology*, *31*, 1–11. DOI: https://doi.org/10.1016/j.cub.2020.11.031.

Twomey, T., Kawabata Duncan, K. J., Hogan, J. S. et al. (2013). Dissociating visual form from lexical frequency using Japanese. *Brain and Language*, *125*(2), 184–193. DOI: https://doi.org/10.1016/j.bandl.2012.02.003.

van den Bunt, M. R., Groen, M. A., Ito, T. et al. (2016). Increased response to altered auditory feedback in dyslexia: A weaker sensorimotor magnet implied in the phonological deficit. *Journal of Speech, Language, and Hearing Research*, *60*(3): 654–667. DOI: https://doi.org/10.1044/2016_JSLHR-L-16-0201.

van den Bunt, M. R., Groen, M. A., van der Kleij, S. W. et al. (2018). Deficient response to altered auditory feedback in dyslexia. *Developmental Neuropsychology*, *43*(7), 622–641. DOI: https://doi.org/10.1080/87565641.2018.1495723. PMID: 28257585; PMCID: PMC5544192.

Verhoeven, L., & van Leeuwe, J. (2012). The simple view of second language reading throughout the primary grades. *Reading and Writing*, *25*(8), 1805–1818. DOI: https://doi.org/10.1007/s11145-011-9346-3.

Wandell, B. A., & Yeatman, J. D. (2013). Biological development of reading circuits. *Current Opinion in Neurobiology*, *23*(2), 261–268. DOI: https://doi.org/10.1016/j.conb.2012.12.005.

Wang, J., Joanisse, M. F., & Booth, J. R. (2018). Reading skill related to left ventral occipitotemporal cortex during a phonological awareness task in 5–6-year old children. *Developmental Cognitive Neuroscience*, *30*, 116–122. DOI: https://doi.org/10.1016/j.dcn.2018.01.011.

Wang, J., Joanisse, M. F., & Booth, J. R. (2020). Neural representations of phonology in temporal cortex scaffold longitudinal reading gains in 5- to 7-year-old children. *NeuroImage*, *207*(June 2019), 116359. DOI: https://doi.org/10.1016/j.neuroimage.2019.116359.

Watanabe, T., Sasaki, Y., Shibata, K., & Kawato, M. (2018). Advances in fMRI real-time neurofeedback. *Trends in Cognitive Sciences*, *22*(8), P738. DOI: https://doi.org/https://doi.org/10.1016/j.tics.2018.05.007.

Whitehurst, G. J., & Lonigan, C. J. (1998). Child development and emergent literacy. *Child Development*, *69*(3), 848–872. DOI: https://doi.org/10.1111/j.1467-8624.1998.tb06247.x.

Wolf, S., & McCoy, D. C. (2019). Household socioeconomic status and parental investments: Direct and indirect relations with school readiness in Ghana. *Child Development*, *90*(1), 260–278. DOI: https://doi.org/10.1111/cdev.12899.

Yamada, Y., Stevens, C., Dow, M. et al. (2011). Emergence of the neural network for reading in five-year-old beginning readers of different levels of pre-literacy abilities: An fMRI study. *NeuroImage*, *57*(3), 704–713. DOI: https://doi.org/10.1016/j.neuroimage.2010.10.057.

Yap, M. J., & Balota, D. A. (2015). Visual word recognition. In A. Pollatsek & R. Treiman (Eds.), *The Oxford Handbook of Reading* (pp. 26–43). Oxford: Oxford University Press.

Yeatman, J. D., Dougherty, R. F., Ben-Shachar, M., & Wandell, B. A. (2012). Development of white matter and reading skills. *Proceedings of the National*

Academy of Sciences of the United States of America, 109(44), E3045–53. DOI: https://doi.org/10.1073/pnas.1206792109.

Yu, X., Raney, T., Perdue, M. V. et al. (2018). Emergence of the neural network underlying phonological processing from the prereading to the emergent reading stage: A longitudinal study. *Human Brain Mapping, 39*(5), 2047–2063. DOI: https://doi.org/10.1002/hbm.23985.

Ziegler, J. C., Bertrand, D., Tóth, D. et al. (2010). Orthographic depth and its impact on universal predictors of reading: A cross-language investigation. *Psychological Science, 21*(4), 551–559. DOI: https://doi.org/10.1177/0956797610363406.

13 Genetics and Literacy Development

Elena L. Grigorenko

13.1 Introduction

Reading is fascinating to think about. It represents a facet of human civilization that emerged relatively late (compared to, say, tools) yet is a skill required by modern society. The ability to read, coupled with the ability to write, substantiates literacy in its narrow definition. Defined broadly as "the ability to identify, understand, interpret, create, communicate, and compute using printed and written materials associated with varying contexts" (Montoya, 2018, p. 1), literacy remains a centerpiece, pointing to the very nature of the materials and the mastery of them. To reiterate: The referred materials should be printed and/or written and, therefore, require the mastery of reading skills. At the societal level, literacy rates determine the level of prosperity of a country and its place in the hierarchy of today's world. At the group level, these rates differentiate ethnic, religious, or other groups and correlate with the socioeconomic position of a group. At the individual level, literacy (or reading and writing proficiency) is a powerful predictor of educational attainment (Park & Kyei, 2011), labor market placement (Cherry & Vignoles, 2020), and happiness (Angner et al., 2009). It is hard to think of another single skill that is as influential and important at the societal level as individual literacy. Consider physical aptitude or vocal capacity – both are highly appreciated, but neither is so valued that it functions as a gatekeeper to the higher levels of today's society.

The fascination of reading has many angles. One such angle is the societal "decision" – or rather the conclusion of over a hundred years spent constructing "a social world in which much value is located in the individual" (Soysal & Strang, 1989, p. 279) – to develop a system of state-run mass education that places its main emphasis on reading (Cipolla, 1969).[1] As a result, the skill that for centuries had been acquired by only a few became available to and required by billions of people. This transformation generated two challenges. The first was to develop a systematic (stage-based) and effective (quick and inexpensive) way of teaching

---

[1] It has been argued that there is a direct connection between the importance of individualized communication with God through reading of the Bible in Protestantism and the demand for literacy in the first mass education systems of the world.

reading that could be delivered to **many** people simultaneously. The second was to make sure that reading could be taught to many **different** people because even as long ago as in Plato's Academy, the observation was made that students vary in how they learn to read, although the causes for this variation were contemplated only much later (Kussmaul, 1877).

Another angle is the speed with which the demand for the skill spread throughout the world. From the 48 copies of the Gutenberg Bible printed in 1450 in Latin to the ~227,000 new titles per month in 2020 in all written world languages, this dissemination of written materials assumes a market of eager readers who can consume such titles.[2] Given that most of these consumers were born during the twentieth and twenty-first centuries, reading has truly become a successful enterprise! At the time of writing, for the projected 2020 world population of 7,800,000,000, it was expected there would be ~34.92 new titles for every 100,000 people.

A third angle is the ever-changing texture of reading. From the ancient, as in Egyptian hieroglyphs (2680 BC), to the modern, as in Japanese Kanji, to the alphabetical-abstract phone–grapheme mapping that we see in the majority of today's languages, especially those that first came to be written relatively recently (such as Ndebele in the 1960s); from oral, as in St. Augustine's *Confessions* (by St. Ambrose in the middle 300s AD), to silent reading which is the form that proficient reading is generally considered to take today; from unfolded and fully sentenced, as in most printed materials such as books, mass media, and formal documents, to folded and abbreviated, as in today's texting and symbolic prints such as NASDAQ information – reading has changed with the demands of the civilization that produced and uses it.

If my readers think that these characteristics of reading are not relevant to the discussion of its genetic bases, they are mistaken. All of these considerations, when contemplated holistically, define the parameters of the genetic system that is the foundation of literacy in general and (a)typical reading and writing in particular.[3] Yet it is a distal one, with the proximal foundation being the brain. In short, the genetic bases of (a)typical reading and writing are nothing more than the genetic bases of a brain that, pressured by the demands and opportunities imposed by modern society, has turned itself into a reading and writing (i.e., literate) brain.

13.2 Familiality, Heritability, and the Relative Risks of (A)Typical Reading

As soon as industrialized societies established the requirement that their members should attain certain levels of literacy and numeracy in exchange for

---

[2] www.worldometers.info/books.
[3] In this chapter, the terms atypical reading, reading difficulties, Specific Reading Disability (SRD), and dyslexia are used interchangeably.

a commitment to mass education, it became evident that there was great variation in the efficiency and quality of how children mastered these skills (Kerr, 1897). In families educated by the same pedagogy delivered by the same teacher in the same classroom, students varied in their reading and writing skills.[4] Very early on in the research into the causes of this variation, the word "congenital" was used (Fisher, 1905, 1910; Hinshelwood, 1900, 1902, 1907; Stephenson, 1904, 1907; Thomas, 1905), although an articulated position on the role of genes was introduced much later (Hallgren, 1950), following an accumulation of facts substantiating the critical role of the brain in the manifestation of reading difficulties (Orton, 1939).

Thus, since the second half of the last century, the field has attempted to understand how these "genetic factors," deemed by Hallgren (1950) as important to the development of reading difficulties, actually trigger these difficulties. This quest has been as systematic as it could be, given that at various points, it was inevitably limited by (1) the sophistication (or rather lack thereof) of the diagnostic materials necessary for defining phenotypes for genetically informed studies of reading difficulties; (2) the availability and cost of the molecular-genetic technologies that permit the specification of the genetic mechanisms thought to be of importance; and (3) the availability of computational methods, computer power and time to both estimate the role of the genome and connect reading and reading-related phenotypes to genetic influences.[5] Because the capacity for all three was low until the 1980s, studies conducted between 1950 and 1980 generated a diverse array of findings, underscoring the importance of genetic factors but doing so with relative imprecision and lack of specification (Bakwin, 1973; Finucci et al., 1976; Hermann, 1956; Norrie, 1939; Weinschenk, 1965; Zerbin-Rüdin, 1967). As theoretical and corresponding measurement developments accumulated by the early 1980s, some seminal articles set up the spiral development of the field. Among others, the following pioneering publications should be mentioned.

The publication by Lewitter et al. (Lewitter, DeFries, & Elston, 1980) set off a line of important research by looking for the amount and type of reading difficulties aggregating in families, which had also been reported in earlier works (Fisher, 1905, 1910; Hinshelwood, 1900, 1902, 1907; Stephenson, 1904, 1907; Thomas, 1905). This research was done in a systematic way by carrying out formal segregation analyses and fitting different genetic models. However,

---

[4] Importantly, as writing is typically mastered after reading, and writing's facets (e.g., calligraphy, spelling, grammar, and compositional skills) are studied substantially less than, and often together with, reading's facets (e.g., phonemic, phonological, orthographic, and morphological awareness and comprehension), this chapter is focused primarily on reading, with writing being referenced only when the relevant literature permits.

[5] Here I refer to known correlates of reading, such as, for example, indicators of phonemic, phonological, orthographic, and morphological awareness.

the attempt to identify this single model was not successful, as a variety of models were reported to fit the data. Specifically, major gene models (recessive [Lewitter et al., 1980], dominant [Gilger et al., 1994; Pennington et al., 1991], and additive [Pennington et al., 1991]) and polygenic models (Pennington et al., 1991) were reported to be plausible based on their fit with various sets of family data. Although none of these early observations have been maintained, this line of research has been highly important. First, these early researchers were able, given the status of the corresponding assessments, to define reading difficulties not only through categorical clinical decisions (i.e., qualitative phenotypes) but also through continuous indicators (quantitative phenotypes). Second, these analyses generated such diverse patterns of results that they have shed light on the heterogeneity of the genetic mechanisms of reading and reading disability. It was initially assumed that these analyses had captured all types of these mechanisms, as different families might indeed present examples of different modes of genetic transmission. Yet, the current consensus, based on the usage of newly developed analytical approaches, promotes oligogenic models of inheritance for both reading and reading-related traits; these models involve many genes exerting moderate to low effects (Hsu et al., 2002; Naples et al., 2009; Wijsman et al., 2000). Third, given the availability of many samples in the field, estimates of relative risk (Ziegler et al., 2005) consistent with heritability estimates (i.e., the proportion of the phenotypic variance controlled by genetic factors) for (a)typical reading and related traits have been generated.

The article by LaBuda et al. (DeFries, Fulker, & LaBuda, 1987) introduced the complexity of quantitative genetics into previously simplistic models of variance decomposition and set off a plethora of ever-more-sophisticated reports of the heritability of reading and reading-related skills. As the field has grown and acquired remarkable – both with respect to phenotypic-behavioral characterization and the sheer number of participants – genetically informed samples (i.e., samples structured by known degrees of biological relatedness – twins or other siblings, nuclear and extended families), it has been able to provide information on several important issues. Thus, compared to early twin studies, there are much more precise estimates of heritability for both reading performance and reading-related skills. In fact, the corresponding literature is so large that it could be meta-analyzed, and such analyses have indicated that heritability estimates, when error variance is taken into account, range between 41 and 74 percent for reading and up to 90 percent for reading-related processes (Grigorenko, 2004). Heritability estimates are reportedly not modulated by sex (Hawke et al., 2007).

Yet, a host of variables do appear to differentiate heritability estimates, such as age (Byrne et al., 2009; Harlaar et al., 2014; Soden et al., 2015) and ethnicity (Grigorenko et al., 2006). Moreover, there is an observation that heritability estimates vary across the severity of difficulties, both for reading skills (Hawke et al., 2007) and for reading-related indicators, such as IQ (Wadsworth, Olson, & DeFries, 2010), and working and short-term memory (van Leeuwen et al., 2009). Heritability estimates appear to increase across the lifespan, although nonlinearly, as children get older (Byrne et al., 2005; Kovas et al., 2013; Lewis et al., 2018; Samuelsson et al., 2007; Soden et al., 2015; Wadsworth et al., 2001); yet, this might not be the case for all indicators of reading (Tosto et al., 2017). Importantly, although reading is an acquired skill, its developmental stability is largely driven by genetic factors (Harlaar et al., 2014; Soden et al., 2015). Interestingly, parental correlations on reading-related skills indicate the presence of assortative mating for some (Naples et al., 2009; Swagerman et al., 2017; van Bergen et al., 2017) reading-related variables, which might have important applied implications. Among other findings, there are some that reflect the fundamental assumption of quantitative genetics; specifically, that heritability reflects the influence of the genome that is unleashed when the environment is optimized and homogenized to be most beneficial for those who develop reading and reading-related skills. This phenomenon has been demonstrated in the literature on reading with regard to teaching instruction (Taylor et al., 2010), parental education (Friend et al., 2009), and SES (Hart et al., 2013, 2014). Similarly, there are observations that heritability estimates are higher in societies with an egalitarian educational system, which reduces environmental variance (Grasby et al., 2019; van Leeuwen et al., 2009). Of note is that, when considered meta-analytically, such variables as publication year, grade level, project, zygosity methods, and response type moderate heritability estimates obtained in twin studies (Little, Haughbrook, & Hart, 2017). Importantly, it has been demonstrated that children's reading ability determines how much they choose to read, not the other way around (Zeeuw et al., 2018), although reading exposure does strengthen reading skills. Although researched substantially less, the etiology of writing appears to mirror the etiology of reading (Olson et al., 2013).

Last but not least, the report by Smith et al. (Smith et al., 1983) marked the first attempt to materialize the very elusive genetic factors and to translate the heritability of reading) and reading-related skills into specific molecular mechanisms. This report triggered the ongoing quest for the molecules and their pathways that lay the ground for the sociocultural construction of the literate brain.

This chapter was written and accepted for publication in October 2020, but the book had taken some time to come to production. For an update on this section, see Elliott & Grigorenko (2023), the Dyslexia Debate. Cambridge, UK: Cambridge University Press.

13.3 Structural DNA Variation and (A)Typical Reading

As is the case for many other complex disorders, the field of molecular-genetic research within (a)typical reading is dominated by two major models of the overall genetic architecture of complex human traits. These models differ fundamentally both in their specification of the disability and their interpretation of normal variation in reading performance.

Up to now, the field of genetic studies of specific reading disability (SRD[6]), commonly known as dyslexia (see Rigatti et al., Chapter 12 in this volume), has been dominated by the common disorder–common variant (CDCV) hypothesis (Schork et al., 2009), according to which SRD arises in the polygenic background: the inheritance of multiple common genetic risk variants are individually characterized by small effect sizes, but they collectively represent a certain liability threshold above which the disability is manifested. It is also assumed that some of these risk variants are general to all facets of SRD and, perhaps, to SRD and other learning disabilities (Plomin & Kovas, 2005), whereas others are SRD specific and even reading-component specific (Naples et al., 2009). These partial overlaps of risk variants can explain substantial, but far from 1, genetic correlations between different reading-related componential processes, both in typical reading and SRD. When other sources of variance (e.g., age, ethnicity, SES, quality of teaching) are considered, they can also explain differential heritability estimates for different reading-related componential processes and their fluctuations. Finally, the CDCV hypothesis assumes continuity between typical and atypical states (i.e., a single underlying trait that defines various states), as the common risk variants are present in the general population at the levels below the liability threshold, and this presence guarantees a continuity of reading performance.

On the contrary, the common disorder–rare variant (CDRV) hypothesis (Schork et al., 2009) assumes that each case (or almost each case) is caused by a single rare variant of large effect size and that these variants can occur in different genes in different families/individuals. This hypothesis can explain the robust findings of the genetic underpinning for specific families and the lack of generalizability of these findings to heterogeneous SRD samples. Although both hypotheses and their multiple versions are implicitly present in the literature on SRD, they have not been systematically tested. This is especially the case for the CDRV hypothesis, as the supporting evidence is circumstantial rather than systematic. In order to describe the frontiers of research with regard to both hypotheses, a brief introduction on the terminology, conceptual apparatus, and common grounds upon which the corresponding studies have been generated is needed.

---

[6] There are no molecular-genetic studies of Specific Writing Disability (SWD) per se to be cited here, although different SWD-related phenotypes, such as spelling, are often used in molecular-genetic studies of SRD.

The decade of studies into the genetic architecture of common human traits/disorders, which unfolded after the release of the first draft of the human genome, has led to a number of realizations. Specifically, it has become evident that the statistical power of genome-wide association (GWA) studies of complex traits/diseases, even with sample sizes considerably larger than employed previously (e.g., thousands of cases and controls), remains low (Manolio, Brooks, & Collins, 2008; Rodriguez-Murillo & Greenberg, 2008; Tenesa, Farrington, & Prendergast, 2008; The Wellcome Trust Case Control Consortium, 2007). Two leading explanations have been put forth to explain this lack of power and progress in identifying causal common variants for common traits/disorders.

One points to the small genetic effects, thought to be significant for susceptibility loci associated with complex traits/diseases, for example, odds ratios of 1.1–1.5 (Ioannidis, Trikalinos, & Khoury, 2006; Manolio et al., 2008). The other effect is the remarkable heterogeneous genetic mechanisms underlying what are perceived as homogeneous behaviorally common traits/diseases (Munson et al., 2008; Ring et al., 2008; Simms et al., 2009; Sutcliffe, 2008; Weiss, 2009). To address the issue of effect sizes, even larger samples have been called for (Manolio, 2010), although there have been some disagreements regarding the potential yield of these calls (Stein & Elston, 2009). To understand the heterogeneity, there has been a growing interest in the role of rare genetic variants in the etiology of complex disorders (Ahituv et al., 2007; Cohen et al., 2004; Cohen et al., 2006; Ji et al., 2008; Romeo et al., 2007; Romeo et al., 2009; Zhu et al., 2010). The impact of a rare variant is often circumscribed to specific isolated families or even specific individuals. This, in turn, assumes the presence of many heterogeneous rare variants, both transmitted in families and arising *de novo*, the large-effect (Gorlov, Gorlova et al., 2008) impact of which triggers homogeneous (or semihomogeneous) behavior manifestations. Capitalizing on these observations, a number of theoretical analyses (Pritchard, 2001; Pritchard & Cox, 2002; Reich & Lander, 2001) and simulation studies (Peng & Kimmel, 2007; Pritchard, 2001; Reich & Lander, 2001) of the genetics of common diseases/disorders have been conducted.

Numerous interesting observations have been made in this research (Peng & Kimmel, 2007). One of these, which is particularly pertinent to this discussion, is that if the genetic etiology of a common disease/disorder assumes the involvement of multiple loci (i.e., if one of the major assumptions of the CDCV hypothesis is invoked), then a diverse allelic spectrum with rare causal alleles should be anticipated for at least some of these loci (i.e., one of the major assumptions of the CDRV is summoned as well). This diversity is substantiated by the existence of a much larger than anticipated array of normal genetic/genomic variation that has to be taken into account when searching for the candidate genes or functional elements associated with common traits/disorders (Conrad et al., 2009).

More specifically, the central assumption dominating the field upon the completion of the first draft of the human genome (Lander et al., 2001) was that delineating the main type of genomic/genetic variation between two individual human beings would be captured primarily (although not exclusively) by their complement of single nucleotide polymorphisms (SNPs, a common variation in each of the nucleotides, A, T, C, or G, of the DNA sequence). This type of variation was expected to affect about 0.1 percent of the total genomic sequence. Yet, subsequent research has not confirmed that delineation and, instead, has revealed *copy-number-variation* and *structural-variation* (CNV/SV) to be the main sources of variation between humans.[7] Indeed, the completion of additional human genome sequences overrode the initial estimate of 0.1 percent and stipulated that the degree of variation between two "normal" individual genomes is much larger. The nature of this variation is very complex: In addition to SNPs, each genome contains an abundance of very small insertions and deletions (indels, the insertion or the deletion of bases in the DNA sequence longer than 1 nucleotide), and a large amount of CNV/SV, where entire blocks of the DNA sequence, ranging in size from just 1 kb to several mb, have been inserted, deleted, inverted, or translocated (Conrad et al., 2009).

To illustrate, about 45 percent of the human genome consists of transposons and other retroelements such as LINE-1 and Alu sequences (Lander et al., 2001). In our understanding of the formation and role of CNV/SV, such retroelements are multifunctional. Specifically, their excision from one position or insertion into another constitutes a smaller CNV in itself. Yet, simultaneously, retroelements are frequently clustered around the ends (breakpoints) of larger CNV/SV, leading to the hypothesis that they can give rise to larger events through mechanisms such as nonallelic homologous recombination, NAHR (Kim et al., 2008), a mechanism that is thought to be responsible for genomic syndromes such as DiGeorge Syndrome (Dittwald et al., 2013), the core of whose manifestation includes, among other features, learning difficulties.

The role of transposable elements in evolution in general and in human evolution, in particular, has long been recognized (Skipper et al., 2013). Recent literature has accumulated evidence regarding the potentially important role of transposable elements (activity). Their role appears to be important in both typical and atypical pathways of development, especially in the nervous system differentiation (Duranthon et al., 2012). Transposition events can interfere with the function of the genome by inserting themselves directly into transcribed sequences, disrupting genes themselves or their regulatory elements (or nearby

---

[7] Structural-variations are comprised of CNVs such as deletions and insertions, as well as copy-number-neutral events such as inversions and balanced translocations.

elements), and thereby altering their activity. The quest to understand the role of transposable elements in a genome-wide fashion is ongoing and has only become possible with modern genomic technology. Currently, it is estimated that about 0.05 percent of all transposable elements are still capable of transposition and that about thirty-five to fifty subfamilies of Alu, LINE-1, and SVA elements remain actively mobile (Dewannieux & Heidmann, 2013).

Parallel to this fundamental general realization depicting the nature of normal variation in the human genome is the appearance of an increasing number of studies that link not only point mutations and functional SNPs but also events such as CNV/SV to phenotypic effects, both in atypically and typically developing individuals. Yet, technology is only now becoming available that may allow the linking of comprehensively mapped genotypes consisting of all classes/sizes of variation events to clinical phenotypes. Normal human genomic variation has to be taken into account when trying to understand complex traits/disorders, both in terms of causative and modifying events, if indeed a complex trait/disorder is caused not by a single genetic event of strong effect but a combination of variants each of small effect, or by a rare variant of medium-strong effect embedded in a background of modifying normal variants (i.e., the merge of CDCV and CDRV hypothesis). The data on both normal and disorder-related human genomic variation have been rapidly accumulating through large-scope collaborative efforts (e.g., 1000 Genomes Project, 100,000 Genomes Project).

The chapter so far, I hope, has illustrated the "repertoire" available to the genome to control both typical and atypical development. Clearly, reading development is not an exception and, as it appears now, the genome has possibly exercised many of its tricks in substantiating the diversity in the human brain structure and function, which is reflected, in turn, in the diversity of human development in general and reading development in particular. Next, I will present a brief overview of the relevant literature that attempts to illustrate how the two hypotheses, CDCV and CDRV, may be exemplified in the current literature on the molecular-genetic bases of typical and atypical reading.

The CDCV hypothesis has capitalized on the frequent manifestation of reading difficulties in the general population, while the other, CDRC, has capitalized on the infrequent manifestation of severe reading difficulties in extended families highly dense with SRD. These studies (Grigorenko, 2005) can be subdivided into a number of major overlapping categories by the type of samples they engage with (i.e., genetically unrelated cases/probands and matched controls or family units such as siblings or nuclear and extended families) and by the type of genetic units they target (i.e., specific genes, specific genetic regions, or the whole genome). For all approaches combined, there are references to at least twenty (Schumacher et al., 2007) potential genetic susceptibility loci (i.e., regions of the genome that have demonstrated a statistically significant linkage to SRD; typically these regions involve more than one and often hundreds of genes) and about a dozen "official" (Grigorenko & Naples, 2009; Peterson & Pennington, 2012) candidate genes (i.e., genes located within susceptibility loci that have been statistically associated with SRD). Yet, none of these loci or genes have been either fully accepted or fully rejected by the field. Moreover, new regions and candidate genes are being presented on a regular basis, and both lists are likely to continue expanding (Becker et al., 2017; Rubenstein et al., 2011).

Numerous genome-wide screens for SRD and reading- (and writing)-related components have been reported (Brkanac et al., 2008; de Kovel et al., 2004; Eicher et al., 2013; Fagerheim et al., 1999; Field et al., 2013; Fisher et al., 2002; Gialluisi et al., 2014; Gialluisi et al., 2019; Igo et al., 2006; Kaminen et al., 2003; Luciano et al., 2013; Meaburn et al., 2008; Nopola-Hemmi et al., 2002; Price et al., 2020; Raskind et al., 2005; Roeske et al., 2011; Svensson, 2011; Truong et al., 2017). These studies, driven by the CDCV hypothesis, utilized hundreds of thousands of genetic markers as technology and cost permitted. These studies have generated numerous suggestive findings, but the overwhelming majority of them are inconsistent, with a low replicability coefficient and small effects. In discussing this pattern of results, typically, a reference is made to the low statistical power (as evidenced through relatively small sample sizes) of the original whole-genome studies (Gialluisi et al., 2019), although newer studies with large samples (Gialluisi et al., 2019; Price et al., 2020) still produce inconsistent results, suggesting that the difficulty in creating a texture of replicable findings is related not only to the issue of statistical power but likely also to some other issues, such as the overall credibility of the CDCV hypothesis (Gibson, 2012) or the categorization of developmental disorders (Peters & Ansari, 2019). There are also studies that focus on particular regions of the genome (Deffenbacher et al., 2004; Francks et al., 2004). The selection of these regions is typically determined either by a previous whole-genome scan or by a theoretical hypothesis capitalizing on SRD and its componential processes (Skiba et al., 2011).[8]

Yet, some of the studies settled on candidate regions through different means, such as a known chromosomal aberration, that is, through the verification of the CDRV hypothesis. Denmark, for example, has a health policy of screening all newborns for macro-chromosomal changes (e.g., large rearrangements). In these

---

[8] For example, one early study (Cardon et al., 1994, 1995) focused on the short arm of chromosome 6 (6p) – specifically, on the Human Leukocyte Antigen (HLA) region – assuming that there were connections between RD and left-handedness, and left-handedness and autoimmune functioning. Neither of the connections has been confirmed, but the region 6p21, identified as a result of this study, remains a prominent player in the field, harboring two candidate genes for RD, *DCDC2*, and *KIAA0319*.

cases, researchers can screen individuals who have such rearrangements for the presence of SRD (Buonincontri et al., 2011). The hypothesis is that a gene affected by such an aberration is somehow related to SRD. In addition, as the ultimate goal of this work is to identify specific genes whose functions are related to the transformation of a brain into a reading brain, a number of candidate genes for reading difficulties have been identified – *ROBO1* (Hannula-Jouppi et al., 2005), *DYX1C1* (Taipale et al., 2003), and *SEMA6D*[9] (Ercan-Sencicek et al., 2012). All of these genes have been detected through studies of single extended families (Taipale et al., 2003) or individual cases (Ercan-Sencicek et al., 2012).[10] Systematic explorations of the importance of different types of structural variation in the field of reading have been few and – on large events, that is, insertions and deletions larger than 1mb (Girirajan et al., 2011) and copy number variants, CNV – smaller in size, with a median total length of ~640 kb covered by CNVs per sample, or ~479 kb, considering only CNVs annotated to genes (Gialluisi et al., 2016). It is important to stress that large structural variants are relatively rare (e.g., <1 percent of the general population), and the underlying assumption here is that the identification of such rare variants will provide a clue for subsequent studies of the gene(s) affected by this structural alteration or the pathway in which this gene(s) is(are) involved. It is especially relevant to investigations of the genetic bases of complex traits such as reading abilities or disabilities. The idea is that once a rare variant is identified and associated with a particular trait (e.g., reading), there is a need to investigate common variance in the gene/region that was impacted by this rare variant. In the field of reading, an example of such a transition from a rare variant to a continuous trait is the research on *ROBO1* (Bates, Luciano, Montgomery et al., 2011).

As we have indicated, there are "official" candidate genes being evaluated as causal genes for DD and reading-related difficulties in at least two independent studies or datasets. These include:
- *DYX1C1*, now referred to as *DNAAF4* (Currier et al., 2011; Taipale et al., 2003) at 15q21;
- *KIAA0319* (Cope et al., 2005; Dennis et al., 2009; Francks et al., 2004; Harold et al., 2006; Sánchez-Morán et al., 2018) at 6p22;
- *DCDC2* (Li et al., 2018; Marino et al., 2012; Meng et al., 2005; Riva et al., 2019; Schumacher et al., 2006) at 6p22;
- *ROBO1* (Bates, Luciano, Medland et al., 2011; Hannula-Jouppi et al., 2005; Tran et al., 2014) at 3p12,

---

[9] Semaphorins are a large family of proteins, including both secreted and membrane-associated proteins, many of which have been implicated as inhibitors or chemorepellents in axon pathfinding, fasciculation and branching, and target selection (www.ncbi.nlm.nih.gov/gene/80031).

[10] In this particular case, the proband was originally referred to the Yale Child Study Center at the age of three, as a child with developmental language disorders, but later, at the age of twelve, he presented with a reading comprehension disorder with intact decoding skills.

- *GRIN2B* (Ludwig et al., 2010; Mascheretti et al., 2015) at 12p13;
- *FOXP2* (Peter et al., 2011; Sánchez-Morán et al., 2018; Wilcke et al., 2012) at 7q21.1;
- *CNTNAP2* at 7q25 (Newbury et al., 2011; Peter et al., 2011; Vernes et al., 2008).

However, more genes have been reported as putative additions to this list (e.g., Buonincontri et al., 2011; Ercan-Sencicek et al., 2012; Newbury et al., 2011; Scerri et al., 2010). At this point, the field contains both support and lack of support for the involvement of each of these genes; thus, the findings are somewhat difficult to interpret. In addition, there is an ongoing debate regarding the specificity of the impact of SRD-related genes. There is growing evidence that a high degree of pleiotropy is exerted by at least some of these genes. Thus, the *DYX1C1/DNAAF4* gene has been implicated in ciliary dyskinesia (PCD) – a disorder manifested through chronic airway disease, laterality defects, and male infertility (Tarkar et al., 2013). The *DCDC2* gene has been shown to play a role in kidney disease (Schueler et al., 2015). Importantly, many of the "SRD (which can also be SWD)" genes have been implicated in other neurodevelopmental and psychiatric disorders. Specifically, *KIAA0319* has been featured in speech and sound disorders (SSD) (Eicher et al., 2015), language difficulties (Rice, Smith, & Gayán, 2009), ADHD (Mascheretti et al., 2017), and Autism Spectrum Disorder (ASD) (Eicher & Gruen, 2015). *DCDC2* has been associated with disorders such as SSD (Eicher et al., 2015) and ADHD (Mascheretti et al., 2017), but also with general cognitive ability (Davies et al., 2018). *ROBO1* has been identified as an ASD-associated gene (Anitha et al., 2008; Iossifov et al., 2012), and its pathway, SLIT/ROBO, has been featured in the literature on schizophrenia (Brennand et al., 2011). Clearly, more time and effort will be needed to understand each gene's involvement with reading and its related processes.

13.4 Conclusions and Discussion

In this brief chapter, I have attempted to trace the evolution of the genetic bases of (a)typical reading and writing, that is, the two fundamental skills that underlie the acquisition of literacy. While summarizing and interpreting the literature, I have underscored the general differentiation of the CDCV and CDRV hypotheses and lines of research into the following bases: from simplistic to complex, from one kind to many kinds, from deterministic to highly probabilistic, and from responsive to environmental pressures. These two hypotheses still dominate the literature, so there is a growing understanding that they are likely to only partially capture the complexities of the genetic mechanisms involved in the manifestation of complex human traits and the related neurodevelopmental disorders.

Given the impetus behind this volume, two issues appear to be particularly important to consider. The first issue pertains to the universality of the mechanisms discussed in this chapter regarding the linguistic and cultural diversity in which global literacy exists. Notably, the overwhelming majority of both quantitative and molecular-genetic studies of reading and writing have been carried out with English- (or, less frequently, other European languages-) speaking samples and in high- and middle-income countries. When considered collectively, they reflect a pattern of results that demonstrates enough conversion to believe that, fundamentally, the genetic mechanisms that set up the brain for the acquisition of reading and writing are the same. Yet, the field is still at the very beginning of the inquiry into these mechanisms and their specificity and/or generality. Clearly, more studies in non-European languages that have writing systems around the world will be necessary to appraise the extent of the universality of the genetic mechanisms that preconfigure the human brain for acquiring literacies in their narrow and broad definitions.

Relatedly, more studies are needed to sample not only different languages but also different countries and cultures. This might appear counterintuitive as the focus is on genetic mechanisms, but two considerations are particularly important here. The first pertains to the nature of quantitative genetic approaches that generate heritability estimates. As the phenotypic variability for any trait within the corresponding framework is always fixed at 100 percent, the variability of its sources, additively, is also fixed at 100 percent. To illustrate, the variability in schooling in high-income countries is substantially lower than that in lower-income countries, so it is likely that the distribution of heritability and environmentality (the estimate of the importance of merged, that is, all contributing environments) will also be different. When environmental variability is constrained and every child gets quality schooling, individual differences will be more sensitive to the influences of genetic factors. When environmental variability is huge, and some children go to high-quality private schools, whereas others do not go to school at all, the environment overrides the genetic variation. The propensity of a human brain to transform into a literate brain then depends on print exposure and effective teachers because children cannot learn to read and write without being taught how to read and write. Also, essentially, the role of the genetic mechanism in reshaping the illiterate brain of a young child into the literate brain of an adult only establishes the range of individual differences for the parameters defining this transformation (e.g., the maximum and minimum speed and accuracy with which people as sampled from the general population, however defined, can acquire the skills of reading and writing); it does not determine the mean value in the population. That mean value is established and constantly redefined by a society which forms expectations regarding the types and depth of orthographies it requires (see Perfetti & Verhoeven, Chapter 11 in this volume). And most importantly, these expectations are translated from societies to their child-members by educators; collectively, teachers in their well-organized evidence-based classroom can continuously move this mean up, substantially and perhaps indefinitely!

I started this chapter with the features of reading (and writing) that I find fascinating and highlighted the very quick ascent of reading to the pinnacle of the hierarchy of human skills, its universal value among millions of people, and its ever-changing texture. For these features to be present, the brain must exercise plasticity in its absolute essence. And for the brain to become a reading and writing brain (and a literate brain) with ever-expanding capacities for literacy (as I believe literacy will diversify its presentation and, likely, become more and more central to human civilization), it has to be substantiated by a set of diverse genetic/genomic mechanisms that are multiple, complex, and elegant. These mechanisms can and must be cataloged. Just give the field some time.

Author Note

This work was supported by the US National Institutes of Health, awards P50 HD052117 (PI: Fletcher), P20 HD091005 (PI: Grigorenko), and P50 HD052120 (PI: Wagner). Grantees are encouraged to express their professional judgment; this essay does not necessarily represent the policies or positions of the NIH. I would like to thank Ms. Nicole Guha for her editorial support.

References

Ahituv, N., Kavaslar, N., Schackwitz, W. et al. (2007). Medical sequencing at the extremes of human body mass. *The American Journal of Human Genetics*, *80*, 779–791. DOI: https://doi.org/10.1086/513471.

Angner, E., Miller, M. J., Ray, M. N., Saag, K. G., & Allison, J. J. (2009). Health literacy and happiness: A community-based study. *Social Indicators Research*, *95*, 325–338. DOI: https://doi.org/10.1007/s11205-009-9462-5.

Anitha, A., Nakamura, K., Yamada, K. et al. (2008). Genetic analyses of Roundabout (ROBO) axon guidance receptors in autism. *American Journal of Medical Genetics Part B: Neuropsychiatric Genetics*, *147B*, 1019–1027. DOI: https://doi.org/10.1002/ajmg.b.30697.

Bakwin, H. (1973). Reading disability in twins. *Developmental Medicine and Child Neurology*, *15*, 184–187.

Bates, T. C., Luciano, M., Medland, S. E. et al. (2011). Genetic variance in a component of the language acquisition device: ROBO1 polymorphisms associated with phonological buffer deficits. *Behavior Genetics*, *41*, 50–57. DOI: https://doi.org/10.1007/s10519-010-9402-9.

Bates, T. C., Luciano, M., Montgomery, G. W., Wright, M. J., & Martin, N. G. (2011). Genes for a component of the language acquisition mechanism: ROBO1 polymorphisms associated with phonological buffer deficit. *Behavior Genetics*, *41*, 50–57.

Becker, N., Vasconcelos, M., Oliveira, V. et al. (2017). Genetic and environmental risk factors for developmental dyslexia in children: Systematic review of the last decade. *Developmental Neuropsychology*, *42*, 423–445. DOI: https://doi.org/10.1080/87565 641.2017.1374960.

Brennand, K. J., Simone, A., Jou, J. et al. (2011). Modelling schizophrenia using human induced pluripotent stem cells. *Nature*, *473*, 221–225. DOI: https://doi.org/10.1038 /nature09915.

Brkanac, Z., Chapman, N. H., Igo, R. P. Jr. et al. (2008). Genome scan of a nonword repetition phenotype in families with dyslexia: Evidence for multiple loci. *Behavior Genetics*, *38*, 462–475.

Buonincontri, R., Bache, I., Silahtaroglu, A. et al. (2011). A cohort of balanced reciprocal translocations associated with dyslexia: identification of two putative candidate genes at DYX1. *Behavior Genetics*, *41*, 125–133.

Byrne, B., Coventry, W. L., Olson, R. K. et al. (2009). Genetic and environmental influences on aspects of literacy and language in early childhood: Continuity and change from preschool to Grade 2. *Journal of Neurolinguistics*, *22*, 219–236. DOI: https://doi.org/10.1016/j.jneuroling.2008.09.003.

Byrne, B., Wadsworth, S., Corley, R. et al. (2005). Longitudinal twin study of early literacy development: Preschool and kindergarten phases. *Scientific Studies of Reading*, *9*, 219–235.

Cardon, L. R., Smith, S. D., Fulker, D. W. et al. (1994). Quantitative trait locus for reading disability on chromosome 6. *Science*, *226*, 276–279.

Cardon, L. R., Smith, S. D., Fulker, D. W. et al. (1995). Quantitative trait locus for reading disability: correction. *Science*, *268*, 1553.

Cherry, G., & Vignoles, A. (2020). What is the economic value of literacy and numeracy? *IZA World of Labor*, 229. DOI: https://doi.org/10.15185/izawol.229.v2.

Cipolla, C. M. (1969). *Literacy and Development in the West*. Harmondsworth: Penguin Books.

Cohen, J. C., Kiss, R. S., Pertsemlidis, A. et al. (2004). Multiple rare alleles contribute to low plasma levels of HDL cholesterol. *Science*, *305*, 869–872.

Cohen, J. C., Pertsemlidis, A., Fahmi, S. et al. (2006). Multiple rare variants in NPC1L1 associated with reduced sterol absorption and plasma low-density lipoprotein levels. *Proceedings of the National Academy of Sciences of the United States of America*, *103*, 1810–1815. DOI: https://doi.org/10.1073/pnas.0508483103.

Conrad, D. F., Pinto, D., Redon, R. et al. (2009). Origins and functional impact of copy number variation in the human genome. *Nature*. Advance online publication.

Cope, N., Harold, D., Hill, G. et al. (2005). Strong evidence that KIAA0319 on chromosome 6p is a susceptibility gene for developmental dyslexia. *American Journal of Human Genetics*, *76*, 581–591.

Currier, T. A., Etchegaray, M. A., Haight, J. L., Galaburda, A. M., & Rosen, G. D. (2011). The effects of embryonic knockdown of the candidate dyslexia susceptibility gene homologue Dyx1c1 on the distribution of GABAergic neurons in the cerebral cortex. *Neuroscience*, *172*, 535–546. DOI: http://dx.doi.org/10.1016/j.neuroscience.2010 .11.002.

Davies, G., Lam, M., Harris, S. E. et al. (2018). Study of 300,486 individuals identifies 148 independent genetic loci influencing general cognitive function. *Nature Communications*, *9*, 2098. DOI: https://doi.org/10.1038/s41467-018-04362-x.

de Kovel, C. G. F., Hol, F. A., Heister, J. et al. (2004). Genomewide scan identifies susceptibility locus for dyslexia on Xq27 in an extended Dutch family. *Journal of Medical Genetics*, *41*, 652–657.

Deffenbacher, K. E., Kenyon, J. B., Hoover, D. M. et al. (2004). Refinement of the 6p21.3 quantitative trait locus influencing dyslexia: linkage and association analyses. *Human Genetics*, *115*, 128–138.

DeFries, J. C., Fulker, D. W., & LaBuda, M. C. (1987). Evidence for a genetic aetiology in reading disability of twins. *Nature*, *329*, 537–539.

Dennis, M. Y., Paracchini, S., Scerri, T. S. et al. (2009). A common variant associated with dyslexia reduces expression of the KIAA0319 gene. *PLoS Genetics*, *5*, e1000436.

Dewannieux, M., & Heidmann, T. (2013). Endogenous retroviruses: Acquisition, amplification and taming of genome invaders. *Current Opinion in Virology*, *3*, 646–656. DOI: http://dx.doi.org/10.1016/j.coviro.2013.08.005.

Dittwald, P., Gambin, T., Szafranski, P. et al. (2013). NAHR-mediated copy-number variants in a clinical population: Mechanistic insights into both genomic disorders and Mendelizing traits. *Genome Research*, *23*, 1395–1409. DOI: https://doi.org/10.1101/gr.152454.112.

Duranthon, V., Beaujean, N., Brunner, M. et al. (2012). On the emerging role of rabbit as human disease model and the instrumental role of novel transgenic tools. *Transgenic Research*, *21*, 699–713.

Eicher, J. D., & Gruen, J. R. (2015). Language impairment and dyslexia genes influence language skills in children with autism spectrum disorders. *Autism Research*, *8*, 229–234. DOI: https://doi.org/10.1002/aur.1436.

Eicher, J. D., Powers, N. R., Miller, L. L., et al. for the Pediatric Imaging, Neurocognition Genetics, Study. (2013). Genome-wide association study of shared components of reading disability and language impairment. *Genes, Brain and Behavior*, *12*, 792–801. DOI: https://doi.org/10.1111/gbb.12085.

Eicher, J. D., Stein, C. M., Deng, F. et al. (2015). The DYX2 locus and neurochemical signaling genes contribute to speech sound disorder and related neurocognitive domains. *Genes, Brain and Behavior*, *14*(4), 377–385. DOI: https://doi.org/10.1111/gbb.12214.

Ercan-Sencicek, A. G., Davis Wright, N. R., Sanders, S. S. et al. (2012). A balanced t(10;15) translocation in a male patient with developmental language disorder. *European Journal of Medical Genetics*, *55*, 128–131.

Fagerheim, T., Raeymaekers, P., Tonnessen, F. E. et al. (1999). A new gene (DYX3) for dyslexia is located on chromosome 2. *Journal of Medical Genetics*, *35*, 664–669.

Field, L. L., Shumansky, K., Ryan, J. et al. (2013). Dense-map genome scan for dyslexia supports loci at 4q13, 16p12, 17q22; suggests novel locus at 7q36. *Genes, Brain and Behavior*, *12*, 56–69. DOI: https://doi.org/10.1111/gbb.12003.

Finucci, J. M., Guthrie, J. T., Childs, A. L., Abbey, H., & Childs, B. (1976). The genetics of specific reading disability. *Annual Review of Human Genetics*, *40*, 1–23.

Fisher, J. H. (1905). Case of congenital word-blindness (inability to learn to read). *Ophthalmology Review*, *24*, 315–318.

Fisher, J. H. (1910). Congenital world blindness (inability to learn to read). *Transactions of the Ophthalmological Societies of the United Kingdom, 30,* 216–225.

Fisher, S. E., Francks, C., Marlow, A. J. et al. (2002). Independent genome-wide scans identify a chromosome 18 quantitative-trait locus influencing dyslexia. *Nature Genetics, 30,* 86–91.

Francks, C., Paracchini, S., Smith, S. D. et al. (2004). A 77-kilobase region on chromosome 6p22.2 is associated with dyslexia in families from the United Kingdom and from the United States. *American Journal of Human Genetics, 75,* 1046–1058.

Friend, A., DeFries, J., Olson, R. et al. (2009). Heritability of high reading ability and its interaction with parental education. *Behavior Genetics, 39,* 427–436.

Gialluisi, A., Andlauer, T. F M, Mirza-Schreiber, N. et al. (2019). Genome-wide association scan identifies new variants associated with a cognitive predictor of dyslexia. *Translational Psychiatry, 9,* 77. DOI: https://doi.org/10.1038/s41398-019-0402-0.

Gialluisi, A., Newbury, D. F., Wilcutt, E. G. et al. (2014). Genome-wide screening for DNA variants associated with reading and language traits. *Genes, Brain and Behavior, 13,* 686–701. DOI: https://doi.org/10.1111/gbb.12158.

Gialluisi, A., Visconti, A., Willcutt, E. G. et al. (2016). Investigating the effects of copy number variants on reading and language performance. *Journal of Neurodevelopmental Disorders, 8,* 17. DOI: https://doi.org/10.1186/s11689-016-9147-8.

Gibson, G. (2012). Rare and common variants: Twenty arguments. *Nature Reviews Genetics, 13,* 135–145. DOI: https://doi.org/10.1038/nrg3118.

Gilger, J. W., Borecki, I. B., DeFries, J. C., & Pennington, B. F. (1994). Commingling and segregation analysis of reading performance in families of normal reading probands. *Behavior Genetics, 24,* 345–355.

Girirajan, S., Brkanac, Z., Coe, B. P. et al. (2011). Relative burden of large CNVs on a range of neurodevelopmental phenotypes. *PLOS GENET, 7,* e1002334. DOI: https://doi.org/10.1371/journal.pgen.1002334.

Gorlov, I. P., Gorlova, O. Y., Sunyaev, S. R., Spitz, M. R., & Amos, C. I. (2008). Shifting paradigm of association studies: Value of rare single-nucleotide polymorphisms. *The American Journal of Human Genetics, 82,* 100–112. DOI: https://doi.org/10.1016/j.ajhg.2007.09.006.

Grasby, K. L., Coventry, W. L., Byrne, B., & Olson, R. K. (2019). Little evidence that socioeconomic status modifies heritability of literacy and numeracy in Australia. *Child Development, 90,* 623–637. DOI: https://doi.org/10.1111/cdev.12920.

Grigorenko, E. L. (2004). Genetic bases of developmental dyslexia: A capsule review of heritability estimates. *Enfance, 3,* 273–287.

Grigorenko, E. L. (2005). A conservative meta-analysis of linkage and linkage-association studies of developmental dyslexia. *Scientific Studies of Reading, 9,* 285–316.

Grigorenko, E. L., & Naples, A. J. (2009). The devil is in the details: Decoding the genetics of reading. In P. McCardle & K. Pugh (eds.), *Helping Children Learn to Read: Current Issues and New Directions in the Integration of Cognition, Neurobiology and Genetics of Reading and Dyslexia* (pp. 133–148). New York: Psychological Press.

Grigorenko, E. L., Ngorosho, D., Jukes, M., & Bundy, D. (2006). Reading in able and disabled readers from around the world: Same or different? An illustration from a study of reading-related processes in a Swahili sample of siblings. *Journal of Reading Research, 29*, 104–123.

Hallgren, B. (1950). Specific dyslexia (congenital word-blindness): A clinical and genetic study. *Acta Psychiatrica et Neurologica Supplementum, 65*, 1–287.

Hannula-Jouppi, K., Kaminen-Ahola, N., Taipale, M. et al. (2005). The axon guidance receptor gene *ROBO1* is a candidate dene for developmental dyslexia. *PLoS, 1*, e50.

Harlaar, N., Trzaskowski, M., Dale, P. S., & Plomin, R. (2014). Word reading fluency: Role of genome-wide single-nucleotide polymorphisms in developmental stability and correlations with print exposure. *Child Development, 85*(3), 1190–1205. DOI: https://doi.org/10.1111/cdev.12207.

Harold, D., Paracchini, S., Scerri, T. et al. (2006). Further evidence that the KIAA0319 gene confers susceptibility to developmental dyslexia. *Molecular Psychiatry, 11*, 1085–1091.

Hart, S. A., Soden, B., Johnson, W., Schatschneider, C., & Taylor, J. (2013). Expanding the environment: Gene × school-level SES interaction on reading comprehension. *Journal of Child Psychology and Psychiatry, 54*, 1047–1055. DOI: https://doi.org/10.1111/jcpp.12083.

Hart, S. A., Soden, B., Johnson, W., Schatschneider, C., & Taylor, J. (2014). Erratum. *Journal of Child Psychology & Psychiatry, 55*(8), 955–956. DOI: https://doi.org/10.1111/jcpp.12276.

Hawke, J. L., Wadsworth, S. J., Olson, R. K., & DeFries, J. C. (2007). Etiology of reading difficulties as a function of gender and severity. *Reading and Writing, 20*, 13–25.

Hermann, K. (1956). Congenital word-blindness: Poor readers in the light of Gerstmann's syndrome. *Acta Psychiatrica et Neurologica Scandinavica, 31*, 177–184.

Hinshelwood, J. (1900). Congenital word-blindness. *Lancet, 155*, 1506–1508.

Hinshelwood, J. (1902). Congenital word-blindness, with reports of two cases. *Ophthalmology Review, 21*, 91–99.

Hinshelwood, J. (1907). Four cases of congenital word-blindness occurring in the same family. *British Medical Journal, 1*, 608–609.

Hsu, L., Wijsman, E., Berninger, V., & Thomson, J. (2002). Familial aggregation of dyslexia phenotypes. II: Paired correlated measures. *American Journal of Medical Genetics. Neuropsychiatric Genetics, 114*, 471–478.

Igo, R. P. Jr., Chapman, N. H., Berninger, V. W. et al. (2006). Genomewide scan for real-word reading subphenotypes of dyslexia: Novel chromosome 13 locus and genetic complexity. *American Journal of Medical Genetics (Neuropsychiatric Genetics), 141*, 15–27.

Ioannidis, J. P. A., Trikalinos, T. A., & Khoury, M. J. (2006). Implications of small effect sizes of individual genetic variants on the design and interpretation of genetic association studies of complex diseases. *American Journal of Epidemiology, 164*, 609–614. DOI: https://doi.org/10.1093/aje/kwj259.

Iossifov, I., Ronemus, M., Levy, D. et al. (2012). De novo gene disruptions in children on the autistic spectrum. *Neuron, 74*, 285–299. DOI: https://doi.org/10.1016/j.neuron.2012.04.009.

Ji, W., Foo, J. N., O'Roak, B. J. et al. (2008). Rare independent mutations in renal salt handling genes contribute to blood pressure variation. *Nature Genetics*, *40*, 592–599. DOI: https://doi.org/10.1038/ng.118.

Kaminen, N., Hannula-Jouppi, K., Kestila, M. et al. (2003). A genome scan for developmental dyslexia confirms linkage to chromosome 2p11 and suggests a new locus on 7q32. *Journal of Medical Genetics*, *40*, 340–345.

Kerr, J. (1897). School hygiene, in its mental, moral, and physical aspects. *Journal of the Royal Statistical Society*, *60*, 613–680.

Kim, P. M., Lam, H. Y., Urban, A. E. et al. (2008). Analysis of copy number variants and segmental duplications in the human genome: Evidence for a change in the process of formation in recent evolutionary history. *Genome Res*, *18*(12), 1865–1874.

Kovas, Y., Voronin, I., Kaydalov, A. et al. (2013). Literacy and numeracy are more heritable than intelligence in primary school. *Psychological Science*, *24*, 2048–2056. DOI: https://doi.org/10.1177/0956797613486982.

Kussmaul, A. (1877). Word deafness and word blindness. In H. von Ziemssen & J. A. T. McCreery (eds.), *Cyclopaedia of the Practice of Medicine* (pp. 770–778). New York: William Wood.

Lander, E. S., Linton, L. M., Birren, B. et al. (2001). Initial sequencing and analysis of the human genome. *Nature*, *409*(6822), 860–921. DOI: https://doi.org/10.1038/35057062.

Lewis, B. A., Freebairn, L., Tag, J., Benchek et al. (2018). Heritability and longitudinal outcomes of spelling skills in individuals with histories of early speech and language disorders. *Learning and Individual Differences*, *65*, 1–11. DOI: https://doi.org/10.1016/j.lindif.2018.05.001.

Lewitter, F. I., DeFries, J. C., & Elston, R. C. (1980). Genetic models of reading disability. *Behavior Genetics*, *10*, 9–30.

Li, M., Malins, J. G., DeMille, M. M. C. et al. (2018). A molecular-genetic and imaging-genetic approach to specific comprehension difficulties in children. *NPJ Science of Learning*, *3*, article no. 20. DOI: https://doi.org/10.1038/s41539-018-0034-9.

Little, C. W., Haughbrook, R., & Hart, S. A. (2017). Cross-study differences in the etiology of reading comprehension: a meta-analytical review of twin studies. *Behavior Genetics*, *47*(1), 52–76. DOI: https://doi.org/10.1007/s10519-016-9810-6.

Luciano, M., Evans, D. M., Hansell, N. K. et al. (2013). A genome-wide association study for reading and language abilities in two population cohorts. *Genes, Brain and Behavior*, *12*, 645–652. DOI: https://doi.org/10.1111/gbb.12053.

Ludwig, K., Roeske, D., Herms, S. et al. (2010). Variation in GRIN2B contributes to weak performance in verbal short-term memory in children with dyslexia. *American Journal of Medical Genetics. Part B, Neuropsychiatric Genetics*, 153B, 503–511.

Manolio, T. A. (2010). Genomewide association studies and assessment of the risk of disease. *New England Journal of Medicine*, *363*, 166–176. DOI: https://doi.org/10.1056/NEJMra0905980.

Manolio, T. A., Brooks, L. D., & Collins, F. S. (2008). A HapMap harvest of insights into the genetics of common disease. *Journal of Clinical Investigation*, *118*, 1590–1605. DOI: https://doi.org/10.1172/jci34772.

Marino, C., Meng, H., Mascheretti, S. et al. (2012). DCDC2 genetic variants and susceptibility to developmental dyslexia. *Psychiatric Genetics*, *22*, 25–30. DOI: https://doi.org/10.1097/YPG.0b013e32834acdb2.

Mascheretti, S., Facoetti, A., Giorda, R. et al. (2015). GRIN2B mediates susceptibility to intelligence quotient and cognitive impairments in developmental dyslexia. *Psychiatric Genetics*, *25*, 9–20. DOI: https://doi.org/10.1097/ypg.0000000000000068.

Mascheretti, S., Trezzi, V., Giorda, R. et al. (2017). Complex effects of dyslexia risk factors account for ADHD traits: Evidence from two independent samples. *Journal of Child Psychology and Psychiatry*, *58*, 75–82. DOI: https://doi.org/10.1111/jcpp.12612.

Meaburn, E., Harlaar, N., Craig, I., Schalkwyk, L., & Plomin, R. (2008). Quantitative trait locus association scan of early reading disability and ability using pooled DNA and 100 K SNP microarrays in a sample of 5760 children. *Molecular Psychiatry*, *13*, 729–740. DOI: https://doi.org/10.1038/sj.mp.4002063.

Meng, H., Smith, S. D., Hager, K. et al. (2005). DCDC2 is associated with reading disability and modulates neuronal development in the brain. *Proceedings of the National Academy of Sciences of the United States of America*, *102*, 17053–17058.

Montoya, S. (2018). *Defining Literacy*. New York: UNESCO Institute for Statistics, UNESCO.

Munson, J., Dawson, G., Sterling, L. et al. (2008). Evidence for latent classes of IQ in young children with autism spectrum disorder. *American Journal of Mental Retardation*, *113*, 439–452.

Naples, A. J., Chang, J. T., Katz, L., & Grigorenko, E. L. (2009). Same or different? Insights into the etiology of phonological awareness and rapid naming. *Biological Psychology*, *80*, 226–239.

Newbury, D. F., Paracchini, S., Scerri, T. S. et al. (2011). Investigation of dyslexia and SLI risk-variants in reading- and language-impaired subjects. *Behavior Genetics*, *41*, 90–104.

Nopola-Hemmi, J., Myllyluoma, B., Voutilainen, A. et al. (2002). Familial dyslexia: Neurocognitive and genetic correlation in a large Finnish family. *Developmental Medicine and Child Neurology*, *44*, 580–586.

Norrie, E. (1939). *Om ordblindhet*. Copenhagen: Munkgaard.

Olson, R. K., Hulslander, J., Christopher, M. E. et al. (2013). Genetic and environmental influences on writing and their relations to language and reading. *Annals of Dyslexia*, *63*, 25–43. DOI: https://doi.org/10.1007/s11881-011-0055-z.

Orton, S. T. (1939). A neurological explanation of the reading disability. *Education Record*, *12*, 58–68.

Park, H., & Kyei, P. (2011). Literacy gaps by educational attainment: A cross-national analysis. *Social forces; a scientific medium of social study and interpretation*, *89*, 879–904. DOI: https://doi.org/10.1353/sof.2011.0025.

Peng, B., & Kimmel, M. (2007). Simulations provide support for the common disease-common variant hypothesis. *Genetics*, *175*, 763–776. DOI: https://doi.org/10.1534/genetics.106.058164.

Pennington, B. F., Gilger, J. W., Pauls, D. et al. (1991). Evidence for major gene transmission of developmental dyslexia. *JAMA*, *266*, 1527–1534.

Peter, B., Raskind, W., Matsushita, M. et al. (2011). Replication of *CNTNAP2* association with nonword repetition and support for *FOXP2* association with timed reading and motor activities in a dyslexia family sample. *Journal of Neurodevelopmental Disorders*, *3*, 39–49. DOI: https://doi.org/10.1007/s11689-010-9065-0.

Peters, L., & Ansari, D. (2019). Are specific learning disorders truly specific, and are they disorders? *Trends in Neuroscience and Education*, *17*, 100115. DOI: https://doi.org/10.1016/j.tine.2019.100115.

Peterson, R. L., & Pennington, B. F. (2012). Developmental dyslexia. *The Lancet*, *379*, 1997–2007.

Plomin, R., & Kovas, Y. (2005). Generalist genes and learning disabilities. *Psychological Bulletin*, *131*, 592–617.

Price, K. M., Wigg, K. G., Feng, Y. et al. (2020). Genome-wide association study of word reading: Overlap with risk genes for neurodevelopmental disorders. *Genes, Brain and Behavior* (July 19, 2020)(6):e12648. DOI: https://doi.org/10.1111/gbb.12648.Epub2020Mar27.PMID:32108986.

Pritchard, J. K. (2001). Are rare variants responsible for susceptibility to complex diseases? *The American Journal of Human Genetics*, *69*, 124–137. DOI: https://doi.org/10.1086/321272.

Pritchard, J. K., & Cox, N. J. (2002). The allelic architecture of human disease genes: common disease–common variant ... or not? *Human Molecular Genetics*, *11*, 2417–2423. DOI: https://doi.org/10.1093/hmg/11.20.2417.

Raskind, W. H., Igo, R. P. Jr., Chapman, N. H. et al. (2005). A genome scan in multigenerational families with dyslexia: Identification of a novel locus on chromosome 2q that contributes to phonological decoding efficiency. *Molecular Psychiatry*, *10*, 699–711.

Reich, D. E., & Lander, E. S. (2001). On the allelic spectrum of human disease. *Trends in Genetics*, *17*, 502–510. DOI: https://doi.org/10.1016/S0168-9525(01)02410-6.

Rice, M. L., Smith, S. D., & Gayán, J. (2009). Convergent genetic linkage and association to language, speech and reading measures in families of probands with Specific Language Impairment. *Journal of Neurodevelopmental Disorders*, *1*, 264–282.

Ring, H., Woodbury-Smith, M., Watson, P., Wheelwright, S., & Baron-Cohen, S. (2008). Clinical heterogeneity among people with high functioning autism spectrum conditions: Evidence favouring a continuous severity gradient. *Behavioral & Brain Functions*, *4*, 11.

Riva, V., Mozzi, A., Forni, D. et al. (2019). The influence of DCDC2 risk genetic variants on reading: Testing main and haplotypic effects. *Neuropsychologia*, *130*, 52–58. DOI: https://doi.org/10.1016/j.neuropsychologia.2018.05.021.

Rodriguez-Murillo, L., & Greenberg, D. A. (2008). Genetic association analysis: A primer on how it works, its strengths and its weaknesses. *International Journal of Andrology*, *31*, 546–556. DOI: https://doi.org/10.1111/j.1365-2605.2008.00896.x.

Roeske, D., Ludwig, K. U., Neuhoff, N. et al. (2011). First genome-wide association scan on neurophysiological endophenotypes points to trans-regulation effects on SLC2A3 in dyslexic children. *Molecular Psychiatry*, *16*, 97–107. www.nature.com/mp/journal/v16/n1/suppinfo/mp2009102s1.html.

Romeo, S., Pennacchio, L. A., Fu, Y. et al. (2007). Population-based resequencing of ANGPTL4 uncovers variations that reduce triglycerides and increase HDL. *Nature Genetics*, *39*, 513–516. DOI: https://doi.org/10.1038/ng1984.

Romeo, S., Wu, Y., Kozlitina, J. et al. (2009). Rare loss-of-function mutations in ANGPTL family members contribute to plasma triglyceride levels in humans. *Journal of Clinical Investigation*, *119*, 70–79. DOI: https://doi.org/10.1172/jc137118.

Rubenstein, K., Matsushita, M., Berninger, V. W., Raskind, W. H., & Wijsman, E. M. (2011). Genome scan for spelling deficits: Effects of verbal IQ on models of transmission and trait gene localization. *Behavior Genetics, 41*, 31–42.

Samuelsson, S., Olson, R. K., Wadsworth, S. et al. (2007). Genetic and environmental influences on prereaidng skills and early reading and spelling development in the United States, Australia, and Scandinavia. *Reading & Writing, 20*, 51–75.

Sánchez-Morán, M., Hernández, J. A., Duñabeitia, J. A. et al. (2018). Genetic association study of dyslexia and ADHD candidate genes in a Spanish cohort: Implications of comorbid samples. *PLoS ONE, 13*, e0206431. DOI: https://doi.org/10.1371/journal.pone.0206431.

Scerri, T. S., Paracchini, S., Morris, A. et al. (2010). Identification of candidate genes for dyslexia susceptibility on chromosome 18. *PLoS ONE, 5*(10), e13712. DOI: https://doi.org/10.1371/journal.pone.0013712. Erratum in: *PLoS ONE* (2010) 5 (12). DOI: https://doi.org/10.1371/10.1371/annotation/2294a38b-878d-42f0-9faf-0822db4a0248. Richardson, Alex J [added]. PMID: 21060895; PMCID: PMC2965662.

Schork, N. J., Murray, S. S., Frazer, K. A., & Topol, E. J. (2009). Common vs. rare allele hypotheses for complex diseases. *Current Opinion in Genetics & Development, 19*, 212–219. DOI: https://doi.org/10.1016/j.gde.2009.04.010.

Schueler, M., Braun, D. A., Chandrasekar, G. et al. (2015). DCDC2 mutations cause a renal-hepatic ciliopathy by disrupting Wnt signaling. *American Journal of Human Genetics, 96*, 81–92. DOI: https://doi.org/10.1016/j.ajhg.2014.12.002.

Schumacher, J., Anthoni, H., Dahdouh, F. et al. (2006). Strong genetic evidence of DCDC2 as a susceptibility gene for dyslexia. *American Journal of Human Genetics, 78*, 52–62.

Schumacher, J., Hoffmann, P., Schmal, C., Schulte-Korne, G., & Nothen, M. M. (2007). Genetics of dyslexia: The evolving landscape. *Journal of Medical Genetics, 44*, 289–297.

Simms, M. L., Kemper, T. L., Timbie, C. M., Bauman, M. L., & Blatt, G. J. (2009). The anterior cingulate cortex in autism: heterogeneity of qualitative and quantitative cytoarchitectonic features suggests possible subgroups. *Acta Neuropathologica, 118*, 673–684.

Skiba, T., Landi, N., Wagner, R., & Grigorenko, E. L. (2011). In search of the perfect phenotype: An analysis of linkage and association studies of reading and reading-related processes. *Behavior Genetics, 41*, 6–30.

Skipper, K. A., Andersen, P. R., Sharma, N., & Mikkelsen, J. G. (2013). DNA transposon-based gene vehicles: Scenes from an evolutionary drive. *Journal of Biomedical Science, 20*, 92.

Smith, S. D., Kimberling, W. J., Pennington, B. F., & Lubs, H. A. (1983). Specific reading disability: identification of an inherited form through linkage analyses. *Science, 219*, 1345–1347.

Soden, B., Christopher, M. E., Hulslander, J. et al. (2015). Longitudinal stability in reading comprehension is largely heritable from grades 1 to 6. *PLoS ONE, 10*(1), e0113807. DOI: https://doi.org/10.1371/journal.pone.0113807.

Soysal, Y. N., & Strang, D. (1989). Construction of the first mass education systems in nineteenth-century Europe. *Source: Sociology of Education, 62*, 277–288.

Stein, C. M., & Elston, R. C. (2009). Finding genes underlying human disease. *Clinical Genetics, 75*, 101–106. DOI: https://doi.org/10.1111/j.1399-0004.2008.01083.x.

Stephenson, S. (1904). Congenital word blindness. *Lancet*, *2*, 827–828.
Stephenson, S. (1907). Six cases of congenital word-blindness affecting three generations of one family. *Ophthalmoscope*, *5*, 482–484.
Sutcliffe, J. S. (2008). Heterogeneity and the design of genetic studies in autism. *Autism Research*, *1*, 205–206.
Svensson, I. (2011). Reading and writing disabilities among inmates in correctional settings: A Swedish perspective. *Learning and Individual Differences*, *21*, 19–29.
Swagerman, S. C., van Bergen, E., Dolan, C. V. et al. (2017). Genetic transmission of reading ability. *Brain and Language*, *172*, 3–8. DOI: https://doi.org/10.1016/j.bandl.2015.07.008.
Taipale, M., Kaminen, N., Nopola-Hemmi, J. et al. (2003). A candidate gene for developmental dyslexia encodes a nuclear tetratricopeptide repeat domain protein dynamically regulated in brain. *Proceedings of the National Academy of Sciences of the United States of America*, *100*, 11553–11558.
Tarkar, A., Loges, N. T., Slagle, C. E. et al. (2013). DYX1C1 is required for axonemal dynein assembly and ciliary motility. *Nature Genetics*, *45*, 995–1003. DOI: https://doi.org/10.1038/ng.2707.
Taylor, J., Roehrig, A. D., Soden Hensler, B., Connor, C. M., & Schatschneider, C. (2010). Teacher quality moderates the genetic effects on early reading. *Science*, *328*, 512–514.
Tenesa, A., Farrington, S. M., Prendergast, J. G. D. et al. (2008). Genome-wide association scan identifies a colorectal cancer susceptibility locus on 11q23 and replicates risk loci at 8q24 and 18q21. *Nature Genetics*, *40*, 631–637. DOI: https://doi.org/10.1038/ng.133.
The Wellcome Trust Case Control Consortium. (2007). Genome-wide association study of 14,000 cases of seven common diseases and 3,000 controls. *Nature*, *447*, 661–678.
Thomas, C. J. (1905). Congenital "word-blindness" and its treatment. *Ophthalmoscope*, *3*, 380–385.
Tosto, M. G., Hayiou-Thomas, M. E., Harlaar, N. et al. (2017). The genetic architecture of oral language, reading fluency, and reading comprehension. *Developmental Psychology*, *53*, 1115–1129. DOI: https://doi.org/10.1037/dev0000297.
Tran, C., Wigg, K. G., Zhang, K. et al. (2014). Association of the ROBO1 gene with reading disabilities in a family-based analysis. *Genes, Brain, and Behavior*, *13*, 430–438. DOI: https://doi.org/10.1111/gbb.12126.
Truong, D. T., Adams, A. K., Boada, R. et al. (2017). Multivariate genome-wide association study of rapid automatized naming and rapid alternating stimulus in Hispanic and African American youth. *bioRxiv*, 202929. DOI: https://doi.org/10.1101/202929.
van Bergen, E., van Zuijen, T., Bishop, D., & de Jong, P. F. (2017). Why are home literacy environment and children's reading skills associated? What parental skills reveal. *Reading Research Quarterly*, *52*(2), 147–160. DOI: https://doi.org/10.1002/rrq.160.
van Leeuwen, M., van den Berg, S. M., Peper, J. S., Hulshoff Pol, H. E., & Boomsma, D. I. (2009). Genetic covariance structure of reading, intelligence and memory in children. *Behavior Genetics*, *39*, 245–254. DOI: https://doi.org/10.1007/s10519-009-9264-1.

Vernes, S. C., Newbury, D. F., Abrahams, B. S. et al. (2008). A functional genetic link between distinct developmental language disorders. *New England Journal of Medicine, 359*, 2337–2345. DOI: https://doi.org/10.1056/NEJMoa0802828.

Wadsworth, S., Corley, R., Hewitt, J., & DeFries, J. (2001). Stability of genetic and environmental influences on reading performance at 7, 12, and 16 years of age in the Colorado Adoption Project. *Behavior Genetics, 31*, 353–359.

Wadsworth, S., Olson, R., & DeFries, J. (2010). Differential genetic etiology of reading difficulties as a function of IQ: An update. *Behavior Genetics, 40*, 751–758. DOI: http://dx.doi.org/10.1007/s10519-010-9349-x.

Weinschenk, C. (1965). *Die erbliche Rechtschreibschwäche und ihre sozialpsychiatrischen Auswirkungen*. Bern: Haber.

Weiss, L. A. (2009). Autism genetics: Emerging data from genome-wide copy-number and single nucleotide polymorphism scans. *Expert Review of Molecular Diagnostics, 9*, 795–803.

Wijsman, E. M., Peterson, D., Leutenegger, A. L. et al. (2000). Segregation analysis of phenotypic components of learning disabilities: I. Nonword memory and digit span. *American Journal of Human Genetics, 67*, 631–646.

Wilcke, A., Ligges, C., Burkhardt, J. et al. (2012). Imaging genetics of FOXP2 in dyslexia. *European Journal of Human Genetics, 20*, 224–229. DOI: https://doi.org/10.1038/ejhg.2011.160.

Zeeuw, E. L., Beijsterveldt, C. E. M., Dolan, C. V. et al. (2018). Why do children read more? The influence of reading ability on voluntary reading practices. *Journal of Child Psychology & Psychiatry, 59*(11), 1205–1214. DOI: https://doi.org/10.1111/jcpp.12910.

Zerbin-Rüdin, E. (1967). Kongenitale Wortblindheit oder spezifische dyslexie (congenital word-blindness). *Bulletin of Orton Society, 17*, 47–56.

Zhu, X., Feng, T., Li, Y., Lu, Q., & Elston, R. C. (2010). Detecting rare variants for complex traits using family and unrelated data. *Genetic Epidemiology, 34*, 171–187. DOI: https://doi.org/10.1002/gepi.20449.

Ziegler, A., Konig, I. R., Deimel, W. et al. (2005). Developmental dyslexia–recurrence risk estimates from a German bi-center study using the single proband sib pair design. *Human Heredity, 59*, 136–143.

14 Role of Self-Regulation in the Transition to School

Frederick J. Morrison, Jennie Grammer, William J. Gehring, Lindsay Bell Weixler, and Matthew H. Kim

14.1 Introduction

Over the last two decades, a sizable body of research has documented the importance of the early childhood years as a critical foundation not only for successful transition to school, but for literacy success in elementary school and beyond (for a review, see Morrison, Bachman, & Connor, 2005). Further, a complex set of factors in the child, family, school, and larger sociocultural context, independently and in interaction, shape the growth of early literacy skills over that crucial time period. Recently, attention has focused on a set of skills called self-regulation (also executive function or effortful control), that has been shown to uniquely impact children's literacy development and academic growth across the school years, as well as their success in adult life (Moffitt et al., 2011). With emphasis on the context of the United States (see also Kieffer & Vuković, Chapter 2 in this volume), this chapter focuses on four central questions about self-regulation, a skill set essential to learning. First, how have scientists conceptualized self-regulation? As will be seen, there are multiple perspectives on the labeling of the term as well as on its measurement. Second, what are the extent and nature of individual differences in self-regulation during the transition to school? Third, what is the unique impact of self-regulation on early literacy and later academic achievement? Finally, can self-regulation be modified by appropriate environmental stimulation, especially in the school environment?

14.2 Conceptualizations of Self-Regulation

Self-regulation refers to the ability to modulate one's thoughts, emotions, and social behavior in the service of achieving goals or otherwise acting appropriately. On a theoretical level, self-regulation has been conceptualized as a complex skill set, composed of three fundamental components: attention control/flexibility, working memory, and response inhibition. Understandably, this coordinated skill has been the object of much attention from scientists across a broad range of disciplines. Developmental scientists have focused on growth of executive functioning from infancy to early adulthood (Welsh, 2001). Executive functioning (EF) has been conceptualized as the cognitive underpinning of the more overtly observable manifestations of behavioral, emotional, and social regulation. Along with education researchers, they have sought to understand the interplay between maturational and environmental factors that shape development of executive skills and the role of variability in children's self-control, which emerges even before children start school, and the impact of this interplay on, for instance, American children's poor academic achievement (Duckworth & Seligman, 2006; Matthews, Ponitz, & Morrison, 2009). From a different perspective, neuroscientists studying cognitive-control processes have noted distinct differences between brain areas subserving basic cognitive functions (attention, memory) and those involved in integrating and coordinating attentional and memory skills. More recently they have also explored differences in the neural bases of these skills in children as compared to adults (Welsh, Friedman, & Spieker, 2006). In addition, cognitive scientists have been analyzing the underlying components of executive functioning (attentional control/flexibility, working memory, response inhibition, planning) to ascertain their structure and function (Zelazo, Craik, & Booth, 2004).

In addition to disciplinary differences, a global perspective uncovers insights into self-regulation that are sometimes country- and culture-specific. For example, in a study of five-year-old children in England, Estonia, and the United States, gender differences in each EF subdomain – inhibition, mental flexibility, and working memory – were only present in Estonian children, with girls outperforming boys (OECD, 2020). Differences in the emergence and development of self-regulation between American and British children compared to Chinese and Korean children are also present, noted in a series of studies that we outline later in the chapter. Scholars have examined the extent to which parenting practices, shaped by culturally shared values around childrearing, might contribute to how children self-regulate as well as to the goals that individuals possess with respect to self-regulation (see Jaramillo et al., 2017, for a review). Although the present chapter focuses on the American context, we acknowledge the importance of attending to contextual factors outside the United States in the study of self-regulation.

Until recently, each discipline has been working in relative isolation from the others, with the consequence that definitions and measurement of self-regulation vary widely. The dominant labels are executive function (from neurophysiological and cognitive researchers), self-regulation (from educational and developmental scientists), cognitive control (from neuroscientists), and effortful control (from early childhood researchers). Likewise, the methods of measurement range from highly constrained tasks with simple responses (needed for neurophysiological and cognitive studies), to more child-friendly tasks that mimic real-world behaviors (Simon Says tasks), to more global assessments from parent and teacher rating scales. The proliferation of constructs and tasks has created a kind of "conceptual clutter" and "measurement mayhem" as these disciplines begin to integrate their efforts (Morrison & Grammer, 2016). At present, it is not clear whether these varying terms refer to distinctly different underlying skills or simply reflect the same construct. Likewise, little is known about how the various measures of self-regulation relate to each other or to real-world behaviors (Morrison & Grammer, 2016). In this chapter, we adopt a broad definition that we introduced earlier in this section: Self-regulation refers to the ability to modulate one's thoughts, emotions, and behavior in the service of achieving goals or otherwise acting appropriately.

14.3 Early Variability in Self-Regulation

As for many skills important for academic success, variability in children's self-regulation emerges early and can remain stable throughout the school years and beyond without explicit intervention (Morrison, Ponitz, & McClelland, 2010). Researchers have consistently found that children from families with higher socioeconomic status (SES) outperform lower-SES children on multiple measures of EF (i.e., Hackman & Farah, 2009; Noble, Norman, & Farah, 2005). For example, a study of American kindergartners found that middle-SES children outperformed low-SES children on inhibition and cognitive-flexibility tasks, and further, that SES accounted for 15 percent of the variance of the composite EF score (Noble et al., 2005). Additionally, a study by Matthews et al. (2009) demonstrated wide individual variability even within a sample of middle-SES children. In that study, children were tested at the beginning of kindergarten on two measures: a direct assessment of their response inhibition and a teacher report of their overall self-regulation in the classroom. The direct assessment utilized the Head-Toes-Knees-Shoulders (HTKS) task, in which children, after following a researcher's example of touching their head, toes, and so on, on command, are then instructed to do the opposite, for example, touch their toes when told to touch their head. The Child Behavior Rating Scale (Bronson, Tivnan, & Seppanen, 1995) was given to teachers, one subscale of which was utilized as a measure of self-regulation (example item: this child can complete a task that requires multiple steps). The frequency distribution on the HTKS task mirrored those on the rating scale. Results from teacher ratings are depicted in Figure 14.1. Substantial variability in children's self-regulation ratings at the beginning of the kindergarten year emerged across teachers. Girls were rated higher than boys and look more similar to each other. Strikingly, teachers also rated as lowest in self-regulation a small but notable cluster of boys at the bottom of the distribution.

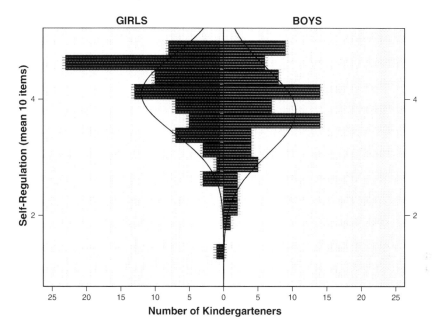

Figure 14.1 Frequency distribution of teacher ratings of self-regulation for males and females at the beginning of the kindergarten year

The pattern of results from this study and others (see Morrison et al., 2010 for a review) corroborate recent findings that meaningful variation in important cognitive skills, including self-regulation, emerge early in development. Further, gender differences in self-regulation favoring girls are evident in early childhood in the United States and may have long-term implications for later development. In that regard, it is noteworthy that a major underlying reason for the gender gap may reside with a group of particularly low-performing boys. Keep in mind that the children in this study all came from middle-SES backgrounds in the United States; including more disadvantaged children would arguably have increased the proportion of low-performing boys. Finally, the close agreement between the direct measure and teacher ratings not only reinforces the overall patterns found but reveals that teacher ratings of self-regulation can accurately mirror direct assessment in a predominantly white middle-class US sample.

Interestingly, gender differences in self-regulation commonly found in American children have not consistently emerged in recent studies of young children in East Asia (Wanless et al., 2013; Weixler, 2012). Wanless et al. found no gender difference in behavioral regulation in young Chinese and Korean children (ages three to six), despite finding a sizeable female advantage among American children. Similarly, Weixler found a substantial female advantage in both attention and working memory in American kindergarteners, but a gender gap was only present in working memory in Chinese children.

Furthermore, young children in China and South Korea are well ahead of typical American and British children in the development of self-regulation skills (Oh & Lewis, 2008; Sabbagh et al., 2006; Weixler, 2012; Yang, Yang, & Lust, 2011). Across multiple domains of self-regulation, Chinese and Korean children outscore their counterparts in the United States and Britain by as much as half to three quarters of a standard deviation. These gaps pervade all socioeconomic levels, and findings from one study indicate that high-SES children in the United States, whose parents typically have graduate degrees and high-status occupations, score similarly to low- and lower-middle-SES Chinese children, whose parents, on average, have a high-school education or less (Weixler, 2012). Though little evidence exists to identify the origins of Chinese and Korean children's early advantage in self-regulation relative to American children, some findings point to cultural differences that include social and family structures, as well as environmental influences, particularly early education, in facilitating the more advanced development of self-regulation in young children in these countries (Tobin, Hsueh, & Karasawa, 2009; Weixler, 2012).

14.4 Self-Regulation and Academic Achievement

Beyond discovery of early variability in self-regulation, accumulating evidence has demonstrated that differences in self-regulation uniquely predict children's emergent literacy skills (Blair & Razza, 2007) as well as their academic achievement across elementary school (McClelland, Acock, & Morrison, 2006; see Morrison et al., 2010 for a review). Some, but not all, studies have shown that self-regulation predicts performance on math tasks more strongly than on reading tasks. This difference may stem, in part, from the fact that elementary math tasks, especially word problems, engage all three self-regulatory skills to a greater degree than beginning reading tasks, which focus primarily on single-word decoding. The sweep of self-regulation is not limited to academic domains or to childhood. A study by Moffitt et al. (2011) found that individual differences in self-control in early childhood predicted patterns of health, wealth, and criminality in adults decades later. Clearly, growth of self-regulation across the lifespan exerts a broad influence on many domains that underlie life success.

For that reason, in part, scientists have been interested in the degree to which self-regulation can be modified. Until recently, conventional wisdom viewed self-regulation as primarily under maturational control. Schools themselves seem to have adopted this view implicitly, because there has been little effort to explicitly teach self-regulation skills in the classroom as part of the school curriculum. This is changing gradually, as schools recognize the potential power of self-regulation in enhancing children's life chances inside and outside the classroom.

Does schooling have a direct effect on growth of self-regulation? Clearly self-regulation improves as children progress through school, and spurts in self-regulation can be seen from preschool to early elementary school. But these changes could all be driven by maturation. We tried to address the causal connection between experiences in school and growth of self-regulation using a natural experiment (Morrison et al., 2005; Morrison et al., 2019). Each year school districts admit students to kindergarten based on a birthdate cutoff that varies widely across localities. The regression discontinuity design (RDD), a quasi-experimental technique, allows us to conduct a natural experiment in which children's experience in school varies as a function of when their birthday falls relative to the school entry cutoff date. Children born prior to the cutoff date are permitted to enter kindergarten, while those born after the date must wait until the following year. Using RDD, it is possible to generate relatively unbiased estimates of the unique effect of schooling without the need for randomization (e.g., Imbens & Lemieux, 2008; Jacob, Zhu, Somers, & Bloom, 2012; Thistlethwaite & Campbell, 1960). A variant of RDD, called the school cutoff method, selects children who cluster very closely around the school cutoff date (by one or two months); we can then effectively equate children on age and compare their growth, using a pre-post design. Differences in growth rates over the school year can be legitimately attributed to schooling-related experiences, though the exact nature of the experience responsible for the differences needs to be separately determined.

Across a number of studies, evidence has accumulated that schooling does in fact have a significant impact on a variety of cognitive, language, and academic skills over the school transition period, generally viewed as three years of age to third grade (Morrison et al., 2005; see Morrison et al., 2019, for a review). Further, research has documented that the extent and timing of the schooling effect varies across different skills (Christian et al., 2000). For example, school cutoff studies have revealed that single-word decoding is influenced both during kindergarten and first grade, but phonemic awareness is uniquely enhanced by schooling experiences much more strongly in first grade. In contrast, the impact of schooling experiences on vocabulary remains mixed, with some studies showing schooling effects on receptive vocabulary (e.g., Weiland & Yoshikawa, 2013; Wong et al., 2008) but no schooling effects on expressive vocabulary (e.g., Christian et al., 2000; Kim & Morrison, 2018; Skibbe et al., 2011).

In an effort to examine schooling effects on growth of self-regulation skills, Burrage et al. (2008) employed the school cutoff method to compare groups of younger kindergarten children and older pre-kindergarten children on two self-regulation skills: working memory (from the Woodcock Johnson-III [WJ-III] battery; Woodcock, McGrew, & Mather, 2001) and response inhibition (HTKS). They also included a measure of word decoding from the WJ-III as a manipulation check. The groups did not differ on maternal education. The results for word decoding revealed that kindergarten children outperformed pre-K children at beginning-of-year testing, revealing a schooling effect during the pre-K year. In addition, a separate effect of the kindergarten year was revealed in a significant group difference favoring kindergarten children at the end of the academic year. The outcomes for working memory demonstrated a strong schooling effect during the pre-K year (beginning-of-year comparison), and while there was not an independent schooling effect during the kindergarten year, the kindergarten children maintained their advantage on the end-of-year posttest. Interestingly, the findings for response inhibition were quite different. Here, there is a marginally significant effect of schooling during the pre-K year, but no evidence of a schooling effect in kindergarten and, in reality, minimal evidence of growth in response inhibition over the two-year period.

Taken together, results for self-regulation mirror those for other skills studied. In these data, schooling experiences do produce significant, unique growth in working memory skills in preschool, but not response inhibition (though other studies find effects for both working memory and response inhibition, as well as attention flexibility, i.e., Weiland & Yoshikawa, 2013). While the reasons for the different patterns remain to be studied, some evidence points to the potential role of classroom experiences. Specifically, Cameron, Connor, and Morrison (2005), using direct classroom observations in first grade, examined teacher's use of orienting and organizing language in directing children's actions. This variable, labeled, "orient-organize," consisted of instructions to the children about what would be happening in the next half-hour, day, or week, and what the children needed to do to prepare. The coding scheme describes "orient-organize" as follows: "the teacher explains to students how they should organize their classwork time (for example, the teacher describes each activity available for 'activity time' or explains that students should work on journaling first, then math, and then free reading); teacher focuses students' attention on the next activity; etc." (Cameron, Connor, & Morrison, 2005). They found that the more time teachers spent in orient-organize instructions, the less time children took to transition between activities. Further, teachers who spent more time in orient-organize instructions in the first half of the school year had children who spent more time managing their own activities in the second half of the year. Connor et al. (2010) found that classroom management that included clear expectations for self-regulated learning led to greater gains in self-regulation for students with initially weaker skills.

We have examined research that demonstrates that EF skills can predict academic outcomes. Before we leave this section, it is important to acknowledge that academic skills and psychological processes may be *bidirectionally related* to each other. The theory of mutualism argues that the development of skills in one domain can influence the development of skills in another domain (van der Maas et al., 2006). In the domain of academic achievement, research has revealed that cognitive abilities and academic skills predict each other in development, and that direct academic instruction can improve reasoning skills (Peng & Kievit, 2020). Empirical research has demonstrated bidirectional links between EF skills and math ability (e.g., Clements, Sarama, & Germeroth, 2016) and science ability (Kim, Bousselot, & Ahmed, 2021). Clearly, additional work is needed to elucidate the nature of the bidirectional links between self-regulation and academic achievement.

14.5 Broadening the Scope: Neurobiological Perspective

Recent investigations have explored individual differences in neurobiological indicators of self-regulation and academic achievement. This exploration into the neural underpinnings of achievement and behavior allows us to better understand the nature and development of self-regulation in young children. Notably, it is possible that development of self-regulation can be observed in the brain before it is manifested in observable behavior, with implications for understanding and training self-regulation (see also Rigatti et al., Chapter 12 in this volume).

Research using the event-related potential (ERP) technique has identified two brain components associated with cognitive processes that occur when individuals make mistakes on inhibitory control tasks. Because self-regulation is especially required in precisely those challenging situations in which controlling one's responses and shifting attention is necessary for optimal performance, error-related ERP components can provide important insights into the nature and development of self-regulation.

The error-related negativity (ERN) is observed as a negative-going deflection in frontal brain locations immediately after an individual makes a mistake on a speeded target discrimination task (see Gehring et al., 2012, for a review). The ERN is thought to reflect conflict monitoring, a component of cognitive-control processes which overlap substantially with self-regulation. The error positivity (Pe) is observed as a slower positive deflection in parietal brain locations between 200 and 500 milliseconds after a mistake. In contrast to the ERN, the Pe is thought to reflect the conscious awareness of the mistake or perhaps response conflict (Overbeek, Nieuwenhuis, & Ridderinkhof, 2005), and has been associated with behavioral changes in task performance associated with committing an error.

We know that individual differences in ERPs are related to meaningful variation in academic achievement in school-aged children and college students, and that a larger ERN and Pe indicate better capacities to engage cognitive-control mechanisms which promote better achievement on academic tasks (Hillman et al., 2012; Hirsh & Inzlicht, 2010). When looking specifically during the transition to school period, findings from a recent investigation indicate that individual differences in early academic outcomes – particularly for reading – are related to the Pe but not to the ERN, and that this relation is positive and nonlinear in nature (Kim et al., 2016). Other work has also linked ERPs with behavior and motivation (e.g., Kim et al., 2017; Lamm, Zelazo, & Lewis, 2006; Moser et al., 2011). It is worth noting that the majority of these investigations have shown links with the Pe and children's school-related skills. This suggests that it is the conscious awareness of having made a mistake that may be more highly related to achievement and motivation. Moreover, these studies indicate that the relation between academics and ERPs depends on development and may be domain-specific, further highlighting the important heterogeneity of effects that is uncovered when brain and behavior are studied in tandem.

Less attention has been focused on whether environmental influences – such as schooling – can influence the magnitude of these ERP components. While research has amply demonstrated contextual influences on behavior and brain development, schooling effects on specific neural indices associated with cognitive control and academic achievement would indicate that the neural correlates of self-regulation might potentially be malleable as a function of school and classroom experiences, thereby transforming the way researchers understand, define, and measure self-regulation. As already mentioned, one potential mechanism might be the nature of teacher instructions to students, such as "orient-organize." Other factors, such as global classroom climate, disciplinary practices, or incentive systems could be potential mechanisms of this effect and should be tested in future research.

Although it is not possible to randomly assign children to enter or not enter school, there are a number of ways to causally examine the role that schooling plays in children's development, such as RDD and the school cutoff method (Morrison, Kim, Connor, & Grammer, 2019). As mentioned previously, both methods leverage the kindergarten entrance age mandated in each country context; by using the birthdate cutoff date, one can compare outcomes for children who are similar in age, but vary in the extent of their experiences in school. Put another way, depending on when they are born, children either enter school or not within a given year. Thus, it is possible to compare the performance of children who were able to go to school versus those who did not, controlling for age.

This comparison is most clear in the children born just before and just after the cutoff: they are virtually identical in age but differ by one year of schooling. As is portrayed in the top panel of Figure 14.2, for the development of some skills such as receptive vocabulary, children's performance depends on age but not schooling experience. Thus, children on either side of the cutoff date (in this case December 1st) look similar in skill level. In contrast, as is demonstrated in the lower panel, for some skills, including alphabet recognition and word decoding (Christian et al., 2000; Morrison, Griffith, & Frazier, 1996), there are discrepancies in the performance of children who have birthdays on either side of the cutoff. When a schooling effect is observed, a gap in performance between children who are oldest relative to youngest for their grade can be seen.

Rather than assuming that children born within the two-month window are identical, a key assumption of the school cutoff technique, RDD can estimate linear or nonlinear regressions for groups who make versus miss the cutoff date for school entry within a prespecified window around the cutoff date (also called a bandwidth). Conditional on the two groups being equivalent on key demographic characteristics, a schooling effect is inferred if the regression lines "jump" at the cutoff date, indicating that the effects for the group who made the cutoff are attributable to schooling experiences and not to some other factor.

In our recent work examining brain and behavioral correlates of children's EF development, we have found preliminary evidence that schooling can explain unique variance in individual differences in ERPs associated with self-regulation. Indeed, using RDD to examine behavioral and ERP data collected from 550 children in kindergarten and first grade, we find an impact of school experience on the differences between the amplitude of the ERN on error and correct trials elicited on a child-friendly go/no-go task. Specifically, experience in the first grade is associated with a 1.11 standard deviation increase in the ERN amplitude related to an additional year in the classroom. Similarly, when considering changes in Pe scores as a function of experience in first grade, we observe a 1.4 standard deviation change in Pe amplitude that is attributable to experience in Grade 1 relative to kindergarten (Grammer, Gehring, & Morrison, 2018).

Although the effects of experience in school can be seen on ERP correlates of children's self-regulation, consistent with other work (Brod, Bunge, & Shing, 2017), in our data we do not observe a commensurate impact of schooling on behavioral indices of these same skills including accuracy and reaction time. Put another way, the impact of school on children's self-regulation cannot be seen when examining children's behavior alone. This finding has potentially

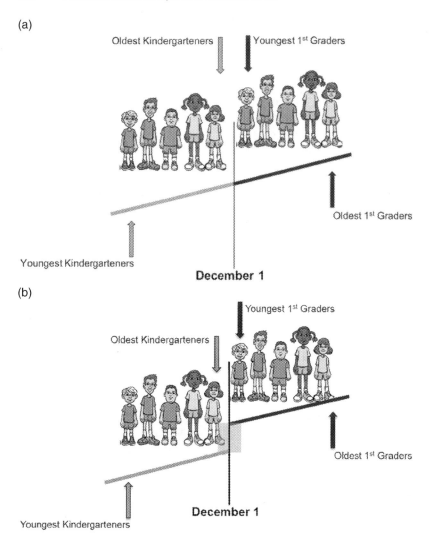

Figure 14.2 In the top panel, there is a linear effect of age, but not schooling. This is typically seen for measures of vocabulary, which appear to be more sensitive to biological maturation compared to schooling. In the bottom panel, there is a linear effect of age as well as a unique effect of schooling. This is shown by the positive slopes for each grade (i.e., an age effect) as well as a jump, or discontinuity, at the cutoff for first-grade children. That is, there is a unique impact of first-grade schooling on the outcome of interest, over and above the effects of age

important implications on our general understanding of the impact that experience in school can have on children's regulation. Self-regulation is particularly challenging to measure across the transition into school for a number of reasons, including tasks that are sensitive to age (i.e., floor and ceiling effects), whether the task taps into discrete dimensions of self-regulation or a global construct, where the task is administered (laboratory vs. school vs. home settings), and even whether the task is administered individually or in group settings (the latter potentially being more ecologically valid as a measure of self-regulation in typical learning environments) (Ahmed, Grammer, & Morrison, 2021). Challenges associated with behavioral measurement may be masking some of the impact in these skills that can be attributed to experiences children have in the classroom. Variations in the association between brain and behavioral measures of self-regulation, particularly in early childhood (Grammer et al., 2014; Grammer et al., 2018), suggest that these two different levels of measurement provide unique information regarding these skills. Thus, by assessing regulation at the behavioral and neurobiological levels, it may be possible to better understand the mechanisms by which experience in school impacts the development of these important skills.

Taken together, these findings related to the neural correlates of self-regulation indicate the substantial heterogeneity that exists in our understanding of self-regulation and related constructs in early childhood. Given the difficulties that the field has experienced with reliably measuring these constructs, it is not surprising that we find added complexity when we also consider the neurobiological correlates of early self-regulation and academic achievement. The field is ripe for further exploration by melding different levels of analysis as researchers seek to better understand the nature and development of self-regulation during the transition to school, with the potential to inform innovative approaches to training and promoting these important skills at an early age.

14.6 Conclusions and Discussion

Like many other skills underlying success in school and later life, individual differences in self-regulation emerge early in development before children enter formal schooling. Mounting evidence documents the strong unique effect of self-regulation on success in school and in later life in the United States and other parts of the world. Of particular interest is a subset of males who comprise the lower end of the distribution of self-regulation skills and who may be at risk for poor developmental outcomes. Despite these strong associations, self-regulation has been shown to be malleable during early development, raising the hope that appropriately timed interventions could improve the self-regulation skills of children at increased risk for poor academic and psychological outcomes. In fact, a host of promising interventions are currently being developed and evaluated. The success of these interventions will spawn new research on how self-regulation develops and when and how it can be modified to help children grow (see Diamond & Lee, 2011).

While research bridging brain and behavior has revealed new insights regarding the impact of schooling on development at multiple levels of analysis, whether and how this knowledge can inform actual instructional practices remains an important question that should be addressed from an interdisciplinary lens. One important area of future research is to identify the classroom-level mechanisms that promote growth in self-regulation skills. Evidence using school cutoff and RDD have demonstrated that schooling has causal impacts on literacy and behavioral skill development, but what it is about schooling that leads to these effects has yet to be determined. Moreover, as we have alluded to, these classroom-level mechanisms may well vary depending on the cultural context in which learning takes place. For example, what are the values, goals, and expectations around learning and achievement that are shared by a given culture, and how do these cultural specifics shape how self-regulation is taught and trained in home and school settings? And which factors appear to be shared across cultures and countries? Demonstrating mere cause–effect relations between schooling and development, while critical, presents only an incomplete picture. In-depth studies are needed to uncover what actually happens in school and classroom environments that promotes growth in literacy and behavioral skills during childhood.

References

Ahmed, S. F., Grammer, J., & Morrison, F. (2021). Cognition in context: Validating group-based executive function assessments in young children. *Journal of Experimental Child Psychology*, *208*, 105131.

Blair, C., & Razza, R. (2007). Relating effortful control, executive function, and false belief understanding to emerging math and literacy ability in kindergarten. *Child Development*, *78*, 647–663.

Brod, G., Bunge, S. A., & Shing, Y. L. (2017). Does one year of schooling improve children's cognitive control and alter associated brain function? *Psychological Science*. DOI: https://doi.org/10.1177/0956797617699838.

Bronson, M. B., Tivnan, T., & Seppanen, P. S. (1995). Relations between teacher and classroom activity variables and the classroom behaviors of preschool children in Chapter 1 funded programs. *Journal of Applied Developmental Psychology*, *16*, 253–282. DOI: https://doi.org/10.1016=0193-3973(95)90035-7.

Burrage, M., Ponitz, C. C., Shah, P. et al. (2008). A natural experiment of schooling effects on executive functions. *Child Neuropsychology*, *14*(6), 510–524.

Cameron, C. E., Connor, C. M., & Morrison, F .J. (2005) Effects of variation in teacher organization on classroom function. *Journal of School Psychology*, *43*, 61–85.

Christian, K., Morrison, F. J., Frazier, J. A., & Massetti, G. (2000). Specificity in the nature and timing of cognitive growth in kindergarten and first grade. *Journal of Cognition and Development, 1*, 429–448. DOI: https://doi.org/10.1207/S15327647JCD0104_04.

Clements, D. H., Sarama, J., & Germeroth, C. (2016). Learning executive function and early mathematics: Directions of causal relations. *Early Childhood Research Quarterly, 36*, 79–90.

Connor, C. M., Ponitz, C. E. C., Phillips, B. et al. (2010). First graders' literacy and self-regulation gains: The effect of individualizing instruction. *Journal of School Psychology, 48*, 433–455.

Diamond, A., & Lee, K. (2011). Interventions shown to aid executive function development in children 4–12 years old. *Science, 333*(6045), 959–964. DOI: https://doi.org/10.1126/science.1204529.

Duckworth, A., & Seligman, M. P. (2006). Self-discipline gives girls the edge: Gender in self-discipline, grades, and achievement test scores. *Journal of Educational Psychology, 98*, 198–208. DOI: https://doi.org/10.1037/0022-0663.98.1.198.

Gehring, W. J., Liu, Y., Orr, J. M., & Carp, J. (2012). The error-related negativity (ERN/Ne). In S. J. Luck & E. S. Kappenman (eds.), *The Oxford Handbook of Event-Related Potential Components* (pp. 231–291). Oxford: Oxford University Press.

Grammer, J. K., Carrasco, M., Gehring, W. J., & Morrison, F. J. (2014). Age-related changes in error processing in young children: A school-based investigation. *Developmental Cognitive Neuroscience, 9*, 93–105.

Grammer, J. K., Gehring, W. J., & Morrison, F. J. (2018). Associations between developmental changes in error-related brain activity and executive functions in early childhood. *Psychophysiology, 55*(3), e13040.

Hackman, D. A., & Farah, M. J. (2009). Socioeconomic status and the developing brain. *Trends in Cognitive Sciences, 13*(2), 65–73. DOI: https://doi.org/10.1016/j.tics.2008.11.003.

Hillman, C. H., Pontifex, M. B., Motl, R. W. et al. (2012). From ERPs to academics. *Developmental Cognitive Neuroscience, 2* (Supplement 1), S90–S98. DOI: https://doi.org/10.1016/j.dcn.2011.07.004.

Hirsh, J. B., & Inzlicht, M. (2010). Error-related negativity predicts academic performance. *Psychophysiology, 47*, 192–196.

Imbens, G. W., & Lemieux, T. (2008). Regression discontinuity designs: A guide to practice. *Journal of Econometrics, 142*, 615–635. DOI: https://doi.org/10.1016/j.jeconom.2007.05.001.

Jacob, R., Zhu, P., Somers, M., & Bloom, H. (2012). A practical guide to regression discontinuity (Working Paper). New York: MDRC.

Jaramillo, J. M., Rendon, M. I., Munoz, L., Weis, M., & Trommsdorff, G. (2017). Children's self-regulation in cultural contexts: The role of parental socialization theories, goals, and practices. *Frontiers in Psychology* (June 6) (8), 923. DOI: https://doi.org/10.3389/fpsyg.2017.00923.PMID:28634460;PMCID:PMC5460587.

Kim, M. H., Bousselot, T., & Ahmed, S. F. (2021). Executive functions and science achievement during the five-to-seven-year shift. *Developmental Psychology, 57*(12), 2119–2133. DOI: https://doi.org/10.1037/dev0001261.

Kim, M. H., Grammer, J. K., Marulis, L. M. et al. (2016). Early math and reading achievement are associated with the error positivity. *Developmental Cognitive Neuroscience, 22*, 18–26.

Kim, M. H., Marulis, L. M., Grammer, J. K., Morrison, F. J., & Gehring, W. J. (2017). Motivational processes from expectancy-value theory are associated with variability in the error positivity in young children. *Journal of Experimental Child Psychology, 155*, 32–47. DOI: https://doi.org/10.1016/j.jecp.2016.10.010.

Kim, M. H., Morrison, F. J. (2018). Schooling effects on literacy skills during the transition to school. *AERA Open, 4*(3), 1–15. https://doi.org/10.1177/2332858418798793.

Lamm, C., Zelazo, P. D., & Lewis, M. D. (2006). Neural correlates of cognitive control in childhood and adolescence: disentangling the contributions of age and executive function. *Neuropsychologia, 44*(11), 2139–2148.

Matthews, J. S., Ponitz, C., & Morrison, F. J. (2009). Early gender differences in self-regulation and academic achievement. *Journal of Educational Psychology, 101*, 689–704. DOI: https://doi.org/10.1037/a0014240.

McClelland, M. M., Acock, A. C., & Morrison, F. J. (2006). The impact of kindergarten learning-related skills on academic trajectories at the end of elementary school. *Early Childhood Research Quarterly, 21*, 471–490.

Moffitt, T. E., Arseneault, L., Belsky, D. et al. (2011). A gradient of childhood self-control predicts health, wealth, and public safety. *PNAS Proceedings Of The National Academy Of Sciences Of The United States Of America, 108*, 2693–2698. DOI: https://doi.org/10.1073/pnas.1010076108.

Morrison, F. J., Bachman, H. J., & Connor, C. M. (2005). *Improving Literacy in America: Guidelines from Research*. New Haven, CT: Yale University Press.

Morrison, F. J., & Grammer, J. K. (2016). Conceptual clutter and measurement mayhem: Proposals for cross disciplinary integration in conceptualizing and measuring executive function. In J. Griffin, P. McCardle, & L. Freund (eds.), *Research Directions in Preschool Executive Functions: Integrating Measurement, Neurodevelopment and Translational Research*. Washington, DC: American Psychological Association.

Morrison, F. J., Griffith, E. M., & Frazier, J. A. (1996). Schooling and the 5 to 7 shift: A natural experiment. In A. J. Sameroff & M. M. Haith (eds.), *The five to seven year shift: The age of reason and responsibility* (pp. 161–186). Chicago: University of Chicago Press.

Morrison, F. J., Kim, M. H., Connor, C. M., & Grammer, J. K. (2019). The causal impact of schooling on children's development: Lessons for developmental science. *Current Directions in Psychological Science, 28*(5), 441–449. DOI: https://doi.org/10.1177/0963721419855661.

Morrison, F. J., Ponitz, C. C., & McClelland, M. M. (2010). Self-regulation and academic achievement in the transition to school. In S. Calkins and M. Bell (eds.), *Child Development at the Intersection of Emotion and Cognition* (pp. 203–224). Washington, DC: American Psychological Association.

Moser, J. S., Schroder, H. S., Heeter, C., Moran, T. P., & Lee, Y-H. (2011). Mind your errors: Evidence for a neural mechanism linking growth mind-set to adaptive posterror adjustments. *Psychological Science, 22*(12), 1484–1489.

Noble, K. G., Norman, M. F., & Farah, M. J. (2005). Neurocognitive correlates of socioeconomic status in kindergarten children. *Developmental Science, 8*(1), 74–87. DOI: https://doi.org/10.1111/j.1467-7687.2005.00394.x.

OECD. (2020). *Early Learning and Child Well-Being: A Study of Five-year-Olds in England, Estonia, and the United States*. Paris: OECD Publishing. DOI: https://doi.org/10.1787/3990407f-en.

Oh, S., & Lewis, C. (2008). Korean preschoolers' advanced inhibitory control and its relation to other executive skills and mental state understanding. *Child Development, 79*(1), 80–99. DOI: https://doi.org/10.1111/j.1467-8624.2007.01112.x.

Overbeek, T. J. M., Nieuwenhuis, S., & Ridderinkhof, K. R. (2005). Dissociable components of error processing: On the functional significance of the Pe vis-à-vis the ERN/Ne. *Journal of Psychophysiology, 19*(4), 319–329. https://doi.org/10.1027/0269-8803.19.4.319.

Peng, P., & Kievit, R. A. (2020). The development of academic achievement and cognitive abilities: A bidirectional perspective. *Child Development Perspectives, 14* (1), 15–20. DOI: https://doi.org/10.1111/cdep.12352.

Sabbagh, M. A., Xu, F., Carlson, S. M., Moses, L. J., & Lee, K. (2006). The development of executive functioning and theory of mind: A comparison of Chinese and US preschoolers. *Psychological Science, 17*(1), 74–81. DOI: https://doi.org/10.1111/j.1467-9280.2005.01667.x.

Skibbe, L. E., Connor, C. M., Morrison, F. J., & Jewkes, A. M. (2011). Schooling effects on preschoolers' self-regulation, early literacy, and language growth. *Early Childhood Research Quarterly, 26*, 42–49. DOI: https://doi.org/10.1016/j.ecresq.2010.05.001.

Thistlethwaite, D. L., & Campbell, D. T. (1960). Regression-discontinuity analysis: An alternative to the ex post facto experiment. *Journal of Educational Psychology, 51*(6), 309–317. DOI: https://doi.org/10.1037/h0044319.

Tobin, J. J., Hsueh, Y., & Karasawa, M. (2009). *Preschool in Three Cultures Revisited: China, Japan, and the United States*. Chicago: University of Chicago Press.

Van der Maas, H. L. J., Dolan, C. V., Grasman, R. P. P. P. et al. (2006). A dynamical model of general intelligence: The positive manifold of intelligence by mutualism. *Psychological Review, 113*, 842–861.

Wanless, S. B., McClelland, M. M., Lan, X. et al. (2013). Gender differences in behavioral regulation in four societies: The US, Taiwan, South Korea, and China. *Early Childhood Research Quarterly, 28*, 621–633. DOI: https://doi.org/10.1016/j.ecresq.2013.04.002.

Weiland, C., & Yoshikawa, H. (2013). Impacts of a prekindergarten program on children's mathematics, language, literacy, executive function, and emotional skills. *Child Development, 84*(6), 2112–30. DOI: https://doi.org/10.1111/cdev.12099.

Weixler, L. B. (2012). The contributions of preschool attendance and kindergarten experience to executive functioning in Chinese and American children. (PhD, University of Michigan.) https://deepblue.lib.umich.edu/handle/2027.42/96108.

Welsh, M. C. (2001). The prefrontal cortex and the development of executive functions. In A. Kalverboer & A. Gramsbergen (eds.), *Handbook of Brain and Behaviour Development* (pp. 767–789). Deventer: Kluwer.

Welsh, M. C., Friedman, S. L., & Spieker, S. J. (2006). Executive functions in developing children: Current conceptualizations and questions for the future. In K. McCartney, D. Phillips, K. McCartney, & D. Phillips (eds.), *Blackwell Handbook of Early Childhood Development* (pp. 167–187). Malden: Blackwell Publishing.

Wong, V. C., Cook, T. D., Barnett, W. S., & Jung, K. (2008). An effectiveness-based evaluation of five state pre-kindergarten programs. *Journal of Policy Analysis and Management, 27*(1), 122–154. DOI: https://doi.org/10.1002/pam.20310.

Woodcock, R. W., McGrew, K. S., Mather, N. (2001). *Woodcock-Johnson III Tests of Achievement*. Itasca, IL:Riverside.

Yang, S., Yang, H., & Lust, B. (2011). Early childhood bilingualism leads to advances in executive attention: Dissociating culture and language. *Bilingualism: Language and Cognition, 14*(03), 412–422. DOI: https://doi.org/10.1017/S1366728910000611.

Zelazo, P., Craik, F. M., & Booth, L. (2004). Executive function across the life span. *Acta Psychologica, 115*, 167–183.

15 Socioeconomic Status, Sociocultural Factors, and Literacy Development

Sonali Nag

15.1 Introduction

A wide range of factors contribute to literacy development and many of these come embedded within the social environment of the child. In this chapter, we review examples of socioeconomic and sociocultural factors, the influence they exert on literacy development, and explanations for these influences. We focus on low-income contexts in developing countries and find the relevant literature to be scattered across multiple lines of investigation. Research on variables with a broad geographic base is reviewed under the themes of socioeconomic status, literacy teaching practices at home, and the dynamics between the home and school language. The level of family income, household wealth, and parental education captures socioeconomic status and are often indicators of children's access to literacy resources. Activities at home include formal and informal teaching moments, and both may nurture literacy learning. Family choices about the language of instruction and teacher attitudes about home languages are examples of the intangible links between home and school language. These factors, which are sources of variability across families and communities, are potentially as important in explaining individual differences in children's literacy attainments as within-child factors such as vocabulary knowledge and listening comprehension skills. The associations of socioeconomic and sociocultural factors with emergent literacy, component skills of literacy, and grade-level achievement tests are also examined. This discussion is framed around findings that are more consistent across contexts, and those that are more mixed. A possibility to consider when socioeconomic and sociocultural factors are unique to specific contexts is that they may similarly explain outcomes. Some of these explanatory mechanisms for the role of socioeconomic and sociocultural factors in literacy learning are listed, and implications for education are discussed. The chapter ends with the proposal that educational practice that is sensitive to socioeconomic and sociocultural disadvantage must prioritize (a) access to resources and (b) instruction that both consolidates skills as well as reduces fragmented development in literacy skills.

15.2 Enabling Conditions for Literacy Development

We were interested in enabling conditions for literacy learning as identified within the psycholinguistic, sociocultural, and pedagogical perspectives. A genetic account of literacy learning is not addressed (see Grigorenko, Chapter 13 in this volume) because this is an understudied area within low-income contexts in developing countries. However, we recognize that genetic factors provide a biological "context" and can thus be a systematic yet unavoidable confound, particularly in the study of sociocultural factors within the home.

Within the psycholinguistic perspective, strong oral language is important throughout literacy development (Turkish: Babayiğit & Stainthorp, 2010; Hindi: Vagh, 2009; Arabic: Elbeheri and Everett, 2007; Bahasa Indonesia: Winskel & Widjaja, 2007; Kannada: Nag & Snowling, 2011). Knowing the structure of words and sentences (phonological, morphological, and syntactic awareness) and the symbols and sounds to represent them (orthographic and phonological knowledge) is important for literacy development. Decoding of single words is effortful in the beginning, and is therefore assumed to take away attention from the process of reading comprehension. Practice improves ease with decoding and this releases more attention for deeper comprehension. With advancing grades, texts become more complex and comprehension-monitoring strategies (such as looking back at the text) become increasingly important for making inferences. Here too, practice deepens the use of these skills (see Perfetti and Verhoeven, Chapter 11 in this volume).

Within the sociocultural perspective, literacy is viewed as playing multiple functions in peoples' lives (e.g., India: Dyer, 2000; Peru: de la Piedra, 2010; South Africa: Mkhize, 2013; Swaziland: Dlamini, 2009). The constructs of cultural and social capital explain why some children have greater access to resources and an environment rich in literacy practices. These advantages may be of recent origin or a privilege accumulated across generations. Home and school languages and cultures also interplay, leading to agreement and disagreement about what is valuable in order to promote literacy. While some processes such as cultural dissonance may occur irrespective of a child's sociodemographic identity, access to school-relevant and literacy-specific resources are systematically lower for those who belong to families with lower economic, social, or cultural power (forty-one countries: Chiu & Chow, 2010). One implication of unequal access and differences in what is valued is that conditions for literacy development also vary.

Within the pedagogical perspective, there is growing evidence of what works in literacy instruction. This evidence base covers a small language set (e.g., see Mol et al., 2008; Nag et al., 2014; National Reading Panel, 2000), but principles may be cautiously drawn from this literature for understudied orthographies and languages. Oral language skills, orthographic knowledge, skills in decoding and comprehension, skills in the mechanics of writing, and expressive writing are important priorities for early years instruction. For the later grades, the focus of instruction shifts to the advancing of expressive oral and written language skills, reading comprehension, and making increasingly complex inferences. While direct instruction with a skilled teacher is important, a lot depends on the support the child receives from the environment. Although much still remains to be understood about the impact on child outcomes of several intricately interconnected environmental attributes (e.g., poverty and urbanicity: Votruba-Drzal, Miller, & Coley, 2016), there is robust evidence that attributes of the home impact language and literacy outcomes. These home attributes overlap with sociodemographic and sociocultural descriptions of the family as well as the literacy practices preferred in the child's school (e.g., Crookston et al., 2014; Eng, Szmodis, & Mulsow, 2014; Nag, Snowling, & Asfaha, 2016).

The sociocultural, psycholinguistic, and pedagogical perspectives intersect. Together they show that enabling conditions are necessary to consolidate language and literacy skills into an efficient system for daily use. Using such a cross-disciplinary framework, we review literature from low-, lower-middle- and upper-middle-income countries published between 1990, the year of the UN Declaration following the Education for All Jomtien Summit, and 2014. We review papers judged as moderate to high in quality and reporting descriptive, associative, or causal evidence about the links between socioeconomic and sociocultural factors and literacy learning. Our interest was to examine effects of particular socioeconomic and sociocultural factors on component skills of literacy in samples matched for grade and examined by linguistic contexts. When thus specified, there were too few studies to allow use of statistical methods such as meta-analysis. Instead, the heterogeneity in this literature is excellent for an interpretative synthesis (Gough, Thomas, & Oliver, 2012). The following synthesis includes multifactorial studies (typically using multilevel/hierarchical modeling) and ethnographies (of classroom, home, or community).

15.3   Role of Socioeconomic Status

Socioeconomic status (SES) is by far the most researched contextual factor (approximately 65 percent of all univariate and multifactorial studies in the review). The assessment of SES is typically made through the sociodemographic indices of family income, household wealth, and education of family members. These measures are reported either individually or as a composite.

The evidence on an association between a composite measure of SES and component skills of language and literacy is consistent (Shure et al., 2014). Among preschoolers, higher SES is associated with higher attainments in vocabulary, expressive language, concepts about print, symbol knowledge, and emergent writing skills. In the early grades, scores are higher on tests of vocabulary, reading accuracy, reading rate, and reading comprehension, and in later grades on reading comprehension and grade-level tests. This higher SES advantage for literacy attainments is irrespective of country, grade, language of instruction, and first- or second-language instruction, and is found in both monoliterate and biliterate groups.

Turning to component measures of SES, there is advantage in higher family income and higher household wealth. Most assets assessed under family wealth are somewhat distant from literacy learning (e.g., water and energy source to dwelling, number of rooms, type of roof) but there are also studies that have used ownership of literacy-relevant possessions such as play materials, study materials, study furniture, televisions, and computers as proxies for both family income and wealth (twenty-five countries: Chudgar & Luschei, 2009). The evidence is mixed for such possessions as predictors. For example, the ownership of a study table showed positive associations with grade-level language tests in five countries but not in another five (sub-Saharan Africa:[1] Smith & Barrett, 2011). Despite significant associations, the ownership of books is no longer a unique predictor of emergent literacy after accounting for a composite of family income and parent education level (South Africa: Willenberg, 2004). In the primary and middle-school years, book ownership is a consistent predictor for reading fluency and performance on grade-level achievement tests both in the home and in another language (e.g., Sri Lanka: Aturupane, Glewwe, & Wisniewski, 2013; Ethiopia: McCormac, 2012; Piper, 2010; six developing countries: Park, 2008; eleven Latin American countries: Willms & Somers, 2001; ten sub-Saharan countries: Smith & Barrett, 2011), but the pattern remains mixed with reading accuracy and reading comprehension (Zimbabwe: Chinyama et al., 2012; India: Sen & Blatchford, 2001). The reasons for the mixed results on ownership advantage are not clear, but evidence from research on shared book reading, for example, suggests that it may be the quality and quantity of use rather than ownership itself that make literacy assets a useful proxy measure of SES.

Family members with a greater number of years of formal education can bring several useful resources to support the child's literacy learning. They may use reading and writing activities at home, showing children the functions of literacy in daily life; they may also have higher levels of vocabulary in the home language and greater proficiency in the school language (e.g., Ecuador: Schady, 2011; Nepal: LeVine et al., 2012). The evidence for an advantage from a higher family education level is, however, also mixed both for the component skills of literacy and within different contexts. The education level of each

---

[1] Communities in each study are identified by country or region. No assumption is being made that the country or region presents a uniform sociocultural context.

parent is often independently associated with primary-school achievement tests (multiple sub-Saharan countries: Smith & Barrett, 2011; Philippines: Huang, 2009; Sri Lanka: Aturupane et al., 2013) but not always (e.g., Guatemala: McEwan & Trowbridge, 2007). Similarly, in the early years, parent education is a predictor of emergent literacy skills in some locations but not in others (India: Vagh, 2009; South Africa: Willenberg, 2004). Ethnographic evidence show that higher family education levels confer family members with the skills and proficiencies to fill gaps in school instruction, but that tutoring beliefs and processes of role allocation also play an influential role in whether home tutoring will be initiated (Nag et al., 2019). Nonetheless, the main trend in the data is that family education level accounts for variation in literacy outcomes in most contexts.

Urbanicity (urban-suburban-rural), attributes of the school, push and pull factors for child labor, and hierarchies of privilege linked to gender, cultural identity, ethnicity, religion, health, and disability are the other social stratifiers found in our review (Shure et al., 2014). The relationship between these characteristics and children's literacy attainments is context sensitive. For example, while a boy advantage in literacy attainment is often reported, this is not a universal. A girl advantage is seen in some communities (e.g., in Madagascar: Fernald et al., 2011; Philippines: Huang, 2009; Sri Lanka: Aturupane et al., 2013; Tanzania: Yu & Thomas, 2008; Vietnam: Griffin and Thanh, 2006), and sometimes the gender advantage switches over depending on age band (e.g., in India: Bandyopadhyay, 2012; Peru: Stevenson, Chen, & Booth, 1990). An urban advantage on grade-level achievement tests is also a strong trend (Bangladesh: Sarker & Davey, 2009; fourteen African countries: Hungi & Thuku, 2010) but in some countries rural disadvantage is reduced by effective schools, and by the level of road connectivity, "modernization" and industrialization because such infrastructure brings better schools for children and employment opportunities for family members, with increased family income, household wealth, and opportunities for further education (e.g., India: Sharma, 1997; Nag, 2007; Belize, Kenya, Nepal: Gauvain & Munroe, 2009; Vietnam: Ikeda, 2010). Meanwhile, urban disadvantage can increase because of greater linguistic diversity in urban than in rural areas and instruction in all home languages not being available (e.g., India: Vagh, 2009). In addition, the disadvantages already accrued because of gender, urbanicity, sociocultural identity, and/or disability multiply when the child is in a lower-SES family.

Overall, therefore, the component SES measures of level of family income, household wealth, and parental education may have direct and/or indirect effect on child outcomes. These measures are indicators of children's access to literacy resources; they are also indicators of whether disadvantage on other social stratifiers will additionally impact literacy outcomes.

15.4 Literacy Teaching Practices at Home

Fifteen multivariate studies show the effects of literacy-focused home interactions on literacy outcomes to vary by context, component skill, and grade of the child. In the preschool years, teaching at home is a predictor of individual differences in emergent writing skills, but not concepts about print, oral language and symbol knowledge (Chile: Strasser & Lissi, 2009; India: Sen & Blatchford, 2001; Vagh, 2009; South Africa: Willenberg, 2004). In the early grades, family members helping with school assignments (homework) is a predictor of the component skills of reading fluency and reading comprehension, but this trend does not recur in multilingual contexts (e.g., Ethiopia: McCormac, 2012; Piper, 2010; India: Sen & Blatchford, 2001). Similarly in the later grades the beneficial effects of help with homework on grade-level achievement or reading comprehension measures are mixed (e.g., sub-Saharan Africa, home tutoring effects are positive for one country, nonsignificant for five, and negative for four: Smith & Barrett, 2011). Ethnographic studies show the reasons for mixed results across country contexts, and include family members not knowing the school language, not having sufficient level of literacy, and issues around role allocation for who-should-do-what to support the child's literacy learning (Nag et al., 2019).

The duration of teaching time supported by the home (i.e., study hours, hours spent on school assignments) also shows mixed effects, with one study not finding confirmation for the hypothesis that too much study time at home has negative literacy outcomes (e.g., Vietnam: Rolleston & Krutikova, 2014; Sri Lanka: Aturupane et al., 2013; Philippines: Huang, 2009). A family's investment in paid tutoring is another attribute of the home. The outcome of such investment on grade-level attainments is nonsignificant once school- and teacher-level effects are taken into account (fourteen African countries: Yu & Thomas, 2008; but see Sri Lanka: Aturupane et al., 2013).

Several family members may be involved in teaching at home. A parent, sibling or another family member as the tutor does not change the pattern of associations with attainments in emergent literacy, but it does for literacy attainments in primary and middle school. Measures of father involvement and sibling involvement, while beneficial in some contexts, can also show nonsignificant or negative effects (e.g., Ethiopia: different trends in McCormac, 2012 and Piper, 2010). A mother-involvement advantage is seen in some contexts, while in others it is nonsignificant (no negative effects reported in this small evidence base). Ineffective routines at home may lead to nonsignificant or negative effects. We did not find this hypothesis assessed in any multifactorial study, but the ethnographies provide a clue: Spontaneous literacy teaching at home is often ambiguous in focus or faithful to routines preferred in school. Meanwhile, school-like home-literacy teaching is

> **Box 1: Ethnographies of classroom literacy practices (from Nag, Snowling, & Asfaha, 2016)**
>
> A review of the "what" and "how" of literacy practices from eleven countries shows that some skills dominate class time. Literacy instruction leans toward developing orthographic knowledge, transcription (handwriting), and presentation skills. Class time is limited for the development of broader language skills and general knowledge, both of which are essential for reading comprehension and narrative writing. Many of the contexts in our review have a rich tradition of sound games, logic games, or folk narratives, but a lively engagement with these cultural-linguistic resources is not observed. Teaching methods are instead restricted to a prescribed textbook, are weak on explanation, and depend substantially on choral lessons, copy writing, and learning from peers. Responsive teaching practices are described, and these are usually around developing orthographic knowledge or presentation skills. Together, these classroom ethnographies suggest that many children are not receiving simultaneous support for the growth of several component skills of language and literacy.

problematic if classroom instruction itself is skewed to promote some skills and neglect others (see Box 1).

Six training interventions with a focus on low-literate family members show positive effects on literacy-supporting attributes of the family member. Significant improvements are seen in confidence in initiating literacy teaching practices at home, and one study shows that these effects are moderated by intensity of participation. When desegregated or qualitative data are available, the data show that tangible home attributes are quick to improve (e.g., frequency and duration of study/tutoring time, number of books, daily monitoring of homework). Effects are minimal or nonsignificant for measures of engagement (e.g., responsive methods for cognitive and language stimulation, estimating children's learning gains over time). It is not clear whether low effects are a matter of dosage and whether longer-term support to family members can improve teaching that demands higher-order proficiencies.

A final point is the need for caution in interpreting trends related to literacy teaching practices at home because of the genetic account of inherited neurocognitive strengths and weaknesses. For example, a within-parent/family member profile of cognitive-linguistic strengths and weaknesses may mediate both literacy teaching practices at home and the within-child profile of strengths and weaknesses for literacy learning, which together then contribute to children's literacy attainments.

15.5 Home Language and School Language

The association of literacy attainments with proficiency and use of the school language is context sensitive. Of twelve multivariate studies, seven find a home language advantage. The quantity of experience of the school language outside of the school is a predictor of performance on grade-level achievement tests and this association is typically found in the later grades (e.g., ten sub-Saharan African countries: Smith & Barrett, 2011; fourteen Southern and Eastern African countries: Yu & Thomas, 2008; Vietnam: Hungi, 2008). Nonsignificant results are reported in studies examining associations with emergent literacy and also literacy tasks in middle school. An explanation for the nonsignificant results is not immediately clear but perhaps these contexts are characterized by limited variability in engagement with children's school learning or in the use of the school language for daily activities (India: Sen & Blatchford, 2001; Vagh, 2009; Morocco: Wagner, 1993; Kenya: Mount-Cors, 2011; Sri Lanka: Aturupane et al., 2013).

Home and school language dynamics also vary across contexts (e.g., Morocco: Wagner, 1993; Kenya: Mount-Cors, 2011, India: Shah-Wundenberg at al., 2012). Families may choose literacy instruction in the dominant language of a region and unwittingly lock themselves out of the child's learning journey because their own proficiency in the school language is limited. Family members sometimes describe teachers as unskilled in language teaching because they show no appreciation for children's emerging proficiency in the school language or the child's effort in learning the new language. Teachers may also ignore home languages, although even in restrictive schools the home language is described as surfacing outside the classroom, or when children are left unsupervised. Finally, when there are instances of bringing the home language into instruction, then code-switching (switching between two languages) is reported and utilized by teachers for explanation (Nag et al., 2016).

Three intervention studies for parents weak in the school language show positive effects (India: Shah-Wundenberg, et al., 2012; Morocco: Rochidi, 2009; Uganda: Parry, Kirabo, & Nakayato, 2014). These interventions span between twelve and twenty-four sessions, with one intervention reporting modest-to-strong beneficial effects (data unavailable for the rest). Qualitative analysis of outcomes also shows increased parental use of code-switches into the school language, greater parental confidence in asking about and praising the child for their schoolwork, and more solution-seeking through materials such as bilingual dictionaries and asking help from others in the environment who are more fluent in the language.

In summary, home language advantage is context sensitive; home languages are often not valued for literacy learning in school; systematic participation from the home is sometimes precluded by low proficiency in the school language; and interventions with parents on skills related to the school language show beneficial outcomes for children's language and literacy skills.

15.6 Explanatory Mechanisms

A possibility to consider is whether the context-sensitive role of socioeconomic and sociocultural factors in literacy learning may be underpinned by common explanatory mechanisms. We examine some of these potential explanatory mechanisms next, with a narrative summary of the studies that informed each mechanism.

Marginalization, alienation from school. Marginalization has many sources and may occur across many contexts. For example, prejudice and teacher insensitivity toward certain cultural groups can lead children away from schools. Equally, there are descriptions of negative attitudes from communities toward the school (e.g., Pakistan: Farah, 1991). Marginalization and alienation from the school system are particularly experienced lower in the sociodemographic hierarchy; for example, by indigenous, nomadic, and migrant families (Bangladesh: Sarker & Davey, 2009; Mexico: Azuara, 2009; India: Dyer, 2000). Language dominance is another source of alienation; this is seen, for instance, when teachers undervalue children's home languages (e.g., Swaziland: Dlamini, 2009). Cultural norms may also snatch away opportunities from select groups. In some countries for example, girls have limited opportunities to practice and maintain their literacy skills outside of school (e.g., Morocco: Spratt, Seckinger, & Wagner, 1991). Thus, prejudice and disregard may take many forms, but a common theme is the experience of marginalization and its potential to push children away from literacy learning.

Limited access, limited variety. Market forces and sociocultural norms influence a child's experience of literacy. In low-income contexts, useful materials and qualified tutors are out of reach because of cost. This leads to a lower variety of learning materials at home (e.g., South Africa: Van Staden & Howie, 2012; Ghana, Zimbabwe: Ngwaru & Opoku-Amankwa, 2010; India: Sen & Blatchford, 2001; multiple countries: Park, 2008; Guatemala: McEwan & Trowbridge, 2007). Similar disadvantages can carry over into schools, including when grade peers also have limited access to opportunities (Bolivia: McEwan & Jimenez, 2002; China, India, Mexico, and Guinea: Carron & Chau, 2009; Vietnam: Rolleston & Krutikova, 2014). Increased cost and reduced variety also occur due to the absence of a vibrant publishing industry for children (e.g., in Quechua: de la Piedra, 2006; in Mayan: Azuara, 2009), and when children live in isolated communities (e.g., India: Sharma, 1997; Vietnam: Ikeda, 2010). Limited access to a variety of literacy artifacts and opportunities are thus a characteristic linked to many sociocultural contexts of disadvantage.

Breaks in literacy instruction. Frequent absence from school disrupts literacy instruction. In high-poverty contexts, "hunger, fee arrears, dirty uniforms due to lack of water, sickness of the child, and absence of mother due to the search for income-generating labour lead to the child missing school" (Kenya: Mount-Cors, 2011, p. 170). Push factors toward school dropout and into child labor are other reasons; here the triggers include culturally entrenched gender roles, and financial urgency (e.g., eleven Latin American countries: Gunnarsson, Orazem, & Sanchez, 2006; Malawi: Nankhuni & Findeis, 2004). Low school attendance may also occur due to seasonal migration for work (e.g., China: Zhao, Valcke, Desoete, & Verhaeghe, 2012; Mexico: Azuara & Reyes, 2011), when school is far from home (Afghanistan: Burde & Linden, 2013; Cambodia: Nonoyama-Tarumi & Bredenberg, 2009) and when children are victims of abuse or are often ill (e.g., Swaziland: Dlamini, 2009). Absence from school is thus a common manifestation of multiple sociocultural processes.

The next two mechanisms are proximal to the very process of literacy learning and are usually discussed in the context of within-child factors. They are, however, equally likely to be triggered by socioeconomic and sociocultural factors.

Shallow consolidation. The pace of literacy learning is speeded up when component skills of literacy become automatic. Orthographic processes in the early years, fluency in the early grades, and reading comprehension and narrative writing throughout development all need time for learning, and well-secured lower-order skills support the development of complex skills. Most factors that slow down the pace of learning exert their influence by disrupting this process of consolidation. Mechanisms like limited access, limited variety, and frequent breaks in instruction place constraints on the practice needed for consolidation. The factors of low socioeconomic status, low skills in family members to teach at home, and language dynamics can also constrain practice.

Fragmented development. Learning stabilizes when all literacy-related skills work together. But a true coherence across spoken and written language as well as the language processing and language production systems appears to be missing for many children. Several studies in the review report a divergent skills profile where children's reading comprehension and expressive writing lag far behind their orthographic knowledge and handwriting (transcription). Such fragmented literacy development, especially of higher-order skills, reduces readiness for further instruction. Skew in explicit instruction may cause this fragmentation in development (Box 1). Put differently, if guided instruction and opportunity to practice is focused only on some skills, then only those skills may develop; this skew may also occur due to family-level factors impacting the focus of home tutoring. For example, when there is a low level of family education, low proficiency among family members in the child's school language, or low availability of literacy artifacts at home, there may be little demand for the child to demonstrate higher-order literacy skills at home; this lack of push within the home may also be a reason why literacy development plateaus in some domains.

In summary, even over-arching sociocultural constructs such as marginalization and alienation from school, are not comprehensive enough explanations for unequal literacy attainments. Instead, a relatively more comprehensive account for the role of socioeconomic and sociocultural factors in low attainments comes from the mechanisms related to poverty, disrupted instruction, and a quality of learning that is shallow and fragmented . These mechanisms appear to explain the nature of associations between socioeconomic and sociocultural resources and literacy development in a wide-ranging set of contexts.

15.7 Future Directions

The evidence base synthesized in this review is reasonable in size but scattered in focus. Some component skills of language and literacy are clearly underrepresented in the literature; more studies are needed that examine oral language, narrative writing, inference making, and affective-motivational skills. A hypothesis that still needs examination is that the impact of sociocultural factors changes over time, and the child's level of attainment and motivation modulates this change. More research focus is also needed on the quality of talk and guided support during literacy teaching sessions at home; this line of research will likely have a greater potential to capture the sociocultural underpinnings of home-literacy practices compared to measures of frequency and duration of tutoring (see also Friedlander and Goldenberg, Chapter 18 and Schwarz, Chapter 19 in this volume). Another important point for the research agenda is to develop multifactorial models to account for the reciprocal influences between sociodemographic variables such as parent education, within-family variables such as proficiency in the school language, and within-child variables such as grade-level achievement. Intra-household analysis, in particular, stands out as a valuable tool in understanding such interactions.

In the area of interventions, robust evidence for what works is needed when enabling conditions are replaced by challenging ones such as weak proficiency in the school language, teachers who have received poor-quality training, parents who are locked out of the child's learning activities, and children whose skills are shaky or fragmented. In addition, interventions that are insensitive to local cultural practices are problematic (see Asfaha and Nag, Chapter 16 in this volume). Such interventions push out local methods and a potential consequence of this insensitivity is the alienating of teachers, families, and children. However, what is to be considered as "culture-sensitive" remains ambiguous but examples of good practice would be including materials that draw upon local oral traditions, and acknowledging teachers' own pedagogical preferences (Tanzania: Jukes, Mgonda, Tibenda, & Sitabkhan, 2023). Another step in this direction is to embed oral language and inference-focused interventions within common classroom practices such as choral lessons, writing for learning, and peer tutoring (Nag et al., 2016). A comparison of effect sizes of such culture-sensitive interventions with a more functional culture-neutral intervention is an important task on the research agenda. This line of research can also review whether established intervention models have been biased by assumptions from a narrow band of sociocultural contexts.

The theoretical framework for synthesizing the literature in this review has been around outcomes specific to children. A sociocultural perspective would further argue that high literacy attainments in children introduce changes in the home and community environment, bringing both tangible and intangible resources for the next generation of learners. This social change is particularly important because deprivation of literacy-enhancing skills, routines, and assets is sometimes a result of historical neglect, making children from some communities more vulnerable to persistent literacy failure. Downstream effects of improved literacy attainments on sociocultural factors are also an important area of research, and developing intergenerational datasets on literacy and livelihoods fits particularly well within this research agenda.

Multilingual contexts, children who are biliterate or for whom the first language of literacy is not the home language, must receive more attention. The literature shows that current models of literacy learning do not adequately address the psycholinguistic complexities of these contexts and that the current conceptualization of socioeconomic and sociocultural variables such as books at home and tutoring at home retains a simplistic focus on just the school language. The popular sociodemographic measure of parent education also needs review. Parent education has been taken as a proxy of the home environment but, as shown above, skills in home tutoring and literacy support are not always better with higher levels of parental education, and the association of parent as tutor is severed altogether when the parent does not know the school language. Finally, one multicountry study measured literacy environments by exploring "quality" of grade peers on literacy-related parameters and found these measures to be predictors of literacy attainment (Rolleston & Krutikova, 2014). More such assessment of the community literacy environment is needed because it informs multifactorial models of literacy learning beyond child, home, and school factors.

15.8 Educational Implications

This review of multifactorial models has shown that family and household attributes are predictors of literacy outcomes beyond school and within-child factors. This is a clear signal that literacy interventions must go beyond a child and school focus and address the broader literacy environment.[2] One approach would be to strengthen the links between the home, where arguably more culture-embedded resources are available (e.g., folk tales, learning routines), and the school, where perhaps the literacy-relevant resources are concentrated (e.g., trained teachers, library books). For this, a serious barrier is the finding that the relationship between the home and school is often uneasy or neglected entirely by the school. Building teacher awareness of tangible and intangible acts of marginalization is an intervention target to consider. This review, for example, shows that many low-income families struggling to subsist, understand the protective role of regular school attendance and strive to keep children healthy and in school. Teachers who are sensitive to these forms of home support could potentially strengthen home–school connections, and thereby enrich the literacy environment for the child. However, we did not find evidence to unequivocally confirm that raising teacher sensitivity will be sufficient for desired outcomes. Teachers also need a comprehensive pedagogical framework to incorporate children's socioeconomic, sociocultural and linguistic resources into structured literacy instruction, and here several interventions are promising (e.g., Bangladesh: Opel, Ameer, & Aboud, 2009; Kenya, Uganda, Zanzibar/Tanzania: Malmberg, Mwaura, & Sylva, 2011).

Reciprocally, intervention with family members is indicated, although an important caveat is that obvious priorities (e.g., their advancing literacy skills, learning the school language) are slow to develop and the family may find it hard to invest in distant targets. There are some indications in the literature of what to focus on in the short term. When children have too few books, then interventions need to target children's language skills (apart from print-related skills), because their exposure to written language usage will be restricted. If book supply to the home is the intervention strategy, then training family members in how to engage children with these books can be recommended. And in a book engagement intervention, it can be argued that parents may

---

[2] A further reason is the finding that language learning is much more sensitive to the quality of out-of-school experiences than mathematics learning is (e.g., Philippines: Huang, 2009)

themselves benefit from role models. Potential interventions that may be evaluated through, for example, effectiveness trials include (a) assisted reading by parent with child, similar to the growing shared book reading and dialogic reading evidence base in high-income contexts, and (b) active listening to child reading, where parents listen to the child read and engage in the text through discussions. Parents listening to children read may be a particularly promising activity in contexts of low literacy or low proficiency in the school language; here, the child leads in reading and translating the text into the home language and the parent leads in connecting the idea units in the text through extended discussion in the home language.

Before closing, a brief summary of the literature on school effects will be useful. This literature shows that a well-functioning and well-resourced school system benefits contexts of inequality, and the learning benefits are particularly more so for the socioeconomic and socioculturally most disadvantaged (e.g., multiple countries: Chudgar & Luschei, 2009; Crookston et al., 2014). Thus, a clear educational implication is the need to develop a social policy that favors distribution of resources to schools for children from low-income homes. A corollary to this investment would be sustained literacy instruction by skilled teachers aiming to consolidate children's skills and prevent fragmentation in skill development as for example seen in analyses of implementation challenges (Nag, 2023). Some priority areas for strengthening foundation skills are oral language, reading comprehension, narrative writing, and inference making. It may be argued that when there are multiple challenging conditions, intervention effects will be small for such higher-order targets, but it is also likely that these interventions could quickly connect with the child's underlying cognitive-linguistic strengths to fill the learning gap left by deprivation or poverty. The findings from randomized controlled trials are mixed; some interventions show unusually high effect sizes (Bangladesh: Opel et al., 2009; Liberia: Piper & Korda, 2011; Turkey: Bekman, Aksu-Koc, & Erguvanli-Taylan, 2011) while others are unremarkable (India: Borkum, He, & Linden, 2012; Uganda, Kenya: Lucas et al., 2014). Although these trials differ in their sample characteristics and primary intervention targets, a discernible trend is for larger effect size when there is more intensive focus on teacher skills and proficiencies.

In conclusion, socioeconomic and sociocultural factors, broadly categorized under socioeconomic status, literacy teaching practices at home, and the home and school language, explain variations in literacy attainments. These factors are often endemic to a social context, and explanatory mechanisms of "why" and "how" they have an influence include themes of alienation from school, limited variety in resources, and breaks in instruction. Divergence in literacy attainments due to socioeconomic and sociocultural factors is also arguably attributable to two further mechanisms, "shallow consolidation" and "fragmented development." These mechanisms are easily triggered in contexts of disadvantage and have an immediacy of impact on literacy attainment. They also provide the first principles for educational practice, which are to prioritize (a) access to resources and (b) instruction that consolidates skills and reduces fragmented development. A further finding is that socioeconomic and sociocultural factors are selective in their impact on component skills of language and literacy (see also Asfaha & Nag, Chapter 16 and Friedlander & Goldenberg, Chapter 18 in this volume). Future research must focus on confirming when causal inferences are warranted.

Acknowledgments

The review was supported by a grant from the Department for International Development (DfID) to M. J. Snowling, SN, S. Chiat, and C. Torgerson, and from the British Academy to SN. Preparation of this chapter was supported by a grant from The Promise Foundation (India).

References

Studies marked with an asterisk are included in this review.

*Aturupane, H., Glewwe, P., & Wisniewski, S. (2013). The impact of school quality, socioeconomic factors, and child health on students' academic performance: Evidence from Sri Lankan primary schools. *Education Economics, 21*(1), 2–37. DOI: https://doi.org/10.1080/09645292.2010.511852.

*Azuara, P. (2009). Literacy practices in a changing cultural context: The literacy development of two emergent Mayan-Spanish bilingual children. *Dissertation Abstracts International Section A: Humanities and Social Sciences, 70*(6-A), 1885.

*Azuara, P., & Reyes, I. (2011). Negotiating worlds: A young Mayan child developing literacy at home and at school in Mexico. *Compare: A Journal of Comparative and International Education, 41*(2), 181–194.

Babayiğit, S., & Stainthorp, R. (2010). Component processes of early reading, spelling, and narrative writing skills in Turkish: A longitudinal study. *Reading and Writing: An Interdisciplinary Journal, 23*(5), 539–568.

*Bandyopadhyay, T. (2012). Gender and school participation: Evidences from Empirical Research in Madhya Pradesh and Chhattisgarh. NUEPA Occasional Paper 41. New Delhi, India: National University of Educational Planning and Administration.

*Bekman, S., Aksu-Koc, A., & Erguvanli-Taylan, E. (2011). Effectiveness of an intervention program for six-year-olds: A summer-school model. *European Early Childhood Education Research Journal, 19*(4), 409–431.

Borkum, E., He, F., & Linden, L. L. (2012). School libraries and language skills in Indian primary schools: A randomized evaluation of the Akshara Library Program.

NBER Working Paper No. 18183 (pp. 0–0): National Bureau of Economic Research. MA 02138-5398.

*Burde, D. & Linden, L. L. (2013). Bringing education to Afghan girls: A randomised controlled trial of village-based schools. *American Economic Journal: Applied Economics*, 5(3), 27–40.

*Carron, G., & Chau, T. N. (2009). *The Quality of Primary Schools in Different Development Contexts*. Paris: UNESCO.

*Chinyama, A., Svesve, B., Gambiza, B. et al. (June 2012). *Literacy Boost Zimbabwe Baseline Report*. Save the Children.

*Chiu, M. M., & Chow, B. W. Y. (2010). Culture, motivation, and reading achievement: High school students in 41 countries. *Learning and Individual Differences*, 20(6), 579–592.

Chudgar, A., & Luschei, T. F. (2009). National income, income inequality, and the importance of schools: A hierarchical cross-national comparison. *American Educational Research Journal*, 46(3), 626–658.

Crookston, B. T., Forste, R., McClellan, C., Georgiadis, A., & Heaton, T. B. (2014). Factors associated with cognitive achievement in late childhood and adolescence: The Young Lives cohort study of children in Ethiopia, India, Peru, and Vietnam. *BMC Pediatrics*, 14, 253. https://bmcpediatr.biomedcentral.com/articles/10.1186/1471-2431-14-253.

*de la Piedra, M. T. (2006). Literacies and Quechua oral language: Connecting sociocultural worlds and linguistic resources for biliteracy development. *Journal of Early Childhood Literacy*, 6(3), 383–406.

*de la Piedra, M. T. (2010). Religious and self-generated Quechua literacy practices in the Peruvian Andes. *International Journal of Bilingual Education and Bilingualism*, 13(1), 99–113.

*Dlamini, S. M. (2009). Early language and literacy learning in a peripheral African setting: A study of children's participation in home and school communicative and literacy practices in and around Manzini, Swaziland. (Unpublished doctoral thesis. University of Cape Town, South Africa.)

*Dyer, C. (2000). "Education for All" and the Rabaris of Kachchh, Western India. *International Journal of Educational Research*, 33(3), 241–251.

*Elbeheri, G., & Everett, J. (2007). Literacy ability and phonological processing skills amongst dyslexic and non-dyslexic Speakers of Arabic. *Reading and Writing: An Interdisciplinary Journal*, 20(3), 273–294.

Eng, S., Szmodis, W., Mulsow, M. (2014). Cambodian parental involvement: The role of parental beliefs, social networks, and trust. *The Elementary School Journal*, 114 (4), 573–594.

*Farah, I. (1991). School ka sabaq: Literacy in a girls' primary school in rural Pakistan. *Working Papers in Educational Linguistics*, 7(2), 59–81.

*Fernald, L. C., Weber, A., Galasso, E., & Ratsifandrihamanana, L. (2011). Socioeconomic gradients and child development in a very low income population: Evidence from Madagascar. *Developmental Science*, 14(4), 832–847.

*Gauvain, M., & Munroe, R. L. (2009). Contributions of societal modernity to cognitive development: A comparison of four cultures. *Child Development*, 80(6), 1628–1642. DOI: https://doi.org/10.1111/j.1467-8624.2009.01358.x.

Gough, D., Thomas, J., & Oliver, S. (2012). Clarifying differences between review designs and methods. *Systematic Reviews*, *1*(28). DOI: https://doi.org/10.1186/2046-4053-1-28.

*Griffin, P., & Thanh, M. T. (2006). Reading achievements of Vietnamese Grade 5 pupils. *Assessment in Education: Principles, Policy and Practice*, *13*(2), 155–177.

*Gunnarsson, V., Orazem, P. F., & Sanchez, M. A. (2006). Child labor and school achievement in Latin America. *World Bank Economic Review*, *20*(1), 31–54.

*Huang, F. (2009). The role of socio-economic status, out- of-school time, and schools: Multi-level assessments of factors associated with academic achievement. (Phd dissertation Curry School of Education University of Virginia.)

*Hungi, N. (2008). Examining differences in mathematics and reading achievement among Grade 5 pupils in Vietnam. *Studies in Educational Evaluation*, *34*(3), 155–164.

*Hungi, N., & Thuku, F. W. (2010). Variations in reading achievement across 14 Southern African school systems: Which factors matter? *International Review of Education*, *56*(1), 63–101.

*Ikeda, M. (2010). Effective primary schools in geographically isolated areas of Vietnam. (Doctoral thesis, Columbia University, USA.) http://search.proquest.com/professional/docview/870287845?accountid=15181.

Jukes, M. C. H., Mgonda, N. L., Tibenda, J. L., & Sitabkhan, Y. (2023). The role of teachers' implicit social goals in pedagogical reforms in Tanzania. *Oxford Review of Education*, *49*(1), 10–28. DOI:https://doi.org/10.1080/03054985.2022.2093178.

* LeVine, R., LeVine, S., Schnell-Anzola, B., Rowe, M. L., & Dexter, E. (2012). *Literacy and Mothering: How Women's Schooling Changes the Lives of the World's Children*. Oxford: Oxford University Press.

Lucas, A. M., McEwan, P. J., Ngwara, M., & Oketch, M. (2014). Improving early-grade literacy in East Africa: Experimental evidence from Kenya and Uganda. *Journal of Policy Analysis and Management*, *33*, 950–976.

Malmberg, L., Mwaura, P., & Sylva, K. (2011). Effects of a preschool intervention on cognitive development among East-African preschool children: A flexibly time-coded growth model. *Early Childhood Research Quarterly*, *26*, 124–133.

McCartney, K., & Dearing, E. (2002). Evaluating effect sizes in the policy arena. *The Evaluation Exchange: Harvard Family Research Project*, *8*(1), 3–29.

*McCormac, M. (2012). Literacy and educational quality improvement in Ethiopia: A mixed method study. (Unpublished doctoral dissertation. Department of Education Leadership, Higher Education and International Education, University of Maryland, USA.)

*McEwan, P. J., & Jimenez, W. (2002). *Indigenous Students in Bolivian Primary Schools: Patterns and Determinants of Inequities. A World Bank Study*. Girls' education working paper series. Washington, DC: World Bank Group.

* McEwan, P. J., & Trowbridge, M. (2007). The achievement of indigenous students in Guatemalan primary schools. *International Journal of Educational Development*, *27*, 61–76.

*Mkhize, D. N. (2013). The nested contexts of language use and literacy learning in a South African fourth grade class: Understanding the dynamics of language and literacy practices. (Doctoral thesis, University of Illinois at Urbana-Champaign, USA.)

Mol, S., Bus, A., de Jong, M., & Smeets, D. (2008). Added value of dialogic parent-child book readings: A meta-analysis. *Early Education and Development, 19*, 7–26.

*Mount-Cors, M. F. (2011). Homing in: Mothers at the heart of health and literacy in coastal Kenya. *Dissertation Abstracts International Section A: Humanities and Social Sciences, 72*(1–A), 137.

*Nag, S. (2007). Early reading in Kannada: The pace of acquisition of orthographic knowledge and phonemic awareness. *Journal of Research in Reading, 30*(1), 7–22.

Nag, S. (2023). Teaching and learning: What matters for intervention. *Oxford Review of Education, 49*(1), 1–9. DOI: https://doi.org/10.1080/03054985.2023.2161197.

Nag, S., Chiat, S., Torgerson, C., & Snowling, M. J. (2014). *Literacy, Foundation Learning and Assessment in Developing Countries: Final Report*. London: EPPI-Centre, Social Science Research Unit, University of London. www.gov.uk/government/uploads/system/uploads/attachment_data/file/305150/Literacy-foundation-learning-assessment.pdf.

Nag, S., & Snowling, M. J. (2011). Cognitive profiles of poor readers of Kannada. *Reading and Writing: An Interdisciplinary Journal, 24*(6), 657–676.

Nag, S., Snowling, M. J., & Asfaha, Y. (2016). Classroom literacy practices in low- and middle-income countries: An interpretative synthesis of ethnographic studies. *Oxford Education Review, 42*(1), 36–54. DOI: https://doi.org/10.1080/03054985.2015.1135115.

Nag, S., Vagh, S. B.,Dulay, K, M. & Snowling, M. J. (2019)). Home language, school language and children's literacy attainments: A systematic review of evidence from low- and middle-income countries. *Review of Education, 7*(1), 91–150. DOI: https://doi.org/10.1002/rev3.3130.

*Nankhuni, F. J., & Findeis, J. L. (2004). Natural resource-collection work and children's schooling in Malawi. *Agricultural Economics, 31*(2–3), 123–134.

National Reading Panel [Institute of Child Health and Human Development]. (2000). *Report of the National Reading Panel. Teaching Children to Read: An Evidence-Based Assessment of the Scientific Research Literature on Reading and Its Implications for Reading Instruction* (NIH Publication No. 00–4769). Washington, DC: US Government Printing Office.

*Ngwaru, J. M., & Opoku-Amankwa, K. (2010). Home and school literacy practices in Africa: Listening to inner voices. *Language and Education, 24*(4), 295–307.

*Nonoyama-Tarumi, Y., & Bredenberg, K. (2009). Impact of school readiness program interventions on children's learning in Cambodia. *International Journal of Educational Development, 29*(1), 39–45.

Opel, A., Ameer, S. S., & Aboud, F. E. (2009). The effect of preschool dialogic reading on vocabulary among rural Bangladeshi children. *International Journal of Educational Research, 48*(1), 12–20.

*Park, H. (2008). Home literacy environments and children's reading performance: A comparative study of 25 countries. *Educational Research and Evaluation, 14*(6), 489–505.

*Parry, K., Kirabo, E., & Nakayato, G. (2014). Working with parents to promote children's literacy: A family literacy project in Uganda. *Multilingual Education*, 4 (13). https://multilingual-education.springeropen.com/articles/10.1186/s13616-014-0013-2.

*Piper, B. (2010). *Ethiopia Early Grade Reading Assessment. Data Analytic Report: Language and Early Learning.* Ed Data II Task Number 7 and Ed Data II Task Number. Addis Ababa: USAID Ethiopia.

*Piper, B., & Korda, M. (2011). *EGRA Plus: Liberia. Program Evaluation Report.* Research Triangle Park, NC: RTI International USA.

*Rochidi, A. (2009). Developing pre-literacy skills via shared book reading: The effect of linguistic distance in a diglossic context. *Dissertation Abstracts International: Section B: The Sciences and Engineering, 70*(8–B), 4801.

*Rolleston, C., & Krutikova, S. (2014). Equalising opportunity? School quality and home disadvantage in Vietnam. *Oxford Review of Education, 40*(1), 112–131.

*Sarker, P., & Davey, G. (2009). Exclusion of indigenous children from primary education in the Rajshahi Division of Northwestern Bangladesh. *International Journal of Inclusive Education, 13*(1), 1–11.

*Sen, R., & Blatchford, P. (2001). Reading in a second language: Factors associated with progress in young children. *Educational Psychology, 21*(2), 189–202.

*Schady, N. (2011). Parents' education, mothers' vocabulary, and cognitive development in early childhood: Longitudinal evidence from Ecuador. *American Journal of Public Health, 101*(12), 2299–2307.

* Shah-Wundenberg, M., Wyse, D., & Chaplain, R. (2012). Parents helping their children to read: The effectiveness of paired reading and hearing reading in a developing country context. *Journal of Early Childhood Literacy, 13*(4), 471–500.

*Sharma, R. (1997). Dynamics of learning three R's in Madhya Pradesh. *Economic and Political Weekly, 32* (17), 891–901.

Shure, D., Parameshwaran, M., Nag, S. & Snowling, M. J. (2014). *Economic and Social Factors related to Literacy and Foundation Learning.* Technical Report No. 5: Literacy. Foundation Learning and Assessment in Developing Countries. Oxford: University of Oxford.

*Smith, M., & Barrett, A. M. (2011). Capabilities for learning to read: An investigation of social and economic effects for Grade 6 learners in Southern and East Africa. *International Journal of Educational Development, 31*(1), 23–36.

*Spratt, J. E., Seckinger, B., & Wagner, D. A. (1991). Literacy in and out of school: A study of functional literacy in Morocco. *Reading Research Quarterly, 26,* 178–195.

*Stevenson, H. W., Chen, C., & Booth, J. (1990). Influences of schooling and urban-rural residence on gender differences in cognitive abilities and academic achievement. *Sex Roles, 23*(9–10), 535–551.

Strasser,K., & Lissi, M. R. (2009). Home and instruction effects on emergent literacy in a sample of Chilean kindergarten children. *Scientific Studies of Reading, 13*(2), 175–204. DOI: https://doi.org/10.1080/10888430902769525.

*Vagh, S. B. (2009). The role of classroom literacy environments in supporting young children's language and emergent literacy development: A longitudinal study in Mumbai, India. (Doctoral thesis presented to the Faculty of the Graduate School of Education of Harvard University.)

Votruba-Drzal, E., Miller, P., & Coley, R. L. (2016). Poverty, urbanicity, and children's development of early academic skills. *Child Development Perspectives, 10*(1), 3–9.

*Wagner, D. A. (1993). *Literacy, Culture and Development: Becoming Literate in Morocco.* Cambridge: Cambridge University Press.

*Willenberg, I. (2004). Getting set for reading in the Rainbow Nation: Emergent literacy skills and literacy environments of children in South Africa. (Unpublished doctoral dissertation. Harvard Graduate School of Education, Massachusetts.)

*Willms, J., & Somers, M. A. (2001). Family, classroom, and school effects on children's educational outcomes in Latin America. *School Effectiveness and School Improvement, 12*(4), 409–445.

Winskel, H., & Widjaja, V. (2007). Phonological awareness, letter knowledge, and literacy development in Indonesian beginner readers and spellers. *Applied Psycholinguistics, 28*(1), 23–45.

*van Staden, S., & Howie, S. (2012). Reading between the lines: Contributing factors that affect Grade 5 student reading performance as measured across South Africa's 11 languages. *Educational Research and Evaluation, 18*(1), 85–98.

*Yu, G., & Thomas, S. M. (2008). Exploring school effects across Southern and Eastern African school systems and in Tanzania. *Assessment in Education: Principles, Policy & Practice, 15*(3), 283–305.

*Zhao, N. N., Valcke, M., Desoete, A., & Verhaeghe, J. (2012). The quadratic relationship between socioeconomic status and learning performance in China by multilevel analysis: Implications for policies to foster education equity. *International Journal of Educational Development, 32*(3), 412–422.

16 Sensitivity to Contextual Factors in Literacy Interventions in the Global South

Yonas Mesfun Asfaha and Sonali Nag

16.1 Introduction

The 1990s saw a sharp rise in the empirical study of literacy interventions across Asia, Africa, Latin America, and other clusters of countries that together have been called the Global South. Arguably, the impetus was the World Conference on Education for All held in Jomtien (Thailand) in March 1990 (Inter-Agency Commission, 1990). A decade on, the effort was formalized further to achieve the UN Millennium Development Goal (MGD 2) of universal primary education by 2015. Providing primary education at scale meant that literacy instruction at scale took center stage. Alongside this development, the measurement of children's learning was maturing as a field, with initiatives such as the multiagency Learning Metrics Task Force (LMTF, 2012–16) turning exceptionally influential in what would be measured and therefore valued as an indicator of success for an educational intervention. It identified literacy and communication as a learning domain, and the ability to read as one of seven areas of measurement for global tracking. The next goalpost, the UN Sustainable Development Goal (SGD 4), is quality education for all by 2030. It has brought to the fore the need for sensitivity as to what constitutes "quality" and to whom. It is against this background that we review experiments with literacy interventions in the Global South. Rigorous reviews of the experiments under consideration have been reported earlier in the context of literacy and foundation learning in developing countries (Nag et al., 2014; Nag, Snowling et al., 2016). Here, we analyze their sensitivity to contextual and cultural factors. We start with a description of the perspectives that led to the focus areas in our qualitative analysis. Then, we present our methodology of using cultural probes to examine interventions and their evaluation. This is followed by a narrative synthesis of the findings and a discussion about the implications for evaluation of the next generation of literacy interventions.

16.2 Why Contextual and Cultural Sensitivity?

The theoretical roots of a contextual analysis of literacy interventions come from sociocultural perspectives on literacy learning, including the "literacy as social practices" account. Within these perspectives, language is considered as a fluid and messy construct, power relations exist in the social contexts where children's language and literacy learning occur, and cultural processes intertwine with teaching-learning processes. Literacy and language education, particularly in bi- and multilingual contexts, are therefore necessarily also influenced by sociolinguistic and sociocultural processes. Such a situated, contextual, and cultural perspective has traditionally recorded the language and literacy practices found in children's schools, classrooms, and homes (e.g., Heath, 1982). The perspective, however, can also be used to problematize and examine the specific language or literacy activities that are chosen and prioritized in an intervention and what is focused on when assessing their effectiveness.

A spotlight on particulars may appear to be at cross-purposes with accounts that solely draw upon universal within-child factors to explain literacy learning. Examples of universal factors include children's phonological awareness, vocabulary knowledge, and grammar knowledge. These are seen as the cognitive-linguistic foundations that support decoding and reading comprehension across linguistic contexts. Other within-child factors include speed of processing, executive functions, working memory, visual processing, and inference making. The language, the writing system, and whether the learner is a novice or an expert may define the strength of associations between these factors and component skills of literacy (e.g., Eritrean and Ethiopic scripts: Asfaha, Kurvers, & Kroon, 2009; South and Southeast Asian scripts: Nag, 2017). Since one explanatory model is not enough to capture language, script, and learner variety, the most tenable account is a moderate rather than a strong universalist view of literacy learning. A further issue in favor of the universal account is its explanatory power in terms of children's literacy attainments as well as of why some activities support learning better than others. These explanations of why there are individual differences in attainments and selective intervention effects are, however, not exhaustive; not all aspects of literacy outcomes can be explained by within-child factors (e.g., the role of socioeconomic status: Hungi & Thuku, 2010; Lervåg et al., 2019; "opportunities to learn" in school and home: Rolleston & Krutikova, 2014; home practices: Dulay, Cheung, & McBride, 2019; Mount-Cors, 2011; Puranik et al., 2018). Thus, an account that includes contextual factors improves our understanding of outcomes.

16.2.1 Experiments and Confidence Expressed by Researchers

Methodologically rigorous intervention trials have been considered essential to assessing the effects of literacy interventions and social policy and reform more broadly (Banerjee & Duflo, 2011; Snowling & Hulme, 2011). These are experimental studies that measure the effect on clearly isolated and specified variable(s) (e.g., children's decoding efficiency) of a well-controlled and carefully manipulated independent variable (the target intervention). Confidence in inferences of causality (the intervention led to the recorded change in the variable), is greatest when it is a randomized controlled trial (RCT), and the use of this design to assess literacy interventions in the Global South has grown.

Randomized controlled trials have been harnessed to understand what the specific causal pathways might be to change. However, this experimental design has been criticized for its reductionist approach and poor attention to contexts of intervention. Despite their rigor, RCTs have failed to provide the level of information within education that the method has provided within, for example, health, nutrition, sanitation, finance, and agriculture. One concern is that the evaluations are in the short term, while longer timescales are needed to better understand the enduring effects of an educational intervention. Incorporating a longer timescale within the RCT is an issue of study design, and there is good reason to believe that longitudinal datasets, despite their rarity within education, can be achieved within the Global South (e.g., Turkey: Kağitçibaşi et al., 2009; India, Vietnam, Peru, and Ethiopia: the Young Lives datasets). The second concern is that measurement has progressed regarding within-child variables but not regarding contextual variables such as quality of teaching and how interventions are reinterpreted by key stakeholders and implementers. A third concern is for experimental trials to more robustly incorporate insights from qualitative methodologies. Examples of qualitative methods include interviews, open-ended field notes, and ethnographic studies. Combining the RCT with qualitative data sources can also help push the focus beyond within-child cognitive-linguistic variables to contextual data such as, for example, sociolinguistic, sociocultural, socioeconomic, institutional, and implementation- and opportunity-related variables. A succinct summary of why the contextual and mixed-methods approach matters is found in the following:

[D]espite a current emphasis in research and policy on attempting to determine *what works*, contexts matter. The fact that contextual influences are multiple and complex makes the work of reading researchers more difficult, and pushes the field to remember that the focus needs to be on *what works, for whom, when, why, and how*. (Kamil et al., 2011, p. xxiv; emphasis in original)

This type of research design assumes an added urgency when considering intervention studies in the Global South. First, many of the interventions we reviewed in middle- and low-income countries were imported programs that were first developed in high-income countries, prompting questions about contextual appropriateness. Second, researchers of reviewed studies expressed confidence in an adapted intervention, and we were interested in examining whether this reported confidence in the intervention had been assessed in the context of the local culture, language, and educational practices.

16.2.2 Sociocultural Responses to Including Context in Literacy Research

Central to the discussion of context is culture that may be said to refer to "the daily patterns of living (cultural practices) that allow individuals to relate to the surrounding social order" (Rueda, 2011, p. 85). Put simply, culture encompasses everyday activities and provides individuals with historically situated patterns for action. Culture is dynamic and it can be assumed that there are many cultures, rather than one grand culture, within a social group. This attention to daily practices can be considered as a response from the sociocultural perspectives to literacy research to calls for avoiding the potential for a "reductionist" approach when mounting an RCT. Studies of cultural factors have focused on how these factors influence school-based acquisition of literacy and learning achievement. These studies most often engage with disadvantaged communities of learners to correct the view that cultures of disadvantaged communities show deficits and to posit that their cultural heritage is a positive resource to harness for learning (e.g., Asfaha & Kroon, 2011; de la Piedra, 2010; Mount-Cors, 2011).

A main concern in this perspective is how students outside the school or mainstream culture face obstacles in achievement when compared with those from within that culture. It is hypothesized that these cultural differences might have an effect on intrapersonal cognitive, motivational, and affective conditions and on interpersonal contexts and settings, "serving to facilitate or constrain participation and interaction" (Rueda, 2011, p. 92). Within this perspective, teachers are therefore urged to practice cultural responsiveness, where they accept and use students' home language and literacy practices and interact with students in ways consistent with the latter's home values (Mount-Cors, 2011; Zhao et al., 2012), and realize that "storytelling and question answering" and the role played by peer learning may be different in different cultures (Nag, Snowling, & Asfaha, 2016; Rueda, 2011). The use of culturally relevant materials and content and deployment of culturally familiar materials are argued to have a positive impact on children's motivation and achievement (Li, 2011; Watanabe, 2015).

Although the bulk of the studies in the sociocultural perspective to literacy have been qualitative in methodological approach, quantitative and mixed-methods studies that examine the linkages between cultural factors and literacy learning outcomes are becoming available. For example, Li (2011) described studies that attempted to measure cultural discontinuities between home and school contexts using a factorial analysis, in order to then use the cultural discontinuity scores to study associations with school achievement.

16.2.3 Literacy as Social Practice

The focus on context in literacy learning and research necessarily leads one to look at how literacy is viewed as a social practice in what has come to be called New Literacy Studies (Street, 1984; 1995). Street argued that the social context for literacy learning varied and "that there are different literacy practices that carry with them different values and affordances" (Street, 2016, p. 336). Within this perspective, the inherently context-free cognitive-linguistic view of literacy learning is contrasted with an "ideological" view, where the focus is on power relations such as those present between the learner and the teacher, the learner and the interventionist, and the learner and the policymaker, to list a few. These power relations are linked to purpose and meaning and what may be considered normative, and include beliefs about specific practices, and how these interact with social stratifiers such as the learner (and the other's) gender, race, age, and health status. One outcome of analysis of power in literacy practices is the critical view on how the literacy that is taught in formal school settings is privileged as the "universal standard"(Street, 2016, p. 337) and the status of out-of-school literacy is no longer valued. While we acknowledge that more needs to be done in the Global South to understand the learning and knowledge gathered by children outside institutionalized school curricula, this is not the focus of this chapter and hence will not be taken up for further discussion (see Nag, Chapter 15 and Friedlander & Goldenberg, Chapter 18 in this volume).

16.2.4 Sociolinguistic and Ethnographic Perspectives on Diversity

Concepts such as diversity and multiculturalism are limited in their power to explain the complexity of different settings (e.g., the multilingual urban centers in the UK: Blackledge & Creese, 2017). Since similar complexities pre-existed in the margins, as well as in mainstream settings, there is a realization that discussions of diversity in reified terms such as language, ethnicity, and race fail to capture the "diversification of diversity" or extreme diversity across the Global South. In addition, our views of linguistic and literacy learning contexts have been informed by conceptualizations of language, multilingualism, and social uses of language within sociolinguistics and ethnographic research, and the intensification of diversity from the mobility accompanying within-country economic shifts and broader globalization, as captured in diaspora research.

Sociolinguistic-ethnographic perspectives view language, in addition to its structural aspects, as something essentially social, and as a fluid and messy construct that lacks a clear boundary when viewed in relation to other languages. Multilingual encounters are constructed in such a way as to unveil the connotations of power or hierarchical relations apparent in the social world. For example, the choice of one or the other national language as school language or as a target of intervention is seldom neutral and carries different implications to different language groups. What is needed is, then, a broader, open yet critical, gaze at how people from different backgrounds come to interact in everyday encounters with each other and with reading and writing (after Blackledge & Creese, 2017).

One indication of the incorporation of context and culture is when literacy interventions acknowledge and are responsive to local factors. For example, all reading programs, irrespective of whether they focus on phonics, whole language, or a mix of the two approaches, are necessarily delivered within the "real-world" milieu of historical, cultural, and linguistic processes (e.g., postcolonial; strong oral tradition; home languages unrecognized in school). We therefore conducted a cultural "audit" of intervention studies published between 1991 and 2016 in low- and middle-income countries. For global literacy, 1990 is the landmark year when the World Conference on Education for All in Jomtien, Thailand (the Inter-Agency Commission, 1990) triggered an international movement to provide literacy instruction (and more) to all children. We first identified contextual factors that were described as important within the sociocultural literature, drawing especially on ethnographies. Intervention studies were reviewed for how these cultural and contextual elements were accounted for in the intervention design, assessment tool, analytic plans, and the interpretation of results. Since all interventions in the review were methodologically high-quality experimental studies, identifying what these studies considered important or relevant to report was seen as indicative of the theoretical and implementational importance given to local factors. The nature of coverage, and thus "cultural sensitivity" in these experiments, has the potential to inform the future design of interventions and also the theoretical underpinnings of literacy research in the Global South.

16.3 Qualitative Analysis of Cultural Probes in Intervention Design and Assessment

16.3.1 Research Questions

Our qualitative review aimed to answer the following questions:
* Are contextual/cultural factors represented in evaluation studies of literacy interventions?
* What are the main representations of these factors?
* Are there gaps in representation of these factors?

Randomized controlled experiments conducted in countries identified as low- and middle-income (World Bank, OECD) provided the database for the review. To examine our questions about representations of contextual and cultural factors, we created a template to guide our cultural probes. We looked for the treatment of contextual factors in three sections of the intervention evaluation reports: (a) the design of the intervention; (b) the assessments used; and (c) the analysis processes. We also noted information not covered by these categories, under issues related to "language" and "other." Assessors (usually the two authors or the first author and a social and cultural psychologist) independently looked for the ways that studies dealt with language diversity, local practices of education, and other cultural elements in different stages of the intervention study. Since the language in which the literacy intervention is carried out has important implications for learning, whether home or school, minority or dominant, foreign or national, we examined how this was recognized in the design of the interventions. Similarly, local educational practices such as choral singing and cultural elements in local games or folk tales may constitute important factors in a particular context (after Nag, Snowling et al., 2016), and we probed whether these were represented in literacy interventions and studies of their effectiveness, and if so, how. We also looked to see how social stratifiers, including gender, income, rural–urban settings, and nomadic-settled lifestyle, were acknowledged. Therefore, our cultural probes aimed to capture contextual factors in the design of interventions, the assessments used in evaluating the interventions, and the analysis of results of the assessment. The thematic analysis of the cultural probe data from across interventions broadly linked to two issues: the language context (e.g., use of folk tales) and the culture and context, not related to language but still relevant (e.g., asking men to run assessments in a conservative school for girls). These qualitative data form the basis of this chapter.

The RCTs for our analysis were published over twenty-six years from 1991 to 2016. All reported an intervention conducted in a low- and middle-income country and had a thematic focus on literacy and foundation learning. These were experiments that had already been reviewed for methodological quality based on the principles of appropriateness, rigor, validity, reliability, openness, transparency and cogency, and clarity of conceptual framing (Nag et al., 2014). Only studies that demonstrated adherence to these principles and were rated as high or moderate-high are included in the current review.

16.3.2 Focus on Randomized Controlled Experiments

The review is based on twenty RCTs reporting seventeen interventions in nine countries. The duration of interventions ranged from four weeks to two years, and the focus of intervention was literacy and numeracy skills (eleven interventions), language skills (four), and school readiness (two). The facilitators were teachers (fourteen), trained volunteers (three), trained facilitators (one), and others such as specialist trainers, school management staff, government officials, and personnel from an agency external to the school system (six). For details see Table 16.1.

Table 16.1 Included randomized controlled experiments by intervention focus, duration, student, and facilitator details

Author, date, Country	Intervention focus	Duration	Level/age targeted	Facilitator	Sample
Abrami et al. (2016), Kenya	Interactive, multimedia literacy instruction	13 weeks (90 minutes weekly lessons)	Grade 2 (7–10 years)	Trained teachers with support from trainers	354 students
Banerjee et al. (2007) (First randomized experiment), India	Remedial instruction on basic literacy and numeracy	2 hours per day for 1 year	Grades 3 & 4 (7–9 years)	Trained volunteers	98 schools
Banerjee et al. (2016), India	Math and literacy instruction; teacher training; materials support	40 days of "learning camps" plus 10-day summer camps	Grades 1–5 (6–12 years)**	Trained teachers, volunteers, government officials	1,156 schools; 35,044 students
Borzekowski & Henry (2010), Indonesia	Educational multimedia targeting language and life skills (*Jalan Sesama* videos)	14 weeks (1 episode per week)	Preschool (3–6 years)	School teachers	160 children; 160 parents
Brooker & Halliday (2015) & Jukes et al. (2016), Kenya	Enhanced literacy instruction	2 years	Grade 1 (90 percent: 7–10 years)**	Teachers and health workers	101 schools; 5233 students
Davidson & Hobbs (2013) and Piper & Korda (2011), Liberia	"teaching literacy using whole-class instruction, prescriptive lesson plans and close monitoring and supervision"(p. 291)	18 months	Grades 2 and 3, (average 12–13 years old)** Grades 1–6**	Trained teachers; coaches	176 schools; 2,988 students; Second intervention = 30 schools

Dowd et al. (2016), *Ethiopia*	Enhanced ELM instruction comprising 50 early literacy & 50 math games	5 months	Preschool (5–6 years)	Trained facilitators	36 Early Childhood centers; 451 students
Gomez Franco (2014), *Chile*	Read-aloud program	1 year	Preschool (3–5 years)	Trained teachers	92 pre-kindergarten classrooms
He, Linden, & McLeod (2008), (First randomized experiment) *India*	Computer-assisted learning (CAL) English program with activities, games, and materials support	1 year	Grades 2 & 3 (6–9 years)*	Trained teachers; outside agency	Experimental grp.: 97 classes; 2,699 students Control grp.: 97 classes; 2,618 students
He, Linden, & McLeod (2009), (First randomized experiment) *India*	Intervention with stories, flashcards, and charts	6 weeks	Grade 1 (4–5 years)	Trained instructors	67 schools; 2,089 students
Kerwin & Thornton (2015), *Uganda*	Mother-tongue instruction, teacher support, & teacher training	1 year	Grades 1–3 (7–9 years)	Trained teachers	38 schools; 1,900 students
Lakshminarayana et al. (2013), *India*	Afterschool remedial math and language support; additional material support for girls	18 months	Grades 2–4 (4–12 years)	Trained community volunteers	Experimental grp.: 107 villages (54 villages received an additional intervention component) Control grp.: 107 villages Total: 4,461 students

Table 16.1 (cont.)

Author, date, Country	Intervention focus	Duration	Level/age targeted	Facilitator	Sample
Lucas et al. (2014), Oketch et al. (2014), *Kenya, Uganda*	Teacher training on "scaffolding approach" to literacy instruction," mentoring of teachers, and material support	Around 18 months	Grades 1–3 (average 6–9 years)*	trained teachers, head teachers, and school management	Kenya: Experimental grp: 3,574 students Control grp.: 3,441 students Uganda: Experimental grp: 3,441; Control: 3,576
Opel, Ameer, & Aboud (2009), *Bangladesh*	Whole-class dialogic reading	4 weeks	Preschool (5–6 years)	Trained preschool teachers	80 students
Ozler et al. (2016), *Malawi*	Teacher training; teacher incentives; parent education	About 6 weeks of teacher training	Preschool (3–5 years)	Trained teachers	189 Community-based Child Care Centers; 5011 children
Piper et al. (2014), *Kenya*	Curriculum, teaching materials and teaching practices aligned with current research; teacher training; materials support	1 year	Grades 1 & 2 (6–8 years)	Trained teachers	73 schools; 2,082 students
Piper et al. (2016), *Kenya*	Mother-tongue literacy instruction	1 year (150 days of instruction)	Grades 1 &2 (7–9 years)	Trained teachers	414 schools; 1,850 students

* Inferred age band.
** Several older children, for example, "most primary grade classrooms are filled with overage students" (Davidson & Hobbs, 2013, p. 285).

16.4 Global Findings on Reform Programs in Literacy Education

The twenty interventions under review attempted to introduce reform programs in literacy education in nine countries in the Global South. We examined how contextual realities were reflected in the design of these interventions, the assessments used in their evaluation, the analysis of results from these assessments, and any other specific intervention-relevant aspect of a particular study.

16.4.1 Nature and Origins of Interventions

The reviewed interventions showed modest localization embedded within a lot of borrowings. The main target of these interventions was increasing the literacy skills of young learners mostly between ages three and nine. Intervention components included provision of teaching materials, introducing best practices in teaching literacy, and/or teacher preparation. A typical description of such an intervention can be found from a study in Kenya, where the literacy intervention was designed to align local teaching practices with "successful models of literacy acquisition in an alphabetic language" in order to tackle "perceived barriers to successful instruction" (Brooker & Halliday, 2015, p. 3). In addition, at least in this same project from Kenya, the intervention "sought to build on effective instructional practices that were already in use locally" (Jukes et al., 2016, p. 451).

However, for most interventions, the ideas introduced in the reforms came from outside the intervention country, mainly from a high-income country in the West. Usually, the central ideas were either borrowed from high-income countries and adapted locally by research teams, or were globally promoted by international agencies and accepted by local NGOs. For example, the multimedia program ABRACADABRA (A Balanced Reading Approach for Children Always Designed to Achieve Best Results for All), also known as ABRA, was based on "systematic reviews of evidence about what works in reading and spelling" by the National Reading Panel that was tasked to address local needs in the United States (Abrami et al., 2016, p. 947). An intervention in Ethiopia was based on an Emergent Literacy and Math (ELM) program developed by the international NGO Save the Children, and provided resources for reading, play, and cooperative games to support literacy and math skills and physical and socio-emotional development (Dowd et al., 2016). Sometimes, explicit geographic reference was made to the origin of the best practices espoused by the intervention. A study in Chile with three-to-five-year-olds, for example, relied in its rationale for intervention development on recommended practices in the United States (Gomez Franco, 2014).

In other cases, we found acknowledgment of the need to bring local practices in line with internationally proven practices "by aligning curriculum and teacher practices with current research" (Kenya: Piper et al., 2014, p. 11). Similar references to the global literature are found in several other studies (e.g., Jukes et al., 2016; Opel et al., 2009). Against this background, adaptations of imported interventions to achieve cultural appropriateness aimed to give due consideration to local cultures and languages. The Primary Math and Reading intervention in Kenya, PRIMR, for example, included locally relevant stories in the literacy intervention (Piper, Zuilkowski, & Mugenda, 2014), and local languages in the consent forms and interview guides (e.g., Afaan Oromo in Ethiopia, Dowd et al., 2016). A match of intervention language with home language was found in a Bangla dialogic story-reading intervention by Opel et al. (2009); all the children and teachers in the study spoke Bangla at home and the Bangla books used for the interventions were locally produced. Taken together, while the effort to adapt foreign ideas into local contexts was present in more than half of the interventions we reviewed, the representation of contextual factors was limited by the inadequacies of definitions of what constitutes the local.

16.4.2 Assessments Used to Evaluate Interventions

Measurement of change is a core element of intervention studies, and we found a preference for globally available assessment frameworks. Prominent among these were the Early Grade Reading Assessment (the United States), the Early Grade Mathematics Assessment (the United States), the Schedule of Early Number Assessment (Australia), and the Reading Recovery Observation Survey (New Zealand). In addition, the use of the Picture Vocabulary subscale of the Woodcock–Muñoz Language Survey Revised (Chile: Gomez Franco, 2014) and the related Peabody Picture Vocabulary Test (Malawi: Ozler, Fernald, Kariger et al., 2016) confirms the popularity of the Peabody-inspired vocabulary tests in interventions in the Global South (Nag, 2016).

Locally produced assessments were available but uncommon, and varied in depth of localization. An example of a more extensive attempt at creating "culturally appropriate" tests is the Malawi Development Assessment Tool (MDAT), for rural Malawi (Ozler et al., 2016). The language, fine motor/perception, gross motor, and personal-social subscales of the MDAT used locally available materials. For example, the language subscale contains items asking the child to explain the use of objects by showing locally available objects "such as a small, homemade broom (used for sweeping), and a matchbox (containing matches, used for lighting stove)," and replaced "apple" with "papaya," "a fruit that is well known throughout the country, and was estimated to be of similar difficulty as the word 'apple' would be in the United States" (Ozler et al., 2016, pp. 56, 57). Dowd et al. (2016) reported similar adaptations using only objects familiar to the child such as rocks, beads, beans, or bottle caps. Translations were, however, by far the most common adaptation. A little over half of the interventions we reviewed (nine interventions) adapted borrowed tests into local intervention languages, with only one third (29 percent, or five) developing own assessments whether in a local language (three interventions) or English (two). Lucas et al. (2014), for example, developed test items in English first and then translated these into the languages of instruction in project sites (Kenya: Swahili; Uganda: Lango).

Two other points are noteworthy: assumptions of when language adaptation is not needed and decisions of when local languages do not need to be the target language. First, close to one fourth of interventions (23.5 percent, or four) retained the language of borrowed assessments because school languages in chosen countries were similar; English (three interventions) and Spanish (one). Here the assumption that the assessment tool did not need language adaptation appeared to be made despite the body of evidence showing how language varieties change across geographies (e.g., World Englishes: Rose & Galloway, 2019). The exception was the acknowledgment that borrowing a North American reading achievement measure would "lack cultural sensitivity to adequately capture the development of reading skills in Kenyan students" (Abrami et al., 2016, p. 962). Second, Davidson and Hobbs (2013) noted that public schools in Liberia use English as a language of instruction and the researchers felt they had to go along with this policy. In this and seven other studies in our review, where English was the language of intervention and assessment, it is not always clear what the roles of the local languages were in administering the assessment. In at least one study, the local language, Marathi, was used to explain a question set even if said in English first (He et al., 2008). In summary, our review suggests variable engagement with the idea of localization of assessment tools coupled with reduced transparency in reporting of localization protocols.

16.4.3   Treatment of Languages and Language Diversity

A further dimension we examined is related to local and nonstandard language varieties in intervention sites. Two interventions aimed at directly developing local-language literacy (Kenya: Piper, Zuilkowski, & Ong'ele, 2016; Uganda: Kerwin & Thornton, 2015). Sometimes the focus on local languages included working, as Kerwin and Thornton (2015) noted in their study in Uganda, to raise awareness by "engaging with parents and the local community to communicate the benefits of mother tongue instruction" (p. 4). However, most interventions (47 percent, or eight interventions) dealt with colonial languages (English, Spanish). In the rest, literacy instruction was in a local language: Telugu, Bangla, Hindi (in two interventions), Swahili (four), Chichewa, Leblango, Afaan Oromo, Bahasa Indonesia, Javanese, Sundanese, Lango,

Marathi (two each), and Urdu, Kikamba, and Lubukusu (one each). Many of the interventions dealt with more than one of these languages (e.g., parallel programs in Lango and Swahili in Lucas et al. 2014: Uganda and Kenya) or two-language interventions covering a local language and English (e.g., Swahili and English in Brooker & Halliday, 2015: Kenya). However, the bias in intervention language is either for a national or state language, or languages that have regional dominance even if they are without official status. This skew, arguably, reflects local school provision, the neglect of mother-tongue education, or the absence of a more differentiated language education policy (see also Verhoeven & Severing, Chapter 4; Nakamura & Holla, Chapter 8, and Morgan et al., Chapter 10 in this volume). It was also not clear in many cases (35 percent, or six interventions) whether the intervention language was the language of most of the students involved in the experimental intervention. For example, in a multimedia intervention using television programming, Borzekowski and Henry (2010) used local languages for the intervention but failed to make clear which of the home languages of participants (Sundanese, Bahasa, Javanese) were used. This remains unclear also with relation to the language of measurement and how the analyses factor in home languages to interpret the results. Thus, the reviewed studies, even if methodologically rated as rigorous, fall short in reporting of the language profile of participating children in literacy interventions. This is clearly identified as an area that needs researcher attention.

16.4.4 Treatment of Local Literacy Resources and Practices

Unlike the mixed views on local languages, many studies portray local literacy practices in a mostly negative light. Echoing debates in the global literature cited in the first section, some experiments that we reviewed acknowledged study limitations (e.g., with comprehension measures in Gomez Franco, 2014), short-lived gains (e.g., limited impact on vocabulary of dialogic reading in Opel et al., 2009), and reservations about scalability. Traditional literacy and educational practices inside the contexts of these studies were sometimes cited as the *cause* behind these problems. For example, business-as-usual educational practices were described as reasons behind a perceived lack of scalability in a study in India: "The key challenge to mainstreaming the program in government schools was the tendency to revert back to the traditional curriculum and school organization" (Banerjee et al., 2016, p. 27). Another example from Kenya cited the reason behind lack of intervention effects on "vocabulary-related skills such as decoding and sight-reading" as the "emphasis in the Kenyan curriculum on this aspect of reading" (Abrami et al., 2016, p. 961).

Some studies tried to take advantage of local resources. In an intervention from India, Banerjee et al. (2007) reported on a remedial program where volunteer young women, the *Balsakhi*, worked to improve the basic skills of children who were underachieving in Grades 3 or 4. The intervention was based on human resources drawn from the same communities, thus, arguably, ensuring that students shared a common background with the facilitators even if not with the designated schoolteachers. In another study, researchers used community mobilization in selecting community volunteers (India: Lakshminarayana et al., 2013). These practices may appear as culturally responsive although the influx of an untrained volunteer teaching workforce might destabilize already fragile education systems in these contexts (Nag et al., 2014).

16.4.5 Gaps in the Representation of Contextual Factors in Interventions

One focus of our review was the treatment of languages in the intervention areas. The main reason for this was the role of language in literacy learning and the relevance of sociolinguistic dynamics of power and identity in multilingual contexts of interventions. Although half of the interventions deal with English and the rest with local languages, many of them (35 percent of all the interventions) fail to mention whether the languages of their interventions are indeed the home languages of the entire student body in their study areas. For example, an intervention from India stated the programs evaluated were "implemented in northern states of India, in which Hindi is the primary written and spoken language" (Banerjee et al., 2016, p. 8). There is no acknowledgment that Hindi was not the home language of all the students in the study, an inference easily made given the linguistic diversity of the said region.

The Northern Uganda Literacy Project (NULP) employed mother-tongue literacy instruction, teacher support, and a training model to improve Leblango, local-language, and also English instruction and learning. In a section reporting the mixed results from the intervention, the authors had to go as far as to point out that Leblango learning has no detrimental effect on English learning, stating that "there is no evidence that the NULP harms students' progress in learning English" (Kerwin & Thornton, 2015, p. 19). And in an intervention on the use of the mother tongue, the intervention reserved less than 20 percent of the training time for "strategies for teaching in the mother tongue" (Piper et al., 2016, p. 787). Many of the interventions (47 percent) were in the global language of English. However, a corollary sociolinguistic discussion related to its use in middle- and low-income countries (e.g., as a source of inequality) was usually absent. In place of this, occasionally the studies mentioned the perception among educators that the use of local languages might be harmful to the development of the school language, English (Kerwin & Thornton, 2015). Lucas et al. (2014) observed similar attitudes among Kenyan teachers as they often used English in their classrooms, despite the official Swahili-medium early primary education policy.

Another issue is related to the potential of cross-language analysis to highlight both the universal aspects of reading and the language- and orthography-specific peculiarities that aid or hamper implementation of a literacy intervention. In their study, Brooker and Halliday (2015) stated that "developing oral language skills is prioritised over teaching the relationships between sounds and symbols" in the instructional tradition in the intervention site, Kenya, and a training program was designed based on this, "but would encourage the explicit and systematic teaching of letter-sound relationships" (p. 9). This was based on the premise that "[l]earning to read any alphabetic system depends on understanding the relationship between sounds and the letters that represent them" (Brooker & Halliday, 2015, p. 8). This centering of the alphabetic principle is presented with little acknowledgment of cross-linguistic processes or systematic comparisons with the co-occurring local languages such as the syllable-timed Swahili. Similarly, Piper, Zuilkowski, and Mugenda (2014, p. 14) noted that "existing books on the Kenyan market placed very little emphasis on letters, phonological awareness, or decoding in either language [English or Kiswahili]." Little again is said about how such concepts as phonological awareness might be applicable to literacy in the local languages as well as to literacy in English and that many teachers struggle with these concepts in mixed and other language contexts. Teachers in these contexts find it difficult to naturalize the largely English-based alphabetic principles and teaching methods but perhaps this is because they often have first languages (or know multiple languages) with simple syllable structures and pre-service training without the Anglocentric focus on phoneme-based instructions. These experiential, sociolinguistic, and psycholinguistic debates about literacy development were underrepresented in the studies we reviewed.

16.5 Conclusions and Discussion

Substantial distance still needs to be covered to avoid reductionist knowledge transfer of what works for literacy interventions in the Global South. There is clearly a need to re-explore and address the potential conflicts and differences between new interventions and existing practices. We have seen that RCTs rated for their methodological rigor fall short in their consideration of contextual factors for the design, assessment, and analysis of the intervention results. Insight about the need for cultural sensitivity was often reported after the intervention rather than before the intervention. Drawing from sociocultural and critical sociolinguistic perspectives has enabled us to point not only to these representations but also to the gaps in the representations of linguistic diversity in the contexts of these interventions (see also Nag, Chapter 15 in this volume). These gaps also include failure to account for the relevance of universal features alongside specific features of reading in the local languages. In addition to language diversity, contextual factors may also include local literacy and educational practices and resources (such as folktales, playful activities, games, and riddles) and many other customs that have the potential to affect the viability of an intervention. Taken together, our review has indicated the need to draw from multiple disciplines in the effort to map important contextual factors.

The reform agenda inherent in intervention studies is clearly paralleled by social change agendas espoused by all the different approaches we consulted to develop the framework of analysis of sensitivity to cultural and contextual factors in intervention studies. However, these arguments of change may risk confrontation with the tendency of culture to maintain the status quo and to retain practices in communities against the reform agendas of interventions. Equally important is the role of individual agency in maintaining traditions or introducing changes. These apparent contradictions may need to be reconciled in further research. The value of cultural sensitivity inquiries needs to be acknowledged in positioning these competing tendencies in such a way as to resolve the potential conflicts that may arise from intervening in specific cultural contexts. Doing this creates room to improve the impacts of interventions and their effect on learning, a goal shared by all the studies reviewed here and enshrined in the UN's SDGs. Combining quantitative and qualitative data in educational experiments and furthering the debate on how far to tolerate hybridity of methods, methodologies, and philosophies within reform agendas for global literacy development are essential in order to ensure sustainable impact.

The contexts of intervention in the high-quality studies reviewed here reveal a complex web of cultural elements which have featured in different sections in the evaluation reports of these interventions. A much more complex picture is also generated by consulting theoretical discussions around contextual factors in multilingual literacy contexts. For example, the "diversification of diversity" alluded to by sociolinguists and linguistic ethnographers provides for linguistic diversity that even goes down to the level of questioning language boundaries and adopts analytical perspectives that center power relations among groups in multilingual contexts. Such levels of analysis are largely absent in the interventions reviewed here. This then leads to the question of what levels of representation of cultural or linguistic diversities are possible or necessary for interventions to achieve cultural sensitivity. It is against this background that we propose that the outcomes of literacy interventions may be better understood if attention is paid to local, contextual factors alongside universal factors. Thus, rather than assuming that supporting the universal within-child factors will provide "certainties" for literacy learning, we argue for intervention evaluations to recognize and record the situated aspect of learning.

References

Studies marked with an asterisk are included in this review.

*Abrami, P. C., Wade, A. C., Lysenko, L., Marsh, J., & Gioko, A. (2016). Using educational technology to develop early literacy skills in Sub-Saharan Africa. *Education and Information Technologies*, *21*, 945–964. DOI: http://dx.doi.org/10.1007/s10639-014-9362-4.

Asfaha, Y. M., & Kroon, S. (2011). Multilingual education policy in practice: classroom literacy instruction in different scripts in Eritrea. *Compare: A Journal of Comparative and International Education*, *41*(2), 229–246.

Asfaha, Y. M., Kurvers, J., & Kroon, S. (2009). Grain size in script and teaching: A comparative study on literacy acquisition in Ge'ez and Latin. *Applied Psycholinguistics*, *30*(4), 709–724.

*Banerjee, A. V., Banerji, R., Berry, J. et al. (2016). *Mainstreaming an Effective Intervention: Evidence from Randomized Evaluations of "Teaching at the Right Level" in India*. (No. w22746). National Bureau of Economic Research, Inc., USA.

*Banerjee, A. V., Cole, S., Duflo, E., & Linden, L. (2007). Remedying education: Evidence from two randomized experiments in India. *The Quarterly Journal of Economics*, *122*(3), 1235–1264.

Banerjee, A. V. & Duflo, E. (2011). *Poor Economics: A Radical Rethinking of the Way to Fight Global Poverty*. Philadelphia, PA: Penguin Books.

Blackledge, A., & Creese, A. (2017). Language and superdiversity: An interdisciplinary perspective. *Tilburg Papers in Culture Studies*, No. 187. https://research.tilburguniversity.edu/en/publications/language-and-superdiversity-an-interdisciplinary-perspective.

*Borzekowski, D. L. G., & Henry, H. K. (2010). The impact of Jalan Sesama on the educational and healthy development of Indonesian preschool children: An experimental study. *International Journal of Behavioral Development*, *35*(2), 169–179.

*Brooker, S., & Halliday, K. (2015). *Impact of Malaria Control and Enhanced Literacy Instruction on Educational Outcomes among School Children in Kenya: A Multi-Sectoral, Prospective, Randomised Evaluation*. 3ie Impact Evaluation Report 18. New Delhi: International Initiative for Impact Evaluation (3ie).

*Davidson, M., & Hobbs, J. (2013). Delivering reading intervention to the poorest children: The case of Liberia and EGRA-Plus, a primary grade reading assessment and intervention. *International Journal of Educational Development*, *33*(3), 283–293.

de la Piedra, M. T. (2010). Religious and self-generated Quechua literacy practices in the Peruvian Andes. *International Journal of Bilingual Education and Bilingualism*, *13*(1), 99–113.

*Dowd, A. M., Borisova, I., Amente, A., & Yenew, A. (2016) Realizing capabilities in Ethiopia: Maximizing early childhood investment for impact and equity. *Journal of Human Development and Capabilities*, *17*(4), 477–493. DOI: https://doi.org/10.1080/19452829.2016.1225702.

Dulay, K. M., Cheung, S. K., & McBride, C. (2019). Intergenerational transmission of literacy skills among Filipino families. *Developmental Science*, *22*(5), 1–14. DOI: https://doi.org/10.1111/desc.12859.

*Gomez Franco, L. E. (2014). Exploring teachers' read-aloud practices as predictors of children's language skills: The case of low-income Chilean preschool classrooms. (Lynch School of Education, Boston College, PhD dissertation.)

*He, F., Linden, L. L., & MacLeod, M. (2008). How to teach English in India: Testing the relative productivity of instruction methods within the Pratham English language education program. (New York: Columbia University. Mimeographed document.)

*He, F., Linden, L. L., & MacLeod, M. (2009). *A Better Way to Teach Children to Read? Evidence From a Randomized Controlled Trial*. Cambridge, MA: Abdul Latif Jameel Poverty Action Lab (JPAL).

Heath, S. B. (1982). What no bedtime story means: Narrative skills at home and school. *Language in Society*, *11*(1), 49–76.

Hungi, N., & Thuku, F. W. (2010). Variations in reading achievement across 14 Southern African school systems: Which factors matter? *International Review of Education*, *56*(1), 63–101.

Inter-Agency Commission. (1990). *World Conference on Education for All: Meeting Basic Learning Needs, 5–9 March 1990, Jomtien, Thailand. Final Report*. New York: Inter-Agency Commission, WCEFA (UNDP, UNESCO, UNICEF, World Bank). https://unesdoc.unesco.org/ark:/48223/pf0000097551.

*Jukes, M. C. H., Turner, E. L., Dubeck, M. M. et al. (2016). Improving literacy instruction in Kenya through teacher professional development and text messages support: A cluster randomised trial. *Journal of Research on Educational Effectiveness*, *10*(3), 449–481. DOI: https://doi.org/10.1080/19345747.2016.1221487.

Kağitçibaşi, C., Sunar, D., Bekman, S., Baydar, N., & Cemalcilar, Z. (2009). Continuing effects of early enrichment in adult life: The Turkish Early Enrichment Project 22 years later. *Journal of Applied Developmental Psychology*, *30*(6), 764–779.

Kamil, M. L., Afflerbach, P. P., Pearson, P. D., & Moje, E. B. (2011). Reading research in a changing era: An introduction to the *Handbook of Reading Research, Volume IV*. In M. L. Kamil, P. P. Afflerbach, P. D. Pearson, and E. B. Moje (eds.), *Handbook of Reading Research*, Vol. 4 (pp. xiii–xxvi). New York: Routledge.

*Kerwin, J. T., & Thornton, R. (2015). *Making the Grade: Understanding What Works for Teaching Literacy in Rural Uganda*. Population Studies Center Research Report, 15(842).

*Lakshminarayana, R., Eble, A., Bhakta, P. et al. (2013). The Support to Rural India's Public Education System (STRIPES) Trial: A cluster randomised controlled trial of supplementary teaching, learning material and material support. *PLoS ONE*, *8* (7), e65775. DOI: https://doi.org/10.1371/journal.pone.0065775.

Lervåg, A., Dolean, D., Tincas, I., & Melby-Lervåg, M. (2019). Socioeconomic background, nonverbal IQ and school absence affects the development of vocabulary and reading comprehension in children living in severe poverty. *Developmental Science*; *22*:e12858. DOI: https://doi.org/10.1111/desc.12858.

Li, G. (2011). The role of culture in literacy, learning, and teaching. In M. L. Kamil, P. P. Afflerbach, P. D. Pearson, & E. B. Moje (eds.), *Handbook of Reading Research*, Vol. 4 (pp. 515–538). New York: Routledge.

*Lucas, A. M., McEwan, P. J., Ngware, M., & Oketch, M. (2014). Improving early grade literacy in East Africa: Experimental evidence from Kenya and Uganda. *Journal of Policy Analysis and Management*, *33*(4), 950–976.

Mount-Cors, M. F. (2011). Homing in: Mothers at the heart of health and literacy in Coastal Kenya. *Dissertation Abstracts International Section A: Humanities and Social Sciences*, 72(1-A), 137.

Nag, S. (2016). *Assessment of Literacy and Foundation Learning in Developing Countries: Final Report*. London: HEART series.

Nag, S. (2017). The Akshara languages of South Asia: Literacy acquisition and development. In C. Perfetti & L. Verhoeven (eds.), *Learning to Read across Languages and Writing Systems: An International Handbook*. Cambridge: Cambridge University Press.

Nag, S., Chiat, S., Torgerson, C., & Snowling, M. J. (2014). *Literacy, Foundation Learning and Assessment in Developing Countries: Final Report*. London:EPPI-Centre, Social Science Research Unit, University of London.

Nag, S., Snowling, M. J., & Asfaha, Y. (2016). Classroom literacy practices in low- and middle-income countries: An interpretative synthesis of ethnographic studies. *Oxford Education Review*, 42(1), 36–54. DOI: https://doi.org/10.1080/03054985.2015.1135115.

Nag, S., Torgerson, C., Asfaha, Y. et al. (2016). Literacy and foundation learning in low- and middle-income countries: A synthesis of intervention studies. Paper presented at the 23rd Annual Meeting of the Society for the Scientific Study of Reading, July 13–16, University of Porto, Portugal.

*Oketch, M., Ngware, M., Mutisya, M., Kassahun, A., Abuya, B., & Musyoka, P. (2014). When to randomize: Lessons from independent impact evaluation of Reading to Learn (RtL) programme to improve literacy and numeracy in Kenya and Uganda. *Peabody Journal of Education*, 89(1), 17–42.

*Opel, A., Ameer, S. S., & Aboud, F. E. (2009). The effect of preschool dialogic reading on vocabulary among rural Bangladeshi children. *International Journal of Educational Research*, 48,12–20.

*Ozler, B., Fernald, L. C., Kariger, P. K. et al. (2016). *Combining Preschool Teacher Training with Parenting Education: A Cluster-Randomized Controlled Trial* (No. 7817). Washington, DC: The World Bank.

*Piper, B., & Korda, M. (2011). EGRA Plus: Liberia. Program *Evaluation Report*. RTI International, USA.

*Piper, B., Zuilkowski, S. S., & Mugenda, A. (2014). Improving reading outcomes in Kenya: First-year effects of the PRIMR initiative. *International Journal of Educational Development*, 37, 11–21.

*Piper, B., Zuilkowski, S. S., & Ong'ele, S. (2016). Implementing mother tongue instruction in the real world: Results from a medium-scale randomized controlled trial in Kenya. *Comparative Education Review*, 60(4), 776–807.

Puranik, C. S., Phillips, B. M., Lonigan, C. J., & Gibson, E. (2018).Home literacy practices and preschool children's emergent writing skills: An initial investigation. *Early Childhood Research Quarterly*, 42, 228–238.

Rolleston, C., & Krutikova, S. (2014). Equalising opportunity? School quality and home disadvantage in Vietnam. *Oxford Review of Education*, 40(1), 112-131. DOI: https://doi.org/10.1080/03054985.2013.875261.

Rose, H., & Galloway, N. (2019). *Global Englishes for Language Teaching*. Cambridge: Cambridge University Press.

Rueda, R. (2011). Cultural perspectives in reading: Theory and research. In M. L. Kamil, P. P. Afflerbach, P. D. Pearson, and E. B. Moje (eds.), *Handbook of Reading Research* (Vol. 4, pp. 84–103). New York: Routledge.

Snowling, M. J., & Hulme, C. (2011). Evidence-based interventions for reading and language difficulties: Creating a virtuous circle. *British Journal of Educational Psychology, 81*(1), 1–23.

Street, B. V. (1984). *Literacy in Theory and Practice*. Cambridge: Cambridge University Press.

Street, B. V (1995). *Social Literacies: Critical Approaches to Literacy in Development, Ethnography and Education*. New York: Routledge.

Street, B. V. (2016). Learning to read from a social practice view: Ethnography, schooling and adult learning. *Prospects*, 46, 335–344.

Watanabe, L. M. (2015). *Books for Botswana: Developing Reading, and Writing Informational Texts with Young Children*. East Lansing, MI: Michigan State University.

Zhao, N. N., Valcke, M., Desoete, A., & Verhaeghe, J. (2012). The quadratic relationship between socioeconomic status and learning performance in China by multilevel analysis: Implications for policies to foster education equity. *International Journal of Educational Development, 32*(3), 412–422.

17 How Teachers Contribute to Children's Literacy Success

David K. Dickinson, Carol McDonald Connor [†], and Elizabeth Burke Hadley

17.1 Introduction

It might seem odd to even ask how teachers contribute to children's efforts to learn to read. To many it is self-evident that they do this by teaching children to recognize printed symbols, associate them with sounds, and assemble the sounds into words that unlock the meaning of written texts; keeping in mind that texts vary not only in the spoken language they represent but also in the symbol system that represents sounds, syllables, and words. Of course, that response is correct to a degree, but it overlooks the critical roles of teachers in facilitating students' skill using academic language, the type of language required for long-term reading success. It also misses the efforts of teachers to help children move from decoding print into words to the construction of mental models that represent the information in texts. Another question that is of concern to policymakers is how much difference teachers make in students' learning, especially because around the world, large sums are being spent on efforts to teach language and literacy. Much of that money is paying teachers and some is going toward attempts to improve instruction. How do we determine whether this is a good use of money? Promises that come easily to the lips of politicians, such as assurances that all children will read at grade level by a particular age, have been shown to be of little value because they represent unattainable hyperbole. We argue instead that what is needed is a sense of the amount of variability in literacy skills that is attributable to teachers' efforts, because that can supply a basis for rational goal setting. Finally, and most pressing, is the need to determine where to focus our efforts: What specific features of classroom instruction make a significant difference in student's acquisition of literacy-related competencies? And what can we learn by examining how children learn to read across the world?

In this chapter we first introduce the theoretical framework we use to understand reading and its development, which is generally consistent across languages, although how language is represented in print may vary. In so doing, we emphasize the central role of oral language and highlight the extraordinary importance of the early years in shaping later reading success. We briefly discuss the complex layering of factors that shape instruction and learning and then examine the amount of variability we can attribute to teachers. We address this issue by drawing on research done from a social-policy perspective. We will see that the answer to the question of teacher effects is hugely affected by the context in which learning occurs. In well-resourced countries, effects of teachers and teaching are important, but relatively subtle, whereas they are much more obvious in countries with few resources or substantial social challenges. We then turn to discussion of the role of teachers in supporting acquisition of the language skills required for reading comprehension as we draw on a relatively small set of studies from around the world that examine the nuances of teacher–child conversations in a detailed manner. Finally, we turn to what many consider to be the heart of reading instruction – teaching children to translate printed words into meaning. We conclude with a consideration of what we see as promising ways of improving instruction.

17.2 Becoming Literate across Languages

Virtually universal across all languages, one of the most tested and supported conceptualizations of reading is the Simple View of Reading (SVR) (Tunmer & Chapman, 2012; Tunmer & Hoover, 1992). The SVR and related perspectives (Language and Reading Research Consortium et al., 2015; Vellutino et al., 2007) conceptualize reading comprehension as the product of language comprehension and decoding. Perhaps the greatest difference across different languages around the world is how symbols (e.g., graphemes) represents the sounds of the language, which directly relates to decoding – matching symbols to the phonemes, syllables, morphemes, and words they represent (see Perfetti & Verhoeven, Chapter 11 in this volume). For example, languages that use the Roman alphabet (e.g., English, Spanish, German, French) use letter symbols to represent phonemes whereas logographic writing systems such as Mandarin and Cantonese use symbols to represent morphemes with diacritics to indicate phonemes (Lin et al., 2010). Moreover, orthography across languages differs in the extent to which there is a one-to-one correspondence between phonemes and graphemes. For example, in Spanish, once one learns the grapheme–phoneme correspondences, one can easily decode the written words. In contrast, in English, which is a polyglot, grapheme–phoneme relations are influenced by the various languages that provided the loan words to English. For example, the /f/ phoneme can be represented by the grapheme "f" as in "farm," which has its roots in old French, or the grapheme "ph" as in "photo," which comes from the Greek word for light. Thus, given the variety in writing systems and the languages using them, we can expect variations in the way decoding is taught.

Language comprehension draws on vocabulary (Language and Reading Research Consortium et al., 2015), syntactic knowledge (Cooper et al., 2002; Craig, Connor, & Washington, 2003; Swanson et al., 2008), and discourse-level skills such as the ability to understand narratives (Dickinson, Hofer, et al., 2019; Garcia & Cain, 2014; Nation & Snowling, 2004; Vellutino et al., 2007). Of course, there are other important sources of influence on how and how well children learn to read. These include home language and literacy environment, family and community resources and priorities, and biological and genetic individual differences, and importantly for this chapter, the school and classroom learning environment, which is largely – but not completely – the prerogative of the teacher (Connor, 2016).

Becoming literate means mastering how to attach meaning to symbols, which represent sounds, such as in English (Wagner & Torgesen, 1987) and morphemes as well as sounds, such as in Chinese (Lin et al., 2010), and combining them to create meaningful words. This is no easy task because, unlike oral language, which has evolved in humans over millennia, writing – and hence reading – is a recent human invention dating back only about 5,000 years, by some calculations. Thus, humans must be explicitly taught how to decode and then connect their linguistic system to the symbols they have decoded. The text-specific processes required to learn to read English, for example, include being able to becoming phonologically aware; learning the alphabetic principle that letters stand for phonemes that are blended to represent oral language (Ehri, 2002); and learning to use the morphological structure of English to decode and infer meaning. Writing reverses this process and may be more difficult to teach because it is generative. Thus teaching, whether formal in school, or informal outside the school (e.g., at home), is crucial if children are going to learn to read. In contrast, learning to read Chinese requires students to memorize many characters, which represent syllables (Lin et al., 2010). For this reason, phonological awareness is not as predictive of later reading development as it is for English students – although it still predicts some variability in reading.

In alphabetic languages, language, decoding, and phonological-awareness abilities play a major role in determining the skill level of beginning readers, and early competencies are highly predictive of later abilities. Language ability is highly related to reading comprehension ability (Catts et al., 1999; Catts, Adolf, & Weismer, 2006; Cutting & Scarborough, 2006; Dickinson & Porche, 2011; Dickinson & Tabors, 2001; NICHD ECCRN, 2005; Storch & Whitehurst, 2002b) and language ability measured in the later preschool and early school years is a remarkably strong predictor of later language (Dickinson & McCabe, 2001; Dickinson & Porche, 2011; Storch & Whitehurst, 2002). This appears to be the case across all languages.

Literacy draws on language abilities that have been emerging since birth and print-related competencies that begin emerging in the years prior to formal schooling when children are in literacy-rich environments. These language abilities are of pivotal importance to later reading development and reading comprehension (Dickinson, Nesbitt et al., 2019; Dickinson & Porche, 2011; Storch & Whitehurst, 2002). Teachers play a critical role in introducing children to new vocabulary and new ways of using language, and they teach critical information about how symbols and sounds are associated and how meaning can be constructed from texts. But the early age at which language-learning trajectories emerge (Fernald, Weisman, & Weisleder, 2013) and the strong year-to-year stability in language and code-related abilities lead to the question, "To what extent do teachers affect the trajectory of children's acquisition of these abilities given their genetic predispositions?"

17.3 A Global Perspective on Instruction

The impact of education and specific types of instruction on children's life prospects varies greatly depending on where they live. Variability in instructional quality affects learning outcomes, and the size of these effects are most noteworthy in the least economically developed countries. The most fundamental issue affecting the education of children is the fact that there are roughly 58 million children who do not attend school and 100 million who fail to complete primary education (UNESCO, 2015). Over 250 million school-aged children are not acquiring basic reading skills (UNESCO, 2014b), either because they stop attending school (120 million), or because they fail to achieve basic learning benchmarks despite having remained in school. These problems vary enormously by region. Whereas 96 percent of the children in Western Europe and the US attain minimum benchmarks by Grade 4, only one third of children in South and West Asia and two fifths in sub-Saharan Africa do so (UNESCO, 2014b). Many countries track their educational success using two major international assessments, the Program for International Student Assessment (PISA) and Trends in International Mathematics and Science Study (TIMSS). Both have shown variability in students' reading skills over the past decade and are correlated with the countries' economic growth (Hanushek & Woessmann, 2012). Many countries have low levels of literacy. For example, the United Nations reports that over 200 million children in sub-Saharan African are unable to read at basic levels (UNESCO, 2017a & 2017b). This is also the case in Central and Southern Asia, where more than 80 percent of children cannot read well.

Low reading attainments impact overall education outcomes, and education has major economic consequences, with these being especially profound for low- and middle-income countries. For example, between 1965 and 2005 in

Latin America and the Caribbean, the average number of years of schooling rose from 3.6 to 7.5. That increase is estimated to have contributed two thirds of the average annual growth rate in GDP per capita of 2.8 percent between 2005 and 2010 (UNESCO, 2014a). One major avenue to addressing these inequities is to improve the quality of classroom instruction through teacher training and the provision of instructional guidance and materials.

17.3.1 Instructional Interventions

Efforts to increase educational levels and, in particular reading skills, take many forms. One approach has been to develop instructional interventions designed to target reading achievement. In one study, eighteen early-reading-grade interventions that included experimental or quasi-experimental designs that were implemented in the Middle East, North Africa, sub-Saharan Africa, East Asia, and the Pacific were reviewed (Graham & Kelly, 2018). Oral reading fluency, letter–sound knowledge, and comprehension were measured, and positive effects were found for most interventions, with moderate-sized effects on reading fluency (0.38) and reading comprehension (0.34) and large effects on letter–sound knowledge (0.63). Effects were largest and most consistently seen for interventions that targeted second graders. Despite these promising results, across all grade levels, most students remained well below the range of correct words per minute required for fluency (Graham & Kelly, 2018). Elements that were typically included in these interventions were teacher training and provision of structured materials. The potential utility of carefully structured material was revealed by a remedial reading intervention delivered in third and fourth grades for one hour a week in Papua New Guinea (Macdonald & Vu, 2018). Reflecting the results of other interventions, its effects were strongest for foundational skills (e.g., initial sound recognition: effect size of 0.63). There were smaller effects on word reading and comprehension, with girls outpacing boys.

17.3.2 Mother-Tongue Instruction

In 2005, 50 percent of the world's out-of-school children lived in communities where the language of school did not match the language used in the home (see also Verhoeven & Severing, Chapter 4; Nakamura & Holla, Chapter 8, and Morgan et al., Chapter 10 in this volume). A response to this challenge that has been adopted in many countries is to provide initial instruction in the child's first language. That approach has had positive effects on educational outcomes in several countries. For example, in Mali there have been efforts to shift from mother-tongue instruction in the early grades to French in later grades. A World Bank report stated that children in schools employing that gradual approach achieved scores that averaged 32 percent higher than those in French-only schools, and that mother-tongue instruction was associated with improved literacy levels in Brazil, Portugal, and Burkina Faso (Bender et al., 2005). A six-year study in Nigeria compared students who had mother-tongue instruction with those who were taught in English. Those who received mother-tongue instruction performed better in English and content subjects (Heugh, 2011). Ramachandran (2017) compared the educational records of students in who attended primary school (ages seven to fourteen) from different regions in Ethiopia that had adopted mother-tongue instruction at different times. Those receiving instruction in their own language had an 18 percent higher probability of being able to read an entire sentence and were 25 percent more likely to report reading newspapers, suggesting they might be more inclined to be politically engaged. Those who received mother-tongue instruction also were 17 percent more likely to read pamphlets and posters about family planning, suggesting they were more inclined to seek information from print and were more integrated into professionalized delivery of healthcare.

While mother-tongue instruction holds promise, it may not be feasible. Providing instruction in multiple languages can be complex. For example, New Guinea is delivering instruction in 380 languages using a desktop publishing system. Mali is teaching in eleven different languages. Another challenge is that parents are sometimes resistant to having their children taught in their mother tongue because they want them to acquire the national language as quickly as possible (Bender et al., 2005; Nag et al., 2019).

A systematic review of twenty-six years of research on home-language instruction in low- and middle-income countries was conducted by Nag et al. (2019), drawing on quantitative and ethnographic studies. In their quantitative analyses, in addition to examining language of instruction they also considered home-based variability related to book ownership, home tutoring, and adult literacy practices. They examined effects on literacy home-language instruction while controlling for demographic covariates (e.g., socioeconomic status, mothers' education, and ethnicity) and home supports for language and literacy. Between Grades 2 and 6 they found a strong trend indicating enhanced reading levels associated with home-language instruction in twenty-six of twenty-nine countries, but effects on component skills such as decoding and comprehension were more variable. Incorporating ethnographic studies, they found varying and complex patterns of effects of early interventions and concluded that the evidence is not robust enough to support the strong version of the home-language-advantage hypothesis. Rather, the correlational evidence points to a multifactorial model of the relationship between Home Language and Literacy Environment (HLLE) and child outcomes. One implication of this finding is that within-child factors such as the oral language foundation for literacy learning are not the only mechanisms to consider when a child is slow to gain mastery in literacy tasks. Contextual factors, including home language, matter (pp. 136–137). The language of instruction has also been a matter of great interest in the United States, where many Spanish-speaking children have begun attending school. Most schools in the United States deliver instruction only in English, but in some cases, children are initially taught in Spanish or in dual-language schools where English and Spanish are used. Dual-language approaches have been found to be successful (Nakamoto, Lindsey, & Manis, 2012; Slavin & Cheung, 2005). However, just as has been found around the world, there are challenges associated with dual-language approaches. One problem is that the quality of instruction in the minority language may not be of high caliber, and there can be detrimental effects on intergroup relations (Valdes, 1997).

17.4 Trends in Instruction in Strong Economies: United States as a Case Study

17.4.1 Student Outcomes

Countries with strong economies have tracked their success in providing high-quality schooling. For example, the United States has tracked student achievement since 1971, beginning during an era when there was generalized alarm about the success of US schools in educating the nation's children. These data make clear that while progress has been made, it has been slow and incremental. Results are grouped into categories reflecting different levels of reading sophistication (National Center for Educational Statistics, 2013). Level 150 describes basic reading; children can follow brief written directions; children can match phrases and sentences to pictures. Readers at Level 200 can understand specific information or sequential information; they can locate facts from paragraphs and combine ideas to make inferences about short simple passages. At Level 250, readers are able to interrelate ideas as they make sense of longer passages, identify main ideas within them, and make generalizations. Levels 300 and 350 describe more refined abilities to understand complex material. Several trends are evident from examining results for the three age groups tested: nine-, thirteen-, and seventeen-year-olds, between 1971 and 2012. First, educational reform efforts have had an impact because the largest gains have been among children from Hispanic and Black families and the weaker readers, groups that have been of special concern. Children at the tenth and twenty-fifth percentile made gains near four times larger than the stronger readers. From these 2012 data we draw conclusions that are important in our consideration of the effects of teachers: (1) nearly all children (96 percent or more) had learned to read simple passages; (2) improvement efforts had moved children from basic comprehension skills relative to their age cohort to stronger but still restricted comprehension ability; and (3) the education system was relatively unsuccessful at nurturing students' abilities to understand complex material. As we discuss later, this ceiling effect may reflect limitations in the school system in terms of building the broad knowledge and language and inferential thinking skills required for advanced reading comprehension.

17.4.2 Examining the Effects of Schooling

Educational policy researchers have long sought to understand the extent to which schools affect students' learning. In the United States, ever since the Coleman report (Coleman, 1966) on schooling, it has been clear that influences outside of school (e.g., families, socioeconomic status) have much stronger effects on student's learning than do schools, and that variation associated with schools is largely accounted for by teacher effects. Goldhaber (2002) reviewed work on teacher effects and concluded that about 60 percent of the variability in student performance is associated with home characteristics while 8.5 percent is related to teacher characteristics. Rowan, Correnti, and Miller (2002) concluded that teachers account for between 4 and 16 percent of the variance in elementary grade students' reading. Of particular importance is the fact that the strongest effects were consistently seen among disadvantaged urban Black and Hispanic student populations (0.26 to 0.46), with the strongest effects being on English vocabulary, the language of instruction (Nye, Konstantopoulos, & Hedges, 2004). Most data come from correlational studies, but in Tennessee, kindergarten students in seventy-nine schools were randomly assigned to classrooms as part of an experiment examining the impact of class size on learning (Nye et al., 2004). Examination of teacher effects on reading found increasing effects of teachers (6.6 percent in Grade 1, 6.8 percent in Grade 2, and 7.4 percent in Grade 3). Teacher education and experience did not account for variance, but SES was important, as teacher effects in first and second grade were especially strong in low-SES schools (9.8 and 7.9 percent respectively).

Additional evidence regarding teacher effects comes from effects to determine the "added value" of having a strong teacher. These approaches use students' performance on state-mandated tests and compare performance of children across classrooms while controlling for covarying factors that account for success to determine the extent to which being in a particular teacher's classroom results in better-than-average performance. Lauen and Henry (2015) conducted such an analysis using end-of-year state assessment data from fifth- through eighth-grade teachers in North Carolina between 2008 and 2009 and between 2012 and 2013 using a sample of 1,000–4,000 teachers at each grade per year. They identified teachers who exceeded, met, or failed to meet expected levels of added value. Teachers who exceeded (top 20 percent) and those who met (next 60 percent) expectations had students who made more progress, with about 8 percent of the variance in student outcomes being attributable to teacher effects. It is noteworthy that this is nearly the same estimate of the effect of variance in teacher quality that was arrived at by the International Longitudinal Twins Study (ILTS; Taylor et al., 2010). The effects of teacher quality accounted for in the Taylor et al. (2010) study show roughly four times more variance in reading than was accounted for by other environmental factors. What this suggests is that, when children come from varied backgrounds, the importance of strong teachers is increased, as indicated by the fact the variance in reading performance associated with teachers is greater than when the population served is more homogeneous. The genetic studies also reveal that genetic factors are more predictive of progress when teaching quality is strong, because children are able to make the most of their learning potential; thus, genetic variance plays a greater role in determining success. Importantly, with the heterogeneous sample in the Taylor et al. (2010) study, researchers found much stronger evidence of genetic effects in classrooms of effective teachers.

Thus, in the United States in the mid-to-late-twentieth and early-twenty-first centuries, about 8 percent of the variance in student performance on standardized measures of academic achievement can be attributed to teachers. The Florida study additionally indicates that the genetic potential of many students is not being fully realized because they are not taught by highly effective teachers.

These studies of schooling effects may underestimate the impact of schooling on children from low-SES homes because they are based on tests given to students who have attended reasonably high-quality schools for several years; they are limited in their ability to consider effects associate with preschool and kindergarten. Effects of the quality of instruction may be especially strong in countries with few resources, where the contrast in educational approaches between high- and low-quality schools is more dramatic.

Knowing that teachers have an impact on student outcomes, the natural next question is, can we identify factors that account for this variability? Nye et al. (2004) found that teacher education and experience were not predictive of student outcomes. Similarly, Goldhaber's (2002) study of elementary grade students found that 8.5 percent of the variance in student outcomes was accounted for by schools and teachers. When they attempted to identify variables that account for this variance, they could only account for 3 percent using variables such as class size, school demographic characteristics, and teacher characteristics (experience, education level and performance) on vocabulary tests. Much of the remaining school-related variance is presumably related to differences in teacher quality. However, 97 percent of the variability in student outcomes was unaccounted for, suggesting that considerable variation is attributable to children's abilities and variation in home and community supports for learning. To better understand teacher variables that affect learning, we next examine the instruction teachers deliver, as we seek to pinpoint specific teaching practices that account for the variation in student growth.

17.5 Teacher Effects on Language Learning

Specific teacher language practices in preschool can have far-reaching effects on children's reading-related competencies. The Home-School Study of Language and Literacy Development (Dickinson, 2001; Dickinson & Tabors, 2001) was the first in the United States to report detailed information about the kinds of interactions in preschool that produce lasting effects on children's language and literacy development. Researchers followed children from preschool through elementary school, recording and coding a full day of teacher–child conversations in preschool, then assessing children in kindergarten and fourth grade on language and vocabulary. Correlational analyses revealed that when preschool teachers talked more with children during free play, and used more sophisticated vocabulary, children's reading comprehension was stronger in fourth grade . Strong and lasting effects were also present for cognitively challenging talk during preschool book reading, explaining 50 percent of variance in vocabulary scores in kindergarten (Dickinson & Smith, 1994), and with kindergarten vocabulary in turn predicting fourth-grade vocabulary (Dickinson & Porche, 2011). These findings suggest that young children's reading skills benefit throughout their early elementary years from the springboard of a rich language environment in preschool.

Results from the Home-School Study have been replicated by a relatively small number of more recent studies in the United States and other countries (most robustly in Chile and Norway) that examine the specific features of classroom instruction that support language and literacy growth, albeit in the shorter term. Chile in particular has been the site of recent sustained language-intervention efforts, due to the government's investment in research and professional development aimed at increasing the quality of early-childhood education (Leyva et al., 2015; Yoshikawa et al., 2015). The detailed intervention work in Chile, including video recordings and coding of teacher language practices, allows for an understanding of whether certain teacher language practices observed in US settings are similarly beneficial in the different linguistic and cultural context of Chile, a developing Latin American country (e.g., Bowne, Yoshikawa, & Snow, 2016). We turn first to the studies that examine these features in pre-K and kindergarten settings, especially highlighting the elements of varied, sophisticated vocabulary, cognitively challenging talk, certain vocabulary instructional practices, and encouraging child talk.

17.6 Teacher Effects on Oral Language

17.6.1 Amount, Diversity, and Syntactic Complexity of Teacher Talk

In general, the sheer amount of teacher talk in early-childhood classrooms has a relatively small impact on children's vocabulary growth, both in the United States (Bowers & Vasilyeva, 2011; Dickinson & Tabors, 2001) and in other countries (Chile; Strasser & Lissi, 2009), with some indications that a high ratio of teacher-to-child talk may even have a detrimental effect because of decreased opportunities for children to actively practice their language skills (Dickinson & Porche, 2011; Gámez & Lesaux, 2015). Studies have also found that the amount of sophisticated vocabulary teachers use is a more important factor than the amount of talk (Dickinson, 2001). The picture shifts for children whose home language differs from the language of instruction, for whom exposure to teacher talk is a powerful source of input in learning a new language. Exposure to more teacher talk has been found to support vocabulary growth in dual-language learners (DLL) in early childhood in both Norway (Aukrust, 2007; Rydland, Grover, & Lawrence, 2014) and the United States (Bowers & Vasilyeva, 2011). One particularly striking study was conducted with Turkish DLLs in Norwegian preschools (Rydland et al., 2014). Researchers observed preschoolers as they interacted with teachers in group settings and with peers and found that the amount of teacher talk and the variability of words used by peers helped predict age-five Norwegian vocabulary scores, taking into account neighborhood and parental factors. Remarkably, these effects persisted up to age ten; during the primary grades, only parental education accounted for the language growth trajectories. The absence of classroom effects suggests that Norwegian classrooms, like US ones (Pianta et al., 2007), provide relatively weak support for oral language development in the primary grades, although large-scale studies of classroom language quality in Norway are needed to better understand the current language environment. Available studies in secondary (Westergård, Ertesvåg, & Rafaelsen, 2019) and early-childhood classrooms in Norway (Bjørnestad et al., 2019) report that the quality of teacher–child interactions, as characterized by indicators such as teachers' responsiveness, support for language, and emotional support, is relatively low.

When teachers' talk is examined in a fine-grained manner, consistent patterns emerge, such as the beneficial effect of using a wide variety of words, including words that are relatively rare and sophisticated. In the United States, the number of word types used by preschool teachers was positively related to vocabulary growth (Bowers & Vasilyeva, 2011), and preschool teachers' use of sophisticated vocabulary during free play has been shown to predict fourth-grade reading comprehension (Dickinson & Porche, 2011). Teachers' lexical diversity has positive effects for DLL children as well, with the density of word types used by teachers predicting first-grade vocabulary in DLL Turkish children in Norway (Aukrust & Rydland, 2011). In this study of DLLs in Norway, total tokens was a stronger predictor than word types, but both were strongly correlated, a finding that is common among studies of classroom language. Studies in US bilingual kindergarten classrooms have also found positive effects of both Spanish and English lexical diversity on DLL children's vocabulary growth in both languages (Gámez, 2015; Gámez & Levine, 2013).

Even teachers' sentence structure impacts children's language growth, with more complex utterances supporting syntactic growth in US preschoolers (Huttenlocher et al., 2002). A more nuanced story emerges for DLL children, with research suggesting that teachers' use of complex syntax supports students' vocabulary growth, but only if the length of utterances is tailored to match or slightly exceed children's language level (Bowers & Vasilyeva, 2011; Gámez, 2015; Gámez & Levine, 2013).

Unfortunately, certain features of teacher talk such as amount, lexical diversity, and syntactic complexity may be largely unconscious and quite difficult to change. The way teachers talk is engrained by years of practice and shaped by cultural and environmental factors, so that asking teachers to add more clauses to their sentences or use a greater variety of words throughout the school day may not be feasible. But while talk varies widely among teachers – some talk more and use more varied and sophisticated words than others – there is also considerable variation in speech within individual teachers. This is especially evident when examining teachers' speech across different settings in the school day, with certain contexts lending themselves more naturally to rich talk than others. A study looking at the language use of Head Start teachers in the United States found that teachers used more syntactic complexity and greater lexical diversity during book reading than in group content instruction or small group instruction (Dickinson et al., 2014). Group discussions about theme-related content included significantly more sophisticated word types and tokens than the other two settings. To better support children's language development, then, engaging in activities such as science investigations and book reading might naturally result in use of more varied and sophisticated talk by teachers and students.

17.6.2 Cognitively Challenging Talk

Certain types of conversations between teachers and children support literacy growth, with compelling evidence across nations that cognitively challenging talk has an especially beneficial effect. Cognitively challenging talk denotes conversation between teachers and children that involves analysis, prediction, and discussion of word meanings (Dickinson & Porche, 2011; Dickinson &

Smith, 1994), and is related to a number of similar terms: inferential talk (Mascareño et al., 2016; Zucker et al., 2013), instructional language quality (Hindman & Wasik, 2013), high-level strategies (Gómez, Valsilyeva, & Dulaney, 2017), and discourse complexity (Aukrust & Rydland, 2011). While these terms are not synonymous, we group them together here to highlight their shared feature: they involve active exchanges between teachers and children that include analysis and discussion of topics beyond the here and now. These conversations, especially in a book-reading setting, have a powerful effect on preschool children's vocabulary, both in the short term and when the effect is traced longitudinally (Dickinson & Porche, 2011).

Certain kinds of cognitively challenging talk help to support vocabulary growth. In one study of Head Start classrooms, teachers' talk about the story was positively related to vocabulary growth. Children were most likely to benefit from comments that were responsive to their comments or questions (Barnes, Dickinson, & Grifenhagen, 2016). Children with stronger initial vocabularies showed the most gains. A follow-up examination of these interactions found that the semantic content of teachers' comments was predictive of growth across the academic year (Barnes & Dickinson, 2016). Comments that involved a moderate degree of challenge (i.e., giving, explaining, defining, and recalling the text) were associated with growth, whereas neither low-level comments (describing and labeling) nor high-demand comments (e.g., modeling categorizing, inferential thinking) had such effects.

The benefits of cognitively challenging talk have been extensively documented in US contexts, but these findings have also been replicated in both Chile and Norway. In Chilean preschools, teacher–child inferential talk during book reading was positively related to growth in child vocabulary in kindergarten (Mascareño et al., 2016). Additionally, teachers who engaged in professional development activities in language and literacy were more likely to use higher-level strategies such as analyzing events and making predictions during shared book reading (Gómez et al., 2017). In Norwegian DLL preschool classrooms, cognitively challenging talk during circle time was a predictor of first-grade vocabulary (Aukrust & Rydland, 2011).

Cognitively challenging talk is also beneficial for DLLs. Hindman and Wasik (2015) examined the effects of instructional language on a subsample of DLL Head Start children from their previous study (Hindman & Wasik 2013), again examining effects of instructional language on children's vocabulary growth. They found that instructional quality predicted both Spanish and English vocabulary learning for Spanish-speaking DLLs. For English vocabulary, this relationship was significantly greater for DLL children with the lowest levels of initial English vocabulary knowledge. Considered in tandem with the findings from the authors' previous study (Hindman & Wasik 2013), these results demonstrate that rich interactions about decontextualized topics are beneficial both for English-only children and DLLs who enter school with low levels of English proficiency, and that these conversations should be a key practice in classrooms designed to support these children.

17.6.3 Specific Features of Vocabulary Instruction

Purposefully and systematically teaching new words has been shown to support children's vocabulary growth in a variety of international contexts, including US (Wasik, Bond, & Hindman, 2006), Chilean (Bowne et al., 2016; Pallante & Kim, 2013), and Greek (Chlapana & Tafa, 2014) early-childhood classrooms. A small number of additional studies have examined in detail some specific features of vocabulary instruction that may be especially beneficial. A study in US preschool and kindergarten classrooms examined the types of vocabulary instruction that predicted children's vocabulary growth, as well as how such instruction differentially impacted children with varying levels of language skills (Silverman & Crandell, 2010). Defining words and applying them in new contexts predicted higher vocabulary scores for all children, but had a greater effect for those with greater vocabulary knowledge. Using vocabulary words during code-related activities was also positively related to vocabulary knowledge. Finally, acting out words was positively related to vocabulary growth for children with low initial vocabulary knowledge, but negatively related for children with high initial vocabulary.

Observations of Chilean kindergarten teachers participating in a language and literacy intervention found that conceptual information about new vocabulary words (e.g., information about word meaning, examples, and facts) was significantly related to growth in children's vocabulary. Interestingly, this conceptual information was provided more frequently in science, math, and nonliteracy content areas than in literacy activities, including book reading (Bowne, Yoshikawa, & Snow, 2017). These studies point to the importance of considering science, social studies, and math discussions as rich, often underused sites for vocabulary instruction, and possible leverage points for interventions.

17.6.4 Encouraging Child Talk

A final feature of early-childhood classrooms that predicts language growth is child involvement in classroom conversations, whether with other children or with teachers. In Norwegian preschools, peer talk during play predicted DLL children's L2 vocabularies at age five (Rydland et al., 2014), and the vocabulary diversity and syntactic complexity of peers' speech in bilingual US classrooms were positively associated with both DLL and English-only children's growth in vocabulary and syntax (Gámez et al., 2019). Belonging to a peer group with higher language skills helped support the language of children with lower language skills and low-SES backgrounds in Norwegian childcare centers (Ribeiro, Zachrisson, & Dearing, 2017).

Other evidence of the importance of considering child involvement came from a preschool intervention that included a curriculum with strong support for building language and emergent literacy skills (Schickedanz & Dickinson, 2005), as well as professional development workshops and in-class coaching for teachers throughout the year. Data were collected each of three years and were analyzed using a regression discontinuity design that provides causal evidence of instructional effects. The study found marked improvement in the language and emergent reading abilities of DLLs and English-only speakers (Wilson, Dickinson, & Rowe, 2013). Of particular importance was the finding that the level of child involvement during book reading helped account for these beneficial effects. The presence of child involvement may serve as a marker that teachers' language is appropriately matched to children's language level and that children are regularly invited to participate in classroom conversations.

17.6.5 Effects of Teacher–Child Interaction in Primary Grades

The effects of teacher–child conversations on language and literacy development have been less frequently studied in the elementary years, but the small number of such studies indicates that specific discourse moves by teachers can support children's growth in vocabulary and reading comprehension. One line of research examines the language of second and third-grade teachers in Reading First schools during literacy lessons (Carlisle, Kelcey, & Berebitsky, 2013;). This series of studies found that teachers' discourse had a significant effect on students' vocabulary and reading comprehension. Specifically, during talk about texts, teachers' use of language that supported students' cognitive engagement and built on their background knowledge accounted for a third to a half of the variance in children's reading comprehension and vocabulary (Dwyer et al., 2016). In reading comprehension lessons, teachers who spent relatively more time on teacher-directed instruction (strategies such as modeling and explaining) and fostering discussion contributed significantly to students' growth in reading comprehension. Effects for teacher-directed instruction were strongest for children from low-income homes. Finally, when examining teachers' support for vocabulary across literacy lessons, researchers found that a 1-standard-deviation (SD) increase in teachers' vocabulary support strategies such as defining words, using them in context, asking students to share definitions or contextual uses, or fostering discussion was associated with a 0.11 SD increase on a standardized measure of reading comprehension (Carlisle et al., 2013).

17.6.6 Summary of Research on Teacher–Child Interactions

Several conclusions can be drawn from these studies. First, there are a number of specific language practices that have been found to foster language growth across ages, languages, and countries, such as teachers encouraging discussion of topics beyond the here and now and systematically teaching new vocabulary words. Second, many beneficial practices are even *more* helpful for DLLs and those from low-income homes. Unfortunately, these language exchanges are relatively rare in early-childhood classrooms, and the quality of vocabulary instruction is higher in classrooms serving higher-SES children than in those serving low-SES children (Wright & Neuman, 2014). Such differential instructional practice will tend to exacerbate the already existing inequities present at school entry. Third, the language background, abilities, and engagement of children need to be considered.

17.7 Teacher Effects on Learning to Read

In many nations, most children are taught how to read early in life, with formal instruction beginning around the age of five or six years. There is clear evidence that, in countries where instruction begins at age five, children who are not reading proficiently by the time they are seven or eight are much less likely to gain proficiency (Spira, Bracken, & Fischel, 2005), that consistently high-quality reading instruction from the ages of six through eight years provides stronger student reading outcomes (Connor et al., 2013), and that early effective instruction has a lasting impact on students outcomes (Konstantopoulos & Chung, 2011). Our understanding about the written structure of different languages (e.g., English vs. Spanish vs. Mandarin), cognitive development, how children learn to read, and the kinds of instructional strategies and learning environments that support this learning has expanded rapidly in the past decade and there is a greater appreciation for the complexity of learning to read, the multiple cognitive and social processes that are brought to this task, and of the fact that the effect of specific instructional strategies depends on the skills children bring to the classroom (Connor, 2016).

17.7.1 Evidence-Based Reading Instruction

Several major publications greatly influenced approaches to teaching reading: *The Teaching Gap* (Stigler & Hiebert, 1999); the National Reading Panel report (NICHD National Reading Panel, 2000) and the National Early Literacy Panel report (2008), among others. *The Teaching Gap* analyzed data from the video studies of instruction from the TIMSS and PIRLS[1] to investigate how professionals teach in Japan, Taiwan, China, and the United States. Instruction varies from country to country and the authors described this as a cultural phenomenon. That is, within a country, teaching across classrooms looks very similar – but between countries, it can vary significantly. Although the study focused on the teaching of math, many of the findings are applicable to the teaching of reading.

The Progress in International Reading Literacy Study (PIRLS) offers international data on how well nine-year-olds are reading. Data came from 61 countries, included over 300,000 4th graders and 16,000 teachers (Mullis et al., 2017). It revealed that approximately half (twenty-four) of the countries successfully taught 96 percent of their children to read at basic levels. The PIRLS report concluded that across countries, a number of school and home factors contributed to children's achievement. Important school factors included school safety and resources, regular attendance, amount of instructional time devoted to reading, and having teachers who understand curricular goals and are effective in implementing the curriculum.

Across languages and nations, there is compelling research supporting the finding that basic instruction in reading must include systematic and explicit instruction in sound–symbol association and how to blend these sound-symbols to create meaningful words, regardless of the language children are speaking. In the United States, the National Reading Panel meta-analysis also revealed that most students required systematic and explicit instruction in the alphabetic principle and the use of phonics methods to achieve proficient reading skills. The report highlighted five core areas of instruction – phonological awareness, phonics, fluency, vocabulary, and comprehension. Recently, writing has been added to create six core areas. Stuebing et al. (2008) and Foorman and Connor (2010) provide excellent discussions of the report's findings.

Most of the recent research on code-based interventions has focused on children who do not make adequate gains in reading skills even when they receive classroom instruction that is generally effective for their peers. For example, a recent study in the United States showed that the sooner six-year-olds who, based on assessment, were at greater risk for reading difficulties received more intensive systematic and explicit decoding instruction, the better were their reading attainments (Al Otaiba et al., 2014). A synthesis of reading research (Connor et al., 2014) provided several recommendations including: (1) using assessment for screening, progress monitoring, and to inform individualized (or personalized) instruction for children; (2) increasing the intensity of explicit instruction when children are not progressing as well as their

[1] http://timss.bc.edu/.

peers; and (3) providing ongoing professional development to teachers focused on developing their specialized knowledge about reading and reading instruction, and how to combine multiple strategies.

A recent meta-analysis of interventions that incorporated multiple components of reading (e.g., language, print, and cognitive skills), in low- and middle-income countries (Kim et al., 2020), noted that we cannot assume that instructional practices that are effective in developed countries will be effective in low- and middle-income countries. This is because schools are often underresourced (e.g., no electricity, few books, no furniture), have fewer opportunities for professional development and mentoring (Lee & Zuilkowski, 2015) and struggle with absenteeism (Benavot & Gad, 2004; Dubeck, Jukes, & Okello, 2012). Results from the meta-analysis (Kim, Lee, & Zuilkowski, 2020) reveal that overall, multicomponent reading instruction is effective ($d = 0.30$), but there was wide variability, with almost 20 percent of the results negative. Challenges included large class size, absenteeism, implementation, and fidelity, and reverting to old ineffective practices. Of particular interest was the difference in effect sizes by reading outcome. The largest average effect was for emergent literacy skills (0.40), then word reading (0.32), reading fluency (0.28), reading comprehension (0.25), and oral language (0.20). As the authors note, "The differential effects of multicomponent intervention on various reading and language outcomes are in line with evidence from developed countries (e.g., Wanzek & Vaughn, 2007)." In other words, the pattern of effects in low and middle-income countries was consistent with those in a US context, where lower-level decoding skills were easier to improve than higher-level comprehension and language skills (e.g., Kim et al., 2016).

17.7.2 Individualized Student Instruction

Accumulating research suggests that the effect of particular types of instruction (code-focused instruction with the teacher, meaning-focused instruction with the teacher, and code- and meaning-focused instruction completed independently or with peers) depends on the language, decoding, and comprehension skills children bring to the classroom. There are also interaction effects on student learning of child characteristic by type of instruction (Connor, Morrison, & Katch, 2004; Connor et al., 2013). For example, sustained independent silent reading (SISR) was once a preferred method for teaching reading in the United States – children spent several hours per week reading a book of their choice, silently and on their own. And for students with strong vocabulary and decoding skills, more time in SISR predicted greater reading gains by the end of the school year. However, for students with weak vocabulary skills, more time in SISR predicted much weaker reading-skill gains (Connor et al., 2004). Instead, when provided with more time in code-focused instruction with the teacher– and small amounts of SISR with increasing amounts over the school year – the children made strong gains. Using these data along with others, we developed empirically derived computer algorithms, called dynamic forecasting intervention models, similar to those developed by meteorologists, to compute recommended amounts and types of reading instruction (Connor et al., 2011). Teachers access the recommended amounts using the technology platform called Assessment-to-instruction or A2i. The more precisely the teachers provided each student with the recommended amounts and the more they used A2i, the stronger were the students' literacy gains. We called this individualizing student instruction (ISI), but the general approach has also been called personalized instruction.

What does effective ISI in early reading instruction look like? Envision a first-grade classroom at a high-poverty school in the United States where children are about six years old. Children seem to be milling about when you enter the classroom, but they soon settle down and begin working at various stations throughout the room. You see a phonics/spelling station, a writing station, a computer station with educational programs, and a book-reading corner with cozy beanbag chairs. Some children are talking and working together. You also notice that each child has a colored folder – blue, green, yellow, orange. These folders are aligned with the students' flexible learning groups (Wharton-McDonald, Pressley, & Hampston, 1998) recommended by the assessments the teacher administered. Four children with their purple folders are at the teacher table. As you listen, they are discussing how to turn the word "pin" into the word "pan." When the group decides that the "i" should be replaced with an "a," they change the letters on their whiteboard. After about five minutes, the teacher rings a bell and says, go to your next station. The children who were with the teacher scatter to the other stations with their folders, open them, and begin to work. At the same time, five children join the teacher at the teacher station. Other children go to the station chart to see where they are supposed to go next. The children soon settle down and the personalized lessons are provided at the different stations.

The teacher has used assessment information to assess and track her students' progress and to develop personalized lessons for them (Connor et al., 2013). She uses the plan to make sure that each student has learning opportunities that were selected based on their assessed learning needs and thus are appropriately challenging for them (hence the colored folders containing personalized learning materials). She has strategized with her literacy coach and other teachers in a professional learning community (PLC) (Bos et al., 1999) at her school about how to meet the needs of certain challenging students – when you observed the classroom, the child who used to be highly disruptive was not noticeable. Her students spend most of their time in meaningful instruction, can work independently, and know how to use the station chart to find their next station. They work appropriately on their own or with peers, and do not interrupt the teacher when she is at the teacher station with other students. By the end of the school year, the students will be generally reading at or above grade level and will have a good head start on a successful school career (Connor et al., 2011).

Given the within-classroom variability in students' achievement levels found in most classrooms, it is likely that individualized instruction will be effective in other countries as well. However, it is important to note the very real barriers to implementing individualized instruction in lower- and middle-income countries. For example, class sizes in some sub-Saharan African countries can be prohibitively high for individualized instruction, with average teacher–student ratios of 1:61 in Eritrea, 1:142 in Liberia, and 1:49 in Sierra Leone (UNESCO, 2017a). The resources of literacy coaches and PLCs that many teachers can draw on in the US or a developed country are not yet available in many countries, and coaching and PLC opportunities that may work well in the United States or Europe may not transfer appropriately to a different historical, social, and cultural context (UNESCO, 2003).

17.8 Implications for Educational Practice

Evidence from education and policy research makes clear that the quality of teachers' instruction matters for helping children learn to their full potential. Several characteristics of instruction have been identified that are associated with enhanced learning, many of which can be implemented internationally:
- provide systematic early reading instruction (ages five to eight);
- use a curriculum that includes well-structured materials that teach sound–symbol associations explicitly;
- train teachers in use of the instructional materials and support them in learning to use them effectively;
- provide teachers with strategies for assessing children and encourage individualization, which includes increased intensity for struggling readers;
- encourage teachers to provide good models of adult language, including sophisticated syntax and varied vocabulary;
- encourage teachers to engage students in extended conversations in which students play an important role;
- provide opportunities for children to engage with teachers in conversations about novel information and concepts, and by talking about past experiences, engaging in debates about topics of interest to the students, and talking about language and the meanings of words;
- read aloud to children and use books as starting points for systematic vocabulary instruction and conversations that deepen comprehension;
- use instruction in which the complexity of the teacher's language is not so great as to exceed children's ability to understand, but also models and encourage mature language use.

Possibly the most malleable targets for improvement are those associated with methods of basic reading and writing instruction. Cross-national studies provide examples of effective methods, and publishers have made available material that can guide teachers toward adoption of desired practices. Personalizing or individualizing this instruction based on students' assessed learning needs will be challenging in countries with very large class sizes, but strategies should be implemented to help teachers better match instruction to students' needs. How teachers talk with children across the day affects their language development, and enhancing children's oral language can help foster improved comprehension once children have mastered the challenges of decoding. Use of mother-tongue instruction will increase the ability of teachers to build children's oral language and associated world knowledge. Decades of research and practice have identified methods that are effective in teaching children basic reading skills, which are the foundation of learning to read proficiently with understanding. The new frontier is the development of methods, practices and technologies that will enable teachers to adopt uses of language that, in turn, enable children to acquire the sophisticated language competence needed for advanced reading comprehension.

References

Al Otaiba, S., Connor, C. M., Folsom, J. S. et al. (2014). To wait in Tier 1 or intervene immediately: A randomized experiment examining first-grade response to intervention in reading. *Exceptional Children*, *81*(1), 11–27. DOI: https://doi.org/10.1177/0014402914532234.

Aukrust, V. G. (2007). Young children acquiring second language vocabulary in preschool group-time: Does amount, diversity, and discourse complexity of teacher talk matter? *Journal of Research in Childhood Education*, *22*(1), 17–37. DOI: https://doi.org/10.1080/02568540709594610.

Aukrust, V. G., & Rydland, V. (2011). Preschool classroom conversations as long-term resources for second language and literacy acquisition. *Journal of Applied Developmental Psychology*, *32*(4), 198–207. DOI: https://doi.org/10.1016/j.appdev.2011.01.002.

Barnes, E. M., & Dickinson, D. K. (2016). The impact of teachers' commenting strategies on children's vocabulary growth. *Exceptionality*, *25*(3), 186–206. DOI: https://doi.org/10.1080/09362835.2016.1196447.

Barnes, E. M., Dickinson, D. K., & Grifenhagen, J. B. (2016). The role of teachers' comments during book reading in children's vocabulary growth. *The Journal of Educational Research*, 1–13. DOI: https://doi.org/10.1080/00220671.2015.1134422.

Benavot, A., & Gad, L. (2004). Actual instructional time in African primary schools: factors that reduce school quality in developing countries. *Prospects*, *34*(3), 291–310.

Bender, P., Dutcher, N., Klaus, D., Shore, J., & Tesar, C. (2005). *In Their Own Language: Education for all (English)*. Washington, DC: World Bank Group. http://documents.worldbank.org/curated/en/374241468763515925/In-their-own-language-education-for-all.

Bjørnestad, E., Broekhuizen, M. L., Os, E., & Baustad, A. G. (2019). Interaction quality in Norwegian ECEC for toddlers measured with the caregiver interaction profile (CIP) Scales. *Scandinavian Journal of Educational Research*, 1–20.

Bos, C., Mather, N., Narr, R. F., & Babur, N. (1999). Interactive, collaborative professional development in early literacy instruction: Supporting the balancing act. *Learning Disabilities Research and Practice*, 14(4), 227–238.

Bowers, E. P., & Vasilyeva, M. (2011). The relation between teacher input and lexical growth of preschoolers. *Applied Psycholinguistics*, 32(1), 221–241. DOI: https://doi.org/10.1017/s0142716410000354.

Bowne, J. B., Yoshikawa, H., & Snow, C. E. (2016). Relationships of teachers' language and explicit vocabulary instruction to students' vocabulary growth in kindergarten. *Reading Research Quarterly*, 1–23. DOI: https://doi.org/10.1002/rrq.151.

Bowne, J. B., Yoshikawa, H., & Snow, C. E. (2017). Relationships of teachers' language and explicit vocabulary instruction to students' vocabulary growth in kindergarten. *Reading Research Quarterly*, 52(1), 7–29. DOI: https://doi.org/10.1002/rrq.151.

Carlisle, J., Kelcey, B., & Berebitsky, D. (2013). Teachers' support of students' vocabulary learning during literacy instruction in high poverty elementary schools. *American Educational Research Journal*, 50(6), 1360–1391.

Catts, H. W., Adolf, S. M., & Weismer, S. E. (2006). Language deficits in poor comprehenders: A case for the simple view of reading. *Journal of Speech, Language, and Hearing Research*, 49(2), 278–293.

Catts, H. W., Fey, M. E., Zhang, X., & Tomblin, J. B. (1999). Language basis of reading and reading disabilities: Evidence from a longitudinal investigation. *Scientific Studies of Reading*, 3, 331–361. DOI: http://dx.doi.org/10.1207/s1532799xssr0304

Chlapana, E., & Tafa, E. (2014). Effective practices to enhance immigrant kindergarteners' second language vocabulary learning through storybook reading. *Reading and writing*, 27(9), 1619–1640.

Coleman, J. S. (1966). *Equality of Educational Opportunity* (summary report). Washington: US Department of Health, Education, and Welfare, Office of Education.

Connor, C. M. (2016). A lattice model of the development of reading comprehension. *Child Development Perspectives*, 10(4), 269–274. DOI: https://doi.org/10.1111/cdep.12200.

Connor, C. M., Alberto, P. A., Compton, D. L., & O'Connor, R. E. (2014). *Improving Reading Outcomes for Students with or at Risk for Reading Disabilities: A Synthesis of the Contributions from the Institute of Education Sciences Research Centers*. Washington, DC: US Department of Education. http://ies.ed.gov/ncser/pubs/20143000/.

Connor, C. M., Morrison, F. J., Fishman, B. et al. (2013). A longitudinal cluster-randomized control study on the accumulating effects of individualized literacy instruction on students' reading from 1st through 3rd grade. *Psychological Science*, 24(8), 1408–1419. DOI: https://doi.org/10.1177/0956797612472204.

Connor, C. M., Morrison, F. J., & Katch, L. E. (2004). Beyond the reading wars: Exploring the effect of child-instruction interactions on growth in early reading. *Scientific Studies of Reading*, *8*(4), 305–336.

Connor, C. M., Morrison, F. J., Schatschneider, C. et al. (2011). Effective classroom instruction: Implications of child characteristic by instruction interactions on first graders' word reading achievement. *Journal of Research on Educational Effectiveness*, *4*(3), 173–207. DOI: https://doi.org/10.1080/19345747.2010.510179.

Cooper, D. H., Roth, F. P., Speece, D. L., & Schatschneider, C. (2002). The contribution of oral language skills to the development of phonological awareness. *Applied Psycholinguistics*, *23*(3), 399–416. DOI: https://doi.org/10.1017/s0142716402003053.

Craig, H. K., Connor, C. M., & Washington, J. A. (2003). Early positive predictors of later reading comprehension for African American students: A preliminary investigation. *Language Speech and Hearing Services in Schools*, *34*(1), 31–43. DOI: https://doi.org/10.1044/0161-1461(2003/004).

Cutting, L. E., & Scarborough, H. S. (2006). Prediction of reading comprehension: Relative contributions of word recognition, language proficiency, and other cognitive skills can depend on how comprehension is measured. *Scientific Studies of Reading*, *10*(3), 277–299. DOI: https://doi.org/10.1207/s1532799xssr1003_5.

Dickinson, D. K. (2001). Putting the pieces together: The impact of preschool on children's language and literacy development in kindergarten. In D. K. Dickinson & P. O. Tabors (eds.), *Beginning Literacy with Language: Young Children Learning at Home and School* (pp. 257–287). Baltimore, MD: Brookes Publishing.

Dickinson, D. K., Hofer, K. G., Barnes, E. M., & Grifenhagen, J. F. (2014). Examining teachers' language in Head Start classrooms from a Systemic Linguistics Approach. *Early Childhood Research Quarterly*, *29*(3), 231–244. https://doi.org/10.1016/j.ecresq.2014.02.006.

Dickinson, D. K., Hofer, K. G., & Rivera, B. L. (2019). The developing language foundation for reading comprehension: Vocabulary, complex syntax and extended discourse from preschool to grade one. In E. Veneziano & A. Nicolopoulou (eds.), *Narrative, Literacy and Other Skills: Studies in Interventions*. Amsterdam: John Benjamin.

Dickinson, D. K., & McCabe, A. (2001). Bringing it all together: The multiple origins, skills and environmental supports of early literacy. *Learning Disabilities Research and Practice*, *16*(4), 186–202. DOI: http://dx.doi.org/10.1111/0938-8982.00019.

Dickinson, D. K., Nesbitt, K. T., & Hofer, K. G. (2019). Effects of language on initial reading: Direct and indirect associations between code and language from preschool to first grade. *Early Childhood Research Quarterly*, *49*(42), 122–137. DOI: https://doi.org/10.1016/j.ecresq.2019.04.005.

Dickinson, D. K., & Porche, M. V. (2011). Relation between language experiences in preschool classrooms and children's kindergarten and fourth-grade language and reading abilities. *Child Development*, *82*(3), 870–886. DOI: https://doi.org/10.1111/j.1467-8624.2011.01576.x.

Dickinson, D. K., & Smith, M. W. (1994). Long-term effects of preschool teachers' book readings on low-income children's vocabulary and story comprehension. *Reading Research Quarterly*, *29*(2), 105–122. www.jstor.org/stable/747807.

Dickinson, D. K., & Tabors, P. O. (eds.). (2001). *Beginning Literacy with Language: Young Children Learning at Home and School*. Baltimore, MD: Brookes Publishing.

Dubeck, M. M., Jukes, M. C., & Okello, G. (2012). Early primary literacy instruction in Kenya. *Comparative Education Review*, *56*(1), 48–68.

Dwyer, J., Kelcey, B., Berebitsky, D., & Carlisle, J. F. (2016). A study of teachers' discourse moves that support text-based discussions. *The Elementary School Journal*, *117*(2), 285–309.

Ehri, L. C. (2002). Phases of acquisition in learning to read words and implications for teaching. In R. Stainthorp & P. Tomlinson (eds.), *Learning and Teaching Reading* (pp. 7–28). London: British Journal of Educational Psychology Monograph Series II.

Fernald, A., Marchman, V. A., & Weisleder, A. (2013). SES differences in language processing skill and vocabulary are evident at 18 months. *Developmental Science*, *16* (2), 234–248. DOI: https://doi.org/10.1111/desc.12019.

Foorman, B. R., & Connor, C. M. (2010). Primary reading. In A. G. Kamhi & P. D. Pearson (eds.), *Handbook of Reading Research* (4th ed.). Mahwah, NJ: Lawrence Erlbaum.

Gámez, P. B. (2015). Classroom-based English exposure and English language learners' expressive language skills. *Early Childhood Research Quarterly*, *31*, 135–146.

Gámez, P. B., Griskell, H. L., Sobrevilla, Y. N., and Vazquez, M. (2019). Dual language and English-only learners' expressive and receptive language skills and exposure to peers' language. *Child Development*, 90, 471–479. DOI: https://doi.org/10.1111/cdev.13197.

Gámez, P. B., & Lesaux, N. K. (2015). Early-adolescents' reading comprehension and the stability of the middle school classroom-language environment. *Developmental Psychology*, *51*(4), 447–458. https://doi.org/10.1037/a0038868.

Gámez, P. B., & Levine, S. C. (2013). Oral language skills of Spanish-speaking English language learners: The impact of high-quality native language exposure. *Applied Psycholinguistics*, *34*(4), 673–696. DOI: https://doi.org/10.1017/s0142716411000919.

Garcia, R. J., & Cain, K. (2014). Decoding and reading comprehension: A meta-analysis to identify which reader and assessment characteristics influence the strength of the relationship in English. *Review of Educational Research*, *84*(1), 74–111. DOI: https://doi.org/10.3102/0034654313499616.

Goldhaber, D. (2002). The mystery of good teaching. *Education Next* (Spring), 50–55. www.educationnext.org.

Gómez, L. E., Vasilyeva, M., & Dulaney, A. (2017). Preschool teachers' read-aloud practices in Chile as predictors of children's vocabulary. *Journal of Applied Developmental Psychology*, *52*, 149–158. https://doi.org/10.1016/j.appdev.2017.07.005.

Graham, J., & Kelly, S. (2018). *How Effective Are Early Grade Reading Interventions? A Review of the Evidence* (Policy Research Working Paper No. 8292). World Bank, Washington, DC. https://openknowledge.worldbank.org/handle/10986/29127.

Hanushek, E. A. & Woessmann, L. (2012). Do better schools lead to more growth? Cognitive skills, economic outcomes, and causation. *Journal of Economic Growth*, *17*(4), 267–321.

Heugh, K. (2011). Theory and practice – language education models in Africa: Research, design, decision-making and outcomes. In A. Ouane & C. Glanz (eds.), *Optimising Learning, Education and Publishing in Africa: The Language Factor* (pp. 105–156).

Hindman, A. H., & Wasik, B. A. (2013). Vocabulary learning in Head Start: Nature and extent of classroom instruction and its contributions to children's learning. *Journal of School Psychology*, *51*(3), 387–405. https://doi.org/10.1016/j.jsp.2013.01.001.

Hindman, A. H., & Wasik, B. A. (2015). Building vocabulary in two languages: An examination of Spanish-speaking dual language learners in Head Start. *Early Childhood Research Quarterly*, *31*, 19–33. DOI: https://doi.org/10.1016/j.ecresq.2014.12.006.

Huttenlocher, J., Vasilyeva, M., Cymerman, E., & Levine, S. (2002). Language input and child syntax. *Cognitive Psychology*, *45*(3), 337–374. DOI: https://doi.org/10.1016/S0010-0285(02)00500-5.

Kim, Y.-S. G., Boyle, H., Zuilkowski, S., & Nakamura, P. (2016). *The Landscape Report on Early Grade Literacy Skills*. Washington, DC: United States Agency for International Development (USAID). https://globalreadingnetwork.net/publications-and-research/landscape-report-early-grade-literacy.

Kim, Y.-S. G., Lee, H., & Zuilkowski, S. S. (2020). Impact of literacy interventions on reading skills in low- and middle-income countries: A meta-analysis. *Child Development*, 91: 638–660. DOI: https://doi.org/10.1111/cdev.13204.

Konstantopoulos, S., & Chung, N. (2011). The persistence of teacher effects in elementary grades. *American Educational Research Journal*, *48*(2), 361–386. DOI: https://doi.org/10.3102/0002831210382888.

Language and Reading Research Consortium, Cain, K., Catts, H. et al. (2015). Learning to read: Should we keep things simple? *Reading Research Quarterly*, *50*(2), 151–169. DOI: https://doi.org/10.1002/rrq.99.

Lauen, D. L. L., & Henry, G. T. (2015). *The Distribution of Teachers in North Carolina, 2009–2013 Research Brief*. Vanderbilt University. http://cerenc.org/wp-content/uploads/2015/08/0-FINAL-final-TQ-Distribution-report-8-6-15.pdf.

Lee, J., & Zuilkowski, S. S. (2015). 'Making do': Teachers' coping strategies for dealing with textbook shortages in urban Zambia. *Teaching and Teacher Education*, *48*, 117–128. DOI: https://doi.org/10.1016/j.tate.2015.02.008.

Leyva, D., Weiland, C., Barata, M., Yoshikawa, H., Snow, C., & Trevino, E. (2015). Teacher-child interactions in Chile and their associations with prekindergarten outcomes. *Child Development*, *86*, 781–799.

Lin, D., McBride-Chang, C., Shu, H. et al. (2010). Small wins big. *Psychological Science*, *21*(8), 1117–1122. DOI: https://doi.org/10.1177/0956797610375447.

Macdonald, K., & Vu, B. T. (2018). *A Randomized Evaluation of a Low-Cost and Highly Scripted Teaching Method to Improve Basic Early Grade Reading Skills in Papua New Guinea*. Washington, DC: World Bank. http://documents1.worldbank.org/curated/ar/247501525353958692/pdf/WPS8427.pdf.

Mascareño, M., Snow, C. E., Deunk, M. I., & Bosker, R. J. (2016). Language complexity during read-alouds and kindergartners' vocabulary and symbolic understanding. *Journal of Applied Developmental Psychology*, *44*, 39–51. DOI: https://doi.org/10.1016/j.appdev.2016.02.001.

Mullis, I. V. S., Martin, M. O., Foy, P., & Hooper, M. (2017). PIRLS 2016 International results in reading. Boston College, TIMSS & PIRLS International Study Center (website). http://timssandpirls.bc.edu/pirls2016/international-results/

Nag, S., Vagh, S. B., Dulay, K. M., & Snowling, M. J. (2019). Home language, school language and children's literacy attainments: A systematic review of evidence from low- and middle-income countries. *Review of Education: An Interdisciplinary*

Journal of Major Studies in Education, 7(1), 91–150. DOI: https://doi.org/10.1002/rev3.3130.

Nakamoto, J., Lindsey, K. A., & Manis, F. R. (2012). Development of reading skills from K-3 in Spanish-speaking English language learners following three programs of instruction. *Reading and Writing, 25*(2), 537–567. DOI: https://doi.org/10.1007/s11145-010-9285-4.

Nation, K., & Snowling, M. J. (2004). Beyond phonological skills: broader language skills contribute to the development of reading. *Journal of Research in Reading, 27*(4), 342–356. DOI: https://doi.org/10.1111/j.1467-9817.2004.00238.x.

National Center for Educational Statistics. (2013). *The Nation's Report Card: Trends in Academic Progress, 2012.* Washington, DC: US Department of Education. http://nces.ed.gov/nationsreportcard/pubs/main2012/2013456.aspx.

National Early Literacy Panel. (2008). *Developing Early Literacy: Report of the National Early Literacy Panel.* Washington, DC: National Institute for Literacy and the National Center for Family Literacy.

NICHD ECCRN. (2005). Pathways to reading: The role of oral language in the transition to reading. *Developmental Psychology, 41*(2), 428–442. DOI: http://dx.doi.org/10.1037/0012-1649.41.2.428.

NICHD National Reading Panel. (2000). *Teaching Children to Read: An Evidence-Based Assessment of the Scientific Research Literature on Reading and Its Implications For Reading Instruction.* Washington, DC:US DHHS, PHS, NICHD.

Nye, B., Konstantopoulos, S., & Hedges, L. V. (2004). How large are teacher effects? *Educational Evaluation and Policy Analysis, 26*(3), 237–257. DOI: https://doi.org/10.3102/01623737026003237.

Pallante, D. H., & Kim, Y. S. (2013). The effect of a multicomponent literacy instruction model on literacy growth for kindergartners and first-grade students in Chile. *International Journal of Psychology, 48*(5), 747–761.

Pianta, R. C., Belsky, J., Houts, R., & Morrison, F. (2007). Opportunities to learn in America's elementary classrooms. *Science, 315*(5820), 1795.

Ramachandran, R. (2017). Language use in education and human capital formation: Evidence from the Ethiopian educational reform. *World Development, 98*, 195–213. DOI: https://doi.org/10.1016/j.worlddev.2017.04.029.

Ribeiro, L. A., Zachrisson, H. D., & Dearing, E. (2017). Peer effects on the development of language skills in Norwegian childcare centers. *Early Childhood Research Quarterly, 41*, 1–12. DOI: https://doi.org/10.1016/j.ecresq.2017.05.003.

Rowan, B., Correnti, R., & Miller, R. J. (2002). What large-scale, survey research tells us about teacher effects on student achievement: Insights from the prospects study of elementary schools. *Teachers College Record, 104*(8), 1525–1567. DOI: https://doi.org/10.1111/1467-9620.00212.

Rydland, V., Grover, V., & Lawrence, J. (2014). The second-language vocabulary trajectories of Turkish immigrant children in Norway from ages five to ten: The role of preschool talk exposure, maternal education, and co-ethnic concentration in the neighborhood. *Journal of Child Language, 41*(2), 352–381. DOI: https://doi.org/10.1017/S0305000912000712.

Schickedanz, J., & Dickinson, D. K. (2005). *Opening the World of Learning: A Comprehensive Literacy Program.* Parsippany, NJ: Pearson Early Learning.

Silverman, R., & Crandell, J. D. (2010). Vocabulary practices in prekindergarten and kindergarten classrooms. *Reading Research Quarterly, 45*(3), 318–340.

Slavin, R. E., & Cheung, A. (2005). A synthesis of research on language of reading instruction for English Language Learners. *Review of Educational Research, 75*(2), 247–284.

Spira, E. G., Bracken, S. S., & Fischel, J. E. (2005). Predicting improvement after first-grade reading difficulties: The effects of oral language, emergent literacy, and behavior skills. *Developmental Psychology, 41*(1), 225–234.

Stigler, J. W., & Hiebert, J. (1999). *The Teaching Gap*. New York: Free Press.

Storch, S. A., & Whitehurst, G. J. (2002). Oral language and code-related precursors to reading: Evidence from a longitudinal structural model. *Developmental Psychology, 38*(6), 934–947. DOI: https://doi.org/10.1037//0012-1649.38.6.934.

Strasser, K., & Lissi, M. R. (2009). Home and instruction effects on emergent literacy in a sample of Chilean kindergarten children. *Scientific Studies of Reading, 13*(2), 175–204. DOI: https://doi.org/10.1080/10888430902769525.

Stuebing, K. K., Barth, A. E., Cirino, P. T., Francis, D. J., & Fletcher, J. M. (2008). A response to recent reanalyses of the National Reading Panel Report: Effects of systematic phonics instruction are practically significant. *Journal of Educational Psychology, 100*(1), 123–134.

Swanson, H. L., Rosston, K., Gerber, M., & Solari, E. (2008). Influence of oral language and phonological awareness on children's bilingual reading. *Journal of School Psychology, 46*(4), 413–429. DOI: https://doi.org/10.1016/j.jsp.2007.07.002.

Taylor, J., Roehrig, A. D., Hensler, B. S., Connor, C. M., & Schatschneider, C. (2010). Teacher quality moderates the genetic effects on early reading. *Science, 328*, 512–514.

Tunmer, W. E., & Chapman, J. W. (2012). The simple view of reading redux: Vocabulary knowledge and the independent components hypothesis. *Journal of Learning Disabilities, 45*(5), 453–466. DOI: https://doi.org/10.1177/0022219411432685.

Tunmer, W. E., & Hoover, W. A. (1992). Cognitive and linguistic factors in learning to read. In P. B. Gough, L. C. Ehri, & R. Treiman (eds.), *Reading Acquisition* (pp. 175–214). Hillsdale, NJ: Erlbaum.

UNESCO. (2003). *Teacher Professional Development: An International Review of the Literature*. Paris: UNESCO. https://unesdoc.unesco.org/ark:/48223/pf0000133010?posInSet=3&queryId=bf873b49-024f-4531-a330-b85eee8a19f8.

UNESCO. (2014a). *Sustainable Development Begins with Education: How Education Can Contribute to the Proposed Post-2015 Goals*. Paris:UNESCO. http://unesdoc.unesco.org/images/0023/002305/230508e.pdf.

UNESCO. (2014b). *Teaching and Learning: Achieving Quality for All*. Paris: UNESCO. https://en.unesco.org/gem-report/report/2014/teaching-and-learning-achieving-quality-all.

UNESCO. (2015). *Education for All: 2000–2015: Achievements and Challenges*. Paris: UNESCO. https://en.unesco.org/gem-report/report/2015/education-all-2000-2015-achievements-and-challenges.

UNESCO. (2017a). *Global Education Monitoring Report 2017/18: Accountability in Education*. Paris:UNESCO.

UNESCO. (2017b). More than one-half of children and adolescents are not learning worldwide (Fact Sheet No. 46). Paris: UNESCO. http://uis.unesco.org/sites/default/files/documents/fs46-more-than-half-children-not-learning-en-2017.pdf.

Valdes, G. (1997). Dual-language immersion programs: A cautionary note concerning the education of language-minority students. *Harvard Educational Review, 67*(3), 391–429. DOI: https://doi.org/10.17763/haer.67.3.n5q175qp86120948.

Vellutino, F. R., Tunmer, W. E., Jaccard, J. J., & Chen, R. S. (2007). Components of reading ability: Multivariate evidence for a convergent skills model of reading development. *Scientific Studies of Reading, 11*(1), 3–32. DOI: http://dx.doi.org/10.1080/10888430709336632.

Wagner, R. K., & Torgesen, J. K. (1987). The nature of phonological processing and its causal role in the acquisition of reading skills. *Psychological Bulletin, 101*, 192–212.

Wanzek, J., & Vaughn, S. (2007). Research-based implications from extensive early reading interventions. *School Psychology Review, 36*(4), 541–561.

Wasik, B. A., Bond, M. A., & Hindman, A. (2006). The effects of a language and literacy intervention on Head Start children and teachers. *Journal of Educational Psychology, 98*(1), 63–74. psyh. DOI: https://doi.org/10.1037/0022-0663.98.1.63.

Westergård, E., Ertesvåg, S. K., & Rafaelsen, F. (2019). A preliminary validity of the classroom assessment scoring system in Norwegian lower-secondary schools. *Scandinavian Journal of Educational Research, 63*(4), 566–584. DOI: https://doi.org/10.1080/00313831.2017.1415964.

Wharton-McDonald, R., Pressley, M., & Hampston, J. M. (1998). Literacy instruction in nine first-grade classrooms: Teacher characteristics and student achievement. *Elementary School Journal, 99*(2), 101–128.

Wilson, S. J., Dickinson, D. K., & Rowe, D. W. (2013). Impact of an Early Reading First program on the language and literacy achievement of children from diverse language backgrounds. *Early Childhood Research Quarterly, 28*(3), 578–592. DOI: https://doi.org/10.1016/j.ecresq.2013.03.006.

Wright, T. S., & Neuman, S. B. (2014). Paucity and disparity in kindergarten oral vocabulary instruction. *Journal of Literacy Research, 46*(3), DOI: https://doi.org/10.1177/1086296x14551474.

Yoshikawa, H., Leyva, D., Snow, C. E. et al. (2015). Experimental impacts of a teacher professional development program in Chile on preschool classroom quality and child outcomes. *Developmental Psychology, 51*, 309–322.

Zucker, T. A., Cabell, S. Q., Justice, L. M., Pentimonti, J. M., & Kaderavek, J. N. (2013). The role of frequent, interactive prekindergarten shared reading in the longitudinal development of language and literacy skills. *Developmental Psychology, 49*(8), 1425.

18 The Literacy Ecology of the Home
The Case of Rural Rwanda

Elliott Friedlander and Claude Goldenberg

18.1 Introduction

> Schooling is not the same thing as learning.
> World Development Report, 2018: *Learning to Realize Education's Promise* (World Bank, 2018)

In the past thirty years, following the widespread introduction of free primary education in lower- and middle-income countries, primary school enrollments skyrocketed (UNESCO, 2015). This increase in enrollment did not necessarily come with improvements in learning. Both small-scale and nationally representative reading assessments revealed that children in the early primary years still struggle with basic reading skills, despite several years of schooling (Gove & Cvelich, 2011). For example, cross-sectional data collected over ten years show ever-expanding primary enrollments accompanied by ever-declining average literacy skills for millions of Indian children (ASER, 2015). With these findings emerging across lower- and middle-income countries, the international education community has turned its attention from ensuring unfettered access to primary education toward addressing the learning crisis and actually improving student achievement (see Nag, Chapter 15 and Asfaha & Nag, Chapter 16 this volume). Nearly all of this attention focuses on the school. Indeed, despite the opening sentence (cited as the epigraph to this chapter) to the World Bank's 2018 World Development Report, the 240-page report spends a mere 100 words reviewing evidence around the role of the home in primary-school-goers' achievement (World Bank, 2018).

In this chapter, we report on the role of the home in children's learning, even in extremely rural, impoverished areas of lower- and middle-income countries. We use both quantitative and qualitative data collected as part of a larger randomized control trial of a literacy intervention in eastern Africa (Friedlander et al., 2019; Friedlander & Goldenberg, 2016). First, we describe the Literacy Ecology (LE) theoretical framework. Second, we report survey, ethnographic, and child reading data from a rural district in Rwanda that illustrate connections between home and community literacy and children's early reading achievement. We conclude by exploring future directions and implications of the findings for efforts in lower- and middle-income countries to improve children's early literacy attainment.

18.2 Previous Research on Ecological Factors in Learning to Read

Funders have urged educators to devise interventions using research-based best practices to address the learning crisis. In response, over the past two decades educational researchers have rigorously evaluated revamped teacher training, new curricular materials, empowered school management committees, and other attempts to improve student outcomes (Ganimian & Murnane, 2016; McEwan, 2015). These efforts have been based on documented or presumed linkages between school-based inputs such as teacher training on the one hand and student outcomes such as improved achievement on the other. Such linkages between home or community inputs and student learning outcomes are not nearly as prevalent in lower- and middle-income-country research literature. Several recent reviews and meta-analyses point out this conspicuous gap in the type of education interventions in the developing world: Very few seek to enlist home and community resources to improve children's learning trajectories (Cao et al., 2014).

The rarely documented efforts at researching the role of the family in children's learning usually target the homes of children too young for primary school. In one review (Nag et al., 2018) of 260 studies set in lower- and middle-income countries, published between 1990 and 2013, only 5 included attempts to improve children's learning experiences at home, and none of these included primary-school-aged children. In another review of 223 education interventions in developing lower- and middle-income countries, the interventions explicitly occurred outside of and independent of the school. One strategy, *improving parenting practices*, was found to have a positive impact on child outcomes, especially for the youngest children. The other strategy, *increased resources in students' homes*, superficially appears a good candidate for out-of-school supports to learning. However, the review states this strategy largely revolved around provision of computers and tablets and had little observable impact. Based on these reviews, it seems that holistic home interventions targeting the family and broader community have not been widely implemented, much less evaluated. One notable exception to this gap in the literature is the Literacy Boost program, created by the international nongovernmental organization Save the Children. Reports and articles published by Save the Children find significant links between children's home environment and reading achievement (Dowd et al., 2017).

Great variation exists in the literature on high-income countries that examines the role of the home and family in children's learning. Differences in research methods, outcomes, and participant demographics make direct comparisons among studies difficult. Yet overall, most of the literature in high-income countries has reported generally positive relationships between the quality of children's home experiences and their learning (Barton & Hamilton, 1998; Evans, Shaw, & Bell, 2000; Goldenberg, 1987; Heath, 1983; Leseman & de Jong, 1998; Park, 2008; Purcell-Gates, 1996; Snow, Burns, & Griffin, 1998). Taylor's rhetorical question highlights why the positive relationship between the home and children's literacy development is to be expected: The question emerges of whether we can seriously expect children who have never experienced or have limited experience of reading and writing as complex cultural activities to successfully learn to read and write from the narrowly defined pedagogical practices in our schools (Taylor, 1983, p. 91).

Yet despite the wealth of research on the relationship between the home and children's academic learning in high-income countries, and suggestive studies in lower- and middle-income countries (Chansa-Kabali & Westerholm, 2014; Dowd, Wiener, & Mabeti, 2010; Friedlander, 2013; Kalia & Reese, 2009; Nath, Guajardo, & Hossain, 2013; Wagner, 1993), researchers remain skeptical that a robust relationship even *exists* between children's home experiences and their academic achievement in lower- and middle-income countries. For example, according to Cao et al., "in the developing world context, the link between household characteristics and reading outcomes is much less clear than in developed countries" (Cao et al., 2014, p. 14). The absence of concerted efforts to improve children's achievement-related learning opportunities in lower- and middle-income-country homes and communities reflects the doubts surrounding the significance of these influences for children's school learning (Kim et al., 2016).

18.3 The Literacy Ecology Framework

We approach the subject of children's home and community contexts from an ecological systems perspective (Bronfenbrenner, 1979). Ecological systems theory posits that an individual's development is a function of reciprocal and interactive relationships among nested systems in which an individual is situated and the individual's own psychological processes (Bronfenbrenner, 1979).

Readers may be familiar with the term "home literacy environment," which has been defined as the availability of material resources, the press for academic achievement, the amount of shared book reading, the value placed on reading, and opportunities for verbal interaction (Hess & Holloway, 1984). Reformulating the definition of the home literacy environment using an ecological systems lens strengthens the conceptualization by accounting for the reciprocal interaction between the child and the nested ecosystems in which the child develops. This reciprocal interaction necessarily involves the intrinsic processes of children's learning and development, which then helps account for the internal disposition (e.g., abilities, interest, motivation) of the individual child. These dispositions will mediate the home literacy environment and therefore should be accounted for in any analysis of the home context. In other words, child characteristics are *part of* the literacy ecology, not separate from it. Moreover, the very term "*home* literacy environment" limits the focus of inquiry to environmental contributions in the home. Particularly in rural lower- and middle-income country contexts, a child's "home" may have a very different connotation than it does in high-income countries. That is to say, in a lower-income-country setting, the influence of the child's neighbors and community may play a much larger and more influential role in the life of a child than in that of a child living in a high-income-country context.

Following this literacy ecology framework, reading development can be understood as dependent on three sets of factors: individual child characteristics, characteristics of the child's home and community, and features of the child's school. In this chapter, we focus on the first two sets of factors, individual child factors and home and community factors. For more on school-related factors, see Friedlander et al. (2019).

18.4 Ecological Factors in Learning to Read: The Case of Rwanda

18.4.1 Design of the Study

In this section, we use quantitative data to understand relationships among children's LE and their early (Primary 1) reading development in Rwanda. The data came from two sources: a reading skills assessment of Primary 1 students and LE surveys of the children's caregivers. The qualitative data come from a series of weeklong ethnographies conducted by a Rwandan collaborator (Tusiime, Friedlander, & Malik, 2014). We collected the data during September and October 2013.

We assessed students on a range of Kinyarwanda language and literacy skills using individually administered assessments. For our analysis, we use four of the subtests as outcome variables: (1) letter identification, (2) decoding, (3) reading, fluency, and (4) reading comprehension. All outcomes were continuous and measured as percentage correct, with the exception of fluency, which was measured as the number of words correctly read in one minute on a Primary 1-leveled passage. We selected these outcomes to represent a range of reading skills, from basic to more advanced.

Following the reading-skills data collection, we asked the caregivers of a subset of children to participate in an LE survey. The LE survey contained 113 items and covered a wide range of questions regarding the role and use of literacy in the home, both by the caregiver and the entire family. A total of 466 caregivers participated in the LE survey, and we matched caregiver responses with the reading-assessment data of their children using individual identifiers. In so doing, we were able to estimate the degree of association between the nonschool LE and children's reading abilities.

18.4.2 The Five Factors of the Nonschool Literacy Ecology

Our first step in our analysis was identifying the factors of the literacy ecology. To do so, we conducted an exploratory factor analysis to identify potential underlying factors of the nonschool literacy ecology in rural Rwanda. For more on data reduction and factor loading, see Friedlander (2015). Our analysis of the caregiver reported data yielded five factors: (1) literacy interactions at home (hereafter *Literacy Interactions*), (2) caregiver competency in literacy (*Caregiver Competency*), (3) reading materials, (4) religious reading activities (*Religious Reading*), and (5) child interest/engagement (*Child Interest*). The first four factors relate to the home and community, while the fifth factor relates to the individual child. Table 18.1 contains the factor names with brief descriptions.

Literacy Interactions includes variables related to the verbal and reading activities at home, and measures of family size and years of schooling. *Caregiver Competency* includes, among others, two observed variables on whether the responder could read and sign the informed consent form independently and whether the caregiver reported that he/she had learned to read from his/her teacher. *Reading Materials* is a straightforward grouping of variables that index the total amount of different types of reading and writing materials available at home, excluding religious print materials. This last set of materials loaded most highly onto the fourth factor, *Religious Reading*, and includes items that relate both to the respondents' own use of literacy for religious purposes and whether the respondent engages the child with religious

Table 18.1 *Variables loading onto each factor*

Factor name	Factor description
Literacy Interactions	The types and frequency of literacy interactions occurring at home as reported by the caregiver.
Caregiver Competency	Caregiver's ability to read independently, as observed by the data collector and reported by the caregiver.
Reading Materials	The number of reading materials at home as reported by the caregiver.
Religious Reading	The religious-related activities occurring at home and materials found in the home, as reported by caregiver.
Child Interest	Child's interest and engagement with literacy, as reported by the caregiver.

reading materials. The fifth factor, *Child Interest,* consists primarily of observations of the focus child's interest in and habits around reading, as reported by the caregiver. Loading highly but negatively onto *Interest* is also a variable indicating that a caregiver reported not helping his/her child to learn.

18.4.3 Relation between Ecological Factors and Literacy Outcomes

In order to assess the relationship between children's literacy ecologies and their reading skills, we fitted several multivariate regression models using the LE factors to predict child reading scores. Every regression controlled for the child's sex, age, socioeconomic status, and whether the focus child reported repeating Primary 1. We clustered standard errors at the school level to account for students nested in schools.

The results in Table 18.2 indicate that, on average, when controlling for relevant background characteristics, *Literacy Interactions* and *Child Interest* most highly and consistently predicted reading achievement across all outcomes. *Caregiver Competency* also significantly predicted all outcomes except reading fluency. Neither *Reading Materials* nor *Religious Reading* predicted any reading outcomes.

The findings from Table 18.2 support many of the findings in both the high-income and the lower- and middle-income-country research on the LE.

Table 18.2 *Multivariate regressions using LE factors to predict reading achievement (N=466)*

Factors	Letter identification β (SE)	Decoding β (SE)	Reading fluency β (SE)	Reading comprehension β (SE)
Literacy Interactions	0.042** (0.013)	0.024** (0.009)	0.811* (0.353)	0.025* (0.009)
Caregiver Competency	0.041** (0.014)	0.022* (0.010)	0.663 (0.391)	0.023* (0.011)
Reading Materials	0.017 (0.011)	0.018 (0.012)	0.523 (0.399)	0.016 (0.011)
Religious Reading	−0.011 (0.013)	−0.009 (.008)	−0.307 (0.395)	−0.014 (0.008)
Child Interest	0.037* (0.014)	0.024** (0.008)	0.680* (0.311)	0.024* (0.010)
R^2-squared	0.126	0.142	0.090	.110
Adjusted R^2	0.109	0.125	0.073	.092

Standard errors clustered at the school level in parentheses. β = beta coefficient. SE = Standard Error. All models control for gender, age, whether the child repeated Primary 1, and socioeconomic status. * $p<.05$, ** $p<.01$, *** $p<.001$

Interactions demonstrated significant links to literacy learning in the same way as reported in studies on shared book reading (for example, Bus, van IJzendoorn, & Pellegrini, 1995), verbal interactions (Hart & Risley, 1995), and support for studying or help with homework (Zevenbergen et al., 1997). The findings concerning the *Competency* factor also concur with high-income country research findings (Neuman, 1996). The *Interest* factor significantly predicted reading achievement in a manner similar to research carried out in high-income countries (Baker & Wigfield, 1999). Finally, the *Materials* factor did not significantly predict any of the outcomes, likely due to issues of collinearity.

18.5 Explanatory Mechanisms

To explore possible explanatory mechanisms for the findings presented above, we turn to qualitative data describing the literacy ecologies of two girls living in rural Rwanda. First we provide details on the two girls who were observed, the families of those girls, and the villages in which they lived. We then present the qualitative data on the factors of their respective literacy ecologies, highlighting instances that demonstrate the various significant relationships that we presented in the previous section.

A lecturer at the University of Rwanda – College of Education (referred to by his initials, MT) collected the qualitative data. He visited the homes of two students for one week each during the final months of 2013. We randomly selected two female students from the population of homes that participated in the LE survey and who had indicated they would be willing to participate in the observation. We refer to these two girls by the pseudonyms of Flora and Jolly. The observer followed the girls during their daily routines in the village. Observations occurred in November and December, following the end of the academic year in October. The two girls were observed by MT from approximately sunrise to sunset. He conducted planned interviews with participants and kept detailed notes on unplanned discussions and exchanges he had with the girls, family members, neighbors, community members, neighborhood youth, and local leaders. During the interviews and unplanned discussions, MT inquired about the interviewees' perceptions of ways in which activities in the home and broader community may have related to literacy practices.

In order to triangulate data from home observations and interviews with family members, MT visited key places in the village outside of the participants' homes thought to be representative of their nonschool LE outside the home. He collected data in spaces that each child frequented regularly, including the farmers' market, the local church, each child's school, trading centers, water-collection centers, the woods where children spent time, played, and gathered firewood, and the monthly village-wide communal work projects and meetings. We coded MT's notes and observations using codes that corresponded to each factor. The coded notes were then compared to the significant associations resulting from the multivariate regression analyses.

18.5.1 Introducing Flora and Jolly

Flora lived on a steep, relatively isolated hillside with her parents, two younger brothers, an aunt, and a grandmother. Flora and her siblings spent most of the observation week performing chores under the supervision of her grandmother and aunt. Flora's parents were at home rarely during the observations, as they were either tending their fields or in the market selling produce. Jolly lived in a planned settlement with her parents, six siblings, and a man who performed domestic duties. Jolly spent much of the observation time playing with friends and siblings. Jolly's mother was home for many of the observations, but her father, who usually works as a primary school teacher, was away from home while marking examinations for the national primary school leavers' exam.

Despite living in the same district in Rwanda, the two communities in which the girls lived were very different. Jolly's village was located in a planned community, called an *umudugudu*. In the *umudugudu*, there are government-built low-cost homes for people to buy or be resettled in for free. Usually within the *umudugudu* or in close proximity to it there is a school (depending on the population size, it may be both a primary school and a secondary school), water, electricity, retail shops and other related infrastructure. This was the case for Jolly's *umudugudu*. Jolly's village appeared full of children playing and singing together or simply roaming the paths between houses. This was in sharp contrast to Flora's village, which offered less opportunity for social interaction, as houses were isolated on hillsides. Jolly's village also had two shops that sold a few basic items, which meant that Jolly and her family did not have the same long commute as Flora's family did to access basic necessities. In comparison with Flora's area, a large number of educated people resided in Jolly's village. Jolly's neighbor, for instance, had two sons who studied at university level, and Jolly's own sisters had also completed university. The presence of these more educated individuals, in addition to the higher socioeconomic status of the village and the ease with which the *umudugudu* could be accessed, provided a seemingly better environment to support the education of young children.

18.5.2 Reading Skills of Flora and Jolly

Crucial for this chapter, Flora and Jolly also differed in another important aspect: their reading skills. When MT asked Flora to recite the Kinyarwanda alphabet, she was able to recite up to the letter "k" before mixing up the sequence of letters. He asked Flora if she would like to write something in his book. While she could write various letters and numbers, it was clear that

410   *Elliott Friedlander & Claude Goldenberg*

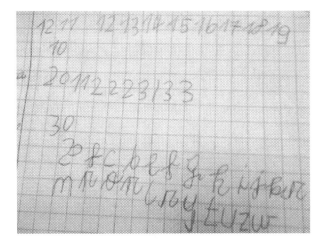

Figure 18.1 Flora's writing sample

Figure 18.2 Jolly writing in MT's notebook

she struggled with the alphabet and distinguishing between certain letters. Her writing sample is reproduced in Figure 18.1.

Jolly, on the other hand, was an extremely proficient reader and writer. She was the family scorekeeper when playing cards and could read simple sentences in Kinyarwanda. At one point, while MT conversed with Jolly's mother, Jolly took MT's notebook (see Figure 18.2) and wrote:

The Literacy Ecology of the Home: Rural Rwanda 411

Uyu mugaboyaje hano arimoguhamagaraterefone. Arimokuvugana na mama. Yaje kurebakodukubagaga

This man who came here was talking on phone a few minutes ago, now he is talking with my mother. He came here to find out whether we are calm and disciplined.

Table 18.3 provides a snapshot of the two girls' out-of-school literacy ecologies in the form of values for the variables that make up each literacy ecology factor.

18.5.3 Literacy Ecology Factors in the Lives of Flora and Jolly

18.5.3.1 Literacy Interactions As reported in Table 18.2, the *Literacy Interactions* factor significantly predicted every reading outcome. One would therefore expect that MT would observe few or no reading interactions in the home of the struggling reader, Flora, but would observe many in the home of Jolly, the good reader. As expected, the qualitative data showed precisely this (see Table 18.3). But the differences in literacy interactions in the two girls' homes extended more deeply into differences between the children's home literacy ecologies.

Flora's father stated that, due to a lack of resources, Flora had never seen him read. When asked what role parents play in their children's learning,

Table 18.3 *Evidence of the five LE factors in the qualitative data*

Factor	Selected variables	Flora	Jolly
	Family size	7	10
	N of family who can read and write	1	8
Literacy	N of family who read to child	0	≥ 1
Interactions	N of family who help child study	0	≥ 1
	N of family who talk to child	0	10
	Years of family schooling total	~4	70 or more
	Years of schooling – average	≤ 1	≥ 9
Caregiver Competency	Can read and write well	neither parent	both parents
Reading Materials	Books/writing materials	0	many
Religious Reading	Religious reading activities occur at home	no evidence	no evidence
	Total N of religious texts at home	2	no evidence
	Child likes to read	no evidence	no evidence
	Child asks what writing says	no	yes
Child Interest	Child asks for parents to read to her	no	no
	Caregiver reports helping the child learn	no	yes
	Caregiver has seen child pretend to read	no evidence	yes

her father mentioned the importance of providing children with books and pens and sending them to school. At no point did anyone in Flora's family mention reading to Flora or helping her to study as important actions in helping Flora to learn. Flora herself reported that during the school year, her considerable workload was identical to that when not in school, and there was little time for homework and no one at home to help her; her homework was usually completed with the help of friends on the way to school.

The absence of reading interactions clearly indexes a great deal more than the absence of children reading, being read to, and the presence of individuals with whom these interactions can and do occur – which are, to be sure, important influences in themselves. Absence of reading interactions also indicates familial attitudes and assumptions about the family's role in children's literacy development. The families demonstrate that they prioritize children's education by incurring the opportunity costs of sending a child to school. However, Flora's family did not see themselves as having a role in Flora's children's education beyond sending her to school. That is, the school, and education more broadly, are unfamiliar places, seen as being for people with skills that Flora's parents do not possess. Hence, they do not feel empowered to make concerted efforts to improve Flora's literacy and learning. This likely explains the depressed achievement we observed in literacy skills. The lack of emphasis on homework in the home is also likely to depress Flora's achievement, particularly if she is already struggling with basic literacy skills.

During the week MT spent with Flora, he witnessed no spontaneous literacy interactions in the home. This includes both interactions involving the written word and verbal exchanges. The one literacy-related activity, when Flora wrote the letters and numbers shown in Picture 1, occurred only after MT asked Flora if she would like to write in his book. Even verbal exchanges between Flora and her elders were limited. One rainy morning, while the family waited inside for the rain to pass before starting to work, MT attempted to speak with Flora's father. Each time MT did so, Flora's father told all the children to leave the room. Even when MT assured her father that they could continue the conversations in the children's presence, her father insisted,

Ntabgo ari umuco mwiza, abana ntibakagombye gusangira ibiganiro nabanti bakuru.

It's not good manners, children should not be involved in the discussions with adults.

In this traditional family, not only did Flora experience very few literacy interactions; in addition, she lived in a microsystem that explicitly limited children's opportunities for meaningful verbal interactions with adults. This in itself is likely to have unfavorable consequences for cognitive and academic development over and above the consequences of minimal literacy interactions. Jolly's home, on the other hand, was relatively full of *Literacy Interactions*. Jolly's mother informed MT that during school terms, her children have specific time set aside for homework and reading, and that she even kept her children awake to study late into the evening. Jolly's parents also encouraged Jolly to spend time reading, even when it meant that Jolly's chores would be neglected. In one instance, Jolly's mother volunteered to shine the pile of shoes that Jolly was shining, so that Jolly could spend time reading instead. At another point, when Jolly realized that her father would soon be home after a long time away, Jolly started sorting books in the family home, informing MT that she was planning to start reading when her father returned. The main literacy interaction that MT directly observed was card-playing, which necessitated keeping score on a piece of paper. Despite the limited nature of this literacy interaction, the activity was infused with opportunities for verbal interaction. During a conversation with MT, Jolly's mother said:

Nkunda gukina amacarita n'abana bangye. Bituma ntagira irungu cyangwa ngo njye kunywa cyangwa ngo ndyame kunywa. Bituma nasabaana nabana bangye nkamenye nibibazo bafite mumashuri nkabasha kubagir anama.

I love playing cards with my children. I don't get bored and go to the local bar to drink or even sleep during the day. It is also an opportunity to bond with my children and know the details about their educational problems and provide help.

The observer never heard Jolly's parents express the belief that children should not be involved in discussions with adults. To the contrary, as this last quote indicates, Jolly's mother relished and sought out opportunities for this type of engagement with her children. Moreover, Jolly's parents placed a great deal of value on literacy activities and interactions, as demonstrated in their encouragement, and even directives, for Jolly to spend time reading.

In summary, the differences between Jolly and Flora's families in the frequency of literacy interactions was stark enough, but the contrast extended to the very ecosystems that supported – or failed to support – those interactions. The priority assigned to literacy by the adults, the corresponding prioritization of children's time, the opportunities for adult–child interactions, all held in place by material conditions and parents' stated values and priorities, created strikingly different literacy ecologies for the two girls. These contrasts help us understand not only that *Literacy Interactions* indexed a deeper constellation of factors in each child's home literacy ecologies but also why it robustly predicted each of the four reading measures administered to children.

18.5.3.2 Caregiver Competency The quantitative results on *Caregiver Competency* suggest that children with better reading skills have caregivers with greater literacy competency. Therefore one would expect a significant difference between the caregivers of Flora and Jolly in terms of *Caregiver Competency*. Over the course of the week, MT did not observe great competency in literacy on the part of Flora's caregivers. In terms of raw numbers, Table 18.3 indicates that MT found no evidence of any literacy *Caregiver Competency* in Flora's parents. Flora's mother cited a lack of books as the greatest challenge to reading, but then added the following, indicating that what she doesn't know prevents her from actively supporting her daughter's literacy development:

Biga ibintu ntazi. Ntabwo nzi igifaransa n'icyongereza.

They study some things that I don't know. I don't know French and English.

When MT suggested that her help in Kinyarwanda would benefit Flora, she responded:

Yego nzabikora ariko hashize igihe kirekire narataye ishuri. Hari amagambo amwe n'amwe angora gusoma.

Yes, I will but it has been long since I dropped out of school. There are some words that are difficult for me to read.

In addition to very limited literacy skills, Flora's mother revealed a lack of confidence in her ability to do anything that would support, in any way, Flora's reading and writing skills. Similarly, Flora's father did not demonstrate a high degree of *Caregiver Competency* in literacy. He mentioned to MT that Flora had never seen him read anything. Considering that he dropped out of school in Primary 2, it was not clear whether this lack of reading was a consequence of no materials to read or a lack of proficiency in reading. No matter the cause, it was clear that Flora's caregivers did not possess strong competency in reading nor dispositions that would lead them to encourage or support Flora's literacy development.

Jolly's father ranked highly on the *Caregiver Competency* factor, particularly when compared to Flora's parents. Jolly's father was a teacher and required that his children learn to read from young ages. The primary evidence of his *Caregiver Competency* stems from his profession as a teacher. In addition to the literacy activities required of a teacher, he also served on the national examination board, marking national exams for students around the country. This provided further evidence of his literacy competency. From the data collected, it was more difficult to assess the *Caregiver Competency* of Jolly's mother. The existing data certainly place her higher than Flora's parents, as she served on a sector administrative committee. She also read and signed the consent forms provided. However, even if Jolly's mother lacked a high level of literacy competency, her repeated statements concerning her commitment to the education of her children and the high levels of education achieved by her other children as well as her siblings (many of whom completed tertiary education) likely balance out any lack of *Caregiver Competency* on Jolly's mother's part.

Similar to *Literacy Interactions*, qualitative evidence on *Caregiver Competency* reveals the profound differences between the two girls' home literacy ecologies that help explain the differences in children's reading abilities. Flora's parents did not display any overt competency in reading, nor did they reveal attitudes and behaviors that would support and encourage their daughter's literacy growth. Flora's mother cited her own lack of knowledge and skills and seemed to doubt that she had any capacity to help Flora with what she was learning in school, even through encouragement or support. Jolly's parents, in contrast, both ranked highly on the *Caregiver Competency* factor, but also showed positive attitudes about their own abilities to play a meaningful role in their children's learning. Jolly's mother came across as a more assured person who felt that she had something important to contribute to Jolly's education, whereas statements from Flora's mother betray a passivity and resignation that are unlikely to benefit Flora's education.

18.5.3.3 Reading Materials In contrast to the *Literacy Interactions* and *Caregiver Competency* factors, *Reading Materials* (an index of the number of different types of reading and writing materials present in the home), did not significantly relate to reading achievement in the multivariate regressions. Yet there was a large difference between Jolly's and Flora's print environments. How does one explain the lack of significant association between materials and children's reading in the quantitative data, while the two case studies demonstrated a great contrast in reading materials?

Taking both the quantitative and qualitative data into account suggests the following: It is not that materials do not matter; they do. *Reading Materials* are indeed necessary. But they are not a *sufficient* condition for the sorts of *Literacy Interactions* that influence children's reading achievement. Most of the *Literacy Interactions* observed in Jolly's home would not have been possible without the presence of abundant materials. At the same time, because of the strong and statistically significant association between *Reading Materials* and *Literacy Interactions* (r=0.35) the absence of a significant association between materials and achievement is almost certainly the result of collinearity[1]. That is, *Literacy Interactions* are correlated with *Reading Materials* and account for more variance. But it would be wrong to conclude that *Reading Materials* is not a meaningful factor in the out-of-school LE. The contrast between the *Reading Materials* in Jolly and Flora's homes, the use of those materials in the *Literacy*

---

[1] A full table of correlations among literacy ecology factors is available from the first author.

Figure 18.3 Flora holding her exercise book

Interactions observed in Jolly's home, and the absence of both materials and interactions in Flora's home suggest materials are indeed important nonschool influences on children's reading growth.

By any standard, the print environment in Flora's home was poor. Flora only had access to one piece of writing: her school notebook (see Figure 18.3). Flora's exercise book was only produced when MT asked Flora whether she had any books. When he asked to see it, Flora and her brother spent five to ten minutes looking for the book, finally locating it sandwiched between two sacks of grain. It was clear the exercise book was only used for school. Over the course of the weeklong observation, besides Flora's notebook, MT only observed two other distinct print materials in Flora's family's possession: a small Bible, and a sheet of paper with a prayer written on it that was kept by Flora's aunt.

Jolly, on the other hand, lived in an extremely print-rich environment (see Figure 18.4). In Jolly's home, MT found a large stack of books: textbooks, teacher's guides, and even photocopies of books. Jolly's father brought these materials home from school for his children to use. Her father also regularly brought home chalk, and created a smooth surface close to the ground on the side of the family home to allow children to practice their writing. As the family lived in an *umudugudu* and shops were close by, there were also manufactured products with print on them. MT even found print in an unlikely place: old school notebooks were found in the family's pit latrine. Whether these last materials were actually read is difficult to determine, but their presence in the most unlikely of places demonstrated the degree to which Jolly was surrounded by print. Indeed, the print was so abundant that MT witnessed Jolly tearing a piece of paper from her older sister's notebook to clean her shoes. By comparison, Flora's one notebook, in which she wrote her math notes in the front, Kinyarwanda notes in the back, and English notes in the middle, was a

Figure 18.4 A stack of books in Jolly's house

treasured item, covered with paper salvaged from an old cement bag to protect it from the elements during her long walk to school.

In summary, the qualitative evidence regarding *Reading Materials* helps to understand the quantitative finding of no association, net other factors, between *Reading Materials* and reading achievement. The qualitative data show a dramatic difference in the amount of print materials in the home of Jolly, a skilled beginning reader, in contrast to the home of Flora, a struggling reader. This contrast suggests a "necessary but not sufficient" relationship between materials and reading achievement: Materials are necessary; indeed most of the interactions MT observed could not have occurred without literacy materials. But the interactions are what directly link to improved reading outcomes. Once interactions are entered into the regression models, materials appear to drop away as predictors of reading outcomes. But it would be a mistake to conclude they do not matter. They do – but only if used for literacy interactions.

18.5.3.4 Religious Reading The *Religious Reading* factor, like *Reading Materials*, did not demonstrate significant associations with reading achievement, when controlling for other factors, in the quantitative data.

The ethnographic data suggests one reason why not – there was little variability and few religious reading activities occurring in the homes. This finding was corroborated by the statistical sample, which revealed very infrequent religious reading and no association with any measure of child literacy. Thus, the explanation for lack of association between *Religious Reading* and child literacy is in contrast to the explanation for lack of association between *Reading Materials* and child literacy. The presence of *Reading Materials* was strikingly different in the two girls' homes, but its association with reading outcomes was statistically masked by *Literacy Interactions*. The presence of *Religious Reading* in the two homes – and among the sample as a whole – was close to nil.

MT observed very few religious reading activities in either of the homes or villages. MT accompanied Flora's family to Sunday services at the parish church. Flora's aunt brought a small Bible with her, one of only two Bibles that MT saw among the roughly 300-person congregation. A few minutes into the service, the majority of children went outside to play, and did not witness the aforementioned Bible passage being read aloud. During the service, individuals came to the altar and read selected Bible passages. However, the congregation was never asked to read along while the passages were read aloud. There was no other evidence of literacy activities during the church service. Jolly's family did not attend church services on the week of the observation. In Jolly's home, MT did not observe any religious-related reading activities, nor religious texts in the home.

In summary, the *Religious Reading* factor showed no links with reading achievement, neither in the qualitative nor quantitative data. The most likely explanation is that *Religious Reading* appears to happen very infrequently, and even when it does occur, children are only indirectly exposed to activities that involve *Religious Reading* materials.

18.5.3.5 Child Interest   The *Child Interest* factor significantly predicted all reading outcomes in the quantitative analysis. The home ethnographies of the two girls found the same association between interest and reading achievement. During the week MT spent with Flora, MT witnessed no acts and had no discussions with Flora that would indicate that she had any interest in reading, or motivation to read. The only variable that loaded onto this factor and for which evidence existed in Flora's LE was reports by the caregiver that he/she did not help the child to learn. Discussions with Flora's parents indicated that they did not see a role for themselves in Flora's learning.

Although noticeably more than what Flora demonstrated, Jolly displayed only modest motivation to read or interest in reading. At times, Jolly's mother urged Jolly to stop playing cards and to read a book instead. However, these urgings went unheeded by Jolly. Four separate incidents that relate to motivation stand out in the data as relating to Jolly's *Child Interest*. The first was already reported during the description of the children's reading skills. Jolly independently took MT's notebook and wrote a sentence in it without being prompted. The second instance was Jolly asking MT about the meaning of the words "NIU Huskies" that were written on MT's shirt. The third instance occurred when Jolly proudly asked MT to watch her write her name. The fourth and final instance occurred on the eve of her father's return to the house after an extended period away from home while marking national exams. With her father's impending arrival, Jolly started sorting the stack of papers and books in the living room, setting aside a pile for her to read either with or in the presence of her father. When MT asked Jolly what she was doing, she explained that she would want to read these books once her father returned home. In short, her interest and motivation in the activity was inspired not by an intrinsic drive or interest in reading itself. Rather, the knowledge of her father's arrival spurred her into engaging with the materials. Limited as these displays of interest were, they were considerably more than was observed during observations at Flora's home.

MT saw no evidence that Flora took interest in engaging in literacy activities. Thus, to the extent that participating in these activities helps promote literacy skills, Flora's lack of self-motivated literacy engagement meant fewer opportunities for literacy development. Jolly's interest and engagement in reading, although modest, provide some indication of the mechanisms through which *Child Interest* might be encouraged in the literacy ecology of the home. In Jolly's home, the father had set up a very clear culture of reading, which encouraged and motivated Jolly to engage in and practice reading. The data are less clear regarding Jolly's interest in reading engagement, or a broader literacy motivation on Jolly's part that is intrinsic to Jolly herself. The qualitative data suggest that the routines and expectations in Jolly's home – the literacy ecology microsystem – seemed to be what drove her interest and engagement in reading. That interest and engagement, although extrinsically fueled, are likely to have helped Jolly further develop her emerging literacy skills.

18.6 Conclusions and Discussion

This chapter has explored the home literacy ecology of early grade students in Rwanda. Using parent surveys, we identified five distinct factors of children's literacy ecology: *Literacy Interactions, Caregiver Competency, Reading Materials, Religious-Related Reading,* and *Child Interest*. Using the LE factors to predict reading achievement, we found that the *Literacy Interactions* at home, *Child Interest*, and to a slightly lesser degree *Caregiver Competency* all significantly predicted children's reading achievement, while *Reading*

Materials and *Religious-Related Reading* bore no relationship to reading achievement.

The qualitative data illustrate the quantitative relationships we found. Flora, a struggling reader, lives in a household with few or no habitual literacy interactions. Her parents are functionally illiterate, and without any children's books or role models, Flora does not demonstrate significant interest in literacy. On the other hand, Jolly, who is able to read and write in an age-appropriate manner, lives in a household with abundant, casual literacy interactions. Her parents both read, and she has access to reading materials. Jolly does seem slightly interested in reading, but her interest could be the result of extrinsic motivation to please her father.

Our findings largely agree with findings from the existing research on the home literacy ecology in both high-income countries and, to a lesser extent, low- and middle-income countries. The significant associations we found between the literacy-related characteristics of the home and reading achievement echo existing research, both qualitative and quantitative, that underlines the importance of the home in children's learning development (Friedlander, 2013; Heath, 1983; Hess & Holloway, 1984; Sénéchal & LeFevre, 2014; Snow et al., 1998).

Our findings also provide evidence that support some of the relationships between individual children, the home, and children's reading achievement that underlie the Literacy Ecology framework. The quantitative findings certainly suggest that children's interest is directly related to their reading achievement, as do the factors of the home and community literacy ecology. As to the reciprocal nature, or the directionality of the relationship between the individual child and the factors of the home and community literacy ecology, we are unable to make any claims from our quantitative analysis.

Unlike other chapters in this volume, the data in this chapter cannot speak to specific neurocognitive constraints that may affect the Literacy Ecology or children's reading development. That said, it is reasonable to expect that neurocognitive constraints could attenuate the relationships between the LE and reading development. For example, children with poor phonological sensitivities will have a more difficult time acquiring reading skills, even in a home with ample literacy interactions. The same is likely true for children with relatively weak short-term memories. Follow-up data collection not reported in this chapter showed that a large number of children made very poor progress in reading, to the point of being nonreaders after two years of schooling (Friedlander & Goldenberg, 2016). To what extent nonschool literacy ecologies can be augmented and used to help children at risk for poor reading outcomes despite neurocognitive constraints is one of the many questions in need of addressing.

Another question that should be further explored is the role that religion currently plays, and could play, in children's literacy development and the overall enrichment of the literacy ecology. This is important to explore as religion plays a much more central role in rural community life in lower- and middle-income countries, particularly those in Central and South America and in Africa. By and large, the religious organizations have clear hierarchies, with revered leaders and sophisticated communication systems. Moreover, religion is of paramount importance to large swathes of the population. Future research would do well to explore how educators and researchers could partner with religious organizations to help improve the literacy ecology in homes and communities.

The data in this study were collected in a small geographical area, one of Rwanda's thirty districts. At this point, it is not possible to state categorically that these findings apply to the entirety of lower- and middle-income countries. But the findings do suggest that even in places that are impoverished, and do not have a great deal of access to print or a culture of reading, the nonschool literacy ecology plays a role in children's reading development. The next step for research will be to test whether interventions aimed at improving the literacy ecology of the home and wider community lead to improvements in children's learning. The qualitative data suggest some of the challenges interventions will face. The LE factors we found to be associated with one or more reading outcomes are actually indicators of much deeper, complex, and possibly hard-to-change material and cultural conditions that define children's literacy ecologies outside of school. Thus, for example, reading interactions in the home could be increased, but doing so might require not just introducing more reading materials but also challenging basic beliefs some parents hold about the relative priority of school and household work or whether adult–child conversations are appropriate.

Long-term studies of intervention efficacy and sustainability are needed to justify investment outside the school. Investing in the nonschool LE will require working not simply with the education system, but also with a variety of institutions and actors to achieve lasting change. The upfront investment in doing so may be high. But over the long term, parents and family members stay relatively constant, while teachers and textbooks tend to have high attrition rates. Encouraging widespread literacy requires a cultural change as much as it requires changes in pedagogy and curricula. Investments in the family and community may trump all rate-of-return analyses, but research is needed to investigate this proposition.

For now, this research has important implications for educational improvement efforts across lower-income countries. Current efforts to address the learning crisis, for the most part, are still confined to the schools. But primary schools in lower-income countries are only open officially for a small percentage of the time a child is awake in a year (for example, Rwandan schools are only open for 15 percent of a child's year). If schools, governments, donor agencies, and education-focused organizations are truly interested in helping all children learn to read, the most obvious implication is that efforts must expand beyond the school walls. Doing so has the potential to capitalize far more of the time available for children to learn. Failure to do so will likely lead to more lackluster results and a generation of school-attenders who cannot read as well as they must if they are to help propel large-scale development and economic and social progress in their countries. When education efforts fully expand outside of school, it will take much more than just the Ministry of Education to support learning and literacy. Coordinated partnerships between the Ministry of Education and Ministries of Health, Infrastructure, Social Affairs, Youth, Culture, and others will need to provide children with the support and scaffolding needed to learn.

The findings of this chapter lend credence to the idea that research performed in high-income countries has solid applications in lower- and middle-income-country research. But this does not mean all findings apply appropriately, nor that the research from high-income countries covers the ways literacy and learning can be supported. Our findings also call for an expansion in the way we think about learning institutions, the literacy ecology, and improving all children's learning. The strong links between the nonschool LE and reading achievement call for more research into the home and community LE, and more programs that seek to address literacy improvement both inside and outside the school walls. The task for education systems, governments, and development partners is to use the entire spectrum of that research to achieve the goal of universal early-grades literacy and learning.

References

ASER. (2015). *Trends Over Time 2006–2014*. New Delhi: ASER.

Baker, L., & Wigfield, A. (1999). Dimensions of children's motivation for reading and their relations to reading activity and reading achievement. *Reading Research Quarterly, 34*(1996), 452–477. DOI: https://doi.org/10.1598/RRQ.34.4.4.

Barton, D., & Hamilton, M. (1998). *Local Literacies: Reading and Writing in One Community*. London: Routledge.

Bronfenbrenner, U. (1979). *The Ecology of Human Development: Experiments by Nature and Design*. Cambridge, MA: Harvard University Press.

Bus, A. G., van IJzendoorn, M. H., & Pellegrini, A. D. (1995). Joint book reading makes for success in learning to read: A meta-analysis on intergenerational transmission of literacy. *Review of Educational Research, 65*(1), 1–21. DOI: https://doi.org/10.3102/00346543065001001.

Cao, Y., Ramesh, A., Menendez, A., & Dayaratna, V. (2014). *Out-of-School Parental and Community Involvement Interventions: A Literature Review*. Chicago: NORC – University of Chicago.

Chansa-Kabali, T., & Westerholm, J. (2014). The role of family on pathways to acquiring early reading skills in Lusaka's low-income communities. *Human Technology: An Interdisciplinary Journal on Humans in ICT Environments, 10*(1), 5–21.

Dowd, A. J., Friedlander, E. W., Jonason, C. et al. (2017). Lifewide learning for early reading development. *New Directions for Child and Adolescent Development, 155*, 31–49. DOI: https://doi.org/10.1002/cad.20193.

Dowd, A. J., Wiener, K., & Mabeti, F. (2010). *Malawi Literacy Boost 2009 Year 1 Report*. Washington, DC: Save the Children.

Evans, M. A., Shaw, D., & Bell, M. (2000). Home literacy activities and their influence on early literacy skills. *Canadian Journal of Experimental Psychology, 54*(2), 65–75. DOI: https://doi.org/10.1037/h0087330.

Friedlander, E. W. (2013). Environmental factors associated with early reading achievement in the developing world: A cross-national study. *International Journal of Educational Research, 57*, 25–38. DOI: https://doi.org/10.1016/j.ijer.2012.10.006.

Friedlander, E. W. (2015). Towards learning for all: Understanding the literacy ecology of rural Rwanda. (Unpublished doctoral dissertation, Stanford University, Stanford, CA.) purl.stanford.edu/vx971nt5655

Friedlander, E. W., Arshan, N., Zhou, S., & Goldenberg, C. (2019). Lifewide or school-only learning: Approaches to addressing the developing world's learning crisis. *American Educational Research Journal, 56*(2), 333–367. DOI: https://doi.org/10.3102/0002831218792841.

Friedlander, E. W., & Goldenberg, C. N. (eds.). (2016). *Literacy Boost in Rwanda: Impact Evaluation of a Two Year Randomized Control Trial*. Stanford, CA: Stanford University.

Ganimian, A. J., & Murnane, R. J. (2016). Improving education in developing countries: Lessons from rigorous impact evaluations. *Review of Educational Research, 86*(3), 1–37. DOI: https://doi.org/10.3102/0034654315627499.

Goldenberg, C. N. (1987). Low-income hispanic parents' contributions to their first-grade children's word-recognition skills. *Anthropology & Education Quarterly, 18* (3), 149–179. DOI: https://doi.org/10.1525/aeq.1987.18.3.05x1130l.

Gove, A., & Cvelich, P. (2011). *Early Reading: Igniting Education for All: A Report by the Early Grade Learning Community of Practice*. Research Triangle Park, NC: Research Triangle Institute. www.rti.org/sites/default/files/resources/early-reading-report-revised.pdf.

Hart, B., & Risley, T. R. (1995). *Meaningful Differences in the Everyday Experience of Young American Children*. Baltimore, MD: Paul H. Brookes Publishing.

Heath, S. B. (1983). *Ways with Words: Language, Life and Work in Communities and Classrooms*. Cambridge: Cambridge University Press.

Hess, R. D., & Holloway, S. D. (1984). Family and school as educational institutions. *Review of Child Development Research, 7*, 179–222.

Kalia, V., & Reese, E. (2009). Relations between Indian children's home literacy environment and their English oral language and literacy skills. *Scientific Studies of Reading, 13*(2), 122–145. DOI: https://doi.org/10.1080/10888430902769517.

Kim, Y.-S. G., Boyle, H. N., Zuilkowski, S. S., & Nakamura, P. (2016). *Landscape Report on Early Grade Literacy*. Washington, DC: USAID. https://allchildrenreading.org/resources/usaid-landscape-report-early-grade-literacy/.

Leseman, P. P. M., & de Jong, P. F. (1998). Home literacy: Opportunity, instruction, cooperation, and social-emotional quality predicting reading achievement. *Reading Research Quarterly*, *33*(3), 294–318. DOI: https://doi.org/10.1598/RRQ.33.3.3.

McEwan, P. J. (2015). Improving learning in primary schools of developing countries: A meta-analysis of randomized experiments. *Review of Educational Research*, *85*(3), 353–394. DOI: https://doi.org/10.3102/0034654314553127.

Nag, S., Vagh, S. B., Dulay, K. M., & Snowling, M. J. (2018). Home language, school language and children's literacy attainments: A systematic review of evidence from low- and middle-income countries. *Review of Education, rev*3.3130. DOI: https://doi.org/10.1002/rev3.3130.

Nath, B. D., Guajardo, J., & Hossain, M. (2013). *Literacy & Numeracy Boost Bangladesh Baseline July 2013*. Washington, DC: Save the Children.

Neuman, S. B. (1996). Children engaging in storybook reading: The influence of access to print resources, opportunity, and parental interaction. *Early Childhood Research Quarterly*, *11*(4), 495–513. DOI: https://doi.org/10.1016/S0885-2006(96)90019-8.

Park, H. (2008). Home literacy environments and children's reading performance: a comparative study of 25 countries. *Educational Research and Evaluation*, *14*(6), 489–505. DOI: https://doi.org/10.1080/13803610802576734.

Purcell-Gates, V. (1996). Stories, coupons, and the TV Guide: Relationships between home literacy experiences and emergent literacy knowledge. *Reading Research Quarterly*, *31*(4), 406–428.

Sénéchal, M., & LeFevre, J.-A. (2014). Continuity and change in the home literacy environment as predictors of growth in vocabulary and reading. *Child Development*, *85*(4), 1552–1568. DOI: https://doi.org/10.1111/cdev.12222.

Snow, C. E., Burns, M. S., & Griffin, P. (1998). *Preventing Reading Difficulties in Young Children*. Washington, DC: National Academy of Sciences.

Taylor, D. (1983). *Family Literacy: Young Children Learning to Read and Write*. Portsmouth, NH: Heinemann Educational Books.

Tusiime, M., Friedlander, E. W., & Malik, S. S. (2014). *Literacy Boost Rwanda: Literacy Ethnography Report*. Stanford, CA: Stanford University. http://unesdoc.unesco.org/images/0022/002256/225654e.pdf.

UNESCO. (2015). *EFA Global Monitoring Report 2000–2015: Achievements and Challenges*. Paris:UNESCO. http://unesdoc.unesco.org/images/0023/002322/232205e.pdf

Wagner, D. A. (1993). *Literacy, Culture and Development: Becoming Literate in Morocco*. London: Cambridge University Press.

World Bank. (2018). *World Development Report 2018: Learning to Realize Education's Promise*. Washington, DC: World Bank. DOI: https://doi.org/10.1596/978-1-4648-1096-1.

Zevenbergen, A. A., Whitehurst, G. J., Epstein, J. N., et al. (1997). Outcomes of an emergent literacy intervention in head start homes and classrooms. *Journal of Educational Psychology*, *86*(4), 547–555. DOI: https://doi.org/10.1207/s19309325nhsa0101_16.

19 Parental Literacy Support in Monolingual and Bilingual Contexts

Mila Schwartz

19.1 Introduction

Children's formal literacy instruction at school differs from their exposure to literacy-related activities in the home context. At school, literacy is acquired through structured activities, whereas at home, an exposure to literacy may be supported in the informal context of spontaneous daily parent–child communications and games aimed primarily at providing emotional care and supporting harmonious child development. These informal home activities often start before children enter preschool and are related to emergent literacy skills development. Emergent literacy refers to skills, knowledge, and beliefs that develop before the formal acquisition of reading and writing (e.g., Sénéchal et al., 2001).

This chapter focuses on early literacy acquisition as embedded in specific social contexts such as children's home environment. During the last three decades, the role of parental support, or family support when persons other than parents are involved in promoting children's literacy at home, has been broadly examined within a monolingual context (e.g., Aram & Levin, 2011; Bus, van IJzendoorn, & Pellegrini, 1995; Sénéchal & LeFevre, 2002). Concerning a bilingual context, numerous studies have shown that literacy acquisition in minority languages in a home or community setting might serve as a springboard for literacy acquisition in the second language (e.g., Dressler & Kamil, 2006; Schwarz, Kahn-Horwich, & Share, 2014; Schwarz, 2020). However, less is known on parental support of biliteracy among language-minority children. Thus, together with home support in the monolingual context, this chapter addresses research evidence on literacy practices in different languages provided by family members to children growing up in bilingual or multilingual homes. We start out with a brief overview of prominent theoretical frameworks that outline parental support and literacy development among children. In addition, drawing mainly on examples from North America, Israel, and other high-income country contexts, research on parental support in a monolingual context and in a bilingual context is dealt with (see also Friedlander & Goldenberg, Chapter 18; Kieffer & Vuković, Chapter 2 and Morgan et al., Chapter 10 in this volume). Finally, educational implications are given.

19.2 Theoretical Framework

19.2.1 Vygotsky's Sociocultural Theory

Children acquire written-language conventions through assistance from others (family members, teachers, and peers) in specific sociocultural contexts. During this process, children's literacy skills develop further through their use of tools available in the environment such as books, electronic devices, and greeting cards. In this regard, two related notions, *Zone of Proximal Development* and *scaffolding*, should be addressed. These notions were proposed by Lev Vygotsky and elaborated by Jerome Bruner (1986). Vygotsky (1978) viewed the concept of scaffolding as synonymous with adult–child interaction. This interaction occurs within the Zone of Proximal Development, defined as "the distance between the actual developmental level as determined by independent problem solving, and the level of potential development as determined by problem solving under adult guidance or in cooperation with the more capable peers" (Vygotsky, 1978, p. 86).

Scaffolding could be provided to the child by simplifying the task through breaking it down into smaller steps/pieces and by providing behavioral modeling, that is, demonstrating to the child how to complete the task's stages. For example, Aram and Levin (2001) analyzed the nature of mothers' scaffolding of their preschool children's writing. The researchers observed how mothers instructed the child to divide the word into the sounds, created a connection between phoneme and grapheme, and then taught the child to produce the graphic form of the letter. I illustrate how, through home literacy practices, parents and other family members provide scaffolding for children's literacy acquisition within monolingual and bilingual contexts.

19.2.2 Family Language and Literacy Policy Model

In line with Bronfenbrenner's (1992) ecological theory, which looks at the child's development within his or her close and distant interactions, the parents are most proximal to the child and hence, have the largest effect on his or her development. The family is a critical area for studying intergenerational heritage language transmission because of its essential role in forming the child's early linguistic environment. Narrowly defined, the heritage language is a language other than the dominant community language and is spoken in the child's home (Montrul, 2008; Polinsky & Kagan, 2015). In this chapter, the notion of the heritage language is superficially equivalent to the minority language or L1. The maintenance of heritage language has been explored primarily within the family language policy model (e.g., Kopeliovich, 2013; Schwartz, 2010). This model derives from Fishman's (1991) reversing language shift model, in which it is argued that language survival requires explicit efforts to be made to retain ethnic languages at the family and community levels, and from Spolsky's (2004) model of language policy.

There is a general agreement that the association with intimacy and privacy makes the family particularly important in providing playful activities associated with language and emergent literacy development. Drawing on this assumption, this chapter proposes to extend the family language policy model by including within it a *literacy component*. The family language policy model suggests L1 maintenance and development; however, some studies point out that language-minority parents might use L1 at home, but not support literacy acquisition in L1 at home or in a community context (e.g., Schwartz, Leikin, & Share, 2005). Hence, I suggest distinguishing between two notions, *family language policy* and *family language and literacy policy* (hereafter FLLP) by putting an emphasis on literacy as a distinct and designated component of this policy.

Our focus is on an FLLP with the following components: (1) *family language and literacy ideology*, or the family's beliefs and attitudes toward first and second languages and literacy and their use at home and in diverse community and social contexts; (2) *family language and literacy management*, or the specific efforts made to influence language and literacy practices through planning (e.g., a decision to support emergent literacy in L1), and (3) *family language and literacy practices*, or the daily home practices, focusing on language and emergent literacy in L1 and L2 (e.g., teaching the child the letters of alphabet, writing a birthday party invitation card together with the child). The aim of family language and literacy practices in the heritage language is to meet social needs such as communication with family members living abroad, and religious observance. In addition, through literacy practices with the child in the heritage language, the family members support intergenerational transmission of "historically accumulated and culturally developed bodies of knowledge and skills essential for household or individual functioning and well-being" (p. 133, Moll et al., 1992). In the context of the FLLP, "funds of knowledge" refers to family and community literacy and cultural practices, which are linked to the child's literacy development in monolingual and bilingual contexts.

19.2.3 Role of the Home Literacy Environment

The FLLP includes the concept of the *home literacy environment* (HLE), which can be defined as the experiences and attitudes regarding literacy and its acquisition that children encounter within the home (e.g., Leseman & de

Jong, 1998; Serpell, Baker, & Sonnenschein, 2005). Serpell et al. (2005) expanded this definition by a notion, *the intimate culture of child's home*, defined as a confluence of parental beliefs about literacy, literacy activities, and parent–child interactive processes during these activities. This concept also includes family literacy practices (e.g., joint book reading and teaching letter names) and devices (e.g., storybooks, experiential and paper-pencil games, computer games, and TV programs) used in the family, which promote emergent literacy and literacy development (Aram & Levin, 2011). Family literacy practices, such as joint parent–child book reading, are particularly important, since they arouse children's interest in literacy and provide them with knowledge of the world. More specifically, this joint literacy activity makes children familiar with story structure and the written-language register (Bus, van IJzendoorn, & Pellegrini, 1995). In addition, the concept of HLE encompasses a socio-emotional aspect of the intimate parent–child interactions and time spent together, which has an inevitable impact on the child's emotional development as well as on cognitive and linguistic development (de Jong & Leseman, 2001; Serpell et al., 2005).

19.2.4 Toward an Ecological Approach

Language ecology can be defined as "the study of interactions between any given language and its environment" (Haugen, 1972, p. 325). According to this definition, a language does not exist independently of its environment but in interaction with it. The research on language ecology relates, among others, to environmental factors promoting language and literacy development. We address the interaction between such environmental factors as parental attitudes toward home literacy support, characteristics of the parent–child emotional relationship, and the literacy activities at home and in school, in both monolingual and bilingual contexts (Aram & Levin, 2001; Leseman & de Jong, 1998; Kopeliovich, 2013; Reyes & Azuara, 2008).

Regarding a monolingual context, most research on parental support of home literacy practices presented here are quantitative longitudinal studies. These studies are aimed at examining the impact of parental beliefs and the HLE on children's emergent literacy acquisition and development. The picture is different in a bilingual context as most existing studies applied longitudinal ethnographic observation as the main methodological approach. This difference in the methodological approaches could be attributed to a fact that even though bilingual and biliterate children exist in every corner of the world, in each country, they have unique experiences depending on educational policy, country of origin, the status of their language, societal attitudes toward bilingualism, and unique characteristics of their ethno-linguistic community. Furthermore, recent research points out that overarching pan-group labels such as "Latino" or "Asian," which are frequently used to refer to the immigrant population in the United States, for example, do not refer to homogeneous groups (Winsler et al., 2014). For example, the stereotype about high-achieving children characterizing primarily the Chinese culture is often attributed to all Asian children, even though they come from different countries and cultures across the Asian region (Lim & Lim, 2003; Winsler et al., 2014). In addition, even Chinese immigrants do not represent a homogeneous community. High-achieving students in the Chinese community usually come from middle-class families with educated parents, often university graduates and academics. Because of their attainments, the school system tends to overlook the needs of children from low-income Chinese families with less educated parents who speak limited English and cannot support L2 literacy development at home (e.g., Shah, 2011).

Turning back to the longitudinal ethnographic observations of the HLE in the bilingual context, I assert that this methodological approach offers rich data on the nature of parent–child interaction (e.g., scaffolding questions, writing mediation, praise) including emotional contact (e.g., affectionate touch, gestures, smiling) during language and literacy activities (Gregory, 1998). Nonetheless, we can find promise in current efforts to apply quantitative methods in a bilingual context as well, which will be addressed further later in this chapter.

19.3 Parental Support in a Monolingual Context

19.3.1 Parental Beliefs

Parental support of children's literacy development is inevitably connected to components of the FLPP such as the parents' literacy beliefs about how children acquire literacy and their own role in this process (e.g., Serpell et al., 2005; Weigel, Martin, & Bennett, 2006). In other words, parents' literacy practices as a part of their family literacy policy and child's HLE may be viewed as a realization of parental beliefs. Two studies will be used to illustrate this point.

Weigel et al. (2006) found that profiles of mothers' beliefs regarding the literacy development of their preschool children related to the child's HLE. Data was collected from seventy-nine mothers and their children in the United States. Most mothers had a European descent with diverse educational levels ranging from high school to a university degree. In this study, two parental-belief profiles emerged – "facilitative" and "conventional." The facilitative profile characterized mothers who believed in the importance of providing their children with diverse learning opportunities at home (e.g., shared book reading, telling stories, and playing language games with children) as a springboard for future literacy success in school, and in their own active role in this process. In addition, the mothers who tended to hold facilitative orientations reported having higher education levels and made more statements about their previous positive educational experience and extensive personal engagement in reading than mothers with conventional orientations.

The conventional profile described mothers who reported being unable to support their children's literacy development at home due to lack of time and limited availability of books. They perceived schools as playing the most important role in teaching children and tended to spend less time with their children on shared-literacy activities. Accordingly, the mothers in the conventional group reported that they were less engaged in storytelling, shared book reading, and other emergent literacy activities than the mothers in the facilitative group.

In another comprehensive research project conducted in the United States, Serpell et al. (2005) showed that parental beliefs about the best way to assist their child in literacy acquisition and development were correlated with the literacy practices reported by the parents and observed by the researchers. In this longitudinal study, the researchers followed sixty-three children and their families from low-income and middle-income backgrounds over five years, from when the children were aged four to the end of the third grade at the age of nine. Much of the researchers' focus was on the home environments in which the children grew up with different levels of individual parental literacy. The two main orientations of parental beliefs were identified: entertainment orientation, which stressed making the parent–child literacy interaction enjoyable for the child and focusing on the child's agency in the process of literacy development; and skills orientation, which stressed direct emergent literacy-skill teaching. In the following subsection, I elaborate on research findings regarding a link between these orientations, parental literacy practices at home, and children's literacy development at preschool and school.

19.3.2 Home Literacy Practices

Several large-scale longitudinal research projects have underscored the importance of the HLE for children's literacy acquisition and development (see also Friedlander & Goldenberg, Chapter 18 in this volume). The impact of HLE on children's literacy development has been mainly evaluated on three parameters: (1) the presence of literacy resources at home while observing their use during joint parent–child literacy interactions; (2) the frequency of children's engagement in literacy-related practices, and (3) parents' familiarity with children's storybooks (e.g., Bus, van IJzendoorn, & Pellegrini, 1995; Korat & Levin, 2001; Stanovich & West, 1989).

Some studies focused on measuring HLE through the presence at home of literacy devices such as adults' and children's books, which, in Western culture, is inevitably linked to parents' socioeconomic status (SES). For instance, Korat and Levin (2001) found the expected differences in the number of books in the families with low and middle SES in Israel: Low-SES homes had 124 adult books and 51 children's books on average, as opposed to middle-SES homes, which owned 309 adult books and 86 children's books on average.

Regarding possible effect of the number of books at home on children's reading skills, Lau and McBride-Chang (2005) showed that this home environmental factor significantly contributed to second-graders' reading performance in Chinese-character recognition in Hong Kong, even when vocabulary knowledge and maternal education were statistically controlled. In this context, a recent study of van Bergen, van Zuijen, Bishop, and de Long (2017) showed that the association between the number of books at home and the children's reading ability might be explained by a third variable such as genetic predisposition to poor reading passing from parent to child. In this study, the data was obtained from 101 Dutch-speaking families (from both parents and their child with an age range of seven to seventeen years old) in the Netherlands. The finding was that the number of books in the home predicted child reading over and above parental reading fluency. However, this effect was rather "modest once parental skills had been controlled, consistent with a mixture of cultural and genetic transmission" (p. 155). That is, the genetic predisposition to slow reading fluency may also influence the parental motivation to buy books for the home.

Parental literacy practices as part of the family literacy policy and a child's HLE at preschool period have been substantially researched. Some studies took a focused approach to studying the nature of relations between a specific and central parental literacy activity and the children's literacy development. Examples include a focus on shared storybook reading and its frequency and children's literacy development (Bus, van IJzendoorn, & Pellegrini, 1995), a focus on children's active participation in interactive book reading and the child's expressive vocabulary (Mol, Bus, de Jong, & Smeets, 2008), and a focus on shared writing activity, parental scaffolding, and children's literacy development (Aram & Levin, 2004). Bus et al. (1995) conducted a comprehensive meta-analysis of sixteen studies on joint book reading and language development, sixteen studies on joint book reading and emergent literacy, and nine studies on joint book reading and reading achievement. The analysis showed that, on the whole, this type of parental support explained 8 percent of the variance in language (Cohen's $d=0.67$), phonological processing (Cohen's $d=0.58$), and reading achievement (Cohen's $d=0.55$). The strength of the influence of the parent–child joint book reading on the children's reading skills was even stronger than the influence of one of the most powerful predictors of reading problems, the nonword reading deficit, which explained approximately 6 percent of the variance between normal readers and readers with disabilities. In addition, as suggested by the researchers, the frequency of the joint book reading was a main factor necessary for the success of this type of parental support. This factor significantly affected children's literacy skills even in the lower-SES families with low parental literacy.

Aram and Levin (2001; 2004) examined another specific parental literacy activity, joint writing, in light of Vygotsky's (1978) concept of scaffolding strategies activating the child's Zone of Proximal Development (ZPD). When analyzing the nature of parental writing support, researchers focus on the way that the parent introduces the child to the writing system (e.g. for the alphabetic writing system, there is a focus on segmenting the word into its phonemes, connecting each phoneme to a letter name, and printing the letter) and refers to the conventions of writing. In monolingual families, these features of joint writing activities have been found to relate to children's early literacy (Skibbe et al., 2013) and predict children's acquisition of reading and writing in different orthographies (Aram & Levin, 2004; Skibbe et al., 2013).

For example, Aram and Levin (2001) assessed a link between the quality of maternal mediation of writing and preschool child's (five-and-a-half to six years old) emergent literacy skills by asking children to write words and names and asking their mothers to help them. Forty-one low-SES and low-educational-level mothers and their children living in Israel were recruited to participate in the study. The researchers distinguished between two types of maternal mediation to the child identified using the literate scale, which was composed of levels of grapho-phonemic mediation and reference to orthographic rules, and printing mediation, which included level of mother's scaffolding of child's letter writing. It was found that the mother's level of literate mediation at preschool age was strongly connected to the child's emergent literacy level, measured by independent word writing and recognition, phonological awareness, and orthographic awareness, after controlling for the SES of the family. Moreover, the study showed that mothers who mediated children's writing within the child's Zone of Proximal Development (Vygotsky, 1978) – challenging the child and providing help when the challenge was difficult – were more aware of their children's literacy levels and cognitive abilities.

19.3.3 Modeling Parental Literacy Support

A causal model of the relationship between parental literacy practices, emergent literacy development, and literacy achievements during the first three years of schooling has been proposed by Sénéchal and LeFevre (2002). They distinguished between two types of parental literacy practices, joint book reading, and direct "teaching" of emergent literacy abilities such as invented spelling and letter-name memorization. Based on data collected among children from middle–high-SES homes, they found distinct causal pathways between these two types of parental literacy practices and different reading components. They uncovered a direct causal pathway from frequency of joint parent–child book reading to language development (vocabulary and listening comprehension) skills at the start of first grade. This, in turn, predicted reading comprehension at the end of third grade. At the same time, frequency of the "teaching" of parental emergent literacy skills was found to be related to word-decoding skills at the end of first grade.

These findings were further empirically supported and extended by Hood, Conlon, and Andrews (2008), who included spelling as an independent variable in the model. Based on data collected in a large-scale three-year longitudinal study in Australia, Hood et al. (2008) showed that the parental direct "teaching" practices indirectly affected word reading and spelling in first and second grade *via* their relationship with emergent literacy skills. Furthermore, in line with Sénéchal and LeFevre's study, no significant correlation was found between joint book reading and later reading and spelling skills. In addition, in line with Bus et al. (1995), Hood et al. (2008) found that effects of home literacy practices did not differ among families with a diverse range of SES.

In their comprehensive five-year longitudinal project, Serpell et al. (2005) investigated the relationship between parental literacy beliefs and practices, emergent literacy development, and literacy achievements during the first three years of schooling. Two types of parental literacy practices were distinguished. The first type had an entertainment orientation and made the literacy experience pleasant through the child's active engagement in literacy-related games and telling stories. The second type was oriented more toward skills such as using workbooks and flashcards and teaching children to recognize letters and to write their names, in a school-like, instructing manner.

It was found that in homes where, during the preschool period, parents believed that the HLE should be a source of entertainment, children's literacy development was considerably assisted. The parental entertainment orientation was significantly related to emergent literacy skills during the preschool period, word recognition in first and second grade, and reading comprehension in third grade. At the same time, no significant relationships were found between parental skills orientation and literacy skills. Regarding SES, this project showed that middle-income parents were more entertainment-oriented while low-income parents advocated a more skill-oriented approach. Differences were also found in the frequency with which children were exposed to certain types of text. Thus, children from low-income homes were less familiar with more developmentally advanced texts, such as storybooks and chapter books, and read picture books more frequently, even when they were in third grade. To recap, this project highlighted the role of the nature of children's literacy experience at home as having a direct impact on literacy development. Socioeconomic status was not directly related to this development, but had an indirect influence on the children's HLE.

Thus, Serpell et al. (2005) highlighted that the HLE measured at preschool ages, rather than SES, was a factor significantly predicting word reading and reading comprehension when children were in third grade. However, Phillips (2010) drew attention to the fact that low-SES families cannot be viewed as a homogeneous group. This researcher critically addressed the mistaken assumptions of many educators and educational policymakers that there is an overwhelming deficiency of literacy practices and low interest in children's literacy development in low-income families (Phillips, 2010). In Western countries today, even families with low SES and a low level of parental education own children's books and basic writing tools (crayons, pencils, and paper). However, children from low-SES homes differ from children from high-SES homes in their literacy home experiences such as in the frequency of joint storybook reading and quality of parental mediation during joint literacy activities, which were found to influence children's literacy abilities (e.g., Aram & Levin, 2001; Leseman & de Jong, 1998; Korat & Levin, 2001).

In addition, drawing on a distinction between such entertainment-oriented activities as joint book reading and nursery-rhyme singing and more structured and skill-oriented "teaching" activities such as letter learning and writing practice, another question attracts the attention of practitioners in particular: Should parents be encouraged to provide more emergent literacy activities at home such as letter naming and invented spelling rather than enjoyable joint book reading with the child, or vice versa? Summarizing what we have learned thus far in addressing this question, it is evident that the way parents initiate activities with their children and the children's place in this initiative might reflect their beliefs about what it means to be literate and how literacy is acquired, and their own role and their child's role in this process. Some empirical evidence exists also regarding the link between SES and parental preference for one of the two types of practices (e.g., Serpell et al., 2005). Additionally, both these types are linked to literacy acquisition, but the magnitude of their impact depends on its underlying components of literacy and language, namely decoding, spelling accuracy, and fluency versus vocabulary and reading comprehension. Researchers and practitioners need to encourage more enjoyable and playful methods for structured and "teaching"-oriented activities at home. They need to induce awareness among parents that joint parent–child book reading as well as other types of activities constitute quality time spent together, which is essential for children's socio-emotional well-being and security.

Importantly, an analysis of the current research on the FLLP, including HLE and children's literacy development suggests that such factors as SES, parental education, cultural and linguistic variations, and the quantity and quality of literacy devices available at home have been inconsistently addressed and produced contradictory data. In this context, Burgess (2005) claimed that a complex network of environmental and attitudinal factors and not just SES explained the quality of the HLE. Further, only a few studies have addressed the important environmental and attitudinal factor of the quality of the socio-emotional interaction during joint parent–child literacy activities. One notable exception is by de Jong and Leseman (2001), who conducted a longitudinal research project over five years in the Netherlands. The study examined how the HLE, including the nature of the socio-emotional interactions during mother–child shared-literacy activities, affects the development of word decoding and reading comprehension in an ethnically and social-economically heterogeneous sample of sixty-nine children and their mothers, coming from a native Dutch background and from immigrant Surinamese and Turkish backgrounds. The researchers found that the quality of socio-emotional interaction style (e.g., supportive presence, respect for the child's autonomy, confidence in the success of the ongoing interaction) during joint parent–child activities such as book reading and problem solving measured at preschool ages was related to children's reading comprehension at school up to third grade.

Finally, from the previous subsections overwhelming use is made of quantitative methods of data collection. At the same time, alongside the quantitative analysis, it was the use of qualitative analysis of observation data that permitted detailed inferences about the form and content of verbal interaction (e.g., scaffolding questions, writing mediation, praise) and non-verbal interactions (e.g., affectionate touch, gestures, smiling) between parents and children during joint literacy activities (Aram and Levin, 2001; Gregory, 1998).

19.4 Parental Support in a Bilingual Context

19.4.1 Family Language and Literacy Policy in a Bilingual Context

Family language and literacy policy in the bilingual context is affected by general language policies in particular families. Many immigrant and minority-language parents feel strongly about teaching their children the heritage language and literacy as a way of transmitting their values and traditions, strengthening their ethnic identity, and keeping in touch with monolingual relatives (Schwartz, 2010). Similar to the monolingual context, in bilingual families, parents' literacy beliefs and practices are interrelated as components of their FLLP, and children's biliterate development can be viewed as a realization of this interaction.

In a twelve-year-long research project, Kopeliovich (2013), as a parent-researcher, presented her experience of raising a bilingual Russian–Hebrew-speaking family in Israel. She incorporated a new perspective, of parents as language and literacy teachers in the bilingual family. Drawing on an ecological approach toward childhood literacy and biliteracy, she asserted that teaching literacy in the heritage language at home should be based on two related principles. The first principle is teaching within a bilingual biliterate mode (e.g., creative translation of literary texts from Russian to Hebrew and vice versa, highlighting structural differences between the languages and stimulating the development of metalinguistic awareness). The second principle is parental management of a multidimensional and flexible FLLP, which assumes a positive emotional coloring of home literacy activities and "unbiased attitude to diverse languages that enter the household and respect for the language preferences of the children" (Kopeliovich, 2013, p. 251). These parental beliefs in the bilingual biliterate mode and a flexible language policy at home can be expected to result in the child's metalinguistic awareness of word structure and print conventions.

Similarly, Li (2007) found that FLLP played a critical role in children's biliteracy development in Mandarin or Cantonese (L1) and English (L2). This one-year, ethnographic study examined how parents' attitudes toward biliteracy development are related to practices at home. The study focused on three Chinese immigrant families with first- and second-grade children in Vancouver, an ideal location for biliteracy development due to the high density of Chinese immigrants and good economic prospects for bilinguals. Semi-structured interviews revealed that the parents had different perceptions of literacy learning in L1 and L2. Thus, in two cases, the findings showed some discrepancy between the parents' overall positive view of biliteracy and their home practices. In one of these families, parents believed that Chinese learning would be a barrier to the child's English development. In a second family, the parents did not believe that young children could acquire two languages and cultures simultaneously. In a third case, the parents believed that their children's acquisition of literacy skills in Chinese at home would have a positive impact on their progress in English literacy. Their beliefs led to their child's positive attitude toward biliteracy. This diversity in the FLLPs was attributed to intrafamily factors such as parents' perceptions of their minority status in the host society and proficiency levels in the two languages, as well as several school and societal factors, such as a lack of interest in children's linguistic resources among mainstream teachers and lack of understanding on the part of policymakers of how individual learners' language socialization is shaped through their biliterate development.

19.4.2 Home Biliteracy Practices

Home biliteracy practices assume more significance for intergenerational transmission of L1 literacy than L2 literacy. Since schools are not always willing or lack resources to support L1 literacy, the responsibility falls on parents and other family members to provide the support. Duursma et al. (2007) found that Spanish (L1)-speaking children in bilingual programs were able to acquire English (L2) literacy solely through instruction at school but relied on home support for Spanish (L1) literacy. Schwarzer (2001) observed the literacy practices of his trilingual daughter at home and in school in the United States (with Hebrew and Spanish as heritage languages and English as the socially dominant language). He reported that although the child was in a Spanish–English bilingual elementary program, writing and reading instruction at school was provided mostly in English, with few opportunities to practice Spanish. Her Hebrew literacy development was supported only at home.

Research on a link between the type of maternal writing mediation and the child's emergent literacy skills, conducted within the monolingual context, became a source of inspiration for exploring the nature of these relationships within a bilingual biliterate context. Recently, Minkov (2021) investigated the connection between the mother's mediation strategies and the child's emergent biliteracy in Russian–Hebrew-speaking families in Israel by using quantitative methodology. More specifically, the study established the links between such characteristics of FLLP as the mothers' attitudes toward emergent biliteracy, their planned activities, writing mediation, language practices, and the emergent literacy of the children in both Russian, as a heritage language, and Hebrew as a dominant language of the society. It has been found that writing support given in one of the child's languages explained a significant amount of variance in the child's emergent literacy skills in the target language as well as cross-linguistically, namely, in another language. Minkov explained this cross-linguistic predictability in light of the consistency of the mother's behavior during writing mediation. Thus, the writing support given by the mothers in two languages was highly correlated across languages; that is, the mother tended to show the same level of mediation. For example, by mediating the child's writing on a phonological level, the mother separated the word into syllables and sounds or encouraged the children to do so in both languages. In addition, the study showed that during writing mediation the mothers were sensitive to the orthographic characteristics of each language. Hence, in Hebrew they were sensitive to consonant-vowel structure as the smallest instructional unit versus the Russian phoneme (consonants and vowels) being the smallest instructional unit.

Several studies have found that biliteracy development may scaffold L2 literacy acquisition (Li, 2007; Reyes, 2006; Ruiz, 1984). Through biliteracy practices at home, children begin to develop metalinguistic awareness, which is defined by psycholinguists as a person's explicit knowledge about language, knowledge that can be brought into awareness, verbally reported, and declaratively presented (Bialystok, 2001; Bruck & Genesee, 1995). Recent longitudinal ethnographic studies give examples of how home literacy practices induce children to compare the prominent characteristics of their languages and notice different aspects of oral language (e.g., phonemes, morphemes) and print (Kenner & Gregory, 2012). Metalinguistic awareness, in turn, enhances biliteracy development. Even if parents focus exclusively on L1 literacy, this still may produce positive effects on children's L2 literacy acquisition (Hancock, 2002; Reese et al., 2000) by increasing metalinguistic awareness, providing necessary tools and skills for the acquisition of L2 literacy, and building the children's confidence in their ability to learn.

In a longitudinal ethnographic research project, Reyes (2006) examined emergent literacy practices at home among first-generation Mexican families living in Arizona. The study showed that four-year-old children in these families learned to represent ideas in writing in Spanish and English simultaneously. Reyes (2006) demonstrated also how home and community environments (supermarket, local library, tax office, clothing store) supported the development of the concept of print in two languages. Through their exposure to different prints, children developed differential hypotheses about L1 and L2 orthographies. For example, when four-year-old Adam was asked by the researcher to identify which words were written in Spanish, he explicitly noted the letter patterns used in Spanish, such as double *rr* in the word *perro* "dog" and Ñ as in the word *niña* "girl," but not in English. Reyes (2006) concluded that the diverse literacy practices in use at home and in the community enabled children to practice in their Zone of Proximal Development and provided them with the "opportunity to transact with two overlapping and interactive literate worlds" (p. 286).

Another example is Schwarzer (2001), a parent-researcher with longitudinal experience in encouraging the triliterate development of his daughter, Noa, in the United States. As noted above, Noa was enrolled in a bilingual English–Spanish-speaking school and was exposed to literacy in Hebrew at home. Like Reyes's (2006) findings, this study showed how a six-year-old girl growing up in a triliterate environment provided her own hypotheses about how to spell in her three languages and to compare three scripts. She raised questions about spelling in these three scripts and understood that two of them, English and Spanish, had similarities, whereas the Hebrew script was quite different. Even with minimum experience with writing in Hebrew (a total of six instances during one research year), Noa was aware that at the end of a word, the Hebrew letter ה /h/

"hei" is silent and appears frequently in that position because of its morphological role as indicator of a feminine noun (pp. 122–123).

Parental approaches toward biliteracy practices at home often have a tendency to incorporate practical steps for realizing the intergenerational transmission of heritage language through planned and structured literacy activities (e.g., Schwarzer, 2001). Other case studies present a tendency for spontaneous literacy activities drawing on daily faith practices and reading sacred texts with family members (e.g., Reyes, 2006). Both planned and spontaneous activities were described by Kopeliovich's (2013) longitudinal ethnographic study with a focus on parents as teachers. The study showed that parents can plan, regulate, assess, and negotiate explicit systematic literacy activities (home lessons of the heritage language, thematic units of study, creative-writing projects), enhancing their FLLP goals. Alongside the planned literacy activities, the parents as teacher-researchers observed and collected data on their children's initiations of spontaneous literacy activities such as children writing notes to parents or siblings, letters, and samples of independent writing in each of the languages or in both languages combined. Particularly interesting artifacts were related to the children's games: doctor's prescriptions, lists of dolls and stuffed animals attending a "kindergarten," lesson plans and worksheets for younger siblings, maps related to imaginary lands, a peace treaty signed after a big quarrel, and a dictionary of a language invented by the children (p. 252). It is therefore clear that within their FLLP, parents as agents might build a creative HLE that supports intergenerational heritage language transmission as well as other languages the child may acquire later in life.

19.4.3 Modeling Parental Biliteracy Support

Recent research shows that within immigrant families, family literacy support might be bidirectional (e.g., Gregory, 2001, 2004). Based on longitudinal home observations of children's emergent biliteracy in Spanish and English, Reyes (2006) revealed that, through participating in diverse literacy practices, family members supported not only the child but also each other in biliteracy development. This role was defined by Reyes as bidirectional. Thus, parents and older siblings served as experts and scaffolded L1 print knowledge but became novice learners when performing English (L2) literacy practices together.

Furthermore, research has shown that limited proficiency in the L2 does not prevent parents from helping their children develop L2 and L3 literacy skills (e.g., Caesar & Nelson, 2013; Riches & Curdt-Christiansen, 2010). In a study of Chinese parents in Montreal, Riches and Curdt-Christiansen (2010) observed that educated middle-SES parents helped their children with English homework and read books with them. They also purchased French reading materials, hired tutors to help their children learn French, and some of them even took French classes to help their children.

As in the monolingual context, it would be a mistake to generalize that minority parents with lower SES and education levels do not invest in their children's literacy development. Several studies showed that Spanish-speaking parents from lower-SES backgrounds might be eager to be involved and help their children with L2 literacy acquisition at home (Anderson & Minke, 2007; Caesar & Nelson, 2013; Walker et al., 2013). However, minority parents, especially with lower SES, might have trouble communicating with schools due to a lack of common educational and cultural values (Hidalgo, 1993).

To summarize, the studies reported showed that emergent biliteracy is a result of family policy with proactive biliteracy management embedded into an ecological perspective, considering different intra- and interfamily factors. This biliteracy management can be expressed by planned literacy activities initiated by family members as well as spontaneous literacy activities "embedded in meaningful contexts" and initiated by the child (Reyes & Azuara, 2008, p. 392). Children's exposure to the concept of print in different languages at home and in community environments helps them to develop hypotheses about L1 and L2 scripts. The observations showed that children's home experience with writing and reading in different languages might draw their attention to the degree of orthographic and linguistic proximity between the languages, facilitating their literacy development in both languages.

19.5 Conclusions and Discussion

The longitudinal ethnographic observations and data triangulation presented in the previous sections enabled exploration of parent–child literacy interactions in naturalistic activities relevant to the children's daily lives. Exploration of these behaviors is not always possible based on the structured task-based approach, such as asking parents to dictate specific word pairs to their child or to fill out questionnaires about their FLLP. At the same time, a mixed-methods approach might help to generalize the qualitative data, to a degree, such as frequency of some observed phenomenon of family literacy activities in the home and to provide a panoramic view of the situation under study (Marsland et al., 1999). As noted by Mackey and Gass (2005), in qualitative research, quantification permits more precise examination of the occurrence of the phenomenon, such as its regularity, and facilitates subsequent drawing of inferences.

Additional questions can be asked about the longitudinal consequences of FLLP and the way it changes over time and possible directions in modifying the FLLP as children grow older. It is reasonable to assume that the parents' biliteracy practices with preschool children differ from those used with elementary-school children and adolescents. Given that the role of peers in the language socialization of bilingual children increases with age, it would be important to observe, for example, parents' tendency to seek suitable environments for L1 literacy support as children grow older.

With an eye on educational implications, it is important to note that in both monolingual and bilingual contexts, parents have been observed during many literacy practices in their homes, in addition to being asked to provide a self-report about these practices. However, as Phillips (2010) found, teachers frequently consider structured knowledge of print concepts as essential for success and largely ignore such spontaneous literacy practices as reading the Bible and searching for supermarket coupons. Teachers should be open to acknowledging that parental beliefs about literacy development might not be narrow, with a focus on learning the alphabet and shared book reading (Schwarzer, 2001). Thus, it is also important for teachers to view literacy development not only in terms of how print works, but on the where, why, and when; that is, literacy in all its manifestations in a broader social sense (Schwarzer, 2001).

Monolingual teachers do not have to become fluent in their students' languages to acknowledge their cultures and to foster bi- and multiliteracy in the classroom (Schwarzer, 2001). Despite speaking only one language, they can still find ways to demonstrate the value and importance of diversity. Creating a multilingual environment is also beneficial for monolingual students because it raises their language awareness and helps them develop metalinguistic skills (Armand & Dagenais, 2005). Teachers can illustrate a multiliterate print atmosphere in the classroom or encourage students to construct bilingual books and journals, or to address cards to the family in their heritage languages (e.g., Chatzidaki, 2015). Teachers can also recruit the help of parents, older siblings, and community members to create multilingual projects together with the students. Taking time to know children's interests and connecting their home experience (funds of knowledge) to their school experience might be very beneficial for their literacy acquisition. The "language awareness" project (Hélot & Young, 2005; Young & Hélot, 2003) is an example of how immigrant languages can be placed on an equal footing in a school context and how children can be educated to the linguistic and cultural wealth that is present in their classrooms and in their communities. This has been achieved in the "language awareness" project conducted by teachers and parents in a primary school in Alsace, where a variety of languages and cultures were presented to pupils. Language awareness has been promoted by raising children's curiosity about languages that are present in their multilingual classrooms by means of exposure to a variety of writing systems and different alphabets that their peers experience at home.

References

Anderson, K. J., & Minke, K. M. (2007). Parent involvement in education: Toward an understanding of parents' decision making. *Journal of Educational Research, 100*, 311–323.

Aram, D., & Levin, I. (2001). Mother–child joint writing in low SES: Sociocultural factors, maternal mediation, and emergent literacy. *Cognitive Development, 16*, 831–852.

Aram, D., & Levin, I. (2004). The role of maternal mediation of writing to kindergartners in promoting literacy achievements in second grade: A longitudinal perspective. *Reading and Writing: An Interdisciplinary Journal, 17*, 387–409.

Aram, D., & Levin, I. (2011). Home support of children in the writing process: Contributions to early literacy. In S. Neuman, & D. Dickinson (eds.), *Handbook of Early Literacy Research* (Vol. 3, pp. 189–199). New York: Guilford.

Armand, F., & Dagenais, D. (2005). Languages and immigration: Raising awareness of language and linguistic diversity in schools. *Canadian Issuers, Spring*, 99–102.

Bialystok, E. (2001). *Bilingualism in Development*. Cambridge: Cambridge University Press.

Bronfenbrenner, U. (1992). *Ecological Systems Theory*. London: Jessica Kingsley Publishers.

Bruck, M., & Genesee, F. (1995). Phonological awareness in young second language learners. *Journal of Child Language, 22*, 307–324.

Bruner, J. (1986). *Actual Minds, Possible Worlds*. Cambridge, MA: Harvard University Press.

Burgess, S. (2005). The preschool home literacy environment provided by teenage mothers. *Early Child Development and Care, 175*, 249–258.

Bus, A. G., van IJzendoorn, M. H., & Pellegrini, A. D. (1995). Storybook reading makes for success in learning to read: A meta analysis on intergenerational transmission of literacy. *Review of Educational Research, 65*, 1–21.

Caesar, L. G., & Nelson, N. W. (2013). Parental involvement in language and literacy acquisition: A bilingual journaling approach. *Child Language Teaching and Therapy, 30*(3), 317–336.

Chatzidaki, A. (2015). Preparing future teachers for dealing with classroom diversity. In S. Gaviilidou, A. Gkaintartzi, E. Markou, & R. Tsokalidou (eds.), *Proceedings of the 3rd International Conference "Crossroads of Languages and Cultures. Issues of Bi/Multilingualism, Translanguaging and Language Practices in Education"* (pp. 21–37). Thessaloniki: Aristotle University of Thessaloniki.

de Jong, P. F., & Leseman, P. P. M. (2001). Lasting effects of home literacy on reading achievement in school. *Journal of School Psychology, 39*, 389–414.

Dressler, C., & Kamil, M., (2006). First and second-language literacy. In D. August & T. Shanahan (eds.) *Developing Literacy in Second-Language Learners: A Report of the National Literacy Panel on Language-Minority Children and Youth* (pp. 197–238). Mahwah, NJ: Lawrence Erlbaum Associates.

Duursma, E., Romero-Contreras, S., Szuber, A., Proctor, P., & Snow, C. E. (2007). The role of home literacy and language environment on bilinguals' English and Spanish vocabulary development. *Applied Psycholinguistics, 28*, 171–190.

Fishman, J. A. (1991). *Reversing Language Shift: Theoretical and Empirical Foundations of Assistance to Threatened Languages*. Clevedon: Multilingual Matters.

Gregory, E. (1998). Siblings as mediators of literacy in linguistic minority communities. *Language and Education*, *1*(12), 33–55.

Gregory, E. (2001). Sisters and brothers as language and literacy teachers: Synergy between siblings playing and working together. *Journal of Early Childhood Literacy*, *1*, 301–322.

Gregory, E. (2004). "Invisible" teachers of literacy: Collusion between siblings and teachers in creating classroom cultures. *Literacy*, *38*(2), 97–105.

Hancock, D. R. (2002). The effects of native language books on the pre-literacy skill development of language minority kindergartners. *Journal of Research in Childhood Education*, *17*(1), 62–68.

Haugen, E. (1972). *The Ecology of Language: Essays by Einar Haugen*, ed. A. S. Dil. Stanford, CA: Stanford University Press.

Hélot, C., & Young, A. (2005). The notion of diversity in language education: Policy and practice at primary level in France. *Language, Culture and Curriculum*, *18*, 242–257.

Hidalgo, N. (1993) Multicultural teacher introspection. In T. Perry & J. Fraser (eds.), *Freedom's Plow: Teaching in the Multicultural Classroom* (pp. 99–106). New York: Routledge.

Hood, M., Conlon, E., & Andrews, G. (2008). Preschool home literacy practices and children's literacy development: A longitudinal analysis. *Journal of Educational Psychology*, *100*, 252–271.

Kenner, C., & Gregory, E. (2012). Becoming biliterate. In J. Larson & J. Marsh (eds.), *The SAGE Handbook of Early Childhood Literacy* (pp. 364–378). London: SAGE Publications.

Kopeliovich, S. (2013). Happylingual: A family project for enhancing and balancing multilingual development. In M. Schwartz & A. Verschik (eds.), *Successful Family Language Policy* (pp. 249–276). New York: Springer.

Korat, O., & Levin, I. (2001). Maternal beliefs, mother-child interaction, and child's literacy: Comparison of independent and collaborative text writing between two social groups. *Applied Developmental Psychology*, *22*, 397–420.

Lau, J. Y. H., & McBride-Chang, C. (2005). Home literacy and Chines reading in Hong Kong children. *Early Education and Development*, *16*(1), 5–22.

Leseman, P. P. M., & de Jong, P. F. (1998). Home literacy: Opportunity, instruction, cooperation and socio-emotional quality predicting early reading achievement. *Reading Research Quarterly*, *33*, 294–318.

Li, G. (2007). Second language and literacy learning in school and at home: An ethnographic study of Chinese Canadian first graders' experiences. *Literacy Teaching and Learning*, *11*(2), 1–31.

Lim, S., & Lim, B. K. (2003). Parenting style and child outcomes in Chinese and immigrant Chinese families: Current findings and cross-cultural considerations in conceptualization and research. *Marriage & Family Review*, *35*(3–4), 21–43.

Mackey, A., & Gass, S. M. (2005). *Second Language Research: Methodology and Design*. Mahwah, NJ: Lawrence Erlbaum Associates.

Marsland, N., Wilson, I., Abeyasekera, S., & Kleth, U. (1999). *A Methodological Framework for Combining Quantitative and Qualitative Survey Methods*. Reading: Social and Economic Development Department, Natural Resources Institute and the Statistical Services Centre, University of Reading.

Minkov, M. (2021). Early literacy development in immigrant families: How bilingual ideology, management and practice predict children's early literacy. (Unpublished PhD thesis, Tel-Aviv: Tel-Aviv University.)

Mol, S. E., Bus, A. G., DeJong, M. T., & Smeets, D. J. H. (2008). Added value of dialogic parent–child book readings: A meta-analysis. *Early Education & Development, 19*, 7–26.

Moll, L., Amanti, C., Neff, D., & González, N. (1992). Funds of knowledge for teaching: A qualitative approach to developing strategic connections between homes and classrooms. *Theory into Practice, 31*, 132–141.

Montrul, S. (2008). *Incomplete Acquisition in Bilingualism*. Amsterdam: John Benjamins.

Phillips, L. M. (2010). The making of literate families: Considerations of context and misconceptions. In D. Aram & O. Korat (eds.), *Literacy Development and Enhancement across Orthographies and Cultures* (pp. 123–135). Literacy Studies. New York:Springer.

Polinsky, M., & Kagan, O. (2015). Heritage language: In the "wild" and in the classroom. *Language and Linguistic Compass, 1*, 368–395.

Reese, L., Garnier, H., Gallimore, R., & Goldenberg, C. (2000). Longitudinal analysis of the antecedents of emergent Spanish literacy and middle-school English reading achievement of Spanish-speaking students. *American Educational Research Journal, 37*(3), 633–662.

Reyes, I. (2006). Exploring connections between emergent biliteracy and bilingualism. *Journal of Early Childhood Literacy, 6*, 267–292.

Reyes, I., & Azuara, P. (2008). Emergent biliteracy in young Mexican immigrant children. *Reading Research Quarterly, 43*(4), 374–398.

Riches, C., & Curdt-Christiansen, X. L. (2010). A tale of two Montreal communities: Parents' perspectives on their children's language and literacy development in a multilingual context. *The Canadian Modern Language Review, 66*(4), 525–555.

Ruiz, R. (1984). Orientations to language planning. *NABE Journal, 8*, 15–34.

Schwartz, M. (2020). Strategies and practices of home language maintenance. In A. C. Schalley & S. A. Eisenchlas (Eds.), Handbook of Social and Affective Factors in Home Language Maintenance and Development (pp. 194–217). Mouton de Gruyter.

Schwartz, M. (2010). Family language policy: Core issues of an emerging field. *Applied Linguistics Review, 1*(1), 171–192.

Schwartz, M., Kahn-Horwitz, J., & Share, D. L. (2014). Orthographic learning and self-teaching in a bilingual and biliterate context. Journal of Experimental Child Psychology, 117, 45–58.

Schwartz, M., Leikin, M., & Share, D. L. (2005). Bi-literate bilingualism versus mono-literate bilingualism: A longitudinal study of reading acquisition in Hebrew (L2) among Russian-speaking (L1) children. *Written Language and Literacy, 8*, 179–207.

Schwarzer, D. (2001). *Noah's Ark: One Child's Voyage into Multiliteracy*. Portsmouth, NH: Heinemann.

Sénéchal, M., & LeFevre, J. A. (2002). Parental involvement in the development of children's reading skill: A five-year longitudinal study. *Child Development, 73*(2), 445–460.

Sénéchal, M., LeFevre, J., Smith-Chant, B. L., & Colton, K. (2001). On refining theoretical models of emergent literacy: The role of empirical evidence. *Journal of School Psychology*, *39*, 439–460.

Serpell, R., Baker, L., & Sonnenschein, S. (2005). *Becoming Literate in the City: The Baltimore Early Childhood Project*. New York: Cambridge University Press.

Shah, P. G. (2011). Asian Americans' Achievement Advantage: When and Why does it Emerge? (Unpublished PhD thesis, Columbus, OH: Ohio State University.)

Skibbe, L. E., Bindman, S. W., Hindman, A. H., Aram, D., & Morrison, F. J. (2013). Longitudinal relations between parental writing support and preschoolers' language and literacy skills. *Reading Research Quarterly*, *48*, 387–401.

Spolsky, B. (2004). *Language Policy*. Cambridge: Cambridge University Press.

Stanovich, K. E., & West, R. F. (1989). Exposure to print and orthographic processing. *Reading Research Quarterly*, *24*, 402–433.

Taylor, L., Bernhard, J., Garg, S., & Cummins, J. (2008). Affirming plural belonging: Building on students' family-based cultural and linguistic capital through multi-literacies pedagogy. *Journal of Early Childhood Literacy*, *8*(3), 269–294.

Tran, Y. (2014). Addressing reciprocity between families and schools: Why these bridges are instrumental for students' academic success? *Improving schools*, *17*(1), 18–29.

van Bergen, E., van Zuijen, T., Bishop, D., & de Jong, P. F. (2017). Why are home literacy environment and children's reading skills associated? What parental skills reveal. *Reading Research Quarterly*, *52*, 147–160.

Vygotsky, L. S. (1978). *Mind in Society: The Development of Higher Psychological Processes*. Cambridge, MA: Harvard University Press.

Walker, J. M. T., Ice, C. L., Hoover-Dempsey, K. V., & Howard, M. (2013). Latino parents' motivations for involvement in their children's schooling: An exploratory study. *The Elementary School Journal*, *111*(3), 409–429.

Weigel, D. L., Martin, S. S., & Bennett, K. K. (2006). Mothers' literacy beliefs: Connections with the hone literacy environment and pre-school children's literacy development. *Journal of Early Childhood Literacy*, *6*(2), 191–211.

Winsler, A., Burchinal, M. R., Tien, H. et al. (2014). Early development among dual language learners: The roles of language use at home, maternal immigration, country of origin, and socio-demographic variables. *Early Childhood Research Quarterly*, *29*, 750–764.

Young, A., & Hélot, C. (2003). Language awareness and/or language learning in French primary school today. *Journal of Language Awareness*, *12*(3 and 4), 236–246.

20 Global Literacy
Patterns and Variations

Charles Perfetti, Sonali Nag, Kenneth Pugh, and Ludo Verhoeven

In this final chapter, we provide a wide-angle perspective on the major issues that arise when one thinks globally about literacy. In doing so, we draw attention to what we see as convergent higher-level conclusions that emerge from global literacy research, especially some of the observations made by authors of this volume. We begin with an obvious starting point: regional variations in literacy.

20.1 Regional Variations in Global Literacy

The previous chapters report observations from nine areas that cover most of human habitation across the globe, minus some large areas (North Africa, West Asia, Southeast Asia) and all but one of the many island communities around the globe. Overall, we have a strong representation of world regions, even though, in some cases, the information is based on a small fraction of a region's many subregions and communities.

There are two different aspects of regional variation that are relevant for the goal of understanding global literacy issues. One is the detailed analysis of a region as a case study, a description of uniquely identified literacy practices. The second is the identification of literacy practices and outcomes in that region that reflect patterns that are universal or at least largely shared. Both are valuable. The specific observations allow us to learn about, for example, differences in literacy practices within a village in Rwanda, across island communities in the Caribbean, or within bilingual families in Israel. They also allow us to reflect on how these specific differences reflect general principles of a human-ecology analysis of literacy; for example, the fact that the differences observed within a specific Rwandan, Caribbean, or Israeli community mirror sociocultural processes that vary in a similar way in other regions, even though these variations may be expressed differently.

Global Literacy: Patterns and Variations

In what follows, we focus mainly on this second aspect of regional variation, highlighting the shared patterns that we see across regions and suggesting the generalizations, hedges, and universal patterns that emerge.

20.2 Global Patterns and Principles in Literacy Development

Despite many important differences across the globe, literacy development suggests some general patterns that reflect nearly universal developmental phases and shared operating principles.

20.2.1 Operating Principles in Literacy Development

In an earlier volume, Verhoeven and Perfetti (2017) suggested a set of operating principles (OPs) that underlie learning to read. These OPs, based on research across seventeen diverse languages and their writing systems, identified generalizations that applied to those seventeen languages, and by extension, to reading in all languages.

These OPs follow from a zero-order first principle: Learning to read is figuring out (in detail) how one's writing system encodes one's language. The nine general OPs (Verhoeven & Perfetti, 2021) capture the essential features of this learning across three overlapping phases of reading development: (a) preliteracy attention to spoken language and secondarily to written-language signals in the environment; (b) development of word identification and spelling through discovery of the mapping principles of the writing system and acquisition of an orthographic inventory of words that increases with experience, allowing a shift from computation to retrieval as the major procedure for word identification; (c) increasingly fluent comprehension through increased use of linguistic and conceptual knowledge and executive control.

These OPs reflect the perceptual, cognitive, and linguistic demands of written language and apply universally. They are, however, embedded in layers of literacy ecology that affect the opportunity for children to prosper across all three of these phases of development. We interpret the development of literacy as reflecting the cognitive achievements of the OPs, embedded across all its phases in a literacy ecology.

In the following sections, we examine the patterns of literacy development and some of the ways that cognitive outcomes are affected by their ecological embedding.

20.2.2 Role of Language and Writing-System Variation

Only when the study of reading moved beyond research on the alphabetic writing system, mainly English, could the role of writing-system variation be appreciated.

It was predictable that reading is largely the same across writing systems because of the foundational principle of writing systems: They map written forms to language forms, not directly to concepts. Thus, at the highest level, all writing systems follow this principle – and all successful learners figure out, at least implicitly, how their writing system does this. These general ideas, formulated as a universal grammar of reading (Perfetti, 2003), are the starting point for considering how variations in writing systems matter for literacy development.

The general approach for such consideration is the classification of writing systems based on the level of language they map – words, morphemes, syllables, and subsyllabic units including phonemes. With this approach, we can compare literacy development across systems, with a focus on the demands of learning, comparing, for example, the demands of a syllable mapping with those of a phoneme mapping. This binary mapping comparison tends to favor syllabic systems (e.g., Japanese Kana and Cree) in some ways and alphabetic systems in others. Thus, syllable systems provide an easier mapping because spoken syllables are more accessible to consciousness than are phonemes. However, for many languages, alphabets are much more efficient than syllabaries, because the number of graphs is smaller, matching (in a perfect alphabet) the number of phonemes in a language; the number of syllables is always many times larger than the number of phonemes and thus requires more graphs to be learned. The comparative research within this framework provides specific implications for a general theory of reading that includes both universal and writing-specific components that are instantiated in the development of brain specialization for reading (Perfetti, Cao, & Booth, 2013).

Beyond mapping comparisons are other dimensions of writing that are relevant (Daniels & Share, 2018). A particularly important one for the learner is the number of graphs in the writing system. This number is determined by the mapping system – relatively few graphs for abjads and alphabets, more for syllabaries, many more for alphasyllabaries, and the largest number for the Chinese morphosyllabic system (Chang, Chen, & Perfetti, 2017). As is the case with Chinese, the very large inventory of graphs in alphasyllabaries requires an extended learning period over several years (Nag, 2007) This multidimensional framework is valuable in understanding the cognitive demands that writing systems place on learning to read: The mapping level, the consistency of the mapping, the number and corresponding complexity of the graphs – these differ systematically across writing systems and they make a difference for the course of reading development.

The role of the writing system is a bit more complex when considered in specific regional contexts. What determines which system serves a given region or nation? The world's existing writing systems are mainly the result of discovery and borrowing, with some invention, developed over long periods with many modifications. Ideally, one might imagine that languages develop written forms that are well suited to the properties of the language, and there are multiple suggestions that writing systems show such adaptations (Seidenberg, 2011; Frost, 2012; Perfetti & Harris, 2013). However, there are many sociopolitical counterinfluences to idealized language adaptation that are most noticeable when writing systems are imposed from outside. As suggested by Daniels (1992), when nonliterate people developed writing, they tended to adopt syllabaries. When literate people, including colonial powers and missionaries, developed writing, they chose alphabets. A good match with an indigenous language may or may not result. A mismatch between an imposed writing and a native language adds to a literacy challenge. It is true that any writing system can be learned by the speaker of any language. It is also true that learning a mismatched writing system adds to the challenge of literacy acquisition (see Verhoeven & Severing, Chapter 4; Nakamura & Holla, Chapter 8 in this volume).

20.3 Patterns of Literacy Development

Here we consider general patterns observable across the overlapping phases of reading development that we described in the introductory chapter (Chapter 1): early (pre)literacy, learning to read and spell, and advanced literacy.

20.3.1 Early Literacy

We do not expect the pathway through literacy development to vary dramatically across the ecological structures that support the language and preliteracy phases. Early preliteracy experiences are important to start a child on the path to literacy, whether the child lives in Austria, Canada, Mongolia, or Zambia. What varies is not so much the importance of supportive preliteracy experiences, but their quality and quantity. These vary within a region and within a language community as well as across regions. Although effective teaching should and can make up for low-quality preliteracy experiences, high-quality preliteracy experiences increase the literacy odds for any child.

It is important to recognize the role of the immediate social environment – not just parents but the more general role of the child's caregivers, peer environment, and neighborhood. This immediate social environment provides input for language development, especially through vocabulary growth. The knowledge of word forms and their meanings is critical in supporting a child's knowledge of language and concepts. A rich language environment that supports early literacy development can be provided by a community of caregivers, siblings, and other conversation partners. We see dramatic contrasts around the world in these early environments and, importantly, while these contrasts may vary somewhat with regions, what matters most are the specific local ecologies of the home and the local community.

A final observation on the general pattern of early literacy development: The early experiences provided by the family and community environments help develop the cognitive resources that the child has to apply to literacy and the self-regulation that can facilitate the transition from home to school (Morrison et al., Chapter 14 in this volume). They can also stimulate affective and motivational enablers of literacy, especially the child's interest in language and literacy. On the cognitive side, the development of literacy begins early in the life of the child, in the form of natural processes of language development and conceptual development. Vocabulary acquisition is a component of both conceptual and language development and is a critical cognitive component in supporting literacy (see Verhoeven & Perfetti, 2011). On the affective and motivational side, seeking rather than avoiding language and literacy experiences is a disposition that makes a future of literacy engagement more likely.

20.3.2 Learning to Read

For the child learning to read and spell, the key foundational learning occurs through a series of learning episodes that unlock the written code that opens the spoken language and its meanings. This can happen prior to school, but universally it is schooling that provides the needed systematic learning episodes. These learning episodes can include some insights about how the writing system works: "Ah, the symbols stand for little pieces of sound" (or big pieces, or word-like forms). But the real work is acquiring an inventory of these mappings. This gradually increasing inventory, rather than sudden insight, may lead the child to solve the problem of how a writing system works. Either way, the mappings must be learned and applied to specific written forms (see also McBride, Pan, & Mohseni, 2021).

This process occurs around the world in the child's interactions with reading materials and teachers. Whether the child is learning that <t> is /t/ or that <a> is always /a/ (in most European languages), or that <a> is almost never /a/ (in English), the learning episodes may produce both insight into the principles of the system and the acquisition of its specific mappings. Of course, these processes are only the start. Breaking the code but using it on just a few words or even a few hundred words produces an inert knowledge that is well short of functional literacy. For this additional step, increasing opportunities for effective reading practice are essential.

The school and community ecologies are critical for both the initial code-breaking and extended-practice phases of literacy development. So too are the home environments, whose effect begins in the preschool years. As concluded by Friedlander and Goldenberg (Chapter 18, this volume), research in middle- and high-income countries has, on balance, demonstrated the impact of the quality of children's home experiences on their learning. We should expect this relationship to be evidenced in low-income countries as well, because all regions have variability in home experiences. Although research confirming this assumption is thin, the research in rural Rwanda summarized by Friedlander and Goldenberg shows positive relations between home-literacy factors and measures of primary-grade reading skill. For example, literacy interactions, as reported by a caregiver, and the literacy competence of the caregiver predicted a child's basic skills in letter knowledge and decoding. Furthermore, literacy interactions also predicted fluency and comprehension. We can assume that these relations are highly general. They converge with the results of studies in the United States and other middle- and high-income countries in showing a positive role for verbal interactions (e.g., Hart & Risley, 1995; Dickinson & Porche, 2011), and shared book reading (Bus, van IJzendoorn, & Pellegrini, 1995; Noble et al., 2015).

20.3.3 Advanced Literacy

Beyond the achievement of basic literacy is the transition to a more robust functional literacy, one that serves the individual as a participant in a variety of culturally defined literacy activities. The importance of this higher level for both individuals and societies is a worldwide concern. Many children make a start at the decoding and early reading phases of literacy but move only partway to the level of functional literacy implied by current standards.

The concept of functional literacy needs to be contextualized: Functional for what and for whom? These contexts are partly recognized in international assessments that distinguish different literacy contexts, for example, digital literacy, workplace literacy. Still, there is a shared idea across these different contexts: An individual with functional literacy can read and understand written texts and chooses to engage in literacy activities when doing so would be useful. Higher standards, for example, the ability to write a series of coherent paragraphs, are sometimes evoked. A few wide-scope generalizations are possible. On the one hand, the factors that affect basic literacy (e.g., early literacy experiences, SES) also affect this achievement of higher literacy achievements. On the other hand, success in basic literacy does not guarantee success in higher-level functional literacy (see Vágvölgyi et al., 2016, for a review on functional literacy).

The pathway to advanced literacy requires basic reading skill plus motivation and opportunity. Comprehension of written texts is at the heart of advanced literacy because other aspects of functional literacy (reading to follow instructions or to learn something, writing comprehensible messages) depend on it. Comprehension depends on multiple knowledge sources and an array of cognitive processes that operate on them, as described in the Reading Systems Framework (Perfetti & Stafura, 2014). One of these knowledge sources is vocabulary, which combines knowledge of word forms with conceptual knowledge and is a powerful component of reading across languages. Another important source involves knowledge of increasingly complex syntactic constructions. Crucially, these knowledge sources and comprehension processes depend on a reader's deeper engagement with the texts. This engagement depends on a motivation to read (e.g., Wigfield & Guthrie, 1997), which, in turn, depends on many factors in the literacy ecology.

The global variation in comprehension and the low levels of functional literacy even in many middle- and high-income countries reflect many considerations that matter for engagement and opportunity, including SES, language factors, immigration status, schooling quality, access to books, and other factors throughout the literacy ecology. One fact that highlights that low levels of functional literacy are present even in middle- and high-income countries is the finding that, in 2018, around one in five fifteen-year olds in the European Union (EU) could not interpret texts effectively (PISA data, cited by Araújo and Costa, Chapter 5 in this volume). However, the variation across countries within the EU is equally dramatic (from 8 to 26 percent), an indication that there are specific national circumstances and policies that matter.

20.4 Literacy and Schooling

Although the development of literacy begins early through natural processes of language development and conceptual development, it is the factor of school experiences, explicitly designed to teach reading, that we expect to ensure the achievement of literacy. Each classroom within a school is its own literacy ecosystem, with one or more teachers, students, literacy curriculum materials, assessments, and regulated interactions. The classroom itself is embedded within other systems – the school, the community, the larger school administrative units, and local, regional, and national government control agents. The child experiences the classroom directly, but the layered systems have dramatic impacts on what happens there. Most obvious are the financial resources that influence the classroom's educational focus, the teaching, the curriculum materials, and the class size. Additionally, educational goals, achievement standards, teacher training, and other important factors are controlled at various layers in the schooling ecosystem. A national case study of the multiple consequences of broad changes in educational goals and policy is provided for Russia by Velichenkova and Rusetskaya (Chapter 6 in this volume).

20.4.1 Patterns and Variations in School Ecosystems

Expanded schooling is responsible for worldwide increases in literacy, not just in the twenty-first century but even prior to 1800. Across Europe and other areas (generally the Global North), an increase in schooling has continuously brought an increase in literacy. The delivery of basic literacy instruction is the main goal of primary-grade schooling around the world. Beyond this general pattern, variation abounds in multiple ways. To focus on one, we consider the setting of standards and goals.

The EU provides a wide-scope model, developed in accord with the general regional goals the EU community. The countries of the EU share education benchmarks, setting goals for increasing the number of students who achieve at or above benchmarks in reading. Interestingly, the EU also sets goals for post-secondary education, reflecting a shared purpose of preparing people for high-skill jobs. The linkage of educational attainment with economic outcomes (and thus social outcomes as well) may be an important driver of the growth in literacy.

For regional goal setting to be effective, assessments that inform policy-makers about progress are important. International assessments such as the Program for International Student Assessment (PISA) for secondary schools and the Progress in International Reading Literacy Study (PIRLS) for the fourth grade provide results that are used comparatively (across regions and across language, SES and gender demographics) and as policy drivers. Important also is the value of these assessments in research. For example, studies with PIRLS data point to general patterns – for example, cross-national effects of early literacy skills and/or early literacy experiences in predicting fourth-grade achievement (Araújo and Costa, Chapter 5 in this volume).

The European model – goal setting and assessment – has come to be recommended as a way to chart progress and inform policy in the Global North, and increasingly in the Global South. Assessment at scale is thus used to inform national policies from early-childhood to primary-school programs. For example, PIRLS data include the resources schools commit to teaching reading and the extent to which they focus on academic success. However, evidence that instructional factors affect fourth-grade achievement has been weak, leaving little to recommend to schools on basic approaches to reading. This may reflect relative low variance in teaching methods within earlier PIRLS samples, because they were limited to within the EU. The discussion of influential factors is likely to change as cross-national surveys become more varied: More than fifty-five countries participated in the 2018 PIRLS assessments, and more than eighty countries participated in each of the two most recent PISA assessments of fifteen-year-olds. The absence of a systematic cross-national assessment of teaching methods that also accounts for culturally rooted practices is another reason why evidence for recommendations of basic approaches to support foundational literacy in diverse settings is yet to develop.

Of course, participating in an assessment is not enough. Using the assessments to make effective policy is the necessary next step. Among low-and middle-income countries, a 2013 report by the IEA (International Association for the Evaluation of Educational Achievement, 2013) found evidence that assessments (many regional and national as well as international) were used to recommend policy (Best et al., 2013). Data from assessment programs were most often used at the agenda-setting, implementation, and evaluation stages, but less frequently at the policy formulation stage. The largest policy impacts were aimed at teacher quality in preparation and in-service professional development. Curricula and performance standards were also influenced by assessment data. Interestingly, whether policy was affected by the assessments depended on other layers in the school ecosystem – investment priorities, media attention, public opinion, and dissemination to stakeholders.

Overall, the increased use of assessments and their use in literacy policy is a positive indicator that the goals-assessment model can be effective input to policy (thus, a goals-assessment-policy model) to improve literacy outcomes. Still, the larger effect of schooling is the difference between school and no school. Some 59 million primary-age children did not attend school in 2018, according to the most recent data from UNESCO (2019). The same report showed 138 million 15–17-year-olds not in school. The report attributes these high numbers, especially the data on adolescents, to factors of sex, location, and wealth.

20.4.2 Teaching and Teacher Quality

The child's participation in literacy activities in school centers on the classroom teacher. School systems control teacher quality and literacy expertise through their ability to allocate resources and manage instruction. Children in poor areas attending low-resourced schools face correspondingly poor literacy outcomes. Still, poor areas also can have great teachers and we expect such teachers to produce better outcomes for their students.

The specific contribution of the individual teacher within the many-layered factors that affect individual student outcomes (school resources, community SES, classroom makeup, individual student characteristics) can be difficult to assess. Indeed, the teacher qualities that succeed in one situation might fail in another. Illustrating the relation between teacher effects and disadvantage, a review of multiple studies shows that between 4 and 16 percent of the variance in elementary-grade students' reading is accounted for by teacher effects (Rowan, Correnti, & Miller, 2002). These effects are even larger among disadvantaged urban Black and Hispanic student populations (see Dickinson et al., Chapter 17 in this volume).

A particularly important perspective on this question comes from data from the International Longitudinal Twins Study (ILTS), which assesses the contribution of genetic and environmental influences on literacy. Among a heterogeneous sample, teacher effects are much stronger than other environmental factors. Thus, as pointed out by Dickinson et al., when children come from varied backgrounds, the importance of strong teachers is increased. Further, genetic influences are much stronger in classrooms that have effective teachers (Taylor et al., 2010), because effective teaching is a major environmental factor that is "controlled," allowing genetic influences to be observed.

The more specific question is, what makes an effective teacher? Certainly, education and specific preparation in literacy teaching should matter. But unpacking teacher effectiveness through large scale multifactor studies has not been successful at pinpointing specific features. Self-report studies in the United Kingdom indicated that effective teachers taught letter sounds and read aloud to their early-primary-grade students. More detailed studies of teacher interactions with learners can be more revealing, but have come mainly from preschool situations, where one finds generalizations across countries in the effectiveness of specific teacher–child interactions that support learning (e.g., Chile as well as the United States, Leyva et al., 2015).

Our generalization on teaching is this: Despite problems assigning unique value-added effects to teachers in the context of contributions of other layers in the literacy ecosystem, the evidence that teachers make a difference is clear and substantial.

20.4.3 *The Language of Instruction*

Colonial conquests, voluntary migrations, and the political settings of international boundaries ensure that there is no such thing as a monolingual nation. Moreover, communities within nations also tend toward multilingualism. In such communities, instruction in a single school (politically dominant) language means that many children are not being taught in their native or home language. From a strictly cognitive perspective, learning to read in one's "mother tongue" – or at least in a second language that has been mastered – is critical: Learning to read includes learning how a writing system encodes one's language. Beyond this foundational principle are gradations that matter. For one, some children enter a school with some knowledge (as opposed to no knowledge) of the school language. What is nearly impossible with no knowledge becomes merely difficult with some experience with the school language. Second, it is possible for a child to increase its knowledge of the school language itself because of literacy instruction in that language. These gradations are the basic background for the practical questions concerning the language of instruction: Should the home language be used? If not, what can help support literacy? The issues surrounding these questions are varied and complex, as shown across multiple geographical and political contexts, including the Caribbean (Verhoeven & Severing, Chapter 4), Australia (Morgan, Reid, & Freebody, Chapter 10), and India (Nakamura & Holla, Chapter 8) and other areas discussed in chapters of the current volume.

Some countries have established a policy of initial instruction in a child's home language, with a later shift to the dominant language. In Mali, where native language instruction was introduced to precede the later use of French as the school language, children in schools that followed this approach showed substantially higher literacy scores than children in French-only schools (Bender et al., 2005). Positive effects for home-language instruction were also found in studies in Brazil, Portugal, and Burkina Faso. A review by Nag et al. (2019) concluded that, across twenty-six of twenty-nine countries, benefits for home-language instruction occurred between Grades 2 and 6, although the extent of the advantage varied by context. (See Dickinson et al. [Chapter 17 in this volume] for a review of the evidence for home-language effects.)

Thus, both the basic logic of how reading works and the results of research support the positive effects of home-language instruction in school. Prior to school, home support for language development and early literacy can give a child language resources that serve literacy whether or not the home language is used in the school. Having books in the home language in the home, where that is possible, can ease the child's transition to school-language literacy while also strengthening language development.

There are, nevertheless, counter-considerations. For one, the dominant language, not the home language, may be perceived as more valuable, that is, prestigious or economically and socially important. Certainly, governments and school administrators make this argument on behalf of learning in a dominant language rather than home languages. Further, parents themselves often have the same view. India's emphatic multilingualism provides an example of the tension between such perceptions and the case for home language (Nakamura & Holla, Chapter 8 in this volume).

A second complicating factor is how to provide instruction in multiple languages. Bilingual cases with a dominant privileged language and a prominent second language (e.g., English and Spanish in the United States), should be relatively simple to manage for home-language first (or dual-language) instruction. This is not simple in practice, and assuring quality instruction in each of two languages can be a challenge. Moreover, multiple languages, not just two, are common across the world. Mali is teaching in 11 different languages, and New Guinea manages

Global Literacy: Patterns and Variations

instruction in 380 languages through desktop publishing (Dickinson et al., Chapter 17 in this volume). The lesson seems to be that managing home-language support for literacy is challenging, but possible.

20.5 Challenges to Literacy Development

In considering the challenges to literacy development, we elaborate on our framework of literacy ecology as introduced in Chapter 1. Figure 20.1 captures this global literacy framework. It shows literacy development as embedded in language development and that it can be predicted by (a) system factors referring to variations in the linguistic and writing systems, (b) child factors associated with the neurobiological foundation of children's learning capacity, and (c) support factors associated with processes in the home and at school. All these influences exist within a sociopolitical context that exerts influence broadly across the system.

This framework draws attention to the proximal factors influencing literacy development – home and school support – that are enfolded within layer of "sociopolitical context," which has both broad and deep influences on the functioning of the more proximal factors. The challenges to literacy attainment arise from all levels of the literacy ecosystem, from factors intrinsic to the individual child to extrinsic factors that are seemingly very remote from the child's literacy interactions but have large effects mediated through multiple

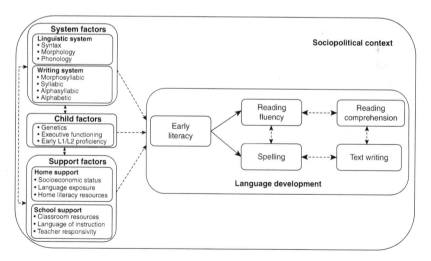

Figure 20.1 The global literacy framework

educational, social, and political structures. We begin with system-based and child-based challenges, with the clear recognition that even these are partly the result of the broader layering of ecosystems that include the child.

20.5.1 Language- and Writing-System-Based Challenges

The challenges of languages and writing systems are complex, not reducible to simple generalizations nor to lists of "top ten" most difficult languages. Claims of learning differences among languages and writing systems abound: English spelling is too complex to learn, alphabets are easiest to learn, Chinese writing is the hardest to learn, and so on. Such claims require context to evaluate and do not stand up as generalizations. For example, language difficulty is about learning a foreign language, which depends very much on its relation to the speaker's native language. For the child acquiring language naturally, differences among languages are negligible and nearly impossible to quantify. Learning a writing system is different, because it must be learned through explicit or implicit teaching rather than naturally. The real challenge for the learner is less about the features of the writing system than about the match between those features and the spoken language. Written Chinese seems to fit better with spoken Chinese than with spoken English, and the reverse is also likely. These observations are caveats to guard against overemphasizing language and writing-systems differences in learning to read. With these caveats, we can better appreciate the differences that matter. There are several that do matter for the learner.

An important one of these is that writing systems differ in graphic efficiency, that is, the number and complexity of their graphs. The more graphs an orthography has, the more demanding it is to learn. The challenge from the size and complexity of the graphic inventory varies – relatively low in the case of alphabetic learning, intermediate in the case of syllabic (e.g., Japanese Kana) and alphasyllabic learning (e.g., Kannada), and high in the case of Chinese. These differences translate to differences in the amount of learning time required to master the inventory of graphs and their mappings to language. Among alphabetic orthographies, the development of reading fluency is affected by syllabic complexity and the transparency of the grapheme–phoneme mappings (see Daniels & Share, 2018). Thus, system-based challenges include not just the graphs but also the mapping principles that govern their link to spoken language. Since writing involves encoded language, not simply encoded speech, it can accommodate not only phonemic but also syllabic and morphological aspects of a language. An optimal writing system – one perfectly tuned to the features of the spoken language – is an ideal that may be approximated in some cases (Frost, 2012) but in general, especially when the writing system is imposed from outside the language community, this is not the case.

20.5.2 Child-Based Challenges

Some factors become, in some sense, enduring characteristics of the child, such as individual learner-cognitive and language abilities, approaches to literacy events, and self-regulation. All these individual characteristics, however, reflect the complex influences of context- and environment-provided literacy ecosystems. Thus, we focus here on brain-based child-based factors that seem intrinsic to the child in a clearer way – although even for these, factors external to the child are important.

20.5.2.1 Reading Disability

Reading disability, or dyslexia, has always been understood as having biological origins, as instantiated by current definitions (Verhoeven, Perfetti, & Pugh, 2019). According to the International Dyslexia Association (https://dyslexiaida.org), dyslexia can be defined as "a specific learning disability that is neurobiological in origin." The definition adds that dyslexia "results from a deficit in the phonological component of language." Dyslexia organizations around the world echo this definition, including those in India, Singapore, Australia, the UK. The Australian Dyslexia Association adds, unhelpfully, "There is no cure for dyslexia since it is a brain-based difference" (Australian Dyslexia Association, 2021).

We need to accept the biological definition, because of the overwhelming evidence of genetic transmission, and also hedge it slightly, because of the incorrect inferences it invites. The first of these is the assumption that a genetic condition cannot be modified. As Grigorenko (Chapter 13, this volume; also, Olson et al., 2019 and others) emphasizes, it is when genetic status is controlled (e.g., in identical twins) that environmental effects are most clearly observed. These effects include teacher effects, as we observed in the preceding section. Environmental interventions to counter the challenges of a biologically based dyslexia not only are possible but have been proved effective.

The second reason for the hedge is that the dyslexia label has been applied unevenly around the globe, within communities, and across demographic groups. Two children may have identical profiles of inaccurate and halting word identification with phonological problems, but only one of them may be considered to have dyslexia, while the other is considered a poor reader or a slow learner. Elliot and Grigorenko (2014) argued, with supporting detail, that the term dyslexia may do more to hide reading problems than to illuminate them. There are many aspects to this issue, but a global perspective brings two into focus: (a) Do our two failing readers benefit from the same focused interventions designed to address decoding? (b) If one of them is poor or from a disadvantaged group, will their reading problem be attributed to low intelligence or low opportunity, while the higher-SES child receives a dyslexia diagnosis? Will they be treated differently because of these attributions? We assume, with or without a special dyslexia label, and consistent with advances in research, that genetic factors place some children at risk of having problems in basic word-reading and spelling processes. Instead of claiming there is not much that can be done about a genetically affected disorder, the response should be to optimize the child's proximal ecosystems, including focused instruction on word reading and phonology.

In the second part of the three-volume series on reading of which this book forms the third part, Perfetti, Verhoeven, and Pugh (2019) concluded that reading problems around the world are associated with multiple cognitive factors. The main one is indeed the phonological deficit, most often expressed in both spoken language and written language. But there are also orthographic and symbol-naming factors that emerge as important in most languages, and especially in nonalphabetic languages that do not demand phoneme-level mapping. Reading problems at the individual-child level thus follow a shared pattern around the globe: that of a prevalent phonological processing problem accompanied by additional problems with other aspects of the word-identification system.

This does not mean there is no global variation in the pattern of child-based reading problems. The genetic approach makes this clear. Schooling in high-income countries is less variable than it is in lower-income countries. This implies that the distribution of heritability and total environment influences are correspondingly different. When most children receive quality schooling, individual differences will tend to reflect the genetic factors. When many children fail to receive quality schooling, environmental variability is large, influenced by the schooling and the more remote ecosystem layers that affect it. For the well-off, schooling may be better as a result of their access to higher-resourced private or public schools. For the poor, however, a lower-quality school may be the best environment possible, compared with dropping out of school or not attending at all. As Grigorenko (Chapter 13 in this volume, p. 304.) concludes: "The propensity of a human brain to transform into a literate brain then depends on print exposure and effective teachers, because children cannot learn to read and write without being taught how to read and write."

We can talk about child-based factors because genes and the neurological development they control are indeed individual. However, in so doing, we do not evade the layered elements of the literacy ecology and their direct influence on "child-based" challenges to literacy.

20.5.2.2 Poverty Challenges to Brain Development If brain function is the signature individual-child factor, then brain development is the primary pathway to a brain that is wired to meet the challenges of learning, including learning to read. Rigatti et al. (Chapter 12 in this volume) provide a general picture of the development of the brain systems that serve language, memory, and vision and become connected to function as reading networks.

However, the development of neural systems is at risk from the effects of environmental stressors. These stressors, which arise from exposure to toxins, malnutrition, and socio-emotional stress, are more frequently experienced by children in poverty. The negative effects of poverty on brain development are becoming well documented and there are plausible links to explain the pathways of these effects. Indeed, atypical patterns of structural brain development mediate the relationship between household poverty and impaired academic performance (Hair et al., 2015).

Socioeconomic status is associated with literacy in multiple ways because it is reflective of multiple layers of the ecosystem (neighborhood, family, school). Part of this association is mediated by brain development. For example, family income is associated with a child's brain surface area, and this association is especially strong for lower-income families – small differences in income are associated with large differences in brain surface area (Noble et al., 2015). Providing a possible explanation for such effects, Merz, Wiltshire, and Noble (2019) observed brain-structure differences in the cortical surface area of left hemisphere brain areas that function in language – larger cortical surfaces for high-SES children than those with lower SES. Further, they found that this SES-left hemisphere association was mediated by measures of language input to the child (number of adult–child conversation turns). Thus, we see here the layered effects of the ecosystem on the brain's readiness for literacy and learning in general.

It is important to point out also that the poverty–brain development relationship is not just about cognitive functioning. The accumulation of socioemotional stressors that can accompany poverty has a negative effect on emotional regulatory systems in the brain that affect later mental health (Hanson et al., 2019). We can expect to find that emotional health is another factor in the child's engagement with literacy activities. Thus, as observed by Rigatti et al. (Chapter 12 in this volume), although brain development is a "child-based" challenge, the challenges to normal brain development arise not just through genetic anomalies, but also from adverse physical and social environments.

20.5.3 Challenges in Literacy Ecological Systems When we think of poverty effects on literacy and schooling, our thoughts are less likely to be on the brain and more likely to be on financial resources that affect educational opportunities. Wealth – familial, regional, national – matters greatly for educational outcomes across the globe. Socioeconomic status consistently correlates with language and literacy skills (Nag, Chapter 15 in this volume; Shure et al., 2014). Further, this relation holds across ages – early childhood, childhood, and adolescence – and schooling across global regions. This pattern does not depend on which indicators of SES are used, as Kieffer and Vuković (Chapter 2 in this volume) conclude in their North American studies.

Schooling provides the institutional center of the literacy ecology: the agencies charged by governments around the world with the delivery of education. Accordingly, we have devoted a previous section to schooling and teaching, the most important way schooling supports the child's learning. Here, in considering the challenges to literacy associated with schooling, we emphasize the risk to those children who must attend poorly resourced schools or learn in conditions that interfere with effective teaching. Effective teaching matters, even when its critical features are less tangible than the specific literacy teaching methods. A few conclusions that affect teaching quality and classroom environment are obvious, some backed clearly by data, some not so clearly. Literacy learning is more at risk when the teacher/student ratio is large, in a class with an attention-dividing environment. Learning is more effective when student attention can be directed to specific learning events – the teacher, a visual display, a book – when teachers are well trained in the basics of literacy instruction, and when instructional methods and curriculum materials are consistent with the sciences of learning and reading.

These proximal factors, situated in the child's immediate learning environment, mediate influences from the higher levels of the schooling ecosystem – in particular, the financial and human resources that can provide safe, supportive physical learning environments and the hiring of trained teachers. Economic disparities around the world cause schooling disparities and thus place many children at risk of poor learning outcomes. Rich countries can pay more for education and usually do; children in poor countries are at risk for low-quality schooling.

Some national comparisons are possible and show an interesting picture of commitment to education. Thirty-seven countries are members of the Organisation for Economic Cooperation and Development (OECD). These countries provide a wide range of per capita wealth, as measured in Gross Domestic Product (GDP). In 2017, the per capita GDP ranged from less than $20,000 US dollars (Colombia) to almost $120,000 (Luxembourg), providing a large-enough wealth range to assess national commitments to education. For elementary- and secondary-school education, the expenditures of these thirty-seven countries were remarkably predictable along a linear function with a correlation of $r=.86$ between per capita GDP and total expenditures (public and private funding) per student (National Center for Education Statistics, 2022). With 74 percent of the variance in student expenditures accounted for by a country's per capita GDP, there can be only small deviations. The two poorest countries (Colombia, Mexico) somewhat underspent relative to their GDP; but so too did two of the three richest countries (Ireland, Switzerland) and a few with midrange economies (Lithuania, Turkey). Only a few countries noticeably overspent on education relative to their wealth, including one of the poorer countries (Portugal), three midrange countries (Korea, Belgium, Austria), and one at the high-wealth end (Norway). Comparable data from more countries in the Global South are needed to get a fuller picture. But for these thirty-seven countries, most of them in the Global North, we see a striking uniformity in the portion of a nation's wealth invested in the education of children in the primary and secondary grades. (Data from 2019 allow a similar conclusion.)

It is important to emphasize that school resources extend beyond the financial, to human resources that are broadly educational – the instructional resources enabled by the sociocultural, linguistic, technological, and strategic structures that characterize a classroom environment and that can be supported or inhibited by school leadership. These depend not only on financial resources but also on the leveraging of available talent and leadership.

20.5.4 *Challenges in Preschool and Home Support*

Preschool. Formal schooling has the role of education guarantor; it is the place where inequities in earlier opportunities are confronted and where all children should have a chance to learn. However, we know that literacy opportunities prior to formal schooling are essential in preparing children for success at school. The effects of inequities are evidenced in the early markers available in preschool settings: Vocabulary, expressive language, and print-related concepts are predicted by SES. As children enter school, SES predicts reading measures including accuracy, rate, and comprehension. Nag (Chapter 15 in this volume) concluded that the SES factor in literacy is universal across nations, grade levels, and language of instruction (i.e., for first or second language). Access to supportive preschool literacy experiences is important in preparing children for formal instruction, but it too is highly dependent on SES in most of the world.

Home and Community. Differences in home environments arise from economic and family-education factors and can be indexed in various ways. One well-known index is the number of books in the home. While such an index might imply differences in literacy events (amount of reading by family members and reading to children), it is more likely to be a stand-in for SES. Indeed, the number of books loses much of its predictive power when SES is controlled. However, the effects of SES itself – and its components of family income and parental education – are also indirect. They are implemented through the language, literacy, and learning opportunities that are greater with higher SES. It is important to recognize that these more direct causes of early literacy support are not totally dependent on economic status. Reading to children, an important preliteracy event, can be done with one or two books;

unopened books on the shelf are not helpful except as indicators of other opportunities that families with education and financial resources can provide to children. Schwartz (Chapter 19 in this volume) shows how parental support can make a difference in children's literacy development in both monolingual and bilingual contexts.

Because home environments are enabling factors in literacy development, the challenge is how to leverage the potential of home environments – even in poor homes – to be actually supportive. Research on home environments in middle- and high-income countries has generally verified that the quality of children's home experiences is related to learning outcomes, including reading scores (e.g., Friedlander and Goldenberg, Chapter 18 in this volume). There has also been considerable research on this relationship in lower-income countries, including a review of data from schools in locations across Africa and Asia (Dowd et al., 2017, Nag et al., 2019). Interestingly, reading scores have also been found to be higher when children participate in community learning activities. However, as Friedlander and Goldenberg (Chapter 18 in this volume) point out, there remains a shortage of systematic intervention studies to provide models and evaluations of home/community interventions. Still, it seems clear that the combination of family and community can provide important resources for early literacy support (see also Nag, Chapter 15 in this volume).

20.6 Literacy Learners and Their Enfolding Ecosystems

We conclude by emphasizing the value of a particular ecological perspective on literacy development. The proximal enablers of successful learning (the child's relevant knowledge, the teacher's effectiveness) must be in central focus. Embracing an ecological perspective without this focus can draw attention away from what can be fixed directly – the learning and teaching events. The array of political and social systems that enfold the child and the school have profound influences on these learning and teaching episodes and need to be addressed. Our perspective – a learning-centered literacy-ecology approach – focuses attention on the enfolding ecosystems and their powerful influences, while keeping the learning events that directly lead to literacy at the center.

Our global literacy framework (Figure 20.1) draws attention to the proximal factors influencing literacy development – home and school support – while leaving the largest enfolding layer of "sociopolitical context" undifferentiated. This lack of differentiation of social-political context is partly because of its complexity and partly because the specific features of context depend on local conditions that reflect factors of social stratification, governance, linguistic, cultural, economic, and political power, and historical developments. Nevertheless, a complete analysis of the contexts of literacy should include a critical evaluation of how ideological beliefs, economic interests, and political agendas drive literacy-support systems around the world (see also Wickins & Sandlin, 2007).

Striving for global literacy, at a meaningful level, involves focusing attention on all these factors in different ways and on different timelines. The nearly universal acceptance of literacy as a human right helps with this. So too does the accumulation of scientific knowledge about the basic nature of literacy across languages and writing systems, its various proximal enablers, and the distal contexts that can support or challenge it.

References

Australian Dyslexia Association. (2021). What is dyslexia? (web page). Sydney: ADA. https://dyslexiaassociation.org.au/what-is-dyslexia/.

Bender, P., Dutcher, N., Klaus, D., Shore, J., & Tesar, C. (2005). *In Their Own Language: Education for All*. Education Notes. Washington, DC: World Bank. http://hdl.handle.net/10986/10331.

Best, M., Knight, P., Lietz, P., Lockwood, C., Nugroho, D., & Tobin, M. (2013). *The Impact of National and International Assessment Programmes on Education Policy, Particularly Policies Regarding Resource Allocation and Teaching and Learning Practices in Developing Countries*. Camberwell, VIC: ACEReSearch. https://research.acer.edu.au/ar_misc/16/.

Bus, A. G., van IJzendoorn, M. H., & Pellegrini, A. D. (1995). Joint book reading makes for success in learning to read: A meta-analysis on intergenerational transmission of literacy. *Review of Educational Research, 65*(1), 1–21. DOI: https://doi.org/10.2307/1170476.

Chang, L.-Y., Chen, Y.-C., & Perfetti, C. A. (2017). GraphCom: A multidimensional measure of graphic complexity applied to 131 written languages. *Behavior Research Methods, 50*, 427–449.

Daniels, P. T. (1992). The syllabic origin of writing and the segmental origin of the alphabet. In P. A. Downing, S. D. Lima, & M. Noonan (eds.), *The Linguistics of Literacy* (pp. 83–110). Amsterdam: John Benjamins.

Daniels, P. T., & Share, D. L. (2018). Writing system variation and its consequences for reading and dyslexia. *Scientific Studies of Reading, 22*(1), 101–116. DOI: https://doi.org/10.1080/10888438.2017.1379082.

Dickinson, D. K., & Porche, M. V. (2011). Relation between language experiences in preschool classrooms and children's kindergarten and fourth-grade language and reading abilities. *Child Development, 82*(3), 870–886. DOI: https://doi.org/10.1111/j.1467-8624.2011.01576.x

Dowd, A. J., Friedlander, E. W., Jonason, C. et al. (2017). Lifewide learning for early reading development. *New Directions for Child and Adolescent Development, 155*, 31–49. DOI: https://doi.org/10.1002/cad.20193.

Elliott, J. G., & Grigorenko, E. L. (2014). *The Dyslexia Debate*. Cambridge: Cambridge University Press. https://doi.org/10.1017/CBO9781139017824.

Frost, R. (2012). Towards a universal model of reading. *Behavioral and Brain Sciences, 35*(5), 263–279. DOI: https//doi.org/10.1017/S0140525X11001841.

Hair, N. L., Hanson, J. L., Wolfe, B. L., & Pollak, S. D. (2015). Association of child poverty, brain development, and academic achievement. *JAMA Pediatrics*, *169*(9), 822–829. DOI: https://doi.org/10.1001/jamapediatrics.2015.1475.

Hanson, J., Albert, W., Skinner, A., Shen, S., Dodge, K., & Lansford, J. (2019). Resting state coupling between the amygdala and ventromedial prefrontal cortex is related to household income in childhood and indexes future psychological vulnerability to stress. *Development and Psychopathology*, *31*(3), 1053–1066. DOI: https://doi.org/10.1017/s0954579419000592.

Hart, B., & Risley, T. R. (1995). *Meaningful Differences in the Everyday Experience of Young American Children*. Baltimore, MD. Paul H. Brookes Publishing Company.

International Association for the Evaluation of Educational Achievement. (2013). *The Impact of National and International Assessment Programmes on Education Policy, Particularly Policies Regarding Resource Allocation and Teaching and Learning Practices in Developing Countries*. Amsterdam: IEA. www.iea.nl/publications/study-reports/international-reports-iea-studies/impact-national-and-international.

Leyva, D., Weiland, C., Barata, M. et al. (2015). Teacher–child interactions in Chile and their associations with prekindergarten outcomes. *Child Development*, *86*(3), 781–799. DOI: https://doi.org/10.1111/cdev.12342

McBride, C., Pan, D. J., & Mohseni, F. (2021). Reading and writing words: A cross-linguistic perspective. *Scientific Studies of Reading*, 26(2), 1–14. DOI: https://doi.org/10.1080/10888438.2021.1920595.

Merz, E. C., Wiltshire, C. A., & Noble, K. G. (2019). Socioeconomic inequality and the developing brain: Spotlight on language and executive function. *Child Development Perspectives*, *13*(1), 15–20. DOI: https://doi.org/10.1111/cdep.12305.

Nag, S. (2007). Early reading in Kannada: The pace of acquisition of orthographic knowledge and phonemic awareness. *Journal of Reading in Research*, *30*, 7–22.

Nag, S, Vagh, S. B., Dulay, K. & Snowling, M. J. (2019). Context and implications: Home language, school language and children's literacy attainments: A systematic review of evidence from low- and middle-income countries. *Review of Education*, 7 (1), 151–155. DOI: https://doi.org/10.1002/rev3.3132.

National Center for Education Statistics. (2022). Education Expenditures by Country. *Condition of Education*. US Department of Education, Institute of Education Sciences. https://nces.ed.gov/programs/coe/indicator/cmd.

Noble, K. G., Houston, S. M., Brito, N. H. et al. (2015). Family income, parental education and brain structure in children and adolescents. *Nature Neuroscience*, *18* (5), 773–778. https://doi.org/10.1038/nn.3983

Olson, R. K., Keenan, J. M., Byrne, B., & Samuelsson, S. (2019). Etiology of developmental dyslexia. In L. Verhoeven, C. Perfetti, & K. Pugh (eds.), *Developmental Dyslexia across Languages and Writing Systems* (pp. 391–412). Cambridge: Cambridge University Press.

Perfetti, C. A. (2003). The universal grammar of reading. *Scientific Studies of Reading*, 7 (1), 3–24. DOI: https://doi.org/10.1207/S1532799XSSR0701_02.

Perfetti, C., Cao, F., & Booth, J. (2013). Specialization and universals in the development of reading skill: How Chinese research informs a universal science of reading. *Scientific Studies of Reading*, *17*(1), 5–21. DOI: https://doi.org/10.1080/10888438.2012.689786.

Perfetti, C. A., & Harris, L. N. (2013). Universal reading processes are modulated by language and writing system. *Language Learning and Development*, 9(4), 296–316.
Perfetti, C., & Stafura, J. (2014). Word knowledge in a theory of reading comprehension. *Scientific Studies of Reading*, 18(1), 22–37. DOI: http://dx.doi.org/10.1080/10888438.2013.827687.
Perfetti, C., Verhoeven, L., & Pugh, K. (2019). Developmental dyslexia across languages and writing systems: The big picture. In L. Verhoeven, C. A. Perfetti, & K. Pugh (eds.), *Developmental Dyslexia across Languages and Writing Systems* (pp. 441–461). Cambridge: Cambridge University Press.
Program for International Student Assessment (PISA). (n.d.). www.oecd.org/pisa/.
Progress in International Reading Literacy Study (PIRLS). (n.d.). https://nces.ed.gov/surveys/pirls/.
Rowan, B., Correnti, R., & Miller, R. J. (2002). *What Large-Scale, Survey Research Tells Us about Teacher Effects on Student Achievement: Insights from the Prospectus Study of Elementary Schools*. Philadelphia: CPRE Research Reports. https://repository.upenn.edu/cpre_researchreports/31.
Seidenberg, M. S. (2011). Reading in different writing systems: One architecture, multiple solutions. In P. McCardle, J. Ren, O. Tzeng, & B. Miller (eds.), *Dyslexia across Languages: Orthography and the Brain-Gene-Behavior Link* (pp. 146–168). New York: Brookes.
Shure, D., Parameshwaran, M., Nag, S. & Snowling, M. J. (2014). *Economic and Social Factors related to Literacy and Foundation Learning, Technical Report No. 5: Literacy, Foundation Learning and Assessment in Developing Countries*. London: DfID.
Taylor, J., Roehrig, A. D., Soden Hensler, B., Connor, C. M., & Schatschneider, C. (2010). Teacher quality moderates the genetic effects on early reading. *Science*, 328 (5977), 512–514. DOI: https://doi.org/10.1126/science.1186149.
UNESCO. (2019). Out of school children and youth. http://uis.unesco.org/en/topic/out-school-children-and-youth.
Vágvölgyi, R., Coldea, A., Dresler, T., Schrader, J., & Nuerk, H. C. (2016). A review about functional illiteracy: Definition, cognitive, linguistic, and numerical aspects. *Frontiers in Psychology*, 7, 1617. DOI: https://doi.org/10.3389/fpsyg.2016.01617.
Verhoeven, L., & Perfetti, C. A. (2011). Introduction to this special issue: Vocabulary growth and reading skill. *Scientific Studies of Reading*, 15(1), 1–7.
Verhoeven, L., & Perfetti, C. (eds.). (2017).*Learning to Read across Languages and writing systems*. Cambridge: Cambridge University Press.
Verhoeven, L., Perfetti, C.A., & Pugh, K. (eds.) (2019). *Developmental Dyslexia across Languages and Writing Systems*. Cambridge: Cambridge University Press.
Verhoeven, L., & Perfetti, C. (2021). Universals in learning to read across languages and writing systems. *Scientific Studies of Reading*, 1–15. DOI: https://doi.org/10.1080/10888438.2021.1938575.
Verhoeven, L., Perfetti, C., & Pugh, K. (2019). Cross-linguistic perspectives on second language reading. *Journal of Neurolinguistics*, 50, 1–6. DOI: https://psycnet.apa.org/doi/10.1016/j.jneuroling.2019.02.001.
Verhoeven, L., & Snow, C. E. (eds.). (2001). Introduction: Literacy and motivation: Bridging cognitive and sociocultural viewpoints. In L. Verhoeven & C. E. Snow

(eds.), *Literacy and Motivation: Reading Engagement in Individuals and Groups.* New York: Routledge. DOI: https://doi.org/10.4324/9781410601735.

Wickins, C., & Sandlin, J. (2007). Literacy for what? Literacy for whom? The politics of literacy education and neocolonialism in UNESCO- and World Bank sponsored literacy programs. *Adult Education Quarterly, 57,* 275–292. https://doi.org/10.1177/0741713607302364.

Wigfield, A., & Guthrie, J. T. (1997). Relations of children's motivation for reading to the amount and breadth or their reading.*Journal of Educational Psychology, 89*(3), 420. DOI: https://doi.org/10.1037/0022-0663.89.3.420.

Index

adolescent reading
    and linguistic diversity, 46–48
    SES factors, 42–43
advanced literacy, 10–13, 15, 451–452
Africa
    early literacy outcomes, 139–141
    language of instruction, 134–138
        data for 20 countries, 135
        effects of mismatch with L1, 143–147
    literacy and schooling, 134–148
akshara. *See also* writing systems
    learning to read, 161–163
Australia
    Aboriginal cultures
        history, 205
        languages, 205–207
        literacy, 208–213
        schooling, 208–211
    demographics, 203–205
    educational policy, 214–215, 222–226
    multilingualism, 217
    migrant communities, 213–216

bilingual education
    Australia, 209–211
    benefits, 73, 75–76, 217
    challenges, 86
    cross-language transfer, 18–19
    Dutch and Papiamentu, 79–82
    sociopolitical perspectives, 21, 36
    varieties, 135
bilingualism
    Australia, 212–213
    benefits, 84
    family language, 435–436
    South America, 57–58
biliteracy, 73, 155, 163–166, 436–440
    akshara and English, 165–166
    challenges, 166
    cross-linguistic transfer, 163–164
    home practices, 435–436

brain development, *see also* neural bases of literacy
    adaptations with literacy, 269–272
    poverty effects, 460–461
    specialization for reading, 270–272

Canada
    United States, comparison with, 35–52
        immigration policy, 37
        reading disparities, 38–39
        SES, 39–43
    SES factors, 41–43
    and vocabulary, 40
Caribbean
    creole languages, 71
        Papiamentu literacy, 76–79
    literacy development, 71–86
    literacy levels, 75–76
Cherokee syllabary, 242–244
China
    Cantonese language, 181
    Chinese writing system, 179–180, *see also* writing systems
    literacy development, 179–191, *see also* learning to read: China
    Mandarin language, 180
Cree syllabary, 244

decoding, *see* learning to read
dyslexia, 13–14
    genetic risk, 297
    global issues, 459–460
    in Chinese, 188–189
    neural basis, 272–273
    Russia, 125–129

Early Childhood Longitudinal Study, 39
early literacy, 7–8, 266, 449–450, *see also* home literacy environment
    brain development, 269–270
    dependence on spoken language, 267–268
    child–teacher conversations, 383

470 *Index*

early literacy (cont.)
    Home-School Study of Language and Literacy, 383
    Russia, 124
    SES factors, 335–336
    shared book reading, 95–96
    teaching at home, 338
East Asia, 191–193
    Confucian tradition, 178
    demographics, 174–175
    literacy education, 178–179
ecological approach, 34–35, 428–429, 436
    applied to education in North America, 35–38
    literacy ecology framework, 404–405
    proximal and enfolding factors, 464–465
education, *see also* schooling
    expenditures
        national comparisons, 462–463
        South America, 60–61
    goal setting, 453–454, *see also* global education goals, UNESCO
    European model, 453–454
    universal primary education, 4–5
educational policy
    Africa, 147–148
    Australia, 222
    biliteracy programs, 74–75
    Caribbean, 84–86
        language planning, 71–72
    China, 178–179, 190
    India, 156–158
    Japan, 179
    language policy, 456–457
    South America, 59–62
effective teaching practices, *see* teaching
Europe
    EU literacy and education levels, 91–93
    migrant students, 98–99
    PIRLS, *see* international assessments
    regional variations in literacy rates, 92–93
executive functioning, 15, *see also* self-regulation

genetic factors, 15, 254, 292–305, 460
    heritability, 293
        dependence on environment, 296
    human genome studies, 299–300
    reading disability, *see* dyslexia
global education goals, 133–134, 353
global literacy framework, 21–22, 457
global regions
    Australia, 203–228
    Canada and United States, 33–52
    Caribbean, 70–86
    East Asia, 174–193
    Europe, 90–111
    Global South, 353–369
    India, 155–167
    Russia, 118–129
    South America, 56–67
    sub-Saharan Africa, 134–148
Global South
    cultural-context limitations, 368–369
    results for nine countries, 358–368
global variations in literacy. *See also* global literacy framework
    global literacy rates, 3–5
    languages and writing systems, 447–449
    regional variations, 446–447
    RCT interventions, 354–356

Hangul, 177, *see also* writing systems
home literacy environment, 17–18, 338–340, 427–428, *see also* language factors
    biliteracy practices, 437–440
    challenges, 463–464
    China, 190–191
    educational implications, 441
    effects on learning, 403–404
    Europe, 108
    Family Language and Literacy Policy (FLLP) model, 426–427
    India, 158
    measures, 430–432
    parental factors, 425–441
        bilingual contexts, 435–440
        parental support, 432–435
    Russia, 122–123
    Rwanda case study, 411–413
home literacy model, 95

immigration
    Australia, 213–217
    East Asia, 175
        rural migration in China, 191
    Europe, 98–99
    North America, 36–37
India
    biliteracy, 157
    education policy, 156–160
    learning to read, 161–163
    literacy levels, 155–156
    multilingualism, 156–160
        language policy, 156–160
indigenous languages
    Africa, 134–135
    Australia, 205–208
    Caribbean, 71
    South America, 57–59

Index

language policy, 58
   support for, 72
writing systems
   imposed writing systems, 250
   invented writing, North America, 242–244
instruction, *see also* teaching
   effective methods, 64–65
   India, 159
   global perspective, 377–378
   individualized, 391–393
   neuroscience implications, 276–278
   preschool, *see also* early literacy
      encouraging child talk, 387–388
   Russian, 120–122
   systematic phonics, 9–10, 390–391
      in Chinese, 10
   South America, 65–66
international assessments
   limitations of large data sets, 51–52
   PIRLS
      Europe, 96–98
         national comparisons, 99–103
         prior to school, 100
         SES, 107
      North America
         language differences, 45
         reading achievement & SES, 41–43, 46–47
      Russia, 125
   PISA
      Australia, 218
      East Asia, 174
      Europe, 98–99, 104–107
         national comparisons, 104–107
         international comparisons, 218–220
      North America, 46–47
      Russia, 125
      South America, 62
      sub-Saharan Africa, 139–146
   International Longitudinal Twins Study, 455
interventions, 378, *see also* instruction
   sociocultural perspectives, 353–354

Japan
   literacy development, 179
   writing systems, 176

Kenya
   literacy interventions, 363
Korea, 174–175
   Hangul writing system, 177
   language, 177

language factors
   family language and literacy policy (FLLP), 435–436
   home language, 44–48
   India, 158
   language exposure, 17, 74
   language of instruction, 18–19
      Africa, 134–139
      home vs school language, 73–75, 378–380, 455–457
         contextual influences in Africa, 340–341
         feasibility issues, 379–380
      policy, 135
   language proficiency, 15–16
   school success, 83–84
language policy, *see* educational policy
learning to read
   Africa, 139–144
   akshara, 160
   child interest, 418–419
   China, 180–186
      character learning, 186–187
      morphological awareness, 182–184
      orthographic knowledge, 184–186
      phonological awareness, 181–182
   decoding, 8–10, 376
      in advanced literacy, 10–13
      and comprehension compared in L1 and L2, 80–81
      cross-linguistic transfer, 165–166
      European comparisons, 94
   Japan, 179
   learning events, 450–451
   morphological processes, 256
      Chinese, 182–184
      Russian, 119–120
   operating principles, 252–257, 447
   phonological awareness, 94–95
   reading comprehension, 6, 10–13, 95, 256–257, 451–452
      and language ability, 376
      Chinese, 187–188
      global variation, 452
      home support, 432–435
      teacher-talk effects, 388
   role of spoken language, 253–254
   Russian, 119–120
   teacher effects, 389–393, *see also* teaching
   word identification, 255–256
lexical quality hypothesis, 15, 186
   applied to Chinese, 186–187
literacy
   achievement levels
      Australia, 218–222

literacy (cont.)
  Caribbean, 75–76
  East Asia, 174
  growth in, 3, 91–93
  India, 155
  as a social practice, 357
  definitions, 2–3, 5, 292
    functional literacy, 451
    PISA definition, 104
  historical context, 292–293
  literacy ecologies
    literacy ecology framework, 34–35
    underlying factors, 406–407
    perspectives on development, 334–335

migrant communities
  Asia, 174, 191
  Australia, 213–214, 217, 226
  Europe, 98–99
  Sweden, 97
Millennium Development Goals, 133, 353

National Reading Panel, 64–65, 334, 390
neural bases of literacy
  Korean, 192
  nonalphabetic reading
    Chinese, 188–190
    Japanese, 192–193
  universal brain network, 257–259
    development of, 269–272

operating principles in literacy development, *See* learning to read
Organisation for Economic Co-operation and Development, *see* international assessments: PISA
orthography, *see* writing systems

parental factors, *see* home literacy environment
poverty, 4, *see also* socioeconomic status
  effects on neural development, 461
  Roma children, 16
  South America Indigenous peoples, 58

randomized controlled trials (RCTs), *see* interventions
reading comprehension, *see* learning to read
Reading Systems Framework, 452
Russia
  instruction, 120–122
  literacy development, 118–127
Russian orthography, *see* writing systems
Rwanda, 402–422
  case study of literacy, 405–419
    educational implications, 419
    literacy outcomes, 407–408

schooling, 346, 452–454, *see also* education
  classroom resources, 19–20, 98
  India, 160
  European comparisons of school effects, 109
scripts, *see also* writing systems
  visual complexity, 247–248
self-regulation, 316–328
  cross-cultural effects, 320
  effects of schooling, 321–323
  ERP studies, 323–324
  gender differences, 319
simple view of reading, 11, 187, 375
sociocultural factors, 341–345, *see also* socioeconomic status, interventions
sociocultural theory, 426
socioeconomic status, 16, 333–345
  educational implications, 345–347
  and influence on literacy, 265, 273–275, 335–337
  across ages and global regions, 461–463
  Australia, 218–221
  Europe, 96, 100–103, 107
  language skills, 39–43
  neural development, 192
  South America, 59–61
  and linguistic diversity, 49–51
  promoting equity, 48–49
sociolinguistic perspectives, 357–358
sociopolitical factors, 20–21
  and writing systems, 449
South America
  demographics, 56–60
    Indigenous population estimates, 57
    national economic differences, 59
  educational achievement data, 62–63
  Indigenous languages, 57–58
  reading instruction, 64–66
  teacher training, 64–66, 75, *see* teacher training: South America
spelling, 9–10, 12
  Chinese, 178, 186–187
  Russian, 119–120
Sustainable Development Goals (SDGs), 133

teaching, 374–394
  effective practices, 20, 393–394
  effects on language learning, 383
  national comparisons, 389–390
  teacher quality, 381–383, 454–455
  teacher talk, 384–385
    cognitively challenging talk, 385–387
  teacher training

Index

need for reading science, 65, 66
South America, 64–66
Uganda, 367–368

Uganda
Northern Uganda Literacy Project, 367
UNESCO
Sustainable Development Goals, 2, 20, 133
United States
Compared with Canada, 35–52
immigration policy, 37
reading disparities, 38–39
instructional outcomes, 380–392
SES factors, 41–43
and vocabulary, 40
universal brain network, *see* neural bases of literacy
universals in literacy development, 6, *see also* learning to read: operating principles

vocabulary
acquisition, 7–8
effects of cognitively challenging talk, 385–387
home language differences, 48
importance for advanced literacy, 15
preschool instruction, 387
SES differences, 40

writing systems, 8–10
adaptations to language, 248–250
akshara orthographies, 155–156, 162
learning to read, 160
Chinese, 175–176, 179–180
influence on reading, 250–252, 458
invented systems, 241–244
Japanese kanji and kana, 176
Korean Hangul, 176–177, 242
mappings and classifications, 245–246
Mongolian, 177
orthographic depth, 93–96
Russian orthography, 118
scripts and visual complexity, 247–248
syllabaries, 242–244

Zambia, 140–145

Printed in the United States
by Baker & Taylor Publisher Services